MACROECONOMICS

MACROECONOMICS

Samuel A. Morley
Vanderbilt University

The Dryden Press
Chicago New York Philadelphia San Francisco
Montreal Toronto London Sydney Tokyo
Mexico City Rio de Janeiro Madrid

Acquisitions Editor: Elizabeth Widdicombe
Project Editor: Nancy Shanahan/Julia Ehresmann
Managing Editor: Jane Perkins
Design Director: Alan Wendt
Production Manager: Mary Jarvis

Text and Cover Designer: Alan Wendt
Copyeditor: Nancy Maybloom
Compositor: York Graphic Services
Text Type: Helvetica

Library of Congress Cataloging in Publication Data

Morley, Samuel A.
Macroeconomics.

1. Macroeconomics. I. Title.
HB172.5.M67 1983 339 83-11703

ISBN 0-03-059301-8

Printed in the United States of America
456-016-987654321

Address orders to
383 Madison Avenue
New York, NY 10017

Address editorial correspondence to
One Salt Creek Lane
Hinsdale, IL 60521

CBS College Publishing
The Dryden Press
Holt, Rinehart and Winston
Saunders College Publishing

To Monica

The Dryden Press Series in Economics

Breit and Elzinga
The Antitrust Casebook
Breit and Ransom
The Academic Scribblers, Revised Edition
Campbell and Campbell
An Introduction to Money and Banking, Fifth Edition
Dolan
Basic Economics, Third Edition
Dolan
Basic Macroeconomics, Third Edition
Dolan
Basic Microeconomics, Third Edition
Heertje, Rushing, and Skidmore
Economics
Hyman
Public Finance
Johnson and Roberts
Money and Banking: A Market Oriented Approach
Leftwich and Eckert
The Price System and Resource Allocation, Eighth Edition
Lindsay
Applied Price Theory
Morley
Inflation and Unemployment, Second Edition
Morley
Macroeconomics
Nicholson
Intermediate Microeconomics and Its Application, Third Edition
Nicholson
Microeconomic Theory, Second Edition
Pappas and Brigham
Fundamentals of Managerial Economics
Pappas, Brigham, and Hirschey
Managerial Economics, Fourth Edition
Poindexter
Macroeconomics, Second Edition
Puth
American Economic History
Richardson
Urban Economics
Welch and Welch
Economics: Theory and Practice

Preface

The purpose of this book is to enable the reader to understand how the macroeconomy works, why it does not seem to be working as well as it once did, and what we may be able to do about it. The book presents the basic topics that all students of macroeconomics must know: national income accounting, theories of aggregate demand, consumption and investment; and the demand for money. However, because my interest in writing the book was to deal with the unresolved issues that make macroeconomics such a vibrant and contentious field today, I have given the book a policy and supply-side focus.

A great many of the problems we have encountered in recent years have been supply-side problems—for example, the persistence of inflation despite years of slack, a succession of supply shocks, and the slowdown in the growth of productivity. To help the student understand the reasons for these unpleasant phenomena, the text focuses as much as possible on the supply side of the economy. It does so in several ways.

First, the course material is rearranged so as to develop a complete theory of both supply and demand early in the book—by the end of Chapter 7, to be exact. This allows the student to get quickly to key policy issues such as stagflation, supply shocks, inflationary cycles, and the effect of reducing monetary expansion to control inflation.

Second, the text presents and stresses a fundamental disagreement among economists over the appropriate nature of the theory of aggregate supply. This disagreement is between those who think that markets are clear and unemployment is voluntary and those who think that prices are set and unemployment is largely involuntary. This debate has led to an important conflict of opinion over why our inflation has been so stubborn and whether policies to cure recession are necessarily inflationary. Because this conflict over how the supply side operates is so important, the two models are presented separately and compared according to the supply curves and the policies that each implies. This will allow the student to clearly identify the issues behind many of our current policy debates and to understand what the stakes are in the debate.

Third, a good part of Chapter 19 is devoted to an examination of the recent productivity slowdown and all of Chapter 20 to supply-side economics. The latter chapter looks at government monetary and fiscal policies and their effect on the capacity output level of the economy and uses a case study to examine Reaganomics, which has been billed as the nation's first program based on supply-side principles.

Finally, supply-side factors and prices have been incorporated into the analysis of the open economy. This quite dramatically changes some of the conclusions about policy that are made for an open economy when prices are either ignored or assumed to be fixed.

This book reflects my interest in policy issues, presenting whenever possible policy case studies to complement and deepen the student's appreciation of policy questions. One such issue is the control of inflation, a central concern throughout this book. To present that issue I have developed a comprehensive theory of the joint determination of prices, output, and employment in Chapters 6 through 9; I then have used that theory to study how an economy reacts to contractionary monetary or fiscal policy. The lessons of these chapters are reinforced with examples and simulations. Chapter 18 carries on the discussion of inflation control with a consideration of all the different weapons that we might use to control inflation; the chapter includes a case study of our actual experience in the United States in fighting inflation since the mid 1960s.

Several other policy issues are highlighted in this book. Chapter 15 discusses the policy activism debate, and Chapters 16 and 17 are devoted to a discussion of the practical problems of operating fiscal and monetary policies. Different policy rules for monetary and fiscal policies are discussed, as well as implications for policy of the government budget identity. That identity implies that all fiscal policy has a monetary side effect, which is ignored in the standard analysis. For example, the usual treatment of tax cuts ignores the implications of how the resulting deficits are financed. As a result, it seriously underestimates the crowding out of private expenditure caused by the rising deficit. That is because the standard analysis concentrates on the money market and ignores the bond market. But when deficits are financed by bond sales, as they have been to a great extent since 1980, the bond market is crucial. We have learned, to our sorrow, that bond-financed deficits may have a severe effect on interest rates and a perverse effect on the economy—just the opposite of what was expected by policymakers. In order to better understand how all this works, an entire chapter is devoted to portfolio theory and asset markets, both of which allow a full analysis of crowding out, a key feature of the economy since 1980. They also help us to see the effect of monetary policy on the asset and goods markets in both the short run and the long run.

Learning how to control aggregate demand with monetary and fiscal policies should not be the only thing the student learns about demand management. Equally important is the question of when to use contractionary and when to use expansionary policy. On one level, that is a question about how to stabilize the economy, and it is dealt with in the chapter on policy activism. But on a deeper level, it is a question about the use of demand management to fight inflation and recession. If the economy is in a recession, should the government expand the money supply or cut taxes to try to get out of it? Should it use contractionary monetary policy to fight inflation? These are important questions, and ones on which economists disagree. That disagreement stems mainly from the difference of opinion over the correct theory of aggregate supply. Broadly speaking, those who believe that prices are set by sellers think that prices are unresponsive to the level of demand. They tend to favor expansionary policy as an escape from recession, but they frown on contraction as a cure for inflation. Those who think that prices are flexible favor contractionary policy to cure inflation but are afraid of the inflationary costs of expansionary policy.

No one knows for sure which of these groups is right. Nevertheless, it is imperative to understand the issues involved, because that will help to explain why at times the government is reluctant to take steps to get out of recession, and why at other times it consciously pushes the economy into recession. That understanding will also help the student to evaluate the arguments for and against both of these actions and to focus on the normative question of when and if the government should use contractionary policy to fight inflation with recession.

How to Use This Book

I have tried to make this book as simple as I could without sacrificing theoretical correctness. The student who reads it most likely will have had an introductory economics course but even that, strictly speaking, is unnecessary. All the material from the introductory course is reintroduced in the first three chapters, so the book can be read by someone with no previous economics training. Mathematically, the student needs no more than high-school algebra and the ability to work with graphs and figures. Each model or theory is presented in three different ways: verbally, graphically, and algebraically. Each model is reinforced with problem sets. To best understand each example, the student should work out the algebra, derive the graphs, and work the problem sets. The best way to learn to think like a macroeconomist is to start doing macroeconomics.

A number of aids are provided to help the student do that. First, there is a glossary, which defines all the key terms written in boldface type in the text. Second, a set of discussion problems appears at the end of each chapter, which should provide a rich dividend in the student's understanding of how the models work. Third, each chapter contains key concepts, which the student should have fully grasped before continuing on. Finally, a summary for each chapter emphasizes the central points made by the chapter and indicates what is to follow. These summaries should strengthen the student's grasp of the central logic of this book.

Acknowledgments

Many people have generously helped me in the writing of this book. In particular, I would like to thank the following for comments and suggestions that materially improved its quality: Stanley Black, Vanderbilt University; Rendigs Fels, Vanderbilt University; Jeffrey Frankel, University of California at Berkeley; Glenn Hueckle, Purdue University; Woo Jung, Vanderbilt University; Laura LeHaye, University of Illinois, Chicago Circle; Richard Long, Georgia State University; Michael McElroy, North Carolina State University; Virginia Owen, Illinois State University; M. Ray Perryman, Baylor University; and Susan Ranney, University of Michigan. Needless to say, I absolve them of responsibility for any errors that remain.

Next, I wish to thank several classes of patient students who gave me the opportunity to try out new ideas and new ways of presentation and whose comments in several cases found their way directly into this book. Munir Abu-Ghazaleh, Roger Andreae, David Gray, Roberto Martins, Manisri Puntularp, Thurman Senn, and Jonathan Wight were particularly helpful.

Writing a book is never easy—but the people at The Dryden Press made it as easy as possible. In particular, I want to thank Liz Widdicombe, the economics editor, for her enthusiasm and support and my project editors, Julia Ehresmann and Nancy Shanahan, for their assistance in keeping everything on schedule and in providing help and encouragement whenever it was needed. My thanks also to Nancy Maybloom, my careful copyeditor, who turned a manuscript I thought was finished into truly final form. Next, I want to thank my typist, Nancy Latham, for the care she took with this manuscript and for her willingness to put up with impossible deadlines. I also want to thank my son, William J. Morley, for doing all the computer work and the diagrams. I have been lucky to have all of these people to work with.

Finally, I want to thank my family for the amount of time that they gave up to let me write this book. To live with a writer working under a deadline is not much fun. They put up with that cheerfully and unfailingly urged me on. I have been lucky to have such people to live with.

Samuel A. Morley
Nashville, Tennessee
October 1983

Contents

PART FOUR THE COMPONENTS OF AGGREGATE DEMAND

PART FIVE PROBLEMS IN DEMAND MANAGEMENT AND THE CONTROL OF INFLATION

PART ONE

AN OVERVIEW OF MACROECONOMICS

Chapter 1

Introduction

The field of macroeconomics is currently in considerable ferment. Our economic performance since the mid-1970s has been unsatisfactory. We have had far too much inflation and far too much recession, often at the same time. Economists disagree about what is wrong and what we ought to be doing about it.

The purpose of this chapter is to acquaint the reader with the field of macroeconomics and to spell out what we shall be covering together throughout this book. We shall also focus our attention on the significant areas of disagreement among macroeconomists and the policy disputes those disagreements bring about.

What is Macroeconomics?

Macroeconomics is the study of key economic magnitudes, such as prices, income, and employment, measured over the entire economy. "Macro" comes from a Greek word meaning "big," and in this sense it implies economic factors aggregated over all the individuals, business firms, and government units in the economy. Macroeconomics does not tell us what is going on in particular markets. It does not study unemployment rates in Charleston or the price of steel in Pittsburgh. Rather, it treats the entire economy as if it were composed of uniform households, businesses, governments, and markets, for each of which a single wage, unemployment rate, or price level can be derived. Macroeconomics leaves out the differences among firms or markets in order to concentrate on key aggregate factors and the relationships among them. By doing so it loses something in realism—but hopefully, what it loses in realism it more than makes up for in its ability to explain how the economy as a whole operates.

During the last thirty years macroeconomists have developed a coherent explanation for the macroeconomic system. That explanation tells us what determines such important aggregate variables as the inflation rate, unemployment, and the level of output. It also tells us how government actions affect the economy and under what conditions deliberate actions by the government can change the levels of these variables.

Unfortunately, the explanations offered by macroeconomists of how the economy works seem to be much less convincing now than they used to be. Events in the economy since 1970 have all too often confounded economic forecasts and left policymakers puzzled about what to do and what model of the economy to follow. Macroeconomics is in a state of confusion and, some would say, crisis. For the last fifteen years we have been attempting to control inflation and excessive unemployment. As yet we have not succeeded. Recessions follow price explosions with depressing regularity. The United States seems unable to regain the stable, noninflationary growth path it was on before the Vietnam War. Even familiar policies no longer seem to work as expected. For example, President Reagan cut taxes in 1980, promising an era of more rapid growth. Tax cuts had always led to an expansion in the economy. But this time the United States plunged into the most severe recession in forty years. To make matters worse, the government budget deficit since that year seems to have been out of control.

What is wrong? Why is there such a state of confusion among policymakers and the public? We think that the sense of uncertainty comes mainly from a lack of consensus among economists themselves about how our economy works. Because they do not agree they give no clear signal to policymakers about what to do. There are profound differences of opinion about how fiscal and monetary policies work, and particularly on the relationship between them. That is the main source of confusion about the effect of the Reagan tax cut. There are also sharp differences about the supply side of the economy. Some think that demand or supply shocks lead quickly to price adjustments without extended recessions or booms. Others think that most of the supply response is in quantities produced, not prices. These two alternative views lead to sharp disagreements about how to control inflation and recession. Finally, there is an increasingly influential group of economists who argue that economic behavior is significantly affected by public expectations about government policy. This implies that the government is virtually powerless to affect the level of economic activity except in the very short run. It follows that the government should not attempt to engage in countercyclical policy, a position hotly disputed by other economists.

What are we to make of this welter of conflicting ideas? One thing we cannot do is ignore it—the issues are too important. We as informed citizens need to understand the general lines of the alternative opinions of economists about how the economy works, why it does not seem to work as well as it once did, and what we may be able to do about it. Hopefully, this book will help us to do that. It is not going to hide the differences of opinion among economists by presenting only a single explanation for phenomena when in fact there may be several available, each with strong advocates. This book instead will try to reflect the important differences of opinion among economists. It will discuss them, draw out their policy implications, and weigh them against empirical evidence, all with the intention of helping us to understand what economists are arguing about and what are the implications of their arguments for policy.

The unresolved questions of how the economy works and why it isn't working well are important ones. They are going to affect the world in which we live and work. If we resolve them successfully, our economy should get back on a high-employment, low-inflation expansion path. If we do not, we may look forward to a long continuation of stagflation.

Macroeconomic Models

The basic tool of macroeconomics is the **macromodel,** a formal representation of the behavior of firms, households, and government, the three basic units that make up our economy. We will go into a great deal more detail on what models are and how to use them in later chapters, so here we will simply say that a model is a systematic way of representing the behavior of households, firms, and governments in such a way that the outcome for each unit is consistent with its preferences and the constraints to which it is subject.

Models are useful for several reasons. First, they help us to understand how the economy works and the links or feedbacks among different markets and economic units. For example, prices determined in the market for output have an effect on wage demands in the labor market, since workers are interested in the purchasing power of their wages. At the same time, wage demands by workers will have an effect on the prices that firms charge for their products. There is a simultaneous feedback among employment, wages, prices, and output that we need a model to fully capture and examine. That is what a macromodel does.

The main use to which macromodels are put is the isolation of the determinants of important macro variables. A good model will tell us the factors that influence such things as the unemployment rate or inflation. It will give us a prediction for exactly how an economy will react to such changes as an oil-price shock or an increase in taxes, or how much unemployment will decline or prices will rise if the government lowers taxes or raises the money supply. That knowledge is obviously extremely useful.

We can use such predictions as a guide for policymaking. Suppose, for example, that we have a model that tells us how much prices will respond to changes in the money supply. That prediction can be used by government policymakers to decide on the appropriate money supply needed to reach a desired inflation rate. Thus, if our model predicts that the inflation rate will decline by 1 percent for each 1 percent reduction in the money supply, and if inflation is 2 percent higher than desired, the government authorities should reduce the money supply by 2 percent. (This is obviously only an example; authorities would have to worry about the effect of their policy on output and employment, too.) Even if our model is not accurate enough for such exact predictions, it will still tell us the direction in which policy should move. That may be a considerable advantage in complex situations.

Another use for macromodels is to help us to explain and understand the past. Since models give us a measure of cause and effect, they can be used to determine what caused certain events in the past to happen. For example, suppose a model gives us an exact estimate of how much prices go up when the government increases the money supply or how much production responds to tax cuts. With this information, we can ask how much less inflation we would have had if the money supply had expanded more slowly or taxes had been cut in particular historical situations. We do this by running a simulation of the economy using historical values for all variables except the money supply or taxes. These we set at the levels at which we think they should have been set. We then compare our simulated model with actual economic history. The difference between the two isolates the effect of the money supply having been expanded or taxes having been cut at the historical rather than the simulated rate.

In this book we will study several of the main macromodels. At times this may appear to be nothing but a theoretical exercise. But understanding economic theory is never an end in itself—rather, it is a means to help understand how our economy works and what part the government should take in making it work better. Behind each of the models we shall examine is an economic history or reality that they should help us to understand. In order to see more clearly what that reality looks like, consider now the historical time paths of several of the key economic variables that we shall be trying to explain.

Output, Inflation, and Unemployment

The basic measure of output or production in an economy is **gross national product,** or GNP. GNP tells at a glance how many goods and services were produced by the economy over a certain time interval. Since GNP is measured in current prices, a good part of any change in GNP may be nothing but a result of changing prices or inflation. If one is interested in tracking production over time, price changes should be netted out. As we shall see in the next chapter, one does this by dividing or deflating by a price index. The result, GNP/P, is called **real GNP;** it is a measure of the value of production at constant prices. When real GNP rises or falls, one knows that production itself has gone up or down.

The solid red line in diagram (a) of Figure 1.1 shows us what has happened to real GNP in the United States since 1900. As the reader can see, there has been a striking increase in that variable. Despite severe depression in the 1930s and a slowdown since 1973, real GNP has grown by more than ten times since 1900, which is an average annual growth rate of 3 percent.

To get more perspective on that performance, we show the growth rate of real GNP relative to **capacity GNP.** Capacity GNP is a measure of how much the economy could produce if all idle resources were put to use. Capacity GNP is based on an estimate of the full employment labor force and average labor productivity. Economists estimate the labor force, subtract what they call frictional (normal) unemployment, and then apply an estimate of average labor productivity to the resulting working labor force to get their best guess of how much the economy could have produced had it operated at the frictional level of unemployment. That is capacity GNP.

Several conclusions are suggested by the comparison between actual real and capacity GNP in diagram (a). First, almost all the growth in real GNP in the last 80 years has been due to a growth in capacity GNP. This says that supply-side

Figure 1.1
Output, Inflation, and Unemployment in the United States (1900–1982)

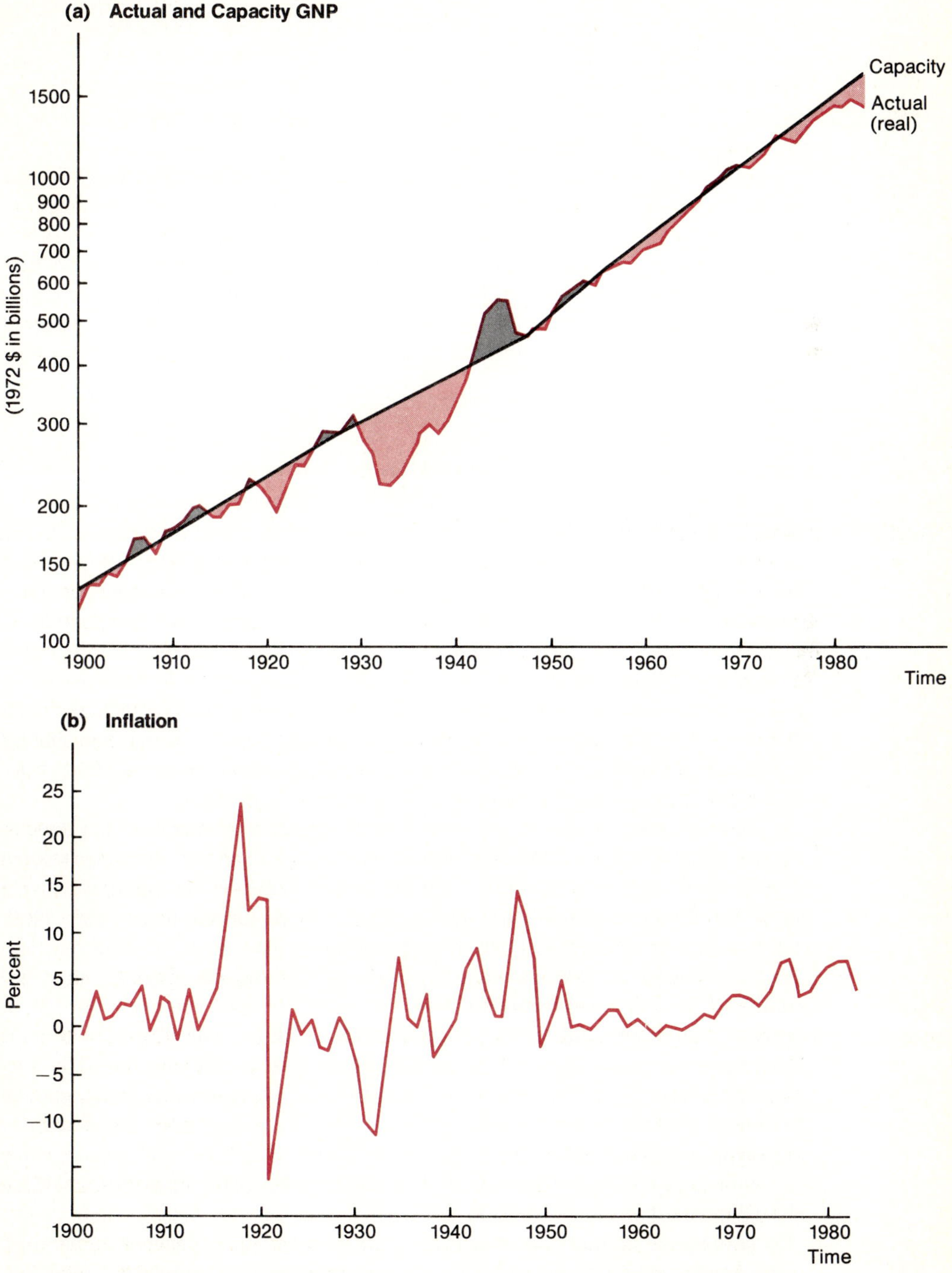

Figure 1.1 *(continued)*

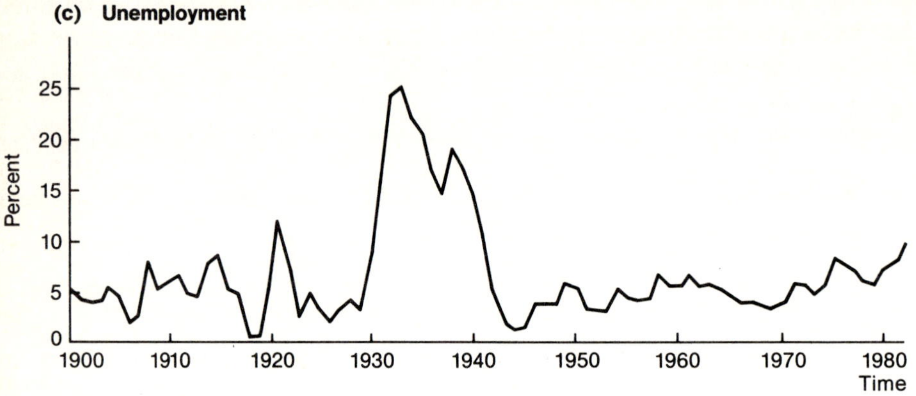

factors are the key to growth in the long run. Second, there are three periods when we operated far short of our potential: the 1930s, the years from 1954 to 1963, and the period since 1975. By contrast, there are five periods when we operated above our normal capacity. Four of these were during wars: World War I, 1917—1919; World War II, 1941–1945; the Korean War, 1950–1953; and the Vietnam War, 1965–1970. The only nonwar period is the late 1920s' boom episode. For some reason, war is the only time when we are willing (or able) to operate the economy at or above its capacity output level

We turn now to the historical record of inflation and unemployment, shown in diagrams (b) and (c) of Figure 1.1. Inflation is measured as the percentage change in the price index for GNP, while the unemployment rate is the percentage of the labor force actively seeking but not finding work.

First, compare diagrams (b) and (c) to diagram (a). As one would expect, there is a clear negative relationship between the unemployment rate and the level of real GNP. Periods of low GNP are periods of high unemployment, and vice versa. What is more interesting is the relationship of the output and unemployment series to inflation. All of the periods of high output are also periods of relatively high rates of inflation. Both world wars and the Vietnam War caused very sharp increases in inflation rates, although in the World War II period some of that inflation seems to have been delayed by wage and price controls until after the war. The clear lesson appears to be that excess demand leads to high inflation. The only possible exception to that rule is the Korean War, when a relatively successful system of controls helped to avoid the high inflation that generally accompanies low levels of unemployment.

Now look at the reverse side of this inflation-output-unemployment relationship. What happens to the inflation rate when output is below its potential or unemployment above normal? As we can see, until the mid1970s recessions were always accompanied by a decline in the inflation rate. That was true in the late

1920s, the 1930s, and the late 1950s. This fact, plus the high rate of inflation associated with booms, led economists to assert that there is a negative relationship between the inflation rate and unemployment, a relationship known as the *Phillips curve*, named after its discoverer, A. W. Phillips. The importance of the Phillips curve is what it seems to imply for policy, namely, a trade-off between inflation and unemployment. The historical fact that periods of low (high) inflation have also been periods of high (low) unemployment has led many people to reach two important conclusions: (1) high levels of employment and periods of rapid growth lead to inflation, and (2) reducing inflation requires suffering recession and high unemployment. Much of our macropolicy in the postwar period has been based on these two simple assertions.

Macroeconomics in the 1970s: Crisis or Hope?

Unfortunately for economists, the period since 1970 has been different than any that went before. It has eliminated the Phillips curve, at least as a basis for policymaking. For the first time since economists started keeping records, a significant increase in the unemployment rate has not brought down the inflation rate. Quite the contrary: The inflation rate has actually increased at the same time that unemployment has stayed above the norms for any other period since 1940. Since the 1970s, the U. S. economy has been in a period of extended stagflation, a period when inflation and unemployment have been simultaneously at high levels. This has presented a major, unpleasant problem for macroeconomists, one their theories have seemed poorly equipped to handle.

As far as we can tell, what has happened is a combination of unexpected changes on the supply side of the economy. Oil-price shocks, greater wage and price rigidity, more pessimistic projections of inflation, and declining increments in worker productivity have all tended to raise prices even in the midst of recession. These events have forced macroeconomists to think far more carefully about their theories of aggregate supply. The new supply-side theories being developed show great promise in helping to understand what has gone wrong in our economy during these last ten years. We will incorporate several of these new theories in the economic models that we build in later chapters.

Because of the economic difficulties that the United States has been through in recent years, there appears to be a popular perception that we no longer know how to manage the economy—in particular, that we are incapable of getting out of recessions once they have started, or of stopping booms until they have generated runaway inflation. How different the situation is now from the one twenty years ago! At that time macroeconomists under President Kennedy prescribed a tax cut to get the economy moving again. The tax cut was duly passed in 1964 and, true to prediction, the economy did go into an extended five-year boom. The economy seemed to be controllable, and macroeconomists seemed to know how to control it. There is little of that confidence today—indeed, there is talk of a "crisis" in economic policymaking.

Yet we can hope that the perception of confusion and uncertainty is overemphasized. We will attempt to show that the history our economy has traced out is largely consistent with our models and explainable by them. Granted, we must make some changes to take account of new elements on the supply side, particularly fuel prices and expectations. We used to not have to worry about these elements, because they didn't change much. But they do now, so their roles must be specifically addressed.

We must also incorporate interactions between monetary policy and fiscal policy. These were ignored in many older models, with the result that the net effect of changes in taxes has been widely misunderstood. This includes President Johnson's 1968 surtax and the recent tax cut under President Reagan. People who expected such fiscal policy measures to have effects independent of whatever monetary policies were being followed were disappointed. Tax cuts in 1981–1982, a period of tight money, did not get the country moving. They did not give us a boom—nor should they have been expected to. Fiscal and monetary policies are tied together by something called the *government budget identity,* about which we will learn a good deal more in later chapters. The main implication of that identity is that the net effect of fiscal policy on the economy depends upon how it is financed. The models that we shall develop in this book will all incorporate the government budget identity, so that we shall better understand what can be expected of fiscal and monetary policies, whether acting alone or together.

Aggregate Supply and Demand

The basic building blocks for our models are the notions of **aggregate supply** and **aggregate demand.** Aggregate demand relates the quantity of output demanded to price. That relationship is a negative one, because higher prices reduce real money balances, drive up interest rates, and raise the real burden of taxes. All tend to reduce demand. By contrast, supply is thought to be positively related to output, because business should be willing to sell more at higher prices. These aggregate demand and supply relationships are summarized in Figure 1.2, a figure with which we will work a good deal in this book.

Most economists agree on the general shapes of the aggregate supply and demand curves, the former being upward sloping, the latter downward sloping. What they don't agree on is the degree of slope of the two curves, particularly the supply curve. One group thinks that the supply curve is relatively steep, as shown in diagram (a), perhaps even vertical; another group thinks it is relatively flat, particularly at low levels of output, as shown in diagram (b). On this simple difference, many important points of policy hinge. Let us look at several of them in particular.

First, how does an economy react to expansionary government policy? To expand the economy the government either increases the money supply, lowers taxes, or increases government expenditure. Under most conditions this should increase aggregate demand. This is shown in Figure 1.3, where the aggregate demand curve shifts out to the right to the dashed lines. But the net effect of the expansion on output and prices depends on the shape of the aggregate supply curve. If it is steep, expansionary policy primarily raises prices; there is only a

Figure 1.2
The Aggregate Supply and Demand Curves

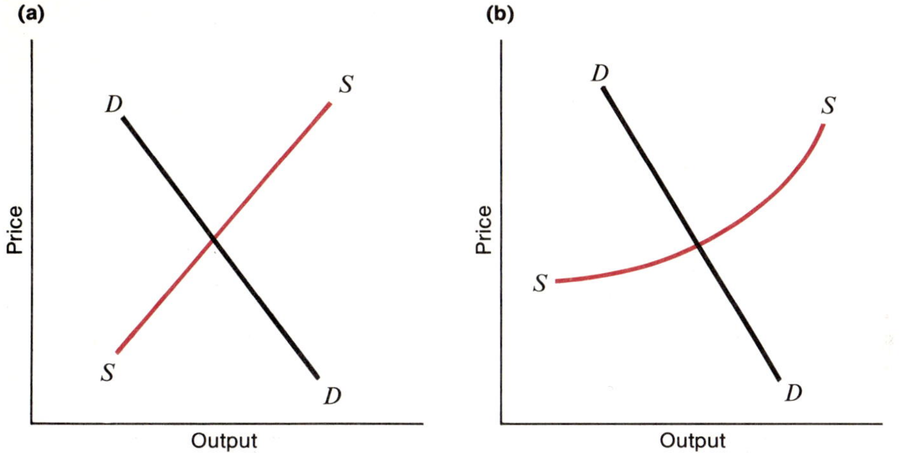

Figure 1.3
The Effect of an Increase in Aggregate Demand

An increase in aggregate demand shifts the demand curve to the right, from DD to $D'D'$. However, the effect of this change on prices and output depends on the shape of the aggregate supply curve. In either type of economy, the change will increase output from Y to Y' and increase prices from P to P'. However, the rise in prices will be greater and the rise in output will be smaller in the economy with the steeper supply curve.

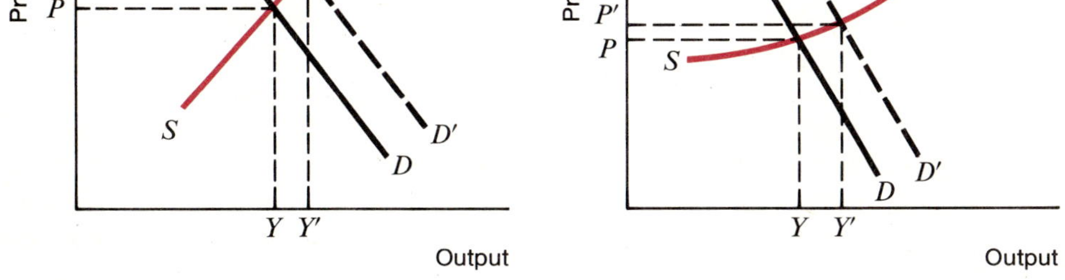

moderate increase in output. However, if the supply curve is flat, the same expansion does not increase prices at all; it increases output, presumably just what the action was intended to accomplish. Since no government would increase demand in order to raise prices, we conclude that expansionary demand policy will be effective only when the supply curve is relatively flat. People who favor expansionary government policy to combat recession are acting on the belief that the supply curve is flat. Those who oppose such actions generally argue that expansions cause inflation. Implicitly or explicitly, their argument is based on the assumption that the aggregate supply curve is steep.

Exactly the same sort of difference of opinion occurs over contractionary government policy. Governments reduce aggregate demand in order to fight inflation. They do so by reducing the money supply, lowering government spending, or raising taxes. Each shifts the aggregate demand curve to the left, as shown in Figure 1.4. Again, the effect of the policy depends on the **shape of the aggregate** supply curve. If it is flat, the policy simply causes a recession; there is little, if any, reduction in prices. Only if the supply curve is steep do prices decline in response to contractionary policy. Since the government would not cause a recession except in the hope of curing inflation, we conclude that contractionary policy makes sense only when the supply curve is upward sloping, not when it is flat.

To summarize: Those who believe the supply curve is flat will be in favor of expansionary government policy to combat recession, but they will be against restrictive demand management to fight inflation. Those who think the supply curve is upward sloping favor contractionary policy to cure inflation but are unenthusiastic about expansionary policy in a recession.

We have just had a vivid and extended example in the United States of this difference of opinion about the shape of the aggregate supply curve. It took place in 1982 and 1983. By the summer of 1982, the U. S. economy had been in a severe recession for at least two years. The unemployment rate was headed for a postwar record. Despite these indications of economic distress, there was a strong debate among policymakers about whether the government should take steps to combat the recession by either expanding the money supply, cutting taxes, or increasing government spending. Those who were opposed to such expansionary measures argued that if we were to allow the economy to expand, we would surely undo all the progress that had been made on inflation during the recession. In other words, they thought that expansion would be inflationary. The advocates of expansion argued that, given the depth of the recession, inflation rates would not increase because of faster growth provided that the expansion was not carried too far. The opponents of expansion won that argument, which meant that the recovery from the recession was slow and cautious, which of course prolonged the period of high unemployment. Had the other side won, we would have come out of the recession faster—but perhaps with a much higher rate of inflation. Thus, we can see that how an economy responds to changes in aggregate demand, whether by price or output changes, has very important implications for the way the government makes its policy and for whether the economy has a tendency toward recession or inflation.

Which shape does the supply curve in our economy have? That would seem to be an easy question to answer by empirical investigation, but in fact it is not.

Figure 1.4
The Effect of a Reduction in Aggregate Demand

Here we show a reduction in aggregate demand. The demand curve shifts to the left. In each economy output falls from Y to Y' and prices fall from P to P'. However, in the economy with the flatter supply curve, the decline in output is greater and the decline in prices is smaller than would be the case if the supply curve were steeper, as it is for the economy portrayed in (a).

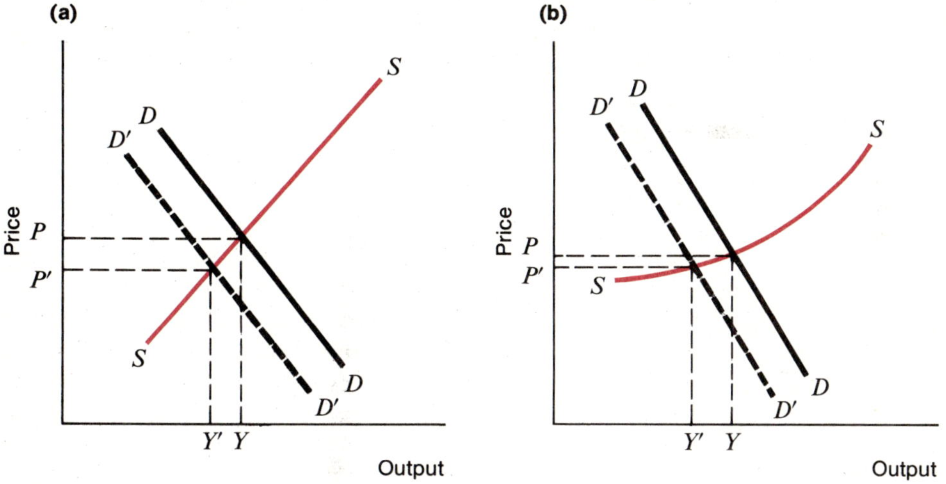

First of all, the shape of the supply curve depends on the time horizon of the model. Most economists would agree that prices are inflexible over a period as short as one week, but almost no one would expect much inflexibility over five years. Thus, the shape of the supply curve depends crucially on its time scale. Accurate determination of supply curve slope has been further complicated by such factors as oil price shocks, which have shifted the curves.

Given the policy relevance of the supply curve shape, we shall present two alternative theories of supply—one for a flat supply curve, the other for an upward-sloping curve. Comparing the policy implications of each curve will be a great help in understanding the debate over how much government should do to help the economy get out of recession and what are the best ways of fighting inflation.

Organization of the Book

Chapters 1–5 of the book develop a model of aggregate demand. This model shows the interactions between financial markets and goods markets, and it is a good vehicle for understanding how monetary and fiscal policies work and the interactions between them. Chapters 6–10 add the supply side to the model. They show how conditions in the labor market critically influence the economy's supply curve. Because of its importance to determining how the economy operates, we have developed two alternative models for aggregate supply, which we present in Chapters 6 and 7: the partial equilibrium theory and the disequilibrium theory. Each corresponds to one of the supply curves shown in Figure 1.2.

Any macroeconomic theory must be capable of explaining why economies have booms and recessions instead of steady growth. Our two theories do this in very different ways. The partial equilibrium theory is based on the notion that workers make errors when they forecast future prices. When this happens the economy has either a boom or a recession, because the forecasting errors cause workers to demand wages that are inconsistent with the full employment level of prices. As we shall see, if workers overforecast future inflation they demand too-high wages, and the economy is pushed into recession. If they underforecast inflation, the economy has a boom.

The other supply theory is based on markup pricing and rigid wages. Under this theory the aggregate supply curve is relatively flat at less than full employment, because costs in a significant portion of the economy are negatively related to output. Hence, when there is a reduction in aggregate demand there will be an immediate decline in output and employment, rather than a reduction in price.

Having developed these two models, we then use them, in Chapters 8–9, to show how each economy reacts to changes in aggregate demand. Each economy will have a cycle in response to a change in demand. However, we show that the cycles last longer in the markup price economy and involve wider fluctuations from the full employment level of output. In other words, it appears that economies with markup pricing are likely to be less stable than economies where prices are more sensitive to the level of output. We then go on to ask how the two types of economy react to supply shocks or attempts by the government to reduce inflation. As one might expect, it is relatively difficult to control inflation or absorb supply-side shocks in the markup pricing economy. For when aggregate demand is reduced, output tends to decline more than prices. Inflation control means long periods of recession in this type of economy. Of course, inflation control also causes recessions in the partial equilibrium economy, but they are shorter because prices are more responsive to slack in the economy.

In Chapter 10 we show what our two theories imply about the Phillips curve, the relationship between inflation and unemployment. We show that the Phillips curve is analogous to our supply curves; thus, the markup pricing economy tends to have relatively flatter Phillips curves. That means that unemployment reduces inflation less rapidly in the markup pricing economy, which is what makes counterinflationary policy so costly. When the Phillips curve or the supply curve is flat, it takes a lot of idle capacity and unemployment to reduce inflation.

In Chapters 11–14 of the book we develop in more detail the theories underlying the most important behavioral relationships in our model. Chapters 11 and 12 examine alternative theories of consumption and investment. Chapters 13 and 14 derive the demand for money in the context of a complete theory of the public demand for different assets. We then use the theory to show how changes in the supplies of different assets, such as government bonds, or changes in the public's preferences lead to changes in the relative prices of different assets, which in turn cause increases or reductions in investment.

In the next section of the book we address several important policy questions. The first, discussed in Chapter 15, is the extent to which the government should attempt to stabilize the economy through discretionary monetary and fiscal policies. For a long time, many economists have argued that the government has done more harm than good when it has tried to stabilize the economy. Poor forecasts, bad judgment, and political pressures have all combined to cause many unfortunate policy mistakes. Recently a very significant theoretical development called *rational expectations* has reinforced this view. According to rational expectations theory, government policymakers can influence the level of activity in the economy only when their actions are unexpected. But if they try to follow any sort of stabilization rule, the public will eventually learn the rule—at which point policymakers will no longer be able to stabilize the economy by following the rule. It would be far better, argue the rational expectations economists, to force government policymakers to follow some sort of rigid rule. An example of the sort of rule they have in mind is to have the money supply expand at a constant rate regardless of conditions in the economy. That would at least guarantee that the government itself would not be an additional source of instability in the economy.

In Chapters 16 and 17, we take up specific problems in the operation of fiscal and monetary policies. First, we discuss various measures and goals for fiscal policy. Next, we examine the necessary link between fiscal and monetary policies imposed by the government budget identity. Almost all fiscal actions have monetary side effects; similarly, monetary policy has an impact on the government deficit. Because of this, we argue that monetary and fiscal policies should be coordinated in order to conduct a sensible and coherent macroeconomic policy.

Chapter 18 takes up the problem of controlling inflation. Drawing out the implications of previous chapters, we show that the difficulty of the task depends on the flatness of the supply curve or the insensitivity of prices and wages to the level of aggregate demand. In a lengthy study we examine U. S. experience with antiinflation policy and conclude that the empirical evidence points to a quite flat supply curve. If that is the case, controlling inflation by recession will always be exceedingly expensive in the United States. We also consider indexing and forms of wage-price controls as alternative ways to either live with or control inflation without recession.

Chapters 19–22 contain three additions to the basic model developed earlier in the book. Chapters 19 and 20 are extensions of the theories of aggregate supply. In Chapter 19 we develop a theory for the growth of potential income in an economy over time. We show how per capita income in the long run is related to the economy's capital intensity and propensity to save. In Chapter 20 we look more carefully at supply-side economics, which we describe as the effect of government policy on the level of capacity output. We show that supply-side questions are actually far broader than those raised in the Reagan economic program, which focuses exclusively on regulation and taxes. But monetary policy and demand management in general also have an effect on capacity, because both affect capital formation. Whether tax cuts are a more potent stimulus to investment than expansionary monetary policy is a question that we cannot answer. But it is quite clear that no supply-side policy works well in recession. Finally, in Chapters 21–22, we broaden our model to include the foreign sector. We show how the balance of payments imposes constraints on policymakers and in what ways monetary and fiscal policies are different in open and closed economies.

Summary

In this chapter we took an introductory tour of the subject matter of macroeconomics. First, we defined the field and showed that it is principally concerned with determining such aggregate economic variables as GNP, prices, and employment. The main tool that macroeconomists use for that purpose is the macromodel, which is an internally consistent set of relationships or equations that is used to examine the main factors determining the key macro variables. Macromodels are also useful to government policymakers, because they show the effects of government policy on the economy. They therefore have come to be used as an instrument to help control the economy.

Next, we looked at our actual economic record since 1900 in order to know the general historical behavior of the variables—GNP, prices, and employment—that our macromodels will have to explain. It is clear from that record that the period since 1970 has not been a particularly good one for the U. S economy. Rising inflation forced us twice during that decade to endure severe recession in order to bring the price spiral under control. That experience, coupled with the difficulties of controlling aggregate demand in an inflationary environment, has brought to the surface some important differences of opinion among economists. We pointed out three such disputes: the first over the shape of the aggregate supply curve, the second over the interaction and coordination of monetary and fiscal policies, and the third over the role and formation of price expectations in the economy. Each of these issues has important implications for the logic of our macromodels and for policymaking. These we shall examine more thoroughly in the following chapters.

Key Concepts

macroeconomics
macromodel
gross national product
real GNP
capacity GNP
aggregate supply and demand
shape of aggregate supply curve

Chapter 2

Measuring National Income and Prices

As we indicated in the last chapter, our basic concern in this text is to understand how output, employment, and the price level are determined in the economy. In order to do that, it is useful to first know how output and prices are measured. This will be the purpose of this chapter.

GNP: Measurement and Significance

The basic measure of output in our economy is **gross national product,** or GNP. GNP is defined as the value of goods and services produced for sale in the economy over a period of time. Thus, GNP is a measure of salable production, or of the flow of output over a time interval. To some extent what the GNP accountants choose to regard as salable is arbitrary. For example, we do not count the value of work performed by housewives as part of GNP, but we do count the same work if performed by paid housekeepers. The same is true for home gardeners and do-it-yourselfers as opposed to truck gardeners and professional home repairpersons.

The general criterion for whether a particular activity is or is not included in GNP is whether it is produced for sale. However, there are two important exceptions to this production-for-sale rule: housing and government activities. If a house is rented, the value of rental payments is included in GNP, for rent is a measure of the value of the services produced by a house. But what about owner-occupied housing? This type of housing clearly provides exactly the same sort of services that rental housing does. Therefore, it should be and it is handled in an equivalent

Table 2.1
GNP in the Bread Economy

	Sales	Purchases	Value Added
Bread industry	$1,000,000	$500,000	$ 500,000
Flour industry	500,000	250,000	250,000
Wheat	250,000	—	250,000
Total value of production			$1,000,000

manner.[1] The hypothetical value of rental payments is calculated for owner-occupied housing and is added to GNP. The other major GNP component that is not produced for sale is the activities of the government. The value of government activities is assumed to be equal to the salaries of government employees. Thus, whenever government employees get raises, GNP goes up.

In order to actually calculate GNP, one cannot simply add up the total value of sales in the economy, even though that may seem logical in view of the definition of GNP as the value of salable production. First, many sales are secondhand products, such as cars or houses. Since these are not produced during the measurement period, they do not count in GNP. The second reason that we cannot simply add up total sales in the economy is **double counting.** Many products, such as steel plates or flour, are intermediate goods sold by one producer to another producer for use in the production process. If we were to take the total sales of both producers as a measure of their combined output, we would double-count the value of intermediate products. Consequently, when we measure GNP, we have the choice of either counting the value added in each establishment or counting only the total value of *final* goods, by which we mean goods sold to final users.

As an example of the two possible ways of measuring output, consider the wheat, flour, and bread example shown in Table 2.1. For simplicity, suppose that all flour is sold to bakers and all wheat is sold to flour millers. In that case, production and sales in a hypothetical economy would be as shown in Table 2.1.

The total value of production in the economy is $1,000,000. That can be measured either by adding up the values of the three industries or by calculating the value of final sales—in this case, equal to the value of bread produced by the economy. Obviously, to add up the gross sales of the three sectors (column 1)

[1] In effect, the home-owning household is treated as a business that rents to itself. The imputed rental payments are included in household income and household consumption. Other consumer durables are not treated in this way even though they have exactly the same characteristics as housing.

would seriously overestimate the value of production, because it would double-count the value of wheat and flour, the intermediate inputs.

GNP: Not a Measure of Welfare

Why do we care about GNP? What does it tell us? That may seem like a foolish question in a macroeconomics book but, in fact, it is not. GNP is a measure of production. It tells us how much the economy produced during a certain time period. As such, it is a good proxy for employment. However, it is not a very good measure of welfare, even though it is often used as if it were. For example, it is common to compare GNP across countries, or in the same country over time, the implication being that a higher value of GNP indicates an improvement in welfare. But it is quite possible for a rise in GNP to make the inhabitants of a country worse off. Let us see why.

First, GNP does not assign a value to time. Thus, GNP might be increased by people who are working longer hours. This is what actually happened in our economy during World War II. Were the people better off? They had more goods but less leisure. The GNP measure picks up the value of the extra goods, but it ignores the value of leisure. This is relevant in the United States because, over the last 20 years, the average number of hours that we work to produce our GNP has dropped by over four hours per week. A true measure of welfare would make some allowance for the fact that we are now able to produce both more goods and more leisure than we used to.

While the average workweek has fallen in recent years, the number of people in the labor force has risen dramatically. In 1927, only one woman in three was in the labor force; by 1980, over one half of the women were working. GNP does not include the value of nonmarket activity, such as housework. Thus, when women go into the labor force, GNP goes up. But the value of the housework that they used to do has been lost. A proper welfare measure would have a negative offset for the value of time no longer used for nonmarket activities.

A second reason that GNP is a poor measure of welfare is the treatment of depreciation on the capital stock. Depreciation is an estimate of the amount of capital that is worn out or used up in the process of production. A measure of welfare should subtract from production what is necessary to maintain the capital stock. We do this in a crude way by subtracting depreciation from GNP to get **net national product,** or NNP. NNP is a better measure of welfare than GNP, but still it totally ignores depreciation of our inherited stock of natural capital. By natural capital, we mean our country's endowment of natural resources, such as rivers, clean air, and fertile land. The destruction of these resources, caused by production, should be subtracted from GNP just as depreciation is, if we wish to convert GNP from a measure of production to a measure of welfare.

Suppose, for example, that we cut down all our forests in order to produce extra GNP. Granted, our production would be higher: We would have more lumber. But we would also have no forests. The GNP accounts would pick up the value of the extra lumber, but it would make no offsetting depreciation entry for the loss of forests. The same is true with our air and rivers. Both GNP and NNP ignore the reduction in the value of natural capital that occurs during the process of production.

To some extent, the depletion or depreciation of our natural capital is an inevitable result of production. In 1600, the colonists found a continent with an incomparable abundance of natural capital. Over the last 300 years, each generation has added to the stock of man-made capital to be passed on to succeeding generations but has used up the natural capital. NNP picks up the positive contribution of investment but ignores altogether the negative effect of the latter. Whether the first outweighs the second is an important intergenerational welfare question.

Still another factor that ought to be taken into consideration is the distribution of income. Generally it is believed that the less equal the distribution, the lower the level of welfare generated by a given level of income. If a country achieves a rapid growth in GNP at the cost of a rise in income inequality, welfare will probably rise by a good deal less than real income.

Several years ago, William Nordhaus and James Tobin attempted to construct a measure of economic welfare for the United States.[2] Starting with net national product, they added an imputed value for leisure time. They then subtracted expenditures on such things as crime prevention and national defense, on the grounds that such expenditures had been forced on us by the fact that the world had become a more dangerous place in which to live. We were spending more just to maintain our previous level of safety, but this did not make us better off. Finally, they made a small correction for the fact that more of our production was taking place in crowded, polluted, and noisy city environments. Nordhaus and Tobin did not make a correction for the depreciation of our national resource base.

While there is a good deal of arbitrariness in the Nordhaus-Tobin measure of welfare, it is interesting to see the comparison of trends in their measure with trends in NNP. Between 1929 and 1965, NNP in real terms grew by 3.1 percent per year. The welfare measure grew more slowly, at about 2 percent per year. Real product growth rates quite clearly overstate the growth rate of welfare. Indeed, if depreciation of natural resources were included, the net growth rate of welfare may well have been negative, especially in recent years.

The Circular Flow of Income and Expenditure

We return now to the technical problem of measuring GNP. Since GNP is the value of production, we can measure it as either the sum of payments to someone or as the sum of final sales to someone. It will be our purpose in this section to see how

[2]William D. Nordhaus and James Tobin, *Is Growth Obsolete?* (Washington, D.C.: National Bureau of Economic Research, General Series 96, 1972).

Table 2.2
The Components of GNP, 1982

(Payments Side)	($ in billions)
GNP	$3057.5
less: Depreciation	−356.8
equals:	
NNP	2700.7
less: Indirect taxes, business transfers, and government subsidy to public enterprise	−264.3
equals:	
National income	2436.4
less:	
Retained earnings and foreign dividends	−35.3
Corporate profits taxes and social security	−312.5
plus: Government transfers and interest	408.7
Household interest and business transfers	72.3
equals:	
Personal income	2569.6
less: Personal tax payments	−397.2
equals:	
Disposable Personal Income	$2172.4

Note: Figures may not exactly coincide with Figure 2.1, because of rounding.

GNP is divided up among households, business, and government and how these three, in turn, complete the circular flow of income by their respective purchases from business.

To visualize the circular flow, we show what has been inelegantly termed a "plumbing" diagram of the U. S. economy in Figure 2.1. Assuming for the moment that all productive activity takes place in business, we can measure GNP as either the sum of business outlays to the factors of production or as business sales of final goods. These two must be equal, because profits are defined as a residual. We start on the righthand side of the diagram, with GNP broken down by payments. Then we trace out the various subtractions from GNP by government and business, which reduce GNP to disposable income, the net income from production available to households to save or spend. There are several intermediate definitional levels of income generated by this process, each of which is shown and defined in Table 2.2. However, before entering this maze of national income accounting, remember that the important thing to keep in mind is the various items that make up the difference between total and disposable income.

Figure 2.1
Circular Flow of Income, 1980

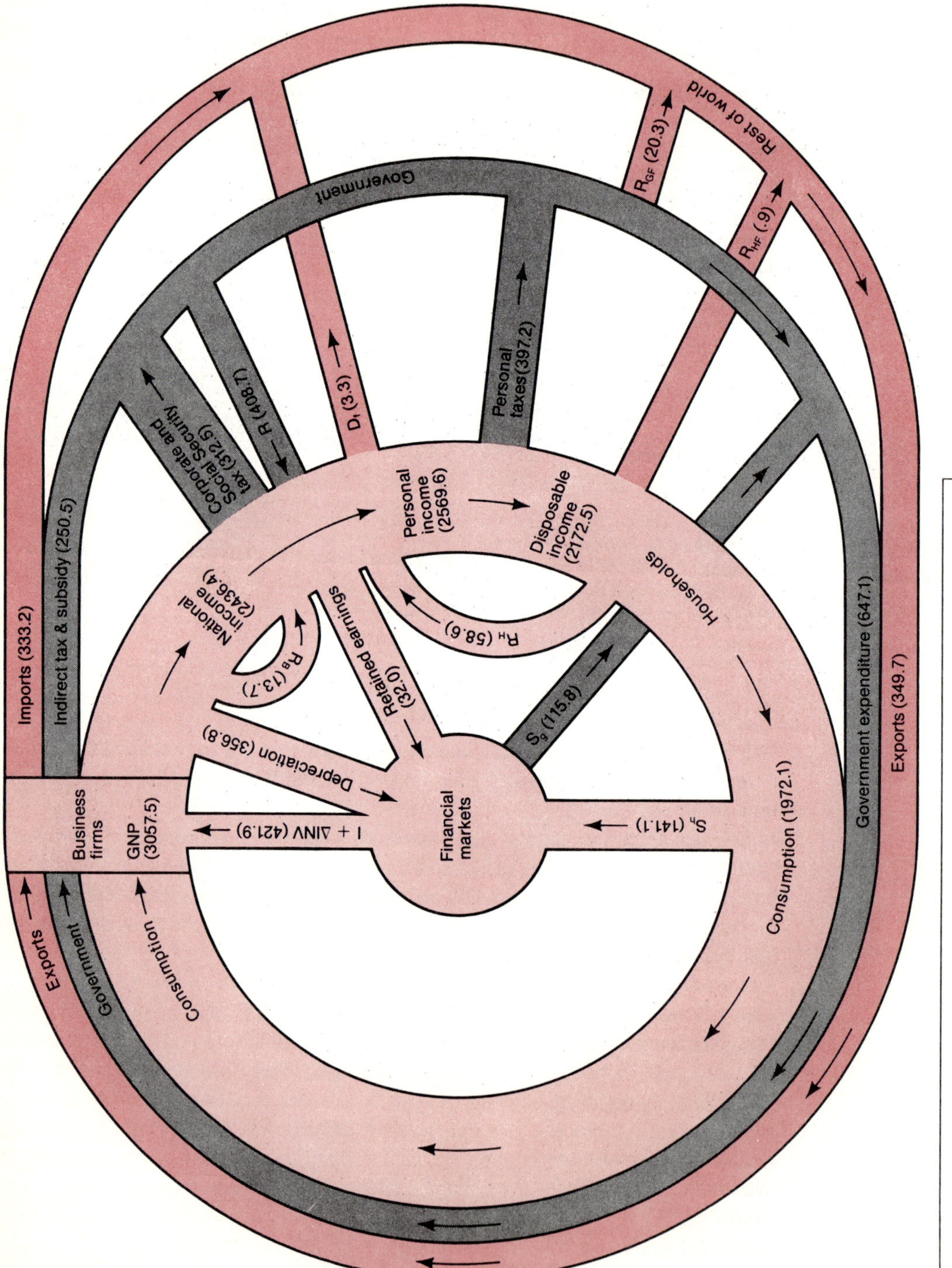

R_B = Business transfers
R = Government transfer payments plus interest
R_H = Household interest payments
R_{HF} = Household transfer payments to rest of world
R_{GF} = Government transfer and interest payments to rest of world
D_F = Dividend payments to rest of world
S_g = Government saving

The value of production, or GNP, is shown at the top of the diagram. By definition it can be decomposed into either payments or sales. (Right- and left-hand sides of diagram). If you follow the payments flow around the diagram, you will see the main diversions from the income stream to the government in the form of taxes, and to business in the form of depreciation and retained earnings. What is left is disposable income with which households may either spend on consumption, save, or make interest payments. An important reverse flow from the government to individuals is transfer payments (R), equal to $408.7 billion in 1982. As you can see, in 1982 the government did not raise enough in taxes to pay for both its expenditures plus its transfers. Thus it had to borrow $115.8 billion from the financial markets. The financial markets are also the source of financing for private investment.

Source: *Economic Report of the President,* (Washington, D.C., 1981).

From GNP to National Income

National income is the sum of payments to the three factors—labor, land, and capital—that combine to produce output. It is calculated by subtracting depreciation, indirect business taxes, and business transfers from GNP and adding subsidies on government enterprise. As we have already seen, depreciation is an estimate of the amount of capital that is worn out or used up in the process of production. It cannot be counted as the income of any of the three factors. Similarly, indirect business taxes, which are sales, luxury, and excise taxes collected by business and paid to government, are subtracted because even though they are part of the gross value of production, they are not paid to any of the three factors of production. Government subsidies to public enterprises are added because here the factors of production receive more than the value of their output; that is, subsidized government enterprises run at a loss.

The breakdown of national income for the United States in 1982 is shown in Table 2.3. As the reader can see, the great bulk of our national income is devoted to labor payments. Despite many people's intuitive feelings to the contrary, less than one dollar in five in the United States goes as payment for the use of capital. We have included the income of self-employed proprietors as a separate line because it is impossible to know what part of their income is a return to labor and what part is a return to the capital they invest in their businesses.

Table 2.3
Distribution of National Income by Factor Share, 1982

	($ in billions)	
	Amount	**Share**
Labor		
Compensation of employees	$1855.9	76.2%
Land		
Rental income of persons	34.1	1.4
Profits		
Corporate profits	161.1	6.6
Interest payments	265.3	10.9
Proprietors income	120.1	4.9
National Income	$2436.5	100.0%

From National Income to Personal Disposable Income

We now complete the division of GNP into business, household, and government income by analyzing the path from national income to **personal disposable income,** which is the household share of GNP. To get disposable income from national income, we subtract retained earnings of business and tax payments to the government by both corporations and individuals, and we add what are called **government transfers.**

Retained earnings of business is the difference between net profit after taxes and dividend payments. In 1982, business earned a net profit before taxes of $161.1 billion. It paid $58.8 billion in taxes to the government and $70.3 billion in dividends to households and foreigners, and it retained the rest, $32.0 billion, for reinvestment. Retained earnings plus the reserve for depreciation is what we will call **gross business saving.**

Transfers are payments by the government to households or individuals not connected with services rendered. They include things like medicare payments, social security benefits, welfare, and food stamps. Interest payments are another type of transfer. They are payments by the government to households on outstanding debt. Transfers are like negative taxes, a large offset to the high level of taxes that we pay to our government. Summing together all the withdrawals and adding the transfers, we are left with a disposable personal income of roughly $2,172 billion, which is approximately 71 percent of GNP. (See Table 2.4.)

Table 2.4
Division of GNP among Households, Business, and Government ($ in billions)

		Share
To business		
Depreciation	$356.8	
Retained earnings and foreign dividends	35.3	
Total	392.1	12.8%
To government		
Indirect taxes	250.6	
Social security + profits	312.5	
Personal income tax	397.2	
Transfers and interest	−408.7	
Total	551.6	18.0
Interest payments by households	−58.6	−1.9
To households		
Disposable Income	2172.5	71.1
Total GNP	$3057.5	100.0%

Note: In Tables 2.4 through 2.9, totals may not agree because of rounding.

The Breakdown of GNP by Recipient Unit and Use

Payment Side

On the payment side, GNP is divided among households, business, and the government. This separation is shown schematically in Table 2.4. One of the striking features of the table is the government accounts. The government collects a very large sum in taxes, almost one-third of GNP, to be exact. But it gives over 40 percent of those taxes back to the private sector in the form of transfers and interest. In effect, a large part of government taxes goes to redistribute income in the private sector rather than to buy goods and services.

Sales Side

We now turn to the sales side of the economic system. Here we shall measure GNP as the value of all final goods produced in the economy. The national income accountants have divided up GNP into four types of goods. We describe each of them in turn.

Consumption As the reader can see in Figure 2.1, the provision of consumption goods ($1972.1 billion, or 64.5 percent of GNP) is the largest use of our productive capacity. Consumption is defined as the sum of newly produced durable and nondurable goods and services purchased by households. It includes haircuts, movies, automobiles, TVs, and so on. It does not include purchases of used goods, such as antiques or cars, because these are not newly produced. In the aggregate, such goods net out because for every purchaser in the private sector there must also be a seller. Purchasers of used goods simply transfer the ownership of assets in the private sector.

Consumption measures expenditures on newly produced commodities by households with one exception—housing. Housing is treated as a capital good in the national accounts, which means that housing construction is considered to be investment, rather than consumption. A capital good is a durable good that yields services over time. Most capital goods—such as factories and machine tools—are used in the process of production. Housing yields its services directly to the owner, but in every key respect conforms to the definition of a capital good. Logically, automobiles and other durables ought also to be included among household capital goods, but they are not.

The part of GNP received by households, as we have seen, is personal disposable income. Households save part, spend part on interest payments, and spend the rest on consumption. In 1982, the allocation was as shown in Table 2.5.

What is immediately apparent from Table 2.5 is the small share of saving in personal disposable income. As we shall see in Chapter 11, saving is beginning to rebound after reaching very low levels in 1980. But even under the best of circumstances, it has never amounted to more than 7–8 percent of disposable income. Furthermore, there has been a sharp rise in both household indebtedness and interest rates in recent years, with the result that interest payments by households now take a sizable fraction of income that used to be saved.

Investment The second component of GNP is **investment** ($421.9 billion, or 13.8 percent of GNP), defined as the total production of new capital goods plus any change in inventories. Recall that capital goods are durable producer goods, including housing. The sum of all capital goods in the economy is called the **capital stock.** It is made up of all our factories, machines, roads, dams, and housing.

Investment is the addition that we make to the capital stock in any year. It is the part of production that we set aside to replace and expand the stock of man-made capital to be used in the future. In recent years, people have been paying more attention to investment, because it is the component of GNP that has most to do with our ability to grow, to provide new jobs, and to increase worker productivity. As we shall see, economic growth and a rising standard of living both require a rising stock of capital, because it is new machines that make possible new and more productive ways of making things. All of these desirable outcomes require a high level of investment.

Yet, the level of investment in the United States is lower than in virtually any other developed country. Gross investment in 1982 amounted to only 13.8 percent of GNP, compared to an investment ratio of 23 percent in Canada, 24 percent in

Table 2.5
Allocation of Disposable Income, 1982 ($ in billions)

	Amount	Share of Disposable Income
Consumption	$1972.1	90.8%
Saving	141.1	6.5
Interest payments	58.6	2.7
Payments to rest of world	.9	
Total of disposable income	$2172.7	100.0%

Note: Because of rounding, total does not agree exactly with Table 2.4.

Table 2.6
Components of Investment, 1982 ($ in billions)

Fixed investment	
Nonhousing	$347.5
Housing	95.8
Total	443.3
Change in inventories	−21.4
Total investment	$421.9
Reserve for depreciation	$356.8

France, 22 percent in Germany, and 32 percent in Japan.[3] But that isn't all. These figures include replacement. No one knows exactly what actual capital depreciation is, but it must consume a large part—at least one-half—of our gross investment. Furthermore, as Table 2.6 indicates, a substantial part of the remainder is devoted to housing. On balance, the amount of net investment on additions to plant and equipment must be quite small. It is this fact which has led recent administrations to look for ways to stimulate additional investment.

Government Expenditure Government expenditure on goods and services ($647.1 billion, or 21.2 percent of GNP) is the third component of GNP. Note that this category includes *only* government expenditures on such things as salaries of government employees and soldiers, tanks, battleships, and dams. It does not include transfer payments, such as welfare or retirement. That is because transfers are not part of production. Thus, there are two distinct notions of government

[3]These figures are for 1977.

Table 2.7
Government Expenditures as a Fraction of GNP (various years)

	Purchases of Goods and Services as a Fraction of GNP		Government Transfers as a Fraction of GNP
	Federal	State and Local	
1960	10.6%	9.2%	5.3%
1964	10.2	10.1	5.5
1968	11.2	11.6	6.5
1972	8.6	12.8	8.4
1976	7.5	13.6	10.8
1980	7.6	12.8	10.8
1982	8.4	12.7	13.4

Source: *Economic Report of the President,* (Washington, D.C., 1983).

expenditure, which are important to distinguish. One is the total number of dollars spent by the government. The other is government expenditure on goods and services. The first category is equal to the second, plus transfers. The former is the concept one needs to use when calculating government deficits. But, from the national-accounts perspective, it is only government expenditure on goods and services that is relevant, because it measures the fraction of production that goes to the government.

In the United States, government transfer payments are very large, but the government expenditure share of GNP is not. The government taxes away from us about one dollar out of every three that we earn, but on goods and services it spends only about one dollar in five of GNP (see Table 2.7). Those who think that government is too big tend to look at the gross burden of taxes, which is 31.4 percent of GNP. Those who think it is too small subtract transfers and point out that the government spends around 21 percent of GNP, which is small compared to other countries. Whatever the case, it is important to realize that in the United States the tax system is being used to substantially redistribute income among households in the private sector.

Since the 1970s, many people have become convinced that in the United States the government has grown much too fast relative to GNP, and that it now controls too large a fraction of our productive resources. When thinking about this issue, it is crucial to distinguish between what the government spends on goods and services and what it spends on transfers. It is the latter category that has been growing in recent years, not the former. Furthermore, it is state and local government expenditures that have been growing in relative terms, not the federal government's. This can be clearly seen in Table 2.7. All this should be kept in mind when we send politicians to Washington to cut expenditures. The main place where Washington can cut is in transfer payments. To reduce the fraction of goods

Table 2.8
Government Expenditures as a Fraction of GNP, 1977, in Various Countries

U.S.	18%
U.K.	21
Germany	20
Sweden	28
France	16
Japan	11
Switzerland	13

Source: World Bank, *World Development Report 1979.*

and services going to the government, we would be better off sending our cost-cutters to the states and the cities.

To put the size of government in perspective, refer to Table 2.8, which shows some comparative data from other western countries. As the reader can see, the United States is not really out of line with other countries, particularly considering the size of U. S. defense expenditures (about 6 percent of GNP) relative to other countries. Whether one thinks we have too much or too little government spending, international evidence shows that we do not spend more on government than the other industrialized countries, particularly when defense is excluded.

Net Exports The final category of goods into which we will divide GNP is net exports, defined as exports and imports. Exports ($349.7 billion, or 11.4 percent of GNP) include all sales of goods and services to foreigners. Imports ($332.2 billion, or 10.9 percent of GNP) are purchases of goods and services from foreigners. Imports are a net subtraction from total sales. If they are final goods, like Datsuns or French wine, they directly satisfy the demand by U. S. purchasers for final goods. If they are intermediate goods, such as crude oil, they are included in the value of domestic final goods and have to be subtracted in calculating the value of domestic production. In either case, it is customary to subtract imports from exports to get the net effect of the foreign sector on demand. For the United States, exports have exceeded imports for most of the postwar period, adding slightly to domestic demand.

A Fundamental Identity

We are now ready to combine the two sides of the GNP accounts into one single equation. Since the value of what is produced is paid out to either business, government, or households, and since these must either spend their receipts on output or save them, we shall be able to derive a very important identity between investment and saving.

Taking the sales side first, we divided GNP into consumption goods, investment goods, government, and net exports:

(2.1) $$Y \equiv C + I + \Delta INV + G + E - M.$$

Y = GNP
C = consumption
I = fixed investment
ΔINV = change in inventories
G = government expenditure on goods and services
E = exports
M = imports

We write this equation with an $\equiv$, which means that the relationship is always true, by definition. Y is equal to GNP, the value of production in the economy. All the items on the right-hand side of Equation (2.1), except ΔINV, are elements of final sales. We could, therefore, rewrite Equation (2.1), as:

(2.2) $$\text{Production} \equiv GNP \equiv Y \equiv \text{Sales} + \Delta INV.$$

Equation (2.2) says that the value of production equals the value of sales plus inventory changes. When production exceeds sales, inventories rise and the term ΔINV is positive. When production is less than sales, inventories fall.

Going back to our plumbing diagram, Figure 2.1, we showed how GNP was divided up among households, business, and government. Combining all the different components of taxes into one item, T, we have:

(2.3) $$Y \equiv Y_D + T - R + S_b - R_H + D_f.$$

Y_D = personal disposable income
T = total tax payments
R = transfers plus interest
S_b = gross business saving = retained earnings plus depreciation
R_H = interest payments by households
D_f = dividend payments to foreigners

Now we set Equation (2.3) equal to Equation (2.1) to get:

(2.4) $$C + I + \Delta INV + G + E - M = Y_D + T - R + S_b - R_H - D_f$$

We are now going to rewrite Equation (2.4) in terms of four sources of saving. In order to do that we first define what these four sources are. They are:

1. Household saving: the difference between disposable income and expenditures on consumption, interest payments, and transfers to foreigners (R_{HF}).

$$S_h = Y_D - C - R_H - R_{HF}$$

2. Government saving: the difference between government tax receipts and its total expenditure including G, R, and transfers to foreigners (R_{GF}).

$$S_g = T - R - G - R_{GH}$$

3. Business saving: the sum of depreciation plus retained earnings.

4. Foreign saving: the sum of imports plus all transfer payments and dividends less exports.

$$S_f = M - E + D_f + R_{HF} + R_{GF}$$

Now we are ready to rewrite Equation (2.4). First collect terms in a way which makes the relationship between investment and total saving clearer.

(2.4a) $$I + \Delta INV \equiv \overbrace{\{Y_D - C - R_H\}}^{S_h + R_{HF}} + \overbrace{\{T - R - G\}}^{S_g + R_{GF}} + S_b + M - E + D_f$$

(2.4b) $$\equiv S_h + S_g + S_b + \overbrace{\{M - E + D_f + R_{HF} + R_{GF}\}}^{S_f}$$

(2.4c) $$\equiv S_h + S_g + S_b + S_f$$

(2.5) $$I + \Delta INV \equiv S_T$$

From the definitions of S_h and S_g one can see that the first two bracketed terms in Equation (2.4a) are just household and government saving plus foreign transfers. Hence if we rewrite the equation inserting these terms, we see at once that the entire right hand side of the equation is decomposable into three domestic sources of saving, plus four terms which we shall call *foreign saving*. It measures the difference between imports plus transfers and exports. If imports are greater than exports, domestic investment does not have to be matched by domestic saving. In effect, some investment goods can be made available from abroad through imports, rather than by the government or households holding down their expenditures, so that the investment goods might be produced domestically. In that case, investment is matched by foreign, rather than domestic, saving. In the U. S. economy, S_f is generally quite small, so that one can almost say that investment must be matched by some form of domestic saving.

Equation 2.5 is a fundamental identity in economics. It tells us that by definition, in any economy, total investment including inventory changes must be matched by some form of saving. Furthermore that saving must come from one of four sources, three domestic and one foreign. Let us see how Equation (2.5) was satisfied in 1982. Again using Table 2.4 and the data presented in Figure 2.1, we can derive Table 2.9. It tells us clearly that the main source of saving to finance investment in the United States is business saving. Household saving just barely offsets the negative saving (deficit) of the government.

Now look back at the financial market in the center of Figure 2.1. Private and business saving are inflows of funds to the capital market. Investment and govern-

Table 2.9
Components of Saving, 1982 ($ in billions)

Household		
Y_D	$2172.5	
less: C	−1972.1	
less: R_H	− 58.6	
less: R_F	− .9	
equals: S_h	141.2	$141.2 Household saving
Government		
T (net of subsidies to government enterprise)	960.2	
less: G	−647.1	
less: R_{GH}	−408.7	
less: R_{GF}	− 20.3	
equals: S_g	−115.8	−115.8 Government saving
Business		
Depreciation	356.8	
Retained earnings (Net of D_f)	32.0	
equals: S_b	388.8	388.8 Business saving
Foreign sector		
M	333.2	
less: E	−349.7	
plus: R_{GF}	20.3	
plus: R_F	.9	
plus: D_F	3.3	
equals: S_F	8.0	8.0 Foreign saving
Statistical discrepancy		− .3
Total		421.9 Gross investment

D_f = Dividend payments to foreigners
R_F = Household transfers to foreigners
R_{GF} = Government interest and transfer payments to foreigners

ment deficits are outflows. The function of the financial markets, which we examine more closely in Chapters 13 and 14, is to match savers and borrowers. One major borrower is private investors. Another, unfortunately, is the government. Rather than being a source of saving, the government ran a large deficit which had to be financed by diverting private saving away from private investors. One could say that government borrowing crowded private investors out of the financial markets. Large government deficits have been an unfortunate feature of the U. S. economy in recent years. Unless private saving can be increased to match government deficits, or the deficits themselves can be brought under control, they will crowd out private investment.

We are going to make much use of Equation (2.5) throughout this text. As we shall see in the next chapter, it becomes the basic equilibrium condition of our model of aggregate demand. Also, when we consider the problem of economic growth and how investment should be increased in order to improve productivity, Equation (2.5) reminds us that any such rise in I must be matched by saving. Either business must be allowed to depreciate assets more rapidly, households must be given greater incentives to save, or the government must reduce its deficits through higher taxes or lower levels of expenditures. None of these is easy to accomplish.

Real and Nominal GNP

One of the important corrections that must be made in comparing and interpreting the movement of GNP over time is to separate that part of the change stemming from rising prices from the part due to changing production. GNP is always reported in current dollars. We call this measure **nominal GNP.** But because we are interested in GNP as a measure of production, we want a GNP measure that is independent of prices. This we shall call **real GNP.** Real GNP is defined as the value that GNP would take if prices were constant. Obviously, real GNP is a hypothetical construct. How is it measured?

In a simple economy, one would calculate the value of total production using the prices of some base year. For example, suppose we had an economy producing cars, bread, and oranges in the amounts and prices for 1972 and 1980 shown in Table 2.10.

The top two parts of the table show the nominal GNP for 1972 and 1980 for an economy with rising prices. Nominal GNP rises from \$13 million to \$21,450,000, an increase of 65 percent. What part of that increase is due to rising production and what part to rising prices? To find out, we calculate 1980's GNP in the prices for 1972. It is \$14.3 million. This is what GNP would have been in 1980 had there been no increase in prices. Thus, the increase in real GNP is 10%.[4]

We now use the example to calculate the **GNP deflator,** which is the price index for GNP. The GNP deflator is defined as the ratio of nominal to real GNP and is written:

$$P = \frac{GNP_N}{GNP_{REAL}} \times 100.$$

The GNP deflator tells us how much GNP rose simply because prices went up. In our example, the deflator for 1980 is:

$$P_{1980} = \frac{21{,}450}{14{,}300} \times 100 = 150.$$

[4]The percentage rise in real GNP is the difference between real GNP in 1980 and 1972 expressed as a percentage of 1972; that is,

$$\frac{14{,}300{,}000 - 13{,}000{,}000}{13{,}000{,}000} = .10.$$

Table 2.10
Calculating Real and Nominal GNP

Nominal GNP, 1972

Commodity	Price	Quantity	Sales
Cars	$5,000.00	1,000	$ 5,000,000
Bread	.50	10,000,000	5,000,000
Oranges	.30	10,000,000	3,000,000
Total			$13,000,000

Nominal GNP, 1980

Commodity	Price	Quantity	Sales
Cars	$8,000.00	1,100	$ 8,800,000
Bread	.75	11,000,000	8,250,000
Oranges	.40	11,000,000	4,400,000
Total			$21,450,000

Real GNP in 1980: 1980 Quantity × 1972 Prices

Commodity	Price	Quantity	Sales
Cars	$5,000.00	1,100	$ 5,500,000
Bread	.50	11,000,000	5,500,000
Oranges	.30	11,000,000	3,300,000
Total			$14,300,000 (1980 GNP in 1972 prices)

Another way to think of the deflator is that it measures how much more one would have had to spend to buy 1980's GNP at the prices of 1980 rather than of 1972:

$$\frac{(\$21,450 - \$14,300)}{\$14,300} = .50.$$

Rising prices have caused a 50-percent increase in the cost of 1980's GNP. Accordingly, we say that the GNP deflator has risen by 50 percent between 1972 and 1980.

To summarize this discussion, we have the following important relationship:

(2.6)
$$GNP_{REAL} = \frac{GNP_{NOM}}{P}.$$

In general, it is possible to deflate any nominal magnitude by an appropriate price index to separate out the effect of real changes and inflation. In addition to real GNP, another important real magnitude is the **real wage,** W/P. The expression

Figure 2.2
Real and Nominal GNP, 1947–1982

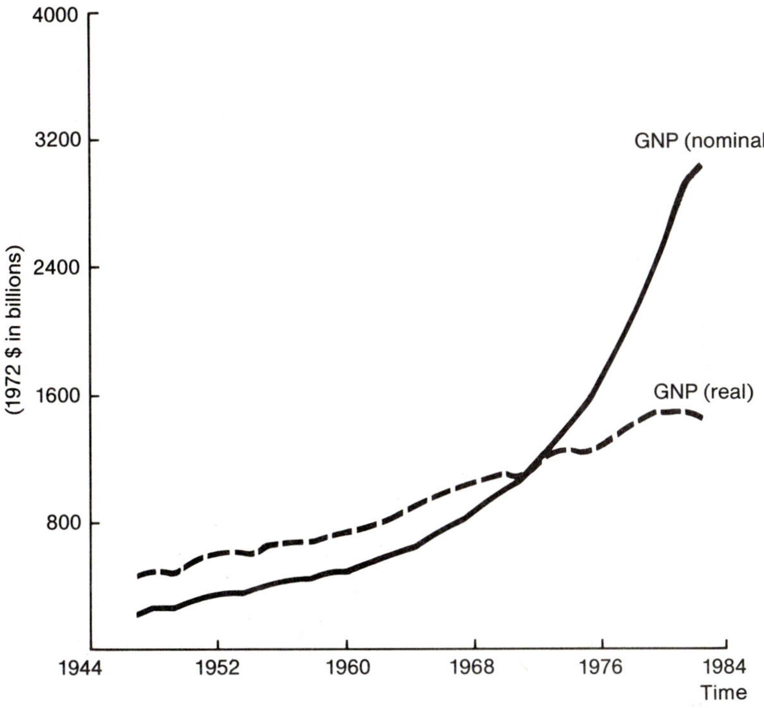

W/P corrects money wages for changes in the cost of living. It tells us the real purchasing power represented by the nominal wage *W*.

When the inflation rate rises, as it has in the United States, real and nominal magnitudes can, and have, moved in the opposite direction, as one can see in Figures 2.2 and 2.3. For example, consider the two GNP series in Figure 2.2. By looking at the real value of GNP, one can see that since 1968 the United States has had three recessions, or periods of falling real output. But these recessions are disguised by rising prices in the nominal GNP line in the figure. The same disparity between real and nominal magnitudes can be seen with even greater clarity in the two wage series in Figure 2.3. Money wages have risen very rapidly every year since 1968. Yet the real wage peaked in 1973. The post–oil-embargo world has been one in which inflation has completely offset any wage increases gained by the U. S. labor force. The dismally flat wage line in Figure 2.3 tells as well as anything the difficulties of the U. S. economy in recent years. No one in our inflationary world can afford not to understand the difference between nominal and real magnitudes. For most purposes, the real value is the more significant of the two.

Figure 2.3
Real and Nominal Wages, 1947–1982

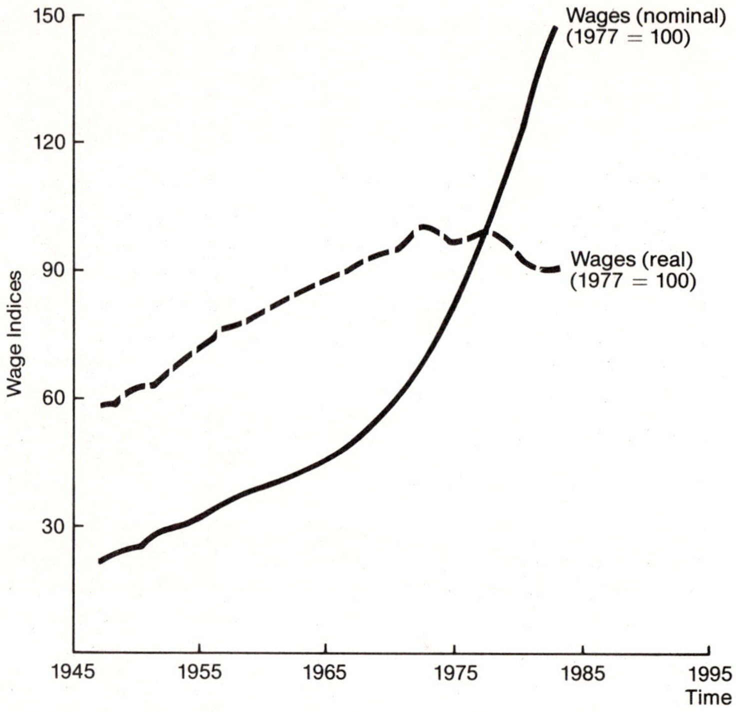

Basic Price Indices

In the United States there are three basic price indices: the **GNP deflator,** the **consumer price index** (CPI), and the **producers price index** (PPI). The GNP deflator, which we have just discussed, is our best measure of the changing prices of currently produced output. Unlike the CPI, this index does not reflect items such as used housing, secondhand cars, or imported oil, all of which directly affect the CPI. The GNP deflator is collected and published quarterly by the Department of Commerce, the agency of the government in charge of all national income accounts. The GNP deflator is the ratio of nominal to real GNP, and the base year used by the Department of Commerce is 1972.

The Consumer Price Index (CPI)

The CPI, calculated and published monthly by the Bureau of Labor Statistics (BLS), measures the cost of a market basket of goods and services purchased by the average urban consumer. Since expenditure patterns change, the weights of the various components of the market basket are periodically updated by means of an extensive consumer survey. The most recent update took place in 1972–1973. Given the market basket, the BLS calculates the CPI by constructing a weighted average of the price indices for each of the components. In this way, individual price changes are weighted according to their importance in the average consumer's budget. Formally, the CPI is:[5]

$$\text{CPI} = \sum_{i=1}^{n} d_i P_i.$$

d_i = share of good i in consumer market basket
P_i = price index for commodity i, base year equal to 100

The CPI is our most closely watched price index, partly because it is our closest measure of changes in the cost of living, but also because it is used to adjust retirement benefits and wage payments for workers with cost-of-living clauses. Currently, more than 8.5 million workers are covered by such agreements, as well as all social security beneficiaries and food stamp recipients.

There has been a good deal of criticism of the CPI in recent years, largely because of its treatment of housing costs. Housing prices and interest rates have both been rising rapidly in recent years. Yet most people own their own homes, and they are not affected on a month-to-month basis by the rise in housing prices. Indeed, one could argue that homeowners benefit from such a housing inflation, since their net worth rises. The problem is, what proportion of households purchase houses each month? In essence, the BLS is accused of overestimating this percentage quite drastically, and thus seriously overstating the true rise in the cost of living to the average household.

The Producers Price Index (PPI)

The producers price index is collected and published monthly by the Bureau of Labor Statistics. It is based on the prices of commodities at the wholesale level. It is not a good measure of the cost of living, because it does not include services such as health, rent, and education. Furthermore, it counts input prices more than once, thus pyramiding the effects of any changes in these prices. For example, a rise in the price of oil shows up directly, then again as a rise in the price of fertilizer and plastic, and finally as a rise in the price of the products using plastics or fertilizers as inputs. Probably indices for individual commodity groups, published as subindices of the PPI, are more useful than the PPI itself.

Summary

The important ideas that you should retain from this chapter are how GNP is measured, how it is split up among households, government, and business, and how in turn their spending completes the circular flow of income. We used the

[5] The symbol Σ means the sum of each of the i elements to the right of the sign.

circular flow to derive a very important identity between total investment in the economy and four sources of saving. What is not consumed by households or spent by the government is saved; what is saved is invested. Any increase in saving must by definition be matched by an increase in investment and any increase in investment by an increase in saving. We shall use this concept in deriving a model of aggregate demand in the next chapter.

Having learned how to measure GNP and how GNP is divided up into various components, we are ready to build a model for GNP. That model will contain both demand and supply features. For convenience in the next several chapters, we shall concentrate first on the demand size. We shall build a mathematical model of aggregate demand. That model will have behavioral equations for household consumption and investment. It will also have to contain equations reflecting the influence of financial markets, because these affect consumption and investment. Subsequently, if the model we shall develop accurately portrays behavior, it should quite accurately predict total demand. If it can do that, it will be a useful tool in helping policymakers to avoid the twin dangers of recession and inflation. With that goal in mind, we turn now to the task of constructing a model of aggregate demand.

Key Concepts

gross national product
double counting
net national product
national income
personal disposable income
government transfers
gross business saving
capital stock
investment
nominal GNP
real GNP
GNP deflator
real wage
consumer price index
producers price index

Problems and Questions for Discussion

1. Which of the following are included as fixed investment in the national accounts?
   a. Ms. Jones's purchase of 100 shares of General Motors stock.
   b. Mr. Smith's purchase of a newly constructed house.
   c. Hertz's purchase of 1000 cars for its rental car fleet.
   d. General Dynamics' acquisition of a smaller company.
   e. Mr. Ralph's purchase of a car for his personal use.
   f. TVA's construction of a nuclear power plant.
   g. Ms. Carroll's deposit of $1000 into her savings account at the bank.
2. Which of the following are included in consumption in the national accounts?
   a. New housing purchases.
   b. Used housing purchases.
   c. New automobile purchases.

d. Value of production of home vegetable gardens.

e. Baby-sitting expenses paid by a family while both parents work.

3. Prove that the difference between saving and fixed investment is equal to the difference between sales and production.

4. Suppose that while on vacation in Florida you find some Spanish gold. Does this discovery increase GNP? Is GNP increased when you sell the gold you have found? If you now go out and celebrate your good luck by purchasing a new Camaro, does that purchase represent an increase in GNP? If so, where has production increased? If not, since your purchase represents an increase in consumption, how is the national accounting identity satisfied?

5. Interest on government debt is treated as a transfer payment. How is interest on private debt handled? Why doesn't disposable income have a term for interest receipts from private debt?

6. Two alternative ways to measure the relative size of government are the ratios G/Y and T/Y. What are the differences between the two? For what purposes might you want to use one ratio or the other? Which do you prefer and why?

7. Suppose that we have the following data for a hypothetical economy:

GNP = \$1000
Gross profits (before depreciation) = \$250
Depreciation = \$100
Dividends = \$100
Taxes = \$250
Government expenditure on goods and services = \$200
Government transfer payments = \$100
Exports = \$100
Imports = \$100
Gross investment = \$150

Using the above information, and assuming business tax payments are zero, calculate the following:

a. NNP
b. Disposable income
c. Business saving
d. Government saving
e. Household saving
f. Foreign saving

To check your answers, show that the four sources of saving are equal to gross investment.

8. Suppose that we have the following two historical series (in billions of dollars):

	Nominal GNP	Real GNP
1979	\$2414	\$1483
1980	2626	1481
1981	2922	1510

What is the value of the GNP price index for 1980 and 1981? What was the rate of inflation between 1979 and 1980? Between 1980 and 1981? What was the rate of growth of real GNP between 1979 and 1980?

9. Suppose that prices and output in a hypothetical economy are the following:

1975

Commodity	Price	Quantity
Meat	$4000	1,000,000 tons
Clothing	500	10,000,000 units
Automobiles	7000	6,000,000 units

1980

Commodity	Price	Quantity
Meat	$4500	1,200,000 tons
Clothing	750	11,100,000 units
Automobiles	7500	5,000,000 units

a. Calculate the increase in real and nominal income between 1975 and 1980.
b. Setting the GNP price index equal to 100 in 1975, what is the value of the price index in 1980?
c. What proportion of the increase in nominal income was caused by an increase in real GNP, and what proportion was due to the change in prices?

PART TWO

THE THEORY OF AGGREGATE DEMAND

Chapter 3

A Model of Aggregate Demand in a Simple Economy

In this chapter we present our first models of aggregate demand. Demand, together with supply, which we will deal with in Chapters 6–9, determines the level of real income, employment, and prices in the economy. Aggregate demand is of course influenced by many things—consumer optimism, government policy, the level of private sector liquidity, and other random factors. As economists, our job is to find an explanation for demand which is simple enough to be useful and yet which reflects as many of the important influences as possible. In this chapter we shall construct several simple models of the demand side of the economy. They will include the link between consumption, income, and taxes, but they will ignore the influence of financial factors on the level of aggregate spending. Those factors will be added to our basic model in Chapter 4.

We convert the demand model into an explanation for real income by making the implicit assumption that supply always reacts passively to the level of real demand in the economy. This is equivalent to assuming that prices are constant, an assumption we shall maintain until Chapter 6, when we begin to consider the determinants of aggregate supply.

The Logic of Macroeconomic Models

To describe and understand macroeconomic processes, our basic tool will be the **macroeconomic model,** or macromodel. A macroeconomic model is a representation of the economy in terms of a set of behavioral equations, definitions, and identities. These equations can be "solved" for an **equilibrium,** which is a set of values for each of the variables in the model that simultaneously satisfies all the equations. The model contains all the relationships that the model builder thinks are essential, and the solution tells hypothetically how the economy will behave when disturbed in certain ways. If the model is a good representation of the economy, it will have a good deal of predictive power. It will approximate, or track, the economy very closely. Obviously, a good model of the economy would be a very useful tool in helping both the government and the private sector to predict the level of economic activity. Indeed, that has been the chief use of most of the macromodels built in recent years. At one time it was hoped that our models would become so accurate that the government could use them to control the economy, by adjusting its spending or taxes in such a way as to offset unwanted fluctuations in private-sector spending. So far, however, our models are not accurate enough to permit this. Many doubt that they will ever be.

In building models, it is useful to distinguish between two types of variables in the equations: *endogenous* and *exogenous*.

Endogenous variables are variables whose values are determined by, or within, the model. Examples in the typical macromodel are income, prices, consumption, and employment.

Exogenous variables are variables whose values are determined outside the model. Some examples of exogenous variables are foreign prices, technology, and weather. The values of exogenous variables are thus independent of the model, whereas the values of endogenous variables are determined by the model and are thus dependent on it.

A particularly important set of exogenous variables consists of those under the control of the government, such as taxes, the money supply, and government expenditure. These variables are exogenous because they are determined by government decision rather than by the economic system. When building a model, the economist can choose whether to treat a particular variable as exogenous or endogenous.

Schematically, one could represent a macromodel as shown in figure 3.1. The model of the economy is a set of equations containing both endogenous and exogenous variables. When one assigns values to each of the exogenous variables, the model can be solved for the equilibrium values of each of the endogenous variables. Equilibrium is therefore the solution of the model. It gives a predicted value for each endogenous variable.

One major use for models is to examine how each endogenous variable reacts to changes in any exogenous variable. To do this, we change the particular exogenous variable whose effect we are investigating and compare the solution values for each endogenous variable. This will be particularly relevant in using government policy variables to control the economy. Economists call this type of methodology **comparative statics.** Comparative statics is the study of the changes in equilibrium caused by changes in exogenous variables. It does not worry about how the economy gets from one equilibrium position to another—that is the province of *dynamics*. For example, suppose the government increases its spending by $1 billion. Comparative statics analysis will tell us what will happen to the economy after all adjustments in production and spending have taken place. Dynamics will tell us exactly how the economy will reach its new equilibrium position; it may even predict how long the process will take.

Figure 3.1
A Schematic of a Macromodel
Given particular values for each exogenous variable, the model determines equilibrium values for each endogenous variable.

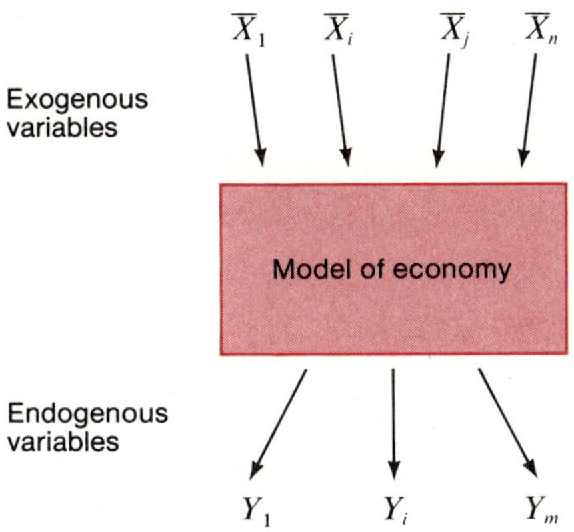

A Simple Model of Real Aggregate Demand

Now that we have had an abstract introduction to what a model is and what it can do, let us construct a simple model of real aggregate demand and see how it works. In Chapter 2 we discussed how aggregate demand is typically divided up into household consumption, business and household investment, government expenditure on goods and services, and net exports. To simplify things at the outset, we shall ignore the foreign sector and write total demand as:

(3.1) $$D = C + \overline{I} + \overline{G}.$$

D = total sales or demand
C = consumption
$\overline{I}$ = gross fixed investment
$\overline{G}$ = government expenditure on goods and services

In this model we shall assume that both investment and government expenditures are exogenous, which we shall indicate by writing a bar over each variable. We are then left with the question of what determines household consumption. (A great deal of research, which we will analyze in Chapter 11, has been devoted to this question.)

Broadly speaking, it appears that the main influence on real consumption is real household disposable income. The consumption of the typical household is positively related to its disposable income. Empirically, a linear relationship of the following type fits the observed data quite well:

(3.2) $$C = \bar{C} + cY_d.$$

$\bar{C}$ = autonomous consumer expenditures
c = marginal propensity to consume = the change in real consumption per unit change in real disposable income
Y_d = real disposable income

Equation (3.2) is called a consumption function. On a graph of consumption and disposable income, it is a straight line with intercept $\bar{C}$ and slope equal to c (see Figure 3.2). The slope of the consumption function, c, is sometimes called the **marginal propensity to consume,** or MPC. The MPC is defined as the change in consumption per unit change in disposable income. The larger the MPC, the steeper will be the consumption function in Figure 3.2.

Consumption depends on disposable income. In this first model, we shall ignore business saving and transfers and set disposable income equal to total production minus taxes. We shall treat taxes as exogenous variables and write the equation for disposable income as:

(3.3) $$Y_d = Y - \bar{T}.$$

Y = total production or income
$\bar{T}$ = taxes

Our final model equation is an equilibrium condition that requires that supply be equal to demand. It is:

(3.4) $$Y = D.$$

Y = production or supply
D = sales or demand

Equation (3.4) says that in equilibrium sales must equal production or, equivalently, that demand must equal supply. If that condition is not met, business will find that it is either accumulating or running down inventories—for by definition, Production = Sales + change in inventory (ΔINV). Therefore, we can write our basic equilibrium condition in a form equivalent to Equation (3.4) as:

(3.4a) $$\Delta INV = \text{Unintended inventory investment} = 0.$$

We shall consider all inventory changes as an indicator of disequilibrium in the economy. When inventories are increasing supply is greater than demand, and one should expect business to cut back on production. When inventories are falling demand is greater than supply, and production should be increased. Both of these patterns are strongly confirmed by observation. In our model we are looking for an equilibrium, by which we mean a point at which we expect income to stay constant. Hence it is natural to use the condition that inventories be constant or, equivalently, that sales equal production (Equation [3.4]) as the basic equilibrium condition.

Figure 3.2
The Consumption Function

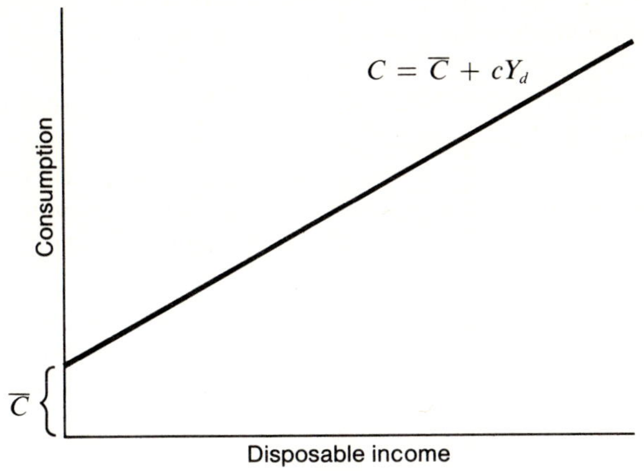

The reader should note that not all inventory changes in an economy are unintended. Business maintains a certain desired ratio of inventory to sales. Whenever sales increase, inventories should increase too. Similarly, inventories may vary with the interest rate. However, in equilibrium, desired inventories will be constant, and therefore our equilibrium condition that $\Delta INV = 0$ is still valid.

In the diagram of sales and production or income in Figure 3.3, Equation (3.4) is represented as a 45° line. Above this line, sales are greater than production, so inventories are falling; below the line, the opposite is true. Any point on the line is an equilibrium in the goods market, because sales equal production. Therefore, if the economy is above the line, we should expect output to be increasing; below the line, it should be falling.

We now have the four basic equations for our model in Figure 3.1. We repeat them for convenience.

(3.1) $$D = C + \overline{I} + \overline{G}.$$

(3.2) $$C = \overline{C} + cY_d.$$

(3.3) $$Y_d = Y - \overline{T}.$$

(3.4) $$Y = D.$$

The endogenous variables are Y_d, C, Y, and D; the exogenous variables are $\overline{T}$, $\overline{G}$, $\overline{I}$, and $\overline{C}$. When we assign values to each of the barred exogenous variables, the model will give us predicted values for each of the four endogenous variables.

Figure 3.3
A Diagram of the Equilibrium Condition in the Goods Market
Above the 45° line demand is greater than supply, or sales are greater than production. Inventories are falling, which should induce producers to increase production. Below the line supply is greater than demand, which should mean a decline in production. The 45° line itself is where production equals sales, or where supply equals demand; unintended inventory investment is zero. This line represents equilibrium in the goods market.

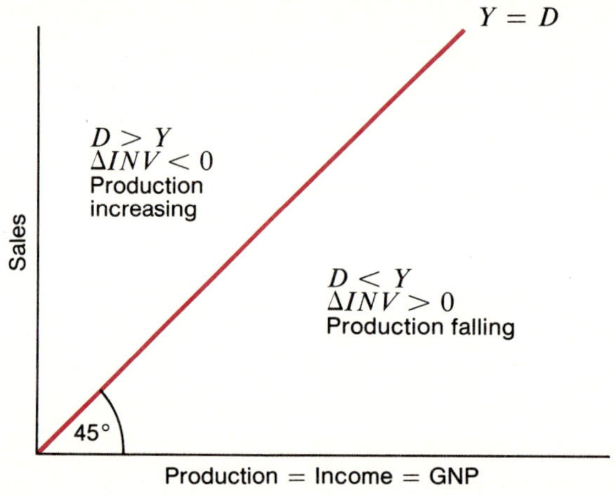

Mathematical Solution of the Model

Let us now see how we can solve our model. This turns out to be an easy task. First, substitute Equation (3.4) into Equation (3.1) to get:

(3.5) $$Y = C + \bar{I} + \bar{G}.$$

Next, substitute Equation (3.2) and Equation (3.3) into Equation (3.5) to get:

(3.6) $$Y = \bar{C} + c(Y - \bar{T}) + \bar{I} + \bar{G}.$$

Finally, simplify Equation (3.6) to get an equation that expresses Y as a function of exogenous variables:

(3.7) $$Y = \frac{\bar{C} - c\bar{T} + \bar{I} + \bar{G}}{1 - c}.$$

Reducing still further, we get:

(3.7a) $$Y = \frac{A}{1 - c}$$

$$A = \bar{C} - c\bar{T} + \bar{I} + \bar{G}.$$

The term A is the sum of all expenditure that does not depend on income. For this reason we shall call A **total autonomous expenditure.**

Equation (3.7) is what economists call a **reduced-form equation,** which means an equation in which one endogenous variable is shown as a function of only exogenous variables. If we assign values to each exogenous variable and if we have values for each behavioral parameter, the reduced-form equation gives us the equilibrium value for one of the endogenous variables. In our case, Equation (3.7) tells us the equilibrium value for income.

There are reduced-form equations for each of the endogenous variables. The equations for consumption and disposable income can be easily obtained by substituting Equation (3.7) into Equations (3.2) and (3.3). Thus, the reduced-form equation for Y_d is:

(3.8) $$Y_d = \frac{\bar{C} + \bar{I} + \bar{G} - \bar{T}}{1 - c}.$$

Similarly, the reduced-form equation for C can be obtained by substituting Equation (3.8) into Equation (3.2):

(3.9) $$C = \frac{\bar{C} + c(\bar{I} + \bar{G} - \bar{T})}{1 - c}.$$

These reduced-form equations will be useful when we analyze the effect on equilibrium of changes in our exogenous variables. First however, we go back and show our equilibrium solution for income in a diagram. To do this, we combine Equations (3.1) through (3.3) to show total demand as a function of income:

$$\begin{aligned} D &= C + \bar{I} + \bar{G} \\ &= \bar{C} + \bar{I} + \bar{G} - c\bar{T} + cY \end{aligned}$$

(3.10) $$D = A + cY.$$

Demand depends on income because consumption depends on income. Equation (3.10) says that total demand is equal to autonomous expenditure plus induced consumption. In Figure 3.4, Equation (3.10) is a straight line with intercept equal to A and slope equal to c, the marginal propensity to consume. Along this line consumers are spending their income according to the consumption function, while G, I, and T are all set at their exogenous levels.

As we saw in Figure 3.3, equilibrium in the commodities market requires that production equal sales, or supply equal demand. All the points for which that is true are on the 45° line. Hence we can immediately deduce that the equilibrium level of income must be at point J, where the demand function D intersects the equilibrium function (the 45° line). At this intersection, income equals Y_0 and consumption equals C.

What would happen if the economy were at some point other than Y_0, for example, Y_1? At Y_1, total demand is H, which is less than production. Businesspeople will find that they are accumulating inventories. They will cut back produc-

Figure 3.4
Goods Market Equilibrium

The line C is the consumption function. It relates consumption to total income. The line D represents total demand. It is simply $C + I + G$. Equilibrium occurs where the line D intersects the 45° line, since there we know that supply equals demand and consumers are on their consumption function. From Figure 3.3 we also know that if the economy is out of equilibrium, it will move back to the equilibrium point, J. This is represented by the arrows in the figure.

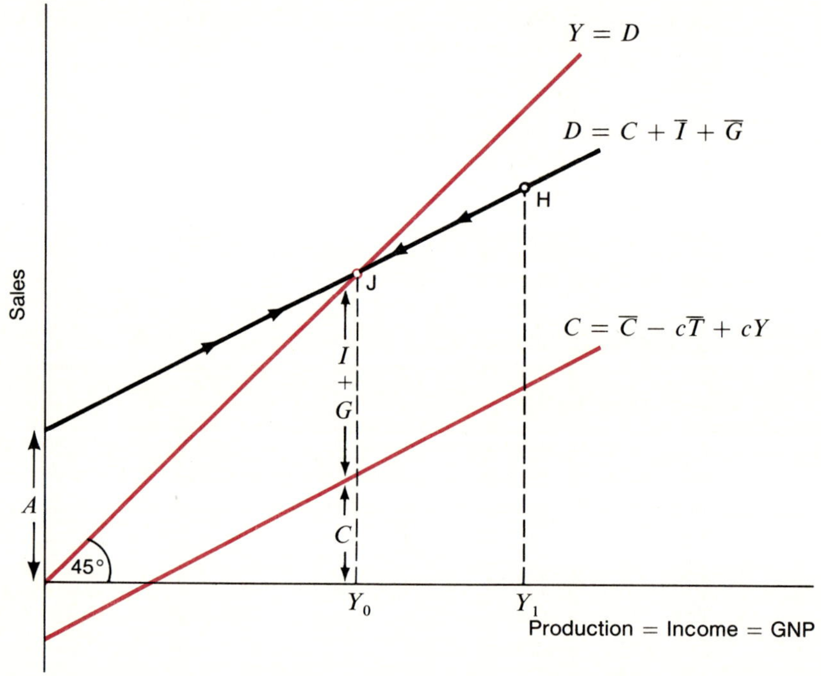

tion, which means that over time the economy will move from Y_1 back toward Y_0. In the opposite situation, to the left of Y_0, businessmen will find that sales exceed production, and they will increase output. Hence whenever the economy is out of equilibrium, inventory changes give the signal that causes production to expand or contract toward equilibrium. This process stops when production reaches Y_0. The arrows on the diagram indicate the direction of movement of the economy when it is out of equilibrium. As the reader can see, no matter where it starts the economy converges on Y_0, which is why that point can be thought of as an equilibrium.

A Numerical Example

In order to see how our model works, we will now construct a numerical example and solve for equilibrium. Suppose the observed levels of the exogenous variables for a hypothetical economy are the following:

$$\bar{T} = 160$$
$$\bar{G} = 100$$
$$\bar{I} = 100$$

Suppose further that from empirical research the consumption function is estimated to be:

$$C = 100 + .75Y_d.$$

To find equilibrium income, we substitute the particular values of our exogenous variables into Equation (3.7):

(3.7)
$$Y = \frac{\bar{C} - c\bar{T} + \bar{I} + \bar{G}}{1 - c}$$
$$Y = \frac{100 - .75(160) + 200}{1 - .75}$$
$$Y = \frac{300 - 120}{.25}$$
$$Y = 720.$$

To check our answer, let us see whether all equations are satisfied. First, calculate consumption and disposable income:

$$C = 100 + .75(Y_d).$$

$$Y_d = Y - 160$$
$$= 720 - 160$$
$$= 560.$$

$$C = 100 + .75(560)$$
$$= 520.$$

Since demand is equal to $C + I + G = 720$, the reader can see that our solution is consistent. Consumers are on the consumption function, and sales are equal to production.

Figure 3.5 shows our diagrammatic representation of the model. The intercept of the demand function is:

$$A = \bar{C} - c\bar{T} + \bar{I} + \bar{G}$$
$$= 300 - 120$$
$$= 180.$$

The slope of the aggregate demand function is .75. For this function, equilibrium is at $Y = 720$.

Figure 3.5
Determining Equilibrium in a Hypothetical Economy

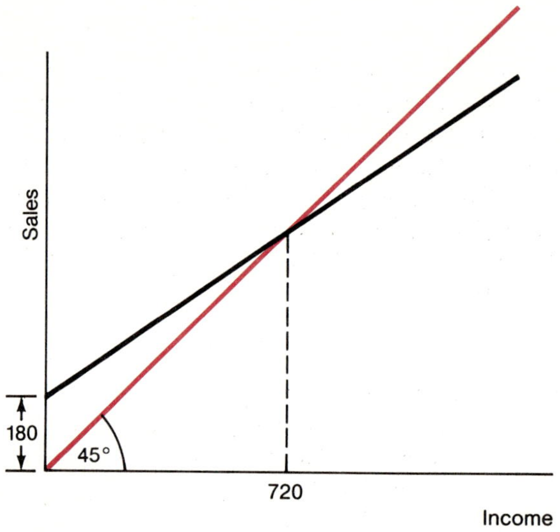

The Multiplier

We have now found equilibrium for our simple macroeconomic model. A natural question to investigate is the effect of changes in exogenous variables on that equilibrium. What, for example, would be the effect of a change in government expenditure or taxes on the level of income in the economy? This question can be easily answered using the reduced-form equation (3.7), repeated here for convenience:

(3.7) $$Y = \frac{\bar{C} - c\bar{T} + \bar{I} + \bar{G}}{1 - c}.$$

We first calculate the effect of a change in G. To do this, calculate the equilibrium level of income for G_0; then do the same for G_1, a different value of G. Then, subtract Y_0 from Y_1 to see the change in equilibrium that is associated with the change in G.

$$Y_0 = \frac{\bar{C} - c\bar{T} + \bar{I} + G_0}{1 - c}.$$

$$Y_1 = \frac{\bar{C} - c\bar{T} + \bar{I} + G_1}{1 - c}.$$

Table 3.1
Multiplier Matrix

Endogenous \ Exogenous	$\bar{G}$	$\bar{I}$	$\bar{C}$	$\bar{T}$
Y	$\frac{1}{1-c}$	$\frac{1}{1-c}$	$\frac{1}{1-c}$	$\frac{-c}{1-c}$
Y_d	$\frac{1}{1-c}$	$\frac{1}{1-c}$	$\frac{1}{1-c}$	$\frac{-1}{1-c}$
C	$\frac{c}{1-c}$	$\frac{c}{1-c}$	$\frac{c}{1-c}$	$\frac{-c}{1-c}$

Therefore:

(3.11) $$Y_1 - Y_0 = \frac{G_1 - G_0}{1 - c}.$$

We shall denote the difference between two values of a variable by a Δ. Thus, we may write Equation (3.11) as:

(3.12) $$\Delta Y = \frac{\Delta G}{1 - c}.$$

From Equation (3.12) we can now derive an expression for the change in Y per change in G. It is written $\Delta Y/\Delta G$, and it is known as a **multiplier.**[1] From Equation (3.12) we see that this multiplier is:

(3.13) $$\frac{\Delta Y}{\Delta G} = \frac{1}{1 - c}.$$

A multiplier is formally defined as a change in an endogenous variable with respect to a one-dollar change in an exogenous variable. There is a multiplier for each endogenous variable with respect to each exogenous variable; in our model, $4 \times 3 = 12$ in all. Many of these multipliers are identical, as we shall see in Table 3.1. We will write the multipliers with subscripts for the particular endogenous and exogenous variables being investigated. Thus, the income-government spending

[1]Readers with a knowledge of calculus will notice that the multiplier is the derivative of an endogenous variable with respect to an exogenous variable in a reduced-form equation. Thus, the income-government multiplier is dY/dG in Equation (3.7).

multiplier is $MULT_{YG}$. Because our model is linear, each multiplier is the coefficient of the particular exogenous variable for the endogenous variable in the reduced-form equation. Thus, the income-government spending multiplier is the coefficient of G in the reduced-form equation for income, Equation (3.7).

Let us now calculate the income-tax multiplier ($MULT_{YT}$). Applying the same technique we just used for G, we have:

$$Y_1 = \frac{\bar{C} - cT_1 + \bar{I} + \bar{G}}{1 - c}$$

$$Y_0 = \frac{\bar{C} - cT_0 + \bar{I} + \bar{G}}{1 - c}$$

(3.14) $$\Delta Y = \frac{-c\,\Delta T}{1 - c}.$$

Hence the tax multiplier ($MULT_{YT}$) is:

(3.15) $$\frac{\Delta Y}{\Delta T} = \frac{-c}{1 - c}.$$

As the reader can see from Equation 3.7, $-c/(1 - c)$ is indeed the coefficient of T in the reduced-form equation of Y.

To calculate the rest of the multipliers in our model, take the reduced-form equation for each endogenous variable and observe the coefficient of each exogenous variable. Each coefficient in each reduced-form equation is a multiplier telling exactly how much a particular endogenous variable will change when a certain exogenous variable is changed by one dollar. Thus, the matrix tells us at a glance what the effect of any variable is on the economy.

In the first row of Table 3.1, many of the multipliers are equal. That is because the effect of an additional unit of exogenous expenditure on income is the same regardless of whether it comes from G, I, or C. One could therefore call $1/(1 - c)$ the income-expenditure multiplier. Looking at the first row of the table, and remembering that c is always less than one for an economy, it can be seen that the income-expenditure multiplier is a good deal larger than one. This implies that if government or investment expenditure increases by one dollar, total demand will go up by some multiple of one dollar. Let us see why and how this happens using our basic equilibrium diagram in Figure 3.6.

In our diagram, suppose an economy starts with government spending G_0 and the demand curve D_0. Equilibrium income will be Y_0. Now let government spending increase to G_1. That will shift the demand curve up to D_1. In the short run, if businessmen do not immediately adjust production sales exceed production, and the economy goes to a disequilibrium point such as A. At A inventories are falling, which should spark an increase in production. But that increase stimulates extra consumption, which raises demand to point B. At B there is still a disequilibrium ($D > Y$), but it is smaller because there has been a leakage out of the extra production into saving. The process continues until the economy reaches a new

Figure 3.6
The Effect of a Change in Government Expenditure on Equilibrium Income

An increase in government expenditure (ΔG) shifts the demand curve up to D_1. Equilibrium income increases from Y_0 to Y_1. The change in income is $(1/MPS)\ \Delta G$. The change in household consumption is equal to $c\ \Delta Y$, and the change in household saving is $(1 - c)\ \Delta Y$. This is just equal to the ΔG itself.

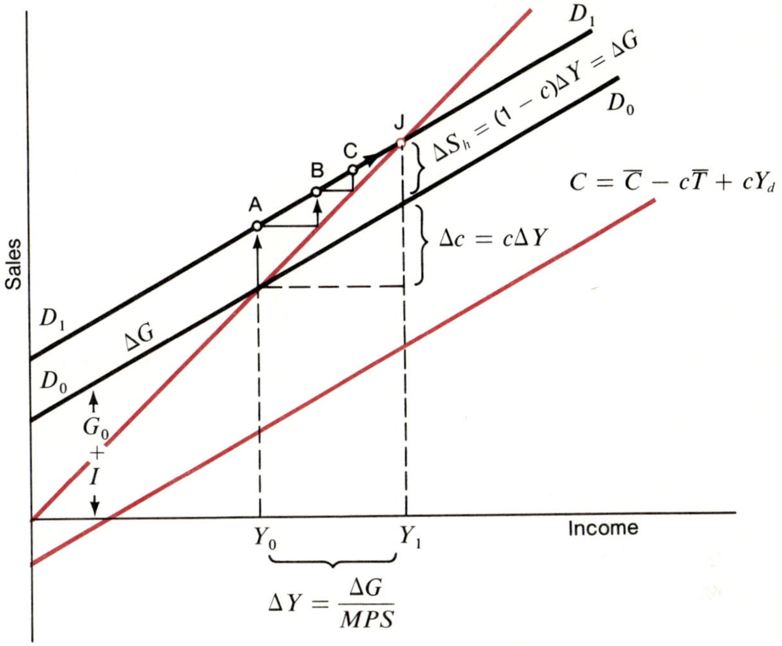

equilibrium at Y_1. The net change in Y is $\Delta G/(1 - c)$. That change is larger than the change in G because the extra income resulting from the initial increase in G induced consumers to spend more, and that in turn required additional production. As we shall see in a moment, the expansion goes on until the leakages into saving exactly match the increase in G.

Equilibrium as the Equality of Saving and Investment

A useful alternative way to think about the equilibrium condition is in terms of the equality of saving and investment. In the previous chapters we derived a fundamental identity that said that total saving must always by definition be equal to total investment including any changes in inventories. We repeat the equation here for reference.

(2.5) $$S_T \equiv I + \Delta INV.$$

In the complete model saving can be broken down into four sources: household, business, government, and foreign. However, in this first simple model we are assuming that both business and foreign saving are zero. Thus, our fundamental identity becomes:

(3.16) $$S_h + S_g \equiv I + \Delta INV.$$
$$S_h = Y_d - T$$
$$S_g = T - G$$

Equation (3.16) is a definitional identity—an equation that is always true. To convert this equation into an alternative equilibrium condition, recall from Equation (3.4a) that equilibrium requires that unintended inventory investment or $\Delta INV = 0$.[2] Therefore, substituting Equation (3.4a) into Equation (3.16), we can express our basic equilibrium condition in the very useful alternative form:

(3.17) $$S_T = I.$$

Equation (3.17) says that in equilibrium total saving must be just equal to intended investment, which we are defining as fixed investment by setting unintended investment equal to ΔINV. Thus, the basic equilibrium condition can be expressed in any of three equivalent forms:

1. $Y = D$.
2. $\Delta INV = 0$.
3. $S_T = I$.

As we shall now see, the third form is particularly useful in understanding why aggregate demand reacts as it does to changes in exogenous expenditure.

Let us look once again at the change in government expenditure and its effect on the level of income. As we have already shown, the net effect on income of a change in G is $\Delta Y = \Delta G/(1 - c)$. Our equilibrium condition tells us that total saving must equal intended investment in equilibrium. Hence it must follow that between equilibrium positions, any change in investment must be matched by an equal change in total saving—that is, $\Delta S_T = \Delta I$. This is always true. An increase in G by one dollar lowers government saving by an equivalent amount, since government saving is defined as $T - G$. If investment does not change, the equilibrium condition says that private saving must go up by an equal amount; that is,

$$\Delta S_h = -\Delta S_G = \Delta G.$$

[2]Recall that we are making the assumption that all inventory investment is unintended. Strictly speaking, the equilibrium condition is that total saving equal intended investment.

Private or household saving depends on income. Hence to increase private saving, income must increase by enough to generate the required amount of saving (ΔG). But by how much does income have to increase to generate that much saving? That depends on the relationship between saving and income. From the definition of household saving we have:

(3.18) $$S_h = Y_d - C.$$

Substituting Equations (3.2) and (3.3) into Equation (3.18) we have:

(3.19) $$S_h = -\bar{C} - (1 - c)\bar{T} + (1 - c)Y.$$

Equation (3.19) gives us the relationship between S_h and Y that we need. It tells us that S_h changes by $(1 - c)$ times any change in income. The term $(1 - c)$ is called the **marginal propensity to save** (MPS) by economists. Formally,

$$MPS = \frac{\Delta S_h}{\Delta Y} = 1 - c.$$

Let us return to the problem of generating $\Delta S_h = \Delta G$. For our equilibrium condition we require $\Delta S_h = \Delta G$. But according to Equation (3.19), $\Delta S_h = (1 - c)\,\Delta Y$. Hence by substitution we get:

$$(1 - c)\,\Delta Y = \Delta G$$

$$\frac{\Delta Y}{\Delta G} = \frac{1}{1 - c}.$$

As we recall from Equation 3.13, this is the income-government multiplier.

Now we see why the income-government multiplier is greater than one. We have to raise S_h by the same amount that government spending increases. But since household saving rises only by some fraction of the change in income (because the MPS < 1), income must rise by more than ΔG in order to generate $\Delta S_h = \Delta G$. The higher the MPS is, the smaller the multiplier will be.[3]

We show this alternative method of deriving equilibrium in terms of saving and investment in Figure 3.7. The upward-sloping function is Equation (3.20). It shows the relationship between total saving (S_T) and income. Equation (3.20) is derivable from our definitions of household and government saving as follows:

$$S_h = Y_d - C$$

$$S_g = T - G$$

$$S_T = S_h + S_g = Y_d - C + T - G$$

[3]Suppose, for example, that the MPS = .25. In order to generate 1 extra dollar of household saving, disposable income would have to rise by 4 dollars.

Figure 3.7
Saving and Investment

Line S shows total saving, government plus private, as a function of income. The equation for the saving function is:

$$S = -\overline{C} + c\overline{T} - \overline{G} + (1 - c)Y.$$

We know that in equilibrium total saving equals investment. Thus, we find equilibrium income at the intersection of the saving and investment lines. A change in G reduces total saving and shifts the whole saving schedule down by ΔG. Since the slope of the saving function is $(1 - c)$, we know that the change in equilibrium income must be $\Delta G/(1 - c)$.

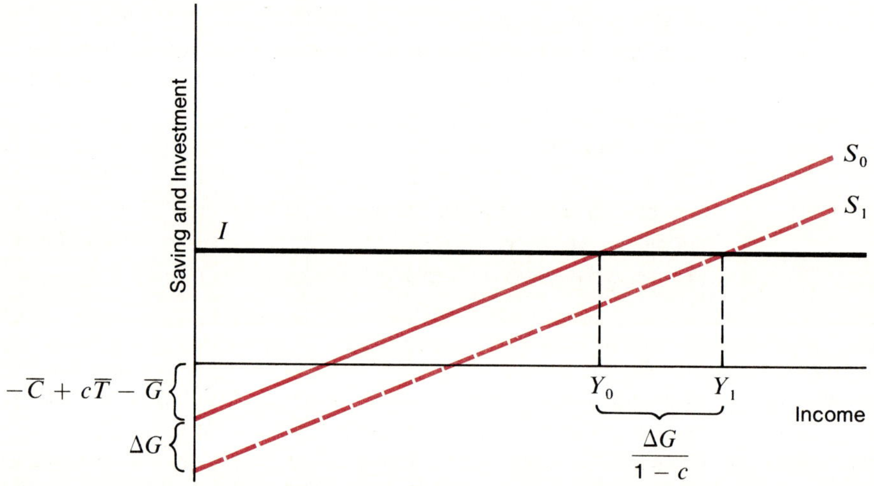

(3.20) $$S_T = -\overline{C} + c\overline{T} - \overline{G} + (1 - c)Y.$$

The slope of the saving function is the amount of saving induced per dollar of income. In this model it is the MPS of households, $1 - c$. The intercept of the saving function is $-\overline{C} + c\overline{T} + \overline{G}$. To find equilibrium we use the requirement that $S_T = I$. Hence equilibrium is at the intersection of the saving function and the horizontal line $I = \overline{I}$.

Now consider the effect of an increase in G. We see from the definition of the intercept that an increase in G reduces total saving, shifting the saving function downward from S_0 to S_1. Equilibrium income rises to Y_1. At that point, induced household saving has risen by exactly the increase in government spending. For note that according to Equation (3.20), $\Delta S_h = (1 - c)\Delta Y$. Hence

$$\Delta S_h = \frac{(1 - c)\,\Delta G}{1 - c} = \Delta G.$$

How a Tax Cut Affects Equilibrium Income

We now turn to a graphical and numerical analysis of the effect of a tax cut. Recall from our multiplier discussion that a tax cut should change the equilibrium level of income by $-c\ \Delta T/(1-c)$ (see Equation [3.15]). We wish to use our two diagrams and a numerical example to see exactly how and why the economy reacts as it does to a cut in taxes.

We show the effect of a tax cut in Figure 3.8. Recall that in (a), the intercept of the aggregate demand curve is $A = \bar{C} - c\bar{T} + \bar{I} + \bar{G}$. Thus, a cut in taxes shifts the curve up by $-c\ \Delta T$ from D_0 to D_1. Equilibrium income rises by $-c\ \Delta T/(1-c)$.

This is somewhat easier to see in (b), where we show saving directly. A fall in taxes reduces government saving by ΔT, but it raises household saving by $(1-c)\ \Delta T$. Total saving falls by the sum of the two effects, $-c\ \Delta T$. In the diagram the total saving function shifts downward by that amount, which can also be shown by using the definition of the intercept of the saving function (see Equation [3.20]).

Since total saving must always be equal to investment in equilibrium and since investment has not changed, income has to rise enough to induce an extra $c\ \Delta T$ of household saving. But, according to the saving function, induced saving is $\Delta S_h = (1-c)\ \Delta Y$. Hence by substitution, $\Delta S_h = (1-c)\ \Delta Y = -c\ \Delta T$. This in turn breaks down directly into the income-tax multiplier:

$$\frac{\Delta Y}{\Delta T} = \frac{-c}{1-c}.$$

Thus, it is always possible to interpret any change in equilibrium income as being that change necessary to bring total saving back into line with intended investment. Any change in an exogenous variable that reduces saving is expansionary (such as a rise in G or a fall in T). It will require an increase in income to induce additional saving to offset the initial reduction.

A Numerical Example

We now show the effect of a tax cut in the numerical example that we developed a few pages back. We showed that for the initial values, $T = 160$, $G = 100$, $I = 100$, and the consumption function $C = 100 + .75Y_d$; the equilibrium level of income is $Y = 720$.

Now suppose that the government lowers taxes by \$10 billion. Let us see what happens to the equilibrium level of income. We shall answer this question in three alternative ways: by solving directly for Y using Equation (3.7), by using the diagram in Figure 3.9, and by using the multiplier.

First, substituting the new value of T into Equation (3.7), we have:

$$Y = \frac{100 - .75(150) + 100 + 100}{.25}$$

$$= 750.$$

The \$10 billion tax cut increases the level of income from \$720 billion to \$750 billion.

Figure 3.8
The Effect of a Tax Cut on Equilibrium Income
A cut in taxes shifts the demand function and savings function by $c\ \Delta T$. Income increases by $1/(1-c)$ times that change.

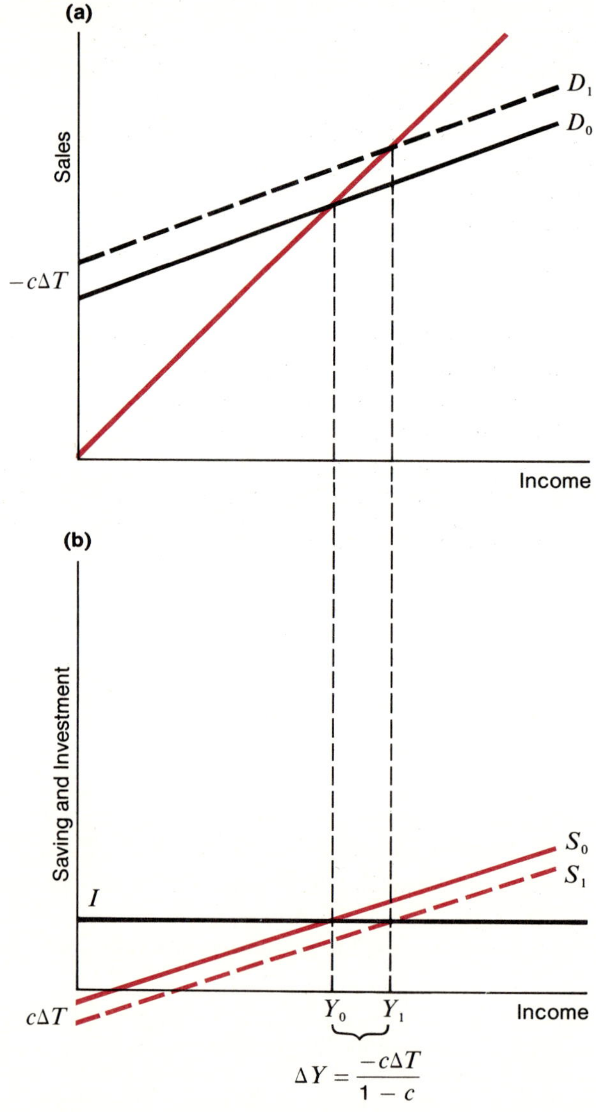

We now show the same solution diagrammatically in Figure 3.9.

In (a), the reduction in taxes shifts the consumption function and aggregate demand up by \$7.5 billion to the dashed line D_1. Why? Because the intercept term A now becomes:

Figure 3.9
Equilibrium in a Hypothetical Economy
A reduction of $10 billion shifts the aggregate demand curve up by $7.5 billion and the aggregate saving curve down by the same amount. This increases equilibrium income by 4 × $7.5 = $30 billion.

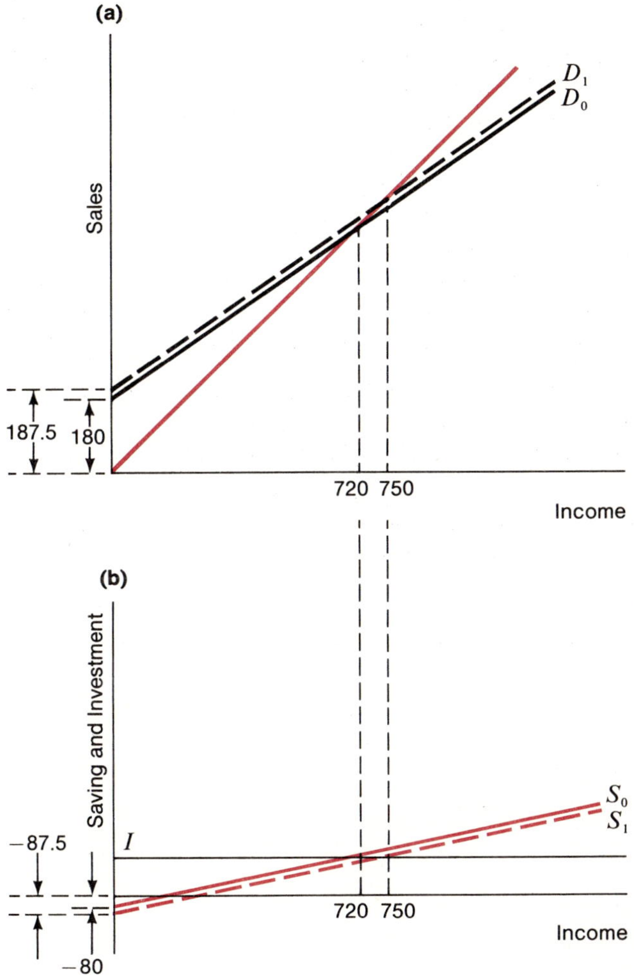

$$A = 100 - .75(150) + 200$$
$$= \$187.5 \text{ billion.}$$

By similar reasoning, the aggregate saving function in (b) shifts downward by the same amount.

A reduction in taxes increases consumption and reduces total saving because it increases disposable income. In the case being analyzed here, Y_d rises by $10 billion. Since the MPC = .75, consumption rises by .75 × \$10 billion = \$7.5 billion. Total saving is a bit more complicated. Since Y_d rises by \$10 billion and consumption by only \$7.5 billion, clearly S_h rises by \$2.5 billion. But S_g falls by the amount of the tax. Hence the effect of the change in taxes on total saving is −\$10 billion + \$2.5 billon = −\$7.5 billion. This is the amount by which the aggregate saving line shifts downward in (b). The new equilibrium may be read off the diagram where the dashed line D_1 intersects the 45° line (at Y = \$750 billion). In (b), equilibrium occurs where the new saving line intersects the line $I = 100$. Thus, a \$10 billion tax reduction increases income in this economy by \$30 billion.

Algebraically, the simplest way to calculate the effect of the change in taxes is to use the multiplier, for by definition that is exactly what it tells us. The income-tax multiplier is, from Equation (3.15),

$$\frac{\Delta Y}{\Delta T} = \frac{-c}{1 - c} = -3.$$

Hence if we reduce taxes by \$10 billion, the multiplier tells us that income will increase by \$30 billion. Thus, the new equilibrium level of income will be \$720 + \$30 = \$750 billion. The reader can verify that this is also the solution of the equilibrium equation for Y (Equation [3.7]), if we substitute T = \$150 billion in place of the original value of \$160 billion.

Once again we can interpret the change in the equilibrium level of income in terms of the necessary equality of savings and investment. As we have seen, a reduction in taxes of \$10 billion reduces total saving by \$7.5 billion. Since investment is unchanged, this is the amount by which private saving must be increased at the new equilibrium. Since we know that the MPS is .25, the necessary increase in income will be 4 × \$7.5 billion = \$30 billion. At this new level of income, S_h will have risen by \$10 billion—\$2.5 billion because of the direct effect of lower taxes on disposable income and \$7.5 billion because the total level of income has increased. Note that the total change in S_h just exactly offsets the \$10 billion reduction in S_g.

Using the Macromodel to Control the Level of Aggregate Demand

We have spent a good deal of time developing a mathematical model of the economy. What good is this model? What can it be used for? Our model is too simple for prediction, but it will show the method by which more realistic models can be used by macroeconomic policymakers in their efforts to control the economy. As we shall see, there are increasing doubts over just how controllable the economy is, but let us ignore these for the moment and take a first look at the use of the macromodel as a policy tool.

In the models of the previous sections, we treated taxes and government expenditure as exogenous variables. Actually these variables are controllable by the government; they are policy variables. To the economic system they are exogenous, but to policymakers these are the levers by which the level of economic activity can be influenced. Decisions regarding the income and expenditure level of the government are called **fiscal policy**. Let us see how fiscal policy works.

In our previous example we saw that for the initial values of G and T, the equilibrium level of income was $720 billion. But let us suppose that the Council of Economic Advisers estimates that the full employment level of output is actually $760 billion. That is, at the current fiscal policy settings, there will be a recession and a $40 billion short-fall in employment and production.

We now want to use our model to tell us what changes to make to get to full employment. To do that, income has to be increased by $40 billion. What change in G would bring that about? If we use the multiplier, that is an easy question to answer. We know that for our particular model the income-government multiplier is

$$\frac{1}{1-c} = \frac{1}{.25} = 4.$$

Income rises by $4 for every $1 increase in government spending. Since we want an increase in income of $40 billion, we should increase government spending by $10 billion, from $100 billion to $110 billion. Readers can confirm for themselves that this change will indeed lead to an income level of $760 billion by substituting the new value of G into Equation (3.7).

It is often difficult to increase G in the short run, because this requires plans, contracts, and congressional approval. Thus, it may be faster for the government to use taxes to induce the change in income.[4] By how much do taxes have to be changed to push income up to $760 billion?

Once again we use the definition of the income-tax multiplier. It tells the change in income per change in taxes. In our model the tax multiplier is $-c/(1-c) = -3$ (see Table 3.1). This means that income rises by $3 per $1 reduction in taxes. Therefore, since we want an increase of $40 billion in income, we should lower taxes by $40 billion/$3 billion = $13.33 billion.

Making Government Revenue Endogenous

In our first model we considered government revenue to be exogenous. But in fact, taxes depend on income. Most of our taxes, such as the personal and corporate income tax, are levied directly on income. Others, such as the property tax and tariffs, tend to rise as income goes up, because rising income increases the value of both property and imports, the base of these two taxes.

Let us suppose, as a first approximation, that total taxes are proportional to income. This results in the following tax function:

[4] Current experience suggests that taxes are just as hard to adjust as government spending.

(3.21) $$T = tY.$$

If we now introduce Equation (3.21) into our model, we have a five-equation system consisting of Equations (3.1)–(3.4) plus (3.21). The complete model with endogenous taxes is therefore:

(3.1) $$D = C + \bar{I} + \bar{G}$$

(3.2) $$C = \bar{C} + cY_d$$

(3.3) $$Y_d = Y - T$$

(3.4) $$Y = D$$

(3.21) $$T = tY$$

The endogenous variables of this new system are C, Y, Y_d, D, and T; the exogenous variables are $\bar{G}$, $\bar{I}$, and $\bar{C}$. We solve for equilibrium in this system just as we did in the original model. Substituting Equations (3.21) and (3.2)–(3.4) into (3.1), we get:

(3.22) $$Y = \frac{\bar{C} + \bar{I} + \bar{G}}{1 - c(1 - t)}$$

Equation (3.22) is the reduced-form equation for income. Like Equation (3.7), of which it is the counterpart for the model with endogenous taxes, Equation (3.22) tells us how equilibrium income depends on the exogenous variables of the model. We can now ask what the income-government multiplier is for the new model. That multiplier MULT_{YG} is the coefficient of G in Equation (3.22). Thus:

(3.23) $$\frac{\Delta Y}{\Delta G} = \frac{1}{1 - c(1 - t)}.$$

Why and how is this new multiplier different from the multiplier in our original model $1/(1 - c)$? We rationalized that multiplier by showing that in equilibrium $I = S_T$, and therefore $\Delta I = \Delta S$. In the original model, $(1 - c)$ was the change in total saving per change in income, or the MPS of the economy. In our new model, both private saving and government saving are affected by a change in income. The expression $1 - c(1 - \text{t})$ is the change in total saving, government and private, per dollar of income.

We can show this by using the definition of total saving:

$$\begin{aligned} S_T &= S_h + S_g \\ &= -\overline{C} + (1 - c)Y_d + T - \overline{G} \\ &= -\overline{C} + (1 - c)(1 - t)Y + tY - \overline{G} \end{aligned}$$

(3.24) $$S_T = -\overline{C} - \overline{G} + (1 - c[1 - t])Y.$$

In this model the change in total saving induced by a change in income is $1 - c(1 - t)$. This expression is what we might call the social marginal propensity to save. It is also the slope of the saving function for the endogenous tax model, as we shall see in a moment.

The multiplier $1/(1 - c[1 - t])$ is smaller than the original one because there are more leakages into saving than there were in the original model. Remember that income has to rise enough to produce the extra saving to match extra government spending. If taxes rise with income, total saving will be more sensitive to income; thus, income will not have to rise as much to reestablish equilibrium. One could say that reducing the multiplier makes income less sensitive to changes in G or I or to any other change in autonomous expenditure. It makes equilibrium less subject to fluctuations. We will discuss this stabilizing property of the tax system in Chapter 5.

We now adapt our two basic diagrams of the economy for the new tax function, shown in Figure 3.10. The aggregate demand curve D, shown in diagram (a), is now:

(3.25) $$\begin{aligned} D &= \overline{C} + \overline{I} + \overline{G} + c(1 - t)Y \\ &= \overline{A} + c(1 - t)Y. \end{aligned}$$

The saving function, shown in diagram (b), is:

$$\begin{aligned} S_T &= S_h + S_g \\ &= -\overline{C} + (1 - c)Y_d + T - \overline{G} \end{aligned}$$

(3.26) $$S_T = -\overline{C} - \overline{G} + (1 - c[1 - t])Y.$$

As the reader can see in Figure 3.10, when taxes are a function of income, the aggregate demand curve is flatter and the aggregate saving curve is steeper than was the case in our first model. The line D has a slope of $c(1 - t)$ in (a), rather than c, as it did in Figure 3.4. Similarly, the saving function in (b) has a slope of $1 - c(1 - t)$ rather than $(1 - c)$. When there are leakages into taxes, induced spending is less and induced saving is greater in response to changes in income.

In this more realistic model, if the government wishes to use taxes to control the level of demand it changes the tax rate, t, rather than T as it did before. Suppose a reduction in demand is desired. Then, the government raises the tax rate from t_0 to t_1. This will rotate the aggregate demand curve down to D_1 in Figure 3.10 and rotate the saving function up to S_1. Equilibrium income falls from Y_0 to Y_1.

Figure 3.10
Equilibrium with Endogenous Taxes

In (a), when taxes are a function of income the slope of the demand curve depends on the tax rate. If the tax rate is increased from t_0 to t_1, the demand curve rotates clockwise. Equilibrium income decreases from Y_0 to Y_1.

In (b), when taxes are a function of income total saving has two components that depend on income: household saving and government saving. As a result, the saving function has a steeper slope than it did in the model with lump sum taxes. A change in the tax rate can be used to change the level of income. Here we show the effect of an increase in the tax rate from t_0 to t_1. The demand function in (a) rotates clockwise and the saving function rotates counterclockwise, and income falls from Y_0 to Y_1.

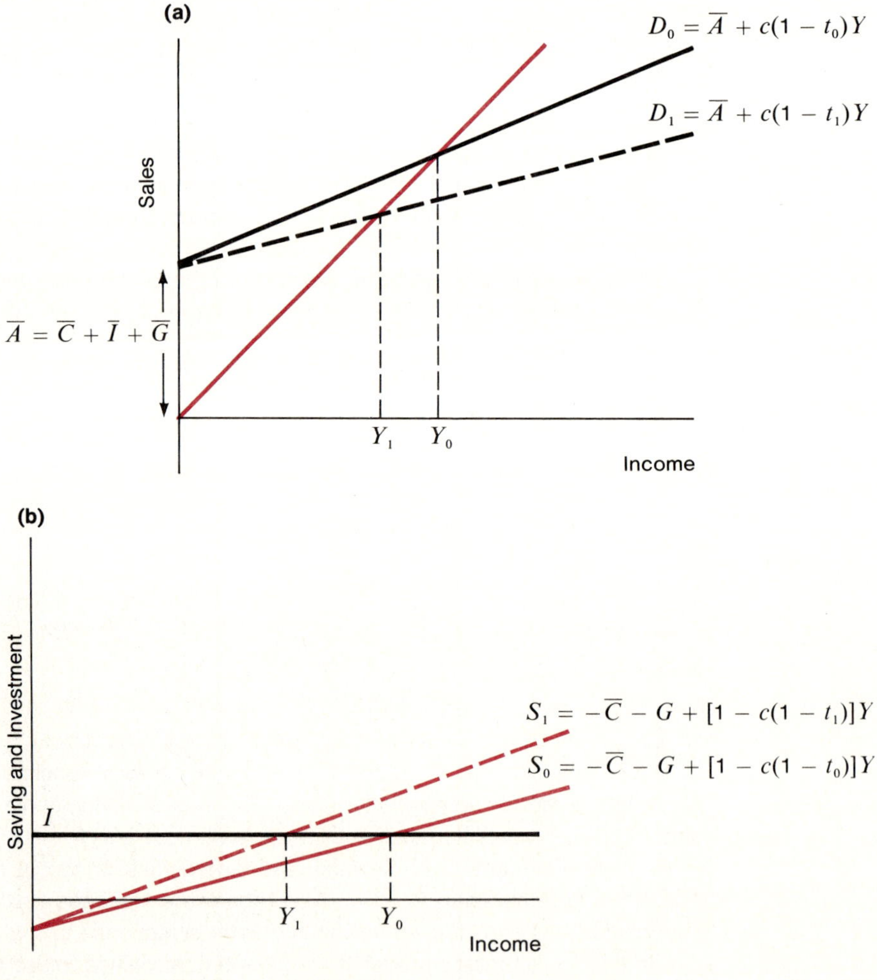

A Rough Estimate of the Expenditure Multiplier for the United States

Let us now try to get a rough idea of the expenditure multiplier for the United States. To do that, we must calculate the MPC of consumers and the net subtraction of both taxes and gross business saving from income. These will tell us how disposable income changes with total income. We will derive very simple estimates based on the GNP data. What we are doing here is econometrics on the back of an envelope, but it will give us a pretty good idea of orders of magnitude and of the overall social marginal propensity to save in the United States.

So with apologies to the model builders and econometricians, let us go ahead. We will take a three-year average of the observations of 1967–1969 and of 1977–1979.[5] Then we will calculate the changes in GNP, disposable income, and consumption. For simplicity, we will lump together business saving and taxes.

Making the necessary calculation, we find that over the ten-year period in question:

$$\Delta Y_d = \$874 \text{ billion}$$
$$\Delta Y = \$1265 \text{ billion}$$
$$\Delta C = \$822 \text{ billion}$$

From this we get

$$c = \frac{\Delta C}{\Delta Y_d} = .94$$

and

$$t = 1 - \frac{\Delta Y_d}{\Delta Y} = .31.$$

Note that t includes both business saving and taxes in this example. Putting these numbers into the multiplier formula, we get:

$$\frac{\Delta Y}{\Delta I} = \frac{1}{1 - c(1 - t)} = \frac{1}{(1 - .94(.69))} = \frac{1}{1 - .65} = \frac{1}{.35} = 2.85.$$

In our economy, this calculation suggests that income is likely to go up by a bit less than 3 times any increase in exogenous expenditure. The actual multiplier is thus quite a bit smaller than it was in our original example. That, of course, is because the leakages into saving are larger in reality than in our example.

Recall that the denominator of the multiplier is the economy-wide MPS. What are the components of this MPS? Together the government and business took \$.31 of each extra dollar of income ($t = .31$). Of this, the government took \$.19

[5]We do that to avoid using artificial peaks and troughs in the data.

and private business \$.12. Thus, only \$.69 out of each additional dollar of GNP was available to households as disposable income. Out of that amount, households saved only 6 percent, or \$.04 ($.06 \times .69$), a very low figure relative to private saving in other countries. In all, then, the economy diverts out of aggregate demand about 35 percent of any change in income (\$.19 to the government +\$.12 to business +\$.04 to household saving). Much of that comes from the tax system.

Even this multiplier estimate probably overstates the net effect on income of any change in exogenous expenditure. For changes in expenditure generally affect the intertest rate which, in turn, affects investment and consumption expenditures. So far we have ignored this feedback relationship between aggregate demand and the interest rate. In the next chapter, we shall expand our model to make the interest rate an endogenous variable. As we shall see, this will have a profound effect on both our multipliers and our model of the economy.

Summary

In this chapter we have constructed our first simple models of the economy and shown how they can be used to predict the effect of changes in exogenous variables or by the government to help control the level of income. In order to make our model more realistic, we need to incorporate the effect of asset markets on the economy and interest rates. We do this in the next two chapters, after which we build a model of the economy that includes both demand and supply.

Key Concepts

macroeconomic model
equilibrium
endogenous variable
exogenous variable
comparative statics
marginal propensity to consume
total autonomous expenditure
reduced-form equation
multiplier
marginal propensity to save
fiscal policy

Problems and Questions for Discussion

1. Consider an economy with the following behavioral equations and identities:

$$
\begin{aligned}
C &= 80 + .80Y_d \\
I &= 100 \\
G &= 100 \\
T &= 100 \\
Y_d &= Y - T
\end{aligned}
$$

a. What are the endogenous and exogenous variables in this model?
b. Derive reduced-form equations for each endogenous variable.
c. What are the equilibrium values for each endogenous variable?

2. What are the multipliers of income and consumption with respect to I, G, and T? How are these multipliers related to the reduced-form equations? Why is the income-government spending multiplier greater than one—that is, why does income go up by more than one dollar when government spending goes up by one dollar?

3. Suppose that government authorities want to increase the level of equilibrium income to \$1200. By how much should they change G? By how much should they change T? Why is the change in T greater than the change in G?

4. Suppose the government increases the value of both G and T by \$20. What will be the new level of equilibrium income? Why is the new level different from the initial level? This exercise demonstrates that balanced-budget fiscal policy measures have an effect on output.

5. Write the aggregate savings function for this model. Show that in equilibrium in Problem 4 total saving equals investment.

6. Questions 6–9 use the data and model shown in Problem 6. Suppose that we have an economy in which tax revenue is endogenous. A model for such an economy is the following:

$$C = 160 + .80Y_d$$
$$I = 100$$
$$G = 100$$
$$T = .20Y$$
$$Y_d = Y - T$$

a. Derive the equilibrium values for each endogenous variable.
b. Derive the multiplier of income with respect to G and I.
c. Why are each of these multipliers lower than the multiplier you obtained in Question 2?

7. a. If you were in charge of fiscal policy, by how much would you increase G in order to increase the equilibrium level of income by \$200?
b. We know that in equilibrium, $S = I$. Therefore, when we increase the equilibrium level of income by 200, $\Delta S = \Delta I$. Show how this equality is satisfied for the increase in G you have chosen in your answer to part a of this question.

8. If you wanted to keep the level of government spending at \$100, but wanted the level of equilibrium income to rise to \$1200, what tax rate would you choose?

9. Suppose that fixed investment increases by \$50. Calculate the new equilibrium level of income and show how the change in investment is matched by changes in household and government saving.

10. President Reagan lowered tax rates in order to increase saving in the economy. Will *total* saving go up if we lower taxes? In your answer, define total saving and show the relationship between it and taxes.

Chapter 4

Money, Interest, and Income

In Chapter 3 we developed a simple model of aggregate demand. We showed there how income depends on saving, investment, and fiscal policy. That model ignored any relationship between interest rates and spending, and yet we know that interest rates do have a strong effect on the spending of both investors and consumers. It must therefore follow that the interest rate has an influence on the level of income. It is this interaction that we shall explore in this chapter.

One purpose for expanding our demand model beyond the simple version presented earlier is to avoid making serious errors by ignoring the interest feedback. A second purpose is to enable us to include assets and monetary policy in our analysis. Assets include such things as money, bonds, machinery, and housing, all components of a nation's wealth. As we shall see, both the level and the composition of the stock of assets have an important influence on the interest rate. Monetary policy works through asset markets, for monetary policy affects the composition of the asset portfolio held by the public. This in turn affects the interest rate and hence the level of aggregate demand.

The IS-LM model that we shall be presenting here is the core of the modern theory of aggregate demand. It provides for the simultaneous determination of interest and income in the goods and money markets and allows us to analyze the effects of both monetary and fiscal policies on the level of economic activity.

The Relationship Between Interest Rates and Aggregate Demand

In Chapter 3 we showed how aggregate demand is a function of investment and autonomous consumer expenditures, both of which were treated as exogenous to, or independent of, the level of aggregate demand. However, both of these variables are influenced by the interest rate. We shall explore the relationship between interest and both consumption and investment more thoroughly in Chapters 11 and 12.

Here we note that interest represents the cost of borrowing. In considering whether to make an investment, investors must compare its expected profitability against the cost of borrowing. The higher the interest rate, the fewer the projects that will be found profitable after payment of borrowing costs. Therefore, we would expect that investment would be negatively related to the interest rate.

The same rationale applies to consumption. For consumers who buy on credit, interest payments are a part of the price of goods. When interest rates go up, purchases on credit become more expensive, and some are likely to be deferred. Hence consumption, like investment, ought to be negatively related to the interest rate.

Let us now translate the relationship between the interest rate and investment and consumption into a series of useful diagrams. In order to do this, we must first establish the **IS curve.**[1]

The IS Curve

The IS curve is defined to be the collection of all pairs of interest rates and income levels at which the goods market is in equilibrium. The IS curve gives the implicit relationship between income and the interest rate under the condition that sales equal production in the goods market. If we were to draw the IS curve, what would it look like? To answer that question, we go back to the equations of Chapter 3.

In Chapter 3 we expressed the goods market equilibrium condition as:

$$Y = C + I + G.$$

Using the simple consumption function, we rewrite this equation[2] as

(4.1) $$Y = \bar{C} + c(Y - \bar{T}) + \bar{I} + \bar{G},$$

or, where

$$A = \bar{C} - c\bar{T} + \bar{I} + \bar{G}$$

(4.2) $$Y = A + cY.$$

[1]The IS and the LM, which will be discussed later in this chapter, refer to the equilibrium conditions in the goods and money markets, respectively. These terms are taken from a path-breaking paper by Sir John Hicks entitled "Mr. Keynes and the Classics: A Suggested Interpretation," *Econometrica* 5 (April 1937): 147–159.

[2]In Chapter 3 we wrote C, I, G, and T with a bar to indicate that they were exogenous variables. Now we will make both $\bar{C}$ and $\bar{I}$ endogenous by incorporating the interest rate into our model.

As we have seen, the element A represents the components of aggregate demand, which are independent of the level of income. However, as we have just discussed, consumption and investment, two of the components of A, are negatively related to the interest rate, r: A rise in r will reduce both $\bar{C}$ and $\bar{I}$. We will write this negative relationship between consumption and investment in a general form as:

(4.3) $$\bar{C} + \bar{I} = -i(r) \quad (i > 0).$$

Substituting Equation (4.3) into Equation (4.2), we show A as a function of G, T, and r:

(4.4) $$A = \bar{G} - c\bar{T} - i(r).$$

Deriving the IS Curve We now use Equation (4.4) to derive the IS curve. Diagram (a) in Figure 4.1 shows how C and I vary with r. Diagram (b) relates $C + I$ to A, and therefore indirectly shows that A varies negatively with r. Diagram (c) is the basic equilibrium diagram from Chapter 3. Here we use it to translate the level of A determined by the interest rate into an equilibrium level of income. For example, if the interest rate is r_0, A is A_0 and equilibrium in the goods market is at Y_0.

Now let us see what happens when interest rates decline. In (a), move from r_0 to r_1. As the reader can see, autonomous expenditure rises from A_0 to A_1. In (c) the entire demand curve shifts up by the change in A, since A is the intercept of the demand function. As a result, equilibrium income rises from Y_0 to Y_1. Thus, we see that a decline in interest rates leads to a rise in aggregate demand.

We now combine these relationships into a diagram of the IS curve, shown in (d). By definition, the IS curve is the collection of all pairs of interest rates and income levels at which the goods market is in equilibrium. Therefore, to construct the IS curve, we simply bring together the pairs of interest rates and income levels that we derived in (a), (b), and (c). As we have already demonstrated, at r_0 income is Y_0; that is point A in the IS diagram. At r_1 income is Y_1; that corresponds to point B. Clearly, if we vary the interest rate we will trace out the negatively sloping line shown in (d). This line is the IS curve. It is a picture of all the pairs of interest rates and levels of income at which the goods market is in equilibrium.

The reason for the negative relationship between income and interest rate should be clear. Rising interest rates reduce investment and increase saving, and that is always contractionary. Either requires a corresponding reduction in saving to keep the goods market in equilibrium. Since saving depends on income, a reduction in saving requires a reduction in income.

The Linear IS Curve Generally, the IS curve is nonlinear because Equation (4.4) is nonlinear. However, for expositional purposes, it is useful to derive the IS curve when Equation (4.4) is linear. In the linear case, Equation (4.4) becomes:

(4.5) $$A = \bar{G} - c\bar{T} - ir.$$

Figure 4.1
Derivation of the IS Curve

Start with interest rate r_0 in (a). Determine $\overline{C} + I$. Part (b) shows the level of autonomous expenditures, A, that corresponds with this amount of $\overline{C} + I$. Then move over to (c), where the level of A determined in (b) is the intercept of the total sales function. Equilibrium income is, as we learned in Chapter 3, the intersection of the total demand function with the 45° line. Hence, for the interest rate r_0, equilibrium income is Y_0. This determines a point, A, on the IS curve in (d). To get to point B, choose the lower interest rate, r_1, and follow the same procedure to get the corresponding equilibrium income, Y_1.This is higher than Y_0 because a lower interest rate leads to higher investment and consumption expenditure.

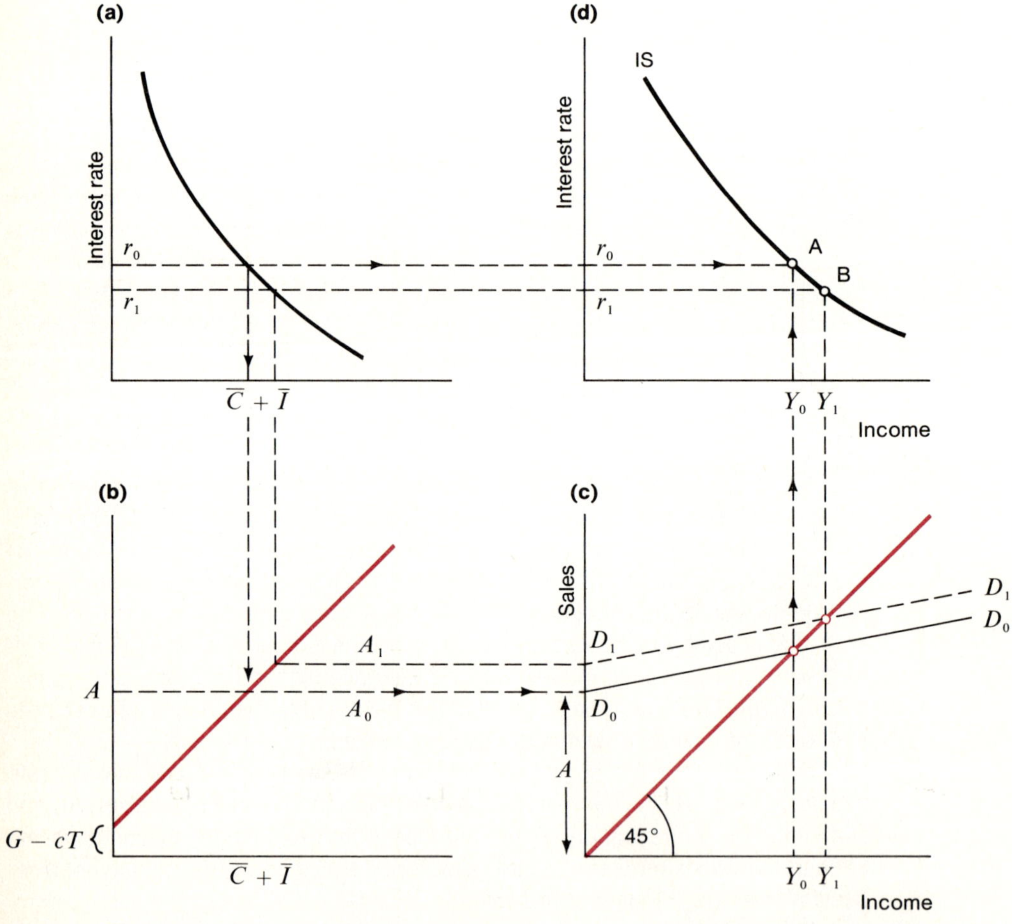

The term $-i$ is a negative linear coefficient that shows the change in A per unit change in the interest rate.

Now we substitute Equation (4.5) into Equation (4.1) and solve for r:

(4.6)
$$Y = \bar{G} - c\bar{T} - ir + cY$$
$$r = \frac{\bar{G} - c\bar{T} - (1 - c)Y}{i}.$$

Equation (4.6) is the IS curve for the linear case. It tells us that the interest rate is related positively to G and negatively to T. It also says that the slope of the IS curve is the coefficient of Y in Equation (4.6), namely, $-(1 - c)/i$, a negative number.

Factors That Influence the Slope and Position of the IS Curve

The slope of the IS curve shows the change in interest that is required to keep saving equal to investment as income changes. It is steep when interest has little effect on autonomous expenditure or when the marginal propensity to save is high. Let us see why.

Suppose, for example, that neither investment nor consumption varies with the interest rate, a situation that is likely to occur in recessions. When that happens, total autonomous spending no longer depends on the interest rate; the curve in (b) of Figure 4.1 is vertical. Thus, when we vary the interest rate, we get no shift in autonomous expenditure and no shift in aggregate demand in (c). That being the case, equilibrium income is also invariant with respect to the interest rate, and we have a vertical IS curve, as shown in Figure 4.2. We conclude, therefore, that the interest sensitivities of consumption and investment affect the slope of the IS curve. The *less* sensitive either is to the interest rate, the *steeper* the resulting IS curve will be.

The dependence of the slope of the IS curve on the interest sensitivity of A can be seen directly in the linear case (see Equation 4.6). The less sensitive A is to r, the smaller i is. Since the slope of the IS curve is $-(1 - c)/i$, it increases as i gets smaller. When i reaches zero, the IS curve becomes vertical.

Another factor that influences the slope of the IS curve is differences in saving propensities. Since the sensitivity of demand to changes in autonomous expenditure is just the inverse of society's marginal propensity to save, it follows that the larger the MPS, the less sensitive demand will be to changes in the interest rate. In terms of Figure 4.1, the size of the MPS affects the slope of our demand function in (c): The higher the MPS, the flatter that function will be. A shift up in autonomous expenditure, due to a fall in the interest rate, will have a smaller impact on demand the flatter the expenditure function in (c). Hence the larger the MPS, the steeper the IS curve.

Again this can be seen directly in the linear model. As we have already indicated, the slope of the IS curve in that model is $-(1 - c)/i$. But since $(1 - c)$ is equal to the marginal propensity to save, s, the slope of the IS curve may be rewritten as $-s/i$. Hence the larger the saving propensity, the steeper the IS curve.

Thus we see two reasons why the IS curve may get steeper.

Figure 4.2
The IS Curve When Investment and Consumption are Independent of the Interest Rate.
The IS curve is steeper the:
more insensitive autonomous expenditure is to the rate of interest.
lower the expenditure multiplier (the higher the MPS).

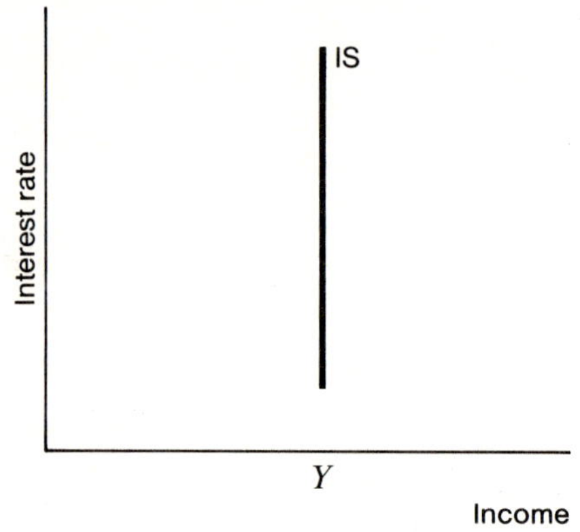

1. If the reaction of autonomous expenditure to changes in the interest rate is small (low value of i), it will take a smaller change in total income to generate the change in total saving required to keep the goods market in equilibrium.

2. If the extra amount of saving per dollar of income is large (high value of s), it will require a smaller addition in total income to generate the extra saving required to balance any extra autonomous expenditure due to declining interest rates.

Since one might expect the interest sensitivity of investment to decline in a recession, we should expect the IS curve to be steeper the lower the level of income— the further to the left in the IS diagram in Figure 4.1. That is why we draw the IS curve in (d) as convex to the origin.

The Effect of Fiscal Policy on the IS Curve

Fiscal policy also affects the IS curve. Take, for example, the positive change in government spending shown in Figure 4.3. This raises the autonomous spending and total sales curves from A_0 to A_1. Keeping the interest rate constant at r_0, we see that equilibrium income would rise from Y_0 to Y_1. Hence, the rise in G shifts the IS curve out from IS_0 to IS_1.

A change in a lump sum tax would have the same effect. A rise in T shifts down the expenditure function in (c). That reduces income, hence shifting the IS curve to the left. A fall in T would have the opposite effect.

The IS Curve When Taxes Are a Function of Income Most tax changes involve tax rates rather than lump sum taxes. What happens to the IS curve when the government changes the tax rate? In Chapter 3 we constructed a model in

Figure 4.3
The IS Curve for Changing G

A change in government expenditure, (ΔG), from G_0 to G_1, shifts the autonomous expenditure up in (b). This shifts up the total demand curve in (c), which increases income from Y_0 to Y_1. Holding the interest rate constant, this means that the IS curve has shifted to the right from IS_0 to IS_1. IS_1 goes through the point r_0, Y_1.

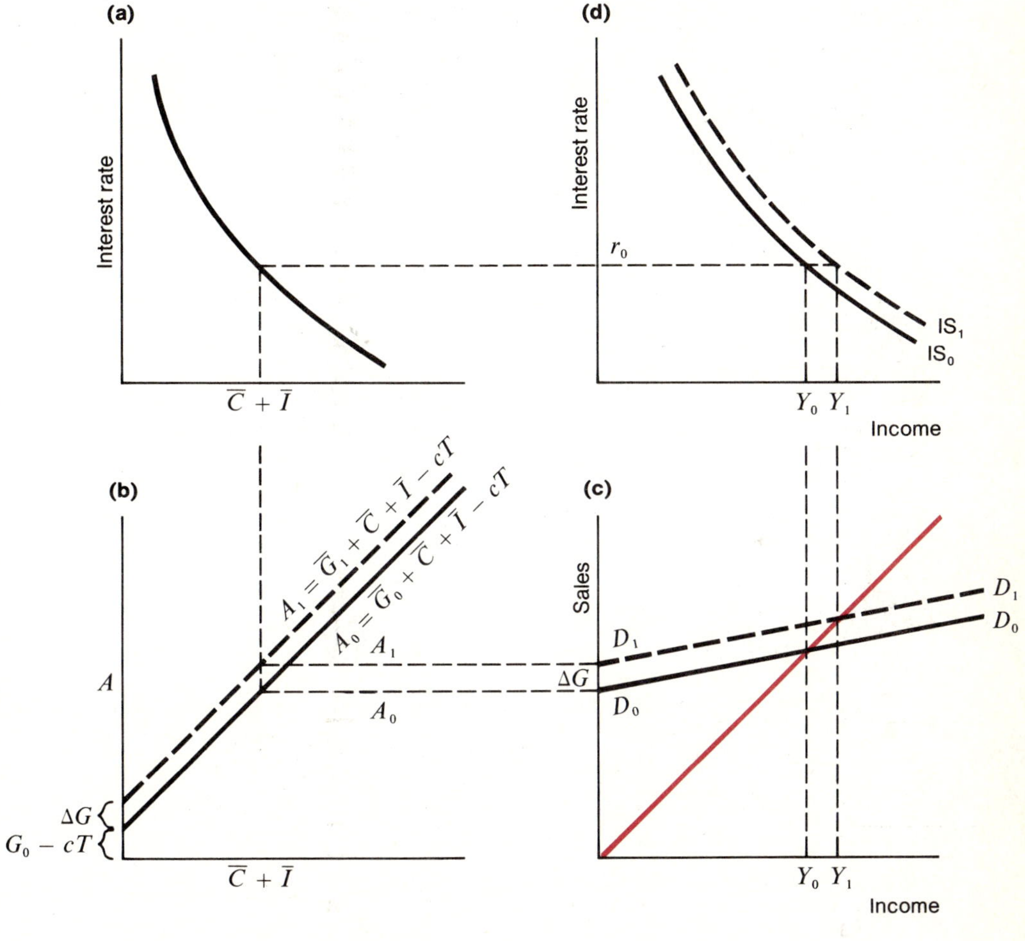

which taxes were a function of income. We now derive the IS curve for this model. We will write the tax function in the simplest possible form as:

(4.7) $$T = tY.$$

If we now substitute Equation (4.7) into Equation (4.1), we get a new expression for both autonomous expenditure and that part of demand which depends on income:

Figure 4.4
The Effect of Lowering the Tax Rate on the IS Curve

Total demand is a function of the tax rate. A reduction in the tax rate rotates the total demand line counterclockwise and raises equilibrium income from Y_0 to Y_1. The IS curve also rotates counterclockwise.

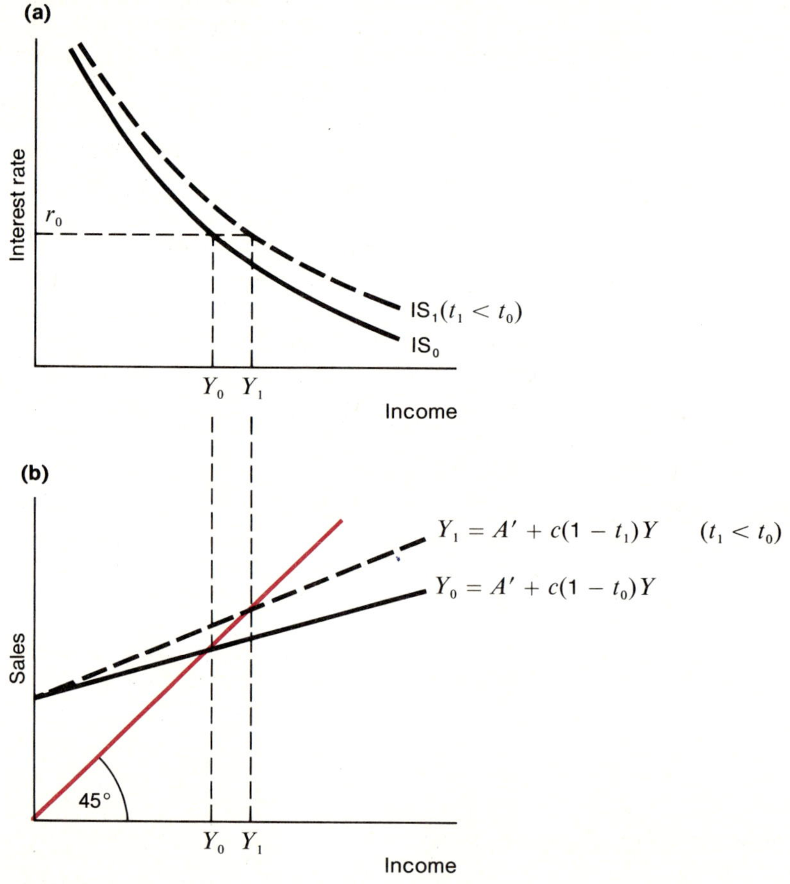

$$Y = \overline{C} + cY - ctY + \overline{I} + \overline{G}.$$

Combining terms, if

$$A' = \overline{C} + \overline{I} + \overline{G},$$

then

(4.8) $$Y = A' + c(1 - t)Y.$$

Autonomous expenditures for this model do not include taxes, since they depend on income. But A' still depends on the interest rate exactly as before. Therefore, using Equation (4.3) we can write A' as a function of G and r:

(4.9) $$A' = \bar{G} - i(r).$$

We now derive the IS curve for this endogenous tax model in Figure 4.4. Diagram (b) shows Equation (4.8). As we learned in Chapter 3, the slope of the demand function shows the amount of induced consumption demand per additional dollar of income; that, according to Equation (4.8), is $c(1 - t)$. Thus, in this model the slope of the demand function depends on the tax rate. If we use the same procedure as earlier to derive the IS curve, we find that the IS curve for this model has the same general shape that it had in our first model. However, that slope depends on the tax rate.

Now let us see what happens when we lower the tax rate. Since the slope of the demand curve is $c(1 - t)$, a reduction in t rotates the demand curve counterclockwise in diagram (b). That in turn rotates the IS curve in a counterclockwise direction and makes the IS curve flatter. In short, the *lower* the tax rate, the *flatter* the IS curve. The reason is that a lower tax rate reduces the society's MPS, making equilibrium income more sensitive to changes in autonomous expenditure.

The following table summarizes the effects of fiscal policy on the IS curve.

Factors	Effect on IS	Net Effect
Rise in G	Shift to right	Expansionary
Fall in G	Shift to left	Contractionary
Rise in T (lump sum tax)	Shift to left	Contractionary
Fall in T	Shift to right	Expansionary
Rise in t (tax rate)	Rotate clockwise	Contractionary
Fall in t	Rotate counterclockwise	Expansionary

Asset Market Equilibrium

We turn now to asset markets and their role in the determination of interest and income. Up to this point we have ignored asset markets and have focused instead on the factors determining the amount of saving and investment in the economy. But households must not only decide how much to save; they must also decide the form in which to hold their accumulated savings. This is a problem in **portfolio theory.** The public holds its wealth, the accumulated result of past saving, in many different forms, from cash and money market certificates to bonds, equities, houses, and gold. Each asset has certain characteristics of safety, risk, and return and a market for which we can analyze supply and demand. Portfolio theory and these characteristics determine the demand for each of the assets. On the supply side, the stock of each asset increases or decreases over time according to processes that differ for each asset. In the short run, the asset markets clear when prices adjust in such a way that the public is just willing to hold its particular portfolio of assets. Over time this portfolio can change, either because of government actions which are called monetary policy, because of government deficits and their financing, or because the price of a reproducible asset has been bid up above its replacement cost.

We shall attempt a more thorough analysis of portfolio theory and the demand for money in Chapters 13 and 14. Here, in order to focus on the main determinants of aggregate demand, we shall present a simplified portfolio theory that will be sufficient to discuss monetary policy and the effect of asset markets on the level of income. To do this we shall somewhat arbitrarily divide the public portfolio of assets into two broad classes: money and all interest-earning assets. We shall define money as cash plus bank checking accounts, ignoring the fact that banks have begun to pay interest on some classes of checking accounts. In making such a division of the total portfolio, we are assuming that all interest-earning assets are broad substitutes. We shall call this second class of assets bonds.

In our classification scheme, the total value of wealth is the sum of money plus bonds:

(4.10) $$W = M + B.$$

The portfolio decision facing the public is: How much of its total portfolio should it hold in interest-earning assets, and how much should it hold in money? In order to understand that decision, we must analyze the public demand for money and bonds. However, we need not analyze the demand for both simultaneously—because of Equation (4.10), either one will be sufficient. For Equation (4.10) is a wealth constraint. It tells us that the public cannot demand more bonds unless it is willing to give up money to pay for them. Nor can it demand more money without being willing to give up bonds. Therefore, if we analyze the demand for money and the total value of wealth is given, we implicitly also know the demand for bonds.

Another way of expressing this idea is to say that if the demand is equal to the supply of money—that is, if there is equilibrium in the money market—the same thing must be true in the bond market. Therefore, in this simplified two-asset world, we can synthesize all of our asset markets into one fundamental analysis of either the money market or the bond market. We shall follow custom in choosing the money market for analysis. The reader should understand that we are implicitly determining demand and supply in the bond market as well, because of the wealth constraint.

The Demand for Money

The demand for money depends on income, interest rates, total wealth, and prices. Let us look at each of these determinants in turn.

The level of real income influences the demand for money because money is used to make purchases. Thus we would expect that the higher the level of income, the greater would be the demand for money.

The interest rate should be negatively related to the demand for money. Recall that money is the non–interest-earning asset in the public portfolio. The interest rate represents the opportunity cost of holding idle cash. Accordingly, the higher the interest rate, the more costly it is to hold money and, therefore, the more bonds and the less money the public should demand. Alternatively, if the interest rate on bonds is low there is little cost in holding money, and the public should therefore demand more of it.

Wealth is positively related to the demand for money. If total wealth rises, one would expect the public to increase its demand for both bonds and money. Indeed, if the interest rate is constant, one might reasonably expect the ratio of money to wealth to remain constant. Suppose, for example, that the public portfolio consists of 25 percent money and 75 percent bonds. Then, if there is a $1 million increase in wealth and no change in the interest rate, one would expect the demand for money to rise by $250,000 and the demand for bonds by $750,000.

Prices are positively related to the demand for money. Since the total volume of transactions in an economy is equal to price times output, a rise in prices, with real income held constant, should increase the need for transactions balances and hence increase the demand for money.

We can summarize this discussion in Equation (4.11), which is a general functional relationship between the demand for money and each of the four factors. The sign over each variable indicates its influence on the demand for nominal money balances.[3]

(4.11)
$$M = m(\overset{+}{P}, \overset{+}{Y}, \overset{-}{r}, \overset{+}{W}).$$

To rewrite Equation (4.11) in real terms, we divide the two nominal variables, M and W, by P:

(4.12)
$$\frac{M}{P} = n\left(\overset{+}{Y}, \overset{-}{r}, \overset{+}{\frac{W}{P}}\right).$$

M/P is called **real money balances.** It is the command over resources represented by a given nominal supply of money. Equation (4.12) says that the demand for real balances is positively related to real income and the real value of wealth and negatively related to the interest rate.

So much for the demand for money. What about the supply of money? In the simple world we are now considering, we shall ignore the complications introduced by fractional reserve banking and say that the nominal money supply, M_s, is controlled by the Federal Reserve. It can change the stock of money held by the public through **open market operations.**

The Federal Reserve has a large quantity of government bonds in its portfolio. An open market operation is the sale or purchase of government bonds by the Fed. When the Fed purchases bonds from the public, it pays for the purchase by increasing the supply of money in public hands. An open market sale of bonds reduces the supply of money. In Chapter 14 we shall go into the entire process of money creation more thoroughly, but for the moment it is sufficient to remember

[3] A fuller discussion of the demand for money will be presented in Chapters 13 and 14.

Figure 4.5
The Money Market

An increase in income increases the demand for money from D_0 to D_1. This raises the equilibrium interest rate from r_0 to r_1.

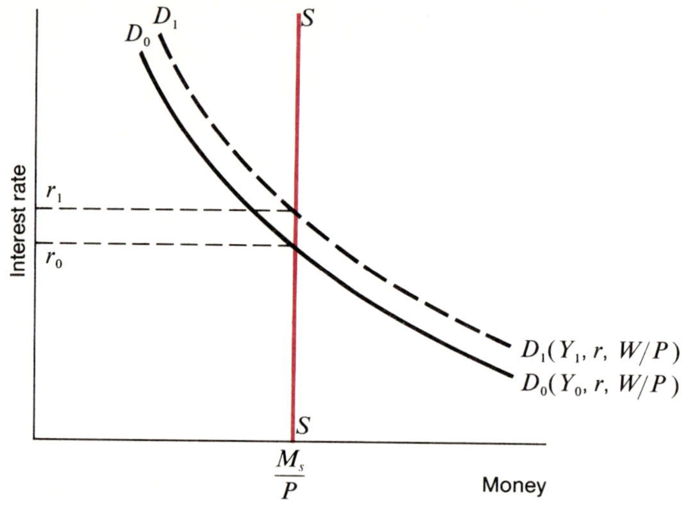

that the Federal Reserve controls the money supply by open market operations. Monetary policy is carried out by the Fed through open market purchases or sales of government bonds, and the money supply is an exogenous policy variable under the control of the Fed.

Equilibrium in the money market requires that demand equal supply. Hence the equilibrium condition is:

$$\frac{M_d}{P} = n\left(Y, r, \frac{W}{P}\right) = \frac{M_s}{P}. \tag{4.13}$$

Let us now put all of these factors together in the form of a diagram of the money market. In Figure 4.5, for given values of Y and W, the demand for real balances can be represented as a negative function of the interest rate. The supply of money is an exogenous policy variable under the control of the Federal Reserve. In the diagram, the supply of real balances is the vertical line SS. Equilibrium in the money market is where supply equals demand, which occurs at r_0.

Figure 4.5 shows only the relationship between the demand and supply of money and the interest rate. Each of the other variables appearing in Equations (4.12) and (4.13) are shift variables in either the demand or the supply of money. For example, an increase in income or wealth increases the demand for money and shifts the demand curve to the right as shown in Figure 4.5. If the M_s does not rise, the rise in Y or W causes an increase in r.

Figure 4.6
The Effect of an Increase in Prices on the Money Market

A rise in prices shifts the money supply curve from S_0S_0 to S_1S_1. But at the same time, it reduces the real value of wealth and therefore reduces the demand for money. However, the demand curve must shift leftward by less than the supply curve. As a result, an increase in prices will raise the interest rate, from r_0 to r_1.

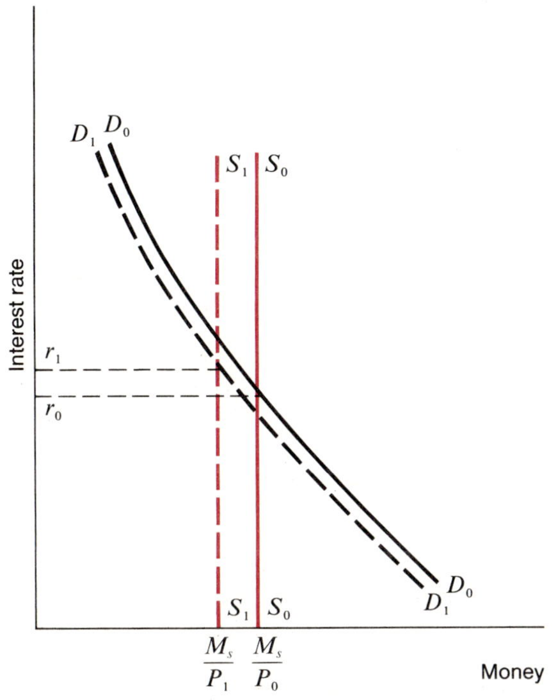

An increase in price, shown in Figure 4.6, is somewhat more complex, for that affects both demand and supply. A rise in price reduces the real supply of money, M_s/P; that shifts the supply curve in the figure to the left. But since the rise in price also reduces the real value of wealth, it also reduces the demand for money.

Which falls more, supply or demand? The answer is that supply does. That is because a reduction in wealth reduces the demand for all assets, not just money. Therefore, a rise in prices causes the supply curve in Figure 4.6 to shift further to the left than the demand curve. The net result is that a rise in prices causes excess demand in the money market and a rise in the interest rate.

The LM Curve

Having presented a thumbnail sketch of portfolio theory and the demand for money, we return now to our analysis of the simultaneous determination of interest and income. To do that, we require that both the money market and the goods market be in equilibrium simultaneously. The IS curve shows the combinations of interest and income at which the goods market is in equilibrium. The **LM curve** shows the same thing for the money market. The LM curve is defined as the collection of all pairs of interest rates and levels of income at which the money market is in equilibrium.

Deriving the LM Curve What does the LM curve look like? To answer that question we use the diagram of the money market to construct the LM curve. Look at Figure 4.7. In (a) we reproduce the money market diagram. If wealth, prices, and income are W_0, P_0, and Y_0, the demand curve for money is D_0D_0 and the equilibrium interest rate is r_0. If income increases to Y_1, the money demand curve shifts out to D_1D_1 and the equilibrium interest rate rises to r_1.

Let us now put this into a diagram of the LM curve, shown in diagram (b). At Y_0, the money market is in equilibrium at the interest rate r_0. Hence, r_0, Y_0 is a point, A, on the LM curve. If income rises to Y_1, there is an increase in the transactions demand for money. Demand rises to D_1D_1, and the market clearing interest rate rises to r_1. Thus, r_1, Y_1 is a second point, B, on the LM curve. Varying Y in this way, one can determine other points on the LM curve.

As the reader can see, the market clearing interest rate rises with income. The LM curve is upward sloping, because a rise in income increases the demand for money. Anything that does this will raise interest rates, at least in the short run.

The Linear LM Curve As in our analysis of the IS curve, it is useful for expositional purposes to derive a specific equation for the LM curve for the case where the demand for money is a linear function of interest, income, and wealth. For that case Equation (4.12) may be written:

$$\frac{M_d}{P} = nY - qr + u\frac{W}{P}. \tag{4.14}$$

The element $-q$ indicates the sensitivity of the demand for money to interest rates. The larger q is, the greater is the interest sensitivity of the demand for money and the flatter the demand curve in the money market.

To derive an algebraic expression for the LM curve for the linear case, substitute Equation (4.14) into Equation (4.13) and solve for r. Thus:

$$\frac{M_s}{P} = nY - qr + u\frac{W}{P}. \tag{4.15}$$

$$r = \frac{nY + u\dfrac{W}{P} - \dfrac{M_s}{P}}{q}. \tag{4.16}$$

The slope of the LM curve in this case is the coefficient of Y, n/q. This coefficient tells us that the slope of the LM curve depends both on the interest sensitivity of the demand for money and on transactions demand. The larger the value of q, the flatter the LM curve. This means that the more interest-sensitive the demand for money, the flatter the LM curve. But since $-q$ is the slope of the demand-for-

Figure 4.7
The Money Market and the LM Curve
In (a), the demand for money is D_0D_0, at income Y_0, and the equilibrium interest rate is r_0; this corresponds to point A on the LM curve in (b). If income is Y_1, the demand for money increases to D_1D_1, and the interest rate rises to r_1; this corresponds to point B on the LM curve. The LM curve is upward sloping, because an increase in income increases the demand for money and raises the interest rate.

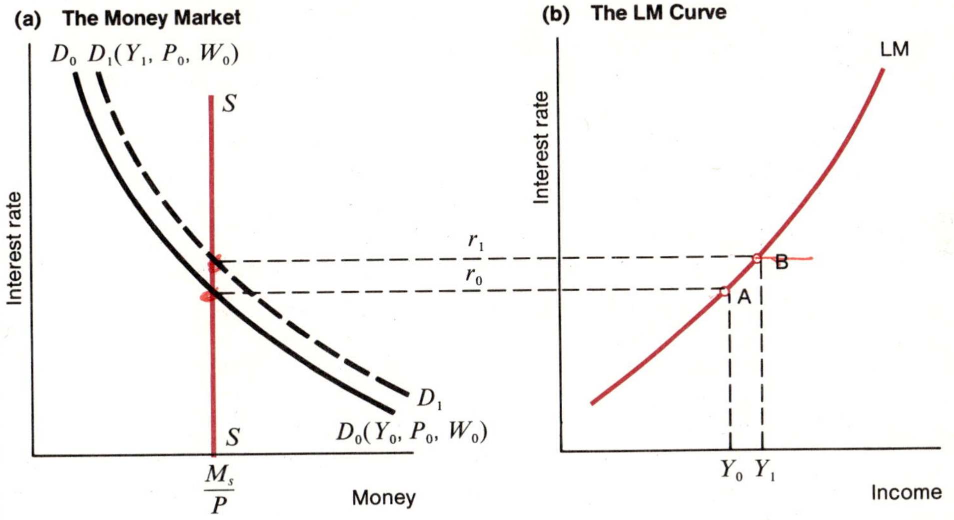

money function itself, we can summarize by saying that the more sensitive the demand for money, the flatter both the LM and the demand-for-money curves will be.

The relationship between interest sensitivity and slope that we have found for the linear case holds true in general. The shape of the LM curve is a mirror image of the underlying demand-for-money curve from which it is derived. The more interest-sensitive the demand for money, the flatter the LM curve.

Factors That Shift the LM Curve

Three factors in our model can shift the LM curve: the money supply, prices, and the supply of bonds. Let us examine each in turn.

The effect of an increase in the money supply is shown in Figure 4.8. First, the increase shifts the vertical supply curve to the right. However, the change in the money supply also increases the demand for money, because money is part of wealth; thus, both the demand curve and the supply curve shift to the right. But which curve shifts more? The answer is, the supply curve. Portfolio theory teaches us that when there is an increase in wealth, the demand for all assets rises, not just the demand for the particular asset whose quantity has increased. Thus, the de-

Figure 4.8
The Effect of a Change in M on the LM Curve

A change in M shifts the money supply to the right. The demand for money shifts also, but by less. That is because we assume that an increase in W increases the demand for all assets, not just money. Since the wealth constraint must be satisfied, we know that $\Delta M_d < \Delta M_s = \Delta W$. Therefore, the increase in M leads to a decline in the interest rate. That tells us that an increase in M shifts the LM down and to the right.

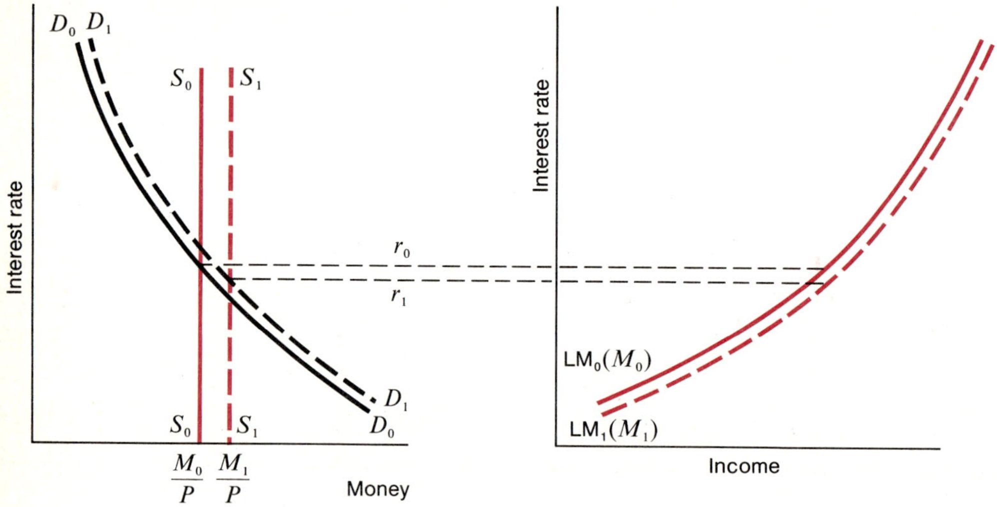

mand for money rises less than the supply, and that causes a decline in the interest rate. To put it another way: The public will not hold the new portfolio, with its higher proportion of money, unless the interest rate on bonds declines. In short, a rise in the money supply drives down the equilibrium interest rate. Given the definition of the LM curve, this implies that the LM curve shifts down and to the right in response to an increase in M_s.

The effect of a change in prices, shown in Figure 4.9, is similar to that of a change in the money supply, since each affects the supply of real balances. For example, a fall in the price level will increase the supply of real balances and the real value of wealth. Both the demand and the supply of money will increase, the latter more than the former, for exactly the same reasons just described in the case of an increase in the money supply. As a result, we know that a reduction in prices shifts the LM to the right while an increase in prices shifts it to the left.

The last factor that can shift the LM curve is a change in total wealth coming from an expansion or contraction in the supply of bonds, holding the money supply constant (see Figure 4.10). Note that this change is not the same as an open market operation, because the latter is a swap of money and bonds by the Fed. The only way that the bond supply can be increased, holding the money supply constant, is for the government to run deficits that it finances by selling bonds.

Figure 4.9
The Effect of a Fall in Prices

A fall in prices increases the real supply of money, thus shifting the M/P line to the right. This shifts the LM curve down and to the right for exactly the same reasons analyzed in the case of an increase in the nominal money supply.

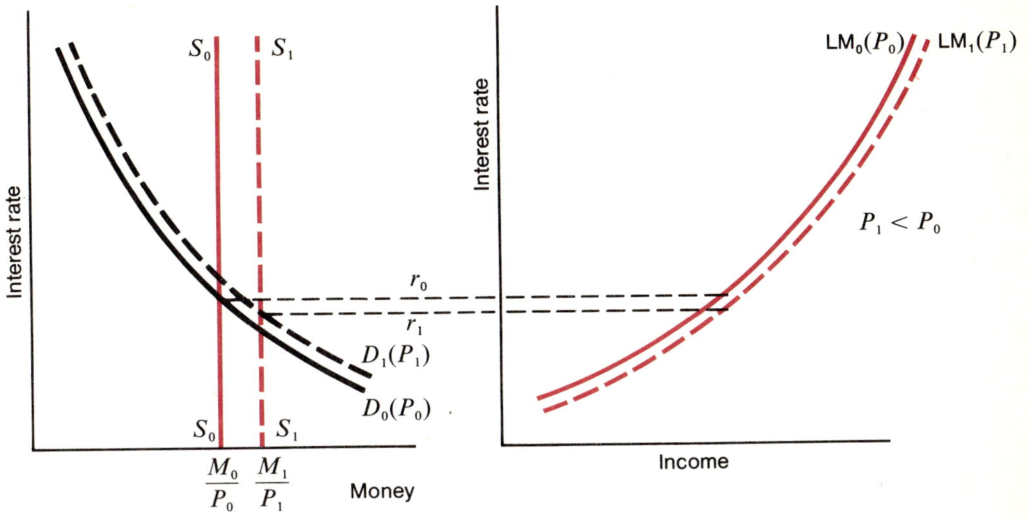

Figure 4.10
The Effect of an Increase in Bonds

An increase in the supply of bonds increases the demand for money. At a given income and price level, the interest rate increases to maintain equilibrium in the money market. That is equivalent to saying that the LM curve shifts up and to the left, from LM_0 to LM_1.

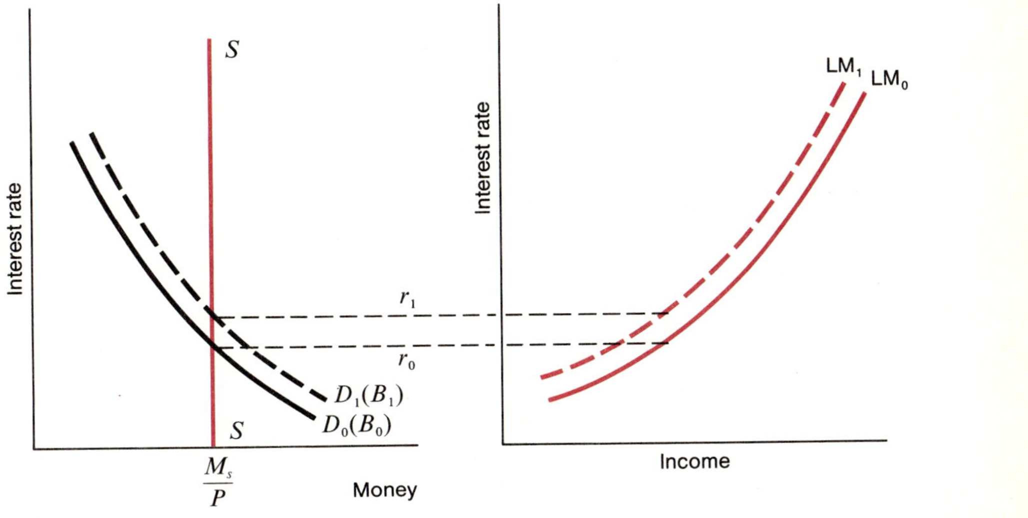

Since bonds are part of wealth, when the bond supply is increased in this way the total value of wealth increases. This increases the demand for money, which in turn drives up the interest rate and shifts the LM curve up and to the left. All this can be seen in Figure 4.10. The increase in the supply of bonds to finance a government deficit increases wealth, thus shifting the LM curve to LM_1. A reduction in the bond supply would have exactly the opposite effect.

The following table summarizes the factors that can affect the LM curve.

Factors	Effect on LM	Net Effect
Rise in M	Shift to right	Expansionary
Fall in M	Shift to left	Contractionary
Rise in B	Shift to left	Contractionary
Fall in B	Shift to right	Expansionary
Rise in P	Shift to left	Contractionary
Fall in P	Shift to right	Expansionary

Equilibrium in the Money and Goods Markets

We now combine our analyses of the money and goods markets to get an equilibrium that simultaneously satisfies both markets. We then examine the dynamic process by which the economy moves from one equilibrium to another. Having done that, we will be ready for a closer look at monetary and fiscal policy and their effects on the economy.

In this chapter we have developed a model in which the interest rate and income are both endogenous variables. We get the equilibrium levels of these two variables simultaneously by requiring that both the goods market and the money market be in equilibrium. Algebraically, we could find the equilibrium values of Y and r by solving simultaneously the equations for the IS and LM curves. However, for the nonlinear case, we will solve this problem using the IS-LM diagram instead. Since the IS and LM curves represent all the equilibrium points in the goods and money markets, the point that simultaneously produces equilibrium in both markets can only be at the intersection of the two curves, point E in Figure 4.11.

Now consider the effect on this equilibrium of an increase in autonomous expenditure.[4] As we learned in our analysis of the IS curve, such a change shifts the IS curve to the right, to the dashed line in Figure 4.11. Two things then happen: Income rises from Y_0 to Y_1, and interest rates rise from r_0 to r_1. At first glance, this result does not appear to be very different from the simple multiplier analysis of Chapter 3.

Yet we learn two interesting things by incorporating the money market into the model. The first is that a rise in autonomous expenditures drives up the interest rate, unless, of course, it is matched by an increase in the money supply. The reason is that any increase in income leads to an increase in the demand for money. Since the supply is fixed, the interest rate must rise.

[4] This increase could come from an increase in G or a reduction in T.

Figure 4.11
The IS-LM Diagram

An increase in A shifts the IS curve out by $\Delta A/(1 - c)$; that is the distance AB. But equilibrium income rises only from A to D. That is because the rise in the interest rate crowds out private expenditure equal to the distance DB.

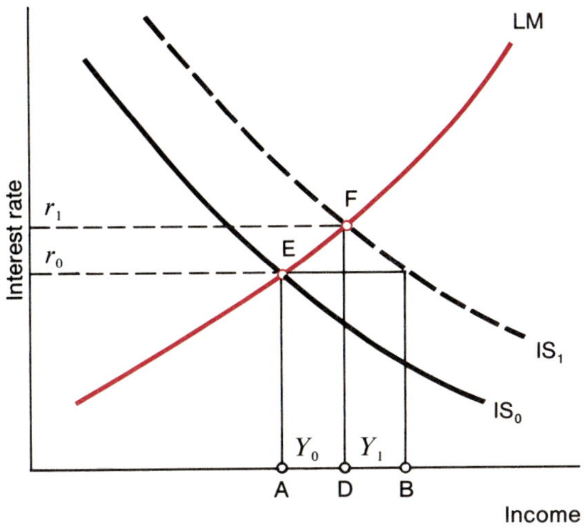

The second thing we learn is that the effect of shifts in autonomous expenditure on income is smaller in the IS-LM model than it was in the simple model of Chapter 3. Let us see why. In Figure 4.11 the rightward shift in the IS curve tells us how much demand would increase if the interest rate did not change. For the model with lump sum taxes, that is exactly the multiplier of Chapter 3 times the change in A. In Figure 4.11 the shift is distance AB, equal to $\Delta A/(1 - c)$. But if the LM curve is upward sloping, the interest rate must change too: It rises from r_0 to r_1. That reduces both consumption and investment expenditure, which reduces aggregate demand and offsets part of the initial rise in A. The offset is the distance BD in Figure 4.11.

What happens here is that a rise in autonomous expenditure increases aggregate demand, but the concomitant rise in the interest rate chokes off interest-sensitive expenditures at the same time. On balance, the net effect of a rise in A is still expansionary, but the size of the effect is smaller than it was in the simple model. Income is less sensitive to shifts in autonomous expenditure in the IS-LM economy, because any increase in aggregate demand also increases the demand for money. That raises the interest rate, which automatically chokes off interest-sensitive expenditures. It should be clear that the steeper the LM curve (the bigger the change in the interest rate), the less income will vary with changes in autonomous expenditures in the goods market.

Dynamic Analysis

We have now shown what happens to the equilibrium income and interest rate in response to a particular disturbance. However, we have not discussed how the economy gets from one equilibrium point to another. That is a problem in dynamics, which can be defined as the study of how an economy moves from one equilibrium to another. To do this, we must consider the characteristics of points that are not on the IS or LM curves.

Consider the four regions into which we have divided Figure 4.12. Any point that is to the right (left) of the IS curve is one at which saving is greater (less) than investment in the goods market. Hence, at any point in either region a or b sales will be less than production, and at any point in region c or d sales will be greater than production.

Similarly, with the money market any point to the right (left) of the LM curve is one at which the demand for money is greater (lower) than the supply, since money demand depends positively on income. We may conclude that there is an excess demand for money in regions b and c and an excess supply in regions a and d.

When there is excess demand in the goods market ($S < I$), production increases; when there is excess supply ($S > I$), production declines. The money market is somewhat more complex. When there is an excess demand for money, people attempt to sell bonds to acquire more money. But since the stock of bonds and money outstanding is fixed, this simply drives down the price of outstanding bonds or, conversely, raises the interest rate. For a bond is a contract promising to pay a fixed number of dollars per year. Secondhand bonds are bought and sold on financial markets, and their price determines the effective interest rate. That is because the effective interest rate is the coupon yield on the bond divided by the price of the bond.[5] Expressed algebraically,

(4.17) $$r = \frac{Co}{P_B}.$$

Co = annual dollar payment to bondholder (coupon)
P_B = market price of outstanding bonds

If there is an increase in the demand for money, the demand for bonds declines. That causes a fall in the prices of outstanding bonds which, according to Equation (4.17), is equivalent to a rise in the interest rate. This is the way that an increase in the demand for money increases the interest rate. When there is an

[5] Bonds are issued at a standard price, usually $1000. At that time, their interest rate and the coupon yield are identical. Subsequently, secondhand bonds may be traded at whatever price they will bring. Then, the effective interest rate is the coupon divided by the current price of the bond. As an example, take a bond issued for $1000, paying a yearly coupon of $80. The original interest rate is 8 percent. Subsequently, if the interest rate rises to 10 percent, investors will be willing to pay only $800 for this bond, since they can buy a new bond earning $100 for $1000. Thus, as the demand for bonds rises the prices of old bonds rise, causing a decline in interest rates. An increase in the demand for money (fall in demand for bonds) has the opposite effect.

Figure 4.12
Disequilibrium Regions

Regions to the right of the LM curve represent excess demand for money. In such cases the interest rate should be rising, which we show by the rising arrows in regions c and b. In regions to the left of the LM curve there is an excess supply of money, and interest rates should be falling. In regions to the right of the IS curve there is an excess supply in the goods market, because saving is greater than investment. We could expect production and income to be falling in such cases, which we show by the westward arrows in regions a and b. To the left of the IS curve, there is excess demand and production is increasing. In this diagram, wherever the economy starts, the arrows indicate that it will go to the equilibrium intersection of the IS and LM curves.

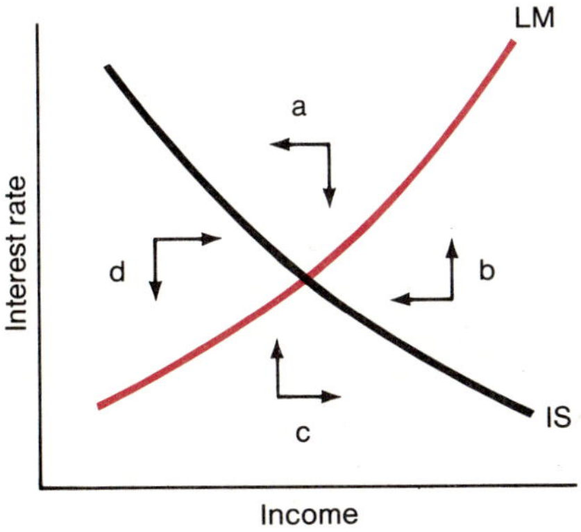

excess demand for money, bondholders attempt to sell bonds, with the result that the price of bonds falls and the interest rate rises. When there is an excess supply of money, there is an excess demand for bonds. Bond prices rise, and the interest rate declines.

We now combine these results, using arrows to indicate the motions that we expect in each of the disequilibrium regions in Figure 4.12. Take, for example, region c. Here there is an excess demand for both money and goods; accordingly, we expect production and interest rates both to be increasing. In region d, there is an excess supply of money and an excess demand for goods. We therefore expect interest rates to fall and production to rise if the economy is temporarily in this area. In Figure 4.12 we indicate the horizontal and vertical movements expected in each region by a pair of arrows. In c the economy will move northeast, in d southeast. We summarize the characteristics of each region in Table 4.1.

Now consider the dynamic pathway by which an economy gets to equilibrium. As before, suppose an autonomous increase in expenditure shifts the IS curve out to IS_1, as shown in Figure 4.13. We know that equilibrium moves from point A to point B. Assuming that the economy starts at the original equilibrium point, A, how does it get to B after the change? After the increase in autonomous expenditure has shifted the IS curve out to IS_1, A is on the border of region c. There is excess

Table 4.1
Characteristics of Disequilibrium Regions

Region	Goods Market	Money Market	Change in Y and r
a	Excess supply	Excess supply	$Y\downarrow, r\downarrow$
b	Excess supply	Excess demand	$Y\downarrow, r\uparrow$
c	Excess demand	Excess demand	$Y\uparrow, r\uparrow$
d	Excess demand	Excess supply	$Y\uparrow, r\downarrow$

Figure 4.13
Dynamic Adjustment to an Increase in Government Spending

An outward shift in the IS curve leads to excess demand for money. As the interest rate rises the economy goes to the new equilibrium, at point B. Since we assume that the money market clears faster than the goods market, the dynamic pathway from point A to point B stays close to the LM curve.

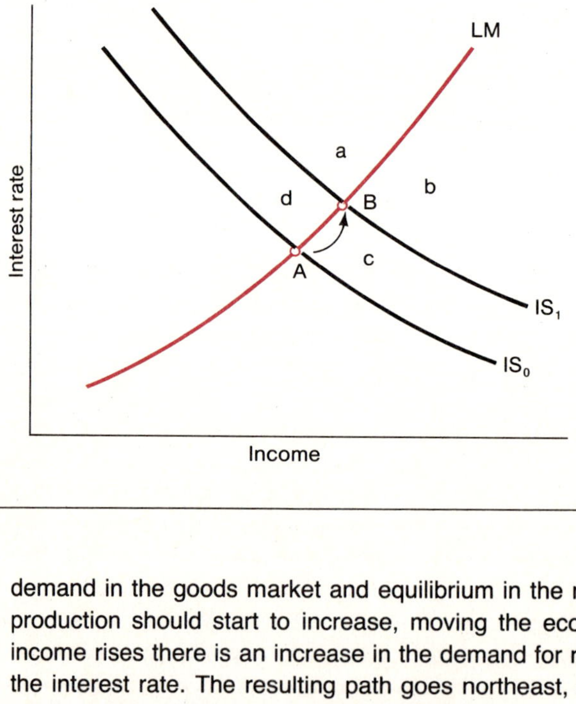

demand in the goods market and equilibrium in the money market. Accordingly, production should start to increase, moving the economy east from A. But as income rises there is an increase in the demand for money, which tends to raise the interest rate. The resulting path goes northeast, as indicated by the arrows, until the new equilibrium is reached at point B.

Relative Adjustment Speeds

We are going to assume that the money market adjusts more rapidly than the goods market. Since it takes time to hire or fire workers and alter production schedules in response to goods market disequilibrium—whereas financial mar-

Figure 4.14
Effect of a Decline in the Money Supply

A decline in M shifts the LM curve to LM_1. However, because we assume that the money market clears faster than the goods market, the economy first goes to point C. At C interest rates have risen enough to make the supply equal to the demand for money at the initial income level. Then, as investment declines, both income and interest rates decline as the economy goes to its new equilibrium at B. The point is that interest rates may well rise and then decline in response to a fall in the money supply.

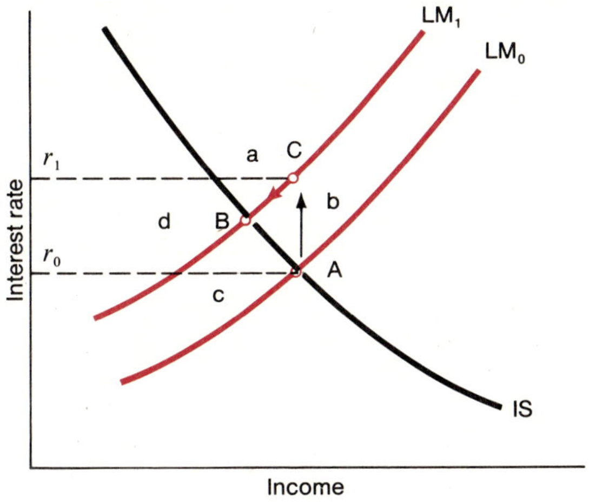

kets should clear rapidly—this seems like a reasonable assumption. It also has some important implications for our dynamic analysis. Basically, it implies that our dynamic adjustment pathways stay close to the LM curve as the economy moves from one equilibrium position to another. This does not affect the dynamic analysis for shifts in the IS curve, but it does when the disturbances are in the LM curve. Let us look more closely at this sort of disturbance.

Suppose that the economy in Figure 4.14 is in full equilibrium at point A but is disturbed by a decline in the money supply. As we have learned, reducing M_s causes the LM curve to shift leftward to LM_1. We also know that the new equilibrium will be at point B, where income is lower and the interest rate is higher. How does the economy get to B? After the reduction in M_s, point A is on the border of region b. The goods market is in equilibrium, but there is an excess demand for money. In general, according to the laws of motion developed in Table 4.1, we know that the economy will move northwest from A to B. However, if we assume that the money market adjusts rapidly, the path is not quite so simple. First, the interest rate rises to r_1; that puts the money market back into equilibrium. But now there is excess supply in the goods market. Investment declines, production drops, and the interest rate gradually drops until a new equilibrium is established at B.

The point of this discussion is that when the money market adjusts more rapidly than the goods market, the interest rate may well rise above its new equilibrium level during the dynamic adjustment process. In other words, in region b the movement may be straight north to the LM curve and then southwest, rather than a gradual change of both interest and income. This particular dynamic pathway will be useful in understanding how the economy responds to monetary disturbances and monetary policy, two subjects we will take up in more detail in the next chapter.

Summary

In this chapter we have combined the goods market and the money market into a simultaneous model of aggregate demand. The model demonstrates how the interest rate feedback affects the impact of changes in government spending or taxes on aggregate demand. It also gives us a framework in which to analyze the effect of monetary policy on the economy. With this framework we are now ready to consider how monetary and fiscal policies can be used to affect the level and the composition of output in the economy. This will be the subject of the next chapter.

Key Concepts

IS curve
portfolio theory
real money balances
open market operation
LM curve
dynamic analysis

Problems and Questions for Discussion

1. Why is the IS curve downward sloping and the LM curve upward sloping?

2. Which of the changes listed below cause a shift in the IS curve and which cause a movement along the IS curve?

- **a.** An increase in G.
- **b.** An increase in the interest rate, leading to a reduction in investment.
- **c.** An increase in income, leading to an increase in consumption.
- **d.** An increase in the money supply.
- **e.** An increase in the marginal propensity to consume.

3. Which of the changes below cause a shift in the LM curve and which cause a movement along the LM curve?

- **a.** An increase in the interest rate, leading to a reduction in the demand for money.
- **b.** An increase in the money supply.
- **c.** An increase in the bond supply.
- **d.** A fall in the price level.
- **e.** An increase in income, leading to an increase in the demand for money.

4. Describe the transmission mechanism by which a change in the money supply leads to an increase in income. Can you think of any circumstances in which the change in M will not lead to a change in Y?

5. The model given in this problem will be used in Questions 5–8. Suppose that an economy has the following behavioral equations and identities for consumption, investment, taxes, and the demand for money. Note that for simplicity we are going to introduce the variable bonds (B), rather than total wealth in the demand for money equation.

$$C = 10 + .8Y_d$$
$$I = 90 - 200r$$
$$T = .2Y$$
$$\frac{M_d}{P} = .4Y - 200r + \frac{.3B}{P}$$
$$Y_d = Y - T$$

Exogenous variables have the following values:

$$M_s = 440$$
$$G = 280$$
$$B = 200$$
$$P = 1.00$$

a. What are the equilibrium conditions for the money and goods markets?
b. Derive and graph the IS and LM curves. What is the algebraic expression for the slope of each curve?
c. Under what conditions would the IS curve be vertical? Under what conditions would the LM curve be flat? Vertical? Explain what those slope conditions imply about the underlying behavioral equations.

6. Using the equations for the IS and LM curves, find the equilibrium values for Y and r. Show this equilibrium on the graph you have made of the IS and LM curves.

7. Show the effect of a change in the tax rate from .20 to .22 on the IS-LM diagram and on the equilibrium levels of Y and r. Why does a rise in tax rates reduce the interest rate?

8. Suppose the money supply increases from 440 to 450. Show the effect of this change on the IS-LM curves and on the equilibrium level of income and interest rates. Assume $t = .2$.

9. Describe the dynamic process by which an economy reaches a new equilibrium after an increase in the money supply.

Chapter 5

Controlling the Level of Aggregate Demand with Monetary and Fiscal Policies

In the last chapter we developed a model with which to analyze how monetary policy and fiscal policy affect the level of aggregate demand. We now use that model to see how and when the two policies can be used. For the moment we shall maintain the assumption that the level of supply adjusts passively to the level of aggregate demand. The supply side will be brought into our analysis in the next chapter.

Monetary Policy

Monetary policy is carried out by expanding or contracting the money supply through open market operations.[1] As we learned in the last chapter, open market operations consist of purchases or sales of government bonds by the Federal Reserve. If the Fed wishes to carry out an expansionary open market operation, it purchases government bonds from the public. This increases the money supply, drives down interest rates, and shifts the LM curve to the right, as shown in Figure 5.1. Under our assumption that the money market adjusts more rapidly than the goods market, the economy moves first from point A to point B. At B the decline in the interest rate stimulates interest-sensitive expenditures, causing investment to rise above saving. At B there is excess demand in the goods market. If supply passively adjusts to the increase in aggregate demand production increases, and the economy expands outward to a new equilibrium at point C in the diagram.

[1] The money supply can also be expanded or contracted by changing the reserve ratio, as we shall see in Chapter 14. That changes the amount of money that can be supported by a given monetary base.

Figure 5.1
Expansionary Monetary Policy

An expansion in the money supply shifts the LM curve to the right. In the short run, interest rates drop as the economy moves from point A to point B. At B there is excess demand in the goods market, so production increases until a new equilibrium is reached at point C.

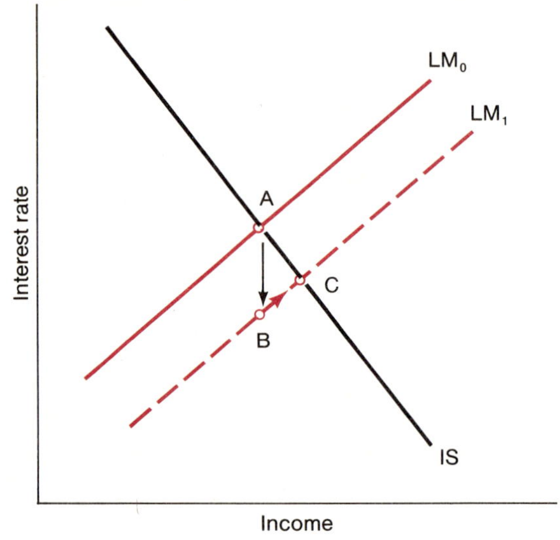

When Monetary Policy Is Ineffective

The effectiveness of monetary policy depends on the slopes of both the IS and LM curves. When either the IS curve is vertical or the LM curve is flat, monetary policy is powerless to change the level of aggregate demand. Let us see why. In Figure 5.2 we show the vertical IS. When the authorities increase the money supply the interest rate drops from r_0 to r_1, but there is no change in spending. The reason is that when the IS curve is vertical, autonomous expenditures do not depend on the rate of interest. Monetary policy works through the interest rate. Therefore, if neither consumption nor investment expenditures are sensitive to the interest rate, monetary policy is ineffective.

The Liquidity Trap Another case in which monetary policy is ineffective occurs when changes in the money supply do not change the interest rate. When this occurs, the LM curve is flat and the economy is in what economists call a **liquidity trap.**[2]

[2]The notion of a liquidity trap was first introduced by John M. Keynes in *The General Theory of Employment, Interest and Money* (London: Macmillan, 1936). It was originally regarded as the chief reason that economies were unable to get out of recession automatically.

Figure 5.2
The Vertical IS Curve

When the IS curve is vertical, monetary policy has no effect on income. That is because changes in the interest rate have no effect on aggregate demand in the goods market.

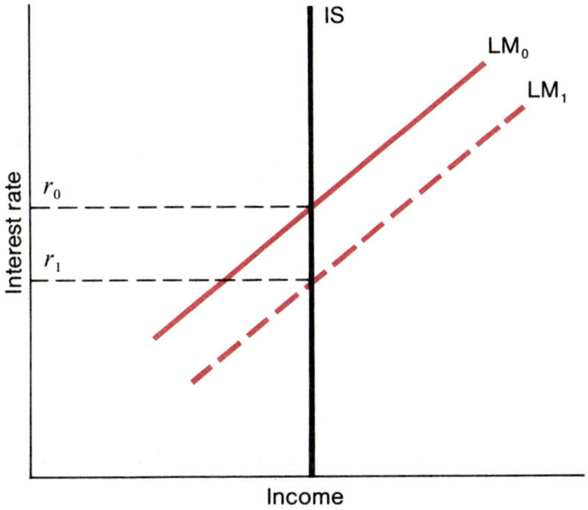

The liquidity trap is shown in Figure 5.3. It occurs at the flat right-hand end of the demand-for-money function. The liquidity trap occurs when the demand for money is so sensitive to the rate of interest that any increase in the money supply is absorbed into idle balances with little or no change in the interest rate. As we shall see further on liquidity traps are thought to occur in depressions, when the interest rate falls to a very low level. When that happens, it is not worthwhile to hold interest-bearing assets.

The liquidity trap portion of the demand-for-money function is reflected in the flat portion of the LM curve in (b), because the LM is a mirror image of the demand for money. When the LM curve is flat, rising income does not drive up the interest rate. The reason is that any increase in transactions balances demanded because of the rise in income can be supplied out of idle balances with no change in the interest rate.

Now consider the effect of expansionary open market operations for an economy in a liquidity trap. The money supply increases from M_0 to M_1; however, the increase in M_s is absorbed into idle balances with no change in the interest rate. As a result, the LM curve does not appear to move. (It shifts to the right as shown by the dashed lines in the diagram, but where it is flat there is no apparent movement.) Since the LM curve does not move, the equilibrium in the goods market is unaffected. The economy stays at point A in the figure. Thus, monetary policy is unable to affect the level of aggregate demand when the economy is in a liquidity trap.

Figure 5.3
The Liquidity Trap

The liquidity trap occurs when the demand for money is very sensitive to the interest rate. When that happens, changes in the supply of money can be absorbed into or out of money balances with no change in *r*. As a result, changes in the money supply have no effect on aggregate spending, and therefore monetary policy is ineffective.

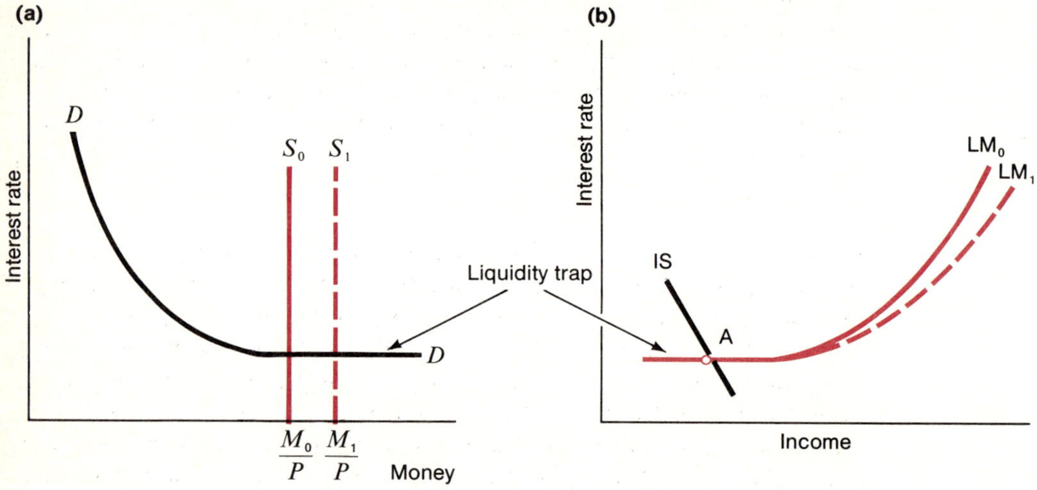

To summarize, monetary policy affects aggregate demand through the interest rate, as shown in the following schematic diagram.

$$\Delta M_s \not\Rightarrow \quad \Delta r \not\Rightarrow \quad \Delta A \Longrightarrow \Delta \textbf{ demand}$$

Liquidity trap (flat LM curve)	Interest-insensitive expenditure (vertical IS curve)

The liquidity trap short-circuits the first link of the chain. Interest-insensitive expenditures break the second. Either is sufficient to destroy the effectiveness of monetary policy.

Fiscal Policy

We turn now to **fiscal policy** and the conditions in which it is effective in changing the level of aggregate spending. As we showed in Chapter 4, fiscal policy affects the IS curve: Increases in government spending and tax reductions shift the IS to the right, and reductions in spending and tax increases shift it to the left. We can now use our complete IS-LM model to analyze the effect of such changes on the level of income. When we do so, we shall see that the effect is a good deal different than it was in the simple model of Chapter 3. Furthermore, there are two cases in which fiscal policy has no effect on the level of aggregate demand. One of these is the exact reverse of the case in which monetary policy is ineffective.

We show the effect of an increase in G in Figure 5.4. The increase in G shifts the IS curve out by distance AB, which is exactly equal to the simple multiplier $1/(1 - c)$ of Chapter 3 times the change in G.[3] As we have already learned, the equilibrium for the economy is at point E. It is clear that the level of income at the new equilibrium point E is smaller than it would be in the simple model. This implies that the effect of G on aggregate demand is smaller in the complete model with money. The reason can be seen in Figure 5.4. When G increases, the increase in income raises the demand for money. That increases the interest rate, which, at least partially, offsets the impact of the original increase in G.

Economists call this the **crowding-out effect.** Raising G, or reducing T, crowds out some private sector expenditure because interest rates are driven up, which reduces investment and consumption. We quantify the crowding-out effect more precisely in Figure 5.4. The rightward shift in the IS curve tells us how much demand would increase *if* interest rates were unchanged; that is distance AB in the diagram. But if the LM curve is upward sloping, the interest rate must change: It rises from r_0 to r_1. That crowds out both consumption and investment and hence reduces aggregate demand (by the amount BC). Thus, the net effect of expansionary fiscal policy is a good deal smaller than it was in the simple model of Chapter 3. What happens is that G increases, which is expansionary, but interest-sensitive private expenditures decline, which partially offsets the expansion. On balance the net effect of expansionary fiscal policy is still positive, but the size of the net fiscal multiplier is a function of conditions in the money market, because these determine the change in the interest rate and hence the amount of crowding out. Looking forward for a moment, it should be clear that the bigger the change in the interest rate (the steeper the LM curve), the larger the amount of autonomous expenditure that will be crowded out, and hence the smaller the net fiscal multiplier.

When Fiscal Policy Is Ineffective

There are two conditions in which fiscal policy is unable to change the level of aggregate demand. In each, crowding out completely offsets the impact of a change in either G or T on aggregate demand. We shall look at the first condition in this section and examine the second, which we shall call asset market crowding out, in the next section.

The most direct and obvious case of complete crowding out occurs when the LM curve is vertical. In that case, the interest rate rises so far in response to expansionary fiscal policy that the increase in G is exactly offset by a reduction in either investment or interest-sensitive consumption. This case is shown in Figure

[3] This is for the model with lump sum taxes.

Figure 5.4
Crowding Out in the IS-LM Diagram

Here we quantify visually the reduction in the fiscal policy multiplier resulting from the rise in interest rates. Crowding out results from the reduction in autonomous expenditure due to the rise in interest rates. If interest rates did not rise with expansionary fiscal policy, income would rise from point A to point B. That is the direct fiscal policy multiplier discussed in Chapter 3. However, due to the feedback of the money market on interest rates, r rises from r_0 to r_1. That crowds out $\Delta A/\Delta r$, which in turn reduces income from point B to point C. The distance BC is, therefore, the amount of expenditure that is crowded out by the rise in interest rates.

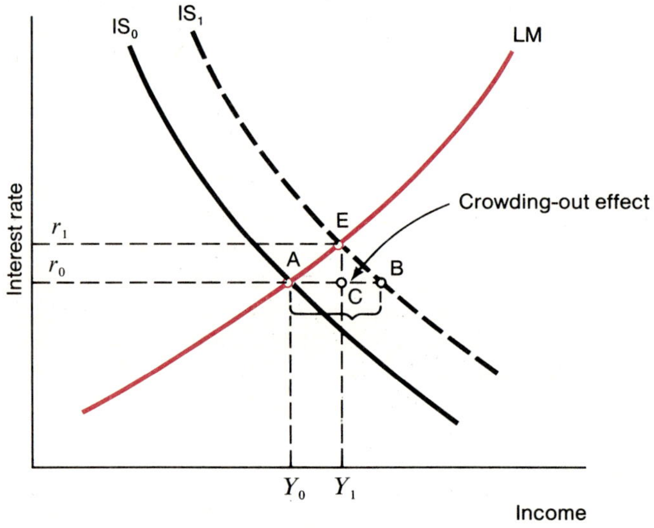

5.5. The IS curve shifts out by $\Delta G/1 - c$. But that increase is matched by a reduction in I and C due to the increase in the interest rate from r_0 to r_1. There is no net increase in demand.

The LM curve is vertical when the demand for money is completely insensitive to the interest rate, depending only on income and wealth. In that case, the money supply will support only one level of income—Y_0 in our diagram. When there is an increase in government expenditure, the interest rate rises far enough to crowd out an equivalent amount of autonomous expenditure.

When we compare situations where monetary policy and fiscal policy are effective or ineffective, a useful pattern emerges. Both policies depend on the interest sensitivity of the demand for money and goods. The greater the interest sensitivity of the demand for money (the flatter the LM curve), the more effective the fiscal policy and the less effective the monetary policy. Conversely, the more interest sensitive the demand for goods (the flatter the IS curve), the more effective the monetary policy and the less effective the fiscal policy.

Figure 5.5
The Vertical LM Curve

When the LM curve is vertical, shifts in the IS curve have no effect on income. That is because the rise in the interest rate is great enough to crowd out an amount of private expenditure equal in size to the initial shift in demand, which is $\Delta G/(1 - c)$.

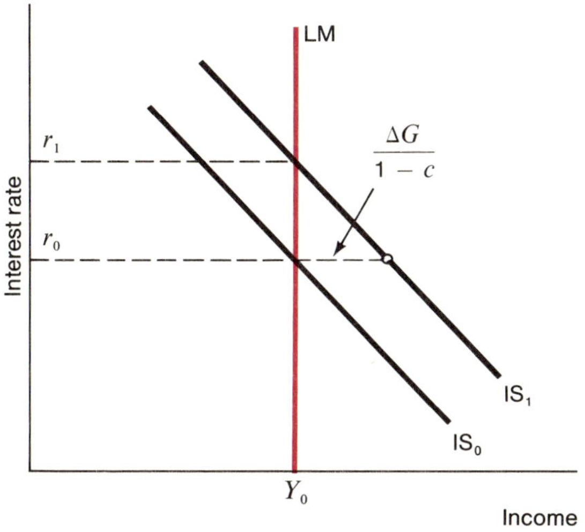

The Asset Market Effect of Deficit Finance

There is a second condition of crowding out resulting from government expenditures, one that comes about when the Treasury sells bonds to finance government deficits. It has been ignored in many textbooks but has become increasingly important in recent years, when very large deficits have been financed by the federal government.[4] Even if the money supply is unchanged, such bond sales tend to increase interest rates and crowd out private sector spending. This type of crowding out is another reason why fiscal policy has less effect on aggregate demand in a monetary economy than it did in the simple model of the goods market that we developed in Chapter 3.

The Government Budget Identity Basic to an understanding of the crowding-out effect of deficit finance is the **government budget identity.** This identity says that government expenditure must be financed by either taxes, bond sales, or the creation of high-powered money. Algebraically, the identity is:

[4] See Carl Christ, "A Simple Macroeconomic Model with a Government Budget Constraint," *Journal of Political Economy* 76 (January-February 1976): 53–67; William L. Silber, "Fiscal Policy in IS-LM Analysis: A Correction," *Journal of Money, Credit and Banking* 2 (November 1970): 461–472; and Alan S. Blinder and Robert M. Solow, "Does Fiscal Policy Matter?" *Journal of Public Economics* 2 (November 1973): 319–337.

(5.1) $$G + R \equiv T + \Delta B + \Delta M.$$

R = transfers
ΔB = change in bonds in public hands
ΔM = change in money[5]

Equation (5.1) is a bookkeeping identity that must be true by definition. It says that government expenditure must be financed either by taxes, by borrowing, or by the creation of money. What sets this identity apart from other budget constraints is the last term on the right, ΔM. All other units must limit their expenditure to revenue, plus borrowing. The federal government can create money to pay for its expenditure as well. Thus, this bookkeeping identity does not appear to be a constraint at all. Yet it does have important implications for the operation of fiscal policy that we now wish to consider.

The government budget identity tells us that deficits can be financed by either selling bonds or printing money. Either choice affects the asset market equilibrium represented by the LM curve. The budget identity reminds us, therefore, that any fiscal policy has monetary side effects, which no government should ignore when it is planning tax revenues and government expenditures.

Let us consider more carefully how the budget identity works. Suppose the government runs a deficit. The Treasury, the financial arm of the federal government, cannot print money directly to cover this deficit. Therefore, when it finds expenditures outrunning revenues, it issues or sells bonds on the bond market. Enter the Federal Reserve, which is both the central bank of the United States and the government's banker. If the Federal Reserve chooses not to support the bond issue by a supportive open market operation, the deficit is bond-financed. The budget identity is satisfied by setting $\Delta M = 0$. Hence, the equation for bond-financed deficits is:

(5.2) $$\Delta B = G + R - T$$

$$\Delta M = 0.$$

Here the stock of government debt in private hands rises by the full amount of the deficit.

But the Federal Reserve may intervene. It may buy an equal number of government bonds to help the Treasury with its debt sales. Generally, the Fed does this to keep bond interest rates from rising. When the Fed intervenes or supports a bond issue in this way, it indirectly buys the bonds from the Treasury. This is called **monetizing the deficit** because, as we shall see in a moment, the effect of the operation is to increase the stock of money in the economy.

In order to understand exactly what happens when the Fed monetizes the deficit, we shall look at an example. Suppose that the government makes a deficit expenditure of $1000 and sells bonds for $1000 to cover the deficit. For simplicity,

[5] In our fractional reserve banking system, the last term is actually high-powered money, but we will ignore this complication here.

Table 5.1
Changes in the Three Balance Sheets When an Increase in G Is Monetized

	Public		Treasury		Fed	
	Asset	**Liability**	**Asset**	**Liability**	**Asset**	**Liability**
Stage A: After bond sale but before government expenditure	+$1000 (new bond) −1000 (old bond)		Federal Reserve account +$1000	Bonds +$1000	Government bonds +$1000	Treasury account +$1000
Net change	——	——	+1000	+1,000	+1000	+1000
Stage B: Effect of ΔG	Money +1000	——	Federal Reserve account −1000	——	——	Treasury account −1000 Currency outstanding +1000
Total change	Money +$1000	——	——	Bonds outstanding +$1000	Bonds +$1000	Currency outstanding +$1000

we shall assume that the bond transactions are made directly with the public. Suppose further that the Fed makes an equivalent bond purchase of $1000 from the public, just exactly matching the Treasury bond sale. Look at Table 5.1 to see what happens to the balance sheets of the Treasury, the public, and the Federal Reserve as a result of these bond transactions and the deficit.

First, note that a balance sheet shows the liabilities and assets owned by an economic unit. (Liabilities are debts owed, while assets are goods and financial instruments owned.) In our simple economic system the two assets are bonds and money, and the total value of the public's assets is just equal to wealth. That is because all debts owed by members of the public cancel out—for they are owed to other members of the public. The main assets of the Federal Reserve are the stock of government bonds that it holds, while its main liabilities are its accounts with the Treasury and the public. (Note that in practice, banks rather than the public have accounts at the Fed.) Finally, the principal liability of the Treasury is its stock of outstanding government debt, and its main asset (in addition to the physical capital owned by the government) is its bank account at the Fed.

With that as a background, consider what happens to the three balance sheets. Stage A shows the change in the balance sheets prior to the change in government spending. The public has acquired a new government bond, by purchase, from the Treasury and sold an equivalent bond to the Fed; on balance, the public balance sheet is unchanged. The Treasury has +\$1000 in its account at the Fed from the proceeds of its bond sale to the public. It also has an additional \$1000 liability on the bond it has issued. The Fed has an additional asset, the government bond it purchased from the bank, and an additional liability, the +\$1000 in the Treasury account.

Now consider the effect of the change in G. The Treasury pays the sellers of government goods or services \$1000. Its account at the Fed is drawn down by \$1000, while the money supply in the hands of the public rises by the same amount. At the Fed, the \$1000 liability is transferred from its Treasury account to its currency account.

When we look at the net effect of this whole operation, summing the stage A and stage B changes in each column, we see that the public is left with +\$1000 of additional money but with its initial stock of bonds. Thus, Equation (5.1) is satisfied, with $\Delta B = 0$ and with M rising by the amount of ΔG. One could say, therefore, that the Fed, by supporting the Treasury debt issue, effectively monetizes the deficit. Algebraically, monetizing the deficit can be expressed as:

(5.3) $$\Delta M = G + R - T$$

$$\Delta B = 0.$$

We have shown that deficit financing must take one of three forms: Either the bond supply increases, the money supply increases, or some combination of the two occurs. In almost every possible case, therefore, deficit financing disturbs asset market equilibrium and moves the LM curve.

A Comparison of Fiscal Policy Financed by Money or Bonds

Consider first the case in which a rise in G is "financed" by an increase in money. This is called monetizing the deficit. As we have already learned, any rise in M shifts the LM curve to the right, which of course increases the expansionary multiplier of the ΔG itself. Look at Figure 5.6. The economy is initially in equilibrium at Y_0. Now assume a ΔG monetized by an equal ΔM. The change in G moves the IS curve out to IS_1, and the rise in M shifts the money supply out to M_1. That in turn shifts the LM curve rightward to LM_1. The net effect of all of these changes is that income rises much further than we would have predicted had we ignored the government budget constraint. Had we done that, we would have predicted that income would rise to Y_1, where IS_1 intersects the original LM curve. But monetizing the deficit shifts the LM out to LM_1, raising equilibrium income all the way to Y_2. Fiscal policy is doubly expansionary when deficits are monetized.

What about the other case, in which deficits are financed by bond sales? This is the case that has not received the attention it deserves, either in the literature or in textbooks. As the reader should be able to guess, we will argue that bond-financed deficits have the opposite effect on the LM curve from monetized deficits.

Figure 5.6
The Effect of Expansionary Fiscal Policy When Deficits are Monetized

Any change in government expenditure or taxes has an effect on the LM curve. Here we show an increase in government spending (or reduction in taxes), financed by increasing M. The rise in G shifts the IS curve out to IS_1. The increase in M shifts the LM curve out to LM_1. Thus, instead of expanding from Y_0 to Y_1, as we would predict if we ignored the effect of how the spending is financed, income increases all the way to Y_2. Monetizing the deficit increases the effectiveness of fiscal policy.

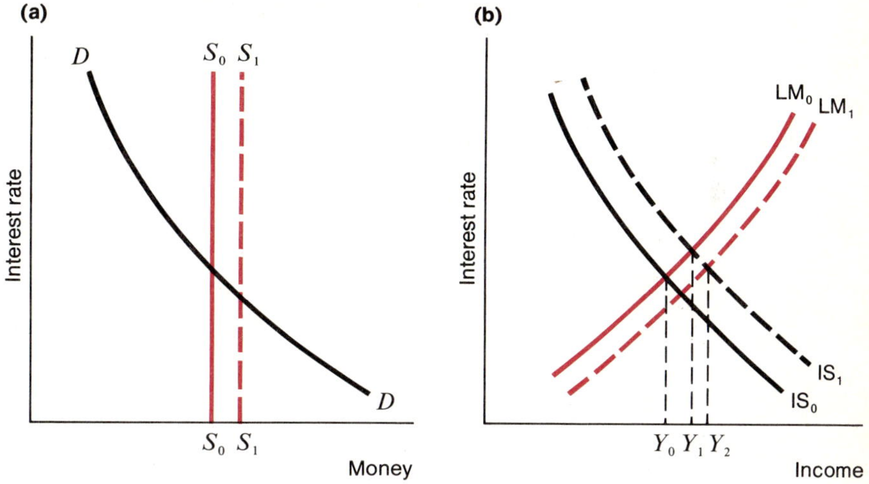

The LM curve shifts back, reducing and perhaps even completely offsetting the direct effect of the expansionary fiscal policy.

We show the net effect of bond-financed fiscal policy in Figure 5.7. An increase in government bonds in public hands increases the value of wealth, which is defined as the sum of money and bonds. This increases the demand for money.[6] Given that M is constant, the interest rate rises; this is true even if income is constant. The government effectively forces the public to change the composition and size of its portfolio. In the short run, equilibrium can be reestablished in the asset market only at a higher interest rate for bonds. To put it another way: The public will hold the additional bonds sold by the government only if the interest rate on bonds goes up. In diagram (a), the effect of the increase in bond supply is

[6] Benjamin Friedman points out that if the government finances its deficits with a short-term debt, which is highly liquid and a close substitute for money, there may be a reduction in the demand for money and an increase in the demand for bonds as a result of government deficits. In this case, rather than crowding out there is "crowding in." Such financing of deficits is expansionary. See Benjamin J. Friedman, "Crowding Out or Crowding In? Economic Consequences of Financing Government Deficits," *Brookings Papers on Economic Activity* (March 1978): 593–655.

Figure 5.7

Crowding Out When Expansionary Fiscal Policy is Financed by Bond Sales

When expansionary fiscal policy is financed by selling bonds, the increase in wealth increases the demand for money. That drives up the interest rate and shifts the LM curve to the left.

Figure 5.7 is a picture of the net effect of expansionary fiscal policy financed by selling bonds. The expansionary fiscal policy shifts the IS curve to IS_1. Because the LM curve has a positive slope, interest rates rise; this crowds out $Y_3 - Y_2$ of private expenditures. But the effect of financing fiscal policy results in a further crowding-out effect, which we call asset-market crowding out. The sale of bonds by the Treasury increases private wealth from W_0 to W_1. That increases the demand for money and drives up the interest rate in (a). As a result, the LM curve shifts to the left in (b), and the final equilibrium income is Y_1 rather than Y_2. The difference, $Y_2 - Y_1$, is asset crowding out. If the increase in the demand for money is big enough, this type of crowding out could completely offset the expansionary fiscal policy.

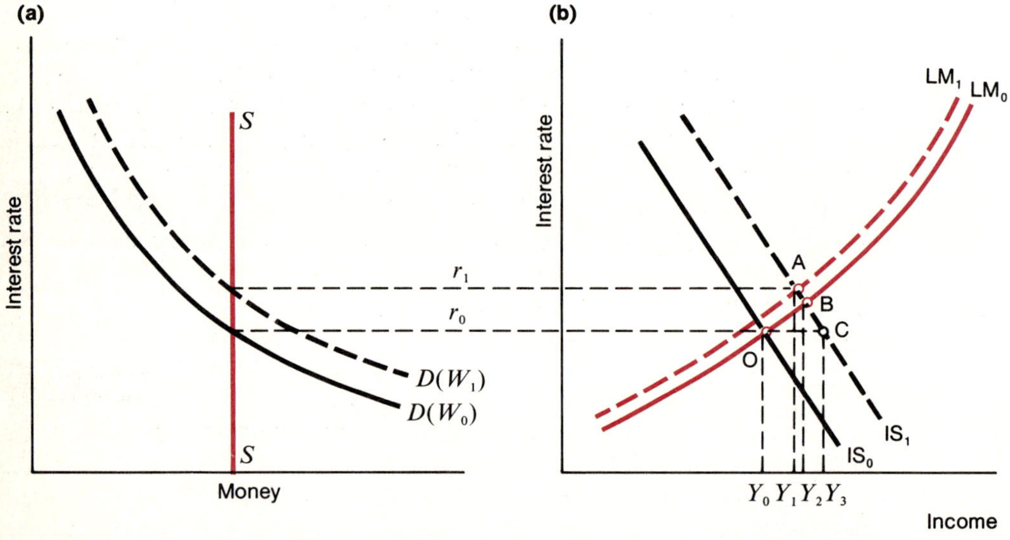

shown by the rightward shift in the demand for money, from $D(W_0)$ to $D(W_1)$. In diagram (b), the increase in the demand for money shifts the LM curve up and to the left, from LM_0 to LM_1. Bond financing is contractionary, because it increases the demand for money. Clearly, the more wealth sensitive the demand for money, the bigger will be the leftward shift in the LM curve.

Diagram (b) allows us to look more carefully at the different types of crowding out. The form of crowding out that we have already analyzed is that resulting from the positive slope of the LM curve. It reduces the expansionary effect of a rise in G from Y_3 to Y_2 (where IS_1 intersects the original LM curve). What we shall call **asset crowding out** is caused by the shift of the LM curve to LM_1 due to bond financing of the deficit. In (b), asset crowding out is the distance $Y_2 - Y_1$.

Note that we are showing one period in what is actually a continuous process. Governments run deficits which they finance by bond sales or monetization over a period of time. Therefore, deficits cause a gradual addition of either money or bonds to the public's portfolio, which will gradually shift the LM curve to either the right or the left. Here we are somewhat arbitrarily cutting the process off at the end of a single period. But in fact, as long as the government continues to run either surpluses or deficits, the public's portfolio of assets and the LM curve will both be continuously changing.

Because of asset market effects, the net impact of fiscal policy depends on how it is financed. Bond financing of expansionary fiscal policy reduces its net effect, because the increase in government bond sales drives up interest rates and crowds out interest-sensitive expenditures in the private sector, such as housing and fixed investment. In fact, as the reader can see from Figure 5.7, the asset effect could be so great that it would completely offset the expansionary direct effect of raising G—that is, the LM curve could shift to the left by just as much as the IS curve shifted to the right. In that case, all that raising G would do would be to crowd out an equivalent amount of private sector demand. Interest rates would be much higher, and the equilibrium level of income might be unchanged at Y_0.

This is the possibility that Milton Friedman was thinking about when he claimed that pure fiscal policy is not a very effective way to change the level of aggregate demand. By pure fiscal policy he meant a change in G or T, with the money supply held constant. We know from the government budget identity that if G increases while the money supply and taxes stay constant, then $\Delta G = \Delta B$. This is a case of bond-financed expansionary fiscal policy. Therefore, when Friedman speaks of pure fiscal policy, he is referring to what we have called bond-financed policy. In the case we have just seen, the direct expansionary effect of fiscal policy on the IS curve is partially, and perhaps even totally, offset by the contractionary effect of bond financing on the LM curve.

Ten years ago, it was fashionable in macroeconomic textbooks to argue about the relative effectiveness of monetary and fiscal policies in terms of the shapes of the IS and LM curves; that is the way we have presented the issue up to this point. Now we will see that the financing question raises a whole new set of issues. Fiscal policy has monetary side effects that either augment or diminish its net effectiveness. When Friedman argues that fiscal policy is not effective, he is not necessarily making the case that the LM curve is vertical or that income taxes do not effect consumption in the short run. Rather, he may be thinking of the offsetting effect that bond financing has on the LM curve.

Case Study

Friedman's Analysis of the Surtax of 1968

Friedman's pessimistic appraisal of the effectiveness of bond-financed fiscal policy is very clear in an analysis that he made of the surtax of 1968. At that time the government, after years of effort, finally raised taxes to reduce aggregate demand. Friedman did not think that the net effect on aggregate demand of this contractionary fiscal policy would be very great. In his words:

Figure 5.8
The Effect of Contractionary Fiscal Policy with a Constant Money Supply

The surtax shifts the IS curve back to IS_1. However, if the monetary base is held constant, the government budget identity tells us that the bond supply must decrease. Thus, there is a decrease in total wealth, which reduces the demand for money, shifting the demand curve in (a) from D_0D_0 to D_1D_1. This is reflected in (b) in the outward shift in the LM curve to LM_1. The net result is that the contractionary effect of fiscal policy is partially offset by the reduced demand for money. Income falls only to Y_1 rather than to Y_2, as might be expected if we ignored the asset market effect. The fall in consumption from the surtax is partially offset by an increase in investment because of the declining interest rates.

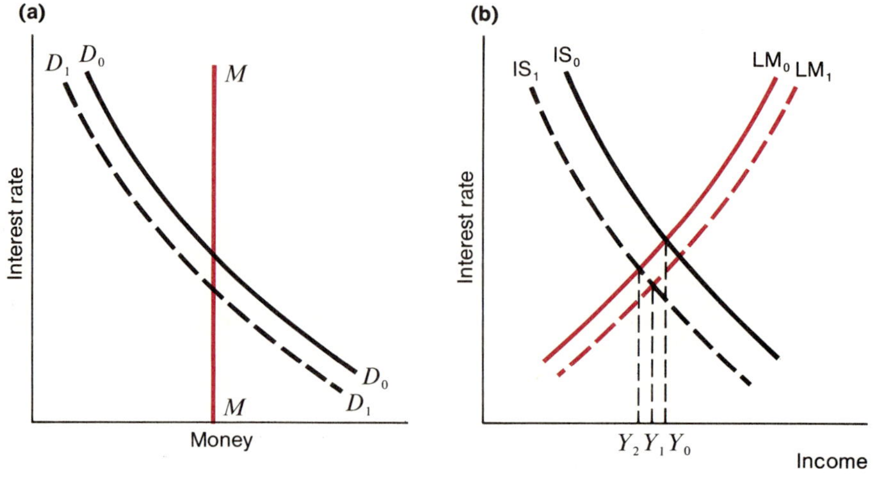

The surtax was sold to a reluctant Congress as the only way to halt inflation. It has now been in effect for over six months. Inflation has not only continued; it has even accelerated.

True proponents grant, the surtax did not even dent inflation. But now, they say, it is taking hold—look at the sharp slowdown in consumption spending in the fourth quarter of 1968. This slowdown provides no evidence that the surtax is affecting the pace of inflation. Those few of us who opposed the surtax granted all along that taxpayers would very likely restrain their spending in response to the surtax. But, we said, that is only half the story. The persons from whom the government would otherwise have had to borrow to finance its expenditures will have more to spend or to lend to others. They will make funds available for additional spending by business enterprises or individuals. Why should total *spending be much affected by the surtax?*

Once again, as so often in the past, what happened to the quantity of money was far more critical . . . than what happened to the level of Federal taxes and spending.[7]

[7] Milton Friedman, "End the Surtax," *Newsweek,* Feb. 10, 1969.

Friedman grants that the surtax will reduce private consumption; the IS curve will shift inward to IS_1, as in Figure 5.8. But if the money supply stays constant (or even increases), the asset market effect causes an expansionary outward shift in the LM curve. Let us see why.

Once again, we use the government budget identity. It tells us that an increase in tax revenues must be reflected either in a reduction of the money supply or in a reduction of the bond supply. If the money supply is held constant (what Friedman called pure fiscal policy), the bond supply must fall (or must grow by less than it would have without the tax cut).

This is the opposite of the expansionary fiscal policy that we have just analyzed. Just as a rise in bonds is contractionary, so retiring bonds is expansionary.[8] In diagram (a) of Figure 5.8, the demand for money falls from D_0 to D_1; in (b), the LM curve shifts out to LM_1 and the interest rate declines. All of these cause an increase in investment. Thus, contraction on the fiscal side is matched by expansion on the asset or monetary side. That is why Friedman says that reduced spending by consumers will be matched by greater spending by investors (because of the decline in interest rates). Hence, the overall level of expenditure may not be very much affected by pure contractionary fiscal policy even though the composition of demand will be. (In Figure 5.8 we show demand falling slightly, from Y_0 to Y_1.)

Summary of Fiscal Policy

Any fiscal policy that is undertaken while the monetary base is held constant is bond financed. Whether expansionary or contractionary, the asset market effect of the change in government debt works at cross-purposes to the direct effect of the fiscal policy change itself. That is one of the reasons why Friedman asserted that pure fiscal policy is not very effective.

Whether the asset market effect fully offsets the shift in the IS caused by the change in G or the change in T is an empirical question, not a theoretical one. Here the evidence suggests that the direct fiscal policy effect is not completely offset by reverse shifts in the LM curve. Furthermore, recent writers have pointed out that the changes in wealth resulting from fiscal policy also affect consumers in a way that will strengthen the direct effect of fiscal policy on the IS curve. For example, increasing the government deficit, whether financed by money or bonds, will increase private sector wealth. According to the consumption theory to be developed in Chapter 11, this will increase consumption. Thus, the IS curve shifts out further than we showed in Chapter 4. In this way the wealth effect on consumption helps to offset the LM shift that occurs in bond-financed fiscal policy.

All in all, it is probably true that expansionary fiscal policy leads to an increase in aggregate demand. However, the net change is much smaller than supposed by

[8] We are ignoring the possible effect of the reduction in wealth on private saving. It could be that the fall in W would increase saving and shift the IS further to the left than the amount shown by the simple tax multiplier. When we say retiring bonds is expansionary, we are referring to its effect on the LM curve.

advocates of fiscal policy, and it is accompanied by a far greater amount of crowding out of private interest-sensitive investment than they have been willing to admit.

To summarize this long discussion, we again distinguish between the two types of fiscal policy: one that is financed by a change in the money supply, or monetized, and one that is bond financed.[9] In monetized fiscal policy, $\Delta M = \Delta G$ or $\Delta M = -\Delta T$. In bond-financed fiscal policy, $\Delta B = \Delta G$ or $\Delta B = -\Delta T$.

When changes in fiscal policy are monetized, the LM curve moves in the same direction as the IS curve. Fiscal policy and the asset market effect of its financing are complementary. Fiscal policy is doubly effective because of the increases or decreases in the money supply caused by the changes in G or T. Friedman would argue that it is the increase in the money supply, rather than the increase in G, that allows the fiscal policy to work in this case. However, when changes in fiscal policy are bond financed, the effect of the change in the supply of bonds on the asset market tends to neutralize the direct effect of fiscal policy on the goods market. The IS and the LM move in opposite directions, which exacerbates crowding out. The more wealth sensitive and the less interest sensitive the demand for money, the greater the shift in the LM curve; hence the greater the total amount of crowding out in response to an increase in G (or a fall in T).

The Quantity Theory and the Relative Importance of Monetary and Fiscal Policies

It will be useful to augment this introduction to monetary and fiscal policy with a discussion of the **quantity theory,** a theory of aggregate demand that forms one of the key theoretical supports for **monetarism.**[10] Monetarism is an important school of economics based on the teachings of Milton Friedman and his followers at the University of Chicago. Monetarists believe that aggregate demand is basically determined by the level of the money supply, and they therefore insist that monetary policy rather than fiscal policy is the key to controlling aggregate demand. By contrast, early Keynesians thought that the demand for money was highly sensitive to interest rates, which implies that aggregate demand is unresponsive to changes in the money supply and therefore responsive to fiscal policy. We now look more carefully at the quantity theory, the basis for the monetarist theory of aggregate demand.

[9] For simplicity, we will assume a balanced budget prior to the change in fiscal policy. In that case, neither M nor B is changing for reasons other than the fiscal measures whose effects we are analyzing.

[10] For a further discussion of the development of the quantity theory, see Thomas M. Havrilesky and John T. Boorman, *Monetary Macroeconomics* (Arlington Heights, IL: AHM Publishing, 1978), 147–167. The fundamental theoretical work incorporating interest rates and portfolio theory was done by Milton Friedman in "The Quantity Theory of Money: A Restatement" in Milton Friedman, ed., *Studies in the Quantity Theory of Money* (Chicago: University of Chicago Press, 1956), 3–25.

The quantity theory asserts that nominal income is a linear function of the money supply. It is expressed formally in Equation (5.4), an equation sometimes called the **equation of exchange:**[11]

(5.4) $$MV = PY.$$

The constant V is called **velocity,** and it is defined as the number of times the average dollar is spent per year. One can interpret Equation (5.4) as either a theory of the demand for money or a theory of aggregate demand.

Note that we can rewrite Equation (5.4) as:

(5.5) $$\frac{M}{P} = \frac{Y}{V}.$$

The right-hand side of Equation (5.5) is another way of writing the demand for money. Early economists thought that V was a constant unaffected by interest rates. If that were the case, Equation (5.5) would say that the demand for money depends only on income. However, modern quantity theorists such as Milton Friedman acknowledge that the demand for money also depends on interest rates and wealth. Since the demand for money is negatively related to the interest rate and positively related to wealth, velocity would be related positively to the interest rate and negatively to wealth. Thus, Equation (5.5) is simply a more specific way of writing our general equation of the demand for money. The only difference between this equation, which is a monetarist demand-for-money equation, and the equations we have been using so far is in the size of the behavioral parameters. There is no important difference of opinion among economists about the form of the equation. Monetarists expect the demand for money, and therefore velocity, to be insensitive to interest rates; Keynesians expected velocity to be highly sensitive to interest rates.

Empirical research, some of which will be referred to in Chapter 14, has pretty much confirmed the monetarists' assertion that the demand for money is not nearly as sensitive to interest rates as the Keynesians had believed it was. But more importantly, it has shown that the demand for money is a stable, predictable function of interest rates and income. The LM curve is relatively steep, although not vertical, and the multiplier of income with respect to money is both larger and more stable than the Keynesians had thought.

Another way to interpret the equation of exchange is as a theory of aggregate demand. To do this we rewrite Equation (5.4) as:

(5.6) $$Y = V\frac{M}{P}.$$

[11] The equation of exchange was developed in Irving Fisher, *The Purchasing Power of Money* (New York: Macmillan, 1911).

Given the dependence of velocity on wealth and the interest rate, we can rewrite Equation (5.6) in a more general functional form as:

(5.7) $$Y = v(\overset{-}{W}, \overset{+}{r})\frac{M}{P}.$$

Equation (5.7) says that real aggregate demand is a function of the money supply, wealth, and the interest rate. This is a monetarist theory of aggregate demand and the basis of the monetarist contention that only money matters in determining the level of aggregate demand. In particular the equation implies that fiscal policy has no effect on aggregate demand unless it changes either the interest rate or the level of wealth. That would be easy to explain in an economy with a vertical LM curve, where velocity is not a function of the interest rate. However, Friedman insists that the quantity theory is equally applicable when the demand for money is sensitive to the interest rate, due to fiscal crowding out and the government budget identity. According to Friedman, changes in fiscal policy not accompanied by changes in the money supply are debt financed. This, as we have seen, shifts the LM curve in exactly the opposite direction as the IS curve and offsets the direct effect of fiscal policy. If the offset is complete, Equation (5.7) is a reasonable equation for aggregate demand. If it is not, demand depends on both monetary policy and fiscal policy.

Virtually all economists accept the general contention of the monetarists that money plays an important role in determining aggregate demand. As Franco Modigliani, a leading Keynesian, put it: "We are all Monetarists—if by Monetarism is meant assigning to the stock of money a major role in determining output and prices."[12] However, Keynesians do not think that money is the only factor that plays a role; they think that fiscal policy also has an effect. They have attempted to show that it is highly unlikely that we live in a world where fiscal crowding out completely offsets the direct effect of fiscal policy. The monetarists have made an important contribution in pointing out that fiscal policy multipliers depend on how fiscal policy is financed. But Keynesians do not believe that the multiplier of bond-financed fiscal policy is zero.

Another area of disagreement between the Keynesians and the monetarists is the so-called transmission mechanism, or the way that changes in the money supply affect aggregate demand. Keynesians argue that money affects the economy through financial markets and the interest rate, basically the approach taken by this book. An increase in the money supply lowers the interest rate, which in turn increases investment; it is the increase in investment that causes income to rise. Typically Keynesians do not think that investment is very sensitive to interest rates, implying that the IS curve is quite steep. Monetarists think that a change in the money supply changes the demand for all goods, not just investment goods. In particular they argue that both investment and consumption expenditures are sensitive to the interest rate, which makes the IS curve a good deal flatter (and mone-

[12] Franco Modigliani, "The Monetarist Controversy or, Should We Forsake Stabilization Policies?" *American Economic Review* 67 (March 1977): 1.

tary policy correspondingly more effective) than it is thought to be by the Keynesians.

Actually, there are two different types of increase in the money supply that should be distinguished here. One is an increase resulting from expansionary open market operations; the other is a government deficit financed by printing money. The first is a pure financial exchange, and it should have its effect on the economy through the interest rate as described above. That effect could be on both investment and consumption.

The second way of increasing the money supply has both a fiscal and a monetary dimension. Monetarists predict that a deficit financed by an expansion in the money supply will increase the demand for all goods and consumption goods in particular. Keynesians would agree on the net effect, but they would explain most of the rise in consumption by the rise in disposable income, not by the increase in consumer cash balances—that is, the Keynesians would attribute most of the increase in consumption to the expansionary fiscal policy that led to an increase in disposable income, not to the increase in the money supply. They would probably expect almost the same increase in consumption from a deficit financed by bonds rather than money. However, in that case, the rise in interest rates would cause a partially offsetting decline in interest-sensitive expenditures, one of which could well be consumption.

Combining Monetary and Fiscal Policies to Alter the Composition and Level of Total Demand

To be successful, macroeconomic policymakers must worry about more than just the level of total income. They must also be concerned with its composition. The composition of output is influenced by the combination of monetary and fiscal policies they choose. Thus, if the world works as our model says it works, it is possible to combine monetary and fiscal policies in such a way that both aggregate demand and its components can be simultaneously determined. Let us see how this can be done.

We can set the stage with an actual policy dilemma. In recent years the rate of capital formation in the United States has been thought by many people to be too low. This has had adverse effects on labor productivity and the competitive position of U. S. exports in the world market. Hence, one goal of policymakers has been to simultaneously increase the fraction of income invested while holding the overall level of aggregate demand constant for fear of inflation. How can this be done?

Consider Figure 5.9. Suppose that the economy is at point A in diagram (b). Suppose further that while the income level at point A, Y_0, is satisfactory the investment, I_0, associated with the interest rate, r_0, is unsatisfactory. The authorities wish to increase investment to I_1 but keep the economy at Y_0. What should they do? To increase investment to I_1, diagram (a) tells us that the interest rate has to be reduced to r_1. How do we accomplish this through monetary or fiscal policy? Obviously, if we were to simply increase the monetary base, shifting the LM curve

Figure 5.9
Increasing the Fraction of Income Invested

To increase investment from I_0 to I_1, interest rates must fall from r_0 to r_1. To keep income at its initial level, Y_0, we have to have simultaneously an expansionary monetary policy and a contractionary fiscal policy, shifting the LM curve outward and the IS curve inward, respectively, so that the intersection of the two curves will be at B.

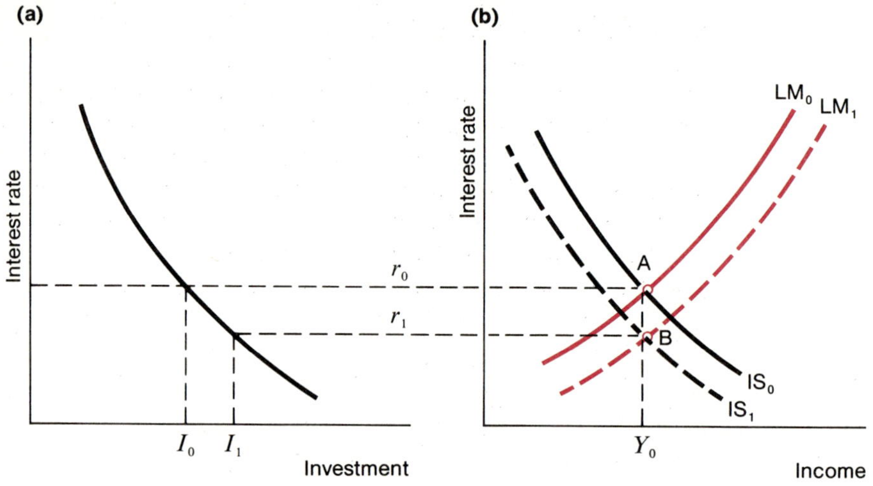

out, income would expand. To keep income constant and yet increase investment to I_1, we have to make the IS and LM curves intersect at point B in diagram (b). That requires an expansionary monetary policy, shifting the LM out, accompanied by a contractionary fiscal policy, shifting the IS back to IS_1.

What we are doing in Figure 5.9 can be seen in the national income identity,

$$Y = C + I + G + E - M.$$

We are raising investment but keeping total income unchanged. Since neither E nor M is changing, this requires a reduction in either government or private consumption. Either G declines or taxes have to be increased enough to drive C down by the change in investment. Either alternative requires a contractionary fiscal policy—an inward shift in the IS curve.

Consider another policy problem. Suppose the government wishes to increase government defense expenditures, give tax reductions to stimulate consumption and saving, and yet hold constant the overall level of aggregate demand. There are basically two ways these three goals can be achieved. The first is by restrictive monetary policy, the second by cutting non-defense government expenditures.

We show the first program in Figure 5.10. Increased defense expenditures and the tax cut shift the IS curve out to IS_1. Other things being equal, this would

Figure 5.10
Increasing G and C without Increasing Income

An increase in government defense expenditure, accompanied by a tax cut to increase consumption, shifts the IS curve from IS_0 to IS_1. This set of policies will increase the government deficit. If that deficit is financed by bond sales, the LM curve will shift to the left. If that is not sufficient to keep income at the desired level, the monetary authorities should engage in contractionary open market operations until the LM curve has shifted to LM_1. At that point, the rise in interest rates will have crowded out as much expenditure as the increase in defense expenditures plus the tax cut.

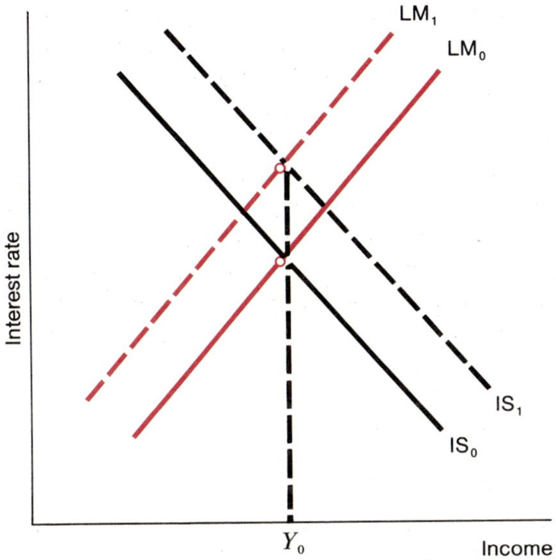

increase the level of aggregate demand. However, the monetary authorities do not monetize the increased government deficit resulting from these two changes in fiscal policy. That shifts the LM curve up and to the left. If the shift is insufficient, the Fed engages in contractionary open market bond sales at the same time to move the LM curve back to where it intersects IS_1 at the desired level of income. In Figure 5.10 the government increases G and C with expansionary fiscal policy and then relies on monetary policy to keep the overall level of demand constant by choking off interest-sensitive expenditures. The rises in C and G crowd out investment and interest-sensitive consumption.

If the government does not wish to crowd out investment when it cuts taxes and increases military expenditure, it must cut non-defense government expenditure by enough to keep the IS curve in its original position. This can be done by reducing either government expenditure on goods and services or government transfer payments. In either case, the cut has to be sufficient to completely offset the expansionary effects of the tax cuts and increased military expenditures. As a practical matter that may not be easy to do.

Table 5.2
Policies Required for Changes in Composition and Level of Income

Effect Desired	Direction in IS-LM Diagram	Policy Required
$\uparrow Y$, $\uparrow I$	SE	Expansionary monetary
$\uparrow Y$, $\downarrow I$, $\uparrow C$ or G	NE	Expansionary fiscal (cut taxes to raise C or raise G)
$\downarrow Y$, $\uparrow I$	SW	Contractionary fiscal
$\downarrow Y$, $\downarrow I$	NW	Contractionary monetary
$\bar{Y}$, $\uparrow I$, $\downarrow C$ or G	S	Contractionary fiscal Expansionary monetary
$\bar{Y}$, $\downarrow I$, $\uparrow C$ or G	N	Expansionary fiscal Contractionary monetary

To summarize, it is possible to move from any point to any other point on the IS-LM diagram by an appropriate combination of monetary and fiscal policies. If the government wishes to increase investment it must lower interest rates, which means moving south in the diagram; if it wishes to increase the level of income, it must move east. We summarize the various choices and the policies required to reach them in Table 5.2.

The national income accounting identity provides an alternative way to think about the implications of Table 5.2. Suppose we wish to move northeast, which means that we wish to increase income and either consumption or government spending. To increase C, we cut taxes. The IS shifts out along the LM curve, and interest rates, income, and consumption all rise. But investment declines (because of the rise in r).[13] Therefore, using the national accounting identity:

$$\Delta Y = \Delta C + \Delta I,$$

we know that the increase in C is greater than the increase in Y, and therefore that investment declines. If the government raises G to achieve the northeast move in the IS-LM curve, both G and C rise but investment is again crowded out. Here the national accounting identity is satisfied as follows:

$$\Delta Y = \Delta C + \Delta G + \Delta I \quad \text{(negative)}$$

We know that consumption rises because income rises, and that increases disposable income, the basic determinant of C. While it is possible that the interest-sensitive component of C could fall by enough to offset the effect of rising Y_d, it

[13] If investment is positively related to output, this statement may not be true.

is unlikely. In general, we may conclude that expansionary fiscal policy always crowds out investment so long as the LM curve is not flat or the loss in taxes is not monetized by the Federal Reserve.[14]

An Algebraic Analysis of the IS-LM Model

So far we have relied on the IS-LM diagram to derive equilibrium income and interest rates and analyze the effects of changes in exogenous variables. For the linear model we can solve the same system algebraically using the equations for the IS and LM curves that we have derived. This will show explicitly the multipliers for an economy with an interest feedback and will also show how the sizes of those multipliers depend on the sizes of certain key behavioral parameters.

Start with the equations for the IS and LM curves, repeated here for convenience. Dropping the bars on G and T, the equation for the IS curve is:

(4.6) $$r = \frac{G - cT - (1 - c)Y}{i}.$$

The equation for the LM curve is:

(4.16) $$r = \frac{nY + u\frac{W}{P} - \frac{M_s}{P}}{q}.$$

Now set Equation (4.6) equal to Equation (4.16) and solve for Y:

(5.8) $$Y = \frac{q(G - cT) - ui\frac{W}{P} + \frac{iM_s}{P}}{q(1 - c) + in}.$$

Equation (5.8) is the equilibrium equation for Y. It shows exactly how income depends on each of the exogenous variables in the model when all interest feedbacks between the money market and autonomous expenditures are included. As in Chapter 3, we can interpret the coefficient of each exogenous variable in the equation as a multiplier that tells exactly how much equilibrium income will change when the exogenous variable changes.

For example, the government expenditure multiplier is:

[14] It is possible to target tax cuts so that they stimulate investment instead of consumption. Accelerated depreciation, reduced corporate income taxes, and investment tax credits are examples of investment-increasing tax cuts. In our discussion we are assuming cuts in personal taxes.

(5.9)
$$\frac{\Delta Y}{\Delta G} = \frac{q}{q(1 - c) + in}.$$

This multiplier is a good deal smaller than the income-government multiplier in Chapter 3, which was $1/(1 - c)$. The reason is the interest feedback: Any increase in income increases the demand for money. That raises interest rates by n/q, which in turn chokes off or crowds out autonomous expenditure.

The monetary multiplier of income is the coefficient of M_s/P in Equation (5.8):

(5.10)
$$\frac{\Delta Y}{\Delta \frac{M_s}{P}} = \frac{i}{q(1 - c) + in}.$$

After inspecting these two multipliers, it should be clear that the more interest sensitive the autonomous expenditures, which translate algebraically into a large value of i and a flat IS curve, the larger the money-income multiplier and the smaller the government spending multiplier.[15] Similarly, the more interest sensitive the demand for money (the larger the value of q and the flatter the LM curve), the more effective the fiscal policy and the less effective the monetary policy.

Two cases are of particular interest: one where the demand for money is very sensitive to the interest rate and the other where it is completely insensitive to it. Each corresponds to a particular value of q: In the first case $q = \infty$, and in the second case $q = 0$. Each also corresponds to a particular shape of the demand-for-money and LM curves. Extreme interest sensitivity ($q = \infty$) means that both the LM and the demand-for-money curves are flat. By contrast, when $q = 0$, both curves are vertical.

Look now at the two multipliers. When $q = \infty$ it is clear, from Equation (5.10), that the money multiplier is zero—that is, monetary policy is totally ineffective. Conversely, the government spending multiplier in Equation 5.9 becomes $1/(1 - c)$, exactly the same multiplier we had in our simple goods market in Chapter 3. The reason is that when $q = \infty$, the interest rate is constant; hence, there is no offsetting interest feedback.

If $q = 0$, the relative effectivenesses of fiscal and monetary policies are reversed. Now the government spending multiplier is zero, while the money multiplier is $1/n$. Here an increase in the money supply causes a rise in income large enough to absorb the entire increase into transactions balances with no help from the interest rate.

Another case where monetary policy is ineffective occurs when the IS curve is vertical. That happens when neither consumption nor investment are affected by the interest rate, or when $i = 0$. From Equation (5.10), it can be seen that the monetary multiplier is zero in this case. At the same time, when $i = 0$ the government expenditure multiplier (Equation [5.9]) simplifies to $1/(1 - c)$, the same value it has in the model without the interest feedback.

[15] From the equation of the IS curve, we see that its slope is $-(1 - c)/i$, which varies inversely with i.

Summary: A Look Ahead

In these first five chapters we have presented a very compact overview of the theory of aggregate demand. We have shown how monetary and fiscal policies affect the economy and have developed the IS-LM framework to consider how conditions in the money and goods markets simultaneously determine aggregate demand and the interest rate. This analysis showed us how to combine monetary and fiscal policies to control both the level and the composition of aggregate demand.

There are two serious shortcomings to this theory. First, it ignores supply. Basically, it assumes that supply adjusts passively to the level of aggregate demand determined in the IS-LM diagram. But supply is not passive. Supply constraints determine how much of changes in demand turn into changes in the price level and how much into changes in production. Up to now we have assumed that all demand changes lead to equivalent production changes. This may have been appropriate once in a recession-prone world with lots of idle capacity, but it certainly is not appropriate now. Ours is a world dominated by such supply constraints as energy, wage demands, and inflation.

We are now going to complete our model of the economy by adding a theory of aggregate supply. This will be the subject of the next four chapters. Having done that, we will be ready to take up the real-world complications that face policymakers. The economy they try to manage is not exactly like our simple model. If it were, their job would be a simple one. Unfortunately, in the real world, policies work with long and variable lags. This requires policymakers to forecast the future in designing their policies. While their forecasting is fairly good, it is nowhere near good enough to achieve policy goals all or even most of the time. Furthermore, some of the behavioral relationships upon which our economic models are built seem to be somewhat unstable. In the recent past, they have exhibited fairly large fluctuations that are not well explained by our theories. We will examine policymaking in the presence of these real-world complications after completing the theory of supply.

Key Concepts

monetary policy
liquidity trap
fiscal policy
crowding-out effect
government budget identity
monetizing the deficit
asset crowding out
quantity theory
monetarism
equation of exchange
velocity

Problems and Questions for Discussion

In the first six questions we incorporate the government budget identity into the behavioral model used in Questions 5–8 of Chapter 4. We repeat the equations of that model for convenience:

$$C = 10 + .8Y_d$$
$$I = 90 - 200r$$
$$T = .2Y$$
$$\frac{M_d}{P} = .4Y - 200r + \frac{.3B}{P}$$
$$Y_d = Y - T \qquad B = 200$$
$$M_s = 440 \qquad P = 1.00$$
$$G = 280$$
$$G = T + \Delta B + \Delta M$$

The budget identity tells us that any change in G not financed by a change in taxes must result in a change in either M or B. We now show that the income-government spending multiplier depends on how changes in government expenditure are financed.

1. Derive the reduced-form equations for Y and r.

2. Calculate the effect on income of a one-dollar increase in G
 a. ignoring the budget constraint (assume $\Delta M = \Delta B = 0$).
 b. assuming the change in G is bond financed (assume $\Delta G = \Delta B$).
 c. assuming the change in G is financed by printing money (assume $\Delta G = \Delta M$).

Draw an IS-LM diagram showing each change.

3. The three effects you have calculated are different income-government spending multipliers. Why are they different from one another and from the multipliers you calculated in Questions 6–9 in Chapter 3?

4. If you have not already done so in your answer to Question 2, how could you obtain the multipliers in that question directly from the reduced-form equation for Y?

5. Using the same procedures used in Questions 2–3, derive and compare the investment-government spending multipliers for
 a. the simple case in which we ignore the government budget identity ($\Delta M = \Delta B = 0$).
 b. bond-financed changes in G ($\Delta B = \Delta G$).
 c. money-financed changes in G ($\Delta M = \Delta G$).

6. Of the above changes in investment in response to a change in G, which shows simple crowding out? Which shows asset crowding out?

7. What is the effect of a reduction in taxes on the economy if the money supply is kept constant? Is the tax cut necessarily expansionary? (Hint: Remember the government budget constraint.)

The following questions test your knowledge of how to use monetary and fiscal policies together to control the level and the composition of aggregate demand.

8. Suppose that you want to increase military expenditure and private investment but keep the level of aggregate demand constant. What combination of monetary and fiscal policies should you use? What will be the effect of your policies on the composition of GNP?

9. Suppose that you want to cut taxes but maintain the levels of both GNP and investment spending. What combination of monetary and fiscal policies should you use? Can you achieve the desired result by the use of fiscal policy alone?

10. In 1980 candidate Reagan proposed to cut taxes by about $50 billion and to cut government expenditures by about $35 billion. Using the IS-LM diagram, show how this program would affect the economy. Will the program increase the share of investment in GNP? Does your answer depend on how the difference between tax cuts and expenditure cuts is financed?

11. Milton Friedman has said that only money matters in determining the level of aggregate demand. Does this mean that the level of government spending or of government deficits has no effect on aggregate demand? Explain.

12. If the government increases the money supply, what do you expect will happen to velocity? Why? Does this mean that monetary policy is ineffective? (That is, does the change in velocity completely offset the change in M?)

13. Under what conditions will fiscal policy be ineffective in changing the level of aggregate demand? Under what conditions will monetary policy be ineffective?

PART THREE

AGGREGATE SUPPLY AND THE JOINT DETERMINATION OF INCOME, PRICE, AND EMPLOYMENT

Chapter 6

The Full and Partial Equilibrium Theories of Prices, Output, and Employment

In the first chapters of this book we concentrated on the determination and control of aggregate demand through monetary and fiscal policies. So far we have ignored aggregate supply. That is equivalent to assuming that prices are constant or that supply factors passively adjust to the level of demand in the economy. This is certainly not realistic, and we are now going to fill in this gap in our theory.

Supply analysis is critical if we are to understand the problem of inflation in our economy. Inflation is the outcome of an interaction between demand and supply. We cannot make intelligent predictions about the effects of changes in demand unless we understand the determinants of supply.

In this chapter, we shall focus on two different theories of aggregate supply. One is what we shall call a full or long-run equilibrium theory. In it, all workers and businesses accurately forecast the level of prices and output and all markets clear. The second theory of supply is a partial or short-run equilibrium theory. Labor and goods markets clear, but workers make forecasting errors in the price level. In the model we shall develop, we will see how these erroneous forecasts cause supply curves to diverge from their full equilibrium levels, contributing to cyclical variations in output and prices.

Yet a third theory of supply is based upon what we shall call a disequilibrium model of the economy. Labor and goods markets are not even in partial equilibrium. Wages and prices are set by sellers and are relatively unresponsive to market conditions, which means that supply may not equal demand. Work on this latter class of model is less advanced than on either of the other two models. Yet the implications of the model for the short-run behavior of the economy are sufficiently useful to merit an extended description. Both the partial equilibrium and the disequilibrium models can be thought of as theories of how an economy behaves in the *short-run*, when either markets do not clear or workers make forecasting errors. The further dynamic question of how the economy gets from the short-run solution to the full equilibrium is one on which a great deal of work is currently proceeding.

Our organization of the various theories of supply will be as follows. In this chapter we shall present the full and partial equilibrium theories of supply. In chapter seven we present the disequilibrium theory and then in the following two chapters, we analyze the dynamic response of the economy to various demand and supply shocks in the two models. As we shall see, the two models lead to significant differences in prediction about the short-run behavior of the economy, particularly in response to anti-inflationary stabilization policy.

The Aggregate Demand Curve

Before turning to the various theories of supply, we restate the theory of aggregate demand developed in Chapters 3–5 in terms of a relationship between price and demand—the aggregate demand curve. The **aggregate demand curve** is the relationship between the quantity of output demanded and the price of output. It tells what happens to aggregate demand when all prices change. You may think that the answer is obvious: If prices rise, surely demand will fall, since that is almost always what happens to the demand for individual commodities when their prices rise. But the answer is not as obvious as it may first appear, for here we are talking about a rise in all prices, not just the price of a single commodity.

The Effects of Price Changes on Aggregate Demand

For any individual commodity, such as beef, demand falls as prices rise precisely because all other prices stay the same. If chicken, pork, bread, and all other prices rise at exactly the same rate, and if the consumer's income rises as well, it is difficult to see why the consumer will buy less beef or any other product. And yet, such a rise in price will reduce aggregate demand. The reason is that rising prices affect the value of wealth, the real supply of money, and the distribution of income. Each of these has a negative effect on aggregate demand.

Consider first the wealth effect. In Chapter 4, we showed that real consumption was positively related to the real value of wealth. Two of the assets in the public portfolio are currency and government bonds. As prices rise, the real value of these two assets falls. Rising prices hurt the holders of government securities, due to the wealth effect. Holders have to save more to compensate for their loss of puchasing power, and their consumption demand should therefore fall as prices rise. Of course, the rise in prices hurts the holders of private debt too, but in this case the loss of the creditor is offset by the gain of the debtor, so that unless the spending behaviors of debtors and creditors differ, the net effect of rising prices on wealth and consumption will be confined to government debt.[1]

[1]There is a debate among economists about whether there really is a wealth effect on government bonds. For if taxpayers consider the future tax liabilities required to pay off the government bonds, then government bonds will not be part of the net stock of wealth. For a discussion of the issue see Robert J. Barro, "Are Government Bonds Net Wealth?" *Journal of Political Economy* 82 (December 1974): 1095–1119.

It could be argued that we should not include government bonds in the wealth effect, because the real value of the future tax liability for repayment of the bonds falls with rising prices. The reduction in future taxes could just offset the loss of purchasing power on the bonds.

The second effect of rising prices on aggregate demand is the reduction of the real supply of money. In Chapter 4 we showed that the LM curve shifted to the left whenever there was a reduction in M/P. Throughout that chapter, we considered only changes in M/P caused by changes in the nominal stock of money. But changes in the price level, holding the nominal stock of money constant, have exactly the same effect. Indeed, holding the money supply constant in the face of rising prices is a form of contractionary monetary policy. It should raise interest rates and reduce all interest-sensitive components of aggregate demand.

The third effect of rising prices on aggregate demand is the change in the distribution of income, both within the private sector and between the private sector and the government. Changes in both may affect the demand for consumption goods. Consider first the inflationary redistribution within the private sector. It is generally believed that inflation helps profits and hurts wages. The evidence from the U. S. economy suggests that inflation at the beginning of expansionary cycles does indeed shift the distribution of income away from labor. If profit earners have less propensity to consume than laborers, transferring income from the latter to the former will reduce aggregate consumption. The same argument can be used for other transfers. Debtors generally gain during an inflation and creditors lose—because debts are specified in dollars. Rising prices change the real purchasing power represented by those dollars. To the extent that debtors have lower spending propensities than creditors this transfer will reduce aggregate consumption.

To our minds, a more significant transfer occurs from the private sector to the government in the form of progressive taxes through what is called **bracket-creep.** Income taxes are specified in dollars, and the rates are progressive. Furthermore, the exemptions are expressed in nominal terms. As prices go up, the exemptions become lower and lower in real terms. An increase in nominal income exactly offset by an increase in prices pushes taxpayers into higher tax brackets with higher tax rates. A greater proportion of this income must be paid to the government as prices rise. Using actual U. S. tax rates from a recent year, an individual with a taxable income of $20,000 pays a tax of $4098. Now suppose that prices and nominal income both rise by 10 percent. This individual's nominal taxable income is now $22,000, and his tax is $4736. In real terms (at prices of the initial year), taxes rise from $4098 to $4736/1.10 = $4305. In other words, the tax receipts of the government rise by more than the cost of living, because the tax system is progressive.

A good example of the effect of inflation on real tax receipts may be seen in the year 1974. During that year personal income rose by 8 percent, but personal income taxes rose by 15 percent. This rise in real tax burden was not caused by a surtax; it was simply the effect of 10-percent inflation on a tax system whose provisions are written in nominal terms. Raising taxes through inflation is a way of increasing government revenues without going through Congress.

Because of the large increases in tax collections due to bracket-creep in the late 1970s, in 1981 President Reagan proposed, and Congress accepted, a fundamental restructuring of our income tax system.[2] Starting in 1984, our tax system will be *indexed*. This means that all the income class limits and exemptions will be automatically adjusted for inflation. This change will eliminate the effect of inflation on taxes and will make aggregate demand far less sensitive to prices than it has been in the past.

To recapitulate, we have found three reasons why rising prices reduce demand: They reduce wealth, which reduces consumption; they reduce the real supply of money, which drives up interest rates and reduces interest-sensitive expenditures; and, in the absence of indexing, they redistribute income to the government.[3]

Deriving Aggregate Demand from the IS-LM Model

We now derive the aggregate demand curve formally from the IS-LM model of Chapter 4. In diagram (a) of Figure 6.1, we show the IS-LM diagram for a certain stock of money, level of government expenditure, tax rate, and price level, P_0. At P_0 aggregate demand is Y_0, the intersection of the solid IS and LM curves. In diagram (b), Y_0P_0 is a point on the aggregate demand curve.

Now suppose that prices rise to P_1. So long as G, M, and t are constant, a rise in prices shifts both the IS and the LM to the left. The LM shifts leftward because M/P falls. The IS curve shifts leftward because of the wealth effect on consumption and because the transfer of income to the government raises the real tax rate. Aggregate demand falls from Y_0 to Y_1. The point P_1Y_1 is thus a second point on the aggregate demand curve in (b). Were we to introduce other price levels and derive aggregate demand from the IS-LM curves, we would trace out the negatively sloped aggregate demand curve in (b). The demand curve with tax indexing will be steeper than the curve without it because indexing will reduce the effect of price on the IS curve.

The Effect of Policy Variables on the Aggregate Demand Curve

It should be obvious that monetary and fiscal policies affect the position of the aggregate demand curve. Expansionary monetary policy shifts the LM curve to the right which, barring a vertical IS curve, increases aggregate demand. Hence, a rise in M shifts DD in Figure 6.1 to the right. Expansionary fiscal policy has the same effect, unless there is complete crowding out or a vertical LM curve. Hence, a rise in government expenditure or a tax cut also shifts DD to the right.

Formally, we write aggregate demand as a function of G, M, t, and P:

(6.1) $$Y_d = d(\overset{+}{G}, \overset{+}{M}, \overset{-}{t}, \overset{-}{P}).$$

[2]The change in the tax system was part of Reagan's Program for Economic Recovery.

[3]Note that we are not considering the effect on demand of changes in future expected inflation. Here we are treating only one-time price changes, which do not change people's expectations about future prices. We discuss the effect of expected inflation on demand in Chapter 14.

Figure 6.1
Deriving Aggregate Demand

A change in price shifts both the IS and LM curves. When prices rise from P_0 to P_1, the LM curve shifts from LM (P_0) to LM (P_1), because the real value of the money supply declines. The IS curve shifts inward as well because of the rise in the real value of taxes due to bracket-creep. The result is that equilibrium income declines from Y_0 to Y_1. The points P_0, Y_0 and P_1, Y_1 are two points on the downward-sloping demand curve in (b).

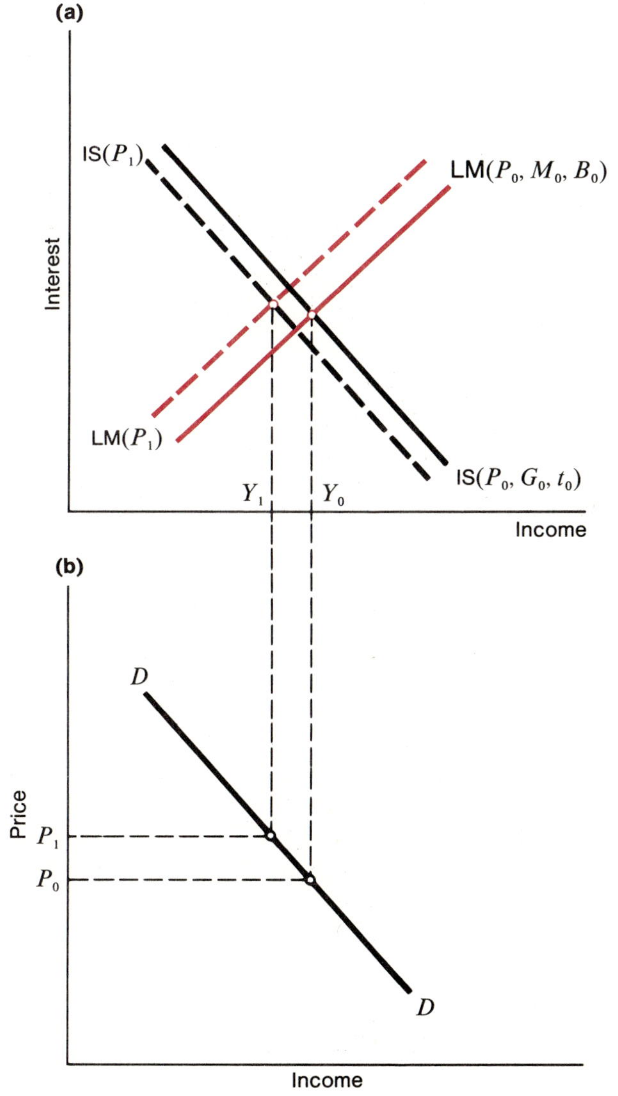

The sign over each variable in the equation indicates the direction of the relationship between it and Y_d. The demand curve DD in Figure 6.1 is simply a picture of the negative relationship between price and demand indicated in Equation (6.1). The other variables in the equation are shift variables in the diagram; they shift DD in the directions indicated by their signs in Equation (6.1). Thus, a rise in G or M shifts DD to the right, and a rise in t shifts DD to the left.

Equation (6.1) tells us how any policy change affects aggregate demand. But we cannot say what happens to income until we know something about aggregate supply. Essentially we are searching for a relationship between price and supply similar to the one that we just found for aggregate demand. This is a subject on which there is profound disagreement among economists. Some think that the supply curve is relatively flat, others think that it is steep. We look now at the theoretical basis for each of these viewpoints.

The Full Equilibrium Theory of Supply

To derive the relationship between the supply of output and price, we look first at the production and pricing decisions of the individual firm and then aggregate across an economy composed of such firms. Our analysis will be for a period short enough for us to assume that the stocks of machines and buildings are both constant. In this model, we will assume a competitive economy in which all firms are price-takers. Hence, to derive a supply curve for the firm, we ask how much the firm would be willing to supply at different prices. But since production depends on the quantity of labor employed, how much the firm is willing to produce will depend on how much it has to pay its workers. Therefore, in order to understand aggregate supply, we must go beyond the product market and analyze the setting of wages as well. To do this, we must broaden our inquiry and examine the labor market, for it is there that the demand and the supply of labor determine the wage rate.

The Demand for Labor

Obviously, the goods and labor markets are interdependent. Since we have to break into this simultaneous production and employment process somewhere, we choose to start with the demand and supply of labor. Imagine a world in which all jobs and all workers are homogeneous. What would be the demand for labor in such a world? That is, how much labor would the typical firm be willing to employ at different wage rates? Just like any other buyer, the employer hires labor services (man-hours) so long as their value to him or her is at least as great as their cost. From a knowledge of the production process, the businessperson knows just how many extra widgets an additional worker can produce. Because he or she also knows the price of widgets, it is possible to calculate the extra revenue that will be received from employing an additional person. The businessperson can then compare the cost of that individual to see if it is profitable to hire him or her. The employer is in business to earn maximum profit and should therefore hire workers only as long as the extra revenue they produce exceeds the wage they must be paid.

Table 6.1
The Production Schedule

Labor Worker-Days	Total Output (Widgets/Day)	MPP (Number of Extra Widgets Produced by Additional Worker)	Price	MRP
1	20	20	$10	$200
2	35	15	10	150
3	45	10	10	100
4	50	5	10	50
5	53	3	10	30
6	55	2	10	20
7	56.5	1.5	10	15

The additional revenue generated by each additional person is called **marginal revenue product** (MRP). It is equal to the **marginal physical product of labor** (MPP), in this case the number of extra widgets multiplied by the price of widgets. Therefore, the profit-maximizing businessperson follows this simple rule: Hire workers until the MRP of the last worker hired is just equal to the wage. This rule, called the **profit maximization rule,** can be written as:

(6.2) $$\text{MRP}_{\text{LAST WORKER}} = \text{Wage}.$$

According to Equation (6.2), if we know the wage rate, the price of widgets, and the marginal physical product of labor in the widget industry, we can predict how many workers the firm will employ and how many widgets will be produced.

Suppose an individual widget maker produces under the conditions shown in Table 6.1. If the wage is $20 per day, the profit-maximizing firm will hire six workers and will produce 55 widgets.[4]

In order to follow the profit maximization rule, the employer must know the MPP of labor—that is, he or she must know the relationship between output and different levels of employment. This relationship is called the **production function** and can be written in a general form as:

(6.3) $$Y_s = y(\overset{+}{N}, \overset{+}{K}).$$

Y_s = output supplied
N = quantity of labor services employed
K = stock of capital (assumed to be constant)

[4]In our example the firm is indifferent as to whether to hire five or six workers, because the numbers we have presented show the MPP as being equal to two widgets for all levels of employment between five and six.

Equation (6.3) says that output rises with the quantity of either capital or labor employed. A typical production function is shown in diagram (a) of Figure 6.2.

We now derive the demand for labor from the production function. Note first that for simplicity we can rewrite Equation (6.2) in an equivalent but more useful form as:

(6.4) $$\frac{W}{P} = MPP_{\text{LAST WORKER}}.$$

In Chapter 2 we called W/P the real wage. It represents the rate of exchange between labor and goods—the amount of goods a businessperson has to give up to buy a day of labor. Thus the profit maximization rule can be restated: Make the marginal physical product of labor just equal to the real wage.

It now remains for us to determine the marginal physical product of labor. It can be derived from the production function. By definition,

$$MPP = \frac{\Delta Y_s}{\Delta N}.$$

Geometrically, the MPP is the slope of the production function in diagram (a) of Figure 6.2. As we have drawn the production function the MPP is positive but decreasing as extra workers are hired.

A falling MPP is only an assumption but a number of important results follow from it, so we should understand its rationale. In drawing up our production schedule, we are assuming that capital and management resources are constant. When the firm hires extra labor, the amount of machinery and management per worker falls. Output per worker should depend positively on capital and management per worker, so the MPP of additional labor should decline. Thus, a falling MPP follows from the fact that the supply of machines is constant at any moment in time. Over time, if the firm invests in new machines the entire production function in diagram (a) will rise, increasing the MPP and allowing the firm to employ more labor.

We can express our assumptions about the MPP formally by writing it as a function of employment and the capital stock:

(6.5) $$MPP = m(\overset{-}{N}, \overset{+}{K}).$$

If we now combine Equations (6.4) and (6.5), we have the firm's demand for labor:

(6.6) $$\frac{W}{P} = m(\overset{-}{N}, \overset{+}{K}).$$

Diagrammatically, Equation (6.6) is the negatively sloped demand curve DD in diagram (b) of Figure 6.2. That demand curve is a visual representation of the MPP schedule derived from the production function and is assumed to be linear. Because the MPP is negatively related to N, employment can increase only if the real

Figure 6.2
Deriving the Labor Demand Curve

The demand curve in (b) is the marginal physical product (MPP) of labor ($\Delta Y_s/\Delta N$). It is the slope of the production function in (a).

(a) The Production Function

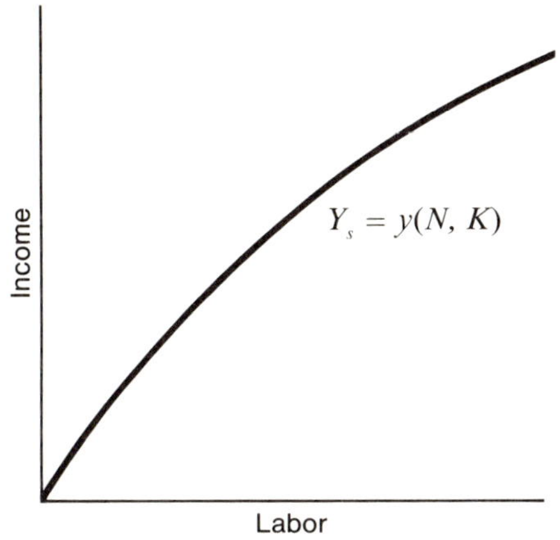

(b) The Labor Demand Curve

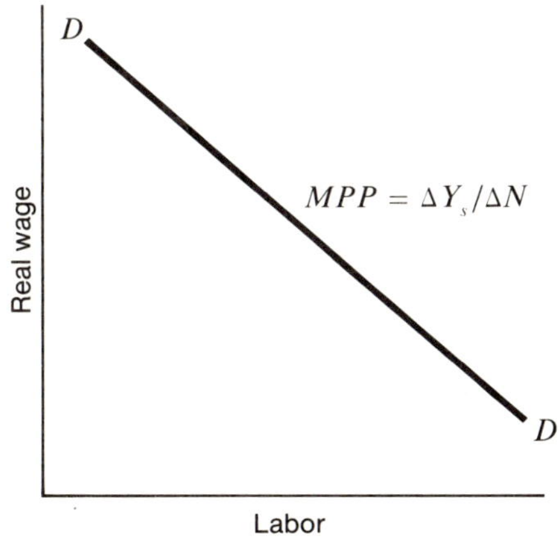

wage declines. Note that the demand for labor does not depend on the level of demand in the economy. It depends only on labor productivity.

Our discussion of labor demand has been carried out at the firm level, but the shape of the labor demand curve for the entire economy should be the same. Each firm maximizes profits by hiring labor until the real wage of the last worker just equals its MPP. If the demand curve for each firm has the same downward slope, this downward slope is preserved when we aggregate over all firms. We can then interpret *DD* in Figure 6.2 as an economy-wide demand curve for labor, which says that employment depends negatively on the real wage. The reason for this is that the capital stock available to the economy is fixed at any moment as it is for the firm. There are only a certain number of machines available to the labor force, so that the additional product of new employment should be falling. Of course, capital formation by the economy over time will push the economy-wide labor demand curve to the right, just as it will for the firm.

The Supply of Labor

Having discussed the aggregate demand curve for labor, we are left with the problem of determining the labor supply curve. Before discussing this problem, however, we should distinguish between two different quantities of labor—hours and people. The two will differ whenever hours per day or days per month change. For convenience, we will assume that the number of hours of labor services each worker provides is fixed. We can then translate the business demand for a number of hours of labor services into a demand for a number of workers. Our labor market diagram will then be shown in terms of number of workers employed instead of number of labor hours. This will simplify the analysis and is also defensible in light of the institutional constraints on the ability to vary the length of the workweek or work-year in response to wage variations.

Consider now the various concepts of labor supply. Labor supply can mean the number of people in the labor force or the number willing to accept job offers. Hence we have two labor supply curves to derive. The first, the supply curve of the labor force, shows the number of workers in the labor force as a function of the wage. The second, which we will call the supply curve of labor, shows the number of workers willing to work at different wage rates. It is this curve that is relevant for production. The difference between the two curves is unemployment.

Labor contracts are expressed in nominal wages, but in reality a worker should be interested in the command over resources that is gained in exchange for giving up leisure. Dollars are not useful in themselves but only for what they will buy. The worker should be thinking of the real, not the nominal, wage. The real wage tells exactly how many goods the worker will receive per day of leisure forgone. The labor supply curve, for whatever concept of supply we adopt, should therefore show the relationship between supply and the real wage.

What does the labor force supply curve look like? It might seem natural to expect that a rise in real wages would bring more people into the labor force; after all, the rise in W/P increases the return to work. But most heads of families are not free to enter or leave the labor force in response to wage variations. They may accept unemployment as they look for a better job, but they do not leave the labor force. The source of any potential fluctuations in the size of the labor force must therefore be sought in the secondary labor force.[5]

[5]For a more complete discussion of the determinants of labor force participation, see Glen G. Cain, "Unemployment and the Labor Force Participation of Secondary Workers," *Industrial and Labor Relations Review* (January 1967): 257–97; and Belton Fleischer, *Labor Economics: Theory and Evidence* (Englewood Cliffs, NJ: Prentice-Hall, 1970), 73–91.

A rise in real wages may well bring nonworkers into the labor force. It is equally possible, however, that as the real wage of the head of the family rises, part of that extra income will be used to buy leisure for family members in the secondary labor force. We have two opposite effects: On the one hand, the rise in real wages makes working more attractive; on the other, it also increases family income and the demand for leisure.

In the absence of any firm conviction or knowledge about which effect dominates, we will assume that one offsets the other. We are thus asserting that a rise in the real wage does not change the number of people in the labor force.

Consider now the labor supply curve. It differs from the labor force supply curve by unemployment. To understand the former curve, we must take a closer look at unemployment. What are its economic determinants, and what is its economic purpose?

A person is voluntarily unemployed when he or she is in the labor force but is devoting full time to seeking a better job. The cost of this unemployment is the wages that would have been earned, and the benefit is the higher-paying job that might be found by further search. This type of unemployment has been called **frictional unemployment.** It stems from imperfections in the labor market. Jobs and workers are not perfectly alike and information about either is not perfect. Workers have an idea of the real wage they should be able to command, but they do not know where a job vacancy for such a wage exists. One way of finding it is to devote full time to a job search. Unemployment provides the time to gather information about the job market in a world where information is costly.

One way of conceptualizing the unemployment decision stems from Phelps.[6] Imagine the economy as a set of separate islands with one factory on each. Information about local island wage rates is perfect, but such information can be obtained for other islands only by visiting each island and sampling its labor market. In other words, to be certain of the opportunities elsewhere, a worker must leave work and travel around the neighboring islands. When is it rational for this individual to become unemployed? It is rational only when the worker believes that the future increase in wages to be gained by moving to another island more than compensates for the days of current wages lost through unemployment. In the rarefied world of perfect information and foresight, unemployment would not occur. Each worker on each island would know exactly what his or her opportunities were. Search and unemployment would be irrational, because all wage rates for equivalent work would be equal. Why, for example, would a carpenter ever quit a job to look for a better-paying one if there were one, economy-wide wage rate for carpenters? Unemployment is rational only where jobs are not all alike and information is not perfect. Unemployment occurs when workers believe they can increase their lifetime earnings by devoting full time to searching for a better-paying job. Note that this sort of frictional unemployment is both voluntary and beneficial to labor, because it is a way of increasing earnings in a world of imperfect and costly information. We should also note that frictional unemployment is not a result of low wages

[6]Among his many writings in this area, see in particular Edmund S. Phelps, *Inflation Policy and Unemployment Theory* (New York: Norton, 1972).

per se but a result of wages being lower than those a person expects to find by looking further.

The frictionally unemployed are a revolving pool of people acquiring information about their opportunities by devoting full time to a search of the job market. They have certain expectations about the level of real wages they desire and should be able to command. Their expectations are based upon what other people in the same profession are earning, hearsay, newspaper advertisements, and other factors. These unemployed will be traveling from job opening to job opening, looking for the job that meets their expectations. Presumably, as their period of unemployment becomes longer, they will scale down those expectations until they finally find an acceptable job.

What would it take to reduce the level of frictional unemployment at any point in time? Remember that each unemployed worker is searching for an acceptable real wage. If there should be a general rise in real wages, some of the unemployed would find jobs and wages meeting or exceeding their expectations. In other words, a rise in the average real wage should reduce the level of frictional unemployment. Conversely we could say that a rise in the real wage increases the number of people actually working.

We can now summarize this long discussion by completing the labor market diagram. In diagram (b) of Figure 6.2, we showed the demand for labor. Now we add two new curves (see Figure 6.3). *NN* is the labor force supply curve. Because, by our assumptions, it is fixed at any point and is not affected by the real wage, it is a vertical line. (The line will be shifting to the right over time as the labor force expands along with the population.) *SS* is the supply curve of labor. It shows the number of people who are willing to work as a function of the real wage. The distance between *SS* and *NN* is voluntary, frictional unemployment. *SS* is upward sloping because of our assertion that as real wages rise, more and more of the unemployed find wage offers in line with their expectations and begin to accept jobs.

Equilibrium in any market is defined as a state in which the quantity supplied equals the quantity demanded, or where the market clears. In the labor market, equilibrium will occur at that real wage rate at which employers are willing to hire all the people willing to work. Geometrically, we are looking for a point on both the supply and the demand curves. In Figure 6.3 this is obviously point A, the intersection of the two curves. At that equilibrium, employment is N_{FE}, unemployment is the distance $N_f - N_{FE}$, and the real wage is W_0/P_0.

If the real wage were lower, there would be an excess demand for labor. Some jobs would be unfilled, because jobholders would have left work to seek higher wages elsewhere. As business tried to fill the vacancies, it would be forced to raise its wage offers. The process would continue until the real wage rose to its equilibrium level W_0/P_0.

It may seem surprising to the reader that unemployment exists in equilibrium. Unemployment would seem to be a symptom of disequilibrium. But the reader should keep in mind that the unemployment we are speaking of here is voluntary, frictional unemployment, which occurs because the labor market is large and heterogeneous and job changes cannot take place instantaneously. Frictional unemployment has been labeled *natural*, or normal, and is estimated at the present time to be between 5.1 and 5.5 percent of the labor force in the United States. When

Figure 6.3
Supply and Demand in the Labor Market

NN is the labor force supply curve. It is assumed to not be a function of the real wage. The labor force is N_f. The horizontal distance between the labor force supply curve and the labor supply curve is unemployment.

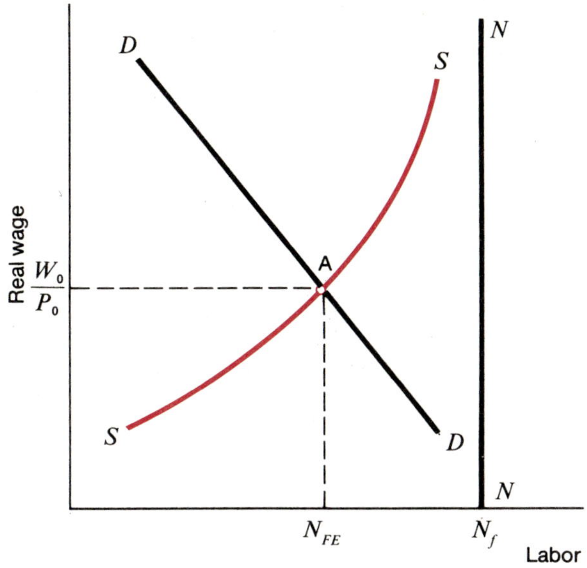

economists speak of full employment, they do not mean that everyone has a job. Rather they mean that unemployment is at its natural level, where all unemployment is frictional or voluntary.[7]

Formally, we can find equilibrium for the labor market as follows. First, we write the labor supply curve as a positive function between the real wage and the labor supply:

(6.7) $$\frac{W}{P} = \overset{+}{s}(N).$$

Then we set supply equal to demand and solve the resulting equation for N. Thus, setting Equation (6.6) equal to Equation (6.7), we get Equation (6.8), which can be solved for the equilibrium level of employment:

(6.8) $$s(N) = m(N, K).$$

[7]The notion of a natural level of unemployment is a somewhat nebulous one. What may be natural in one setting will not be natural in another. Another definition of the natural level is that unemployment rate at which the inflation rate is stable.

Table 6.2
Marginal Revenue Product at Different Prices

Labor	Total Units of Output	MPP	MRP at P = $10	MRP at P = $13.33
5	53.0	3.0	$30.00	$40.00
6	55.0	2.0	20.00	26.67
7	56.5	1.5	15.00	20.00

The Aggregate Supply Curve of the Economy

We return now to our main concern, the aggregate supply curve. It tells us what would happen to output if the prices of all goods changed. Consider the widget maker of the previous section. Let us suppose that the price of widgets rises from $10.00 to $13.33 and *wages do not change*. Table 6.2 shows what happens to MRP. The reader will recall from Table 6.1 that with a wage rate of $20 per day and a widget price of $10, the firm hires six workers and produces 55 widgets. When the price rises to $13.33 it becomes profitable to increase production to 56.5 widgets, because the rise in prices offsets the decline in MPP of the seventh worker. This conclusion should be fairly general. For any firm where the marginal output of additional workers drops, an increase in selling prices enables it to increase output so long as wages do not change.

If the price of labor rises just as fast as prices, there can be no increase in output. Consider our widget maker. At a wage of $20 and a selling price of $13.33, the firm increases its output to 56.5 widgets. But what if workers demand a 33.3-percent increase in wages to compensate for the increase in prices? The new nominal wage rate will be $26.67, but the profit-maximizing ouput will still be 55 widgets. In other words, when nominal wages are allowed to change along with the prices so that real wages are constant, price changes no longer allow firms to change their output.

Is it reasonable to suppose that wages would change along with prices? Economists think that it is. They argue that workers are interested in their real wages because the real wage represents the purchasing power of what they earn. For that reason, we drew the labor supply curve of the previous section in terms of W/P, not W. One should expect, therefore, that any increase in price will be met by an equivalent increase in the money wage rate.

Under these conditions, the somewhat surprising result is that a rise in prices will not lead to an increase in output. The aggregate supply curve will be vertical even though the supply curve for the individual widget maker is upward sloping.

The reason for the vertical supply curve can be seen more clearly in Figure 6.4. Diagrams (a) and (b) show the labor market and the production function, and the curves are identical to those in Figure 6.2. Diagram (c) simply transfers Y from the vertical to the horizontal axis. Diagram (d) is the goods market. We now use Figure 6.4 to understand the vertical supply curve SS in (d).

Figure 6.4
Deriving the Vertical Full-Equilibrium Long-Run Supply Curve

Since both the demand and the supply of labor depend on the real wage, there is only one possible equilibrium in the labor market, namely N_{FE}. But since the capital stock is fixed, that amount of labor can produce only Y_{FE} of income. Variations in the price level have no effect on either employment or output, and therefore the supply curve is a vertical line at Y_{FE} in (d).

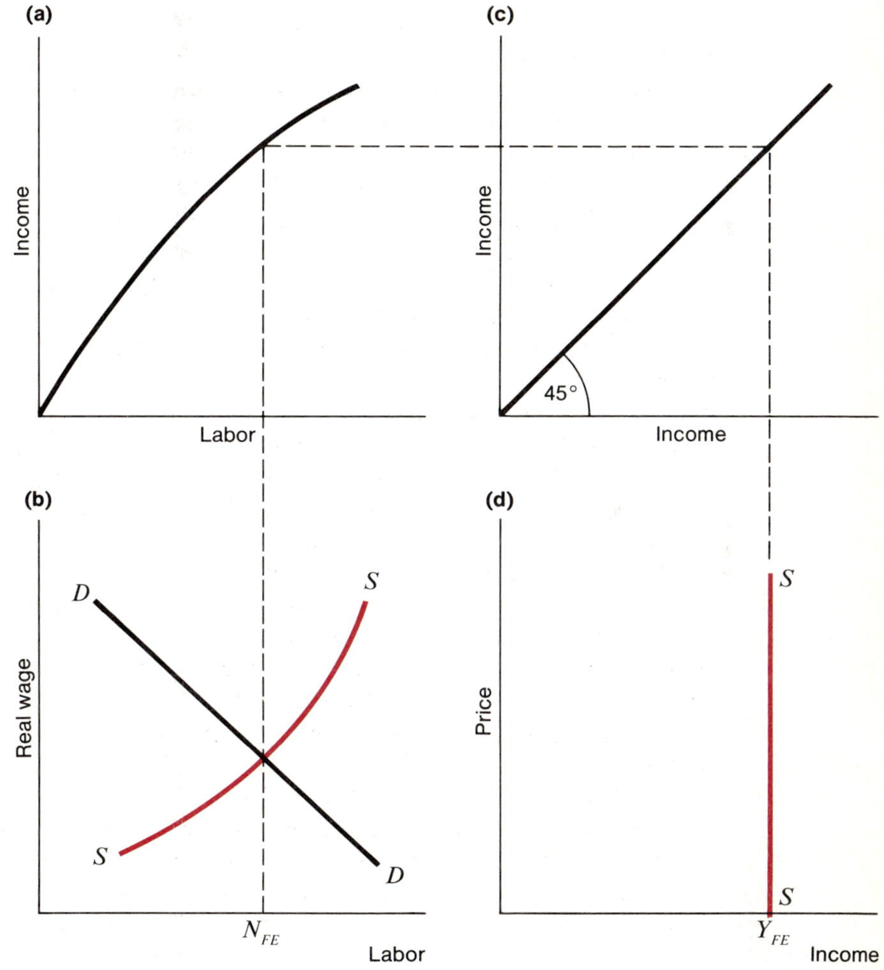

The production function of the economy determines the marginal product of different quantities of labor. If labor thinks in real terms, there is only one possible equilibrium employment level in the labor market, namely, N_{FE}, the intersection of the labor supply and demand curves. N_{FE} is the full equilibrium level of employment, sometimes called by economists the *natural employment level*. No change in price can change this full equilibrium so long as the labor force and employers both think in real terms. But if full equilibrium employment is N_{FE} regardless of the price level, we know from the production function that there is only one possible output level, namely, Y_{FE}, the output producible by N_{FE} workers. Thus, aggregate supply will be Y_{FE}, whatever the price level. In full equilibrium aggregate supply is independent of price, which means that the supply curve is a vertical line at Y_{FE} in diagram (d).

The Partial Equilibrium Aggregate Supply Curve

The main drawback of the theory of aggregate supply we have just developed is that it has no explanation for fluctuations in output and employment. According to that theory there is only one equilibrium, and that is at the full or natural rate of employment. Obviously, this is unrealistic. Economies have booms and recessions, and any macromodel should have an explanation for them.

One such explanation for booms and recessions was developed independently in the late 1960s by Milton Friedman and Edmund Phelps.[8] Friedman and Phelps (hereafter, F-P) set out to explain why economies have booms and recessions when there is a change in demand rather than simply a change in prices as implied by the vertical supply curve. F-P's explanation is based on the notion that even though workers may think in real terms, they are forced to forecast the price level when they enter into long-term contracts. F-P argued that workers are likely to make erroneous price forecasts in the short run. This will have effects on output and employment for as long as the errors persist. We shall call the **F-P model** a partial, or temporary, equilibrium theory of supply. The model retains the equilibrium notion that supply equals demand in all markets, but it brings time into the analysis by acknowledging that in the short run workers may make forecasting errors. When that happens, markets may clear at prices that are equilibrium prices only temporarily. As workers react to forecasting errors, a dynamic adjustment process is initiated by which the economy moves into full equilibrium. During the adjustment process, the economy has the booms and recessions that are observed in the real world.

In the next section we will develop formally the F-P partial equilibrium model. In the full equilibrium model, spelled out in the previous section, we implicitly assume that everyone knows the equilibrium price level and can therefore immediately convert any nominal wage into a real wage. If everyone has perfect foresight about present and future inflation rates, no one will regret his or her decision. But what if those forecasts are wrong?

In the real world, labor contracts often cover a long period. They require forecasts of price changes for more than one market period. Auto workers sign two-year contracts; steel and aluminum workers sign three-year contracts. Even

[8]Edmund S. Phelps, *Inflation Policy and Unemployment Theory*, and Milton Friedman, "The Role of Monetary Policy," *American Economic Review* 58 (March 1968): 1–17.

one-year contracts require price forecasts. Friedman argues that the forecasting problem is more difficult for labor than it is for the firm, because the relevant price to the firm is the price of its product, one single price in a market it knows well. Labor, however, has to worry about the entire cost of living. Remember that workers are interested in the general purchasing power of their wage, and they calculate this by deflating their money wage by a general cost-of-living index. They have to forecast the prices of housing, medical services, food, and all the other products they use. Management has to forecast only one price. In the F-P world, laborers accept job offers contingent upon what they think the real wage is and will be. Yet they probably have a very dim perception of the path of future prices throughout the economy. It is therefore entirely possible that when the future arrives, there will be a difference between the real wage they once thought they would earn and the one they actually earn. In the real world, there is no reason to assume that labor and management base their plans on the same set of price forecasts. There could thus be a difference between the labor supply and demand curves as perceived by management and labor. What occurs in the labor market when these elements of short-run realism are introduced?

The Effect of Unexpected Inflation on Employment and Output

We are now going to investigate the adjustment by the labor and goods markets to an unexpected change in price. To do this, we must distinguish between what we will call the full equilibrium or long-run labor supply curve, which is the supply curve in which labor's price expectations are accurate, and the partial equilibrium or short-run labor supply curve, in which expected and actual prices may be different. The reason we may think of the full and partial equilibrium models as long and short run is that the idea of forecasting errors is inherently a short-run notion. Changes in conditions that cause short-run changes in prices may catch people by surprise and cause them to make forecasting errors. However, given enough time, such errors should be corrected. Thus, one can think of the partial equilibrium model as a short-run model and the full equilibrium model as a long-run one. We shall use the terms full and long-run interchangeably even though it is awkward to think of long-run equilibrium with a constant capital stock.

The labor supply curve that we derived earlier shows the amount of labor that will work at different real wages, under the assumption that labor forecasts prices correctly. We are going to call that a full equilibrium or long-run curve, because in the short run labor may make forecasting errors. What we will call the partial equilibrium or short-run labor supply curve is a relationship that shows the real wage at which various numbers of workers are willing to work when there are forecasting errors. The difference between the two curves results from the difference between expected and actual prices. Short-run equilibrium is always at the intersection of the short-run labor supply curve and the labor demand curve.

To see the effect of forecasting errors on the labor market, imagine an economy in equilibrium with constant prices disturbed by an unexpected rise in government spending. This will cause a rise in prices throughout the economy. Let us suppose that this inflation is entirely unexpected by labor, which is forecasting a continuation of the previous equilibrium price level. If no inflation is expected, the

Figure 6.5
Labor Market When There Is Unexpected Inflation

In the short run, the supply of labor is based on the expected real wage. Therefore, if there is unexpected inflation the short-run supply curve shifts down and to the right, because workers will mistakenly deflate their wage offers by an expected price P_e, which is less than P. They will therefore think that nominal wage offers correspond to a higher real wage than they in fact do. Because of this forecasting error, a greater number of workers will be willing to work for a given real wage (because they think it is a higher real wage).

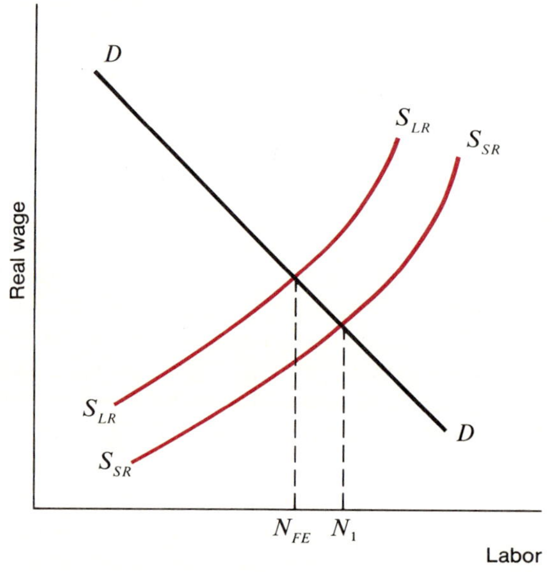

prices used are the equilibrium prices of the previous year. But if prices are rising unexpectedly (that is, if there is unexpected inflation), there will be a difference between what the real wage is perceived to be and the actual wage represented by any nominal wage offer. Labor acts on what it perceives the real wage to be.

Thus, in Figure 6.5 we amend our earlier diagram of the labor market to include the short-run labor supply curve, S_{SR}, in addition to our original supply curve, S_{LR}. Whenever prices rise unexpectedly, S_{SR} lies to the right of S_{LR}. N_{FE} people will continue to work at the old nominal wage even though the rise in prices has reduced the purchasing power that wage represents. It is as if labor is suddenly willing to work for lower real wages.

Suppose that previously the labor market equilibrium was at N_{FE}. Now, owing to the shift in the short-run labor supply curve, employment rises to N_1. Why does that occur? The inflation fools some workers. Take the extra workers between N_{FE} and N_1. These are the people who leave unemployment and go to work because they will receive the increase in nominal wages that they have sought. They do not realize, however, that this increase is being more than offset by rising prices. Management finds that actual real wages are lower and is able to hire more work-

Table 6.3
Effect of Price Increase on MRP

Labor	MRP
4	$66.50
5	40.00
6	26.67
7	20.00

ers, while the workers think, incorrectly as it turns out, that real wages have risen. Unexpected inflation thus appears for employers to be a costless way of increasing unemployment.

We can imagine how the rise in prices causes the increase in employment or the decrease in unemployment. The frictionally unemployed have certain nominal wages at which they are willing to work. If prices are rising employers can afford to raise the nominal wages they pay, and the unemployed workers are likely to find an acceptable wage offer and take jobs. The rise in prices has thus reduced frictional unemployment.

Observe carefully what is taking place. The government spending program causes a rise in prices, increased employment, and a fall in real wages. Consider how this process works at the individual factory. Take our widget firm, for example. We saw that the factory employed six workers at a price of $10 and a wage rate of $20. Suppose that the price of widgets rises to $13.33 and the wage remains at $20. The MRP of any worker will then have risen, producing the revised MRP schedule shown in Table 6.3.

By the rule of equating the real wage to the MPP of the last worker, it is now profitable to employ the seventh worker. The unexpected rise in prices allows for an increase in employment because it shifts the short-run labor supply curve down and to the right.

It should be clear that forecasting errors will have an effect on output, since they change the equilibrium level of employment in the labor market. We show this in Figure 6.6 by means of the same four quadrant diagrams we developed in Figure 6.4.

First we note that the vertical economy supply curve in (d) can now be interpreted as the supply curve in the absence of forecasting errors. For this reason, Friedman called it the long-run supply curve.[9] The economy will be on the long-run supply curve whenever price forecasts by workers are accurate, whatever the absolute level of prices. In the case shown, expected price or $P_e = 100$. Thus, if actual price equals 100, output will be Y_{FE}.

Let us now define a short-run supply curve as the relationship between output and price for a given level of expected prices. We shall construct the curve for $P_e = 100$. As we can see, point A is on that curve. To find other points, imagine first

[9] A better label would be the full equilibrium supply curve.

Figure 6.6
Deriving the Short-Run Aggregate Supply Curve

A rise in prices unexpected by the labor force shifts the short-run labor supply curve to the right, allowing an increase in employment and output. Suppose that workers expect the price to be 100. Then, if the actual price is 100, employment will be N_{FE} and output will be Y_{FE}. Thus, the point $P = 100$, $Y = Y_{FE}$ is on the short-run supply curve. If price rises to P_1, employment will be N_1 and output will be Y_1. Thus, P_1, Y_1 is a second point on the supply curve. The short-run aggregate supply curve therefore shows the relationship between output and price *for a given level of expected price*. Each short-run supply curve intersects the long-run curve at its expected price.

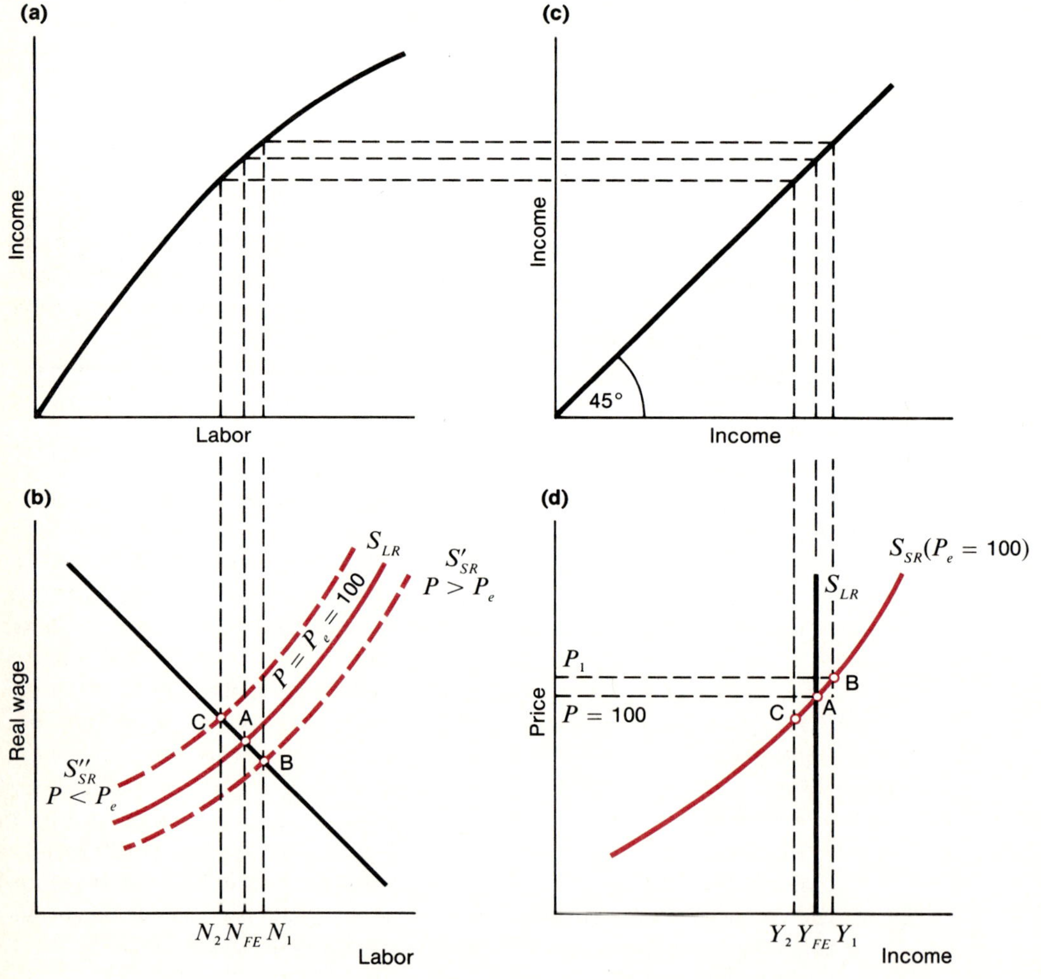

that there is an increase in demand that pushes prices up above 100. In this case, P rises above P_e, which causes the short-run labor supply curve to shift outward to S'_{SR}. As the reader can see, employment rises to N_1 and output rises to Y_1. When P_e is constant, a rise in price leads to an increase in output. Conversely, if P falls below P_e because of a reduction in demand the labor supply curve shifts inward, causing a reduction in both output and employment. In general, if $P > P_e$, short-run supply is greater than full equilibrium or long-run supply ($Y > Y_{FE}$), while if $P < P_e$, $Y < Y_{FE}$.

Looking now at diagram (d), we have found three points on the short-run supply curve. That supply curve is upward sloping rather than vertical. It tells us how much output will be produced at various prices *when workers expect the price to be equal to 100*. There will be a different short-run supply curve for each different level of expected prices. Each short-run curve intersects the full equilibrium curve at the price level expected by labor.

The Partial Equilibrium Theory of the Business Cycle

It remains only to bring demand back into our model to understand the partial equilibrium theory of booms and recessions. In the short run, equilibrium is determined in the goods market by the intersection of a demand curve and a short-run aggregate supply curve.

Suppose we start with an economy on its long-run supply curve as shown in Figure 6.7. Fiscal and monetary policies and private demand are just sufficient to buy up the output supplied at the price level expected by labor. But suppose now that the government increases its expenditure or the Federal Reserve goes on a binge of unexpected money creation. In either case, the demand curve shifts out to D_1D_1. Prices and output both rise, to P_1 and Y_1 respectively. The increase in aggregate demand has caused a boom. Why? Because of unexpected inflation. The extra demand has pushed prices above the level expected by labor; that has enabled employers to raise their nominal wage offers. Because workers do not realize that prices have gone up as well, they interpret the rise in nominal wages as a rise in real wages. That causes an increase in employment. In other words, in the F-P world booms are a result of an unexpected rise in prices that temporarily fools the labor force.

The F-P partial equilibrium theory of recession is parallel to the theory for the boom. Recession occurs when there is a reduction in demand that causes prices to fall below the level expected by labor. Just as in the case of the boom, the recession is caused by the erroneous forecasts in the labor market. However, in this case, since workers have overforecasted the price level, they will unwittingly be making real wage demands that are too high. As a consequence, the short-run labor supply curve will shift to the left, causing a reduction in output and employment.

It is worth noting here that in the partial equilibrium model, all the recessionary unemployment is voluntary. People are unemployed because they think the wage offers they are getting are too low. This differs fundamentally from the view of unemployment that we shall present in the next chapter.

Figure 6.7
A Boom in the F-P Model

A boom in the F-P model is caused by an expansion in aggregate demand. Demand shifts from D_0D_0 to D_1D_1. So long as the rise in price from P_0 to P_1 is unexpected by labor, output increases from Y_{FE} to Y_1.

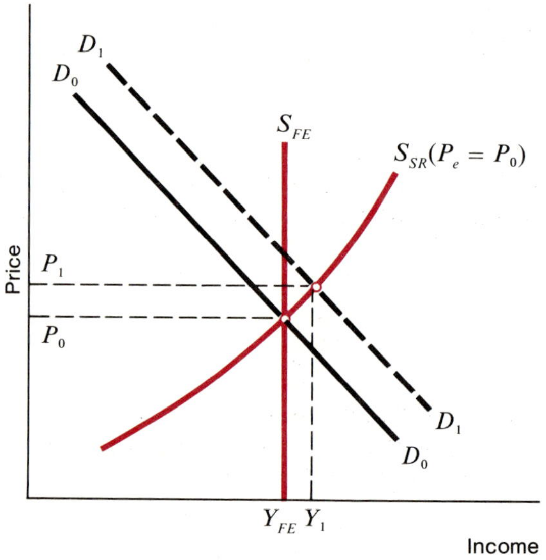

A Formal Derivation of the Partial Equilibrium Short-Run Supply Curve

For those more inclined toward equations than diagrams, we can derive the F-P short-run supply curve algebraically using a simple modification of the earlier labor supply curve. As we have seen, F-P asserted that labor supply is a function of the expected real wage. If we invert Equation (6.7), this behavioral hypothesis can be written as:

(6.9) $$N_s = n\left(\frac{W}{P_e}\right).$$

n = inverse of s in Equation (6.7)
P_e = expected price level
$\frac{W}{P_e}$ = expected real wage

The short-run supply curve differs from the long-run curve (Equation [6.7]) whenever prices are different than expected. It is handy to rewrite Equation (6.9) to show this directly. If we multiply the right-hand side of Equation (6.9) by P/P, we get labor supply as a function of the actual real wage and a new term, P/P_e. Thus:

$$N_s = n\left(\overset{+}{\frac{W}{P_e}}\right)$$

$$N_s = n\left(\overset{+}{\frac{W}{P_e}}\cdot\overset{+}{\frac{P}{P}}\right)$$

(6.10) $$N_s = n\left(\overset{+}{\frac{W}{P}}\cdot\overset{+}{\frac{P}{P_e}}\right).$$

The term P/P_e is the forecasting error of the labor force. Whenever workers underforecast (overforecast) the price level, this term will be greater (less) than one, which means that the short-run labor supply curve will lie to the right (left) of the long-run curve.

We find equilibrium in the labor market by substituting the labor demand curve (Equation [6.6]) into Equation (6.10) to get an implicit relationship between employment and the forecasting error.[10]

(6.11) $$N = n\left(\overset{+}{m}[\overset{-}{N}, \overset{+}{K}]\cdot\overset{+}{\frac{P}{P_e}}\right).$$

To show the positive relationship between employment and the forecasting error more clearly, we can write Equation (6.11) in a simpler form:

(6.12) $$N = l\left(\overset{+}{\frac{P}{P_e}}, \overset{+}{K}\right).$$

Equation (6.12) tells us that employment varies directly with both the unexpected inflation rate and the capital stock. Now substitute Equation (6.12) into the production function to get Equation (6.13):

(6.13) $$Y_s = y\left(\overset{+}{l}\left[\overset{+}{\frac{P}{P_e}}, K\right], \overset{+}{K}\right).$$

[10]Note that because the real wage and employment are related by Equation (6.6), Equation (6.11) is an equation in which only N, K, and P/P_e appear. Thus, it should be possible to rewrite this relationship into a simpler form, as we do in Equation (6.12). The real issue is to show that $\Delta N/(\Delta P/P_e) > 0$. That is clear by inspection of Equation (6.11). The reason is that a rise in unexpected inflation shifts the labor supply curve to the right—or increases N_s in Equation (6.10).

To see the key relationships more easily, we can rewrite Equation (6.13) as [11]

(6.14) $$Y_s = z\left(\overset{+}{\frac{P}{P_e}}, \overset{+}{K}\right).$$

Equation (6.14) is the partial equilibrium short-run supply curve of the economy. It says that in the short run, supply depends positively on price and capital and negatively on expected price. Another way to put this is to say that short-run output depends upon unexpected inflation, for that is what the term P/P_e means. If we set P_e equal to some particular value, as we did in deriving the supply curve in Figure 6.6, then clearly Y_s varies directly with price. This shows that the short-run supply curve is upward sloping.

It is worth noting that the vertical full equilibrium supply curve can be derived from Equation (6.14) by imposing the additional restriction that $P = P_e$. Putting this restriction into Equation (6.14), we get the equation of the full equilibrium supply curve:

(6.15) $$Y_s = z(1, K).$$

Since price does not appear in this equation, we can see at a glance that the full equilibrium supply curve must be vertical.

Summary

This completes our description of the full and partial equilibrium models of the economy. The partial equilibrium aggregate supply curve is upward sloping because in the short run workers may make erroneous forecasts of inflation. When workers underforecast the price level the economy has a boom, because workers inadvertently accept too low a real wage. When they overforecast the price level the economy has a recession. Thus, variations in aggregate demand cause fluctuations in real output rather than simple fluctuations in prices. Eventually, when forecasting errors are corrected, the economy returns to the full equilibrium or long-run aggregate supply curve. That curve is vertical because when both workers and businesspersons think in real terms, changing the level of demand and the level of prices can have no effect on either the level of employment or the level of output. In full equilibrium, production and income are independent of the level of aggregate demand.

[11] Since $\Delta N/(\Delta P/P_e) > 0$ and $\Delta Y/\Delta N > 0$, $\Delta Y/(\Delta P/P_e)$ must also be greater than zero.

Key Concepts

bracket-creep
marginal revenue product
marginal physical product
profit maximization rule
production function
frictional unemployment
F-P model
aggregate demand curve

Problems and Questions for Discussion

1. Using the behavioral model of Chapters 4 and 5:

$$C = 10 + .8Y_d \qquad M_s = 440$$
$$I = 90 - 200r \qquad G = 280$$
$$T = .2Y \qquad B = 200$$
$$\frac{M_d}{P} = .4Y - 200r + .3B/P \qquad P = 1.00$$

a. Derive an algebraic expression for the aggregate demand curve.
b. Graph the expression you have derived.
c. What is the algebraic expression for the slope of the demand curve?
d. Under what conditions would the demand curve be vertical?

2. Show the effect of each of the following changes on the demand curve you have drawn:

a. A rise in T.
b. A reduction in M.
c. A rise in G.
d. A rise in B.

3. The following production data are used in Problems 3–8. Suppose that an economy has the following production function:

Labor Employed	Output
9	90
10	100
11	109
12	117
13	124

a. What is the marginal product of successive units of labor?
b. Derive and graph the demand curve for labor.

4. Suppose the labor supply curve is:

$$L_s = \frac{W}{P} \cdot \frac{P}{P_e}.$$

Derive and graph the full equilibrium supply curve of labor.

5. What is the full equilibrium level of output, employment, and the real wage?

6. Suppose that $P = 122$ and $P_e = 100$.

a. Derive and graph the temporary equilibrium supply curve of labor under those conditions.

b. What are the levels of employment and output?

7. By how far would the price have to rise to employ 12 units of labor if $P_e = 100$? By how far would the price have to fall to reduce employment to 9? What is the output level associated with each of these price levels? Draw a graph of each pair of output and prices. (This curve is the temporary equilibrium supply curve for $P_e = 100$. Notice that it intersects the long-run curve at $P = P_e = 100$.)

8. Suppose that $P_{e,t} = P_{t-1}$, and suppose that actual prices behave as follows:

$P_0 = 100$ $P_3 = 149$
$P_1 = 100$ $P_4 = 149$
$P_2 = 122$

What is the time path of output, employment, and prices for periods 1–4?

9. Why, in full equilibrium, does a change in the price level have no effect on equilibrium employment and output? Why *does* price have such an effect in partial or temporary equilibrium?

10. Under what conditions would we expect to find an increase in the money wage associated with a decrease in the quantity of labor demanded? With an increase in the quantity of labor demanded? With no change?

11. Is it ever rational for a person to become unemployed voluntarily?

a. Under what circumstances would he or she do this?

b. Could we expect a rational but unemployed person to turn down job offers? Why?

12. How might the decision to accept or to leave a job be affected by either anticipated or unanticipated inflation?

Chapter 7

A Disequilibrium Theory of Prices, Output, and Employment

Both of the models that we developed in Chapter 6 assume that markets clear and that all economic agents are price-takers. That means that no supplier of goods or labor is big enough to determine the price at which goods or labor is sold. Instead, prices and wages are assumed to be determined by the requirement that supply equal demand.

Many economists believe that a more realistic model is one that assumes that in fact, sellers set prices and unions set wages. In this model prices and wages are unresponsive to market conditions in the short run. If they are set at too high a level, there will be unemployment and excess supply in the goods market; inventories will pile up before prices begin to decline. As a result markets may not clear, and a disequilibrium may occur in the short run.

In this chapter we shall focus on the disequilibrium theory and its significance in understanding booms and recessions.

A Short-Run Disequilibrium Model of the Economy

To economists who take the disequilibrium view of the economy, the partial equilibrium theory of recession is misleading and unrealistic. According to that theory, recessions occur because there is a lag in the adjustment of expectations about prices—but markets still clear. There are no bread lines or distress sales in the partial equilibrium model. Unemployment may rise above the normal level, but that unemployment is voluntary; it results from an overforecast of the price level. The notion that markets clear in the short run is rejected by disequilibrium economists. They argue that many firms and labor unions have the power to set wages and prices. Furthermore, many contracts last for two or three years. This gives wages and prices an inflexibility with respect to market conditions that makes it likely that neither labor nor product markets will clear in the short run.

The possible inconsistency in wages and prices would not be so serious if there were a single goods and labor market. In such a case prices and wages would converge quite rapidly to the level consistent with full equilibrium. But the modern economy has no such unified market. Price and wage decisions are dispersed across many firms and individuals, none of whom are eager to be the first to adjust their price. This gives to the modern economy a high degree of wage and price rigidity that sharply slows its tendency to return to full equilibrium. Even if a full equilibrium exists, the economy may have little or no tendency to move toward it unless wage and price setters fairly quickly adjust their inconsistent prices toward their full equilibrium levels. This there is no guarantee they will do.

John Maynard Keynes, in his work *The General Theory of Employment, Interest and Money,* made one of the earliest attempts to formalize what we shall call a disequilibrium model of the economy.[1] Writing in the early 1930s in the midst of a catastrophic depression, he attempted to explain why modern economies have depressions. He fundamentally rejected the optimistic view of the partial equilibrium model that markets clear and that deviations from full employment equilibrium are short and self-correcting. He did not think that economic agents were price-takers in the short run. He argued that the dispersion of economic decision making in the modern economy, coupled with the fact that many sellers of labor and goods have market power, is what causes economies to have booms and recessions in response to variations in demand. For these agents often set prices and wages at levels inconsistent with the long-run full equilibrium. When that happens, there is involuntary unemployment until the error is corrected. Furthermore, even though a full equilibrium solution may exist, there may be little tendency for the economy to move toward it. Keynes doubted that recessions were self-correcting, which is why he advocated activist government demand management to improve the performance of the economy.

The disequilibrium model that we shall develop in this chapter represents an amalgam of Keynes's own work and more recent attempts to incorporate other elements of realism as well.[2] The basic feature of any such model is that markets do not necessarily clear in the short run, because wages and prices are set and are unresponsive to market conditions in the short run. Some of the work on the model is still in a formative stage, but the model appears sufficiently promising as an alternative short-run explanation of macroeconomic behavior to merit an extended description. Some might wish to call the model we are about to describe "post-Keynesian" or "neo-Keynesian," because it incorporates wage and price rigidity,

[1] For an interesting modern interpretation of Keynes, see Axel Leijonhufvud, *On Keynesian Economics and the Economics of Keynes* (London: Oxford University Press, 1968).

[2] Our model follows the general lines of disequilibrium models developed in Don Patinkin, *Money, Interest and Prices* (New York: Harper and Row, 1965) and further elaborated in Robert Barro and Herschel Grossman, *Money, Employment and Inflation* (Cambridge, England: Cambridge University Press, 1976).

which is very much in the spirit of Keynes's own approach to the economy.[3]

The Keynesian model used in most textbooks explains recession in a rather peculiar way, by using comparative static equilibrium analysis. The reason this is peculiar is that the model is solved for an equilibrium, implying a point at which the economy comes to a stop. But the Keynesian equilibrium is not a full equilibrium—it is temporary. Some markets do not clear, and therefore there are going to be forces at work changing the equilibrium.[4]

To use an analogy, imagine taking moving pictures of a rock falling. In each frame the rock is stationary, yet over time it is falling. The Keynesian equilibrium is like the individual frames of this movie: It is a still shot of an economy in motion. Unfortunately, the interpreters of Keynes did not pay as much attention to the way the economy moves from one temporary equilibrium to another as they did to the characteristics of the equilibrium itself. This diverted attention from Keynes's effort to develop an approach to the analysis of disequilibrium phenomena.

Money Wage Determination

Keynes made two key empirical points in his analysis of the labor market. The first is that wage bargains are made in nominal, or money, terms rather than in real terms. Workers may think in real terms but labor contracts are not written that way, except in some recent cases where cost-of-living clauses have been included. This seemingly simple fact has far-reaching implications for macroeconomic equilibrium if workers do not react immediately to price level changes. For example, suppose that workers have a contract to work for $5 per hour when the price index is 100. If the price index rises to 125 and they continue to work for $5, their real wage declines to $4; they are supplying the same amount of labor as before at a lower real wage. In terms of the labor market diagram in Figure 6.3 of Chapter 6, the labor supply curve shifts vertically downward. The level of prices in the economy influences the position of the labor supply curve *if labor does not change its wage demand whenever the price level changes*. An increase in demand that raises prices will shift the labor supply curve down and increase employment. We see that if workers do not react to price changes, changes in aggregate demand will lead to changes in employment and output as well as changes in prices.

[3] Another strand of post-Keynesian thought has been developed by Sidney Weintraub and Paul Davidson. See Sidney Weintraub, *A Keynesian Theory of Employment, Growth, and Income Distribution* (Philadelphia: Chilton, 1966) and Paul Davidson, *Money and the Real World* (London: MacMillan, 1973).

[4] Sir John Hicks distinguished between two types of short-run equilibrium, one of which he called flex-price and the other fix-price. In flex-price systems prices adjust to clear markets, but economic actors may be off their supply or demand curves because of expectations errors. The partial equilibrium model of Chapter 6 is an example of a flex-price model. In contrast, fix-price systems have price or wage rigidity in the short run. Markets do not clear, and there is a stock disequilibrium. The Keynesian model is a fix-price model, as is the modified model we are presenting in this chapter. For a further discussion of the nature of equilibrium in macromodels see Sir John Hicks, *Capital and Growth* (New York: Oxford University Press, 1965), chapters 1–3.

Keynes's second main point was that workers are exceedingly reluctant to allow their nominal wages to decline. Wages, he claimed, are inflexible downward. Furthermore, he thought that workers were more likely to resist a reduction in money wages with prices fixed than an equivalent reduction in real wages resulting from a rise in prices with money wages constant. In view of our discussion of the determinants of labor supply, it may seem irrational for labor to distinguish between these two situations, since both lead to the same real wage. However, Keynes did not see this distinction as irrational at all. The money wages of different labor groups determine the distribution of labor income. For one labor union to accede to a reduction in money wages would mean a fall in its relative position within the labor force. An equivalent decline in real wages resulting from a rise in prices affects all workers equally. It reduces real income, but it does not affect the distribution of income among workers. Downward rigidity of wages stems from the importance of the distribution of income to members of the labor force.

From our discussion of the effect of price on the labor market in Chapter 6, it should be clear what will happen if a reduction in aggregate demand forces down the price of output. If money wages are inflexible downward, the fall in price will raise the real wage. Workers will, in effect, be demanding a higher real wage than before. Since the demand for labor is negatively related to the real wage, a fall in price reduces both employment and output. If one accepts the money wage as given, one can say that recession is caused by deficient demand.

In the simple Keynesian model, money wages are treated as exogenous. In our disequilibrium model, we would like to take a somewhat more sophisticated view. While we will retain the assumption that wages are set, we will assume that they are also affected by economic factors. Just like workers in the partial equilibrium model, workers here are concerned with the real, not the money, wage. Wage demands should thus be influenced by either the actual or the expected price. We will assume that wage demands are based on expected price, P_e. But wages are also influenced by conditions in the labor market. High unemployment rates should tend to lower wage demands, low rates to increase them. This will mean that the disequilibrium model's labor supply curve will be upward sloping rather than flat. The steepness of the curve will be determined by the strength of the relationship between wage demands and unemployment. This relationship will play a central role in the entire short-run behavior of the model.

To summarize this discussion, in the disequilibrium model money wages are set, but not necessarily at rates that clear the labor market. Those who set the wages base their demands on what they expect the price level to be and on conditions in the labor market. This means that money wages are neither fully exogenous, as they are in the simple Keynesian model, nor set so that the labor market clears.

We will write the disequilibrium labor supply curve as:

(7.1) $$W = w(\overset{+}{P_e}, \overset{-}{U}).$$

U = unemployment
W = money wage
P_e = expected price

Price Determination

A key feature of the disequilibrium model is **price fixing.** There are many sectors of the U. S. economy that are dominated by a fairly small number of firms that set price and let demand determine the level of output, at least in the short run. Let us divide the economy into two sectors, one a price-setting sector and the other a competitive price-taking sector. Looking first at the price-setters, there is a good deal of evidence that prices are set on the basis of some sort of markup rule. The natural question then arises: What rule do the price-setters use to determine their prices? One response is that they set prices so as to earn a target rate of return on capital on the output that they expect to sell. There is a markup over variable costs equal to required profits per unit of expected output. Mathematically, this **markup pricing** model can be written:

(7.2) $$P = \frac{WN + rK + P_M R}{Q_e}.$$

P = price
W = wage
N = labor units
Q_e = expected output
r = desired profit rate on capital
K = capital invested
P_M = price of raw materials
R = raw materials

The relationship between price and expected output depends upon what happens to the labor output ratio, N/Q, the capital output ratio, K/Q, and the raw material ratio, R/Q, as output varies. We shall assume that R/Q is constant. Under decreasing returns to scale one expects the first two ratios, or a weighted average of the two, to rise as output increases. But a temporary decline is different, because both installed capital and skilled labor are fixed. The firm does not sell its machines or fire workers who are temporarily idle due to demand fluctuations that are expected to be of short duration. That implies that both K/Q and N/Q will rise as sales decline.

Empirically it is a well-established fact that labor productivity falls in recessions and rises in booms; N/Q varies inversely with Q. The reason for this seems to be that firms stockpile skilled labor in recessions that they believe to be temporary. The most persuasive theory of why this is a rational practice has been developed by labor economists and is called the **internal labor market** (ILM) theory.[5]

[5] The fundamental reference for the internal labor market theory is Peter B. Doeringer and Michael T. Piore, *Internal Labor Markets and Manpower Analysis* (Lexington, Mass.: D. C. Heath, 1971). Further work developing the notion of a special connection between the firm and the worker has been published by Costas Azariadis, "Implicit Contracts and Underemployment Equilibrium," *Journal of Political Economy* 83 (December 1975): 1183–1202; Martin N. Baily, "Wages and Employment under Uncertain Demand," *Review of Economic Studies* 41 (January 1974): 37–50; and Walter Oi, "Labor as a Quasi-Fixed Factor," *Journal of Political Economy* 70 (December 1962): 538–555.

Labor Stockpiling

According to ILM theorists, labor is not homogeneous but is differentiated according to acquired skills. Some skills, such as reading, are perfectly general—that is, transferable between jobs. Others are **firm-specific labor skills**—that is, useful only in a particular job. Jobs requiring the latter skills have been labelled **idiosyncratic.**[6] Examples of such jobs might be the operation of a unique machine or the supervision of a particular, unusual group of employees.

How do individuals acquire the skills required by different types of jobs? General skills can be economically taught in schools outside the firm. In contrast, skills required for idiosyncratic jobs probably can be acquired only at the workplace, either through on-the-job training or by observation. Some individuals learn how to do their jobs while doing them; other employees learn how to do a job by watching it being done or perhaps even by doing it on a temporary basis. Such employees are natural replacements when vacancies occur.

Thus, the effect of skill specificity is to segment labor markets. Idiosyncratic jobs tend to be staffed by employees already at the firm; outsiders may not even be considered. Presumably the reason for this is that employees can acquire the specific skills required for an idiosyncratic job at a fraction of the effort and time required of an outsider. The labor market for idiosyncratic jobs tends to be firm-specific or internal.

Of course, workers are idiosyncratic too. Another important feature leading to internal labor markets is the cost of acquiring information about the employee. Many jobs require a high degree of honesty, cooperation, leadership, or judgment. These are qualities that are hard for a firm to evaluate objectively and hard to predict through job interviews. An alternative is to use a job promotion sequence as a screening device. This seems to be particularly important for supervisory and money-handling positions. Internal or firm-specific labor markets are thus a natural development serving to minimize the cost of transferring information about jobs and employees when both are heterogeneous. This segmentation of labor markets has important implications for wage flexibility, as we shall see below.

Firm-specific skills help explain the strong linkage between most workers and their employer. For a variety of reasons, it appears that most workers and firms enter into a longer-term relationship than the standard labor market model implies. There is a fairly strong reluctance on both sides to sever this relationship. The reason is firm-specific job skills. For the worker, a job is more than simply a chance to exchange work for a salary: It also provides the opportunity to learn new job skills, either for his or her own job or for others at the firm. Some jobs, therefore, provide entry to an attractive sequence of future jobs. In such cases, the employee has a strong motivation to remain with the firm. Lifetime earning prospects at the firm should be higher than they would be in another firm because of the specific

[6] The distinction between specific and general skills was introduced by Gary Becker, *Human Capital,* 2d ed. (New York: Columbia University Press, 1975). Further important work has been done in Jacob Mincer, "On the Job Training: Costs, Returns and Some Implications," *Journal of Political Economy* 70 (October 1962): 40–79. The term "idiosyncratic" was introduced in Oliver E. Williamson, Michael Wachter, and John E. Harris, "Understanding the Employment Relation: The Analysis of Idiosyncratic Exchange," *The Bell Journal of Economics* 6 (1975): 250–278.

skills that have been learned, and also because the firm has learned about the employee. By leaving the firm, one loses the promotion possibilities and all the firm-specific skills that have been acquired on the job.

Skill specificity, as we see, creates a presumption that employees will stay with their firms. It should also be true that employees become more valuable to the firm the longer they work. Let us see why. Where employee skills are specific—useless outside the particular firm—it is reasonable to expect that training costs would at least partially be paid for by the firm. Trainees would receive a salary higher than their marginal product during training, which the firm would hope to recoup by paying a salary lower than marginal product over the trainees' future working life at the firm. Thus, specifically trained people should be worth more to the firm than they are paid, and the firm will suffer a capital loss if such people quit. The loss is compounded where employees are acquiring knowledge about other jobs in the firm as they perform their own jobs, for this makes firm employees more trainable and capable of filling vacancies at low cost.

To summarize: When firm-specific skills and information about employees are important, we should observe a strong attachment between the firm and the worker. Valuable knowledge is lost whenever this attachment is broken, either through quitting or through firing. For our purposes here, the main implication of this is in terms of what is called **labor stockpiling,** which means the continued employment of workers at a firm in spite of production levels that do not require their presence. Clearly, labor stockpiling of employees with firm-specific skills is rational for a firm that faces a temporary reduction in demand, since it would have to train a new set of laborers when sales returned to normal levels. If a firm has a multiperiod time horizon, it will accept short-run losses by retaining its skilled labor force in the face of temporary reductions in sales.

We should add here that labor stockpiling may also result from restrictive conditions in labor contracts rather than intertemporal cost minimization. Whatever the cause, stockpiling implies a positive relationship between output and labor productivity. Output per worker will rise in booms and fall in recessions. Empirically, studies of labor productivity show exactly this pattern, which is strong evidence in support of the stockpiling theory.

If both K/Q and N/Q rise when sales decline temporarily, a firm that follows the markup pricing rule and is desirous of maintaining a target rate of return on capital may well raise, not reduce, its prices as sales decline. The businessperson is forced to raise price when capital costs must be spread over fewer units of output. The reader should note that this sort of pricing behavior is not generally consistent with profit maximization, because it does not take into account the effects of price on the level of sales. A monopolist who wishes to maximize profits should find it advantageous to lower prices in the face of falling demand, if fixed capital and labor are significant.

The Disequilibrium Short-Run Aggregate Supply Curve

We will now use the markup pricing equation and our labor stockpiling theory to derive the short-run aggregate supply curve. However, in order to do that we need to know how unemployment is related to output, because that will tell us how wages are related to output. The best-known attempt to measure the unemployment-output relationship was made by Arthur Okun, former chairman of the Council of Economic Advisors.[7] He looked at the historical record prior to 1963 and found that a 3-percent rise in income was generally associated with an approximately 1-percent decline in unemployment. More recent research suggests that this ratio may have fallen to 2:1 since 1970.[8] Furthermore, Okun reasoned that when unemployment is at its long-run full equilibrium level, by definition output also should be at its full equilibrium level. These two findings are expressed in Equation (7.3), which is known as **Okun's law:**

(7.3)
$$U - U_{FE} = \frac{.3(Y_{FE} - Y)}{Y_{FE}}.$$

U_{FE} = full equilibrium unemployment level
Y_{FE} = full equilibrium output level

Let us now draw together this discussion by deriving the relationship between price and output for the price-setting sector of the economy. We repeat Equation (7.2), the markup price equation, for convenience:

(7.2)
$$P = \frac{WN + rK + P_M R}{Q_e}.$$

Consider Figure 7.1. In diagram (a), we show the U-shaped relationship between labor and capital per unit of output implied by the short-term fixity of capital and labor stockpiling. The inflection point comes at what we shall call normal capacity output, Q^*. Diagram (b) shows the positive implicit relationship between the wage rate and output that is derivable from Okun's law and the wage-unemployment relation (Equation 7.1). Note that the curve need not necessarily be linear and will be flatter the weaker the impact of output on employment or of underemployment on the wage rate.

When one puts the U-shaped relationship between factor productivity and output together with the positive relationship between wage rates and output, one gets the **kinked supply curve** shown in (c). That supply curve says that price rises as expected output either rises or falls from Q^*. Below Q^*, price rises to cover the loss in labor productivity due to stockpiling. Above Q^*, it rises both because wages rise with output and because labor productivity probably falls as plants are operated above the capacity for which they were built and as older, less productive plants are pressed into service to meet rising demand.

[7] Arthur M. Okun, "Potential GNP: Its Measurement and Significance," reprinted in Okun's *The Political Economy of Prosperity* (Washington, D.C.: Brookings Institution, 1970), 132–145.

[8] See John A. Tatom, "Economic Growth and Unemployment: A Reappraisal," *Federal Reserve Bank of St. Louis Review* (October 1978): 16–22.

Figure 7.1
Deriving the Short-Run Supply Curve in the Price-Setting Sector

Because both capital and some part of the labor force are fixed factors, costs rise at less than capacity output. They rise at more than capacity output when there are diminishing returns. If wages are related negatively to unemployment and unemployment is related negatively to output (Okun's law), we can derive the relationship in (b) between wages and output. Combining (a) and (b) in the markup pricing equation, we get the U-shaped supply curve in (c). Its downward slope to the left of Q^* is made less steep by the wage relation, and its upward slope to the right of Q^* is made more steep.

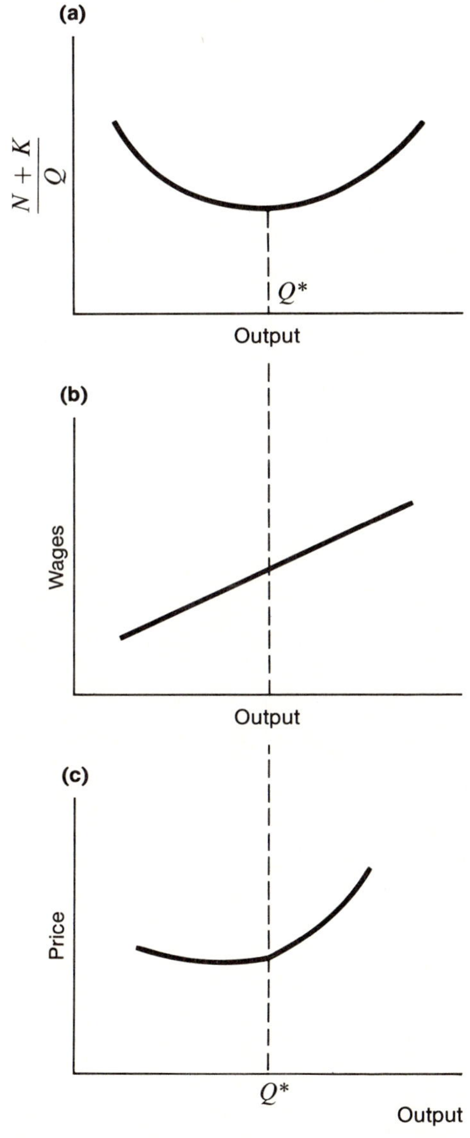

Figure 7.2
Deriving the Aggregate Short-Run Supply Curve for the Economy

The slope of the aggregate economy short-run supply curve is a weighted average of the slopes of the two sectors of which it is composed. It has a change of slope or kink at $Q^* = Y_{FE}$.

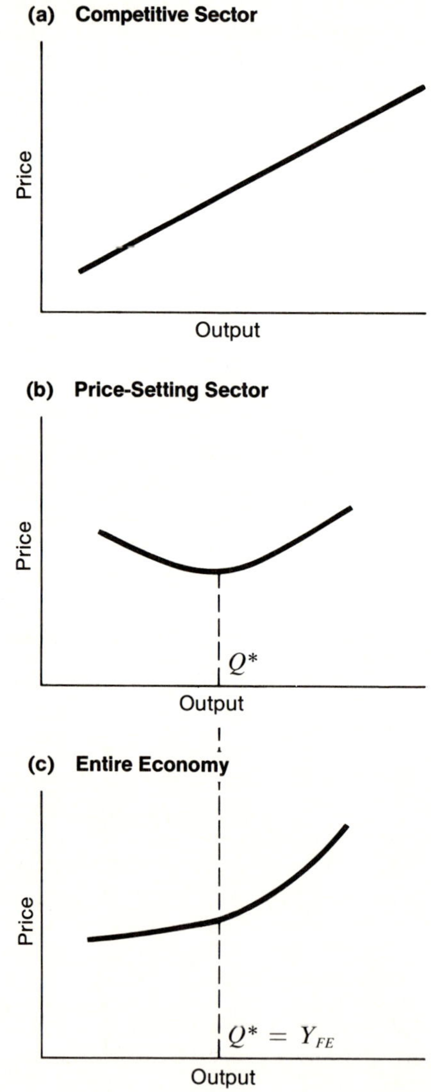

To convert (c) into a supply curve for the price-setters, we have to specify the relationship between expected and actual output. For the remainder of this book, we will define equilibrium as the condition in which expected and actual output are equal, which means that the U-shaped curve in (c) is short-run supply curve. This condition should not blind us to the fact that prices are only indirectly related to output and that the goods markets may not clear, in the sense that the expected level of output may well be less than Q^*.

It remains only to aggregate the competitive and the price-setting sectors of the economy. We shall make the standard assumption that in the competitive part of the economy, short-run supply curves are upward sloping, as in diagram (a) of Figure 7.2.

We now combine the supply curves of the two sectors to get an aggregate supply curve of the general form shown in diagram (c). The curve will have a kink at $Q^* = Y_{FE}$ because that is where a kink occurs in the supply curve of the price-setting sector. Elsewhere, the slope of the aggregate supply curve will be a weighted average of the slopes of the supply curves in the two sectors, the weights being equal to the share of each in total output. Below Y_{FE}, the downward slope of the price-setters' supply curve is either partially or totally offset by the upward slope of supply in the competitive sector, which means that the aggregate supply curve may be either positively or negatively sloped. Above Y_{FE}, aggregate supply is clearly upward sloping. Whatever shape the curve has below Y_{FE}, there will be a significant flattening of the curve—a kink—at Y_{FE} in any economy where price-setting and labor stockpiling are important.

The reader should note that in an actual economy the notion of a particular Y_{FE} is probably an abstraction. Different industries undoubtedly reach capacity at different levels of aggregate output. Consequently, instead of having a discontinuous kink at a certain level of output, the aggregate supply curve probably has a significant change of slope over a certain range of output. Therefore, for the actual economy Y_{FE} should be thought of as a region rather than a point, which means that the slope of the aggregate supply curve may just be sharply increasing in region Y_{FE} rather than actually being kinked at a point. For purposes of our discussion, however, it is useful to treat Y_{FE} as if it were a point.

The Disequilibrium Theory of Booms and Recessions

Having derived the kinked short-run disequilibrium supply curve, it is a simple matter to complete the disequilibium theory of prices and output. We simply complete the goods market diagram by introducing the aggregate demand curve that we derived in Chapter 6. The short-run equilibrium will be at the intersection of these two curves.

Consider Figure 7.3. The two supply curves, S_{SR} and Y_{FE}, are those derived in Figure 7.2. The kink in the short-run curve is at Y_{FE}, the normal capacity output of the economy.

On the demand side, there are no fundamental differences between our two models. Both show that demand is negatively related to prices, which leads to the same downward-sloping demand curve, D_0D_0, for both models. Equilibrium, as usual, is at the intersection of the supply and demand curves. Thus, if demand is D_0D_0, equilibrium will be at point A, the full equilibrium output level of the economy. But suppose aggregate demand falls to D_1D_1. This could happen if government cut spending, if monetary policy became more restrictive, or if spending in the

Figure 7.3
Recession in the Disequilibrium Model

A recession is caused by a reduction in aggregate demand. Demand shifts from D_0D_0 to D_1D_1. Because wages and prices are not perfectly flexible in the short run, output falls from Y_{FE} to Y_1.

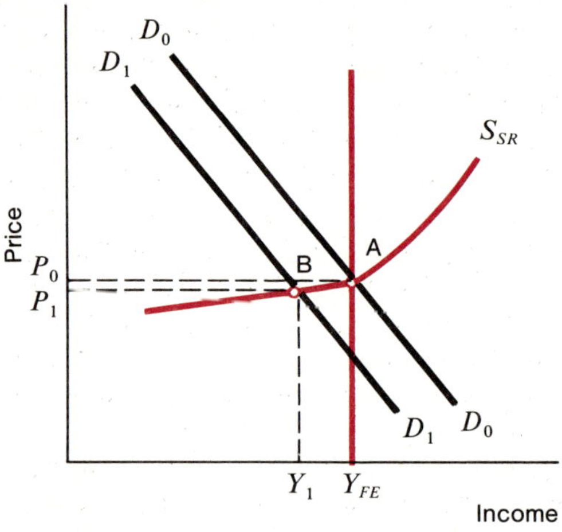

private sector suddenly diminished. According to the diagram, equilibrium falls to point B, the intersection of the new demand curve and the short-run supply curve. Output declines to Y_1, and prices decline slightly to P_1. The reduction in aggregate demand causes the economy to have a recession. Thus the disequilibrium economy, like the partial equilibrium economy, has booms and recessions in response to variations in aggregate demand. Here the recession is caused by the fact that the levels of prices and wages set by workers and firms are inconsistent with the reduced level of aggregate demand represented by D_1D_1.

Figure 7.3 tells us there is a recession when demand falls. We need to know more about the underlying characteristics of this recession, for it is fundamental to the discussion that follows. Therefore, we want to take a closer look at the disequilibrium model labor market to see the implications of markup pricing, wage-setting, and deficient demand for unemployment and the demand for labor.

The Disequilibrium Labor Market

We have assumed that businesspersons set their prices on the basis of the cost of the output they think they can sell. Under these conditions, the firm maximizes profit by minimizing the quantity of labor required to produce that amount of output. What happens in such a world when there is a decline in the money wage? Once prices have been set no change in the money wage, even if it reduces the real wage, has the slightest effect on the demand for labor, because that is determined by the level of expected output. In other words, once prices and output are set, the demand for labor is not the downward-sloping MPP schedule we drew in Chapter 6—instead, it is a vertical line. This changes entirely the short-run "equilibrium" in the labor market. Let us see why.

Consider the labor market in diagram (c) of Figure 7.4. Curve D_0D_0 shows the marginal physical product of labor. This curve is relevant to the determination of a full equilibrium, but it is not relevant in the short run, as we shall see in a moment. On the supply side, we show two vertical supply curves. The first is N_{LF}, the labor force supply curve we discussed in Chapter 6. The second curve is S_{LR}, which we will call the normal, or long-run, labor supply curve. It differs from the labor force curve by the frictional level of unemployment, U_{FE}. As we have drawn the labor market, frictional unemployment does not depend on the real wage. On the surface the supply curve S_{LR} appears to be very similar to that for the F-P model. Appearances, however, are deceiving, as we shall now see.

Full equilibrium in the labor market is at point A, the intersection of S_{LR} and D_0D_0. If we derive the output producible by N_{FE} workers in diagram (a) and transfer it to the goods market, we have the full equilibrium supply curve, a vertical line at Y_{FE}, just as in our previous model. Full equilibrium is attained if aggregate demand is D_0D_0 (diagram d), for this allows price fixers to sell all they wish to, and production levels are just sufficient to employ the entire labor force less frictional unemployment.

But suppose that aggregate demand falls to D_1D_1. According to (d) in Figure 7.4, prices drop slightly to P_1, and production drops to Y_1. What happens to the demand for labor? According to the production function, Y_1 can be produced by N_1 units of labor. No variation in real wages can change that fact. Therefore, in the absence of labor stockpiling, the demand for labor is the vertical line D_1D_1 rather than the MPP schedule, D_0D_0, in diagram (c). D_0D_0 is not relevant in the short run because prices are not flexible. The demand for labor depends on aggregate demand, not the real wage.

If there is stockpiling, employment does not fall as far as N_1; excess labor is carried by the firm. Where is the temporary equilibrium in the labor market? If firms maximize short-run profits and stockpile no labor, they will employ N_1 units of labor and pay a real wage, W/P_1. Equilibrium will be at point B. With stockpiling, equilibrium will be at a point such as C, where $N_2 - N_1$ laborers are surplus to the current level of output.

Note several very important characteristics of the equilibrium at C. First and foremost, it is on neither the long-run labor supply nor the labor demand curve. Second, there is involuntary unemployment in the amount $N_{FE} - N_2$. N_{FE} workers would like to work, but only N_2 can find jobs. In this case, the disequilibrium model differs dramatically from the partial equilibrium model. In the latter unemployment may temporarily rise above U_{FE}, but that unemployment is all voluntary; there is employment for anyone who wants it at a certain real wage. Not so in the disequilibrium model. N_{FE} people wish to work, but wages, prices, and aggregate demand are such that only N_2 can find jobs. What is worse, workers are powerless to improve their situations by unilaterally lowering their wages. For businesspersons simply will not be hiring. They already have more workers than they need, so they are unlikely to hire more, even if the new applicants offer to work for less. The

Figure 7.4
The Effect on the Labor Market of a Reduction in Demand

A reduction in aggregate demand from D_0D_0 to D_1D_1 in the goods market reduces output to Y_1. Since businesspersons fix the level of output and prices, their demand for labor will not be affected by the real wage. The minimum labor required to produce Y_1 is N_1. Hence, if businesspersons want to maximize profits, their demand for labor will be the vertical line D_1D_1 in (c). If there is labor stockpiling they will hold N_2 workers, and equilibrium will be at point C. At C there is job rationing in the sense that businesspersons are not hiring, and there is involuntary unemployment in the amount $N_{FE} - N_2$. Full equilibrium will be reestablished only when prices fall to P_2, shown in (d).

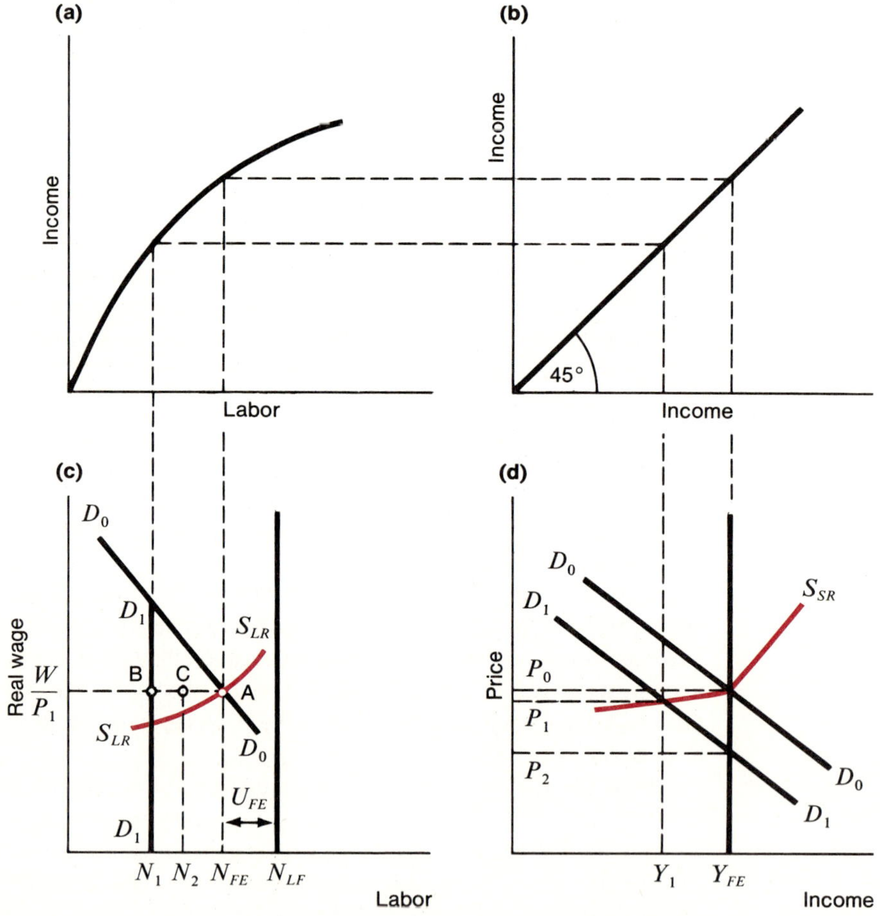

situation is scarcely better for firms. They are paying wages above labor's marginal product and will therefore suffer a reduction in profits. In effect, they are paying for the retention of their labor force. Hence, a reduction in demand is costly to both labor and business.

In the partial equilibrium model, economies have recessions because workers' price expectations are too high. The situation is not too different here. Even if aggregate demand is D_1D_1 as in diagram (d), a full equilibrium does exist at price P_2. If businesspersons would lower their prices and workers would, at the same time, lower their wage demands, the economy would not have to go through a long recession to achieve the same result. But in modern economies, workers cannot be sure that their wage reductions will lead to price reductions. They have no guarantee that employers won't simply use lower wages to raise profits. The same, incidentally, can be said of price-setting businesspersons: They have no guarantee that, if they lower their prices, workers will reduce wage demands. This disconnection between wage and price decisions is one of the great weaknesses of the modern capitalist economy. It tends to make both prices and wages inflexible, and that transforms any fluctuation in demand into a boom or a recession rather than just a variation in the price level. Furthermore, as we shall see in a later chapter, price and wage inflexibility makes it extremely difficult to stop inflations without an extended recession.

Recession Unemployment: Voluntary or Involuntary?

Keynes thought that economies have recessions because demand is insufficient given the level of wages and prices. He labeled the extra unemployment during a recession involuntary, which he defined as any unemployment that would be reduced by a rise in the price level. The same involuntary unemployment is a characteristic of our disequilibrium model.

Many critics of the Keynesian and the disequilibrium analyses contest the idea that the unemployment in a recession is involuntary or that it results from lack of demand. After all, they argue, if the labor force would accept a reduction in money wages equal to any reduction in prices caused by a fall in demand, there need be no involuntary unemployment. For these critics the high rates of unemployment are a result of wage rigidity in the face of fluctuations in aggregate demand, not of the fluctuations themselves. Furthermore, one could argue that the setting of wages at non-market clearing levels must at bottom be due to forecasting errors—for if workers think in real terms, there is only one real wage that clears the labor market. Money wages can only be set at disequilibrium levels by workers who make forecasting errors, in which case the resulting unemployment could be considered voluntary. Looked at in this way, the apparent differences between the partial equilibrium and disequilibrium models seem to disappear.

Logically this observation is correct, yet it misses one of the main points that Keynes and the advocates of disequilibrium-type models are trying to make. In the short run, the disequilibrium dynamics of economies with rigid wages and prices are likely to be different when markets do not clear than they would be if markets did clear. The return to full equilibrium is likely to be slow in disequilibrium economies, as we shall see in the next chapter. This is why Keynes thought that fixing demand and waiting for recession to drive down wages is a very costly and cumbersome way to arrive at full equilibrium. Far better, he reasoned, to accept wage and price stickiness as one of the laws of behavior of the modern economy and adjust our policies to that fact. In particular, he thought it preferable to tailor the level of aggregate demand to the level of prices and wages rather than try to force the latter to conform to a certain level of demand. This insight led Keynes to advocate active demand management to avoid recession, and it is one of the main reasons why Keynesian economics has always been so closely identified with both activist demand management and expansionary monetary and fiscal policies.

While the Keynesian insights have generally been applied to recessionary settings when there is no problem with inflation, we shall see in the next chapter that the implications of the disequilibrium model are equally applicable to stagflation and stabilization.

A Mathematical Version of the Disequilibrium Model

Formally, the short-run disequilibrium model aggregate supply curve can be written:

(7.4) $$P = z(\overset{+}{Y_e}, \overset{+}{Y}, \overset{+}{P_e}\ \overset{?}{K}).$$

In the price-fixing sector, price is set on the basis of expected output and costs. P_e enters the function because of its influence on wages, one of the main components of cost. Capital may raise or lower costs.

We shall assume that actual output is what businesspersons expect it to be, which allows us to rewrite the aggregate supply curve as:

(7.5) $$P = x(\overset{+}{Y}, \overset{+}{P_e}\ \overset{?}{K}).$$

Price is positively related to output in this model, just as it was in the F-P model. However, for the reasons discussed earlier, we shall assume that the supply curve has a significant change of slope (kink) at the full equilibrium or long-run capacity level of the economy. Below the kink, the relationship between price and output is significantly weaker here than in the F-P model—that is, the disequilibrium short-run supply curve is flatter than the F-P supply curve.[9]

On the demand side, we simply reproduce the aggregate demand function of Chapter 6:

(6.1) $$Y_d = d(\overset{+}{M}, \overset{+}{G}, \overset{-}{t}, \overset{-}{P}).$$

[9] Basically the kink expresses the notion that expansions and contractions are fundamentally different. In our model expansions are on the marginal physical product of labor curve, and prices cover rising costs. Contractions involve decisions about dismissing employees already hired. Where stockpiling is important, costs will have a different relationship to output in expansion or contraction.

Finally, we have the equilibrium condition that supply be equal to what businesspersons expect it to be:

(7.6) $$Y_d = Y_e = Y.$$

Note that this condition does not mean that the goods market is in long-run full equilibrium. Rather, it means that the level of output produced, whatever it is, equals the level of output demanded. There are no disequilibrium inventory accumulations here. In that sense, the goods market clears in the disequilibrium model. When we put the last three equations together, we have a system that can be solved for the equilibrium level of income and prices. This equilibrium, it must be remembered, is temporary and short run.

Some Empirical Observations Favoring the Disequilibrium Theory

Obviously the main distinction between our two models is the assumption that prices and wages clear markets in the F-P model and that wages and prices are set, perhaps at levels inconsistent with full equilibrium, in the disequilibrium model. According to the partial equilibrium theory, all unemployment is voluntary. It is due to the refusal of workers to accept jobs principally because the wage rates are mistakenly deflated by too high a price index. Recessions occur when workers overpredict the price index, causing them to turn down nominal wage offers that they would accept had they been correctly informed about prices. That, to many, is not a very accurate description of the labor market of our days.[10] Most of the unemployed do not have an opportunity to turn down job offers at too low a money wage. Wages are inflexible, but during recessions employers are simply not hiring at those wages. They do not lower the wage if a queue of unemployed workers appears outside their gates, but they do not hire either. Unemployed workers do not have the opportunity to make a decision about whether the money wage is too high or too low. The evidence points to job rationing at the going money wage, not voluntary unemployment.

A further empirical contradiction of the F-P model is the behavior of quits. Workers quit a job when they anticipate a better job elsewhere. According to the theory, workers overforecast the price level during recessions. The unemployed refuse jobs because they think the money wage is too low. It would be consistent to expect the employed to think the same thing—that their money wages were not rising fast enough. The quit rate should therefore rise in recessions and fall in booms. But of course it does exactly the opposite. Quits fall during recessions, because employed workers know that there are few alternative job opportunities available, while the opposite occurs during booms.

[10] One of the most eloquent early doubters of the partial equilibrium model as a description of the short-run behavior of the economy was James Tobin, in "Inflation and Unemployment," *American Economic Review* 62 (March 1972): 1–18.

Another important discrepancy between fact and partial equilibrium theory is the relationship between employment and the real wage. Short-run equilibrium is always at the intersection of the short-run labor supply curve and the labor demand curve. Employers are always on their demand curve. Since the labor demand curve is downward sloping, a fall in real wages is required to increase employment. Yet evidence has been accumulating for years that shows unmistakably that real wages and employment are positively correlated, not negatively as the theory predicts. Both go up in booms and down in recessions. This pattern is consistent with our labor stockpiling model.

Summary

This completes our description of the disequilibrium model. The model grew out of an attempt to explain recessions, but it has much wider applicability. The model is based on the notion that both wages and prices are fixed for large parts of the economy, and therefore labor and product markets need not necessarily clear in the short run. Boiled down to essentials, the principal difference between the disequilibrium and the partial equilibrium models is the shape of the short-run aggregate supply curve at less-than-normal or capacity output. In the disequilibrium model it is relatively flat, because of both price fixing and labor stockpiling, whereas in the F-P model it is relatively steep. This apparently small difference leads to large differences in prediction about how economies react to reductions in demand, to stabilization, and to supply shocks, as we shall see in the next two chapters.

Key Concepts

price fixing
markup pricing
internal labor market
firm-specific labor skills
idiosyncratic
labor stockpiling
Okun's law
kinked supply curve

Problems and Questions for Discussion

1. Why is the downward-sloping demand curve for labor not relevant if goods prices are rigid?

2. Compare the partial and disequilibrium theories of how a fall in aggregate demand affects the labor market. Describe some of the empirical predictions of the two theories that differ and that could be tested.

3. A central notion of the disequilibrium model is the setting of wages and prices, possibly at non-market clearing levels. How could a non-market clearing wage be maintained in the face of unemployed workers willing to do work for less? Why would businesspersons ever set prices at so high a level that they were unable to sell all that they could produce?

4. Discuss the role of the internal labor market in the disequilibrium theory of aggregate supply.

5. According to marginal productivity theory, the real wage should go down in booms and up in recessions. Yet empirical observations show that it does exactly the opposite. What is the theoretical reason for expecting the real wage to move countercyclically, and what explanation can you offer for the apparent failure of the theory to predict actual movements of the real wage?

6. Why might one expect the aggregate supply curve to be nonlinear, being significantly flatter at less-than-full employment than it is at full employment or beyond?

7. Problems 7–9 are designed to show how the aggregate supply curve could have a break or change of slope at the full equilibrium level of output. Suppose we have the following disequilibrium model behavioral equations.

Prices are set as a markup over cost:

(a) $$P = \frac{WL + rK}{Q}.$$

(b) $$Q_{FE} = 100.$$

For output less than 100, there is partial labor stockpiling. In this case labor demand is derived from Okun's law:

(c) $$U - U_{FE} = \frac{.3(Q_{FE} - Q)}{Q_{FE}}.$$

For output greater than 100, labor demand is derived from the production function:

(d) $$Q = L^{\frac{1}{2}}K^{\frac{1}{2}}$$

which gives the demand for labor:

(e) $$L = Q^2/K.$$

Wages are a negative function of the unemployment rate:

(f) $$W = \$5 - 10(U - U_{FE}).$$

$$U = \frac{LF - L}{LF} \text{ (the unemployment rate)}$$

$$U_{FE} = \frac{LF - L_{FE}}{LF} \text{ (the full equilibrium unemployment rate)}$$

Initial values are as follows:

$$LF = 107 \qquad r = 10\%$$
$$U_{FE} = 6.54\% \qquad K = 100$$

Calculate the full equilibrium employment, wage rate, and price level.

8. a. If businesspersons expect sales to fall to 80 units, what is the level of employment, the wage rate, and the price?
b. Verify that employment is greater than needed according to Equation (e) in Problem 7. This shows that there is stockpiling at $Q < Q_{FE}$.

9. a. If businesspersons expect output to increase to 103, what are the levels of employment, wages, and prices?
b. Plot the price and output combinations you have found in Problems 8a and 9a on a supply diagram. Your three points are part of an aggregate disequilibrium supply curve. Is the curve nonlinear? If so, where does the change of slope occur? Can you explain why the chango of slope occurs where it does?

Chapter 8

The Inflationary Process

How an Economy Reacts to a One-Time Change in Demand in the Short and Long Run

In the last two chapters we derived two alternative theories of aggregate supply and used them to show how variations in demand may cause a temporary boom or recession as a short-run result. Eventually the economy must return to the full equilibrium supply curve. We would now like to trace out the process by which this return to full equilibrium occurs. To make things simple, we shall ignore additions to the capital stock. Over time such additions gradually move the full equilibrium supply curve. Therefore, if the return to full equilibrium takes an appreciable amount of time, the full equilibrium capacity output may have increased. We shall overlook this complicating factor in the discussion that follows, assuming instead that full equilibrium output is fixed over short-run cycles.

The method of analysis that we will use here is dynamic, because we are examining a succession of short-run equilibria. In our dynamic analysis we are looking for a model that will determine a sequence of levels of output and prices over time rather than for a particular moment. This differs from all the models we have analyzed so far in this book; those have all been static or timeless. We have solved our models for their equilibrium values, but we have not worried about how the economy moved from one equilibrium to another. If we are to understand booms and inflation, we shall have to use a dynamic analysis.

Dynamic Analysis

In order to make **dynamic analysis** easier, economists have adopted a convention. They artificially break up time into periods and study the determinations of prices and output during each period.[1] When they put the periods together, they

[1]See John Hicks, *Capital and Growth,* for a fuller discussion of dynamic analysis in macroeconomics.

have a price path. It is somewhat like making a movie by pasting together a set of still pictures. As we make use of this period analysis here, our problem will be to understand how prices, output, and employment are determined during each period and how the current period is influenced by the past and by expectations about the future. In the partial equilibrium model, the link between the periods will be labor's forecast of prices. When there is an error in forecasting, there will be an adjustment of expected prices. This will change the short-run equilibrium and, if the process is stable, move the economy toward the full equilibrium.

Expected prices are also the link between temporary equilibria in the disequilibrium model. They help determine the level of money wages and thus the position of the aggregate supply curve. However, because the aggregate supply curve is so flat, the correction of inappropriate expectations and wage demands is slow. Thus, the differing shapes of the aggregate supply curves lead to important differences between the way our two short-run models react to disturbances and the length of time it takes to get back to full equilibrium. Generally speaking, disequilibrium models do not correct as rapidly as partial equilibrium models. That means that they return to full equilibrium more slowly and languish in recession longer.

In order to convert the static analysis of the last two chapters into a dynamic analysis, we need to specify how certain variables that were exogenous in the short-run model change from period to period. This is done through **transition equations.**

The transition equations are the mechanism that converts our short-run static analysis into a self-contained dynamic model capable of generating a sequence of short-run, temporary equilibria. In both models the basic transition equation tells how expected prices are adjusted from period to period. Finally, to complete the dynamic model we need a long-run equilibrium condition to tell us the conditions under which the economy comes to a full stop.

The dynamic solution of our models is sequential. The equations of Chapters 6 and 7 are now interpreted as short-run equations, given time subscripts and solved to give a temporary equilibrium for time t. The transition equations tell us how certain variables change from period to period. We then re-solve the short-run equations for period $t + 1$, after substituting in the values of the exogenous variables for that period derived from the transition equations. The process continues until the full equilibrium is reached.

Schematically, the dynamic solution for the two models can be shown in Figure 8.1.

We introduce the dynamic model to see how an economy reacts to changes in demand or supply. As we shall see, the economy follows a typical pattern in reacting to such changes. If there is an increase in demand, prices and output both rise at first as workers are fooled by unexpected inflation. Then as the demand stimulus dies away, or as workers learn about inflation, there is a further rise in prices accompanied by recession. Both of these phases are part of the process by which an economy adjusts over time to changes in demand. In this chapter we shall examine the response to a one-time increase in demand. In the next, we will look at a more realistic case, namely, a change in the rate of growth of demand. We shall also look at the effect of supply-side shocks in that chapter.

Figure 8.1
A Schematic Layout of the Two Dynamic Models

The dynamic multiperiod model is solved in exactly the same way as the models we have used so far. Given values for each exogenous variable, the model determines values for each endogenous variable. Here, however, we must date each of the variables. In addition, some of the exogenous variables are exogenous only because they are functions of variables whose values are determined in previous periods. Expected prices are an example of that type of variable here. They depend on past values of actual prices. The dynamic adjustment of the economy to changes in other exogenous variables is driven by the gradual adjustment of expected prices over time through the transition equation. Each time there is a change in the actual price, the transition equation tells us there will be a change in the expected price, which will in turn change the solution values for all endogenous variables in succeeding periods. The process continues until expected and actual prices are equal, which is the condition for full equilibrium.

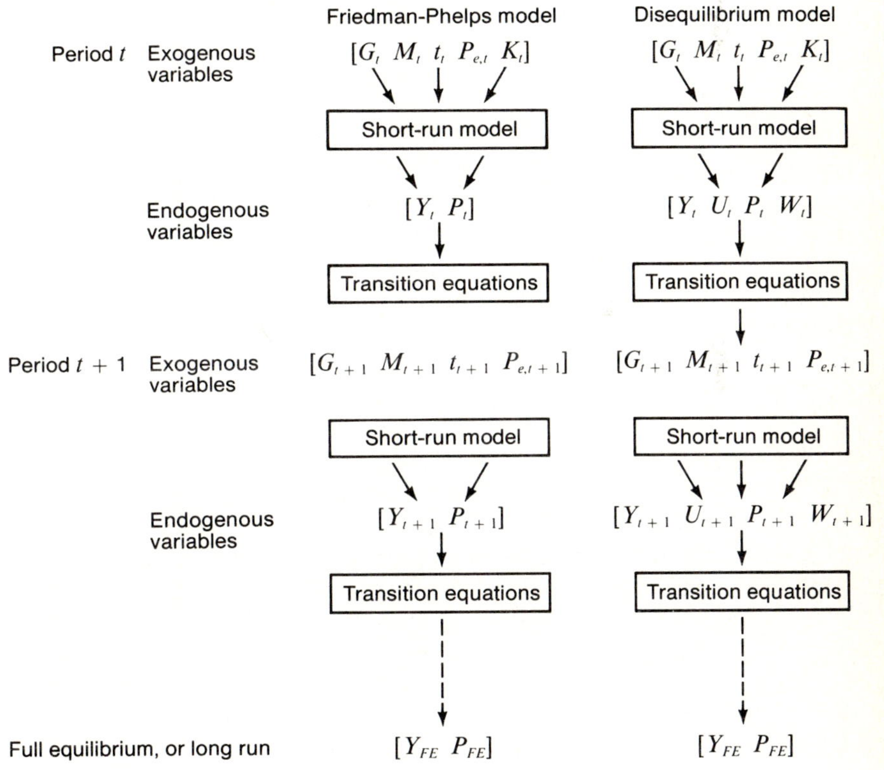

The Effect of a One-Time Increase in Demand in the Partial Equilibrium Model

Suppose that an economy is in full equilibrium. In Figure 8.2, demand is just equal to long-run supply at the price level P_0. Now suppose that there is an unexpected increase in aggregate demand that shifts the demand curve outward to D_1. As we

Figure 8.2
The Effect of an Increase in Demand Where $P_{e,t} = P_{t-1}$ (F-P Model)

Aggregate demand increases from D_0 to D_1. In period 1, equilibrium is at point A; income rises to Y_1, prices to P_1. In period 2, $P_{e,2} = P_1$. This means that the period 2 supply curve intersects the long-run curve at P_1. Equilibrium in period 2 is at point B. Again the supply curve shifts upward, causing subsequent equilibria to move northwest up the demand curve. The process continues until the supply curve intersects the aggregate demand curve D_1 at point C.

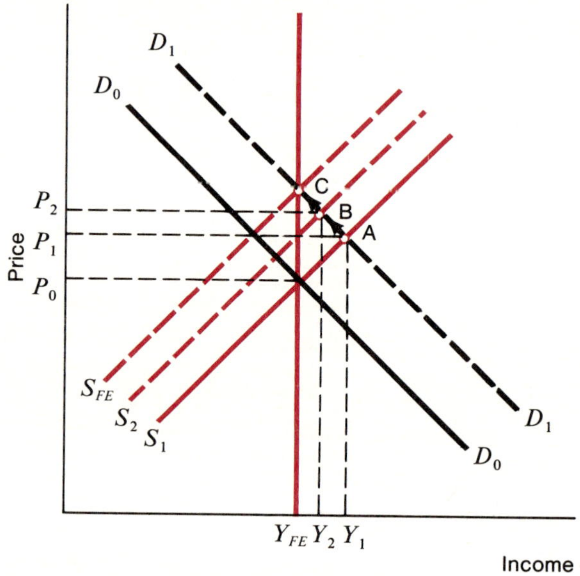

have already seen in previous chapters, the short-run equilibrium is at point A, the intersection of the short-run supply curve and the demand curve. Output expands to Y_1, and prices rise to P_1. Thus, the increase in demand cause an inflation and an expansion in production. This is the first phase in the typical inflationary process. Because it is caused by demand pressure, we might call it the demand-pull, or expansionary, phase.

Of course this cannot be the end of the story. For the rise in prices, which is the reason that output went up, was unexpected by workers. Labor will surely react to its forecasting errors, and that will affect the supply curve, the equilibrium price, and the level of income.

In Chapter 6, we showed that the short-run aggregate supply curve was a function of P_e. But we did not consider how price expectations are formed. This is central to the dynamic version of the partial equilibrium analysis. There are presently two schools of thought on expectations. The first is that expectations are **adaptive,** meaning that they are based on past actual price behavior, adjusted with a lag. The second is that expectations are rational, meaning that they are based on a model of prices rather than past prices. The idea of rational expectations has some extremely powerful implications for the operation of the economy and the role of the government; this we will discuss in Chapter 15.

For the moment let us assume, as Friedman and Phelps did, that expectations are adaptive. Indeed, let us make the simplest possible expectations assumption. Let us suppose that workers predict that prices this period will be equal to prices last period.[2] This expectations assumption leads to the following transition equation:

(8.1) $$P_{e,t} = P_{t-1}.$$

Let us see how the economy shown in Figure 8.2 returns to full equilibrium with this particular transition equation. Recall from Chapter 6 that the short-run supply curve in each period intersects the long-run curve at the level of prices expected by the labor force. Thus in period 1 in Figure 8.2, S_1 intersects the long-run supply curve at P_0. In period 2, according to Equation (8.2), expected price rises to P_1 ($P_{e,2} = P_1$). This implies that the period 2 supply curve shifts upward to S_2. Since the demand curve is still unchanged at D_1, the period 2 equilibrium is at point B. Prices rise to P_2, but output declines from Y_1 to Y_2. The economy is in the second, or stabilization, phase of the inflationary process, in which prices continue to rise but output and employment decline. Without continuing the process in detail it is clear that the supply curve will continue to rise until it intersects D_1 on the long-run supply curve at point C. Prices continue to rise as supply falls back to Y_{FE}.

The condition for full equilibrium is that expected and actual prices be equal. Thus, full equilibrium is reached when prices have risen enough to completely offset the initial increase in demand. At that point, workers are back on their long-run supply curve and output is at the full equilibrium level, Y_{FE}. When one stops to think about it, this is an inevitable result. For if full equilibrium supply is fixed, any change in aggregate demand must cause a price increase just sufficient to offset that change.[3]

The situation differs dramatically when workers learn to forecast inflation. For then an increase in aggregate demand generates an inflationary boom followed by stagflation. To take the simplest possible case, suppose workers expect that inflation this period will be equal to inflation last period. That is, suppose workers predict a continuation of inflation. This form of expectation is expressed in the following transition equation:

(8.2a) $$\left(\frac{\Delta P}{P}\right)_{e,t} = \left(\frac{\Delta P}{P}\right)_{t-1}.$$

This by definition can be written

[2]This is equivalent to assuming that workers expect no future inflation.

[3]Notice that if the cycle has taken a long time, expansions in capacity may actually have increased output during the adjustment period.

(8.2b)
$$\frac{P_{e,t} - P_{t-1}}{P_{t-1}} = \frac{P_{t-1} - P_{t-2}}{P_{t-2}},$$

and, alternatively, as

(8.2c)
$$P_{e,t} = \frac{P_{t-1}^2}{P_{t-2}}.$$

Let us see how the economy would react to the same one-time increase in demand with this new transition equation. In Figure 8.3, the economy again starts the process with an inflationary boom in period 1. However, in period 2, since workers expect a continuation of period 1 inflation, the short-run supply curve shifts much further upward than it did in our first case. And this is not the end of the story. Since there is an inflation in period 2, workers will continue to predict further inflation in period 3. This means that the short-run curve will continue to shift upward beyond the long-run equilibrium point, which, as in the first model, is at C. (The S_3 curve intersects Y_{FE} at $P_{e,3} = P_2^2/P_1 > P_2$.)

As the reader can see from the diagram, prices continue to rise and output falls below Y_{FE} to Y_3. Here we truly have stagflation. Prices are rising, yet the economy is in a recession. Let us see what causes this unfortunate situation.

Just like all recessions in the partial equilibrium model, this one is caused by workers' overforecasting of the inflation rate. In period 3, workers expect prices to rise to $P_{e,3}$. But prices rise less than this. Therefore, workers have unknowingly demanded too high a money wage. Because demand is insufficient businesspersons cannot raise prices high enough to pay such wages, and so they must let some workers go. Unemployment goes up and income goes down.

In subsequent periods, the short-run supply curve will move to the right as shown by the arrows in Figure 8.3 until it finally intersects the long-run curve at point C. These rightward shifts occur as workers correct their overforecasts of inflation. At point C the inflationary process comes to a halt, and the economy is back in full equilibrium. In this case, however, the economy must go through a recession in which unemployment temporarily rises above normal. That recession is required to eliminate the inflation expected by workers.

To recapitulate our results so far: In the F-P partial equilibrium model, economies react to rising demand by a typical cycle of inflation followed by recession. The rise in output that is caused by rising demand is only a short-run result; eventually the economy must return to the long-run supply curve. Therefore, the only permanent result of the rise in demand is a permanent rise in prices. When workers learn to expect inflation, the return to full equilibrium will be more drawn out. Furthermore, it will require a real recession to squeeze the expected inflation out of workers' wage demands.

A Mathematical Representation of the Dynamic Partial Equilibrium Model

Using the demand and supply equations developed in Chapter 6, we can formally write a dynamic version of the Friedman-Phelps model and use it to show how the economy reacts to variations in aggregate demand. The model will have three

Figure 8.3

An Inflationary Process with $\frac{\Delta P}{P_{e,t}} = \frac{\Delta P}{P_{t-1}}$

When workers learn to expect inflation, $P_{e,t}$ will lie above P_{t-1} by the rate of inflation in period $t - 1$. This can be seen in period 3, where the supply curve (S_3) intersects the long-run curve at $P_{e,3} = P_2^2/P_1$. But since the demand curve has shifted up only once, the actual price in period 3 is lower than expected. As a result, the economy sinks into a true recession, with $Y < Y_{FE}$. Subsequently, as workers correct their overforecast of the price level the supply curve will shift back down, and successive equilibria will move southeast down the demand curve D_1D_1 as shown by the arrows, until a new full equilibrium is reached at point C.

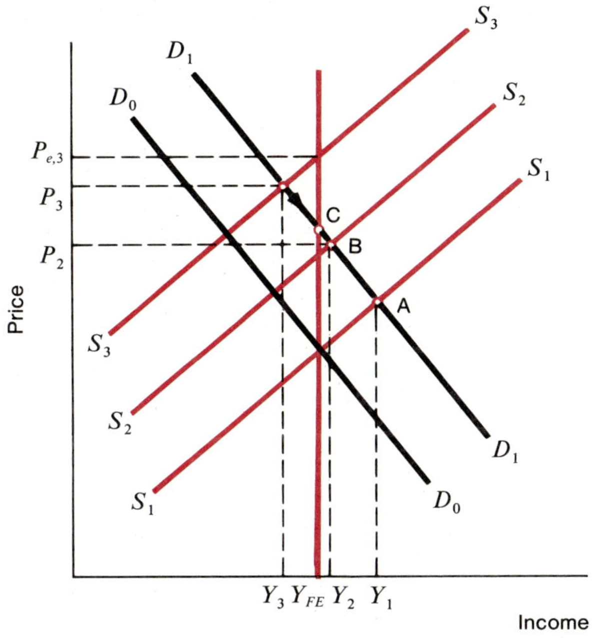

categories of equations: short-run equations to determine equilibrium in each period, transition equations to determine how variables that are exogenous in the short run change from period to period, and equations to show the long-run equilibrium condition.

In this model the short-run equations are those for aggregate supply (Equation [8.3]), aggregate demand (Equation [8.4]), and the short-run equilibrium condition (Equation [8.5]). These equations have time subscripts to indicate that they give us short-run equilibrium at period t. The transition equation tells how price expectations and the capital stock change from period to period. For simplicity we shall assume that the capital stock is constant in the following discussion. Finally, the condition for full or long-run equilibrium states the requirements for the economy to come to a complete stop. In the F-P model, that requires that expected and actual prices be equal.

Mathematically, the complete F-P model can be written as follows:

(8.3) Aggregate Supply

$$Y_{s,t} = z\left(\overset{+}{\frac{P_t}{P_{e,t}}}, \overset{+}{K_t}\right).$$

(8.4) Aggregate Demand

$$Y_{d,t} = d(\overset{+}{G_t}, \overset{+}{M_t}, \overset{-}{T_t}, \overset{-}{P_t}).$$

(8.5) Short-Run Equilibrium Condition

$$Y_{s,t} = Y_{d,t}.$$

(8.6) Transition Equation

$$P_{e,t} = f(P_{t-1}, P_{t-2} \ldots P_{t-n}).$$

(8.7) Long-Run Equilibrium Condition

$$P_e = P.$$

The short-run equations are re-presented here from Chapter 6. The transition equation tells how expected price is formed. When expectations are adaptive, expected price is some function of past actual prices. Logically, the dynamic solution of the model is sequential. In the short-run G, M, T, K, and P_e are exogenous. Given values for each of these variables, we can solve Equations (8.3)–(8.5) for short-run equilibrium values for P, Y_s and Y_d. The value for P is then plugged into the transition equation to get a new value for P_e for the next period. This leads to a new short-run solution for the following period and a new value for P_e. The process goes on until the long-run equilibrium condition is satisfied. If the model is stable, the economy comes to a stop at that point.

A Numerical Example

To familiarize ourselves with dynamic models in general and the F-P model in particular, we now write some specific equations, assign values to the exogenous variables, and trace out the reaction of a hypothetical F-P economy to a one-time increase in demand. In order to focus on the key supply reactions, we shall use a very simple representation of aggregate demand, one in which demand depends only on real balances. This is tantamount to assuming that fiscal policy has no influence on aggregate demand, which is a rather extreme form of monetarism. In our first example, we shall assume that the relationship between money and income is 2 and that workers have the simplest form of price expectations:[4] $P_{e,t} = P_{t-1}$. Under these assumptions, the model is:

[4]Workers expect no inflation.

(8.8) Aggregate Demand

$$Y_{d,t} = \frac{2M_t}{P_t}.$$

(8.9) Aggregate Supply

$$Y_{s,t} = \frac{K_t}{3}\left(\frac{P_t}{P_{e,t}}\right).$$

(8.5) Short-Run Equilibrium Condition

$$Y_{s,t} = Y_{d,t}.$$

(8.10) Transition Equation

$$P_{e,t} = P_{t-1}.$$

(8.7) Long-Run Equilibrium Condition

$$P_e = P.$$

Suppose that we start the model with a capital stock of 3000 and a money supply of 500. Using Equations (8.9) and (8.7), we see that the long-run output of the economy must be 1000. Now use Equation (8.8) to derive an equilibrium price level of 1.00. Thus, for a money supply of 500 and a capital stock of 3000, the long-run equilibrium solution for the economy is $Y = 1000$ and $P = 1.00$.

Let us now investigate how this economy reacts to an increase in demand, represented here by an expansion of the money supply by 50 units, or 10 percent. To get the short-run equilibrium solution, combine Equations (8.8), (8.9), and (8.5) to get:[5]

(8.11) $$Y_t = \sqrt{2000\,\frac{M_t}{P_{e,t}}}.$$

To get P_t, substitute Equation (8.11) back into Equation (8.8):

(8.12) $$P_t = \sqrt{\frac{2M_tP_{e,t}}{1000}}.$$

Using these two short-run equations plus the transition equation (8.10), we can construct Table 8.1 to show exactly how the economy responds to the increase in the money supply.

As the reader can see, the increase in demand first causes a rise in output and prices in period 1. Then as workers' expectations gradually catch up, output falls back toward 1000 and prices rise to the long-run level of 1.10. Table 8.1 is simply a specific example of the general process portrayed in Figure 8.2.

[5]Equations (8.11) and (8.12) are short-run reduced-form equations.

Table 8.1
Dynamic Response to Rise in Money Supply in the F-P Model

Period	M	Y	P	P_e	K
0	500	1000	1.000	1.000	3000
1	550	1049	1.050	1.000	3000
2	550	1023	1.075	1.050	3000
3	550	1011	1.087	1.075	3000
⋮	⋮	⋮	⋮	⋮	⋮
n	550	1000	1.100	1.100	3000

It is worth noting several important characteristics of the long-run full equilibrium solution. For the quantity theory demand curve, the 10-percent increase in the money supply causes an offsetting 10-percent increase in prices. Why? In the long run, income is constrained by the capital stock to be just equal to 1000. That being the case, Equation (8.8) tells us that M/P has to equal 500. This, in turn, implies that any increase in M must lead to an equal proportional increase in P. Increasing the money supply is always inflationary in the F-P world. Furthermore, increasing demand never leads to a permanent increase in output.

The dynamic behavior of the economy is critically dependent on the transition equation. Seemingly slight changes in the formation of expectations have profound effects on the way the economy reacts to disturbances. To see that, let us suppose that workers expect inflation, rather than prices, to continue at last year's level. This assumption, as we have seen, is expressed in the alternate transition equation, Equation (8.2c), which we now put into our model in place of Equation (8.10). Let us now analyze the reaction of our simple economy to the 50-unit increase in the money supply under this new form of expected prices. The only difference between this and the first example is that we use Equation (8.2c) rather than (8.10) to derive the sequence of expected prices.

The dynamic solution for the economy, a specific example of the general dynamic process shown in Figure (8.3), is shown in Table 8.2. As before, the economy starts with rising prices and output, followed by a stabilization phase in which prices rise and output declines. However, unlike the first case, there are several periods during which output falls below the long-run equilibrium level of 1000. That is because there is an inconsistency between workers' forecasts of inflation and the long-run requirement that prices be stable. Recessions are required to eliminate workers' overforecasts of the inflation rate. The dynamic adjustment process is much longer here than it was with the simpler price forecasting rule, and it involves several cycles of rising and falling output before the economy finally reaches the new long-run equilibrium level. Clearly, we could alter the dynamic behavior of the model by changing our transition equation. But under almost any form of adaptive expectations, the economy will go through several cycles on its way to the new full equilibrium position. However, as in the first example, in the long run the only effect of the 10-percent increase in M is a 10-percent increase in prices.

Table 8.2
The Adjustment Process for the F-P Model: An Example

Period	Dollar Supply	Income	Price	Expected Price
1	$500.00	$1000.00	1.000	1.000
2	500.00	1000.00	1.000	1.000
3	500.00	1000.00	1.000	1.000
4	500.00	1000.00	1.000	1.000
5	550.00	1048.81	1.049	1.000
6	550.00	1000.00	1.100	1.100
7	550.00	976.45	1.127	1.154
8	550.00	976.45	1.127	1.154
9	550.00	988.16	1.113	1.127
10	550.00	1000.00	1.100	1.100
11	550.00	1005.97	1.093	1.087
12	550.00	1005.97	1.093	1.087
13	550.00	1002.98	1.097	1.093
14	550.00	1000.00	1.100	1.100
15	550.00	998.51	1.102	1.103
16	550.00	998.51	1.102	1.103
17	550.00	999.26	1.101	1.102
18	550.00	1000.00	1.100	1.100
19	550.00	1000.37	1.100	1.099
20	550.00	1000.37	1.100	1.099
21	550.00	1000.19	1.100	1.100
22	550.00	1000.00	1.100	1.100
23	550.00	999.91	1.100	1.100
24	550.00	999.91	1.100	1.100
25	550.00	999.95	1.100	1.100
26	550.00	1000.00	1.100	1.100
27	550.00	1000.02	1.100	1.100
28	550.00	1000.02	1.100	1.100
29	550.00	1000.01	1.100	1.100
30	550.00	1000.00	1.100	1.100
31	550.00	999.99	1.100	1.100
32	550.00	999.99	1.100	1.100
33	550.00	1000.00	1.100	1.100
34	550.00	1000.00	1.100	1.100
35	550.00	1000.00	1.100	1.100
36	550.00	1000.00	1.100	1.100

The Effect of a One-Time Increase in Demand in the Disequilibrium Model

What we seek to show here is that while the full equilibrium for the two models is identical, there are important differences between them in short-run behavior. These follow directly from the different assumptions about the short-run behavior

Figure 8.4
The Effect of an Increase in Demand Where $P_{e,t} = P_{t-1}$ (Disequilibrium Model)

The adjustment by the economy to a one-time increase in demand in the disequilibrium economy is the same as in the partial equilibrium economy. There is a temporary increase in output and permanently higher prices.

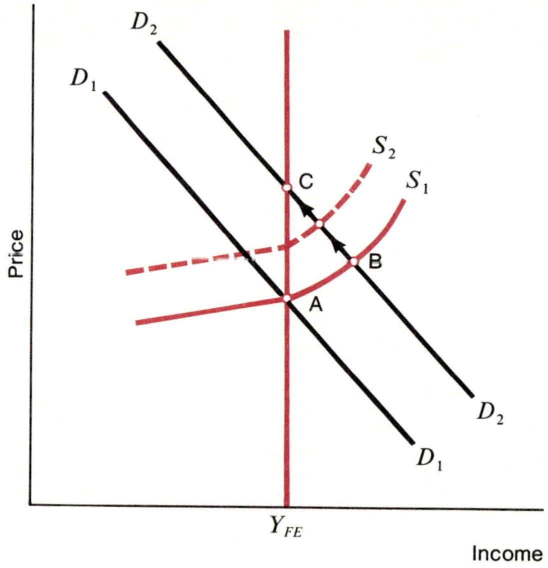

of workers and businesspersons. These differences have profound implications for how the economy operates in the short run and how sensitive it is to fluctuations in demand.

As we saw in Chapter 7, the key feature of the short-run disequilibrium model is that prices are set on the basis of a markup over cost for a large part of the economy, and wages are only weakly related to conditions in the labor market. We summarized all of this in the kinked short-run aggregate supply curve, the kink occurring at or around the long-run supply curve. The question we want to investigate here is how an economy with this sort of supply curve adjusts to changes in aggregate demand. Is its dynamic behavior different from that of a F-P economy?

In order to satisfactorily answer this question, we need to complete the dynamic model whose short-run characteristics were analyzed in Chapter 7. To do that, we must specify the transition equations for the dynamic model. These will tell us how the economy moves from one short-run equilibrium to the next. As we have written the disequilibrium model, the transition equation is exactly the same as in the partial equilibrium F-P model. It specifies the formation of workers' price expectations, a key influence on their wage demands. In the more traditional Keynesian model, wages are entirely exogenous in the short run, and one would need a transition equation for wages. We did not use a fixed wage because we discovered

Figure 8.5
Adjustment to an Increase in Demand Where $\Delta P/P_{e,t} = \Delta P/P$ (Disequilibrium Model)
The general pattern of adjustment to the one-time increase in demand is the same in the disequilibrium and partial-equilibrium models. However, when the supply curve shifts up in period 3, the effect on both output and prices will be greater in the disequilibrium economy. There will be a deeper recession and a greater rise in prices, because the supply curve is so flat for $Y < Y_{FE}$. In the disequilibrium economy, when workers' inflation expectations are inconsistent with aggregate demand, as they are at point C, there will be an extended recession until high rates of unemployment drive down money wage demands.

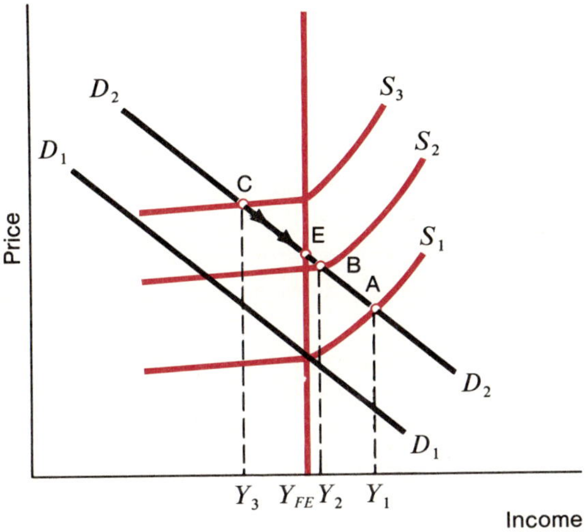

that it tends to be dynamically unstable, which means that the economy does not move back to its full equilibrium after a demand disturbance.

Let us now see how the disequilibrium economy reacts to the same one-time increase in demand that we have already analyzed for the F-P model. See Figure 8.4. Suppose as before that the economy starts in full equilibrium at point A. First, demand increases from D_1 to D_2. In the short run, output and prices rise as the economy moves out to point B. The question now is what happens to the supply curve. As in the F-P model, the short-run supply curve intersects the long-run curve where $P = P_e$. Since there has been an unexpected rise in prices at point B, we should expect a rise in P_e and hence a shift up in the short-run supply curve. Gradually, as P_e rises wage demands catch up with prices, and the supply curve shifts up to its new full equilibrium position at point C. There is little difference between the two models when workers do not forecast inflation.

If workers learn to expect a continuation of inflation, the situation becomes a good deal more complex. We now analyze the reaction of an economy with the transition equation (8.2c) in place of Equation (8.1). Consider Figure 8.5. As before, the economy moves first out to point A. In period 2, however, since workers expect inflation to continue, the short-run supply curve shifts up much further than it did before, to S_2, just as in the temporary equilibrium model. Hence, in period 2 the short-run equilibrium is at point B. Prices continue to rise, but output declines. This unfortunately is not the end of the process. Since there has been further inflation between A and B, the supply curve will shift up again to curve S_3 causing short-run equilibrium to move northwest to point C. Here the economy is in a true recession, not unlike the recession in the F-P model. However, there is an important difference, and that is that the forces driving the economy back to full equilibrium are likely to be much weaker in the disequilibrium model than in the partial equilibrium one, because the short-run supply curve in the former model is so nearly flat. Let us see why.

In the following period, two forces tend to pull the supply curve in opposite directions. On the one hand, workers who are still employed note that inflation has not abated. They will demand higher wages, which tends to raise the supply curve. On the other hand, there is now involuntary unemployment too. That will tend to hold down wage demands. Which of these two influences predominates is obviously an exceedingly important empirical and practical question. If the expected inflation component is greater, the short-run supply curve shifts upward, causing yet another round of stagflation and deepening recession as the economy moves further away from full equilibrium.

Eventually, the negative influence of high unemployment on wage demands should offset the wage-increasing effects of past inflation, allowing the supply curve to decline back to the full equilibrium position at E in Figure 8.5. The point here is that the move back to the full equilibrium may be a very drawn-out affair, requiring many periods to push down wage demands. The flatter the supply curve and the weaker the influence of unemployment on the wage rate, the slower will be the recovery from an inflationary recession in a disequilibrium economy.

A Mathematical Representation of the Dynamic Disequilibrium Model

For comparability it is useful to collect the equations of the complete disequilibrium model together. As in the F-P model, we will have short-run equations to determine temporary equilibrium, the transition equation, and the long-run equilibrium condition equation. The short-run equations, all of which were developed earlier, are re-presented here:

(8.13) Aggregate Supply

$$P_t = x(\overset{+}{Y_t}, \overset{+}{P_{e,t}}, \overset{?}{K_t}).$$

(8.4) Aggregate Demand

$$Y_{d,t} = d(\overset{+}{G_t}, \overset{+}{M_t}, \overset{-}{T_t}, \overset{-}{P_t}).$$

(8.5) Short-Run Equilibrium Condition

$$Y_{s,t} = Y_{d,t}.$$

For the dynamic model we add the transition and long-run equilibrium equations, repeated here for convenience:

(8.6) Transition Equation

$$P_{e,t} = f(P_{t-1}, P_{t-2} \ldots P_{t-n}).$$

(8.7) Long-Run Equilibrium Condition

$$P_e = P.$$

Comparing this system of equations with those of the F-P partial equilibrium model, the reader will note that the only difference between the two is in the short-run supply curve. In this model, price is set on the basis of expected price and output. As we showed in the last chapter, at less than normal output the disequilibrium supply curve is much flatter than the partial equilibrium short-run supply curve. From this single, significant difference stem large disagreements about how economies behave during recessions, as we shall see in the following example.

A Numerical Example

In order to make clear how the disequilibrium model works, and also to show its sensitivity to the slope of the short-run supply curve, we shall present a numerical example just as we did for the partial equilibrium model. As before, let us suppose that aggregate demand is expressed by the simple quantity theory (Equation [8.8]). For simplicity, we shall use a linear supply curve without a kink. Since we are primarily interested in the behavior of the disequilibrium economy in stabilization recessions, this simplification isn't particularly harmful to our understanding. So that the reader can see explicitly the entire price- and wage-setting mechanism, we show separate equations for wages and prices. These can be combined into the short-run supply curve. Prices are based on a simple linear markup over labor costs, where we assume that $N/Q = 1$ and ignore raw materials. Equation (8.15) says that wages are based on expected prices reduced by the excess of unemployment over its frictional or normal level. Equation (8.2c) is the transition equation and expresses our hypothesis about expectations. We will assume, as we did in the second F-P model, that workers expect inflation to continue at the level of the previous period. It should be clear that the equations in the following numerical model are specific examples of the equations shown in the previous section.

(8.8) Aggregate Demand

$$Y_{d,t} = \frac{2M_t}{P_t}.$$

(8.14) Markup Price Equation

$$P_t = 1.1\ W_t.$$

(8.15) Wages

$$W_t = .91(P_{e,t} - [U - U_{FE}]).$$

(8.2c) Transition Equation

$$P_{e,t} = \frac{P_{t-1}^2}{P_{t-2}}.$$

(8.7) Long-Run Equilibrium Condition

$$P_e = P.$$

In order to solve this model it is convenient to use Okun's law (Equation [7.3] from Chapter 7) and Equations (8.14) and (8.15) to derive the short-run aggregate supply curve. Simply substitute Equation (7.3) into Equation (8.15) to get:

(8.16)
$$W_t = .91\left(P_{e,t} + .3\frac{(Y_t - Y_{FE})}{Y_{FE}}\right).$$

Y_{FE} = normal full equilibrium output level

Next, substitute Equation (8.16) into Equation (8.14) to get the short-run supply curve:

(8.17)
$$P_t = P_{e,t} + .33\frac{(Y_t - Y_{FE})}{Y_{FE}}.$$

Equation (8.17) tells us exactly how price varies with output and is a specific example of the general disequilibrium short-run supply curve we wrote as Equation (8.13). It is worth noting that a weaker relationship between wages and unemployment in Equation (8.15) will directly translate into a flatter supply curve (a smaller coefficient on Y_t in Equation [8.17]).

Suppose that we start our disequilibrium model at exactly the same full equilibrium that we did for the F-P model, with a capital stock of 3000 and a money supply of 500. As before, we can see that the long-run equilibrium is $Y = 1000$, $P = 1.00$, and $W = .91$.[6] Note that this wage rate is consistent with the markup pricing equation, Equation (8.14). As before, we now increase the money supply by 50 units and trace out the dynamic reaction by the economy to this disturbance. Table 8.3 gives the time path of income and prices for the disequilibrium model. To more easily compare the short-run responses of the two models, we have also

[6]We get this by remembering that in full equilibrium $Y = Y_{FE}$, $U = U_{FE}$ and $P = P_e$. Thus if price = 1.00 and $M = 500$, Equation (8.8) says that $Y = 1000$. At that price, wages = .91 according to Equation (8.15), which gives a price level of 1.00 by Equation (8.14). Thus, the solution is consistent with all the equations.

Table 8.3
The Adjustment Process for the Disequilibrium Model: An Example

Period	Dollar Supply	Income	Price	Expected Price
1	$500.00	$1000.00	1.000	1.000
2	500.00	1000.00	1.000	1.000
3	500.00	1000.00	1.000	1.000
4	500.00	1000.00	1.000	1.000
5	550.00	1073.84	1.024	1.000
6	550.00	1036.42	1.061	1.049
7	550.00	1000.24	1.100	1.100
8	550.00	972.94	1.131	1.140
9	550.00	957.85	1.148	1.162
10	550.00	955.12	1.152	1.166
11	550.00	962.67	1.143	1.155
12	550.00	976.86	1.126	1.134
13	550.00	993.25	1.107	1.110
14	550.00	1007.59	1.092	1.089
15	550.00	1016.88	1.082	1.076
16	550.00	1019.98	1.078	1.072
17	550.00	1017.60	1.081	1.075
18	550.00	1011.63	1.087	1.084
19	550.00	1004.38	1.095	1.094
20	550.00	997.82	1.102	1.103
21	550.00	993.29	1.107	1.110
22	550.00	991.33	1.110	1.112
23	550.00	991.79	1.109	1.112
24	550.00	994.02	1.107	1.109
25	550.00	997.12	1.103	1.104
26	550.00	1000.17	1.100	1.100
27	550.00	1002.48	1.097	1.096
28	550.00	1003.69	1.096	1.095
29	550.00	1003.75	1.096	1.095
30	550.00	1002.94	1.097	1.096
31	550.00	1001.63	1.098	1.098
32	550.00	1000.25	1.100	1.100
33	550.00	999.13	1.101	1.101
34	550.00	998.47	1.102	1.102
35	550.00	998.31	1.102	1.102
36	550.00	998.58	1.102	1.102
37	550.00	999.12	1.101	1.101
38	550.00	999.73	1.100	1.100
39	550.00	1000.26	1.100	1.100
40	550.00	1000.62	1.099	1.099
41	550.00	1000.74	1.099	1.099
42	550.00	1000.67	1.099	1.099
43	550.00	1000.46	1.099	1.099
44	550.00	1000.19	1.100	1.100

(continued on next page)

Table 8.3 (*continued*)

Period	Dollar Supply	Income	Price	Expected Price
45	550.00	999.94	1.100	1.100
46	550.00	999.76	1.100	1.100
47	550.00	999.68	1.100	1.100
48	550.00	999.69	1.100	1.100
49	550.00	999.77	1.100	1.100
50	550.00	999.88	1.100	1.100
51	550.00	1000.00	1.100	1.100

Figure 8.6
Income Graphs with Fixed Dollar Expansion

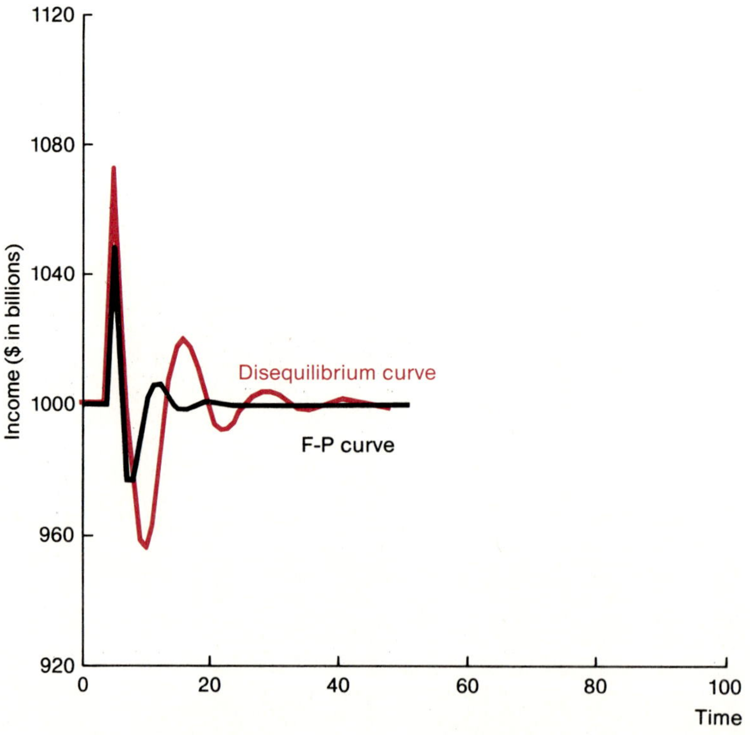

drawn a picture of Tables 8.2 and 8.3 in Figure 8.6. This figure shows us at a glance the different reactions by the two economies to the same stimulus.

It is clear from Figure 8.6 that both models start and end in the same place and both have dynamic cycles as wage demands are brought into line. But the time paths for the two models are quite different. The disequilibrium model has several fairly deep and extended recessions to drive down wage demands. Whereas in the partial equilibrium model output bottoms out at 976 and then rapidly recovers, in the disequilibrium model it falls to 955, and the economy has inflationary recession for six periods in each of its cycles. Were we to assume a flatter supply curve, those recessions would be longer and more severe.[7]

Of course, we must remember that these models are only illustrative examples. But the behavior they exhibit is suggestive. Price and wage rigidity has a profound effect on the dynamic behavior of the economy. The less impact market conditions have on prices and wages, the longer and deeper the period of inflationary stagnation will be. In the case we have been analyzing, the recession is necessary to drive worker wage demands down to a level consistent with price stability. When workers learn to expect inflation, a recession is required. When the recession has only a weak effect on wages, as it does in the disequilibrium model, the length and severity of the recession will be heightened.

A Comparison of the Feedback Mechanism in the Two Models

In the partial equilibrium model, recessions are caused by forecasting errors. They occur whenever prices are lower than workers expect them to be. The economy moves out of a recession as workers bring their price forecasts into line with actual prices. This is the feedback feature that makes recession self-correcting and brings the economy back to long-run equilibrium. This feedback feature is much weaker in the disequilibrium model because the supply curve is so flat. The model's main feedback mechanism is the negative relationship between the wage and the unemployment rate. When an economy is in recession, higher-than-normal levels of unemployment should reduce wage demands and enable businesspersons, whose prices are based on a markup over costs, to lower their prices. Thus, unemployment plays a key role in the dynamic behavior of the disequilibrium economy, just as erroneous price forecasts do in the partial equilibrium model. Which is a more accurate description of our actual economy is an empirical question that we shall discuss further in Chapter 10. Here we can say with fair assurance that the partial equilibrium economy has a stronger self-correcting tendency than the disequilibrium model.

[7]It should be clear that the difference between the short-run behavior of these two models is a result simply of the difference between the slopes of these short-run supply curves. Seemingly small differences in behavior can have quite profound implications for the predicted behavior of the economy.

In the partial equilibrium economy inflation rates fall when there is a recession, because the supply curve is upward sloping. That should lower inflation forecasts and move the economy fairly rapidly toward long-run equilibrium. In the disequilibrium economy this mechanism is virtually absent, because the supply curve is so flat. The main equilibrating factor is the unemployment-wage relationship. Unfortunately, in the modern economy there is a good deal of evidence that this relationship is fairly weak, which implies long periods of **inflationary recession.**

Summary

We have tried to make two main points in this chapter. The first is that economies react to an increase in demand with a typical sequence. First, output and prices rise in a phase that used to be called demand-pull inflation. This is followed by a stabilization phase, in which the economy goes through several further cycles as it approaches its new long-run full equilibrium. In that equilibrium the only permanent effect of the increase in demand is permanently higher prices. In the long run, there can be no trade-off between inflation and output. In talking about the long run, we should emphasize again that we are ignoring changes in the capital stock. If demand fluctuations have an impact on capital formation, as we shall argue in Chapter 19 that they do, then the long-run supply curve is undoubtedly not vertical after all.

The second point is that the dynamic behavior of the economy depends critically upon what type of economy we are in. The less responsive prices and wages are to market conditions, the flatter the short-run supply curve and the more the economy resembles our disequilibrium model. Such models and the economies they represent are less stable than partial equilibrium models. They respond to changes in demand by a protracted sequence of cycles. The flatter the supply curve, the longer the economy takes to bring wages into line with the long-run equilibrium level of prices.

The example we have been using in this chapter to make these points and compare the two models is not a particularly realistic one, because the disturbance is a one-time change in the level of demand. In our inflationary world, a far more likely occurrence would be a change in the rate of growth of demand. We now turn to an analysis of that case.

Key Concepts

dynamic analysis	**adaptive expectations**
transition equations	**inflationary recession**

Problems and Questions for Discussion

1. Why is the period of adjustment to a demand shock larger and the variance in output greater in the disequilibrium than in the partial equilibrium model? What behavioral parameters determine the length and severity of the cycles during the dynamic adjustment process in each model?

2. Why do economies typically have booms in response to an increase in demand? Does this always happen? If not, what is the necessary condition for it to happen?

3. Under what conditions will an increase in aggregate demand lead to a recession sometime during the period of adjustment to a new full equilibrium?

4. Can an economy have a permanent increase in income in response to a permanent increase in the money supply? If so, how? If not, why not?

5. In a partial equilibrium economy, suppose that $P_{e,t} = P_{t-1}$.

a. If actual prices follow the path shown in the diagram, what are the pathways of expected prices and output? Show the two in the same time diagram.

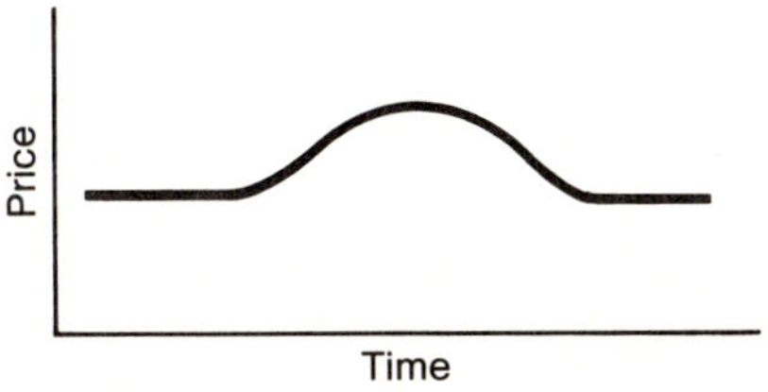

b. How do you know the pathway of output from the information given?

c. Show the same cycle you have drawn in part a in the aggregate goods market diagram. Can you imagine the shifts of demand and supply curves that would give rise to such a cycle?

6. In a partial equilibrium economy, suppose that the expected inflation rate is equal to the previous year's inflation rate.

a. If the actual inflation rate follows the path shown in the diagram, what are the paths of expected inflation and actual output? Draw the two pathways on the diagram.

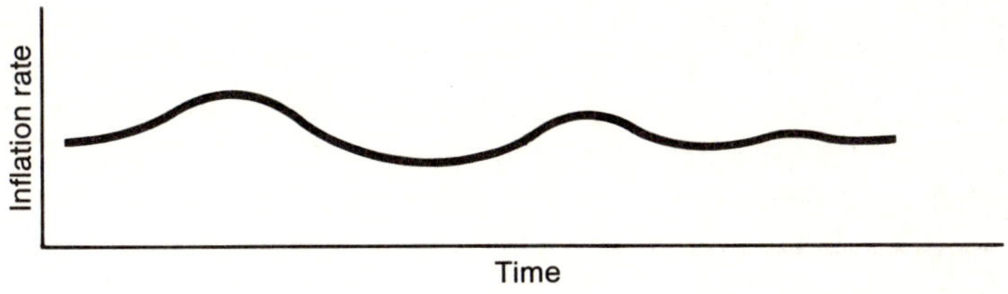

b. Draw the pathway of actual and expected prices levels in part a.

c. Show the cycle you have drawn in parts a and b on the aggregate goods market diagram. What shifts in the demand curve might give rise to such a cycle? How do they compare with the change in demand in Problem 5?

7. Why does the economy have a recession in response to a one-time change in demand when workers learn to expect inflation but not when workers don't expect inflation?

8. Suppose we have an economy in which prices are set as a markup over costs and in which demand is determined according to the quantity theory. For simplicity, we shall assume there is no labor stockpiling. Wage changes are determined by the unemployment rate, but with a one-period lag. The behavioral equations of such a model can be written:

Demand

$$Y_t = \frac{4M_t}{P_t}.$$

Production Function

$$Y_t = 100N_t^{\frac{1}{2}}.$$

Markup Price Function

$$P_t = \frac{1.1WN_t}{Y_t}.$$

Wages

$$W_{t+1} = 9.09 \times P_{t-1} - 10(U_t - U_{FE}).$$

$$U_t = 1 - \frac{N_t}{107} \text{ (unemployment rate)}$$

$$U_{FE} = 1 - \frac{100}{107} = .0654 \text{ (full equilibrium unemployment rate)}$$

Initial values of exogenous variables:

$$M_0 = 2750$$
$$W_0 = 100$$

a. Derive the supply and demand curves for this economy.
b. Combine the supply and demand curves together to get reduced-form equations for Y_t and P_t. (These equations will show Y_t and P_t as functions of M_t and W_t. Note that W_t is exogenous each period because it is determined by lagged values of U and P).
c. What is the transition equation in this model?
d. What is the full equilibrium level of output, prices, employment, and the wage rate?

9. Suppose that the money supply is reduced from 2750 to 2500.
a. Calculate the levels of employment, output, wages, and the price level for two periods after this change.
b. What is the new full equilibrium level of output to which the dynamic adjustment process is leading?
c. What are the characteristics of this new equilibrium compared with the initial equilibrium?

Chapter 9

The Inflationary Process

Demand Cycles, Supply Shocks, and Stabilization

In the last chapter we analyzed the dynamic response of an economy to a one-time increase in demand. While this illustrated the way the dynamic model works, it is not a particularly realistic or useful policy experiment. Economies generally face fluctuations in the rate of growth of demand rather than one-time changes. A particularly common and important pattern is an increase in the rate of growth of demand, followed by a reduction when the government realizes that it has an inflation problem and decides to stabilize. We would like to see how our two different economies react to this sort of disturbance. The experiment we perform in this chapter will illustrate very clearly the problem of reducing the rate of inflation through demand management in a disequilibrium economy.

Another problem, which has become increasingly frequent in recent years, is supply shocks. Rising prices of key inputs to the production process, such as fuel and raw materials, appear to give a strong impetus to inflation. We would like to examine this problem more closely and see how the macroeconomy reacts to supply-side shocks.

The Expansionary Phase of an Inflationary Cycle

The experiment we are about to analyze is one in which the economy starts out in long-run equilibrium with demand expanding at just the rate consistent with price stability. This moving equilibrium is disturbed by an increase in demand that lasts long enough to cause an increase in the inflation rate and in workers' expectations about inflation. Finally, the government, concerned about the acceleration of prices, reduces demand in order to bring the inflation rate back down close to its original level. This scenario fairly accurately describes economic policy in the United States in the period 1964–1970 and again in the period 1976–1981. In both cases, the economy had an initial period of growth accompanied by a rise in the inflation rate. This was followed by a long period of **stagflation,** in which the rate of inflation receded very slowly towards its initial rate. This is a typical pattern in what we shall call the **inflationary cycle.** It is predicted by both of our models, the only difference in each being the length of time it takes for the stabilization recession to do its work of reducing workers' inflation expectations and wage demands.

Let us start by showing the F-P economy in full long-run equilibrium in Figure 9.1. In period 1 the short-run supply and demand curves intersect on the long-run supply curve, and actual and expected prices are equal. Suppose for simplicity that prices are stable, that workers expect no inflation, and that there is no expansion of the long-run supply curve.

Suppose now that in period 2 the government is confronted by the necessity of increasing spending. The most obvious example of such a stimulus might be a war, but any increase in private sector demand would have the same effect. Ideally the government should raise taxes or reduce other spending programs of its own, but let us suppose that it does not. Let us suppose that for three periods, demand grows at 5 percent. We show this growth in demand by a series of 5-percent rightward shifts in the demand curve during periods 2 through 4.

What happens to short-run equilibrium depends on the short-run supply curve. Remember that each period's short-run supply curve intersects the long-run curve at the price level expected by the labor force. Since the economy is in long-run equilibrium in period 1, if expectations are adaptive the short-run supply curve does not move in period 2. Thus, the increase in demand during that period pulls the economy out to point B. Output rises above the long-run level, and prices begin to rise as well. This boom will last only so long as workers' nominal wage demands do not fully reflect the change in prices—that is, so long as some part of the inflation is unexpected.

Let us suppose that in period 3 workers correct their forecasting errors of the previous period but do not expect further inflation—that is, the transition equation in period 3 is:

(9.1) $$P_{e,3} = P_2.$$

In that case, the short-run supply curve moves up to S_3, which intersects the long-run curve at $P_{e,3} = P_2$. In Figure 9.1 we see that period 3 short-run equilibrium is at point C, the intersection of S_3 and D_3. Prices continue to rise at about the same rate they did in period 2; since this inflation is again unexpected by workers, output rises above the boom level it reached during period 2.

Now let us suppose that in period 4, after two periods of unexpected inflation, workers learn to anticipate further inflation. Suppose that they change their price forecasting equation to one that predicts that inflation will continue at the last peri-

Figure 9.1
The Expansionary Phase of the Inflationary Cycle

An unexpected increase in aggregate demand initiates an inflationary cycle. In periods 2 through 4, demand increases by 5 percent per period. Through period 3, workers expect no inflation. They think that prices will be equal to the observed level of the previous year. Since prices were constant in period 1, the period 2 supply curve does not shift. Hence, the increase in aggregate demand leads to short-run equilibrium at point B in period 2. In period 3, the supply curve shifts up by the period 2 inflation. But since there is a further increase in demand in period 3, once again prices increase and output remains above its long-run level. In period 4, workers finally begin to forecast inflation. As a result, the period 4 supply curve shifts up much further than it did in periods 2 and 3. This causes an acceleration of inflation and a simultaneous decline in output—a "stagflation," in the inelegant terminology of the 1970s.

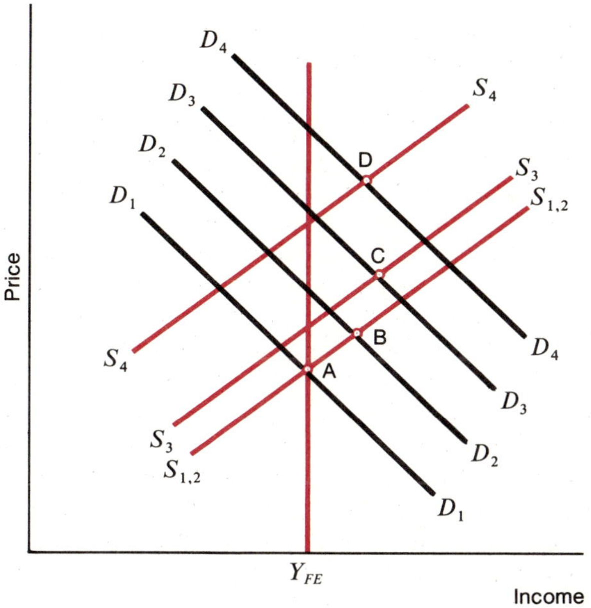

od's rate. As we saw in Chapter 8, this change in behavior leads to the transition equations:[1]

(9.2)
$$\frac{\Delta P}{P_{e,t}} = \frac{\Delta P}{P_{t-1}}.$$

[1]Recall that when expected inflation equals last year's inflation,

$$\frac{P_{e,t} - P_{t-1}}{P_{t-1}} = \frac{P_{t-1} - P_{t-2}}{P_{t-2}},$$

which simplifies to Equation (9.2a) for $t = 4$.

(9.2a) $$P_{e,4} = \frac{P_3^2}{P_2}.$$

In our diagram, this change in expectations has the significant effect of shifting the supply up very much further than it rose in previous periods. S_4 intersects the long-run curve above P_3 by the inflation rate of period 3. The period 4 equilibrium is at point D, a point at which inflation is higher and output is lower than both were in previous periods. The reason for this unfavorable change is that workers are finally learning to forecast inflation more accurately. Such a change in behavior always drives up prices and pushes the economy back toward its long-run output level.

Let us stop and review what has happened during this **expansionary phase** of our inflationary cycle. The increase in the rate of growth of demand led to an increase in both income and prices. At the outset, the increase in prices was a good deal less than the increase in demand because output went up too; there appeared to be a trade-off between output and inflation. However, as workers learned to forecast inflation more accurately, the supposed trade-off began to evaporate. Output fell back toward the long-run level, and the rate of inflation rose toward the 5-percent annual increase in demand. It would be easy to show that if the government were to continue to allow demand to grow at 5 percent, eventually the economy would settle down to a new long-run equilibrium in which output is Y_{FE} and in which prices rise at exactly the rate of growth of demand.

The Stabilization Phase

Rather than let demand continue to grow at 5 percent, let us see what happens under the more realistic assumption that the government, concerned about rising inflation, decides to stabilize. Suppose that the government does this by reducing the growth rate of demand from 5 percent to 2 percent. It should be fairly clear by now that the long-run effect of this change will be a reduction in the inflation rate from 5 percent to 2 percent. However, the interesting question is the short-run effect. For policymakers and politicians, it makes a great deal of difference how the economy gets to this new long-run equilibrium. If the pathway is long and involves many periods of recession, it may be politically difficult to accomplish—and, as we shall now see, there is a very marked difference between the ways that our two models react to stabilization. In predicting behavior in our actual economy, it therefore makes a good deal of difference which is the more realistic of the two models.

Stabilization in the F-P Economy

The **stabilization phase** of the partial equilibrium economy occurs during the reduction of expected inflation to a rate consistent with the expansion of demand. In the case we have been examining, by period 5 workers have learned to expect inflation to continue at 5 percent, the observed rate reached during the expansion phase. Under these expectations, the short-run supply curve will be shifting upward at 5 percent per year. That clearly will not be consistent with a long-run equilibrium in which the demand curve shifts upward by only 2 percent. The stabilization phase of the inflationary cycle goes on until workers' inflation expectations get driven down from 5 percent to 2 percent. Where expectations are formed on the basis of past actual inflation rates, reducing expected inflation requires a number of years in which actual inflation is less than expected. But whenever that happens, as we learned in Chapter 6, the economy is in a recession. Therefore, it follows that reducing inflation requires a recession, unless some other method can be found to reduce expected inflation. We now trace out the stabilization process with the help of our goods market diagram.

We pick up our economy in period 5, the first period in which the government attempts to control inflation by reducing demand growth from 5 percent to 2 percent (see Figure 9.2). This change means that the demand curve in period 5 shifts by only 2 percent above the demand curve of period 4.

Now consider the period 5 supply curve—it will shift much farther up than the demand curve. To see why, recall that the supply curve intersects the long-run curve at the period 5 expected price. That, as implied by Equation (9.2), is the actual price in period 4 times the period 4 inflation rate. Since the period 4 inflation rate is larger than the 2 percent by which demand is now increasing, and since there was an underforecast of inflation in period 4 to correct as well, the supply curve shifts up further than demand in period 5, and equilibrium is at point B. As the reader can see in Figure 9.2, prices go up again, but output begins to decline. Demand expansion is no longer sufficient to accommodate workers' price expectations and wage demands.

The process continues in period 6. Again the demand curve shifts up by 2 percent, while the supply curve shifts up by a much larger amount, reflecting both the underforecast of prices and the high actual inflation of period 5. As we have drawn the diagram, the supply curve shifts up so far that output falls below the long-run level. Government attempts to reduce the inflation push the economy into an inflationary recession.

The reason for the recession is workers' overforecast of the price level. Demand no longer expands rapidly enough to permit the sale of capacity output at the price expected by workers. Because markets are assumed to clear in the F-P model prices fall below $P_{e,6}$, and the economy sinks into a recession. This recession is a necessary part of the process by which the economy reaches a new long-run equilibrium. During recessions, actual inflation rates are less than expected inflation rates. If workers base their predictions on past actual price behavior, the recession will reduce the expected inflation rate. That will moderate the upward shift in the supply curve and lead finally to a new long-run equilibrium.

As we have drawn the process, one can see the slowdown in the upward shift in the supply curve starting in period 7. Workers are still overforecasting the price level, but the errors are smaller, and therefore the economy begins to recover from its inflationary recession. In the diagram the pathway of successive short-run equilibria begins to move northeast. Successive dots in the diagram show the path by which the economy reaches a new long-run equilibrium. From there on, prices rise at 2 percent per period and output is Y_{FE}.

Figure 9.2
Stabilization in a F-P Economy

From period 5 on, demand shifts upward at 2 percent rather than 5 percent. But the supply curve will be shifting upward at the rate of inflation expected by the labor force. Since there was an acceleration of inflation in period 5, the period 6 supply curve shifts up even further than did the period 5 curve. Since demand is only shifting up by 2 percent, equilibrium in period 6 is at point C. Prices continue to rise, but output is now less than Y_{FE}. In succeeding periods, so long as $Y < Y_{FE}$ the actual inflation rate is less than the expected rate. As workers correct their overforecast of prices the upward shifts in the short-run supply curve moderate, and the economy moves back to long-run equilibrium in a succession of damped cycles, as shown in the dashed line at the top of the diagram.

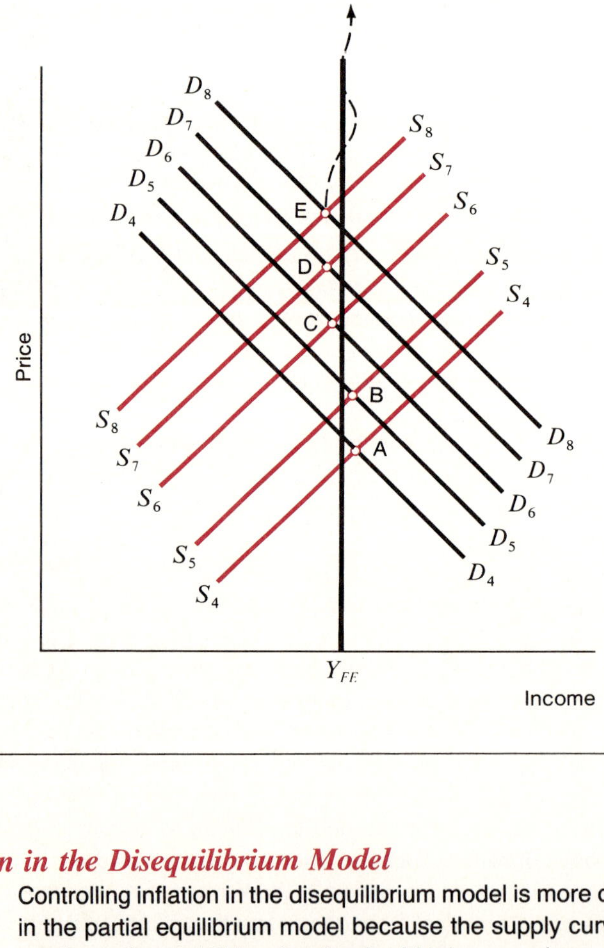

Stabilization in the Disequilibrium Model

Controlling inflation in the disequilibrium model is more drawn out and difficult than in the partial equilibrium model because the supply curve is so much flatter. That weakens the stabilizing feedback of high unemployment on wage and price increases. In the extreme, the feedback may be so weak that the economy is unstable. When that happens, wage demands are never forced down until they are consistent with the slower rate of expansion in demand. We should note that this can only be a problem when a high rate of expected inflation is an important part of each period's wage increases.

Figure 9.3
Stabilization in a Disequilibrium Economy

Stabilization in the disequilibrium economy will take longer and have deeper recessions. The reason can be seen in the diagram. Because the supply curve is virtually flat at less than full employment, supernormal unemployment starting in period 6 has little effect on the price level. Therefore, even though worker wage demands depend on expected prices, just as they do in the F-P model, there is little reduction in expected inflation. Hence, the recession does little to moderate the upward shifts in the supply curve in successive periods. As a result, it takes a higher level of unemployment to begin to force down wage demands and move the economy back toward the long-run equilibrium level of output.

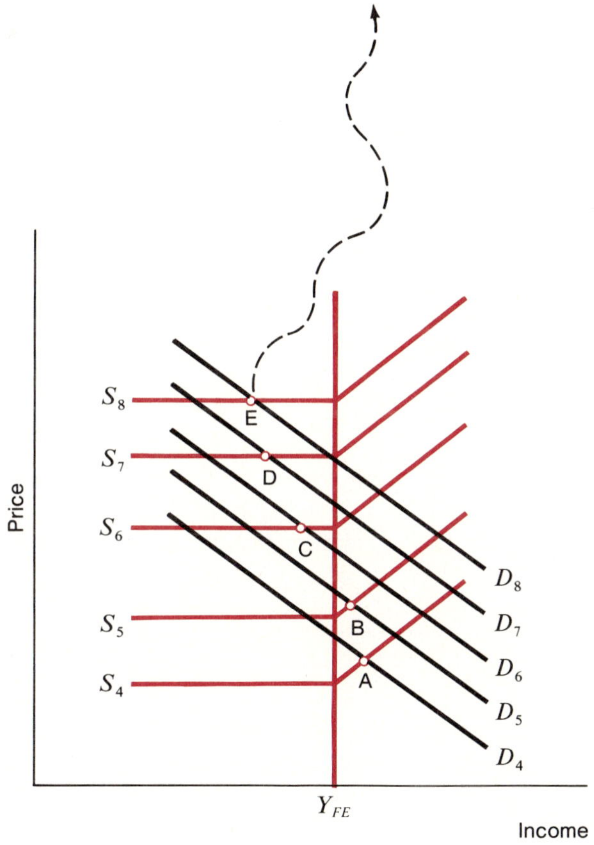

Let us go back to pick up the economy whose expansion phase we analyzed in Figure 9.1. We now want to see how a disequilibrium economy reaches a new long-run equilibrium. The first few periods of the stabilization are shown in Figure 9.3. For simplicity, assume that the disequilibrium supply curves are identical in slope to those in the F-P model for $Y > Y_{FE}$ (above the kink). That implies that the short-run equilibria are identical to those shown in Figure 9.2 up to period 6. But now let us look at what happens from period 7 onward.

Figure 9.4
A Comparison of F-P and Disequilibrium Inflationary Cycles
The inflationary cycle has deeper recessions and is more drawn out in the disequilibrium economy because its supply curve is flatter at less than full employment.

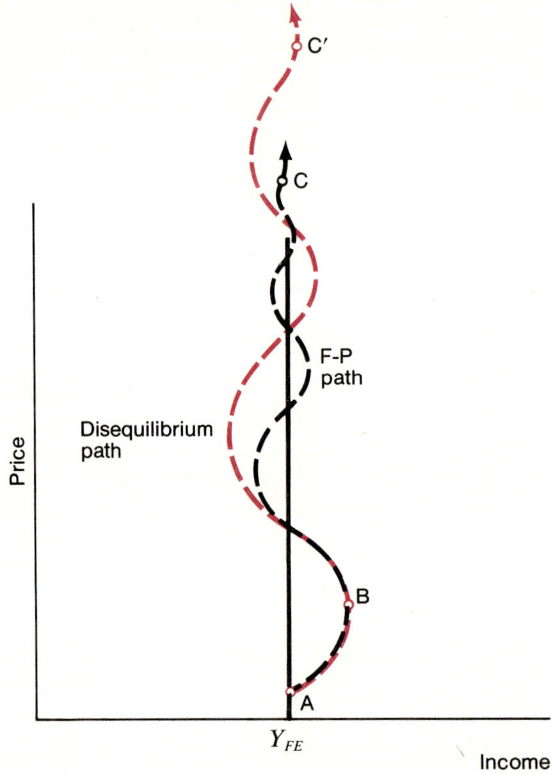

If we assume, as we did in the partial equilibrium model, that workers expect a continuation of inflation, the period 7 supply curve rises by the inflation rate of period 6. But because of government stabilization, demand is now increasing at only 2 percent, rather than 5 percent. Since the supply curve is so nearly flat at less than full employment, almost all of the reduction in demand is reflected in falling output, rather than in prices. Businesspersons find that they cannot sell all they could produce at the prices they feel they must charge to cover costs, because demand is insufficient. As a result, the recession deepens. Yet despite the recession, there is little relief as yet from inflation because prices and wages are so insensitive to demand. Without continuing to describe the process in detail, it is clear that the economy will go through an extended recession as wage demands and prices are gradually brought down to the 2-percent long-run equilibrium growth rate. The weaker the feedback between wages and unemployment, the deeper the recession required to eliminate excessive wage demands.

Looking back over the entire inflationary cycle, we find that in both models the economy goes through an S-shaped path of the type shown in Figure 9.4, just as they both did in response to the one-time increase in demand. And just as before, the only difference between the two models is in the length and severity of the stabilization phase. To generalize, whenever the rate of growth of demand declines unexpectedly, as it did in both of the examples we have been analyzing, there will be a period when wage demands are too high to be consistent with full equilibrium. This will cause a stabilization recession. But when excess supply in goods and labor markets has only a weak influence on wages and prices, it takes a correspondingly greater disequilibrium to move wages and prices down to a lower equilibrium growth rate.

The weak connection between output, wages, and prices in the disequilibrium model makes those who think that it is a realistic description of our economy rather pessimistic about the government's ability to reduce the rate of inflation by reducing the rate of growth of demand. They think that such a policy will only lead to an extended recession, which will usually be terminated by political pressure long before it can have much dampening effect on the inflation rate.

A Comparison of the Inflationary Cycle for the Two Models: A Numerical Example

To gain further understanding of the inflationary process and the difference between stabilization in the partial and disequilibrium models, let us take the two specific numerical models of the economy developed in the last chapter and subject them to the demand cycle we have just been analyzing. We shall expand the money supply by 5 percent for three periods; then we shall reduce the rate of growth to 2 percent and see how our hypothetical economies adjust to this change. The equations of the two models that we use to get equilibrium are exactly the same ones used in Chapter 8, the only difference being the growth rate of the money supply. As before, we shall assume expected inflation is equal to the actual inflation of the previous period.

Sequentially solving the model for Y and P, we derive the dynamic response of the two economies shown in Figure 9.5. As the reader can see, both models go through the typical S-shaped inflation cycle that we have already analyzed theoretically. Both are stable and go back to the long-run equilibrium income level with a permanent inflation rate of 2 percent. The differences between the models are the greater length of the stabilization phase and the greater severity of the cycle in the disequilibrium model. Because its supply curve is so much flatter than that for the F-P model, it takes a far longer time to reduce workers' wage demands. Stabilization causes a 6-percent decline in output that goes on for seven periods, compared to a 2-percent reduction for four periods in the partial equilibrium model.

Figure 9.5
Income Graphs with 2-Percent Dollar Expansion

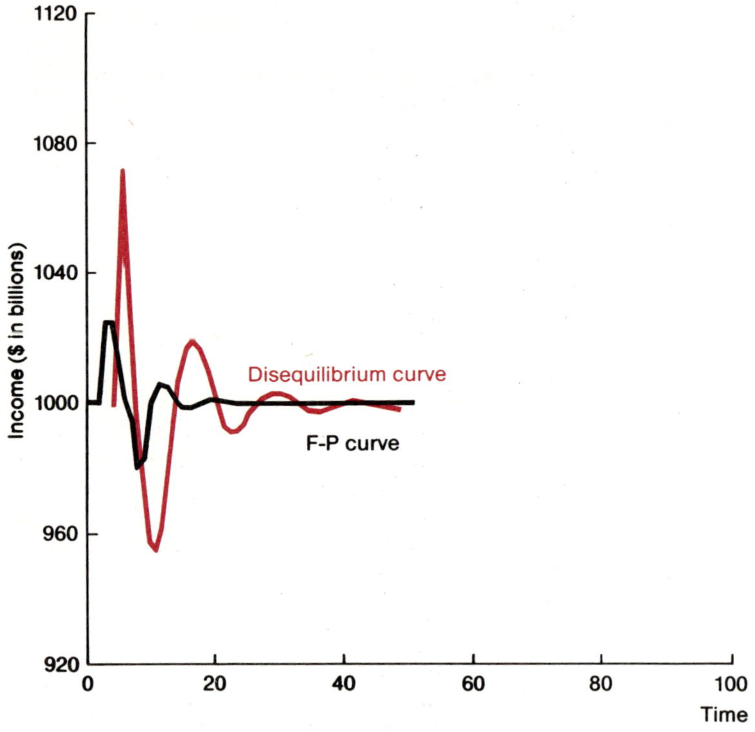

We do not know for sure which is the more realistic of the two models. But we do know that which sort of an economy we live in makes a difference. Stabilization is far more costly, lengthy, and difficult in a disequilibrium-type economy.[2]

Demand-Pull and Cost-Push Inflation

We have split up the inflationary cycle into two parts, the expansionary and stabilization phases. In the former, which extends from point A to point B in Figure 9.4, inflation accelerates and output expands. That is because the acceleration of inflation causes an increase in unexpected inflation. This part of the inflationary cycle

[2]For an alternative description of inflation in modern economies, see Sidney Weintraub, *Capitalism's Inflation and Unemployment Crisis* (Reading, Mass: Addison-Wesley, 1978). See also Arthur Okun, "Inflation: Its Mechanics and Welfare Costs," *Brookings Papers on Economic Activity* (2, 1975): 351–390.

used to be called **demand-pull inflation,** because the rise in prices is caused by an increase in demand relative to supply.

In Figure 9.4 the stabilization phase of the cycle extends all the way from point B to point C′, depending on the model.[3] During the greater part of this phase, workers are demanding catch-up wage increases to compensate them for past unexpected inflation. The supply curve shifts leftward, causing a rise in prices accompanied by falling output. Because wages rise faster than prices during most of the stabilization phase, many people will be tempted to blame the inflation during this phase on excessive wage demands. Indeed, they have even coined a name for this sort of inflation—they call it **cost-push inflation.** The symptoms of cost-push inflation are rising prices and falling output, exactly what we observe through most of the stabilization phase.

However, in the inflationary cycle being analyzed here, it makes little sense to separate the expansionary and the stabilization phases and blame labor's wage demands for the inflation that occurs during the latter. Rather, both stages are part of a single process by which an economy reacts to excess demand. First, the demand curve shifts out, generally because of an increase in government expenditure or an excessive expansion in the money supply; we call this the expansionary phase. Labor's reaction to the initial price increase is a delayed demand for wage adjustments. This causes a leftward shift in the short-run supply curve and the rising wages and prices that have been labeled cost-push inflation. But if we are correct, this cost-push phase is related to or caused by the preceding demand-pull phase. Both phases are parts of the same inflationary cycle.

Case Study

Inflationary Cycles in the United States

One way to test a theoretical model is to test its predictions against actual events in the economy. Our theoretical models of the economy lead us to expect a certain sequence of shifts in the aggregate supply curve over time in response to increases in aggregate demand followed by stabilization. Keep in mind that all we ever observe are the successive intersections of demand and supply curves. Both of our models predict that the economy should follow an S-shaped path in response to such a stimulus. In the post-World War II period, there have been two inflationary cycles that traced out exactly the S-shaped path predicted by our theory.

[3]We are calling this stabilization because it is the part of the inflationary process during which the economy gets back to full equilibrium after an initial disturbance. Since in an actual economy conditions are likely to change before the full cycle is completed, all we are likely to observe of the stabilization is the initial contraction during which wage demands are rising faster than prices and output is falling. That is the pattern that is associated with cost-push inflation.

The first cycle occurred during the 1950s and early 1960s. It was initiated by excess demand during the Korean War and a subsequent capital goods boom in the mid-1950s. In Figure 9.6 we show the historical record of prices and Y/Y_{FE} during this period. As the reader can see, the Korean War period was one of obvious excess demand. However, because wage and price controls were imposed during the war, the rise in prices was less rapid than one might expect.

The five years after 1956 were ones in which a successful attempt was made to wring the inflation out of the system. Fiscal and monetary policies were both restrictive. The full employment surplus was positive from 1954 through 1962, except for two quarters during the recession of 1958.[4] Monetary policy was equally contractionary. Between the end of 1954 and the end of 1960, the nominal money supply increased at an average rate of 3.1 percent per year, which meant that M/P was rising at less than 1 percent per year. The predictable result of these stabilization policies was that the economy went into an extended recession. By the official definition, there were two recessions between 1955 and 1962 but in fact, as the reader can see, the economy operated below Y_{FE} for the entire period.

As our theory predicts, stabilization at first led to stagflation as prices continued to rise while output declined. However, by 1961 the adjustment appears to have been pretty much completed, setting the stage for the great expansion of the 1960s.

The second inflationary cycle took place during the years 1962–1971 (see Figure 9.7). President Johnson advocated, and the Congress passed, a large tax cut in 1964 to get the economy back to full employment after the long Eisenhower-Kennedy stabilization. Helped by supportive monetary policy, the economy moved toward full employment by 1965. At just that moment, the United States became enmeshed in a costly war in Vietnam. But we no longer had the men or machines to supply the extra output required by that conflict. For reasons that continue to be debated by historians, there was no effective reduction in demand until about 1968, when a tax surcharge went into effect and monetary policy finally became more restrictive. The result was a four-year period (1965–1968) during which demand grew far faster than the capacity of the economy (except for a short period of monetary restraint in 1966). The inevitable result was a demand-pull inflationary boom, as the reader can see from Figure 9.7.

When the government belatedly made an attempt to stabilize the economy by raising the tax rate and limiting the growth of money in 1968 and beyond, the economy almost immediately went into a recession. Unemployment rapidly rose from 3.4 percent in 1968 to 6 percent in 1971. But, as our theory predicts, prices continued to rise, presumably as a result of the lagged adjustment of worker expectations.

Frustrated by the slow gains being made against inflation, and worried about the 1972 election, President Nixon cut short the stabilization phase in August of 1971 by imposing the first peacetime wage and price controls in our history. At the

[4]The full employment surplus will be discussed in Chapter 16. It is defined as the surplus the government would run if the economy were on the long-run supply curve, or at full employment. Changes in the full employment surplus are a good indicator of changes in fiscal policy.

Figure 9.6
Inflationary Cycle, 1950–1964

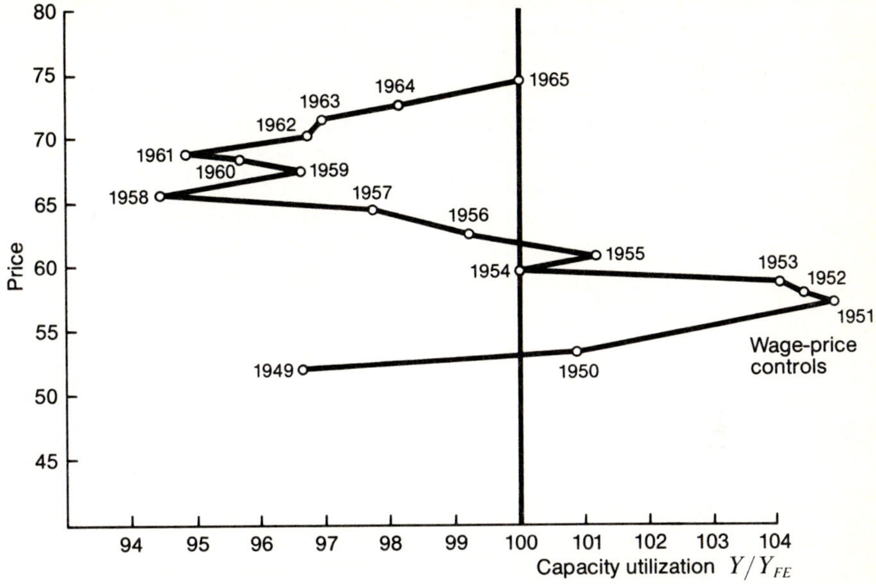

Figure 9.7
The Vietnam War Inflationary Cycle, 1962–1972

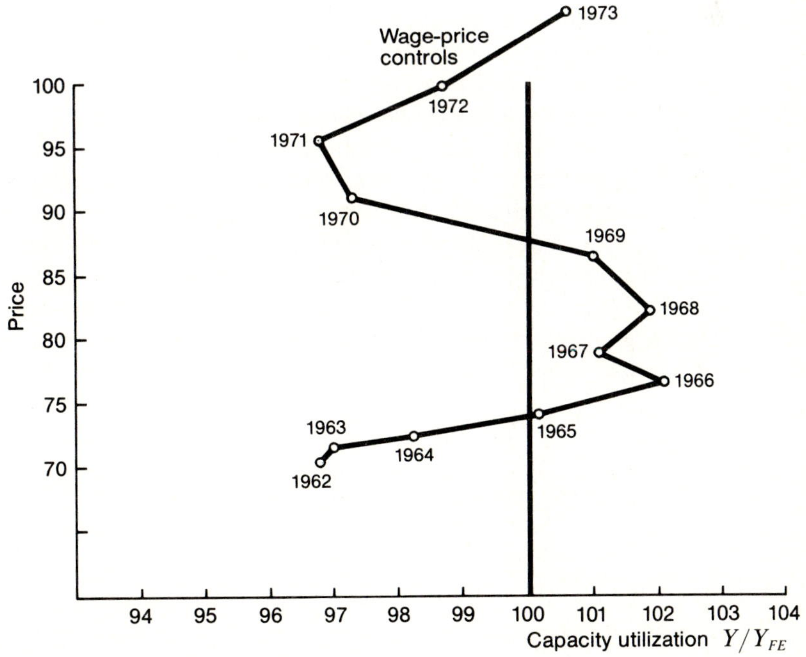

same time both monetary and fiscal policies became far more expansionary, and the economy moved rapidly back toward full employment in 1972 and 1973.

To summarize the experience of these two cycles: Both were started by periods of excess demand, followed by stabilization. In both, an initial period of demand-pull inflation was followed by an extended stabilization (cut off by Nixon's wage and price controls in 1971). During both of those stabilizations prices continued to rise, at times faster than they had during the boom phases. Thus, the S-shaped inflationary cycle, predicted by our theories as the typical response of the economy to growth in demand followed by stabilization, is very close to the actual path of prices and output in two historical instances. Economic history provides strong support for our theory of the inflationary cycle.

Rational Expectations

A key element in our theory of the short run is the behavior of price expectations. Economies move off the long-run supply curve because, even though everyone thinks in real terms, workers make forecasting errors. While our models are quite clear on the effect of forecasting errors on economic activity, they are much less clear on how expectations are actually formed.

In recent years an increasingly influential group of economists have advanced the argument that the adaptive expectations model is unsatisfactory because it does not take into account all the information available to those making wage and price decisions.[5] The adaptive expectations model assumes that prices can best be predicted by knowledge of past prices or inflation rates. But it ignores altogether the influence that current policy may have on prices. In particular, it assumes that workers either ignore or have no knowledge of what determines prices in the economy. Yet, if prices really are determined by some sort of economic model, and if they are influenced by such variables as the supply of money, then rational forecasters ought to be using that information. If they fail to do so their forecasts will contain systematic errors, because they are ignoring information.

These theorists assert that forecasts are based on rational, rather than adaptive, expectations. **Rational expectations** simply means that people use all the available information when forming their expectations. They have a particular model of the economy in mind, and they forecast the likely values of the money supply, government deficit, and any other factors that are likely to have a bearing on the price level.

[5]Most of the rational expectations articles are quite mathematical. A good introduction that isn't too technical is Bennett T. McCallum, "The Significance of Rational Expectations Theory," *Challenge* (January–February 1980): 37–43. See also McCallum's "Rational Expectations and Macroeconomic Stabilization Policy: An Overview," *Journal of Money, Credit and Banking*, vol. 12, pt. 2 (November 1980): 716–747. One of the classic early articles in the area was Thomas J. Sargent and Neil Wallace, "Rational Expectations and the Theory of Economic Policy," *Journal of Monetary Economics* 2 (April 1976): 169–183. We discuss rational expectations further in Chapter 15.

This change from adaptive to rational expectations has a dramatic effect on our model of the economy. Quite simply it implies that if workers forecast exogenous variables correctly, the aggregate short-run supply curve will be vertical. When workers understand the economy there will be no such thing as unexpected inflation, hence no trade-off between prices and output even in the short run, provided that the government does not surprise everyone with an unexpected change in policy.

To see this more clearly, consider the example we used for the F-P model in Chapter 8. It had the following equations:

$$Y = \frac{2M}{P}. \tag{9.3}$$

$$Y = \frac{K}{3}\left(\frac{P}{P_{e,t}}\right). \tag{9.4}$$

$$P_e = \frac{P_{t-1}^2}{P_{t-2}}. \tag{9.5}$$

This generates a reduced-form equation for Y:

$$Y = \sqrt{\frac{2MK}{3P_e}}. \tag{9.6}$$

Our transition equation, Equation (9.5), completely ignores the information contained in the model of the economy, in particular the influence of the money supply on prices. If we suppose that Equation (9.3) is accurate, a far better forecast of prices should be possible than with Equation (9.5).

In particular, a rational expected price should be based on a reduced form for price.[6] It is

$$P_e = \frac{6M_e}{K}. \tag{9.7}$$

M_e = expected money supply

Note that we have pushed the forecast problem back from the price to the values of exogenous variables that influence the price.

Now substitute Equation (9.7) into Equation (9.6) to get:

$$Y = \frac{K}{3}\sqrt{\frac{M}{M_e}}. \tag{9.8}$$

[6]Remember that according to rational expectations, people use a model of the economy to forecast. Since Equation (9.3) is the determinant of prices, that is what forecasters should use.

Equation (9.8) tells us that if workers correctly forecast the money supply, the economy will be on its long-run supply curve. This implies that it is unexpected bursts of money creation that cause short-run booms and unexpected contractions that cause recessions. It is not price behavior that fools workers temporarily—it is erratic demand management by the government.

The reader may be wondering whether the substitution of rational for adaptive expectations would have the same effect in the disequilibrium economy that it has in the partial equilibrium model. The answer is that it would. If one uses the equations of our example and substitutes Equation (9.7) in for P_e, it is possible to show that Y will settle at the long-run equilibrium level so long as workers correctly forecast the money supply. Thus, in either model, rational expectations has a quite dramatic effect on the interpretation of short-run equilibrium.

The rational expectations model has some very important policy implications. First, if the government wants to stabilize, it must first convince the public that it is serious, and then it must follow through on its promises by actually reducing the expansion of demand. If it does that, stabilization need not take nearly as long as implied by the short-run supply curve of either of our models. Rational expectations therefore implies a good deal more wage and price flexibility than adaptive expectations in our models, so long as the government's determination to stabilize is itself credible. In other words, if people believe the government is serious, then stabilization will probably quite rapidly stop inflation.

According to the rational expectations model, most of the inflationary stagnation of recent years is not due to slow adjustment of price expectations. Rather, it is due to the fact that the public must have believed that the money supply was going to grow faster than it did. Workers must have had little faith in the government's protestations that it was trying to control inflation by reducing the expansion in aggregate demand. Wage demands remained high not because of past inflation but because of high expected government deficits and high expected increases in the money supply.[7] For example, in our stabilization policy experiment we increased the rate of monetary expansion from 0 percent to 5 percent and then stabilized by reducing the growth in money to 2 percent. If workers had used Equation (9.3) to predict the price level, and if they had been able to predict the changes in monetary policy, they would not have made the forecasting errors that caused our two economies to have extended cycles in response to changes in the rate of growth of demand.

Our new model has an even more far-reaching implication than those discussed so far. It says that the government cannot systematically affect the level of income in the economy if the public uses rational expectations and is *able to forecast* government policy. This is the basic conclusion of Equation (9.8) for our simple model, and it is true in general for rational expectations models. Only unex-

[7]William Fellner has stressed the credibility aspect of stabilization policy. His argument is that people don't believe that the government is serious about reducing inflation and that is why the expected inflation rate has been so slow to adjust. People's low confidence in government resolve is thus what causes stabilizations, according to Fellner. See William J. Fellner, "The Credibility Effect and Rational Expectations: Implications of the Gramlich Study," *Brookings Papers on Economic Activity* (1, 1979): 167–78.

pected changes in policy will succeed in pushing the economy off the long-run supply curve. Therefore, *if* people form their expectations rationally, activist government demand management is not a very constructive long-run policy.

Many economists are skeptical about the relevance of the rational expectations model. Some point out that it is doubtful that people are so knowledgeable about economic matters that they can predict prices on the basis of an economic model;[8] they probably use some sort of rule of thumb instead. Experience during the most recent recession seems to bear out this claim. Despite the fact that the Fed announced and produced a lower rate of growth of the money supply during a fairly extended period (more than two years), wage settlements still continued to rise at double-digit rates.

Other economists have pointed out that even if expectations are rational, many labor contracts are multiyear. Hence, a change in conditions occurring during a contract would have a short-run effect on output even if workers were to revise their price expectations. In the real world, multiyear contracts and rule-of-thumb price and wage decisions slow down the adjustment of prices and wages to changes in demand. We shall return to rational expectations in our discussion of policy issues in Chapter 15.

Supply-Shock Inflation

The inflations we have analyzed so far have all been started by excess aggregate demand. Such inflations may be prolonged by workers' wage demands once inflationary expectations turn positive, but the initial impetus is an increase in demand too great to be supplied at constant prices. In recent years we have become all too familiar with another form of inflation, one that is started by price increases for key raw materials. We might call this type of inflation **supply-shock inflation,** to indicate that the initial cause of the inflation is a sudden, large leftward shift in the economy supply curve.

Twice in recent years we have experienced just such abrupt interruptions in supply. In early 1973, there was a worldwide crop failure that drove up food prices by over 20 percent in a single quarter in the United States. This was followed in the fall of the same year by the Arab oil embargo and subsequent quadrupling of the price of oil. These two events started a supply-shock inflation epidemic in all western economies. In 1979, as though we needed further instruction in this particular disease, we got another dose of inflation from the supply side when OPEC doubled the price of oil.

We would now like to use the model we have developed to examine the process by which the economy reacts to supply shocks. As we will see, such inflations present policymakers with a dilemma: They must accept either higher prices or a long period of stabilization to drive down domestic real wages.

[8]In particular, see James Tobin, "Are New Classical Models Plausible Enough to Guide Policy," *Journal of Money, Credit and Banking,* vol. 12, pt. 2 (November 1980): 788–800.

Imagine an economy in long-run equilibrium as shown at point A in Figure 9.8. For simplicity, suppose that prices are stable and that there is no productivity growth. What happens if the price of imported oil is suddenly quadrupled, as it was in late 1973 and 1974?

Imported oil is an input into the production process. When its price goes up, both the short- and the long-run supply curves shift to the left as shown in Figure 9.8. The long-run curve shifts for two reasons. First, the United States has to export more to pay for oil. The long-run supply curve shows the amount of *domestic* production available to satisfy demand. If Americans have to sell more abroad to buy oil, domestic supply falls even if production does not. This causes the long-run supply curve to contract. One could think of a rise in the price of oil as a sort of tax by which Americans pay a larger part of their domestic production for imported oil.[9] In the United States, it is estimated that the quadrupling in the price of oil was equivalent to a tax by foreigners of about 1–2 percent of U. S. GNP.

The second reason the long-run curve shifts to the left is that the rise in oil prices requires a reduction in the real wages of U. S. workers. Since businesspersons have to pay more for oil, they will be forced to raise prices even if wages stay constant. That, of course, implies a reduction in the real wage. If the long-run labor supply curve is positively related to the real wage, there will be a long-run reduction in employment and production in response to a rise in the price of oil. This will shift the long-run supply curve even further to the left.

What about the short-run supply curve? Here we have to distinguish between the situations before and after labor reacts to the change in prices. Start with a given level of money wages. Suppose that wages were constant and businesspersons could cover the cost of the oil price hike with a 5-percent increase in prices. In that case, the short-run supply curve would shift to S' in Figure 9.8. This curve has, at most, a temporary significance, because workers have not responded to the necessary decline in their real wages. When they have done this, we will have a whole family of short-run supply curves, each of which intersects the Y'_{FE} at the price level expected by the labor force. We show one such curve in the diagram (S''), that for $P_e = 110$. It is drawn under the assumption that businesspersons must raise their prices by 5 percent to cover oil costs and an additional 5 percent to cover the rise in money wages and the fall in labor productivity that result from labor's delayed reaction to the initial rise in prices. Note that if workers would allow the money wage to decline, the short-run supply curve could just as well shift down as up.

Now let us see what this change in supply does to output and prices. Obviously that depends on what happens to wages and aggregate demand. If both are unchanged, the economy moves from point A to point B. The result of the oil shock is an inflationary recession. Note that the flatter the supply curve, the worse the recession and the greater the rise in prices will be.

[9]The case that we are analyzing here is an example of a general class of factors that contract supply. Another example is a decline in the capital stock. Note that if oil were used not as an input into production but only as a consumer good, there would be no contraction in Y_{FE} if workers were willing to accept the decline in real wages implied by a rise in the price of oil. The same is true for an increase in social security taxes.

Figure 9.8
Supply-Shock Inflation
A rise in oil prices reduces equilibrium output from Y_{FE} to Y'_{FE}. The supply curve S' is drawn assuming money wages are constant. If demand is held constant, the economy moves to point B. The supply shock causes a simultaneous rise in prices and a fall in output. If the government decides to accommodate the price rise, it increases demand to D'. D' intersects the new long-run supply curve, Y'_{FE}, at point C, the intersection of the short-run supply curve S'' that incorporates fully labor's reaction to the oil price increase. Point C is a full equilibrium. Thus, with an accommodating policy, the oil shock causes a permanent increase in prices and loss of output.

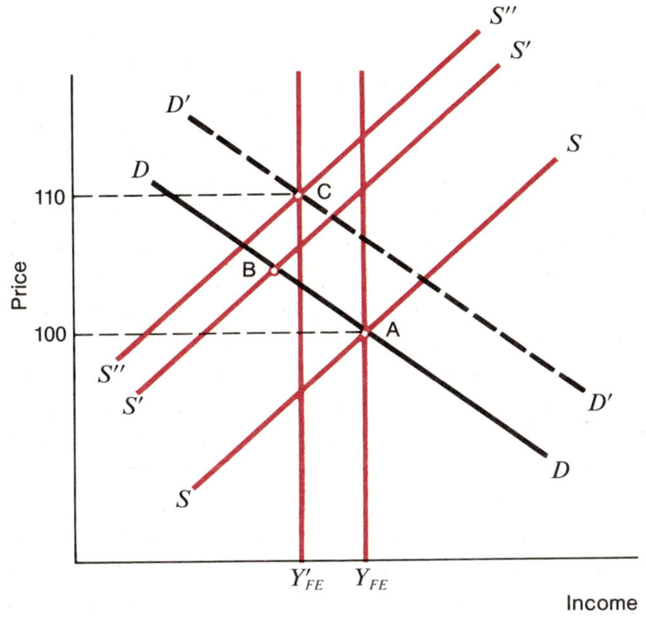

Clearly point B is not a long-run equilibrium, since the economy is off its long-run supply curve. When workers begin to try to adjust their wages to the unforeseen change in prices, there probably will be further inflation.

Accommodating Demand Policy

Essentially there are two ways to get back to full equilibrium. One is to validate the input price increase by allowing aggregate demand to increase. We shall call this an **accommodating demand policy.** In Figure 9.8, the government allows aggregate demand to increase by 10 percent less the percentage reduction in Y_{FE}, shifting DD out to $D'D'$. As a result, the economy moves to point C, perhaps with a delay. In this case, the supply shock causes first a short recession and then a permanent 10-percent increase in prices.

Figure 9.9
Effects of Different Policy Responses to Supply-Shock Inflation

In (a) we show what happens when the government raises demand but workers expect inflation. In that case the supply curve shifts further than S', and the economy has a stabilization recession even though the authorities have increased demand. In (b) the authorities convert a temporary inflation into a permanent one by continuing to increase demand beyond D'. They do this to avoid the stabilization recession shown in (a). In (c) we show what happens when the authorities hold demand constant. Eventually the bulge in prices is eliminated, but the cost is a fairly severe recession. The arrows represent the likely pathway of the disequilibrium economy. As usual, the stabilizations are more severe than they are in F–P-type economies.

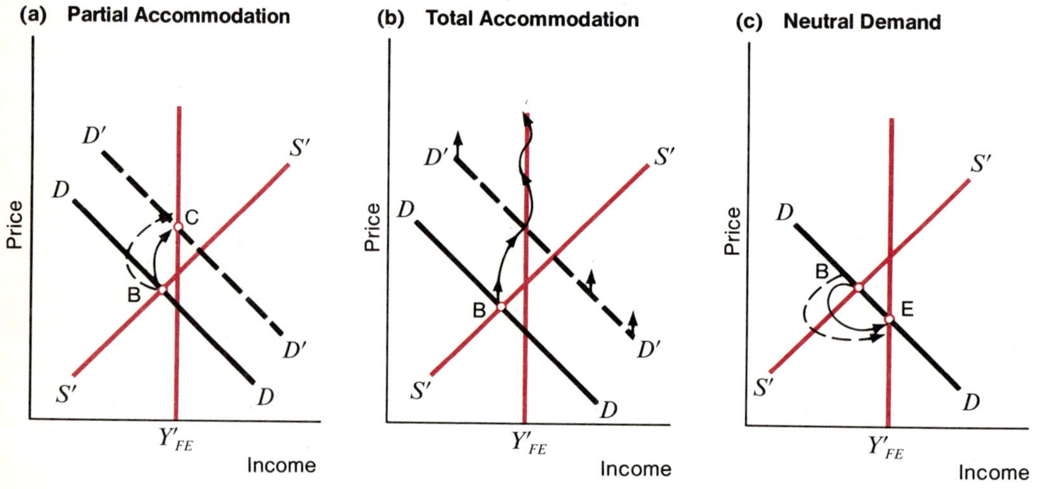

Even with accommodating policy, the return to equilibrium at point C is likely to be accompanied by recessions in economies like the United States where workers have learned to expect inflation. For then the rise in the price index due to the oil shock is likely to be projected forward, in which case workers will demand wage increases to compensate for the expected continuation of inflation. When that happens, the economy does not simply move to point C when demand increases and then stop. Rather, the short-run supply curve will continue to shift upward and to the left, plunging the economy into a further inflationary recession. The authorities then have the choice of holding demand at $D'D'$ and waiting for recessions to squeeze erroneous inflation expectations out of the system or of validating those expectations by allowing a further increase in aggregate demand. If they choose the latter route, they may turn a one-time supply-side shock into a permanently higher rate of inflation.

In diagrams (a) and (b) of Figure 9.9, we show the long-run equilibria that we have been discussing and the pathways that the economy is likely to take in getting to them. We shall call the first partially accommodating, since the authorities allow a one-time increase in demand, and the second totally accommodating. As the reader can see, in the partially accommodating case the final equilibrium is at point

C, but the economy will still have a stabilization recession before it comes to rest if workers adjust upward their expectations about inflation in response to the supply shock.

Authorities are likely to follow the totally accommodating policy in economies where workers build projected inflation into their wage demands and where wages are insensitive to the level of unemployment, because such a policy avoids stabilization recession. In that case, rather than reaching long-run equilibrium at point C and stopping, both the supply curve and the demand curve continue to shift upward. A stabilization recession is avoided, but only at the cost of a permanently higher rate of inflation.

Neutral Demand Policy

Rather than allowing demand to increase, the authorities may elect to hold it constant at its original level. This we shall call a **neutral demand policy,** shown in diagram (c) of Figure 9.9. When the government follows this course, the economy must eventually return to point E. At E prices are slightly higher than they were originally because of the fall in Y_{FE}. However, getting from point B to point E is not likely to be easy. Recall that at point B, workers' wages are based on a constant level of expected prices. When prices rise in response to the oil shock, the immediate reaction of wages is almost certainly going to be a rise, not a decline. And yet, a decline in real wages is necessary in order to get back into long-run equilibrium at point E. The situation will be even worse if workers project the inflation rate forward. If that happens, they are likely to demand wage increases for both the initial and the expected future inflation. This will cause the short-run supply curve to shift further to the left, exacerbating the inflationary recessions.

If the authorities refuse to allow demand to increase, eventually the rising volume of unemployment should begin to force the wage rate down. That will allow the aggregate supply curve to decline until it finally intersects demand at point E. Unfortunately, it may take a long while for this to happen if the economy is one in which unemployment is only weakly related to the wage rate.

In diagram (c) of Figure 9.9, we show the general path by which an economy reacts to a supply shock when the authorities follow a neutral demand policy. There will be a counterclockwise loop, implying further stagflation. As usual, the length and severity of this stabilization period will be longer the flatter the short-run supply curve and the more wages include projected future inflation. In economies with flat supply curves, supply shocks may unleash a long period of stagflation as the economy seeks to find a set of wages and prices acceptable to the authorities and consistent with long-run equilibrium. If the equilibrating forces are weak, wages may never be forced down far enough to get back to full equilibrium output. Supply shocks could quite easily result in a permanent recession or a permanently higher inflation rate.

Stabilization Recessions in Supply-Shock Inflation

In many ways the stabilization required to bring the economy back to the new long-run supply curve is the same as the stabilization phase of the inflationary process. In both cases, the stabilization is necessary to drive down wage demands that are too high. But in one fundamental way, the two stabilizations are different. In the stabilization phase, wage demands are too high because of erroneous expectations, and the stabilization seeks only to *reestablish* the long-run equilibrium real wage. But in the supply-side stabilizations we are analyzing here, real wages must be reduced. If imported energy prices are to rise in real terms, as they must at the new full equilibrium, real wages must decline. Businesspersons can afford to supply the long-run level of output only if the real wage rate declines enough to offset the rise in energy prices. Stabilization will have to go on long enough to force workers to accept this decline in real wages. That is likely to take a long while.

As the reader can see, none of the policy choices facing the government in a supply-shock inflation is very appealing. Both the neutral and the partially accommodating policies require a stabilization recession, and in both of the accommodating policies prices rise above the level reached immediately after the initial disturbance. Supply shocks pose unpleasant policy alternatives for policymakers. They cause either inflation or recessions, and in many cases they may well cause both at the same time.

Structural Inflation

The phenomenon we are examining here is an example of what has been called **structural inflation,** which means inflation caused by supply-side bottlenecks rather than excess demand.[10] Opponents of the structuralist inflation idea follow Milton Friedman in insisting that all inflations, including the one after the oil and food price hikes in 1973, are caused by too fast an expansion of the money supply. Supply bottlenecks force up the relative price of scarce commodities, but that does not mean that all prices have to rise. The aggregate price index goes up only if the monetary authorities accommodate the rise in sectoral prices by expanding the money supply. As we saw in the example, when they do this the economy returns to long-run equilibrium with higher prices and a higher money supply. But if the authorities do not increase the money supply, eventually wages decline enough to allow prices to fall back to their initial level. Thus, the rise in the money supply is a necessary condition for prices to go up. Even though the initial disturbance is not the monetary expansion, a permanent rise in prices will not happen without it. One could say that a supply shock either causes prices to go up or causes an extended recession. Neither is a pleasant alternative.

Structuralists say that growth in the presence of supply bottlenecks causes inflation, while monetarists insist that the cause is excess money creation. In a way, both sides are right. With supply bottlenecks and flat supply curves, either an

[10]There is an enormous body of literature on monetarist versus structuralist theories of inflation. For an early discussion, see the articles in Albert O. Hirschman, ed., *Latin American Issues: Essays and Comments* (New York: Twentieth Century Fund, 1961). A very interesting later contribution, which widens the scope of this discussion and shows that the Latin American experience can happen elsewhere, is in Marcelo Diamand, "Towards a Change in the Economic Paradigm through the Experience of the Developing Countries," *Journal of Development Economics* 5 (March 1978): 19–55.

economy grows with rising prices and a rising money supply or it stagnates with constant prices and money. Thus, structural inflation is the reaction of an economy with flat supply curves to growth with supply-side bottlenecks and permissive monetary authorities.[11]

Case Study

Supply-Shock Inflation, 1972–1978

As we have already indicated, the United States suffered a severe bout of supply-shock inflation in the mid-1970s. In 1972 the economy was in the midst of a boom. Expansionary fiscal and monetary policies had dispelled the stabilization recession of 1969–1971, and wage and price controls seemed, for the moment at least, to be keeping inflation under control. As the reader can see in diagram (b) of Figure 9.10, by the fourth quarter of 1972 the economy was operating above its long-run capacity. At just this moment, two momentous events hit the economy at the same time: President Nixon lifted wage and price controls, and the world experienced a crop failure. During the first quarter of 1973 food prices rose by almost one-fourth, and then nine months later OPEC embargoed its oil and then quadrupled the price.

The effect on the economy of such supply shocks depends critically upon what happens to demand. In this case, the United States chose not to validate the supply-side price increases. Demand management was neutral to contractionary. The fight was led by the Fed. For each of the three years starting in 1973, the money supply fell in real terms, and even by the end of 1978 M/P had not regained the value it had reached six years earlier. This contractionary monetary policy was reinforced by fiscal policy in the key years, 1973 and 1974.

Our theoretical model predicts that restricting demand in the face of a supply shock will lead to stagflation. That is exactly what happened in the United States, according to Figure 9.10. The economy fell into the most severe recession of the postwar period, yet prices continued to rise as workers demanded compensation for rising food and energy costs. The only difference between the actual result and the pathways to equilibrium that we have discussed is that the economy started from a base inflation of about 5 to 6 percent prior to the oil shock, and it returned to that rate of inflation rather than to constant prices.[12]

[11]Following the rational expectations idea, one could argue that the flat supply curves are a result of labor knowing that the monetary authorities don't have the courage to force a stabilization through restrictive monetary policy.

[12]For simplicity, we have kept our diagrammatic analysis in terms of price levels rather than rates of change of prices. That is somewhat awkward when we try to compare our diagram to actual experience, because there appears to be a base or residual inflation rate of about 6 percent. Thus the reader has to bear in mind that the economy does not settle at a point on our diagram. Equilibrium with a constant inflation rate means that the full equilibrium points are moving straight north on our diagram.

Figure 9.10
Hypothetical and Actual Response of the U.S. Economy to Supply Shocks with Neutral to Contractionary Demand Policy

The supply shock of 1973–1974 was met at first with a neutral to contractionary demand-side policy. As our theory predicts, the economy had an inflationary recession. The only difference between the theory and the history is that by 1977 the government, under President Carter, allowed demand to increase before the economy had returned to the original inflation rate. In the United States, therefore, the oil shock led to a higher inflation rate.

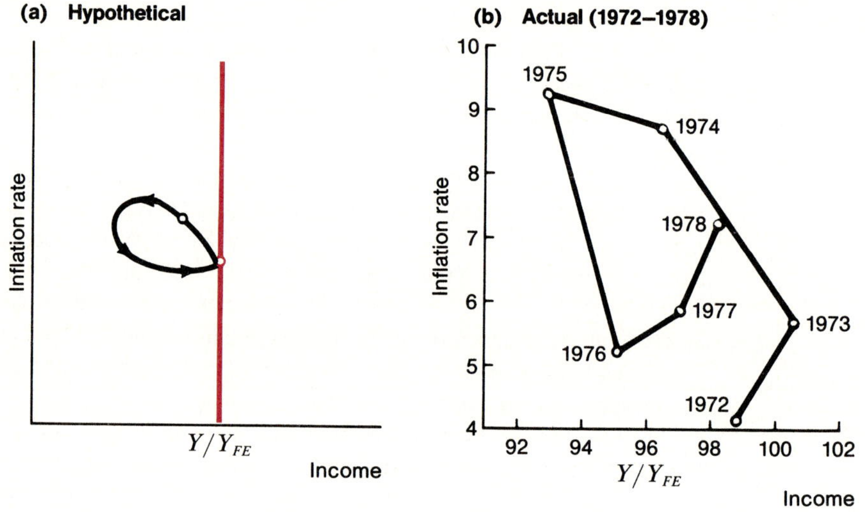

To show the similarity of the actual and predicted experience of the U.S. economy, it is useful to convert our goods market diagram from one relating price and output to one relating output to the rate of inflation. When one does that the counterclockwise loop—that is, the predicted response to neutral or contractionary policy—is exactly what was observed in the U. S. economy from 1974 to 1976 (see Figure 9.10). As the reader can see, the stabilization did not fully eliminate inflation, but it did succeed in limiting the inflationary damage from the oil price hike. After a severe recession, the economy returned to its original rate of inflation.

The only way to cut inflation further would have been an even more prolonged period of recession to force domestic factors of production to accept lower real wages and profits. But the political will to endure such a recession had evaporated. Indeed, the severe recession and uncertain recovery during his presidency probably cost Gerald Ford the election in 1976. Jimmy Carter was elected, at least implicitly, with a promise not to fight inflation any further with recession. As a result, after his election fiscal policy became somewhat more expansionary, and the economy returned slowly to full employment, restrained by a still contractionary Fed under Arthur Burns.

Summary: A Look Ahead

In this chapter we showed how our two model economies react to a change in the growth rate of aggregate demand. Of particular interest—in light of recent U. S. experience—is the effect of slowing down the growth rate of the money supply. We showed that this causes a stabilization recession in either economy as workers adjust to a lower rate of inflation. As expected, the recessions are longer and more severe in the disequilibrium-type economy because of its relatively flat supply curve.

A key role in both of our macromodels is played by expected prices. In this chapter we examined briefly the effect of our assumption about how price expectations are formed. We have assumed that price expectations are adaptive, meaning that they are based on past prices. However, if price expectations are formed rationally, that is, based on a model of the economy rather than the past behavior of prices, the short-run behavior of the economy will be dramatically different. With rational expectations, economies go out of full equilibrium only when the public is unable to predict the values of the exogenous variables that are likely to affect the economy. Specifically, if the public can accurately forecast government policy, there should be no effect on employment or output, no matter what that policy is. Only unexpected changes in policy can have a real impact on the economy.

Finally, in this chapter, we examined the problem of supply-shock inflation. We showed that a supply shock reduces the capacity of the economy. In response the government can do one of the following three things:

a. Hold demand constant (neutral policy). Here there will be a stabilization recession, a permanent drop in output, and a rise in the price level.
b. Increase aggregate demand enough to offset the wage demands resulting from the supply shock (partial accommodation). Here the economy returns to full equilibrium with a less severe recession but also with higher prices than with the neutral policy.
c. Increase the growth rate of aggregate demand enough to accommodate the growth rate of wage demands resulting from the supply shock (full accommodation). Here the economy returns to the full equilibrium more rapidly than in either of the first two cases, but the economy also has a permanently higher inflation rate.

In the last nine chapters we have presented our basic model of the economy in terms of the relationship between supply, demand, and the level of prices. An alternative approach, known as the Phillips curve, makes the relationship between unemployment and changes in the price level the key feature in the analysis of the macroeconomy. Because of the widespread use of the Phillips curve and the social significance of unemployment, we now show the derivation of the Phillips curve for our two alternative models of the economy.

Key Concepts

stagflation
inflationary cycle
expansionary phase
stabilization phase
demand-pull inflation
cost-push inflation
rational expectations
supply-shock inflation
accommodating demand policy
neutral demand policy
structural inflation

Problems and Questions for Discussion

1. According to the temporary equilibrium model, when actual income is less than potential income, the rate of inflation is less than expected. Over time one would then expect inflation rates to be declining. How can one explain the fact that in 1977 and 1978 inflation rates accelerated even though Y was less than Y_{FE}?

2. If the supply curve is flat in the disequilibrium model for $Y < Y_{FE}$, by what process would a recession moderate the inflation rate?

3. Milton Friedman asserts that all inflations are caused by monetary expansion. Using the models we have developed in Chapters 6–9, how would you respond to this assertion? Must an increase in the money supply lead to an increase in prices? Is there a difference between the short and the long run?

4. Discuss the various responses that could be adopted to fight supply-shock inflation. What are the implications of each of your policies for output and the inflation rate?

5. The rise in oil prices in 1973 was like a tax by OPEC on U. S. citizens. The rise in prices in 1973 increased our payments for oil by $18 billion, which was about 1.5 percent of GNP. In responding to this price increase, the U. S. economy endured a severe recession and a period of slow growth in which the accumulated gap between actual and potential output reached over 30 percent of GNP between the years of 1974 and 1978. Why did the United States have to give up 30 percent of GNP in order to pay a tax that did not amount to more than 1–2 percent of GNP?

6. Describe the short- and long-run reactions you expect to occur in an economy in which there is a "once-and-for-all" reduction in the growth rate of the money supply from 10 percent to 5 percent. What will be the differences in response in partial equilibrium and disequilibrium economies?

7. Suppose that your mother calls up to complain to you that President Reagan's plans to run large deficits will be inflationary. Are government deficits always inflationary? If so, why? If not, under what conditions are they inflationary and under what conditions are they not?

8. How might one's beliefs regarding the slope of the aggregate supply curve influence one's policy recommendations during recessions and during inflations?

9. What is the effect on the short-run supply curve of the economy of the substitution of rational for adaptive expectations? Give a verbal description for why the supply curve changes. What policy implications follow from the rational expectations model?

Chapter 10

Unemployment, Inflation, and the Phillips Curve

In this chapter we are going to look more closely at the implications of our models for unemployment. There is a good deal of disagreement among economists over what causes unemployment in our economy, why our unemployment rates are so high, and what, if anything, we can do about it. In this chapter we shall examine the following questions: What is the nature of unemployment? How is the natural rate of unemployment determined, why is it so high, and why is it still growing? Why is there so much teen-age unemployment? We shall also examine the relationship between unemployment and the inflation rate, a relation commonly known as the Phillips curve.

The Definition and Nature of Unemployment in the United States

Unemployment has become an increasingly serious problem in the United States because of its rapid growth since the 1950s. Between 1954 and 1970 the unemployment rate averaged 4.9 percent. Since 1970 it has been above that rate every single year but 1973. At the same time there has been a slow but steady increase in the so-called natural or full equilibrium rate of unemployment. Both of these unfavorable trends are clearly visible in Figure 10.1.

Our statistics on unemployment are based on a rotating sample, run by the U.S. Census Bureau, of about 55,000 households.[1] Each separate household member is asked if he or she was working most or all of the preceding week. The

[1] For more information see *How the Government Measures Unemployment,* BLS Report, no. 505 (Washington, D.C.: U. S. Bureau of Labor Statistics, 1977).

Figure 10.1
Trend in Actual and Natural Rate of Unemployment, 1947–1982

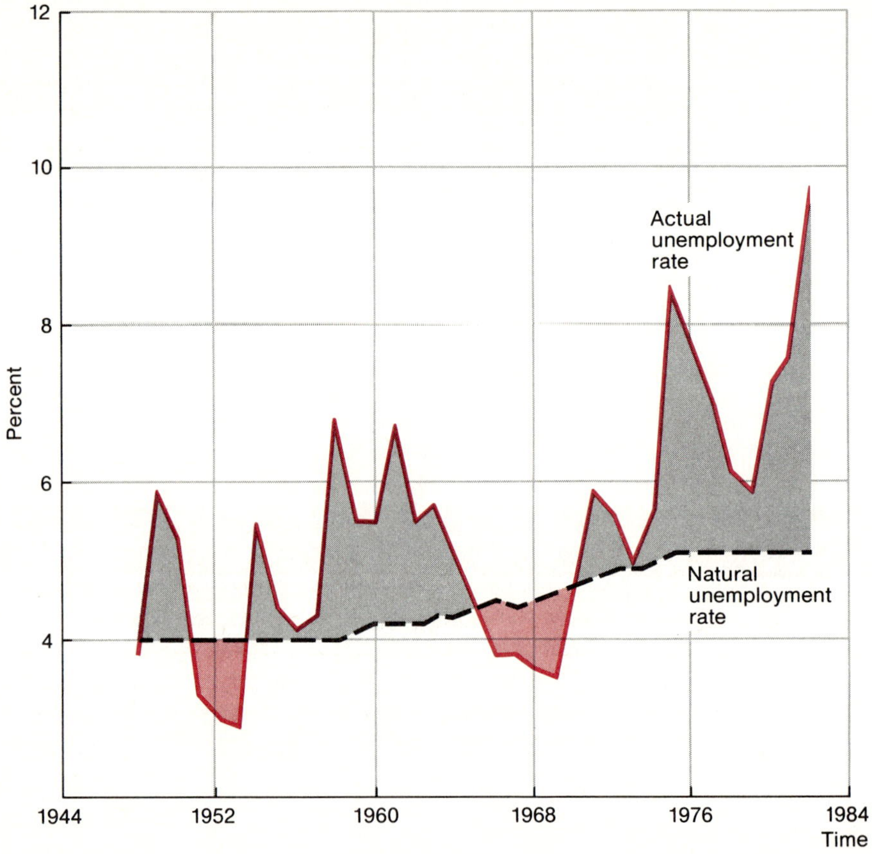

person is counted as employed if he or she did any work for pay, either full or part time, during that week. For those who answer that they were not working, the next question is whether or not they were on layoff or waiting for a job to begin. People in either of these categories are counted as unemployed. For those not working and not on temporary layoff, the next task is to determine whether they should be counted as in the labor force but unemployed or whether they should be counted as out of the labor force. That turns out to be a difficult distinction to draw.

Formally, the distinction between being unemployed and out of the labor force is easy to make. If the person actively searched for work, he or she is counted as unemployed; if not, he or she is left out of the labor force. The difficulty is in determining how actively one has to be searching for work in order to be unemployed. Does asking relatives about job prospects or making a telephone call to a friend about a possible job count as an active job search? The statistics show that the line is a tenuous one, dividing the unemployed from discouraged workers who want work but are not looking actively and hence are not in the labor force. Recent studies indicate that a fairly high proportion of those suffering long spells of unemployment terminate by leaving the labor force and not getting another job. The same is apparently true for teen-agers.[2]

The reason this is important is that reporting only the "actively unemployed" may seriously bias downward the extent of the unemployment problem. Finegan estimates that in the first quarter in 1978 there were about 900,000 of these discouraged workers—defined as people who wanted work but had not looked for work during the four weeks prior to the census interviews. If included among the unemployed, they would have added 1 percent to the 7 percent published unemployment rate.[3] Furthermore, if there is a tendency of the unemployed to leave the labor force, the statistics on the duration of unemployment will be biased as well.

Another point to remember about the unemployment statistics is that they make no distinction between the unemployment of primary wage earners with families and teen-agers seeking part-time work. Yet clearly the distress in the first case is more severe than in the second.

Unemployment by Composition, Duration, and Reason

Having made these cautionary remarks about the unemployment statistics, we shall now look at several different profiles of unemployment. Figure 10.2 shows how the composition of unemployment has changed since 1947. What is immediately evident from that chart is the rise in teen-age, black, and female unemployment as a fraction of the total. Figure 10.3 shows age-sex specific unemployment rates for key subgroups in the population. That diagram eloquently makes the point that unemployment is not borne equally across the population. Blacks, teen-agers, and women all have higher unemployment rates than prime-age males (ages 21–64). Furthermore, these tend to be the groups who are hurt worst by recessions. Look at the large jumps in the unemployment rates relative to the rate for prime-age males during recession years, such as 1958, 1970, and 1975. Finally, note the apparent rising trend of the unemployment rate for blacks relative to the rates for the other groups. For reasons that are not entirely understood, during the recovery in the late 1970s there was little decline in the black unemployment rate even though the rates for all other groups returned to the levels of the early 1970s. Unemployment trends during the 1980–1981 recession only reinforce this picture of the apparently inequitable burden of unemployment.

Another way of looking at the unemployment statistics is by the duration and the reason for unemployment. These are shown in Table 10.1 for the fourth quarter

[2] Kim B. Clark and Laurence H. Summers, "Labor Market Dynamics and Unemployment: A Reconsideration," *Brookings Papers on Economic Activity* (1/1979): 31–33.

[3] T. Aldrich Finegan, "Should Discouraged Workers be Counted as Unemployed?" *Challenge* 21 (November–December 1978): 20–25.

Figure 10.2
Percent of Total Unemployment, 1947–1982

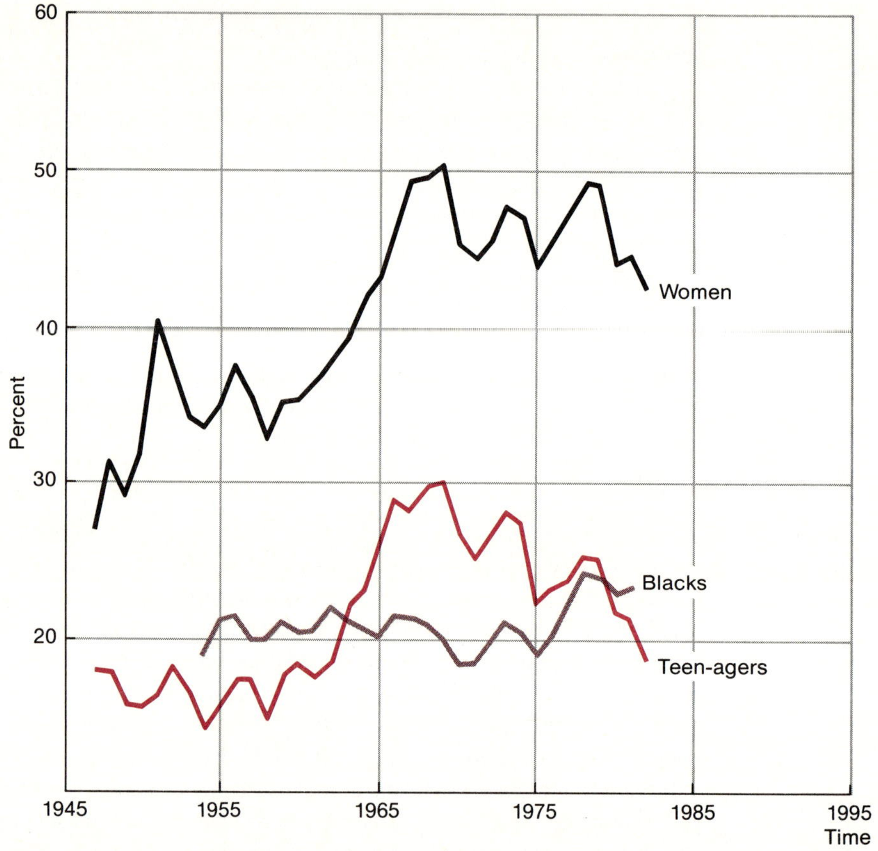

of 1978, a time of relatively full employment, and the fourth quarter of 1980, when the economy had slipped into recession. In 1978 there were 5.9 million unemployed workers. Of those nearly half had been unemployed less than five weeks, a statistic that many people have interpreted as indicating that for most people spells of unemployment are short. Only a small fraction of the unemployed had been unemployed as long as six months.

The evidence from 1978 suggests that most unemployment is short-term turnover, just what one would expect in a labor market where both workers and jobs are heterogeneous and where search takes time. The median duration of unemployment was a low 5.7 weeks, which means that half of the 6 million unemployed had been unemployed for less than that length of time. In short, in 1978 most unemployment does not look like a serious social problem. Granted, there were 530,000 workers who had been looking for work for more than six months. But in a labor force of almost 100 million, that does not seem like such a large number.

Figure 10.3
Incidence of Unemployment by Group, 1947–1982

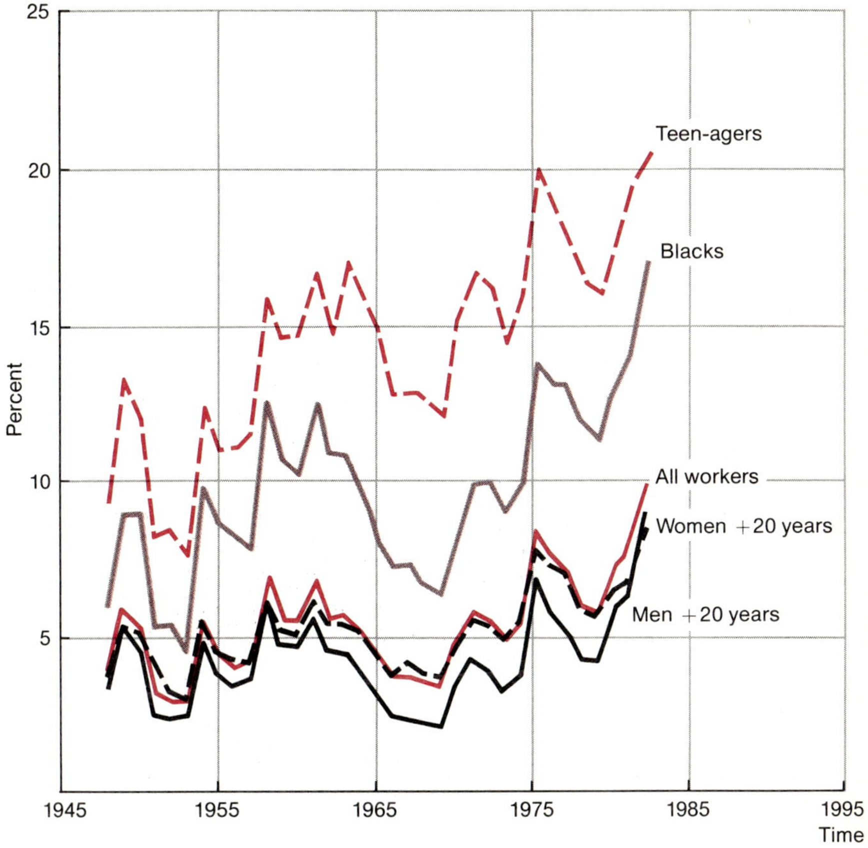

The same general impression of a labor market with a large pass-through of workers who are voluntarily unemployed for short periods of time is reinforced in the bottom half of Table 10.1. There we see the reason for unemployment. Something like 60 percent of the unemployed were either reentering the labor market, seeking their first job, or voluntarily unemployed in the sense of having left their last jobs. Only 30 percent were job losers, the remainder being workers on temporary layoff. Such workers have a high probability of returning to their old jobs.

Before taking a closer look at this relatively optimistic interpretation of these unemployment statistics, consider what happened to unemployment as the economy went into recession in 1980. As expected, the median duration of unemployment lengthened and the proportion unemployed for longer than 15 weeks jumped from 21 percent to 30 percent; indeed, one-half of the 2 million increase in unemployment came from the growth in long-run (over 15 weeks) unemployment. Also as expected, the percent of job losers among the unemployed jumped sharply.

Table 10.1
Unemployment by Duration and Reason, 1978 and 1980

Duration (weeks)	1978 IV (Thousands)	%	1980 IV (Thousands)	%
0–5	2820	48	3136	40
5–14	1863	31	2414	31
15–26	717	12	1233	16
+27	530	9	1100	14
Total	5930		7883	
Mean duration (weeks)	11.2		13.5	
Median duration (weeks)	5.7		7.5	
Reason for unemployment				
Lost last job	2449	41	4231	53
Layoff	718	12	1538	19
Other job loser	1731	29	2693	34
Left last job	853	14	860	11
Reenter labor market	1806	30	1926	24
Seeking first job	846	14	879	11
Total	5954		7896	

Source: U. S. Bureau of Labor Statistics.

The Nature of Unemployment

What do these numbers tell us about the nature of unemployment? The general consensus now appears to be that the bulk of unemployment during relatively tight labor markets is a revolving pool of frictionally unemployed rather than **structural unemployment,** defined as people who are unemployable because their job skills do not match the structure of jobs in the economy at any level of aggregate demand. According to this view, unemployment results from random fluctuations in demand across geographically or functionally separate labor markets. People lose or leave their jobs, and it takes time for them to find new ones.[4]

If this is the nature of most unemployment, it does not seem to be as serious a social problem as the raw percentages of unemployment might suggest. For according to search theory, unemployment is a way of acquiring information about the job market; it is a way of finding the most productive match between heterogeneous workers and jobs. While no one would dismiss the problem of the small

[4] The pioneering study along this line was Robert E. Hall, "Why is the Unemployment Rate so High at Full Employment?" *Brookings Papers on Economic Activity* (3/1970): 369–402. See also Stephen T. Marston, "Employment Instability and High Unemployment Rates," *Brookings Papers on Economic Activity* (1/1976): 169–203, and George L. Perry, "Unemployment Flows in the U. S. Labor Market," *Brookings Papers on Economic Activity* (2/1972): 245–278.

number of long-term unemployed shown in Table 10.1 as irrelevant or even insignificant, the data seem to indicate a labor market that quite successfully generates jobs for nearly all of those who want them. The unemployment problem, according to Robert Hall, is high turnover among certain groups such as teen-agers, females, and blacks, not the lack of jobs per se. As he put it, the problem is not one of finding jobs for groups with high unemployment but rather of finding jobs that are worth keeping.[5]

This optimistic view of unemployment as primarily short term, frictional, and related to search has recently been contested in a provocative paper by Kim Clark and Laurence Summers, two young economists at Harvard.[6] They confirm that most spells of unemployment are relatively brief but argue that this result is misleading, for two reasons. First, the probability of the unemployed finding work is lower the longer one has been unemployed. This means that a high proportion of the total amount of unemployment, measured in numbers of weeks rather than numbers of people, is attributable to people who have experienced long spells of unemployment. In 1974 one-half of the total number of weeks of unemployment came from spells lasting over three months.[7] The second reason is the fact that unemployment often leads to withdrawal from the labor market rather than new employment. This occurred for nearly one-half of the unemployed in 1974. Since many unemployed individuals later reenter the labor market to again actively seek employment, the apparently short average duration of unemployment is somewhat misleading—it could as well result from withdrawal and reentry as from truly short spells of unemployment. Clark and Summers conclude that mean duration of unemployment is not a good indicator of the ease or difficulty of finding work, illustrating as an example that adult men have unemployment spells that are 50 percent larger than teen-agers'. But that isn't because teen-agers find work more easily; it is because the withdrawal rate is so much higher for teen-agers.

While most of the people out of work go back to work soon, it does not follow that most unemployment is frictional. Clark and Summers distinguish between the proportion of spells of unemployment that end within a certain period and the proportion of the total weeks of unemployment contributed by spells of different lengths. In 1974, 60 percent of all unemployment spells were completed within one month. But that does not mean that most unemployment is due to short spells. For at the same time, almost one-half of the total weeks of unemployment was attributable to spells lasting more than three months. What the data show is a heavy concentration of unemployment over a relatively few individuals who suffer long periods before either finding work or leaving the labor force. For example, among adult men almost 50 percent of the total weeks of unemployment in 1974 was attributable to spells lasting four months or more.

In short, Clark and Summers are asserting that quite a large percentage of the total amount of unemployment (in terms of weeks rather than people) is not fric-

[5] Robert E. Hall, op. cit.

[6] Clark and Summers, "Labor Market Dynamics and Unemployment." The account that follows draws heavily on their work.

[7] Clark and Summers, op. cit., p. 19, 24.

tional at all but rather is concentrated among a relatively small number of people who do, in fact, represent a hard-core structural unemployment problem. In 1974, only 2.4 percent of the labor force experienced more than six months of unemployment; yet this group accounted for over 41 percent of the total weeks of unemployment. Even in 1969, when the economy was supposedly at full employment and only frictional unemployment remained according to the natural rate hypothesis, the average person measured as unemployed experienced 5½ months of unemployment.[8]

Clark and Summers also cast doubt on the basic search model rationale for unemployment. First, as is widely recognized, it is not necessary to be unemployed in order to find a new job. Fifty-four percent of those changing jobs do so without a spell of unemployment. Furthermore, it is hardly obvious that search is worthwhile for teen-agers because their job duration is so short. The average teen-age job lasts three months, and the average duration of employment overall is 21 months. There cannot be too much payoff to investment in search when jobs are that short. Adult males theoretically should have the most to gain from job search because their jobs last the longest, yet their unemployment is the lowest of any group. Thus, the basic search idea that unemployed workers reject job offers until they find one exceeding their reservation wage is questionable for the bulk of the unemployed. It is more likely that most people who are unemployed have either just reentered the labor force or just lost their jobs. They are likely to remain unemployed until they find their first job offer.

None of these points reverse the general picture of unemployment in the United States as due mainly to frictional turnover; most unemployment is of that type. Yet the data tend to disguise a fairly sharp dichotomy in the labor market. At the same time that most people find jobs rapidly, there is a small group that does not. Stretches of unemployment are long for this group. This lost work time makes up the bulk of total unemployment measured in time instead of people.

The Natural Rate of Unemployment: Why Is It So High and Why Is It Rising?

The natural or full equilibrium rate of unemployment is a key element in our theory of aggregate supply. On it is based the notion of long-run or full equilibrium output. U_{FE} has been defined as the unemployment rate at which the inflation rate is stable. For this reason, U_{FE} is often referred to as the **nonaccelerating inflation rate of unemployment (NAIRU).**

In the early 1960s, the general consensus was that U_{FE} was probably around 4 percent. That was the rate that Arthur Okun used in 1961 when he estimated the relationship between unemployment and the gap between actual and full employment output.[9] (Okun's law.) He calculated potential GNP by applying a trend growth rate to observed GNP in 1955. Then he estimated the relationship between

[8] Clark and Summers, op. cit., p. 35.

[9] Arthur M. Okun, "Potential GNP: Its Measurement and Significance."

the rate of unemployment and the gap, measured as the difference between potential and actual GNP. His estimate implied that when the gap was zero the unemployment rate was 3.7 percent, quite close to the assumed level of 4 percent for U_{FE}.[10]

Subsequently there has been a good deal of effort devoted to refining the measurement of U_{FE}, and to seeing what current level might be equal to the 4 percent rate of the early 1960s. All observers agree that U_{FE} must have risen since then. The basic reason is changes in the composition of the labor force. Since the early 1960s, the coming to age of the baby-boom generation and the increasing participation of women have raised the aggregate unemployment rate. Both of these groups have much higher turnover and unemployment rates than prime-age males; we have already seen evidence of this in Figure 10.3. Since the aggregate unemployment rate is nothing but a weighted average of the rates for subgroups of the population, when the share of groups such as teen-agers and women increases, aggregate unemployment rates will increase as well.

There have been a number of attempts to measure the effect of these compositional changes in the labor force on U_{FE}.[11] The methodological difficulty in doing so is to capture the interaction between the growth in the size of the teen-age and female labor forces and their observed unemployment rates. Clearly, as the supply of such labor grows, the equilibrium level of unemployment is likely to rise as well.

Michael Wachter has made a quite sophisticated attempt to overcome this difficulty by standardizing the unemployment rates of a large number of different age-sex-race groups against the rate for prime-age males.[12] He then used regression analysis to establish the relationship between the unemployment rates of each subgroup and the rate for prime-age males, in each case adjusting for the change in the labor force share of the group that was occurring over time. He assumed that U_{FE} for prime-age males was 2.9 percent, plugged this number back into each regression to get the hypothetical unemployment rate for each subgroup that corresponded to 2.9 percent, and then constructed a weighted average of these hypothetical rates to get an historical series of U_{FE}.

According to Wachter U_{FE} hit a low of 3.94 percent in 1954 and then rose steadily to a peak of 5.52 percent in 1977. Most other observers appear to agree that the current natural rate of unemployment must be around 5.5 percent.[13] The

[10] Ibid., p. 136.

[11] For a description of these efforts see Joseph Antos, Wesley Mellow, and Jack E. Triplett, "What is a Current Equivalent to Unemployment Rates of the Past?" *Monthly Labor Review* 102 (March 1979): 36–46.

[12] Michael L. Wachter, "The Changing Cyclical Responsiveness of Wage Inflation," *Brookings Papers on Economic Activity* (1 1976): 125–134. See also his article "The Nature of the Unemployment Problem," *Challenge* 21 (May–June 1978): 32–39.

[13] The alert reader will note that Wachter's estimates of U_{FE} are higher than those in Figure 10.1. The data on which that figure is based are taken from the official government estimates of U_{FE} which were used to estimate the full employment level of output and the full employment budget deficit, which we will study in Chapter 16. For purposes of consistency, we have used the official estimates of U_{FE} and Y_{FE} throughout this book. The source of the estimates is Frank DeLeeuw, Thomas M. Holloway, Danvin G. Johnson, David S. McClain, and Charles A. Waite, "The High Employment Budget: New Estimates, 1955–1980," *Survey of Current Business* 60 (November 1980), pp. 13–44.

Table 10.2
Separation Rates per 100 Employees in 1974

U. S.	4.8%
U. K.	2.8
Sweden	2.4
Japan	1.9
Italy	1.4

Source: Roger Kaufman, "Why is the U. S. Unemployment Rate so High?" *Challenge* 21 (May–June 1978): 45.

basic reason that U_{FE} has risen so much is the change in the age-sex composition of the labor force.[14] Although that was unfavorable in the 1970s, it will have a favorable side in the future. For just as the baby-boom generation increased U_{FE} when they were teen-agers, so will their aging cause U_{FE} to fall again in future years. Wachter estimates that U_{FE} will fall to 4.75 percent by the end of the 1980s.

It is well known that the unemployment rate in the United States is high relative to the rates in most other western economies. For example, in 1979, a year of relatively high employment in the United States, our rate was 5.8 percent, and Japan's was 2.1 percent. Some small part of this difference is explained by the different way we treat people on layoff or waiting to start a new job. But by far the biggest reason for the difference is the higher amount of job turnover in the United States. Unlike in the other western economies, there has been a sharp increase in the share of women and teen-agers in the labor force. Both groups have high rates of job turnover and, consequently, high-measured rates of unemployment. This can be seen in Table 10.2, where we show separation rates for different economies for 1974, a relatively good year in the United States.
As the reader can see, there is far more job changing in the United States than in other economies. This evidence on turnover is consistent with Robert Hall's contention that most of our unemployment (he estimated 3 out of 4 percent at full employment) is simply normal turnover.[15]

As we have already noted, some part of that high turnover must be related to the different composition of the United States labor force, in particular the high proportion of teen-agers. In the United States most teen-agers are in school, and those in the labor force tend to work part time. Their attachment to the labor force is not strong, and they tend to have high rates of job turnover and consequently high rates of unemployment. But in Europe, most of the teen-agers who work work full time; they are not in school. Consequently they are likely to have a much

[14] Several other reasons have been advanced for the increase in U_{FE}. Among them are the increase in the coverage of minimum wage legislation in 1967, the increase in the unemployment insurance system, and the requirement introduced in the mid-1970s that welfare mothers register for work. See Joseph Antos, Wesley Mellow and Jack E. Triplett, "What is a Current Equivalent to Unemployment Rates of the Past?" pp. 41–44.

[15] Robert E. Hall, op. cit.

Table 10.3
Labor Force Participation Rates by Sex and Country

	Male Participation Rate (age 15–64 years)		Female Participation Rate (age 15–64 years)	
	1961	**1972**	**1961**	**1972**
U. S.	91.4%	86.4%	43.1%	50.0%
Japan	92.5	89.8	59.9	53.5
W. Germany	95.5	91.7	49.3	47.5
Italy	92.3	81.9	36.6	28.4
U. K.	98.9	92.6	49.3	41.5

Source: Roger Kaufman, "Why is the U. S. Unemployment Rate so High?" *Challenge* 21 (May–June, 1978): 42.

stronger attachment to both the labor force and their jobs. That is undoubtedly why both their turnover and their unemployment rates are lower than those in the United States.

Another interesting fact that comes out of the comparison of the United States with other western economies is that our economy has actually created more employment than the others, which isn't the impression one would get by comparing unemployment rates. But it is so, for the reason that we have increased sharply the number of women in the labor force whereas all other countries have had a decline in the participation of women. This can be seen in Table 10.3. One could say that our employment growth has been very rapid, but the growth in the participation rate has been even more rapid. Thus, despite our relatively high unemployment rates our economy has actually been among the most successful in the western world in creating employment for its labor force.

Unemployment and the Phillips Curve

In this section we return to our two models of the economy to derive a relationship between unemployment and the rate of inflation, a relationship known as the **Phillips curve.** Up until the last few years it appeared to be an empirical fact that when rates of unemployment were high, the rates of change of prices and wages were low, and vice versa. Professor A. W. H. Phillips plotted actual unemployment rates against wage changes for Great Britain from 1861 to 1957 and noticed that over each cycle, the resulting points traced out a rounded L-shaped curve.[16] This

[16] A. W. H. Phillips, "The Relation Between Unemployment and the Rate of Change of Money Wage Rates in the United Kingdom, 1861–1957," *Economica* 25 (November 1958): 283–299.

Figure 10.4
The Phillips Curve

Prior to 1970, there appears to have been a stable negative relationship between the inflation rate and the unemployment rate. This relationship is known as the Phillips curve. However, after the supply shocks of the mid-1970s, it appears that the Phillips curve has shifted upward and to the right. The apparent trade-off between inflation and unemployment implied by the Phillips curve seems to have evaporated.

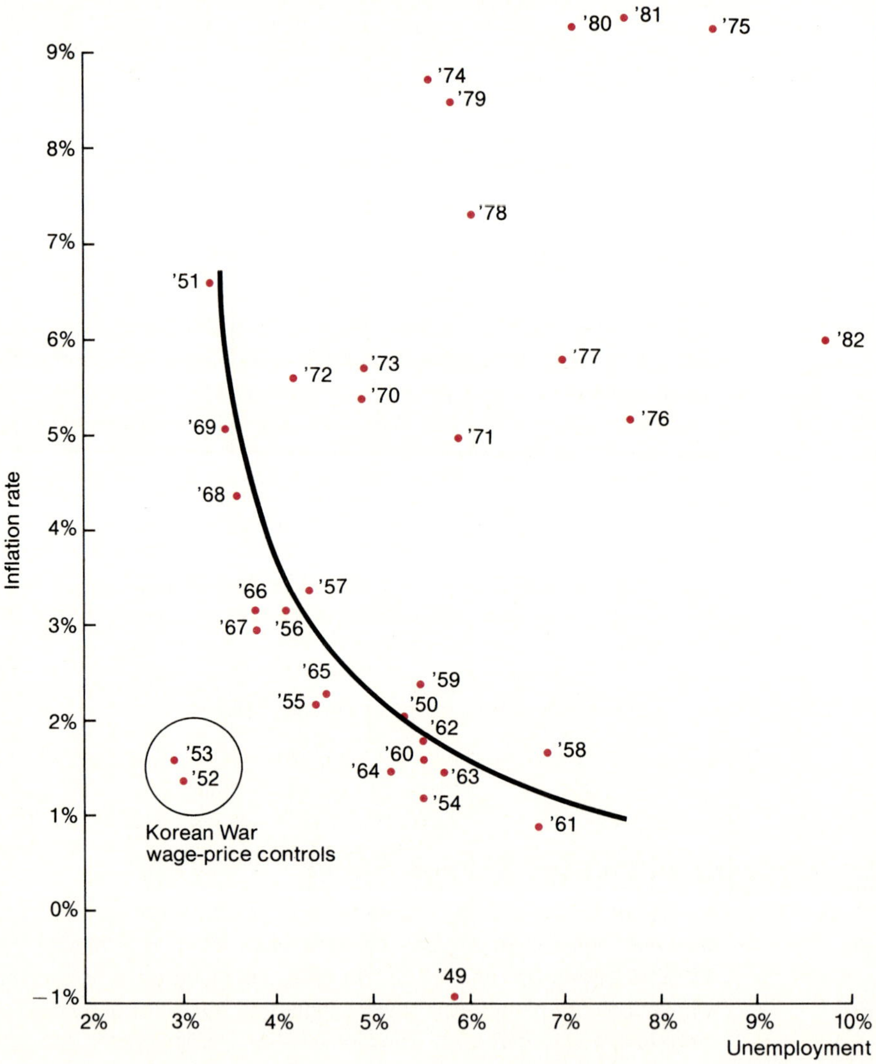

relationship, now known as the Phillips curve, has been confirmed for the United States and extended to price as well as wage changes.

Figure 10.4 summarizes U.S. experience. Up to about 1971 there seems to have been a close-fitting negative relationship between unemployment and the rate of inflation. The economy operated with high unemployment and low inflation in the late 1950s and early 1960s and with the opposite combination in the late 1960s. This appeared to imply that there was a trade-off between inflation and unemployment. If we had too high a rate of unemployment, the Phillips curve seemed to tell us that by expansion we could reduce that rate if we were willing to accept a somewhat higher rate of inflation. Not surprisingly, a political debate raged over what point on the Phillips curve should be chosen as a target for policy-makers.

Friedman and Phelps emphatically contested this interpretation of the historical record. They argued that the Phillips curve was a natural result of labor's short-run forecasting errors. Formally they showed that to each different rate of expected inflation there corresponds one short-run convex Phillips curve. The reason why the curves seem to have been stable in the past is that periods of high inflation used to be followed by stabilizations before price expectations could fully adjust. In this chapter we will examine the F-P argument and show that it is a logical extension of the labor market analysis of Chapters 6 and 7. We will then show how the contrasting views of the partial equilibrium and disequilibrium models are reflected in a disagreement over the shape of the short-run Phillips curve when unemployment rates are above normal.

Deriving the Phillips Curve

In previous chapters we have been concerned with the determination of equilibrium employment and real wage rates. Now our attention is focused on unemployment and inflation rates. Since unemployment is related to employment and output, we should be able to use our models of the economy to derive a Phillips curve.

In order to do that we must first translate our analysis from price levels into rates of inflation. We previously drew our labor and goods markets supply curves in terms of actual and expected price levels. We now wish to convert those diagrams to expected and actual inflation rates. For compactness we shall write Π for the actual and Π_e for the expected inflation rate.

actual inflation $$\frac{(P_t - P_{t-1})}{P_{t-1}} = \Pi_t.$$

expected inflation $$\frac{(P_{e,t} - P_{t-1})}{P_{t-1}} = \Pi_{e,t}.$$

Since the actual price level of the previous year is known, the price forecasting error, which we have written as $P_t/P_{e,t}$ in previous chapters, can be rewritten as the difference between the expected and the actual inflation rates divided by 1 plus the expected inflation rate. This can be shown as follows:

First, divide the numerator and denominator of $P_t/P_{e,t}$ by P_{t-1}:

$$\frac{P_t}{P_{e,t}} = \frac{(P_t/P_{t-1})}{P_{e,t}/P_{t-1}}.$$

But by the definition of Π_t and $\Pi_{e,t}$, the right-hand side of this equation can be rewritten as $(1 + \Pi_t)/1 + \Pi_{e,t}$. Thus, we have:

(10.1) $$\frac{P_t}{P_{e,t}} = \frac{1 + \Pi_t}{1 + \Pi_{e,t}}.$$

Now add and subtract $\Pi_{e,t}$ to the numerator of the right-hand side of Equation (10.1). This gives us:

$$\frac{P_t}{P_{e,t}} = \frac{1 + \Pi_{e,t} + \Pi_t - \Pi_{e,t}}{1 + \Pi_{e,t}}.$$

That simplifies to:

(10.2) $$\frac{P_t}{P_{e,t}} = 1 + \frac{\Pi_t - \Pi_{e,t}}{1 + \Pi_{e,t}}.$$

What we have done in this derivation is convert the ratio of actual to expected prices into an expression involving unexpected inflation. For note that the term $(\Pi_t - \Pi_{e,t})/(1 + \Pi_{e,t})$, the percentage difference between the actual and the expected inflation rate, is what we shall call unexpected inflation (Π_{UN}). That being the case, we can rewrite Equation (10.2) more simply as:

(10.3) $$\frac{P_t}{P_{e,t}} = 1 + \Pi_{UN,t}.$$

Equations (10.2) and (10.3) tell us that when $P_t = P_{e,t}$, expected and actual inflation must be equal. If P_t is greater than $P_{e,t}$, there is unexpected inflation $(\Pi_t > \Pi_{e,t})$. When P_t is smaller than $P_{e,t}$, there is negative unexpected inflation $(\Pi_t < \Pi_{e,t})$.

We now use the equivalence between forecasting errors on prices and inflation rates to derive the short- and long-run Phillips curves. In the partial equilibrium model we wrote the short-run supply curve as Equation (6.14), repeated here for convenience:

(6.14) $$Y_s = z\left(\overset{+}{\frac{P}{P_e}}, \overset{+}{K}\right).$$

Using Equations (10.2) and (10.3), that can be easily converted into a relationship between output and unexpected inflation. We simply substitute Equation (10.2) into Equation (6.14) to get a relationship between output and the unexpected inflation rate:

(10.4)
$$Y = z\left(1 + \frac{\Pi_t - \Pi_{e,t}}{1 + \Pi_{e,t}}, K\right).$$

Or, more simply:

(10.4a)
$$Y = j(\overset{+}{\Pi_{UN}}, \overset{+}{K}).$$

Equation (10.4a) tells us that in the short run output is related to unexpected inflation. Hence, for a given rate of expected inflation, output varies positively with the actual inflation rate.

Figure 10.5 shows the short-run supply curve for $\Pi_{e,0}$. As in our previous analysis, the full equilibrium supply curve is the vertical line Y_{FE}. It is determined by the condition that $P_t = P_e$, which is equivalent to the condition that $\Pi_e = \Pi$, or that unexpected inflation be equal to zero. That being the case, we know that the short-run supply curve drawn in Figure 10.5 must intersect the full equilibrium curve at $\Pi = \Pi_{e,0}$.

In Chapter 6 we learned that there is a short-run supply curve for each expected price level. Here the equivalent relationship is that there is a short-run supply curve for each expected inflation rate. Furthermore, each such supply curve intersects the long-run curve at its expected inflation rate. In general, it is clear that if inflation is higher than expected, output will be higher than Y_{FE}, whereas if it is lower $Y < Y_{FE}$.

Now let us use our new short-run supply curve to derive the Phillips curve. To do that we use Okun's law to determine the relationship between output and unemployment. According to Okun's law, which we re-present here, unemployment is related to the gap between Y and Y_{FE}:

$$U = U_{FE} + e\left(\frac{Y_{FE} - Y}{Y_{FE}}\right)$$

(10.5)
$$U = U_{FE} + e\left(1 - \frac{Y}{Y_{FE}}\right).$$

Now we substitute Equation (10.4) into Equation (10.5), drop K because it is constant, and get an expression for the Phillips curve. It is:

(10.6)
$$U = U_{FE} + e\left(1 - \frac{z(1 + [\Pi_t - \Pi_{e,t}]/[1 + \Pi_{e,t}])}{Y_{FE}}\right).$$

Or, using Equation (10.4a),

(10.6a)
$$U = U_{FE} + e\left(1 - j\,\frac{[\Pi_{UN}]}{Y_{FE}}\right).$$

Let us look more closely at Equation (10.6), the equation of the Phillips curve. First, since both e and z are positive, note that the equation implies a negative relationship between inflation and unemployment. That obviously is because out-

Figure 10.5
The Short-Run Aggregate Supply Curve

The short-run aggregate supply curve can be drawn with respect to inflation. There is a different curve for each rate of expected inflation, and each curve intersects the full equilibrium supply curve at its expected inflation rate. The curve shown is for $\Pi_{e,0}$.

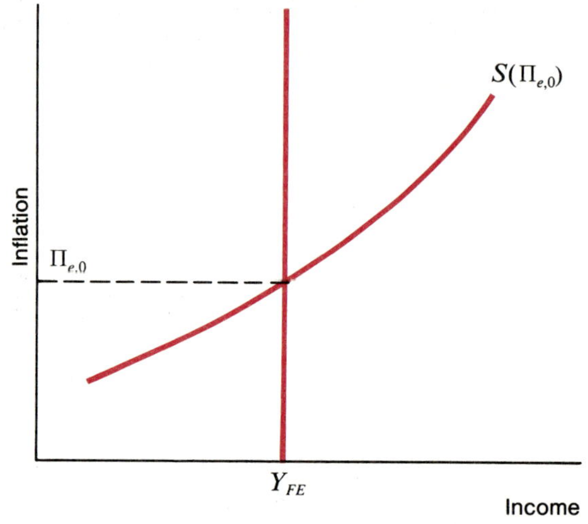

put is positively related to inflation while unemployment is negatively related to output. Secondly, note the all-important term $\Pi_{e,t}$ in the expression. This term tells us that the Phillips curve depends on the expected as well as the actual inflation. Other things being equal, the higher $\Pi_{e,t}$, the higher the level of unemployment. Equivalently, Equation (10.6a) tells us that unemployment is negatively related to unexpected inflation.

Let us now draw a picture of the Phillips curve (see Figure 10.6). Since we are showing the relationship of U and Π explicitly, expected inflation acts as a shift variable. There will be a different short-run Phillips curve for each different level of expected inflation, just as there was a different short-run aggregate supply curve for each Π_e. Clearly the Phillips curve is a downward-sloping function, whose general shape mirrors the aggregate supply curve of the economy. If that curve is steep because z is small in Equation (10.6), the Phillips curve will be steep. If the supply curve is flat (as it is in the disequilibrium model), the Phillips curve will be flat too. For prices act on unemployment through their influence on output. Where prices only weakly affect output, they only weakly affect unemployment as well.

We noted that there is a different short-run Phillips curve for each Π_e. An increase in the expected rate of inflation shifts both the aggregate supply curve and the Phillips curve upward. In Figure 10.6, if expected inflation rises from $\Pi_{e,0}$ to $\Pi_{e,1}$, the Phillips curve shifts upward from PP to $P'P'$.

Figure 10.6
The Phillips Curve

There is a different short-run Phillips curve for each different expected rate of inflation. For a given expected rate, the curve tells us that unemployment is negatively related to the actual inflation rate. The full-equilibrium Phillips curve is the vertical line at U_{FE}, since in full equilibrium changes in prices or inflation rates have no effect on either output or employment. U_{FE} is the full equilibrium, or natural, rate of unemployment. Each short-run curve intersects the full equilibrium curve at the expected inflation rate for which it is drawn. If Π_e rises from $\Pi_{e,0}$ to $\Pi_{e,1}$, the Phillips curve shifts upward.

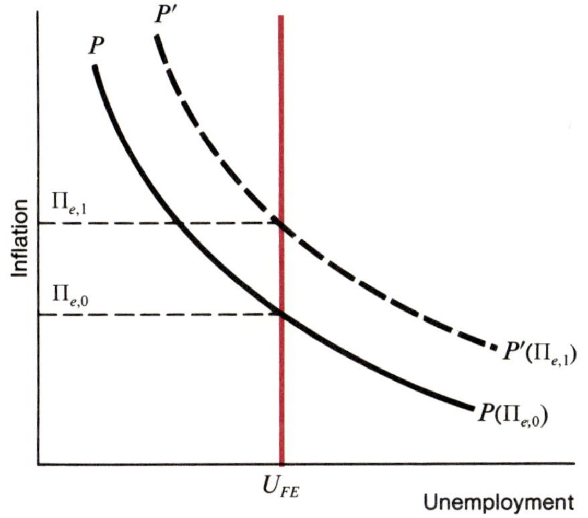

Short-Run versus Full Equilibrium Phillips Curves

In the goods market analysis we saw that there was a big difference between partial and full equilibrium, or between the short and the long run. This same difference shows up in the Phillips curve. Recall that we found that price increases could increase output in the short run. By our reasoning this was because the price increase enabled business to increase nominal wages while still allowing real wages to fall. Because the inflation was unexpected, this situation induced higher-than-equilibrium labor supply and labor demand, a happy but temporary state of affairs. This is exactly what the Phillips curve says: Wage increases reduce unemployment. But if the output-inflation trade-off was short-run and temporary, so should the Phillips curve trade-off between wage boosts and unemployment be short-run. These are merely different views of the same process.

Is there a full equilibrium Phillips curve, and if so, what does it look like? Such a curve would tell us the relationship between unemployment and wage changes when there is no unexpected inflation. For recall that our full equilibrium condition was that $P_e = P$ or, in inflation terms, $\Pi = \Pi_e$. Full equilibrium means no unexpected inflation. Now look back at Equation (10.6). If $\Pi_t = \Pi_{e,t}$, the equation reduces to:

(10.7) $$U = U_{FE} + e\left(1 - \frac{z[1]}{Y_{FE}}\right).$$

But according to the aggregate supply function, when $\Pi = \Pi_e$, $Y = Y_{FE}$. That means that the term $1 - z[1]/Y_{FE}$ is equal to zero, and therefore Equation (10.7), when $\Pi = \Pi_e$, becomes:

(10.8) $$U = U_{FE}.$$

Equation (10.8) is the full equilibrium Phillips curve. In terms of Figure 10.6, the full equilibrium Phillips curve is a vertical line at $U = U_{FE}$. What this vertical line and Equation (10.8) say is that inflation does not affect the levels of employment and unemployment in the economy so long as that inflation is fully anticipated. That is because any change in prices will be immediately offset by an equal increase in nominal wages. In full equilibrium, the only possible equilibrium in the labor market is the intersection of the labor demand and labor supply curves. This determines employment and the real wage. At that real wage a certain additional number of people are seeking work. These are a revolving group of people who have been called frictionally unemployed. We do not expect this unemployment to drop to zero in long-run equilibrium, which is why Friedman called it the "natural" rate of unemployment.

Wage increases by themselves would increase the number of workers willing to work, but businesspeople are not willing to pay the higher wages unless they are offset by price increases. But if they are offset by price increases, no additional workers are willing to work. Therefore, in full equilibrium only one level of unemployment is possible. By the term natural or frictional unemployment we do not mean that this number is fixed and inevitable; increasing information about job vacancies, retraining programs, and so on would tend to lower unemployment. But at any point in time, with given labor market conditions, what we have on the Phillips curve diagram is a vertical line at the natural level of unemployment.

Looking back at the equation for the short-run Phillips curve (Equation [10.6]), we see that each short-run curve intersects the full equilibrium Phillips curve at the rate of expected inflation for which it is drawn. Thus, in Figure 10.6, if both the actual and the expected inflation are equal to $\Pi_{e,0}$, $\Pi_{UN} = 0$, and therefore unemployment will be U_{FE}.

Inflationary Cycles on the Phillips Curve

Consider now the various possible inflationary cycles that we developed and discussed in Chapters 7 and 8. How do these same cycles look in the Phillips curve diagram? The simplest case is the one-time increase in demand, where workers do not adjust their expectations about inflation in response to changes in the actual

Figure 10.7
An Inflationary Cycle with No Adjustment in Expectations

If workers never adjust their expectations of inflation, the economy will stay on the same short-run Phillips curve. An inflationary cycle will then mean a move northwest from point A to point B, during the periods in which $\Pi > \Pi_e$, and then a return to point A, when workers adjust their wage demands to the higher level of prices. To get to point A, the government will probably have to restrain the level of demand through contractionary monetary and fiscal policies.

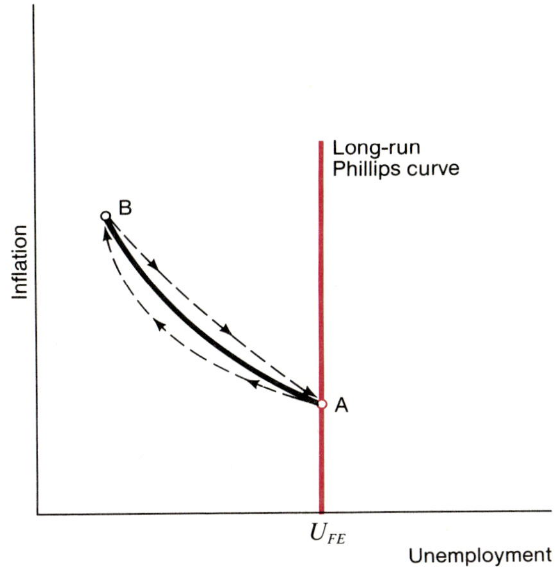

inflation rate. In that case, the expansion phase of the inflation is the leftward movement up a particular short-run Phillips curve from point A to point B in Figure 10.7; the stabilization phase retraces the route back down the curve to its intersection with the full equilibrium curve, from B back to A. Because Π_e does not change, we know that the economy stays on the same short-run curve.

When there is an adjustment of expectations in response to unexpected inflation, either of two different inflationary cycles is possible. As the economy moves up a short-run curve, there will be a gradual shift up to higher and higher curves. Now the authorities have essentially two choices. One is to validate those rising expectations by allowing a further expansion in the money supply; the other is to stabilize the economy by refusing to allow M to increase. If they do the former, they will convert a temporary inflationary bulge into a permanently higher rate of inflation.

We show how such a process works in Figure 10.8. The one-time increase in M causes the economy to move out from point A to point B. At B there is a boom, because there is unexpected inflation. Now if the authorities increase demand again, say at the rate of inflation expected by the labor force, the economy will return to the long-run curve at point C, but there will be a permanently higher rate

Figure 10.8
The Effect of a Permanent Increase in the Rate of Growth of Demand

An increase in demand causes the economy to have a boom so long as inflation expectations do not fully adjust. In the short run, the economy expands to a point such as B. If the authorities continue to expand demand, the economy moves to a new full equilibrium at a point such as C. In effect there has been a trade-off of a temporary boom for a permanently higher inflation rate.

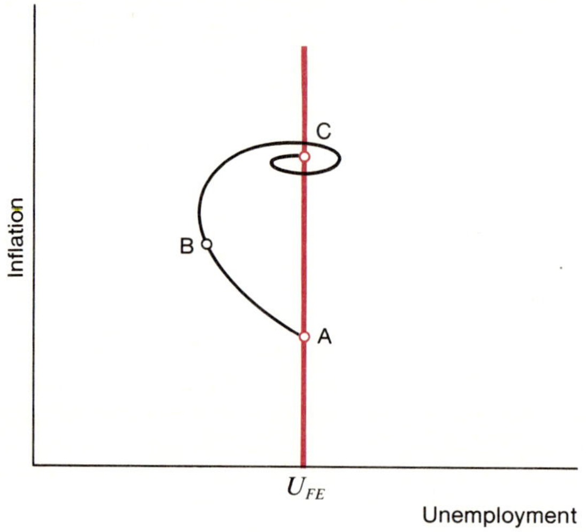

of inflation. It is worth noting that this return will generally not be a smooth one but will follow a path of the sort shown in the figure. In particular, there will be a period during which the inflation rate will be higher than the rate of growth of demand. The reason is that the higher expected inflation will reduce the aggregate demand for money. In order to reduce real balances, there must be a time during which the inflation rate is higher than the rate of growth of money.[17]

Note that during the adjustment to the higher inflation rate, it is possible, and indeed even likely, that the economy will move northeast in the Phillips curve diagram—that is, there will be a period during which inflation and unemployment are both going up at the same time. This is a combination that many people believe the Phillips curve analysis implies cannot happen. That, as we can see, is incorrect: All that is required is an increase in expected inflation greater than the increase in actual inflation. That causes a decline in unexpected inflation, hence a rise in unemployment, even if the actual inflation rate itself is rising. For example, suppose that in a certain year workers expect 2 percent inflation and the actual inflation rate is 6 percent. The unexpected inflation rate is 4 percent and, according to

[17] The rate of growth of M/P is $m - \Pi$, where m is the rate of growth of the nominal money supply.

Equation (10.6), unemployment will be less than normal. But now suppose that in the following year workers raise Π_e to 6 percent. Then, even if the actual inflation rate rises to 7 percent, there will be a rise in unemployment. The economy will move northeast in the Phillips curve diagram. The reason is that the unexpected inflation rate has fallen from 4 percent to 1 percent. It is unexpected inflation that determines the output and employment levels.

We turn now to the stabilization problem. Suppose that the government, having allowed a temporary increase in demand, is unwilling to accept a permanently higher inflation. How can the rate of inflation be brought back to its original level? We know that this requires a reduction in labor's expectations about inflation. If expectations are adaptive, that reduction can only be brought about by a period in which the actual is less than the expected rate of inflation. That, of course, requires that demand growth has to be slowed down—and that, unfortunately, means higher-than-normal unemployment. We analyzed such a case in Chapter 9, when we first increased the rate of growth of the money supply to 5 percent and then reduced the growth rate to 2 percent. We are now looking at the second part of that policy package.

The pathway traced out by the economy will have the general shape shown in Figure 10.9. At the beginning of the process, since the growth rate of demand is lower than the rate of inflation expected by the labor force, the actual will be less than the expected rate of inflation. That, as we know, means that the economy will be in a recession. This recession is necessary to bring Π_e down to a lower level, or to move to a lower short-run Phillips curve. However, during the phase when expectations about inflation are being drawn downward by lower actual inflation rates, workers will be demanding too high a money wage. The expectations error is what causes the recession. Gradually, as Π_e falls, the economy moves to a lower Phillips curve and a new long-run equilibrium at the lower inflation rate $\bar{\Pi}$.[18]

If we combine the two halves of the cycle we have been analyzing here, we have exactly the cycle analyzed in Chapter 9. A clockwise loop in the Phillips curve, from point A to point B and then around back to A, is what one would get in response to a temporary increase in the growth rate of demand followed by a return to the original rate of growth. This clockwise loop is the analogue of the S-shaped cycle that we showed in our diagram of output and price. The correspondence is shown visually in Figure 10.10, for a temporary increase in the growth rate of demand from 2 percent to 5 percent.

Stabilization in a Disequilibrium Economy

In Chapters 7 and 8 we showed that the return to the full equilibrium supply curve is more difficult in a disequilibrium economy because prices and wages are less responsive to demand conditions. In the previous cases, below Y_{FE} the short-run

[18] It can be shown, and should be fairly clear intuitively, that the long-run equilibrium must be at an inflation rate equal to the rate of growth of demand. Hence, when the rate of growth of the money supply falls from 5 percent to 2 percent, the long-run equilibrium inflation rate should decline from 5 percent to 2 percent. The only question is *how* the economy gets from the 5 percent equilibrium to the 2 percent equilibrium.

Figure 10.9
Stabilization in the Phillips Curve

If the authorities wish to reduce the inflation rate from $\Pi_{e,0}$ at point A, they must reduce the rate of growth of demand. If the goal is the inflation rate $\overline{\Pi}$, they must reduce demand growth to that rate. In the short run the actual rate of inflation falls below the rate expected by the labor force, and the economy goes into a recession as it moves out along the short-run Phillips curve $P(\Pi_{e,0})$. As expectations adjust downward, the economy follows the trajectory indicated, ending finally at point B.

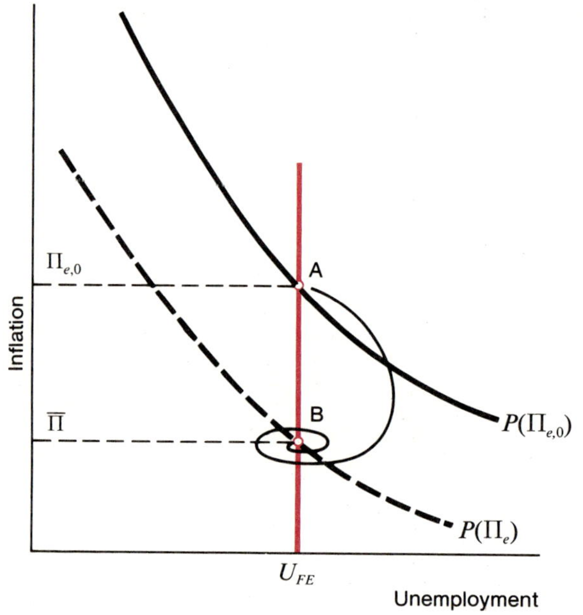

supply curve was flat. Here that translates into kinked Phillips curves, with the kink occurring at U_{FE} (see Figure 10.11). At higher-than-normal unemployment rates, the inflation rate will be relatively insensitive to variations in unemployment.

As one might expect, kinked Phillips curves make inflation reduction lengthy and difficult. For when inflation rates are relatively inflexible in response to falling demand, the rate of inflation will remain virtually constant as the economy goes into recession. Unemployment rises, but the forces drawing down the inflation rate are weak or nonexistent. Markup pricing in the presence of labor stockpiling and idle capacity are the chief factors making prices inflexible downward. Furthermore, if inflation rates do not fall, expectations about inflation cannot be dropping either. That eliminates one source of downward pressure on nominal wages. The only other hope, the unemployed labor force, is also not likely to put effective pressure on the wage rate of the employed. That is partly because firms are not hiring and partly because firms are reluctant to exchange workers with firm-specific skills for new workers, even if those new workers offer to work for less. The economy may

Figure 10.10
The Correspondence between the Aggregate Supply and the Phillips Curve Diagrams

Here we show a complete cycle for an economy in which demand is temporarily increased from a growth rate of 2 percent to a higher rate for several periods after which it returns to the 2-percent rate. The initial expansion causes a boom as the economy moves out to point A. Then, as expectations adjust and as the growth rate of demand is reduced, there is a stabilization recession as the economy moves clockwise in the Phillips curve to point B. If the authorities maintain the 2-percent growth rate in demand, eventually the economy returns to point C, at which it started. In (a), that point C is on the full equilibrium supply curve but inflation is 2 percent, which means that successive short-run equilibria are moving straight north in the diagram.

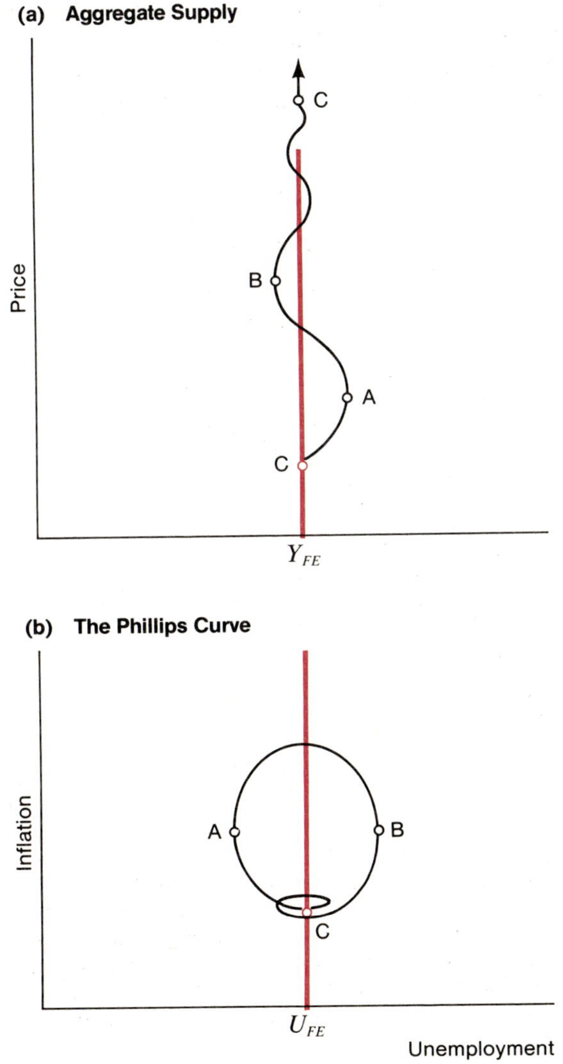

Figure 10.11
The Short-Run Disequilibrium Phillips Curve

The expansion phase is identical to the F-P economy. However, once the economy gets to point B, further stabilization leads mainly to higher unemployment. Because the aggregate supply curve is so flat, there is little further moderation of inflation. Hence, the economy moves straight east to point C on the flat section of the kinked disequilibrium Phillips curve.

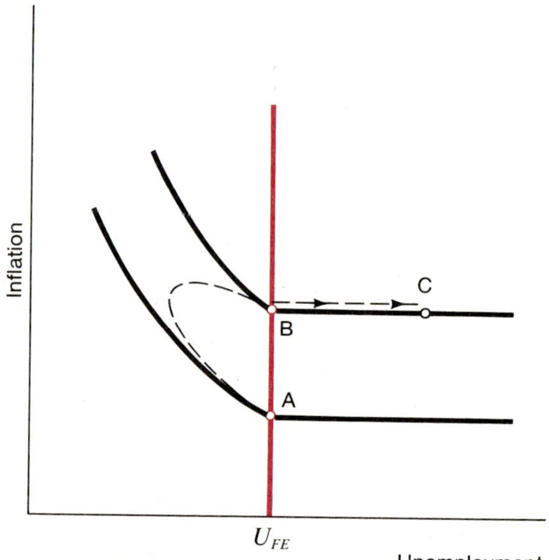

then move out from point B to point C in Figure 10.11, but the forces that help the economy move back to point A in the F-P economy—expectations adjustment, declining marginal cost, and falling rates of wage inflation—may be so weak that the economy comes to rest at point C, a thoroughly unsatisfactory situation from everyone's point of view. Inflation is higher than acceptable to the government stabilizers, and unemployment is higher than normal.

Trade-offs between Inflation and Unemployment

When the Phillips curve was first introduced, economists jumped to the conclusion that its existence implied that there was a trade-off between inflation and unemployment. We now see that the short-run curve implies nothing of the sort. For the short-run curve is drawn for a certain level of expected inflation. If there is a boom caused by unexpected inflation, one should expect labor to adjust upward its expected rate of inflation. Thus, whenever the economy moves to the left up a short-run curve, it will tend to move vertically above the curve to higher curves as expectations adjust.

Our analysis implies that it is not possible for the economy to stay permanently at any point on the short-run Phillips curve except at the long-run natural rate of unemployment. When the government tries to reach any other point and stay at that point, there is a gradually accelerating upward movement above the short-run curve. Here, then, is the answer to the puzzle of why the Phillips curve does not represent viable alternative states of the economy, even though the economy is generally on the curve. The curve is traced during the normal boom-recession inflationary cycle, in which expansion is always followed by stabilization. It is the downturn that reverses the upward adjustment of expectations, so that the economy has remained, more or less, on one curve. You could say, therefore, that the short-run curve has been observable for actual economies exactly because it has never been used as the basis for policymaking. When a government attempts to move an economy out on a short-run curve away from the normal unemployment level, there is a gradual (or perhaps not so gradual) upward movement of the whole curve as the economy adjusts to unexpected inflation. Under such a policy, one would not observe the short-run curve. One cannot use the observed Phillips curve as an indicator of the trade-off between inflation and unemployment.

Summary: A Look Ahead

Our two models of the economy can be translated into a diagram relating the inflation rate to either income or unemployment. The unemployment-inflation relation is known as the Phillips curve. The Phillips curve is the mirror image of the economy's supply curve: The long-run curve is vertical, the short-run curve downward sloping. Like the supply curve, there is a different short-run Phillips curve for each expected rate of inflation. For many years, economists thought that the existence of the short-run Phillips curve indicated a trade-off between inflation and unemployment. We now know that this is incorrect. The apparent trade-off exists only because of short-run forecasting errors. As those errors are corrected, the economy suffers either an acceleration of inflation or a stabilization recession if the authorities try to reduce expected inflation. In either case, the supposed trade-off evaporates into either permanently higher inflation rates or a temporary boom followed by a long recession. The flatter the Phillips curve, the longer such recessions will last.

In the last ten chapters we have presented our basic model of the economy. In order to concentrate on the basic logic and structure of the model, we have refrained from examining closely the different behavioral equations that make up the model. Prior to considering the basic problems of macropolicy, we need to know more about these behavioral equations. Accordingly, in the following chapters we examine theories of consumption, investment, and the demand for money. Having done that, we shall be ready to examine policy issues, such as when and how to control the level of demand and how to stop inflation. These questions will be addressed in Part Four of the book.

Key Concepts

structural unemployment
nonaccelerating inflation rate of unemployment (NAIRU)
Phillips curve
trade-offs between inflation and unemployment

Problems and Questions for Discussion

1. The partial equilibrium model offers an explanation for recession and high unemployment. What is that explanation, and do you think that it is consistent with empirical evidence on the nature of unemployment?

2. Since the short-run Phillips curve is negatively sloped, how is it possible for unemployment and inflation rates to both increase at the same time? Does this constitute refutation of the Phillips curve?

3. Assume an economy in which $\Pi_{e,t} = \Pi_{t-1}$; that is, workers expect inflation to continue at last year's rate. Using the Phillips curve diagram, trace out the reaction by such an economy to an increase in the rate of growth of demand from 0 percent to 6 percent. Describe the characteristics of the long-run equilibrium at this growth rate.

4. We learned that economies typically go through an oscillating decline in the inflation rate in response to a fall in the growth rate of aggregate demand, as shown in the diagram. Show the same adjustment path in the Phillips curve diagram. Be sure to label points A–E in your Phillips curve diagram.

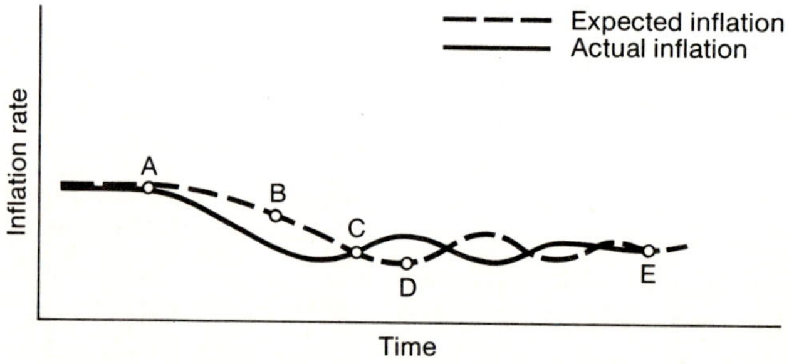

5. Derive a Phillips curve using the aggregate supply analysis of previous chapters and Okun's law.

6. "If, in the past, the government had used the Phillips curve as a guide to policy formulation, we would never have observed such a relation." What does this statement mean, and what does it imply?

7. In the Phillips curve diagram, how might the pathway traced out by an economy in which there is a fast adjustment of expectations differ from that traced out by an economy with slowly adjusting expectations?

8. Under what conditions might there be a decline in unemployment and inflation at the same time (that is, a southwesterly move in the Phillips curve)?

9. If, in the long run, there is no trade-off between inflation and unemployment, then in order to reduce the normal or long-run level of unemployment we should undertake policies designed to shift the long-run Phillips curve to the left. What policies would you suggest to accomplish this goal?

10. Prepare a memo discussing the different possible trade-offs between inflation and unemployment. What policy conclusions about demand management follow from your discussion?

PART FOUR

THE COMPONENTS OF AGGREGATE DEMAND

Chapter 11

The Determinants of Consumption

In Chapters 3–5 we developed a simple model of aggregate demand and used it to demonstrate the logic of demand management by the government. In order to be useful, a model must incorporate all the main determinants of private sector behavior, for if it does not, the model will forecast poorly and be of little use to policymakers. Obviously, our simple model does not pass that test. Its consumption function does not reflect the influence of any variables other than income; it has no explanation for investment, nor does it reflect the influence of asset markets and interest rates on private sector spending. Therefore, if we use the simple model for either policy or prediction, aggregate demand, influenced by excluded variables, will appear to be unstable. To remedy this, we turn now to a closer consideration of the three main components of private sector demand: consumption, investment, and the financial markets.

Errors of Prediction in the Simple Consumption Function

The simple consumption function that we used in Chapter 3 appears to be a reasonable representation of consumer behavior. Numerous cross-section budget studies confirm that consumption is indeed closely related to income. However, there are several empirical observations that are not consistent with the simple theory. First, the ratio of consumption to income has not declined over time as the consumption function implies that it should have. Second, households have not responded to changes in their disposable income resulting from changes in tax rates as the theory predicts. Third, wealth seems to have had a significant influence on consumption on at least two occasions in the postwar period. Fourth, the ratio of consumption to disposable income has varied over the economic cycles.

One important implication of our linear consumption function is that average consumption should decline as income increases. We can see this easily in Equation (11.1) if we divide both sides of the consumption function (Equation [3.2]) by Y_d:

(3.2) $$C = \bar{C} + cY_d.$$

(11.1) $$\frac{C}{Y_d} = \frac{\bar{C}}{Y_d} + c.$$

The right-hand side of Equation (11.1) is average consumption, C/Y_d, a ratio economists call the **average propensity to consume,** or APC. Thus, the equation says that the APC is equal to the MPC (c) plus a number that gets smaller and smaller as disposable income increases. In a household cross-section investigation, we would therefore expect the average consumption to fall as we move from the poorer to the wealthier households. The same should be true for an economy over time. As income increases the size of $\bar{C}/Y_d$ should decline, and the consumption ratio should fall towards the MPC. To put it another way: As income increases, whoever receives that income spends c and saves $(1 - c)$. Thus, over time average spending should get closer and closer to c.

When we turn to the historical record, however, we find that the consumption ratio has not fallen. If anything, it appears to have increased in recent years (see Figure 11.1).

In 1929 consumers were spending about 94 percent of their disposable income. Fifty years later the ratio was almost exactly the same.

A second prediction error with important policy implications has to do with the effect of changes in taxes on consumption. According to the simple consumption function, if the government raises taxes by $10 billion consumption should fall by c times $10 billion. Our theory of using taxes to control the level of aggregate demand is based on this assumption. However, in several recent historical instances, households have failed to act in the manner predicted by the theory.

Consider the celebrated Johnson surtax of 1968. In 1966 the United States was in the midst of the Vietnam War, yet President Johnson was determined to continue with numerous social programs. This guns-plus-butter strategy pushed the U.S. economy into a period of excess demand and accelerating inflation. The administration proposed a tax increase in 1967 to decrease demand. Belatedly, in mid-1968, Congress passed the tax, a 10-percent income surtax. What happened? As the reader can see in Figure 11.1, taxpayers reduced their personal saving in almost exactly the same proportion that their taxes had increased. From 1967 to 1969, tax payments rose by 2 percentage points—from 13 to 15 percent—of personal income, but personal saving fell by almost exactly the same proportion. What this meant was that fiscal policy did not have its expected effect on total demand, for the rise in government saving was almost exactly offset by a decline in household saving.

To put the matter another way, simple calculations of what consumption should have been according to the historical consumption function led to an underestimate of consumption by just about two-thirds of the surtax. This was an error

Figure 11.1
The Savings Ratio in the United States, 1929–1980

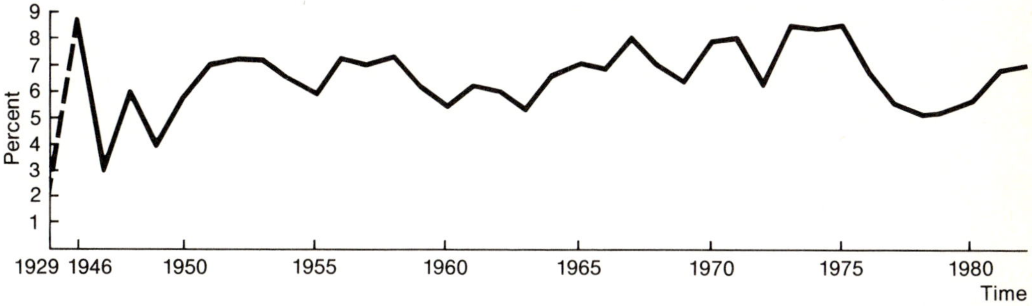

that caused policymakers to overestimate the degree of restraint they were applying to the economy when they raised taxes. The result of that error was a prolongation of the period of excess demand and a worsening of inflation.

A more contemporary error involving consumption occurred in 1979 and 1980. In those years the economy was once again moving into a period of excess demand. Inflation accelerated, reaching 18 percent by mid-1980. Government policymakers wished to slow down the economy. They debated whether another surtax was needed to reduce demand. Noting that inflation itself was increasing the ratio of taxes to disposable income because of bracket creep, they decided that no further action was needed. Because our tax system is progressive, inflation pushes people into higher tax brackets where their average tax burden increases. Inflation acts like an automatic surtax, and should restrain demand just like any other surtax. Because of the inflation tax, economists predicted that consumers would reduce their spending and push the economy into a shallow recession.

Not wishing to exacerbate the recession, and remembering that a presidential election was coming in 1980, the administration proposed no further restrictive tax measures. But once again, as in 1968–1969, consumption failed to respond to the rising burden of taxes. Taxes rose by over 1 percentage point, but saving fell by over 2 percentage points to just a bit over 3 percent of disposable income, the lowest value ever recorded for personal saving in the United States. Once again, the simple relationship between consumption and disposable income failed to predict household behavior, with unpleasant consequences for policymakers. Instead of going into a recession in 1979 as expected, the U. S. economy forged ahead on the strength of rapidly growing consumer demand. By the time the administration realized what had happened, the inflation rate had risen to almost 20 percent. The failure to predict consumption accurately had led to a very costly delay in the application of antiinflation remedies.

In view of these errors of prediction, it is clear that a better model of household consumption is needed, one that can explain these apparently anamolous facts. The two most important attempts to develop more adequate theories of consumption were the **permanent income hypothesis** (PIH), proposed by Milton Friedman during the 1950s, and the **life-cycle hypothesis** (LCH), developed independently by Franco Modigliani, Albert Ando and Richard Brumberg.[1] These two theories were directed towards explaining the first of our prediction errors, that average consumption has not declined over time. But they are also useful in understanding why consumption did not decline in either 1968 or 1979–1980.[2]

The basic idea of both Friedman and Modigliani-Brumberg is that households make a long-run consumption-saving plan, the goal of which is to maximize the utility that they obtain from the use of their lifetime income. Theory tells us that the way to do this is to arrange consumption expenditures so that the utility derived from the last dollar spent is just equal across periods. Otherwise, total consumer welfare could be increased by reducing expenditures in periods when the reward to extra consumption is low and increasing them when the reward is high. According to this approach, saving is the household's way of delaying consumption. It is done because the income stream does not exactly coincide with the preferred consumption stream. Take an obvious and extreme example, retirement. People save for retirement because they prefer to consume less during their working years so as to be able to have something to spend in retirement. Similarly, people such as actors or writers, whose incomes have wide fluctuations, are very likely to save during the good years to smooth out their consumption stream. In both cases, the reason for saving is that households know they will get more satisfaction at the margin if they resist buying steaks during the good years so as to have enough for stew during the bad. Let us now look more closely at these two attempts to model the lifetime consumption plan.

The Permanent Income Hypothesis

Friedman's consumption theory is based on the idea that the household will use saving to smooth out fluctuations in income. Household income is not constant and not known with certainty. Hence, we may divide measured income into two parts, one that Friedman labeled **permanent income,** Y_P, and the other, the variable part, **transitory income,** Y_T, which may be either positive or negative.

[1] Milton Friedman, *A Theory of the Consumption Function* (Princeton, NJ: Princeton University Press, 1957); Franco Modigliani and Richard E. Brumberg, "Utility Analysis and the Consumption Function," in K. K. Kurihara, ed., *Post-Keynesian Economics* (New Brunswick, NJ: Rutgers University Press, 1954); and Albert Ando and Franco Modigliani, "The 'Life Saving: Aggregate Implications and Tests," *American Economic Review* 53 (March 1963), pp. 55–84.

[2] Still another explanation for the relatively flat short-run consumption function is the relative income hypothesis, advanced by James Duesenberry in his *Income, Saving and the Theory of Consumer Behavior* (Cambridge, Mass.: Harvard University Press, 1949). Duesenberry argued that a family's consumption depends on its income relative to other families and also on the family's previous peak income. This theory predicts that consumption falls slowly in recession because of the influence of the previous peak income but that in long-run expansions, families spend a constant k of their income because they emulate the spending patterns of families with the income levels they have just attained.

(11.2) $$Y_M = Y_P + Y_T.$$

Y_M = measured income
Y_P = permanent income
Y_T = transitory income

Friedman reasoned that consumers would base their spending plan on permanent income rather than on measured income. His hypothesis was that consumption would be a constant fraction, k, of permanent income[3]

(11.3) $$C = kY_P.$$

Note that according to this hypothesis, high permanent income households do not save a higher proportion of their income than low income households.

When investigators go out to collect information from households on consumption and income, they do not observe the permanent income of that household; they observe measured income. That means that of two different families, both earning the same income, one may be a very rich family suffering temporary reverses on the stock market, and the other may be a family on welfare who has just won the daily double at Pimlico. According to the Friedman theory, these two families will have very different consumption behaviors even though their measured income is identical. That is because measured income is an imperfect proxy for permanent income. We would like to know if it is possible to derive a formal relationship between measured and permanent income.

Measured and Permanent Income

Friedman assumes that the distribution of transitory income, positive and negative, across families in the economy is random—in particular, independent of Y_P. High income people are neither more nor less likely than low income people to have a good or bad year. He further assumes that the distribution of families is normal across permanent incomes, which means that the number of families in each permanent income class falls as one moves away from the mean income level in either direction.[4]

Now consider an income class above the mean income of the population. It will contain some people from lower permanent income classes who are enjoying a good year, some from higher permanent income classes who are having a bad year, and still others with $Y_T = 0$. Average consumption will be a weighted average of the behavior of these three groups. The first group, with $Y_T > 0$, will have a relatively low level of consumption, because it is based on a level of permanent

[3] In his theory Friedman also distinguished between what he called permanent consumption and transitory consumption and argued that it is permanent consumption that is related to permanent income. We shall ignore this aspect of Friedman's theory in what follows.

[4] By a normal distribution, statisticians mean that a diagram of a number of families at different income levels would look like a bell, centered on the average income of the population. Thus, the further away from the mean within an income class, the smaller the number of families in that class.

income lower than the level temporarily enjoyed. By the same token, those from higher permanent income classes will have relatively high consumption levels. On average, observed consumption will depend on the average number in the group who come from higher and lower income groups.

Algebraically, using Equation (11.3) we may write average consumption of the families in the jth income class as the sum of the consumption of each of the families in the class. This summation is written:

(11.4) $$C_j = \sum_{i=1}^{T} kY_{P,i}.$$

The symbol $\Sigma_{i=1}^{T}$ is simply a shorthand way of saying add up or sum the consumption of each of the families in the income class. Thus, Equation (11.4) means:

$$C_j = kY_{P,1} + kY_{P,2} + \ldots kY_{P,T}.$$

The element $kY_{P,1}$ is the consumption of the first family in income class j, $kY_{P,2}$ is the consumption of the second family, and so on. Altogether there are T families in the jth class, which is why the summation goes from $i = 1$ to $i = T$.

In order to get the average consumption for income class j we divide total consumption by T, the number of consumer units in the income class. Note that we can also move k outside the summation sign, since it is the same value for each of the units in the income class. Thus average consumption, which we write $\bar{C}_j$, is:

(11.5) $$\bar{C}_j = \frac{k \sum_{i=1}^{T} Y_{P,i}}{T}.$$

Now we write an expression for the ratio of consumption to income of the class by dividing average consumption by average measured income:

(11.6) $$\frac{\bar{C}_j}{Y_{M,j}} = \frac{k \sum_{i=1}^{T} Y_{P,i}}{T\,\bar{Y}_{M,j}}.$$

Equation (11.6) says that the average consumption in any income class is equal to k times the ratio of average permanent to average measured income of the group of families in measured income class j. The higher permanent income is relative to measured income, the bigger the average consumption ratio will be. In general, if measured income is a poor proxy for permanent income, the observed ratio C/Y will not be equal to k.

Accepting Friedman's assumption that the population is normally distributed across the permanent income classes, if the jth class being measured in Equation (11.6) is above the mean income of the population, it will contain fewer people from higher classes with negative Y_T than it will people from lower classes with positive Y_T, simply because there are more in the second group than the first. Therefore, the average permanent income of the group will be less than $\bar{Y}_{M,j}$. This in turn

Figure 11.2
The Relationship between Measured Income, Permanent Income, and Consumption

Both consumption and permanent income are functions of measured income. If on average transitory income is zero, average measured and permanent incomes are equal ($\overline{Y}_M = \overline{Y}_P$).

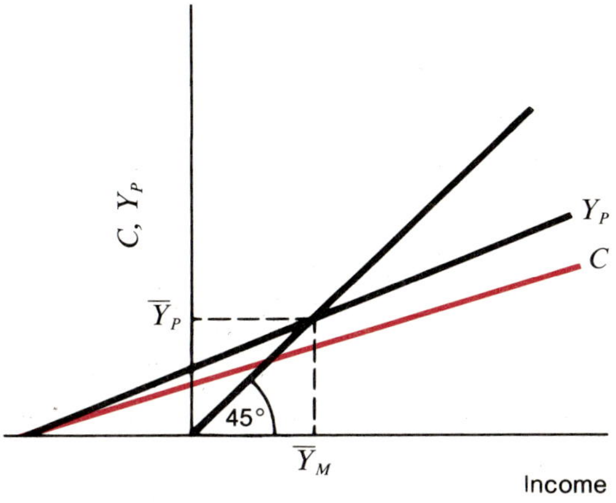

implies that the ratio of consumption to measured income will be less than k.

We now wish to derive visually the relationship between permanent and measured income for a cross section of families, for this will enable us to predict the level of consumption. We know that some of the families in our cross section will have positive transitory income, others negative. Suppose that, on balance, the negative and positive Y_Ts just offset each other so that for the entire cross section average transitory income is zero. This implies, from Equation (11.2), that average measured income of the cross section is equal to its average permanent income; that is,

(11.7) $$\overline{Y}_M = \overline{Y}_P.$$

With the information contained in Equation (11.7) we are now ready to draw the relationship between measured and permanent income for our cross section. (See Figure 11.2.) On the horizontal axis we show Y_M and on the vertical axis, Y_P and C. The line Y_P shows the relationship between measured and permanent income. Because of Equation (11.7) we know that $\overline{Y}_M = \overline{Y}_P$. Therefore, the line Y_P intersects the 45° line at $\overline{Y}_M$. As we move to the right in the figure, Y_P falls below Y_M because of the preponderance of families having temporarily good years over those having bad. That is, the higher the measured income class, the smaller the ratio of permanent to measured income.[5] The greater the variation of income, or

[5] In high measured income levels there will be some millionaires temporarily having bad years and some average income families temporarily having good years. But there will be more of the latter than the former if the distribution of transitory income is random across the population.

Figure 11.3

Consumption Functions for Wage Earners and Farmers

Because wage earners have relatively little income fluctuation, measured income is a good proxy for permanent income. Hence, the relationship between consumption and measured income is close to the permanent consumption function.

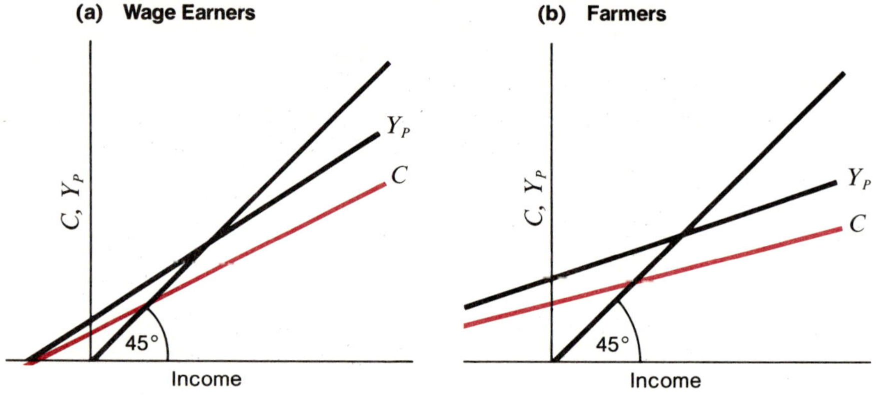

the greater the overall amount of transitory income of the population in question, the flatter the Y_P line should be.

Now consider the relationship of consumption to measured income. It is shown by the line C in Figure 11.2, and it is Friedman's consumption function, Equation (11.3). It lies a distance of kY_P below the permanent income function, expressing Friedman's contention that consumption is a function of Y_P, not of Y_M. We know several things about the consumption function. At the average income of the cross section $\overline{Y}_M$, the ratio of C to Y_M should be just equal to k, since at that income class average transitory income is zero. The lesson to be learned from Figure 11.2 is that in cross-section analysis, consumption will not be proportional to measured income at any point in time, and the MPC will appear to be much less than k. But that is because measured income is only a fair proxy for permanent income, the chief determinant of consumption.

Friedman made a number of ingenious tests of his hypothesis. He took two populations, one of wage earners and the other of farmers and small businesspersons[6] (see Figure 11.3). In the first there is little variation in income, in the second a great deal. Thus, Y_M should be a good proxy for Y_P for wage earners, a poor one for farmers and small businesspersons. Hence, the Y_P line for farmers should be flat, that for wage earners steep. Thus, even if the two populations have the same mean income, one would expect a flatter consumption function for farmers than for wage earners. This has been confirmed in his empirical investigations.

[6] Friedman, op. cit., pp. 69–79.

Another test of the PIH is to compare the consumption of members of different groups with the same income but with different group means, as depicted in Figure 11.4. For example, take the people earning \$20,000 in Mississippi and New York.[7] In the first case, we have an income substantially higher than the mean income of all people in Mississippi, whereas this is close to mean income in New York. Hence, we would expect the ratio of consumption to income to be close to k for New York but very much less than k for the Mississippi group. Why? Because among the people with measured income of \$20,000 in Mississippi, there must be a large number whose permanent income is lower. Hence, the average consumption of the group earning \$20,000 should be far less in Mississippi than in New York. This prediction also was strongly confirmed in Friedman's empirical investigation.

The Aggregate Consumption Function under PIH

So far we have been discussing household cross-section consumption functions. How can all this be translated into an aggregate observed relationship between consumption and income? To do this, we must add together all the individuals to get one observed level of consumption and income. We can then inquire how income and consumption change over time for the economy as a whole. This turns out to be a simple task. Using the same summation technique developed earlier, we add together all of the M households in the economy, each of which determines consumption according to Equation (11.3). Thus, aggregate consumption can be written:

(11.8)
$$\sum_{i=1}^{M} C_i = k \sum_{i=1}^{M} Y_{P,i}.$$

But according to Equation (11.2), permanent income equals measured income less transitory income. Thus, we can rewrite Equation (11.8) as:

(11.9)
$$\sum_{i=1}^{M} C_i = k \left(\sum_{i=1}^{M} Y_{M,i} - \sum_{i=1}^{M} Y_{T,i} \right).$$

If, for the population as a whole, average transitory income is zero, as we have been assuming, the last term on the right-hand side of Equation (11.9) disappears, and we then have the relationship:

(11.10)
$$\sum_{i=1}^{M} C_i = k \sum_{i=1}^{M} Y_{M,i}.$$

But clearly the expressions $\Sigma_{i=1}^{M} C_i$ and $\Sigma_{i=1}^{M} Y_{M,i}$ are simply aggregate consumption and income. Thus, Equation (11.10) tells us that:

[7] Ibid., pp. 79–85.

Figure 11.4
Consumption for Groups with Different Mean Incomes and the Same Measured Income

Groups from populations with different permanent incomes will have different consumption levels, even if they have the same measured income. Here we compare the consumption level of New Yorkers earning the mean income of their population with individuals from Mississippi earning the same amount. We know that the consumption of those New Yorkers is $C = k\overline{Y}_{NY} = k\overline{Y}_M$. But since this measured income is substantially higher than the Mississippi mean income, the Mississippians earning it are likely to have positive transitory income. Therefore, their permanent income must be lower than their measured income. As a result, the consumption level for the Mississippi individuals must be lower than $k\overline{Y}_{NY}$.

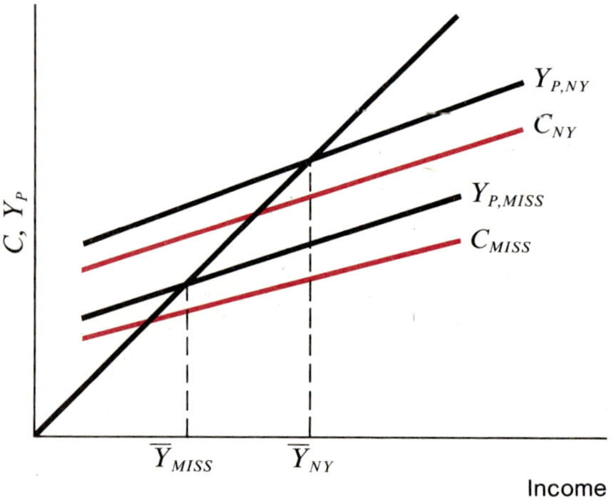

(11.11) $C = kY.$

Equation (11.11) says that in the aggregate, when average transitory income is zero, consumption is proportional to income even if it is not proportional in a cross section. In other words, if the economy is on its long-run equilibrium expansion path, where $\overline{Y}_T = 0$, observed consumption should be k times observed income. Thus the aggregate consumption function will be as shown in Figure 11.5.

There are two points to be noted here. One is that the relationship derived from cross-section analysis may or may not be duplicated in the aggregate. In this case, they are not. In the aggregate, we get the true relationship between C and Y_P because of the key assumption that over the entire population, transitory income washes out. The second point is that the aggregate relationship we have derived here is not necessarily useful for short-run predictive purposes. It gives a prediction of how consumption will behave in the absence of cyclical or policy-caused fluctuations in transitory income. For that reason, it could be thought of as a long-run consumption function.

Of perhaps greater importance and interest is an answer to the question of what happens to aggregate consumption when the economy goes through an

Figure 11.5
The Aggregate Consumption Function
In the aggregate, the relationship between measured income and consumption approximates the consumption function because on the average, $\bar{Y}_T = 0$.

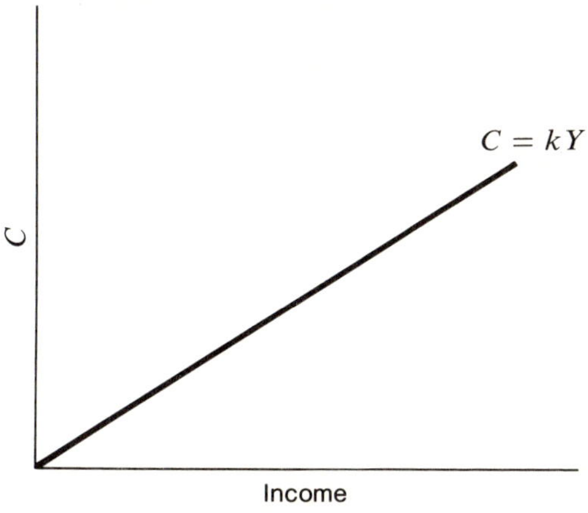

economic cycle. That is, how does consumption change when an economy, shown at point A in Figure 11.6, temporarily goes into recession?

To answer that question, go back to Equation (11.9). If the economy goes into a recession, the assumption that $\Sigma Y_T = 0$ is no longer valid; average transitory income is negative. Using Equation (11.9) we can write aggregate consumption as:

(11.12) $$C = kY - kY_T.$$

Equation (11.12) tells us that when aggregate transitory income (Y_T) is negative, as it would be in a temporary recession, C will be larger than k times measured income. That is, in a recession an economy will trace out a short-run "consumption function" like AC in Figure 11.6.

In reality this line is not a consumption function at all. Although it may look like the cross-section function, it actually has little in common with it. We can see this if we look a bit more closely at the diagram. Suppose the economy starts at the equilibrium point Y_A and then, due to recession, income falls to Y_B. What happens to consumption depends on how much of this decline is temporary and how much is permanent. (This consideration will be important again when we consider the effect of tax cuts on consumption.) If all of the decline is regarded as transitory, consumers will still continue to spend kY_A on consumption, and hence the economy will move from point A to point B. The apparent short-run consumption curve will be flat. If the decline in measured income affects people's perceived permanent income, the consumption level will drop. For example, if as a result of the

Figure 11.6
The Short-Run Aggregate Consumption Function

How consumption varies with income depends on whether fluctuations in income are perceived to be permanent or transitory. If income falls to Y_B but Y_P remains at Y_A, consumption does not decline. The economy moves horizontally to point B. If permanent income falls to Y_C, the economy moves to point C, which implies an upward-sloping consumption function with a slope smaller than k.

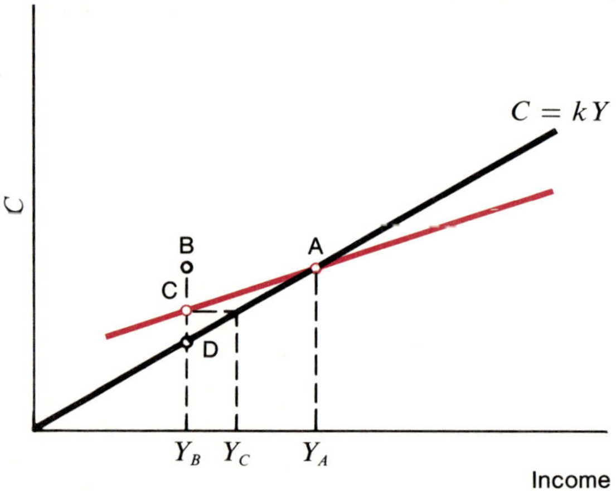

recession permanent income falls to Y_C, consumption will settle at point C, and the economy will have an apparently upward-sloping consumption function. Finally, if permanent income falls all the way to Y_B, consumption will decline to point D, and the economy will trace out the long-run consumption function. Thus, the reader can see that which short-run path the economy traces out in response to disturbances depends crucially on how permanent income responds to changes in measured income.

It has become traditional to suppose that households adjust their permanent income by some sort of adaptive mechanism. One possibility is that permanent income is changed by some fraction of the difference between last period's permanent income and this year's measured income. This behavioral hypothesis can be written:

$$Y_{P,t} = Y_{P,t-1} + a(Y_{M,t} - Y_{P,t-1})$$

$$Y_{P,t} = aY_{M,t} + (1 - a)Y_{P,t-1}. \tag{11.13}$$

If households behave according to Equation (11.13), current permanent income will be a weighted average of past permanent income and this year's measured income. The larger the coefficient a, the bigger the influence of current measured income on permanent income. In the limit if $a = 1$, $Y_{M,t} = Y_{P,t}$.

If we now substitute Equation (11.13) into the Friedman consumption function (Equation [11.3]), we get:

(11.14) $$C = kaY_{M,t} + k(1 - a)Y_{P,t-1}.$$

According to Equation (11.14), the slope of the observed short-run aggregate consumption function is ka. This is flatter than k because a is generally believed to be less than one. Once again measured consumption is relatively weakly related to measured income, because measured income is only a fair proxy for permanent income.

In terms of Figure 11.6, if last year's permanent income is Y_A and measured income this year is Y_B, then if $a = 0$ consumption equals point B, whereas if $a = 1$, consumption = point D. Hence, the more influence measured income has on permanent income (the closer a is to one) the closer the observed consumption function will be to the long-run function.

The Effect of Tax Cuts on Spending According to the PIH

One of the important applications of the PIH is to predict the effect of tax policy on consumer spending. According to the simple model we developed in Chapter 3, consumption should fall by the MPC times the change in disposable income. To make things simple, let us consider the change in taxes as if it were a lump sum tax or transfer. In that case, the predicted change in income is:

$$\frac{\Delta C}{\Delta T} = -\frac{c}{1 - c}.$$

The effect of taxes thus depends on the size of c. Friedman's contribution was to point out that the observed MPC depends crucially on whether changes in taxes are considered to be temporary or permanent. We show the two possible cases in Figure 11.7.

Suppose that the government raises taxes to reduce consumer spending. The surtax reduces disposable income from Y_A to Y_B. How far will consumption fall? That depends on whether consumers think of the surtax as temporary or permanent. If they think that it is temporary, the reduction in permanent income and consumption will be relatively small; the economy will move to a point such as B. In contrast, if the increase is seen as permanent, the reduction in consumption and income will be much greater, and the economy will move to a point such as C. Thus, the observed MPC varies with the perceived degree of permanence of the tax. Where a tax is temporary, households will try to smooth out their consumption. They will draw down saving levels temporarily to maintain consumption levels. That won't happen if the surtax is permanent.

The relevance of all this to tax policy is obvious. If one raises taxes to reduce consumption but announces that the surtaxes are temporary, the demand effect will be small because the observed MPC will be low. If the tax increases are thought of as permanent, the effect on consumption and demand will be much greater.

Figure 11.7
The Effect of Tax Changes on Consumption

The effect of a rise in taxes depends on whether it is perceived as permanent or temporary. The more permanent it is, the closer the effect will be to $\Delta C = k(\Delta Y_d)$. We show two taxes in the diagram. A temporary tax moves consumption to point B, a more permanent tax to point C.

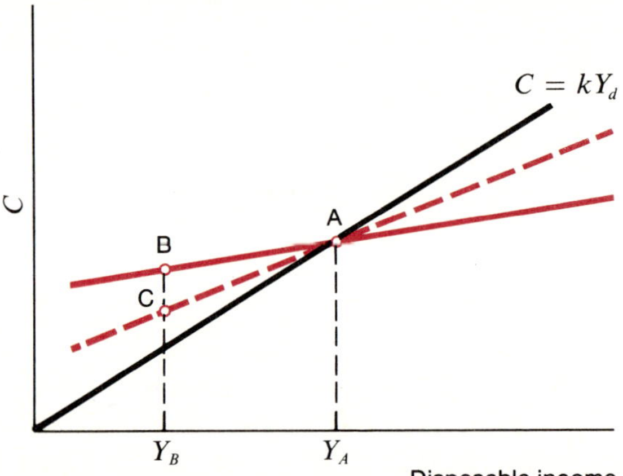

Case Study

The 1968 Surtax, the 1975 Tax Rebate, and the 1964 Tax Cut

There are several striking examples of the difference between the effect on private saving and consumption of temporary and permanent changes in taxes. For example, in 1968 the government passed a surtax to restrain aggregate demand. Like all tax increases, this one was not popular. To sweeten the bitter medicine, the government promised that the tax would be temporary, lasting from January 1968 through June 1969. Announced in this way, the tax was seen as a temporary reduction in income. The PIH predicts that such a change in income should cause households to reduce both saving and consumption so as to spread out the temporary reduction in income over a number of years. That is exactly what consumers did during 1968 and 1969, as the reader can see from Figure 11.8.

Most of the increase in taxes came out of saving and not consumption during the first two years of the tax, which is reflected in the sharp drop in the saving rate during 1968 and the first half of 1969. Eventually, as the surtax was extended for a year to June 1970, consumers did reduce consumption more sharply, but in the first 18 months the nature of the surtax diminished its short-run effect on aggregate demand. Rather than reduce consumption by the MPC, the surtax reduced private saving.

A temporary reduction in the taxes in 1975 had exactly the opposite effect. Saving rates jumped sharply as consumers spread the temporary windfall out, and

Figure 11.8
The Savings Ratio

Changes in taxes which are temporary have only a weak effect on consumption and consequently a large effect on saving. In-this figure we see that the temporary surtax in 1968 caused a reduction in saving for more than a year after its adoption, and the tax rebate of 1975 caused a temporary rise in the saving rate. There was no such change in the saving rate in response to the permanent cut in taxes in 1964.

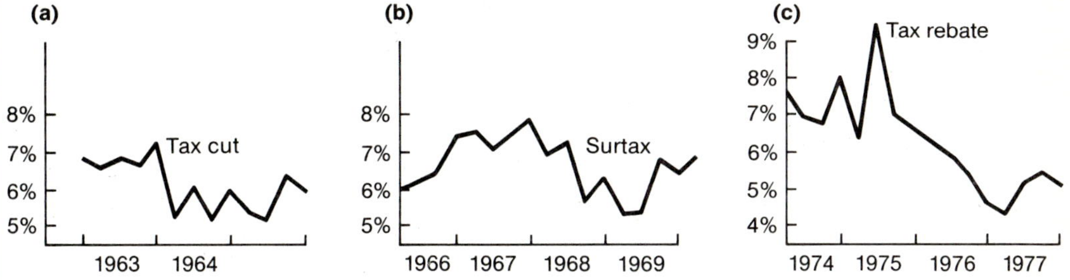

then saving fell slightly in later years as consumers spent the rebate. Both of these events suggest that temporary changes in income tax rates are not a very effective way for the government to influence the level of aggregate demand. In the short run, private and public saving simply move in the opposite direction with little change in the aggregate.

By way of comparison, consider the effect of the permanent tax cut of 1964. This tax cut was designed to overcome a structural tendency to too-high tax receipts at full employment. Consequently, it was a *permanent* tax cut. As the reader can see from Figure 11.8, this tax cut did not cause a big rise in the saving rate when it was introduced in two stages in the second quarter of 1964 and 1965. Because it must have been seen as giving a permanent rise in income, it led to an almost proportional change in consumption, with little effect on the private saving rate.

The Life-Cycle Hypothesis

We turn now to the second major theory of consumption behavior, the life-cycle hypothesis developed by Franco Modigliani, Richard Brumberg and Albert Ando. Like the permanent income hypothesis, the LCH analyzed the consumption-saving decision as part of the effort by households to derive maximum utility from consumption. However, the LCH time horizon is much longer than Friedman's. According to the life-cycle theory, people make a lifetime consumption plan in which they save for retirement. As in the PIH, saving smooths out consumption but in the LCH, earnings variations come not from random shocks but rather from the fact that for most people earning rises to a peak in midlife and then falls toward retirement. People save during the peak earnings years in order to be able to maintain consumption later.

Mathematical Expression of the Life-Cycle Model

Let us now look at this theory more formally. The situation confronting the typical worker is portrayed in Figure 11.9. The individual works for N years and lives for L years, thus spending N-L years in retirement. During his or her working years, income rises to a peak at G, then falls to zero at retirement age N. We have drawn the income profile as the isosceles triangle OGN for simplicity in calculating total income. Obviously, the income profiles vary greatly among different professions, but this does not affect the general point being made here.

The lifetime budget constraint of the worker is that he or she cannot spend more than is earned over a lifetime.[8] If we assume that the marginal utility of consumption in all periods is equal, the worker will wish to consume the same number of dollars in each year. Thus, the problem for the individual is to choose a level, C in diagram (a), such that lifetime consumption just equals total lifetime income. Since income is the area under triangle OGN, and consumption the area in rectangle $OCCL$, the budget constraint is:[9]

(11.15) $$CL = \frac{1}{2} GN,$$

where N is the base and G the altitude of triangle OGN.

(11.16) $$C = \frac{1}{2} \frac{GN}{L}.$$

Let us now define Z as the hypothetical income that, if earned each year over an individual's lifetime, would yield actual lifetime income. By definition Z is what Friedman called permanent income. Using Figure 11.9 we see that Z is determined by the condition:

(11.17) $$ZN = \frac{1}{2} GN.$$

(11.18) $$Z = \frac{1}{2} G.$$

When we substitute Equation (11.18) into Equation (11.16), we get:

[8] We shall ignore here possible interest earnings on savings.

[9] We will assume that all individuals have the same working hours and lifetimes, which allows us to drop subscripts on N and L.

Figure 11.9
The Life-Cycle Consumption Plan

OGN is the earning profile of an individual for a workspan of *N* years. This is equivalent to average earnings of *Z* per year for *N* years where $Z = 1/2\,G$. The budget constraint requires the individual to spend no more than total income over his or her lifetime of *L* years. If consumption is assumed to be equal every year, this budget constraint implies that rectangle $OZZN \geqslant OCCL$.

In (b) we show the net-asset position of the individual over his or her lifetime. Assets are rising whenever saving is positive, which happens between points A and B.

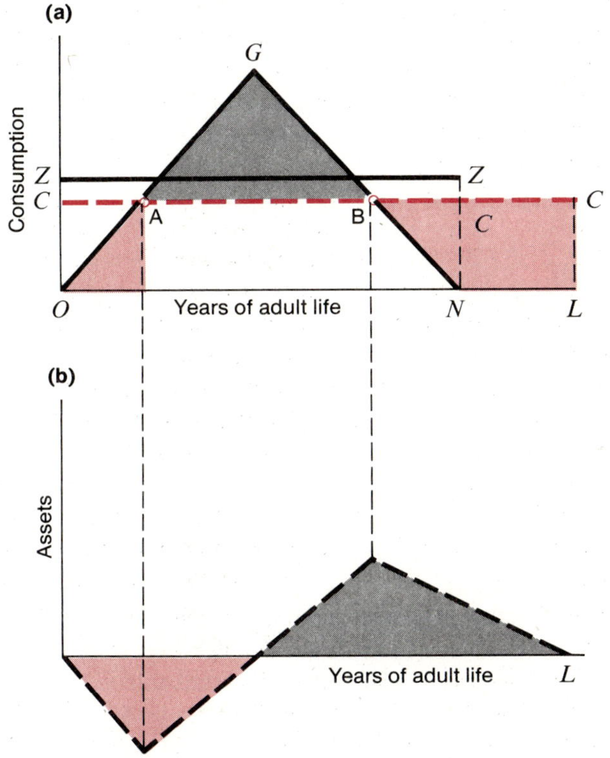

(11.19) $$C = \frac{N}{L} Z.$$

Equation (11.19) says that *C* is proportional to *Z*, the proportion being the ratio of earning years to total lifetime. If we think of *Z* as permanent income, Equation (11.19) gives us an explanation of Friedman's consumption function. His *k* can be interpreted as the ratio of *N* to *L*.

We use Figure 11.9 to see visually what happens to saving and asset accumulation by individuals over their lifetimes. Since saving is the difference between income and consumption, we can see that saving is negative in the two pink areas in diagram (a) and positive in the grey area. Young individuals borrow to finance consumption levels greater than income. Assuming that there are no borrowing constraints, these people go into debt, which we show by the increasingly negative asset positions in (b). Then, as earnings increase, there comes a point (A) where savings finally becomes positive. At that point, the household begins to pay off its debt and build up assets for retirement. The net asset position peaks at the point (B) where the individual again begins to dissave. In the absence of bequests, assets are drawn down to zero at L. The farsighted individual uses his or her last dollars to pay for funeral expenses.

The Role of Wealth in the Life-Cycle Model

We now add wealth to our analysis of life-cycle consumption behavior. Suppose that the individual starts his/her lifetime with some positive level of inherited assets, W. This changes the lifetime budget constraint to:

(11.20) $$CL = ZN + W.$$

We can rewrite this as:

(11.21) $$C = \frac{W + NZ}{L}.$$

Equation (11.21) says that the consumer will raise consumption by W/L above what he or she was able to consume in the absence of wealth. This is a perfectly straightforward implication of the lifetime consumption plan. A consumer splits up any increment of either permanent income or wealth into equal increments to consumption. Here we are looking at the effect of extra wealth at the beginning of adult life. Hence, the additional consumption made possible is W/L.

In general, if there is an addition to wealth at time T, one would expect that consumption would increase each year by an amount $\Delta C = \Delta W/(L - T)$. We show the effect of such a change in Figure 11.10. The household receives an unexpected inheritance at time T. Ignoring the possible interest earnings on the additional wealth, the income stream is unaffected. But the consumption and saving streams are affected. In (a), consumption increases from C to C', which is equal to $\Delta W/(L - T)$. In (b), the wealth position at time T rises by ΔW. But since saving out of income is smaller by the increase in consumption, the net accumulation of assets per period falls. This is shown by the reduced slope of the assets line in (b). Also, of course, the peak in assets occurs earlier in the individual's lifetime. The important lesson to be learned is that an increase in wealth reduces saving. Since assets are intended to finance retirement consumption, any increase in wealth allows the worker to raise planned consumption for each year that he or she expects to live. Wealth, therefore, can have a pronounced effect on the relationship between consumption and income. We will discuss several important examples of the wealth effect in our next case study.

Figure 11.10
The Effect of an Increase in Wealth on Consumption

If an individual receives an addition to wealth at time T, consumption should rise from C to C', which is just equal to the change in wealth divided by the years remaining in the individual's lifetime. Saving is reduced by the same amount. The change in the lifetime wealth profile is shown in diagram (b). The change in wealth shifts the wealth line up at time T. However, since saving is lower, fewer assets are accumulated in subsequent years. In addition, the peak asset level is reached at an earlier age.

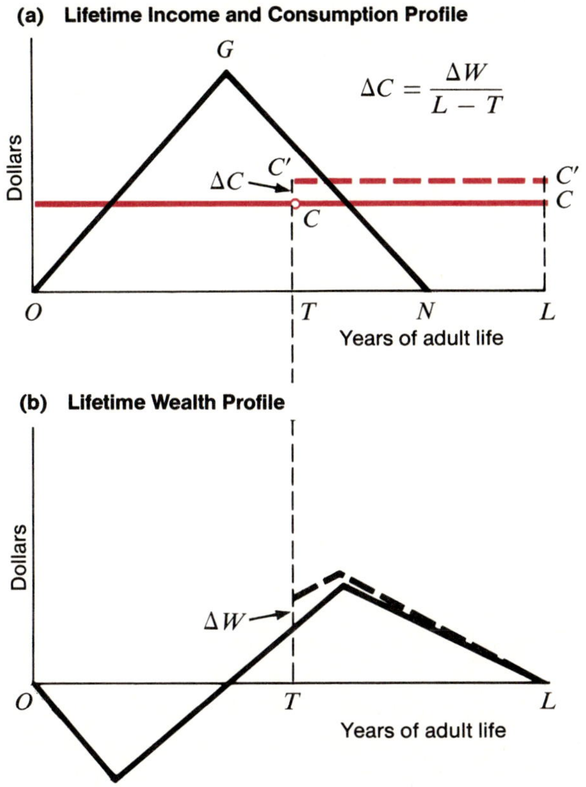

The Aggregate Consumption Function Under LCH

The consumption functions we have been discussing are individual. Since we are concerned with aggregate behavior, we must consider how an economy composed of individuals consuming according to the life-cycle hypothesis would behave. That turns out to be less obvious than it may at first appear.

Consider first the function without wealth, Equation (11.19). If we divide the population into the L age groups and aggregate, we have the following expression for aggregate consumption:

(11.22)
$$C = \sum_{i=1}^{L} Z_i P_i \frac{N}{L}$$
$$= \frac{N}{L} \sum_{i=1}^{L} Z_i P_i.$$

P_i and Z_i are, respectively, the number of individuals and the average income of those in age class i.

Let us now suppose that we have a stationary population and an economy without growth. Under these circumstances, the number of individuals and the lifetime income of those in each income class will be equal. Then Equation (11.22) simplifies to:

(11.23)
$$C = \frac{N}{L}(LZP) = NZP.$$

How does C compare to total income? The rather surprising answer is that they are equal. Total income is equal to average income of each of the age classes up to retirement multiplied by the number in that age group:

(11.24)
$$Y = \sum_{i=1}^{N} Z_i P_i.$$

But under the assumption of constant population and income, Equation (11.24) simplifies to:[10]

(11.24a)
$$Y = NZP.$$
$$Y = C.$$

Thus, even though at the micro level each family saves during its earning years, there is zero saving for the economy as a whole. A moment's thought tells us why. Individuals save for retirement and plan to have no bequests. Hence, the positive saving of the working years is just precisely offset by dissaving during retirement. This is easily seen in Figure 11.9. For a constant population and income, Figure 11.9 is a picture of saving, income, and consumption for each age group in a population at a given moment, as well as of the lifetime plan of the typical individual in the population. Our result says that the positive saving of working years, which is the rectangle $ZCCZ$, is just equal to total dissaving by retired people, rectangle $NCCL$. For the economy as a whole, therefore, net saving is zero.

What then might account for the positive saving that we observe in the economy? Modigliani and his coauthors suggested three reasons. First, population is

[10] If all Z_i and P_i are equal, $\Sigma_{i=1}^{N} Z_i P_i = NZP$.

growing; thus, there are more people in the years of positive saving than there are retired people dissaving. Second, average income is growing; hence, the lifetime expected income of the young is greater than that of the old, so once again positive saving of the young outweighs the dissaving of the retirees. Finally, of course, the time of death is not known with certainty; so people must save enough to guard against the possibility of literally living beyond their means.

Regardless of exactly how individual consumption translates into aggregate consumption, the life-cycle approach gives us valuable insight into the influence of changes in wealth on consumption. We have already seen that an increase in wealth should lead to an increase in consumption and a reduction in saving equal to the increase divided over the individual's lifetime. In the aggregate, the effect of a change in wealth will depend on the average age of the individuals whose wealth increases. If the increase were distributed evenly across the population, average consumption would rise by the change divided by the expected average lifetime of the population.

Case Study

Rising Wealth Reduces Saving After World War II and in 1978–1980

There have been several confirmations of the connection between wealth and consumption. The first is in the years following World War II. During that war the government ran very large deficits, which were financed by selling bonds to the public. Consumption was controlled by taxes and rationing. However, because of the large volume of government debt sold during the war, in 1945 households had a high level of wealth relative to income. Contrary to the expectations of economists, who worried that postwar demand would be insufficient to lead to full employment, consumers engaged in a spending spree. During the years 1947–1949, the saving ratio averaged only 4.3 percent of disposable income, with a historic low of 3.1 percent in 1947 (see Figure 11.1). The rise in wealth and the decline in household stocks of consumer durables caused consumers to raise postwar consumption far above its normal level relative to income, with the result that postwar policymakers had to worry about inflation and excess demand rather than the recession they had feared.

A more recent example of the influence of wealth on consumption occurred during the years 1978–1980. During those three years the economy was expanding toward full employment. Historically, that has always led to an increase in the saving rate. (See 1964–1967 or 1972–1973 in Figure 11.1, for example.) This time no such thing happened. The saving rate hovered at around 5 percent, which is lower than any time since the 1940s.[11] Why?

One very persuasive hypothesis for this striking reversal in saving behavior was that consumers were responding to the large capital gains they were enjoying

[11] The saving rate fell to 3.5 percent in the fourth quarter of 1979, which was a major reason why the economy did not turn down in that quarter.

on their stock of housing.[12] The combination of inflation, the coming of age of the baby-boom generation, and a decline in housing construction helped cause a speculative boom in housing prices. For most families the home is the largest single component of wealth. Thus, the rise in the relative price of housing meant a substantial increase in the real value of wealth. This reduced the need for saving and allowed homeowners to spend a portion of their capital gains on increased consumption. This shift in consumer behavior was so pronounced and significant that it delayed the onset of recession for over a year and complicated enormously the task of the Carter administration in fighting inflation. For during the year when consumers went on their unexpected spending spree and the economy refused to go into recession, the inflation rate accelerated from 11 percent to 13.5 percent. The misforecast of consumer behavior was as responsible as anything for the dismal economic record that helped cause Carter's defeat in the 1980 election.[13]

Saving, Inflation, and the Interest Rate

An important influence on consumption and saving is the inflation rate. When one expects that prices are going to rise, it makes sense to buy now rather than later. Here there are two different types of inflation and two different types of spending to be distinguished.

With regard to inflation, one should distinguish between actual and expected inflation. It is expectations of future inflation that make people spend more today, not simply a rise in prices. Consumption in real terms is probably negatively related to the actual price level or inflation rate, because the real value of wealth is diminished by a rise in prices.[14] But consumption is positively related to the expected rate of inflation. A rise in expected inflation should increase spending, reduce saving, and push the economy IS curve up and to the right.

When one talks about consumption spending, one should distinguish between two forms of expenditure. One is true consumption, by which we mean spending

[12] The major proponent of this hypothesis is Alan Greenspan. See his "Inflation and Economic Activity," *Business Economics* (May 1978): 11–14. An alternative explanation for the rise in consumer spending was suggested by Stephen K. McNees in "The 1979 Consumer Spending Spree: New Era or Last Gasp?" *New England Economic Review* (May–June, 1980): 5–21. He argues that most of the fall in the saving rates was caused by rising energy prices, a form of tax that households treated like any other temporary tax by spreading its effect out and reducing saving rates in the short run.

[13] Yet another example of the effect of changes in wealth on consumption spending took place in the recession of 1974–1975. A sharp decline in the value of financial assets, particularly the stock market, reduced the real value of wealth and caused a significant slowdown in spending. For an interesting discussion of this case see Frederic S. Mishkin, "What Depressed the Consumer? The Household Balance Sheet and the 1973–75 Recession," *Brookings Papers on Economic Activity* (1/1977): 123–164.

[14] Recall from Chapter 6 that we showed that aggregate consumption falls when there is a rise in prices due to what we called the real balance effect—the fall in the real value of money and government bonds. This wealth effect of rising prices forces households to increase their saving to make up inflationary losses in the purchasing power of wealth.

on goods and services that will be used up in the act of consumption. The other is spending on durable goods. A rise in the expected inflation rate may induce savers to make a change in the way they hold their wealth. They may increase the proportion of wealth that they hold in tangible, inflation-proof assets, such as jewelry, art works, and antique cars. Not only are such assets inflation-proof—their enjoyment is not taxed as income. Hence, savers protect their savings from both taxes and inflation if they put saving into such durable consumer goods. The relevance of this to the saving rate is that all purchases of consumer durables, other than housing, are classified as consumption rather than saving. Hence, whenever such an inflationary portfolio switch goes on, it will appear that the saving rate goes down. This factor appears to explain part of the fall in the saving rate during 1979 and 1980.

Another influence on consumption and saving is the interest rate. As we shall see later on, the interest rate is the reward a wealthholder receives for giving an investor the temporary use of his or her purchasing power. Interest can thus be thought of as a reward for saving. One might therefore expect the saving rate to be positively related to the interest rate. However, the situation is not quite so simple. At higher interest rates one does not have to save as much to insure a certain desired level of consumption in retirement. Thus, it is entirely possible that an individual might save less, not more, in response to high interest rates.[15] This issue is an important one, because it bears heavily on the sensitivity of saving to changes in the tax treatment of dividends and interest, a question that has arisen recently in the controversy over supply-side economics. We defer further discussion until Chapter 19, noting here only the fact that the relationship between saving and the rate of interest is theoretically ambiguous. It can only be decided empirically, by observing the behavior of savers.[16]

The Real Interest Rate

In discussing the relationship between saving, expected inflation, and the interest rate, we have separated the influence of the latter two variables. An alternative way to present these relationships is in terms of the so-called **real interest rate.** The real interest rate is defined as the rate of interest minus the inflation rate. In an inflationary environment it is the real, not the nominal, interest rate that measures the reward for saving. For each dollar that an individual saves today, next year he or she gets back $1 + r$, where r is the nominal interest rate. But when there is an inflation, the purchasing power of those dollars is $(1 + r)/(1 + \Pi)$, where Π is the

[15] See William J. Baumol, *Economic Theory and Operations Analysis,* 4th ed. (Englewood Cliffs, NJ: Prentice-Hall, 1977), 653–670, for a good discussion of the saving-interest relationship.

[16] There have been several recent attempts to measure the savings-interest relationship. See E. Philip Howrey and Saul H. Hymans, "The Measurement and Determination of Loanable-Funds Saving," *Brookings Papers on Economic Activity* (3/1978): 655–685; and Michael J. Boskin, "Taxation, Saving and the Rate of Interest," *Journal of Political Economy,* vol. 86 pt. 2 (April 1978): S3–S27. Boskin finds a significant positive relationship while Howrey and Hymans, using a somewhat more restricted definition of saving and post-World War II data, find no relationship at all. One would have to say that the issue is still unresolved.

Table 11.1
Nominal and Real Interest Rates, 1960–1982

	Treasury Bill Rate (3 mos.)	Corporate Bond Rate (Aaa)	Inflation Rate (CPI)	Real rate (col. 2–3)
1960	2.93%	4.41%	1.6%	2.81%
1961	2.38	4.35	1.0	3.35
1962	2.78	4.33	1.1	3.23
1963	3.16	4.26	1.2	3.06
1964	3.55	4.40	1.3	3.10
1965	3.95	4.49	1.7	2.79
1966	4.88	5.13	2.9	2.23
1967	4.32	5.51	2.9	2.61
1968	5.34	6.18	4.2	1.98
1969	6.68	7.03	5.4	1.63
1970	6.46	8.04	5.9	2.14
1971	4.35	7.39	4.3	3.09
1972	4.07	7.21	3.3	3.91
1973	7.04	7.44	6.2	1.24
1974	7.89	8.57	11.0	−2.43
1975	5.84	8.83	9.1	−.27
1976	4.99	8.43	5.8	2.63
1977	5.27	8.02	6.5	1.52
1978	7.22	8.73	7.7	1.03
1979	10.04	9.63	11.3	−1.67
1980	11.51	11.94	14.3	−2.36
1981	14.08	14.17	10.4	3.77
1982	10.69	13.79	6.1	7.69

Source: *Economic Report of the President* (Washington, D. C., 1983).

inflation rate. Therefore, the real reward to saving is $[(1 + r)/(1 + \Pi)]-1$, an expression that is approximately equal to $r - \Pi$, which is what we are calling the real interest rate, r_r.

There is only one small problem with our definition of the real interest rate. When a saver is deciding whether to save or consume, he or she does not know what the inflation rate is going to be in the future. Therefore, he or she is forced to substitute the expected inflation rate for the actual future inflation rate in the above formula, and the real interest rate that results is, in fact, an expected real rate. Therefore, we shall define the real rate as the nominal interest rate less the expected rate of inflation, Π_e:

(11.25) $$r_r = r - \Pi_e.$$

Most recent empirical investigations of saving behavior use the real rate as defined above, not the nominal rate and expected inflation rate separately. But note that the appearance of the real interest rate in the consumption function means that expected inflation affects the IS curve and aggregate demand as well as supply.

Up until 1981, rising inflation rates were not totally reflected in the nominal interest rate, which was held down by the Federal Reserve. As evidence against the belief that expected inflation is highly correlated with actual inflation, the real rate of interest actually became negative during 1979–1980, as the reader can see from Table 11.1. There was a penalty on saving in financial assets. When this happens, savers adjust by putting more of their saving into housing, gold, and other inflation-proof assets. Because many of those assets are classified as consumer goods, measured consumption rises as a fraction of disposable income. Thus, high rates of inflation and negative real interest rates could be another reason for the low saving rate of the 1979–1980 period. Subsequently, in 1981 the real rate rose dramatically to its highest level in the entire postwar period. Perhaps not coincidentally, the saving rate finally began to climb above its 1979 lows.

An Estimatable Consumption Function

As a way of summarizing our discussion of the various determinants of consumption, we present a hybrid consumption function of the type that has been used in most recent empirical work.[17]

(11.26)
$$C_t = a_0 + a_1 Y_{d,t} + a_2 Y_{d,t-1} + a_3 \frac{W_t}{P_t} + a_4 r_r.$$

C_t = real consumption, period t

$Y_{d,t}$ = real disposable income, period t

$\frac{W_t}{P_t}$ = real value of wealth, period t

$r_r = r - \Pi_e$ = real interest rate

Current and lagged real disposable income are in the function because they are the main determinants of permanent income. The real value of wealth enters because of the life-cycle hypothesis. Finally, the real interest rate enters for the reasons discussed in the previous section. From our theory we expect a_1, a_2 and a_3 to be positive. The effect of the real interest rate on consumption (the sign of a_4) cannot be determined a priori.

Summary

Consumption spending is determined according to some form of long-run optimal plan. It is not simply based on current or lagged disposable income. We discussed the two main alternative models. The Friedman permanent income hypothesis

[17] Both the studies cited in footnote 16 used equations similar to Equation 11.26.

predicts that consumption should be a constant fraction of permanent income. However, since household measured income shows random fluctuations around the permanent level, the relationship between consumption and measured income is not constant; it depends on transitory income. This is particularly relevant for fiscal policy. Tax changes will have a small effect on consumption, their primary target, if they are temporary. That is because they do not have a large effect on household permanent income. Households spread the burden of a tax increase across a number of years' consumption, if they expect the tax to be temporary. The policy message is that if the government wishes tax changes to affect aggregate demand, it must convince the private sector that they are permanent. That may be easy to do for tax cuts, but it is not easy for surtaxes.

The life-cycle theory is useful, both for its explicit model of the lifetime consumption plan and because it can be extended naturally to show the influence of changes in wealth on consumption. Since consumers save for retirement, any change in the value of their assets will affect their consumption and saving out of income. We examined two such incidents in the postwar period, the years after World War II and the real estate boom of 1978–1980. In both cases, a rise in household wealth allowed for a significant reduction in saving and caused a boom in aggregate demand.

Key Concepts

average propensity to consume
permanent income hypothesis
life-cycle hypothesis
permanent income
transitory income
real interest rate

Problems and Questions for Discussion

1. In a stationary economy (constant population and constant income), the LCH implies that aggregate saving is zero. Since individuals save in such an economy, how can the aggregate saving rate be zero?

2. Suppose that in the life-cycle model individuals work N years, live L years, earn income Z, and desire a constant level of consumption each year. Derive an expression for the change in consumption that will be caused by a one-year surtax on income. What will be the effect of a permanent increase in the tax rate of the same amount?

3. According to either the LCH or the PIH, would you expect individuals with higher incomes to consume a smaller, a larger, or the same proportion that individuals with lower incomes consume? Explain your answer.

4. Carefully discuss the difference between the cross-section consumption function, $C_i = \bar{C} + cY_{d,i}$, and the aggregate time series consumption function, $C_t = \bar{C} + cY_{d,t}$. Should one expect the parameters $\bar{C}$ and c obtained in cross-section studies to be relevant to the aggregate function? Why or why not?

5. In the PIH, if the aggregate level of transitory income is zero, draw the cross-section consumption function one would observe in an economy, and show what the corresponding point on the aggregate consumption function would be. Explain the position and slope of the curve you have drawn.

6. Why might you expect the consumption function for gamblers to be flatter than the consumption function for bureaucrats? Why might you expect a lawyer to spend more than a secondary-school teacher even if both earned the same income?

7. Why is it that even though the aggregate MPC is less than the APC over time the APC has been roughly constant for almost 100 years?

8. Problems 8 and 9 are designed to illustrate the difference between cross-section and aggregate consumption functions. Assume an economy composed of six individuals, four in their working years and two in retirement. The four working individuals are the following ages, and the six have the following after-tax incomes:

	Income	Consumption
20 years old (1st working year)	$ 3,000	
30 years old (10th working year)	7,000	
40 years old (20th working year)	10,000	
50 years old (30th working year)	5,000	
Retiree 1		$2,000
Retiree 2		4,666

a. Assume that each working individual expects to earn the same income throughout his or her worklife, plans consumption according to the LCH, and has a working life of 40 years followed by 20 years of retirement. What is the consumption level of each working individual? What was the income level of the two retirees during their working lives?

b. Plot the cross-section consumption function for this economy.

c. What is the amount of aggregate consumption? Plot it on your income-consumption diagram. Why isn't the aggregate income-consumption point on the cross-section line?

9. For the economy shown in Problem 8, suppose a one-year 10-percent income tax is levied against all earned income. Calculate the effect of the tax on the consumption of each individual. Show the change in aggregate consumption and disposable income. What is the apparent aggregate MPC? Why is it so much different than the cross-section MPC?

10. Would we expect a change in the value of wealth to change consumption and saving according to consumption theory?

Chapter 12

The Determinants of Investment Spending

We turn now to investment, the second component of private sector spending. Investment includes construction, the production of plant and equipment, and additions to inventory. Smaller than either consumption or government spending, it has averaged about 15 to 16 percent of GNP in the postwar period. Yet despite its relatively small size, investment is an exceedingly important component of aggregate demand. First, it is much more volatile than either consumption or government spending, and its fluctuations have often caused recessions and booms. Therefore, economists, interested in stabilization, need a good model of investment spending so that they may anticipate and perhaps counteract its procyclical fluctuations.

Another reason that investment is important is that both economic growth and improvements in labor productivity depend on it. The capacity of the economy is a function of the labor force and the capital stock. Investment adds to the capital stock. Without investment there are no new factories and machines; without these there is no expansion of output or jobs. How much we as a nation invest determines in the long run how fast we can grow.

Actual Investment Since 1946

Before considering models of investment, let us look for a moment at the postwar record of investment. In Figures 12.1 and 12.2 we show the three components of investment. They are shown separately because each is driven by different forces that require explanation.

Figure 12.1
Components of Investment in 1972 Dollars

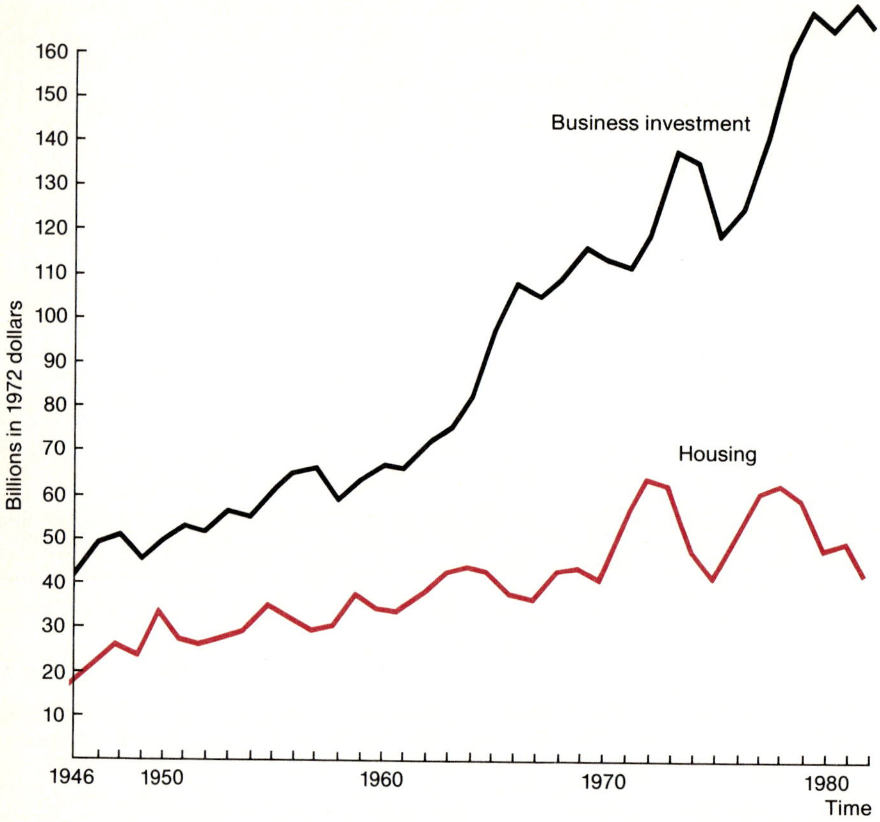

Business Fixed Investment

The first, and perhaps most important, empirical relationship that appears in the data is the positive relationship between business investment and output or capacity utilization. To make this point more forcefully, we have plotted the ratio of actual output to so-called potential output, which one might think of as an indicator of the pressure on capacity. Such periods as the decade from 1954–1964, when capacity utilization was low, were periods when fixed investment grew slowly and hovered around 9 percent of GNP. Such periods as 1964–1974, when the Vietnam War pushed the economy above the normal capacity level, were years when businessmen strove to add to capacity. The same positive association of investment with output shows up in the period when investment fell sharply during the 1974–1975 recession and then recovered along with the economy during the presidency of Jimmy Carter. This observed relationship of investment with output has led to one of the main theories of investment, the **accelerator**.

Figure 12.2
Components of Investment as a Share of GNP, 1946–1982

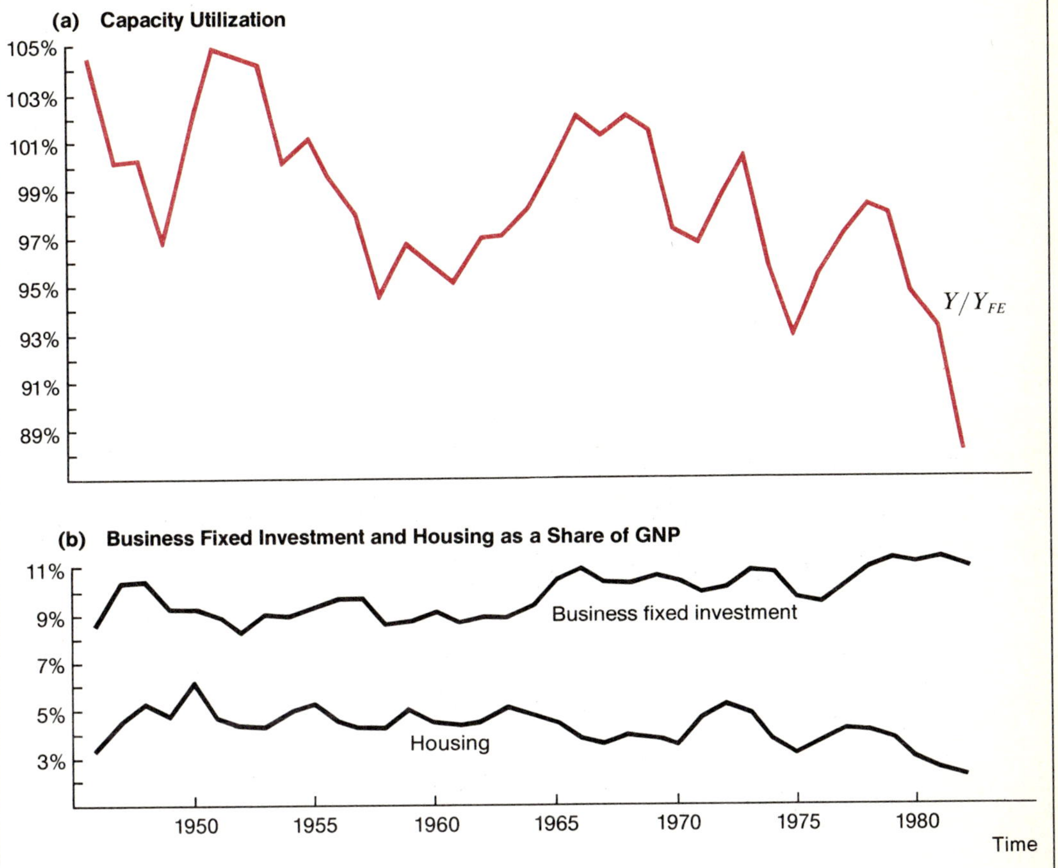

Housing

The second main component of investment is housing. Its association with output is far weaker than fixed investment, since it was relatively high in the 1950s and early 1960s, when output was low, and then fell as a proportion of GNP through the Vietnam War boom years. As we shall see, housing is strongly influenced by the level of interest rates and the availability of credit. When aggregate demand is high there is strong competition for credit, and interest rates are high. In these periods, housing loses out. This is clear in the boom of the 1960s and the recovery period under President Carter. Because of its sensitivity to credit conditions, housing is generally the first component of aggregate demand to turn down in a boom and the first one to turn up in a recession.

This countercyclical tendency has been reinforced by monetary policy. Since 1966 the monetary authorities have, on three different occasions—1966, 1974–

1975, and 1980—attempted to restrain aggregate demand by a tight money policy. As we shall see in Chapter 13, such a policy drives up interest rates. That has a profound effect on housing, because it is largely financed by a set of specialized financial institutions called savings and loan associations. Until recently these institutions had ceilings on the interest rates they could pay depositors. Consequently, when interest rates rose above the ceilings, funds were withdrawn from the savings and loans, a process called **disintermediation.** This severely curtailed credit for construction. As a result, both boom periods and years of restrictive monetary policy have adversely affected housing investment.

Inventory Investment

Inventory investment is a much smaller component of GNP than either of the two we have just discussed. Yet its sharp fluctuations have on several occasions had a profound effect on the level of aggregate demand. Every recession has been marked by a fairly sharp reduction of inventory investment. Two in particular, 1949 and 1974–1975, were clearly exacerbated by sharp reductions of inventories. Equivalently, inventory accumulation has added to excess demand in most booms, particularly those during the Korean and Vietnam Wars. As we shall see, inventories generally rise to excessive levels during the last stages of a boom, and it is the reduction in production to bring them back into line that precipitates recession. When stocks get back to desired levels, production levels are increased and a recovery from recession begins.

In recent years, people have worried a great deal about the low level of investment in the United States, blaming it for declining worker productivity, inability to generate employment, and other assorted ills. But as Figure 12.1 makes clear, that assertion is really true only for residential investment, not for business fixed investment. There have been three postwar periods when fixed investment has risen rapidly in real terms: The first is from 1963–1967, the second is from 1971–1974, and the third is from 1976–1980. These periods were all good for investment because they were periods of growth and expansion. According to the historical record, fixed investment normally is about 10 percent of GNP. It fell short of that level during the period 1949–1963, when there was a good deal of idle capacity, but it has exceeded that level every year but two since 1963. From the figure it is clear that fixed investment has not fallen in the United States despite claims to the contrary. Indeed, the average level of investment during the four years of the Carter presidency (10.7 percent) is the highest for any four-year period in the entire postwar period. It may be that we are investing too little. However, we are now investing more than we were. Therefore, if we wish to find an explanation for low productivity growth, we shall have to look elsewhere. Lack of business investment cannot be the reason.

The component of investment that has fallen in recent years is housing. Buffeted by high interest rates and scarcity of credit, housing has declined sharply from the levels observed in the 1950s, which was about 4.5 percent of GNP. Low rates of housing investment obviously do not have any effect on productivity; they simply insure housing shortages and higher prices in the future. We have already begun to see this as young families find it much more difficult to buy housing. One of the reasons is the diversion of saving away from housing and into both business fixed investment and the financing of government deficits.

Business Fixed Investment

We turn now to explanatory models for the three components of investment. The first is business fixed investment. Since investment is defined as changes in the capital stock, any theory of investment must start with a theory of the **desired capital stock,** K^*. Having determined K^*, the theory then has to explain how the firm acquires the additional capital needed to get from its actual level of capital, K_t, to its desired level, K^*_t. Investment presumably should be some function of the difference between K^*_t and K_t.

The Accelerator Model

The simplest model of investment is the accelerator, developed over 60 years ago by J. M. Clark, who based his theory on the observed relationship between output and investment.[1] He reasoned that firms have a desired relationship between capital and output:

(12.1) $$K^*_t = aY_t.$$

a = desired capital-output ratio
K^* = desired capital

Investment is undertaken whenever the stock of capital that a corporation would like to have on hand at the end of a certain period is greater than the actual stock on hand, less depreciation. If the amount of investment is exactly equal to the difference between these two magnitudes, we can write an expression for gross fixed investment:

(12.2) $$I_t = K^*_t - K_{t-1}(1 - \delta).$$

δ = depreciation rate

Note that in Equation (12.2) we are dating capital as of the end of the period. Thus, the expression $K_{t-1}(1 - \delta)$ is the stock of undepreciated capital inherited from the past and on hand at the beginning of the current period t.

We now define two important relationships. The first tells us that the capital stock at the end of period t is defined to be equal to $K_{t-1}(1 - \delta)$ plus gross investment. Thus:

(12.3) $$K_t = K_{t-1}(1 - \delta) + I_t.$$

[1] J. M. Clark, "Business Acceleration and the Law of Demand," *Journal of Political Economy* 25 (March 1917): 217–235.

The second relationship follows from a key assumption of this simple theory: Investment projects are completed within the period. From this it follows that the actual stock of capital on hand at the end of period t must be just equal to the desired stock of capital: $K_t = K^*_t$ for all t. From this, according to Equation (12.2), it follows that, for all t:

(12.4) $$K_t = aY_t.$$

If we now substitute Equations (12.4) and (12.2) into Equation (12.1), we derive the simple accelerator model:

$$I_t = K^*_t - K^*_{t-1} + \delta K_{t-1}$$

(12.5) $$I_t = a(Y_t - Y_{t-1}) + \delta K_{t-1}.$$

Equation (12.5) says that gross investment is composed of two terms, one depending on the growth of output and the other being replacement. The first term is what we can call **net investment,** or additions to the capital stock. Thus, the accelerator model makes the important assertion that net investment is a function of the growth of output, not the level of output. In a stagnant economy, net investment would fall to zero. There would still be gross investment sufficient to replace capital as it wears out, but the capital stock would be constant, because it would be sufficient to produce the actual, constant level of output.

There are two problems with the simple accelerator. First, it implies a volatility in net investment far higher than observed. Second, it does not allow for the influence of factor prices, particularly wage rates and interest costs. Surely these should have some effect on desired capital. Theorists have offered several reasons why investment is less volatile than the accelerator theory implies. One is that investment projects take much longer than one year to complete. Therefore, even if planned investment were to behave according to the accelerator observed investment would not, simply because only some fraction of projects started each year are completed within the year. We shall use the distinction between planned investment and actual additions to capacity as the basis of the **modified accelerator.**[2]

The Modified Accelerator Model

The key element in the modified accelerator investment model is the distinction we shall draw between **planned investment** and **actual measured investment.** Planned investment, Ip, is the undertaking of an investment project, while measured investment, I, is additions to capacity that result from the plan. Only some fraction of planned investment leads to actual additions to capacity during a given year. For simplicity in what follows, we shall assume that the depreciation rate is

[2]The modified accelerator model that we will present follows closely the investment theory developed by Dale W. Jorgenson in his "Capital Theory and Investment Behavior," *American Economic Review* 53 (May 1963): 247–257.

zero so that we can ignore replacement investment. Net and gross investment will be equal.

Planned Investment As in the simple accelerator, assume that businesses undertake projects equal in value to the difference between their desired and their actual capital plus the backlog of uncompleted projects. Businesses set in motion projects equal to the entire short-fall in capital. That means that by the end of each period, capital on hand, plus the backlog of uncompleted projects, will be just equal to the desired capital stock, from which it follows that new projects will be undertaken only if there is an increase in the desired capital stock. We can write this behavioral hypothesis as Equation (12.6), an equation exactly equivalent to Equation (12.5) except that planned has been substituted for actual investment.

(12.6) $$Ip_t = K^*{}_t - K^*{}_{t-1}.$$

Measured Investment However, it takes time to complete projects. Hence, measured investment I at time t will be different than planned investment. Let a_i be the proportion of any year's projects that are completed after i years. Figure 12.3 shows the profile of a_i. The area under the a_i curve equals one, and the curve tells us that only a small proportion of projects are completed within one year but that almost all projects are completed within three or four years.

With these definitions, we can now write measured investment in any year as the sum of parts of projects initiated in previous years and completed this year:

(12.7) $$I_t = \sum_i a_i \, Ip_{t-i}.$$

As an example of Equation (12.7), suppose that 25 percent of any year's projects are completed the same year, 50 percent the following year, and the final 25 percent in the third year. Then, measured investment or additions to capacity will be 25 percent of last year's projects, plus 50 percent of projects undertaken two years ago, plus 25 percent of projects started three years before. We now substitute Equation (12.6) into Equation (12.7) to show measured investment as a distributed lag function of past changes in the desired capital stock:

(12.8) $$I_t = \sum_i a_i \, \Delta K^*{}_{t-i}.$$

Regardless of how abruptly the desired capital stock may change measured investment will change slowly, because investment takes time. Obviously, Equation (12.8) collapses to the simple accelerator when $a_i = 1$, for then 100 percent of all projects will have been completed within one year.

The Desired Capital Stock It remains now to specify the desired capital stock for this model. This will be more complicated than in the simple accelerator model.

Figure 12.3
Fraction of Projects Completed After i Years

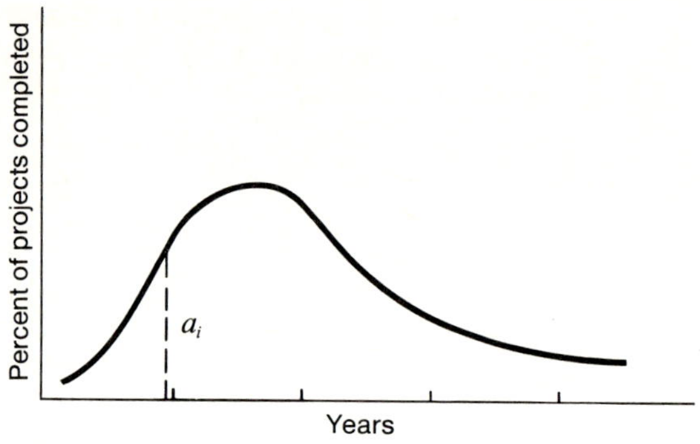

The problem would be simple if capital were rented rather than bought. Then investors would not have to predict the future, for they could maximize profits by renting the optimal quantity of capital and labor services and producing the optimal amount of output. But unfortunately there is no rental market for most capital. Firms therefore must assume that they will have to buy capital goods in order to obtain capital services. But that requires the firm to make a prediction of the level of production expected over the life of the capital good. In other words, because firms buy, not rent, capital, they must base investment decisions on an expected future level of output rather than today's output, as assumed naively by the accelerator theory.

Furthermore, factor prices should have an influence on capital intensity just as wages should on the demand for labor. The cost of capital that is relevant here is called the **user cost.** The user cost is the cost of owning a piece of capital equipment, and it is equal to the interest, plus depreciation on the value of the capital, less capital gains. User cost can be written as:

(12.9) $$rc = r + d - \Pi_{ke}.$$

rc = user cost
r = borrowing rate or cost of funds to investor
d = depreciation rate
Π_{ke} = expected change in price of capital good

A useful alternative interpretation of user cost is in terms of the real rate of interest that we introduced in the last chapter. If we set the expected change in the price of capital goods equal to the expected rate of inflation, then Equation (12.9) says that the user cost of capital is equal to the real rate of interest plus the depreciation rate:

(12.9a) $rc = r_r + d.$

r_r = expected real rate of interest

We turn now to the determinants of the desired stock of capital. In general we should expect K^* to be positively related to the expected level of output and negatively to the user cost of capital. In fact, Jorgenson demonstrates that in equilibrium, the profit-maximizing entrepreneur should make the marginal product of capital just equal to the user cost.[3] Since the marginal product of capital is a negative function of capital, the optimal capital stock should fall as user cost rises:

(12.10) $$K^*_t = g(\overset{-}{rc_t}, \overset{+}{Y_{e,t}}).$$

$Y_{e,t}$ = future level of output expected at time t.

From Equation (12.10) it should be possible to write the *change* in desired capital as some different function of *changes* in user cost and expected income. Equation (12.11) may be anything but simple in practice, and it may require a fairly severe set of assumptions in the form of the function g in Equation (12.10).

(12.11) $$\Delta K^*_t = h(\Delta rc_t, \Delta Y_{e,t}).$$

Measuring Expected Income Turning to the derivation of expected income, we could imagine two types of models. One would have expected income based in some way on past observed income; the other would have it based on a model of the economy. Most estimates of investment have used the simplest possible assumption, namely, that expected sales are equal to actual current sales. This is a fairly naive and extreme solution to the forecasting problem. The more general approach would be to write $Y_{e,t}$ as a weighted average of past actual income:

(12.12) $$Y_{e,t} = \sum_i b_i Y_{t-i}.$$

From Equation (12.12) it follows that the change in expected income is an equivalent function of prior changes in actual income:

(12.13) $$\Delta Y_{e,t} = \sum_i b_i \, \Delta Y_{t-i}.$$

An Estimating Equation for the Modified Accelerator Model We now substitute Equations (12.13) and (12.11) into Equation (12.8) to get an expression for

[3] Ibid.

measured investment as a function of prior changes in actual income and user cost. Note that it probably will not be possible to disentangle the two sets of lag coefficients, the *a*s and the *b*s.

(12.14)
$$I_t = \sum_{i=1}^{n} f_i(\Delta Y_{t-i}, \Delta rc_i).$$

Equation (12.14) is our basic model of fixed investment. It says that investment is based on prior changes in income and user cost. There are two important points here. First, investment is a function of the growth of income, which was exactly the implication of the simple accelerator. Second, investment is influenced by changes in the user cost or the real rate of interest. A decline in the real rate should increase the desired stock of capital and trigger investment. Note that a change in the nominal rate of interest fully reflected in a change in the expected rate of increase of capital goods prices will not have this effect, because it will not change the real rate of interest.

The lags we have introduced in Equation (12.14) only distribute the impact of any period's changes in income or user cost, making investment less volatile than it would be if there were no lags. The length of the lag between the change and observed investment is determined by choosing that lag structure giving the best fit between them. If there is a long lag in the completion of investment projects, the influence of any one year's changes may be felt on investment for a number of years. By the same token, even sharp, short-run fluctuations may have only a small effect on measured investment in the near term.[4]

Case Study

Business Fixed Investment in the 1970s

Peter Clark, in a recent study of business fixed investment in the United States, fit several variants of Equation (12.14) to quarterly data on investment in equipment and nonresidential structures for the period 1954–1972.[5] He used lags up to five years long for both output and user cost changes. He then used his fitted model to predict what each of the components of investment should have been during the period 1973–1978. He was seeking an answer to the question of whether investment had fallen in recent years relative to its performance in the 1954–1972 period.

He found, first of all, that the model without user cost (a modified accelerator) fit the data quite well, and better than any competing model (see Figure 12.4). As

[4]For an excellent survey of econometric studies of fixed investment, see Dale W. Jorgenson, "Econometric Studies of Investment Behavior: A Survey," *Journal of Economic Literature* 9 (December 1971): 1111–1148.

[5]Peter K. Clark, "Investment in the 1970's: Theory, Performance and Prediction," *Brookings Papers on Economic Activity* (1/1979): 73–113.

Figure 12.4
Predicted and Actual Business Fixed Investment, 1973–1978

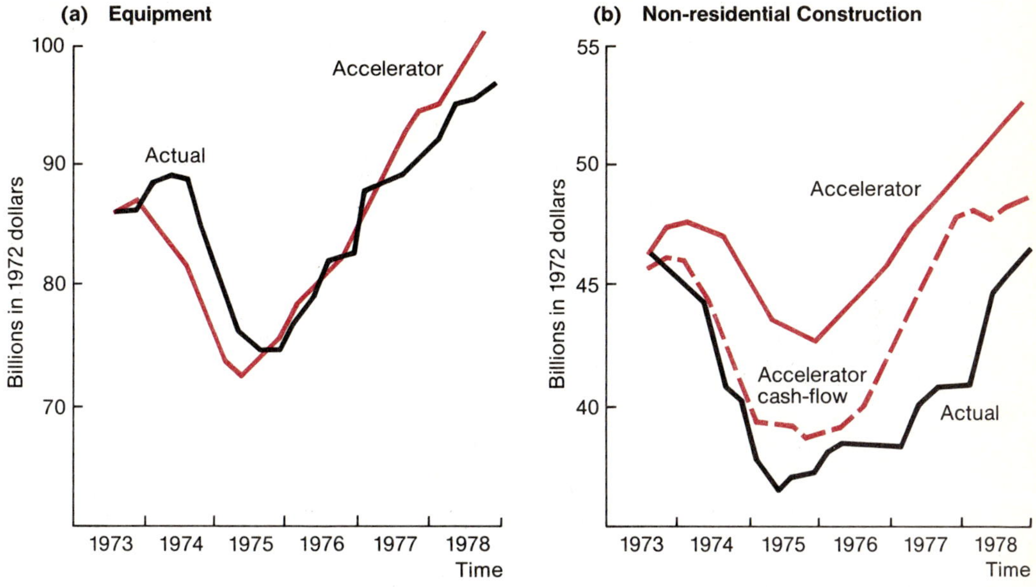

Source: Peter K. Clark, "Investment in the 1970's: Theory Performance and Prediction," Brookings Papers on Economic Activity (1/1979), p. 94.

to why investment had fallen in recent years, he found that such a decline had occurred only in construction, not equipment, investment. Business investment in equipment, which is the sort that should have a big effect on productivity, declined during the sharp recession of 1974–1976, but it declined by less than one would have expected based on the historical record. Furthermore, there was a strong recovery after 1976. Clark concluded that "equipment investment since 1973 has not been lower than what could have been expected."[6]

We made the point at the beginning of this chapter that fixed investment has not declined relative to GNP in recent years—indeed, it has slightly increased. An explanation for this is suggested by Clark's empirical verification of the accelerator model. Investment is high when the economy is growing rapidly, as it did in the mid-1960s, 1972–1974, and 1977–1980. The policy implications of this are clear. If one wishes to raise the ratio of investment to GNP, one must maintain a high and growing level of aggregate demand. Recessions, whether accidental or engineered by the government to control inflation, always have a pronounced effect on capital formation.

[6]Ibid., p. 95.

Housing Investment

The second main component of investment is residential housing. As we noted earlier, housing has a much weaker relationship with output and a far stronger relationship with interest rates than does business investment. Therefore, housing investment appears to be the component of investment demand that is most sensitive to monetary policy.

The theory that we shall develop for investment in housing is different from that for fixed investment. That is because there is a good market for both secondhand and rental housing. The fact that houses can be rented means that the demand for houses cannot be directly derived from the demand for housing services, because the household need not buy the house to obtain the housing service, and the owner need not use the house. The fact that there is a secondhand market for housing means that the prices of used houses will also determine what new houses will sell for. This will in turn determine the amount of new housing construction.

The demand for houses is a part of portfolio theory. Housing is one of the assets in which the public holds its saving. Therefore, as we shall see in the next chapter, the demand for housing should depend on the attractiveness of housing relative to other assets. In choosing a portfolio, wealthholders compare rates of return on alternative assets. The higher the rate of return on other assets, the lower the demand for housing should be. Thus, we would expect housing demand to be negatively related to the interest rate on bonds, bank deposits, and other financial assets.

The Demand for Housing

Housing demand should be positively related to its own rate of return. What exactly is the rate of return on housing? Disregarding tax incentives, the *absolute return* to housing is the rent chargeable on the house plus expected capital gains net of depreciation. Note that this rent may be imputed if the house is occupied by the owner. The *rate of return* on the house is the absolute return divided by the price of housing. Thus we define r_h, the rate of return on housing, as:[7]

(12.15) $$r_h = \frac{\text{rent}}{P_h} - \delta + \Pi_{he}.$$

δ = depreciation rate

Π_{he} = expected appreciation of housing price

P_h = price of housing

[7]We could alternatively have shown demand as a function of the user cost of housing. The user cost would be equal to the borrowing rate, plus depreciation, less expected capital gains on housing. In equilibrium, the user cost times the price of housing should be equal to the imputed value of rent. But if $(r + d - \Pi_{h,e})P_h = \text{rent}$, then $r = \frac{\text{rent}}{P_h} - d + \Pi_{h,e}$, which implies that in equilibrium the borrowing rate for houses should be just equal to r_h, which is just what Equation (12.15) says.

An important, special factor in the housing market is the availability of credit.[8] Housing, because of its long life and ownership by households, is financed to a large extent by a set of specialized financial institutions, the savings and loan associations. Housing loans until very recently were issued at fixed interest rates for long terms. In order to make that sort of financing available, the law allows the savings and loan associations to pay a higher interest rate than banks for time deposits but has limited their lending activities to housing-related loans. Until the recent rise in interest rates, this system generated enough credit to support the housing industry, largely because there were few alternative liquid assets available to the small saver. However, when, in the late 1970s, interest rates rose above the interest rate paid by the savings and loans on deposits, new financial instruments, such as certificates of deposit and money market funds, were created to compete with the savings and loans for funds. Depositors switched their savings out of the savings and loans and over to these new, higher-interest assets, a process called disintermediation.

The result for the housing industry has been very serious. Since the main source of housing finance is the savings and loans, whenever disintermediation occurs loans for housing are drastically curtailed, which causes an abrupt decline in the total demand for housing. Therefore, when market interest rates rise relative to the rates payable by savings and loans, there is a reduction in the credit available for housing and a decline in the demand for housing. This is another reason why the demand for housing should be negatively related to the interest rate.

We can summarize these various determinants of the demand for housing in the following equation:

(12.16) $$D_h = d(\overset{+}{r_h}, \overset{-}{r}).$$

As usual, the sign over each of the rates of return indicates its influence on the demand for housing. For many reasons, it is convenient to split up the different components of r_h and show them separately. Using Equation (12.15), we can then show the demand for housing as a function of housing prices, rents, and expected capital gains on houses. Substituting Equation (12.15) into Equation (12.16), we have the general housing demand equation:

(12.17) $$D_h = h(\overset{-}{P_h}, \overset{+}{\text{rent}}, \overset{+}{\Pi_{he}}, \overset{-}{r}).$$

Demand is negatively related to the price of housing and positively related to average rents and capital gains because the former reduces r_h and the latter two increase it. Bear in mind that we are keeping all other variables constant when we analyze the influence of any particular variable on demand.

[8]For a study of the influence of credit availability on the demand for housing see Dwight M. Jaffee and Kenneth T. Rosen, "Mortgage Credit Availability and Residential Construction," *Brookings Papers on Economic Activity* (2/1979): 333–387.

Figure 12.5
The Housing Market

The demand for the stock of housing in (a) determines the price of housing ($P_{h,0}$) in the short run. At $P_{h,0}$, the housing industry builds I_0 of new houses. These will eventually be added to the stock, shifting the supply curve SS in (a) to the right. A rise in interest rate reduces the demand for houses to $D'D'$. This reduces the price of housing of P_h' and causes a reduction in new construction to I'.

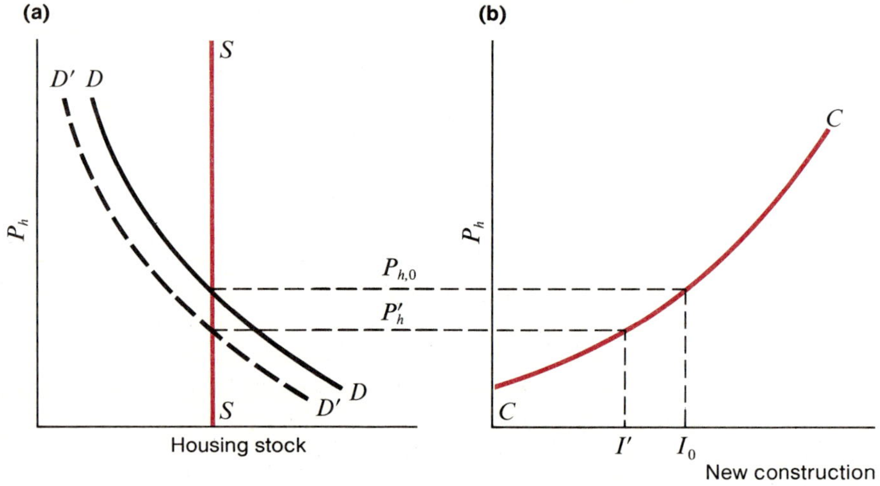

Determination of Housing Investment

We now turn to a diagrammatic analysis of the determination of housing prices and new construction.[9] In diagram (a) of Figure 12.5, we show the market for the stock of housing. The demand curve DD shows explicitly the negative relationship between P_h and the demand for housing incorporated in Equation (12.17). The other variables in Equation (12.17) shift the demand curve right or left in the figure. The stock of houses at any point in time is the vertical line SS in (a). This is a legitimate simplification, because new housing in any period as short as a year or so could not possibly add more than 2 to 3 percent to the stock of houses. Over time, as we shall see, the stock of housing moves to the right whenever there is new construction. In the short run the price of housing, P_h, is set in the housing market at the intersection of the demand and supply curves in Figure (12.5).[10]

New construction or housing investment is shown in diagram (b). The upward-sloping curve, CC, is the supply curve of the construction industry. It shows the amount of new housing that can be constructed at different housing prices.

[9]This stock-flow analysis was first developed by Robert Clower in the little-noticed but very useful paper, "An Investigation into the Dynamics of Investment," *American Economic Review* 44 (March 1954): 64–81.

[10]Note that we are assuming that rents are exogenous. In fact, rents are influenced by income, the age of the population, and several other variables.

Like almost all industry supply curves, this one is upward sloping, which says that the higher the prices of houses relative to other prices, the greater new construction will be. Rising wages or material costs will shift the supply curve CC upward and reduce new construction.

Now consider how the two components of the diagram fit together. The price of housing is, in the short run, determined in the market for the existing stock of houses. Prices settle at the point where demand equals supply, at $P_{h,0}$ in diagram (a). But at that price it is profitable to build new houses—that is, the price of houses is greater than their replacement cost—and, as we can see in (b), I_0 of new houses are built. Over time, as the new investment is added to the housing stock, the supply curve SS in (a) shifts to the right, and new construction declines. In this way new construction adjusts the asset portfolio of the public. Whenever there is an increase in the demand for housing, coming from any of the components in Equation (12.17), the demand curve shifts to the right, causing an increase in P_h. That increase in P_h is the signal that the public would like to hold a larger stock of housing. The economy responds by an increase in new construction, as one can see in (b). This is one of the ways that changes in portfolio preferences have an influence on current production.

One particularly important shift that we wish to consider is an increase in interest rates. According to Equation (12.17), a rise in r reduces the demand for housing, shifting the demand curve in Figure 12.5 to the dashed line $D'D'$. Housing prices decline to P_h', which causes a decline in housing construction from I_0 to I'. In this way, a rise in interest rates reduces housing investment. The interest rate effect may work directly through the influence of other assets on the demand for housing, or it may work through credit availability, which causes a general flow of funds away from the institutions that finance housing.

The negative relationship between housing demand, construction, and the interest rate is the reason why this type of investment has behaved countercyclically over the business cycle. Typically, during an expansion goods market demand increases faster than the money supply, leading to a rise in interest rates. While fixed investment responds positively to the growth in output, construction tends to be crowded out in the late stages of expansion. Conversely, construction is often the first component of aggregate demand to recover during recession. This pattern is particularly pronounced if the government relies on monetary policy for countercyclical stabilization.

Another important influence on the demand for housing is the expected capital gains on houses. According to Equation (12.17), an increase in expected inflation of housing prices should increase the demand for housing and stimulate construction. This occurred during the short-lived housing bubble of 1978–1979, as we shall see in the following case study.

Case Study

Housing in the 1970s

The postwar period has seen a tremendous growth in single-family housing in the United States. Between 1960 and 1979, the rate of homeownership rose from 62 to 65 percent, and the quality of the average home, measured by such things as the number of bedrooms and bathrooms, rose by one quarter.[11] However, construction exhibited increasingly severe cycles during the 1970s. Between 1972 and 1975, housing starts fell by 50 percent. Subsequently, renewed inflation and lower interest rates pushed the housing industry into a new boom, which lasted until the dramatic collapse in 1980. Between 1978 and 1981, the value of construction fell by 50 percent, or $30 billion. There are few other components of GNP that exhibit such violent fluctuations.

A dominant feature of the period since 1963 is the rise in inflation and the public expectations about inflation. Other things being equal, a rise in expected inflation lowers the real rate of interest and increases the demand for housing. Of course the nominal rate of interest has not been constant over this period, but it has not risen by as much as the rise in housing prices. Furthermore, since interest payments are tax deductible, only some fraction of any rise in nominal interest rates represents a true increase in costs. As a result, the rate of return on home ownership rose or, equivalently, the user cost of housing fell by close to 50 percent between the early 1960s and the late 1970s.[12] As our theory would predict, this fall in user cost sparked a dramatic increase in the demand for housing. Hendershott estimates that the price of a constant quality home increased by 199 percent between the first quarter of 1963 and the second quarter of 1979.[13] Since the GNP deflator went up only 130 percent and construction costs only 145 percent, it is quite clear that the relative price of housing was rising, which provided the necessary stimulus to increase new construction.

The increase in expected inflation was an important spur to the demand for housing. However, the main explanation for the severe cycles in housing in the 1970s was cycles in monetary policy. In this period the United States tended to rely on restrictive monetary policy to fight inflation. Both the 1974–1975 and the 1980–1981 recessions were precipitated by tight money and high interest rates. In both cases, housing was one of the major casualities.

In the 1974–1975 episode, rising oil prices and slow monetary growth drove up the nominal interest rate. Even though the rise was not sufficient to offset the inflation (or make the real rate positive), it was enough to cause an outflow of funds from savings and loan institutions and cause a cutback in mortgage lending.[14] The predictable result was a swift collapse in housing demand, housing prices, and construction in 1974–1975 (see Figure 12.6).

Subsequently, expansion during the Carter presidency was fueled by a rising money supply, falling nominal interest rates, and increased availability of mortgage credit. The user cost of homeownership began to fall once again, causing a rise in

[11]See Patric H. Hendershott, "Real User Costs and the Demand for Single-Family Housing," *Brookings Papers on Economic Activity* (2/1980): 401–444.

[12]See footnote 7 for a formal definition of the user cost of housing. The principal reason for the decline in the user cost is the increasing difference over the 1970s between the expected inflation rate or expected price appreciation on housing and the mortgage rate, after taxes.

[13]Hendershott, op. cit., p. 401.

[14]Mortgage rates rose to over 9 percent, but the inflation rate during 1974–1975 was over 10 percent.

Figure 12.6
Housing and Housing Prices, 1953–1982.
P_h—housing prices (CPI)
P—CPI for all items

The relationship between the relative prices of housing and the share of GNP devoted to construction is positive, as our theory predicts, but is not precise. During the period from 1953 to 1965, the relative price of housing was high and the share of residential construction was well over 4 percent. Both housing prices and the construction ratio have fallen sharply during periods of anti-inflationary contraction. Three such periods are 1968–1970; 1973–1975 and 1980–1982. Both have risen sharply during the first stages of recovery, such as during the years 1970–1972 and 1976–1977.

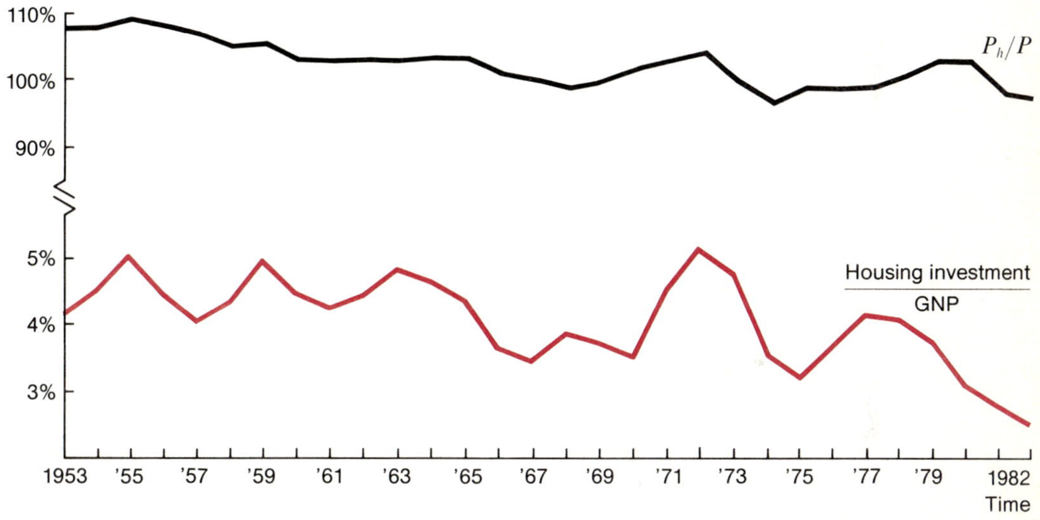

the demand for housing. That, in turn, drove up P_h and sparked a new housing boom.

Between 1975 and 1978, the relative price of housing rose by 14 percent, P_h rose by 23 percent, and new housing starts climbed by 73 percent. All this occurred despite rising nominal interest rates. Changes in the law governing S & Ls allowed these institutions to issue certificates of deposit and pay competitive interest rates for new money. As a result, credit availability became less of a factor than it had been in previous cycles. The typical crowding out of housing investment during expansion was not so pronounced, at least up through 1978.

In 1979 the roof fell in, so to speak, on the housing industry. As inflation once again accelerated in the country, the Federal Reserve tightened up. The money supply, which had grown by 8 percent over the first nine months of 1979, was essentially held constant until May 1980. Mortgage rates reacted sharply, rising from 10.9 percent in April 1979 to 12.9 percent by year's end and finally to almost

17 percent by mid-1980.[15] This, of course, dramatically increased the user cost of homeownership. The result was a collapse in the demand for housing. Prices for the first time in years declined, not only relatively but absolutely as well. Virtually all the gains in the relative price of housing since 1975 were wiped out in the sharp decline of prices in 1980 and 1981. Predictably, new construction fell along with prices. Housing starts fell from an annual rate of 1.5 million units at the end of 1979 to 900,000 units by May 1980, the lowest rate in the entire postwar period. The great 1970s real estate housing bubble was over.

Under the best of circumstances, construction is countercyclical. However, when government countercyclical policy relies mainly on monetary policy, as it did in the 1970s, the typical cycles in the construction sector are amplified. That is because housing is the expenditure most sensitive to interest rate fluctuations. If we continue to depend on monetary policy to stabilize the economy, we can expect housing to continue to bear the main brunt of stabilization.

Inventory Investment

We turn now to inventory investment, the most volatile of the three components of investment. Figure 12.7 shows the procyclical nature of inventories and the very large magnitude of the swings in inventory investment. Businesspersons accumulate inventories in boom years, such as 1950, 1955, or 1966, and then disinvest in recession years, such as 1954, 1958, or 1975. Note the size of the swings in this variable. The fall in 1975 was $18.3 billion dollars, a reduction in demand almost as large as the decline in fixed investment that occurred the same year. Inventory investment has often added to the severity of booms and recessions in the postwar period.

In modeling this variable, it is important to distinguish between intended and unintended inventory investment. We argued, in Chapter 3, that unintended inventory investment was the main indicator of disequilibrium. It is a short-run phenomenon that occurs when sales change prior to an adjustment in production. Thus, at the end of a boom sales may level off, because the monetary authorities apply restrictive monetary policy. If producers are slow to react, inventories will rise. Subsequently, production is sure to decline to bring inventories back into line. We will not model this disequilibrium inventory investment. What we do wish to model is the intended or planned part of inventory investment. We will write intended or planned inventory investment as I_I to distinguish it from unplanned inventory investment, which we have written ΔINV.

[15]For an account of this turbulent period see Albert E. Burger, "What Happened to the Economy in the First Half of 1980?" *Review: Federal Reserve Bank of St. Louis* 62 (August-September 1980): 9–16.

Figure 12.7
Capacity Utilization and Inventory Investment, 1946–1982.

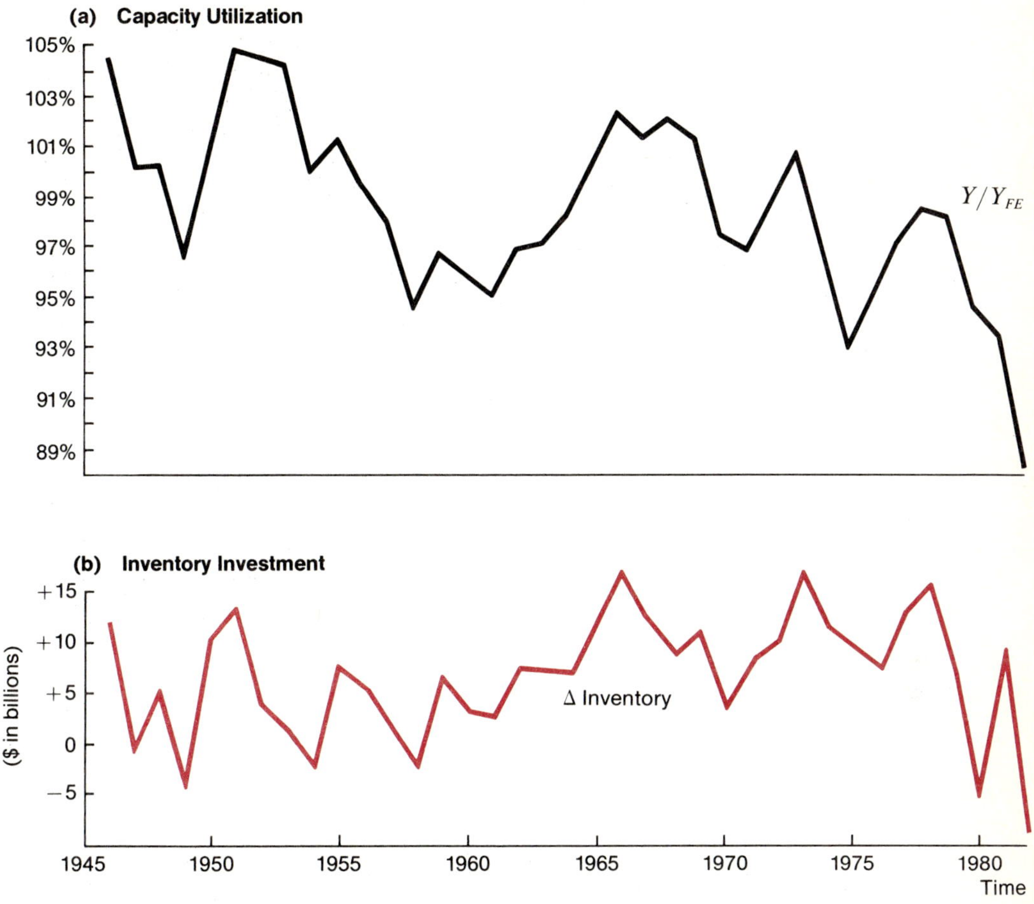

Intended Inventory Investment

Intended inventory investment is a particularly good example of the simple accelerator, because this form of investment does not require a long lead time. It is quick, and therefore it is reasonable to expect it to be finished within a year. Since this is the condition underlying the simple accelerator model, we shall apply that model to explain intended inventory investment.

Businesspersons try to maintain a certain ratio of inventories to sales. One might ask why they do this, since inventories don't appear to yield productive services as do machines and buildings. But, if one stops to think about it, inventories are as much a factor of production as either labor or capital. They are held because of the cost of idle time in production and sales. It is cheaper to keep a stock of spare parts on hand than it is to stop production and procure parts in the case of breakdown. Retailers find it more profitable to have items on hand rather than make customers wait while their orders are purchased or produced. In either case, an inventory saves time, generally substituting for labor.

We can now use the accelerator model of Equations (12.1) through (12.5). The desired stock of inventories is a linear function of output. Thus:

(12.18) $$K^*_{INV,t} = eY_t.$$

$K^*_{INV,t}$ = desired stock of inventory at end of time t
e = inventory-to-sales ratio

Intended inventory investment is equal to the difference between the inventory level on hand and the desired level:

(12.19) $$I_{I,t} = K^*_{INV,t} - K_{INV,t-1}.$$

Inventory adjustments are complete within the year. Therefore, by the end of the period, desired and actual inventories are equal:

(12.20) $$K^*_{INV,t} = K_{INV,t}.$$

Substituting Equations (12.18) and (12.20) into Equation (12.19), it follows that:

(12.21) $$I_{I,t} = e(Y_t - Y_{t-1}).$$

Inventory investment is positive whenever income is going up and is negative when income is falling. This implies extreme volatility in this particular spending stream. Changes in expenditure elsewhere in the economy have a large, procyclical effect on inventory investment.

To get an idea of how volatile inventory investment can be, consider the following example. Suppose we have the following simple model of the economy.

$$C_t = \frac{3}{4}Y_t$$

$$G = 150$$

$$I = 100$$

$$I_{I,t} = .05(Y_t - Y_{t-1})$$

Now if we first solve this system for its permanent equilibrium, where $Y_t = Y_{t-1}$ or where $I_{I,t} = 0$, we will get an equilibrium level of income of \$1000. We now want to see what happens when investment spending rises from 100 to 105. We know that without the complicating factor of inventory adjustment, equilibrium would be 1020 (since the spending multiplier is 4). With inventories, however, the economy overshoots the equilibrium in the short run. This is because there is a positive burst of

Table 12.1
Adjustment to Changes in Autonomous Expenditure with Inventory Investment

	I	G	C	I_I	Y	K_{INV}
Period						
0	100	150	750.00	0	1000.00	50.00
1	105	150	763.75	+1.25	1025.00	51.25
2	105	150	764.06	−0.3125	1018.75	50.93
3	105	150	765.26	+0.08	1020.35	51.02
⋮	⋮	⋮	⋮	⋮	⋮	⋮
n	105	150	765.00	0	1020.00	51.00

Note: The equation for Y_t is:

$$Y_t = \frac{I + G - eY_{t-1}}{1 - c - e}$$

$$Y_t = 5(I + G - eY_{t-1}).$$

From this one sequentially solves for Y_t given a value of Y_{t-1}.

inventory investment, which accentuates the increase in fixed investment. Instead of going to 1020, income goes up 1025 (see Table 12.1). The inventory investment makes the economy more sensitive to disturbances. Eventually, of course, the economy settles back to its equilibrium level of 1020, but that requires a small negative inventory cycle caused by the fact that the economy has to get rid of the excess level of inventories that it accumulates in period 1.

This example is not farfetched. Look back at Figure 12.7. It is quite clear that destabilizing inventory investment took place during both the Korean and Vietnam War booms. It is equally obvious that reductions in excess inventories played a big part in the 1954 and the 1974–1975 recessions. The effect of inventory disinvestment has been particularly pronounced in the last two downturns. Inventory investment and disinvestment amplify any inherent instability in private sector demand, making stabilization by the government that much more difficult.

Summary

In this chapter we have investigated the determinants of the three components of investment. Business investment is quite well explained by a lagged accelerator model containing only past changes in output. This means that business investment is sensitive to how fast the economy grows but appears to be less sensitive to interest rate manipulations by the monetary authorities. Contrary to popular belief, business investment has not really declined in recent years; it is high, relative to both the average of the postwar period and to our explanatory model. There has been a decline in nonresidential construction due to high interest rates and overbuilding in the early 1970s, but this is less significant for productivity growth than for equipment investment. In order to insure a strong investment performance, the surest method is to keep pressure on capacity by maintaining a high and growing level of aggregate demand.

Housing construction is determined by the relationship between the demand and supply for housing. When demand is high, housing prices rise above replacement costs and new construction takes place. The demand for housing is sensitive to interest rates, expected capital gains, and rents. Both demand and construction are particularly sensitive to interest rates, partly because housing is long-lived and partly because a set of specialized institutions, the savings and loans, is the main source of housing finance. Limited until recently in the interest rates they could pay for deposits, savings and loans have always lost funds when interest rates rose very far above their ceilings. As a result, housing has always tended to decline in the late stages of a boom and in periods of monetary contraction, because in both interest rates rise. It is too early to tell how the Monetary Reform Act of 1980 will affect housing finance and construction. We will discuss this act in Chapter 13.

Inventory investment is the most volatile of the types of investment. Because inventory investment does not require a long planning period, it can be explained by a simple accelerator model. When output is growing, inventory investment is positive. However, when the rate of growth of sales declines, inventory accumulation may fall to zero or below. Thus, inventory investment is both highly volatile and procyclical. On many occasions, inventory adjustments have exacerbated shifts in private sector demand, making moderate cycles more severe in both directions than they would otherwise have been.

Key Concepts

accelerator
disintermediation
desired capital stock
net investment
modified accelerator
planned investment
actual measured investment
user cost

Problems and Questions for Discussion

1. Suppose there is an increase in the expected rate of inflation in an economy but the nominal rate of interest is constant. What will be the effect of the change on the desired stock of housing? On the housing investment? Will there be any difference between the short- and the long-run impact of the change in expected inflation?

2. In earlier chapters we treated investment as a function of the rate of interest. According to the theory of investment developed in this chapter, this is not quite correct. Is there a relationship between investment and the rate of interest in a correctly specified theory of investment? If so, what is it? If not, why not?

3. If fixed investment behaves according to the accelerator model, what would you expect the time path of investment to be over the business cycle? Would it be procyclical? Would it help stabilize or destabilize aggregate demand?

4. According to the modified accelerator model, would you expect that expansionary monetary policy would be effective in stimulating investment in a recession? Why or why not?

Problems 5 and 6 are designed to show how the modified accelerator model works.

5. Suppose that a certain economy has the following investment and capital demand equations:

(1) $K^*_t = 3Y_{e,t} - 50i.$

(2) $Y_{e,t} = Y_t.$

K^*_t = desired capital stock at end of time t

$Y_{e,t}$ = expected output at time t

i = nominal interest rate

(3) $I_t = .25I_{P_t} + .50I_{P_{t-1}} + .25I_{P_{t-2}}.$

I_t = measured investment

Ip_t = planned investment

(4) $Ip_t = K^*_t - K^*_{t-1}.$

a. If $Y_{e,t} = 500$ and $i = .10$, what is K^*_t?

b. Suppose that $Y_{e,t}$ rises to 600. What is the new level of K^*_t?

c. Derive the time path of planned and actual investment in response to the change in $Y_{e,t}$.

6. Suppose that the interest rate is reduced from 10 percent to 5 percent in Problem 5 and that $Y_t = 500$.

a. What is the new desired capital stock?

b. Derive the time path of planned and actual investment in response to the change in i_t.

c. Plot the relationship between I_t and i_t that is implied by your answers to part b of this question. This demonstrates the lack of relationship between investment and the rate of interest in the modified accelerator model.

7. Why does housing investment have a countercyclical pattern while fixed investment has a procyclical pattern?

8. The following problem illustrates how an economy has a series of small inventory cycles in response to a change in autonomous expenditure. Suppose an economy has the following behavior equations:

$C_t = 100 + .67Y_t$

$G = 100$

$I = 100$

$K^*_{INV,t} = .08Y_t$

K^*_{INV} = desired stock of inventories

$$I_{I,t} = K^*_{INV,t} - K^*_{INV,t-1}$$

a. What is the equilibrium level of income and K^*_{INV}?
b. Suppose G rises from 100 to 125. What is the new long-run level of income?
c. Trace out the time path of inventory investment and income in response to the change in G.
d. Explain why the economy overshoots the new long-run income level during the adjustment process.

9. If the rate of depreciation is 10 percent, the rate of interest is 7 percent, and the price of machines is expected to rise by 4 percent per year, what is the user cost of capital? What is the real rate of interest? How would user cost be affected by a contraction in the money supply?

10. Compared with other industrialized economies, the rate of gross investment in the United States is low. What factors explain the low rate of capital formation in the United States? Is business investment low? Has investment fallen in recent years? If so, what explanation can you offer for the decline?

Chapter 13

Portfolio Theory

In the last two chapters we showed that consumption and investment are functions of the rate of interest. In this and the next chapter we will focus on the factors that determine the rate of interest. Economists have two different theories of interest rates. Some say that interest rates, being the cost of borrowing, are determined in a market for loanable funds. Others say that interest rates are determined in asset markets, by the stock of assets and the portfolio preferences of the public. In equilibrium the two viewpoints converge, but we think considerable insight is gained by the asset-portfolio view of interest rate determination. We shall therefore use it in our discussion of the interest rate and the analytical link between the asset markets and the demand for current output, particularly investment. Of particular interest is the method by which the government, through monetary policy, influences asset market equilibrium and how this in turn affects investment.

Portfolio Theory and the Demand for Assets

In Chapter 11 we analyzed the household decision about how much to save—that is, how much it should add to its assets. Here we consider the decision about the form in which these assets are to be held. This is a problem in portfolio theory. The public holds its wealth, the result of past saving, in many different forms, including cash, money market certificates, and government bonds on the one hand and over-the-counter stocks, houses, gold, and art objects on the other. Each asset has certain characteristics of safety, risk, and return that makes it attractive to wealthholders.

For each asset we can describe a market and analyze supply and demand. Asset characteristics and portfolio theory will determine public demand.[1] On the supply side, the stock of each asset increases or decreases over time according to processes that are different for each asset. In the short run, the asset markets clear when prices adjust in such a way that the public is just willing to hold the particular portfolio of assets that it has. Over time this portfolio can change, either because of government actions, which we call monetary policy, because of government deficits and their financing, or because the price of a reproducible asset is bid up above its replacement cost.

On the demand side of the asset market there are certain important asset characteristics to consider. The two main asset characteristics that should be important to households are *risk* and *rate of return.* **Risk** may be measured by the uncertainty of the rate of return or the possibility of capital loss. Assuming that households are risk averse, we would expect a positive relationship between the rate of return on an asset and its perceived risk. Money, the least risky asset, has no rate of return; over-the-counter stocks have high average returns, because there is large variation of returns (high risk or uncertainty) for the stocks traded on this market. To put it another way: No one would hold a risky security if its expected return were not higher than a less risky one.

The Wealth Constraint

Before looking more closely at asset demand equations, we start with the fundamental **wealth constraint,** which ties the demand equations together. For each household, the wealth constraint simply says that the total value of all assets is equal to total wealth:

(13.1) $$W = \sum_{i=1}^{T} P_i A_i.$$

P_i = price of ith asset
A_i = quantity held of ith asset

The wealth constraint is of more than accounting significance. For it implies that an increase in the demand for any asset must be matched by a reduction in the demand for some other asset. That is only another way of saying that one cannot demand something without giving something else of equivalent value in payment. Thus, Equation (13.1) implies that:

[1]The portfolio approach to the interaction between the asset market and the goods market was developed by James Tobin in "A General Equilibrium Approach to Monetary Theory," *Journal of Money, Credit and Banking* 1 (February 1969): 15–29. See also James Tobin and William C. Brainard, "Pitfalls in Financial Model Building," *American Economic Review* 68 (May 1968): 99–123.

(13.2)
$$P_i \, \Delta A_i = -\sum_{j=1}^{T} P_j \, \Delta A_j \qquad i \neq j.$$

(13.3)
$$\Delta W = \sum_{i=1}^{T} P_i \, \Delta A_i.$$

Equation (13.2) says that if wealthholders seek an increase in asset i, they have to draw down their holding of the other assets, in their portfolios. Equation (13.3) says that any increase in wealth comes about through additional amounts of some or all of the assets in the portfolio.

The wealth constraint implies that one of the asset demand equations can be derived from the others; it is not independent. For if we know the demand for $T - 1$ assets and we also know the value of wealth, the wealth constraint gives us the demand for the last asset. This has the important implication that if the wealthholder holds the desired amount of $T - 1$ assets, he or she must also be holding the desired amount of the Tth asset.

For example, suppose wealth consists of only two assets: money and bonds. Then, if we know the demand for money and total wealth, we must know the demand for bonds. Furthermore, if the household increases its demand for money, according to Equation (13.2) it must be trying to reduce its holdings of bonds. In this two-asset system, the demand for money and the demand for bonds must be negative images of each other. For anything that increases the demand for money must, by the budget identity, reduce the demand for bonds by an equivalent amount. In a multiasset world, the connections among asset demands are not so simple, but they must still be interdependent.[2] Thus, we may always represent the T asset market by $T - 1$ equations and the wealth constraint.

Inflation Protection

In addition to risk and rate of return, a third important asset characteristic to consider is *inflation protection*. Assets differ widely in the degree to which their real rate of return is affected by inflation.

Money assets, which have a fixed **nominal rate of return,** have a **real rate of return** that is inversely related to expected inflation. Other assets have nominal rates that vary directly with inflation, which means that their real rates tend to be independent of the inflation rate. For example, take housing. The real rate of return on housing is rental payments plus capital gains less depreciation. But since all three of these components tend to rise with the price index, the real rate of return on housing tends to be independent of the inflation rate. When there is an increase in the expected rate of inflation, there should be a shift away from financial assets with fixed nominal rates of return to real assets whose rates tend to rise with inflation. It should follow, therefore, that expected inflation will appear in the de-

[2]By Equation (13.2).

mand function for each asset, its effect being positive for inflation hedges and negative for financial assets that don't offer good inflation protection.

Ranking of Assets by Characteristics

In Table 13.1 we have ranked the various assets available to the public in terms of our three portfolio characteristics: risk, rate of return, and protection against inflation. The ranking is a subjective one, and different asset holders may well see asset characteristics differently. That is one reason why there are willing buyers and sellers for every asset. However they are evaluated, each asset offers a particular combination of characteristics that is attractive to some wealthholders. For example, money, defined as currency plus checking accounts, offers very low rates of return and poor protection against inflation, but it is also low-risk.[3]

We have ordered the assets in Table 13.1 in ascending order of riskiness. Money and short-term bonds are safe assets because there is little uncertainty about their rate of return. By contrast, there is a high degree of uncertainty about the rate of return on corporate equities, long-term bonds, and real estate. That uncertainty arises from two different causes: illiquidity and uncertainty about future prices. Illiquid assets are assets that cannot be sold quickly without a significant price penalty. Most real assets, such as houses, jewelry, and art works, are illiquid in this sense.[4] This makes the price at which they can be sold at any moment highly uncertain. For financial assets, such as corporate equities and bonds, the risk comes from changes in future investor preferences and economic prospects rather than illiquidity. These changes affect the future price at which such assets trade. Thus, even though bonds and equities are liquid assets, a high degree of uncertainty attaches to the price for which they can be sold in the future. Their high rate of return reflects this risk.

Mathematical Formulation of Asset Demand

We will summarize this short discussion in a general equation expressing the determinants of the public's portfolio demand for any particular asset. We shall first write the equation and then discuss each of its elements. Equation (13.4) is the demand for the ith asset. As in previous equations, the signs over each variable indicate how we expect it to influence the demand for the ith asset. A question mark means that we can not predict theoretically whether the variable increases or reduces demand for asset i.

$$D_i = f_i(\overset{+}{r_i}, \overset{-}{r_j}, \overset{-}{\sigma_i}, \overset{+}{\sigma_j}, \overset{?}{\Pi_e}, \overset{+}{W}, \overset{?}{Y}). \tag{13.4}$$

[3]Why, you might ask, would anyone hold money when he or she could hold interest-bearing checkable deposits, the next asset down the list? It has the same risk and inflation protection characteristics, yet offers a higher rate of return. The answer is that there has been a massive switch from money to checkable deposits in recent years, as we shall see in the next chapter.

[4]Gold is an important exception to this rule, because it is a standardized commodity.

Table 13.1
Portfolio Characteristics of Different Assets

	Nominal Rate of Return	Risk	Inflation Protection
Financial Assets			
Money	Low	Low	Low
Checkable deposits	Moderate	Low	Low
Money market certificates	Moderate +	Low +	Low
Short-term bonds	Moderate +	Low +	Low
Long-term government bonds	Moderate-high	Medium +	Low −
Corporate bonds	Moderate-high	Medium +	Low −
Corporate equities	High −	Medium +	High −
Real Assets			
Houses	High	High	High
Gold	Low	Medium	High
Art objects	Low	High	High

r_i = rate of return on asset i
r_j = rate of return on other assets
σ_i = measure of risk on asset i
σ_j = measure of risk on other assets
Π_e = expected inflation
W = total wealth
Y = income

Consider first the rate of return variables, r_i and r_j. For each asset we may define a rate of return, r_i. It is an interest rate in the case of money market certificates or Treasury bills and a pure capital gain in the case of gold coins or art works. For corporate equities, the rate of return is some combination of dividends plus expected capital gains. We hypothesize that the demand for each asset should depend positively on its own rate of return and negatively on the rates of return on competing assets.

The rate of return on most assets is not known with certainty, both because it contains a capital gain or loss term and because of possible future inflation. Accordingly, r_i is the rate that investors expect to earn from asset i. The less certain investors are about its outcome, the more risky the asset i. For a measure of uncertainty we shall write σ_i.[5] σ_i can be thought of as an indicator of the range or variation of possible outcomes. The bigger σ_i, the larger the possible fluctuations in r_i, and hence the more risky the asset. For example, on an investment in porkbellies, the investor may expect to earn 600 percent. But he is also aware that

[5] σ_i is a statistical measure of what is called variance.

he could lose everything because past price fluctuations in porkbellies tell him that the range of outcomes is very wide. We assume that most investors are risk averse. Therefore, a higher σ_i will reduce demand for the ith asset, which is why we show σ_i as having a negative influence on demand in Equation (13.4). For the same reason asset i becomes more attractive, the riskier competing assets are. (i.e., demand for asset i varies positively with σ_j).

Asset demands also depend on expected inflation. As we have already indicated in Table 13.1, some assets offer high protection against inflation while others do not. Therefore, when there is an increase in expected inflation, there ought to be a shift toward inflation-proof assets such as housing or corporate equities and a shift away from money and bonds.[6] Since Equation (13.4) is a general equation valid for both types of assets, the effect of Π_e is uncertain. It will not be uncertain when we write the demand equation for any particular asset. For example, the demand for houses should vary positively and the demand for money negatively with expected inflation.

In addition to rates of return and expected inflation, two other economic variables have an impact on demand. One is the *total value of wealth.* Presumably wealth should be positively related to the demand for all assets because, the structure of yields being held equal, one would expect some of each asset to be added to a portfolio as total wealth increases. Indeed, it might be reasonable to assume that the demand for each portfolio asset would increase in the same proportion as wealth if rates of return did not change. This is an important characteristic. Even if this proportionality condition does not hold, it should still be the case that if the value of wealth is increased through the expansion of any particular asset there should be an increase in the demand for other assets.

The other secondary element influencing asset demands is the level of income. A rise in income means an increase in the level of economic transactions. Transactions are made in money, which is one of the assets in the public portfolio. Hence, one would expect that an increase in income would increase the demand for money.

What about other assets? Here we turn to the wealth constraint. According to Equation (13.2), any change in the demand for money resulting from an increase in income must be offset by a reduction in the demand for some other asset or assets. Therefore, we indicate that the influence of income on the demand for assets in general is uncertain. It will be positive for money and presumably negative for most or all other assets.

Let us now put some content into this general portfolio theory by analyzing the demand and supply of some particularly important classes of assets. In the remainder of this chapter we shall look at three types of assets—government bonds, corporate bonds and stocks, and physical capital, such as housing. The government bond market merits special attention because it is here that the Federal Reserve system engages in open market operations. The corporate asset market

[6] In recent years equities have been a terrible inflation hedge. That is because there has been a rise in interest rates along with the rise in inflation. Because corporate bonds and equities are substitutes, that has tended to depress equity prices.

is important because it directly influences corporate investment. Physical capital markets have become important in recent years because physical capital is such an important hedge against inflation.

The Government Bond Market

Government bonds are a major component of the public portfolio, making up 10 percent of private wealth in 1982. Most of these bonds are issued by the U. S. Treasury to finance government deficits, although some are issued by government agencies, such as FNMA or the TVA. Government bonds are issued in many maturities, from 90-day notes, called bills, to 25-year bonds. For most such bonds there is an active secondary market which, as we shall see, plays a central role in the implementation of monetary policy.

The Relation between Bond Prices and the Interest Rate

In order to understand how the bond market works, one first has to understand what a **bond** is. A bond is a debt agreement between the borrower (seller of the bond) and the holder of the bond, promising to pay the holder a certain fixed number of dollars per year (the coupon) and to pay back the face value of the bond at a specified future date (the retirement date). What is important to us here is that bonds may be bought and sold so that the holder of today need not necessarily be the original bond purchaser (lender). There is a market in what one could call **secondhand bonds.** In that market bond prices are set by supply and demand. Thus, the price of a secondhand bond may rise above or fall below the price at which it was issued. When that happens, the effective interest rate or yield of the bond for today's buyer diverges from the coupon yield.

Bonds are generally issued or sold in units or multiples of $1000. Therefore, at the time of issue the interest rate and the coupon yield of the bond are identical. If we let C be the coupon payment on the bond and $\bar{P}$ be the issue price (usually $1000), then the initial interest rate on the bond is $C/\bar{P}$.

The **effective interest rate,** which we label r_b, may or may not be equal to the coupon yield. That depends on what happens to the price of the bond. The effective rate is the coupon payment divided by the current price of the bond plus or minus capital gains:

(13.5) $$r_b = \frac{C}{P_b} + \Pi_b.$$

r_b = rate of return on bonds
P_b = price of secondhand bonds
Π_b = change in the price of bonds

For short-term bonds, P_b cannot differ very much from the issue price, $\bar{P}$, because each investor knows that within a short period of time the bond will be redeemed for $\bar{P}$. That is why short-term bonds are relatively riskless. But for long-term bonds, the situation is entirely different, as investors have found to their sorrow in recent years. As interest rates have risen, coupons on newly issued bonds have gone up. That has forced down the price of all outstanding government bonds. Losses of 30 to 50 percent of face value have not been uncommon in the government bond market. The reason for this is that new and old bonds are substitutes. Hence, no one would pay P for an old bond, which has a low coupon, when he or she can get a new bond with a higher coupon for the same price. The price on old bonds must be such that investors are indifferent between an old bond paying C_j and a new bond paying C_m. Since they have to pay $1000 for the new bond, the price of the old bond, P_j, is set so that:

(13.6) $$\frac{C_j}{P_j} = \frac{C_m}{1000} = r_b.$$

In Equation (13.6), r_b is the current interest rate on bonds.

Equation 13.6 converts to an important relationship between P_j and r_b:

(13.7) $$P_j = \frac{C_j}{r_b}.$$

Equation (13.7) says that the current price of old bonds is inversely related to the bond interest rate. Of course, the absolute level for any particular bond also depends on its own coupon C_j.

Let us look at a particular bond to see how the process works. Table 13.2 reproduces part of the financial page of *The Wall Street Journal*.

The vital statistics of each bond issue in which there is an active secondary market is quoted every day. The particular bond that is underlined in the table is an issue of the Federal National Mortgage Association (FNMA). It is a 15-year bond issued in 1976 and has a face value of $10,000. It pays the holder $780.00 per year (the coupon rate, 7.8 percent, × $10,000). The bond has a maturity date of October 1991. That is when FNMA will pay back the then holder of the bond the $10,000 it originally borrowed in 1976.

After 1976, the demand for bonds declined while the supply of bonds, largely government bonds to finance deficits in the 1970s, increased. As one would expect, the price of all old bonds has fallen. As one can see from Table 13.2, by 1981 the price of our FNMA 10-91s had fallen from $10,000 to $8616, and the effective interest rate had risen from 7.8 percent to 10.2 percent. Thus, the fall in demand for bonds has led to a reduction in the price of all old bonds or, equivalently, a rise in the effective bond rate of interest (r_b).

The Demand for Government Bonds

Let us consider now the determinants of the demand for government bonds. The demand for such bonds comes from the portfolio preferences of the public and can be represented by one of the general demand equations (see Equation [13.4]).

Table 13.2
Government Bond Quotations

FNMA Rate	Issues Mat	Bid	Asked	Yld
17.50	2-83	100.15	100.19	6.76
7.75	3-83	99.29	100.1	7.32
7.75	3-87	91.12	92.12	10.04
14.30	4-87	112.12	112.28	10.44
11.15	5-87	102.12	102.28	10.38
7.65	6-87	90.24	91.24	10.01
9.10	7-87	94.8	96.8	10.16
15.25	7-87	116	116.16	10.53
14.45	8-87	112.28	113.12	10.66
7.50	10-87	88.24	90.24	9.99
12.13	10-87	105.24	106.8	10.41
10.85	11-87	101.28	102.12	10.20
10.45	1-88	100.28	101	10.19
14.40	2-88	113.24	114.24	10.56
10.50	6-88	100.8	100.24	10.31
16.38	8-88	122.8	123.8	10.71
8.55	9-88	92.8	93.8	10.14
11.00	11-88	101.16	102	10.51
9.30	6-89	95.16	96.16	10.05
12.10	10-89	106.12	106.28	10.63
11.30	12-89	102.20	103.4	10.64
10.90	11-90	101.12	101.28	10.54
7.80	10-91	85.16	86.16	10.17
7.00	2.92	79.28	81.28	10.08
7.05	6.92	79.28	81.28	10.08
10.90	1-93	100.2	100.7	10.87
7.10	12-97	74.8	76.8	10.24

Reprinted by permission of the *Wall Street Journal*.

Substituting the relevant rates of return into Equation (13.4), we have the demand for government bonds:

(13.8) $$D_b = d_b(\overset{+}{r_b}, \overset{-}{r_{bc}}, \overset{-}{r_h}, \overset{-}{\sigma_b}, \overset{-}{\Pi_{be}}, \overset{+}{W}, \overset{-}{Y}).$$

r_b = rate of return on government bonds
r_{bc} = rate of return on corporate bonds and equity
r_h = rate of return on physical capital
Π_{be} = expected change in bond price
σ_b = a measure of riskiness of government bonds

The demand for bonds should be positively related to their own rate of return and negatively related to the rate of return on the competing assets, corporate bonds and physical capital. Demand should be positively related to wealth and negatively related to income, because income induces the public to increase transactions balances at the expense of all competing assets. Demand should also be negatively related to the perceived riskiness of bonds and expected inflation. We can draw Equation (13.8) as the upward-sloping demand curve *DD* in Figure 13.1.

From Equation (13.8) we see that an increase in wealth will increase the demand for government bonds, thus shifting *DD* to the right. An increase in income, in expected inflation, or in rates of return on competing assets will have the opposite effect.

Figure 13.1
The Government Bond Market

In the short run the market clearing rate of return on government bonds is determined in (a), at the intersection of the demand curve and the fixed supply curve. The rate $r_{b,0}$ is what is required to get someone to willingly hold the outstanding stock of bonds. At that rate of return, $0B$ of new bonds will be issued by the government during the current period. Over time these news issues are added to the stock of bonds that the public is forced to hold. In (a), the stock supply curve shifts rightward to S_1S_1, causing an increase in the market clearing rate of return. The process does not converge to a long-run equilibrium solution, since the higher the interest rate the larger the government deficit, and therefore the larger the volume of new issues.

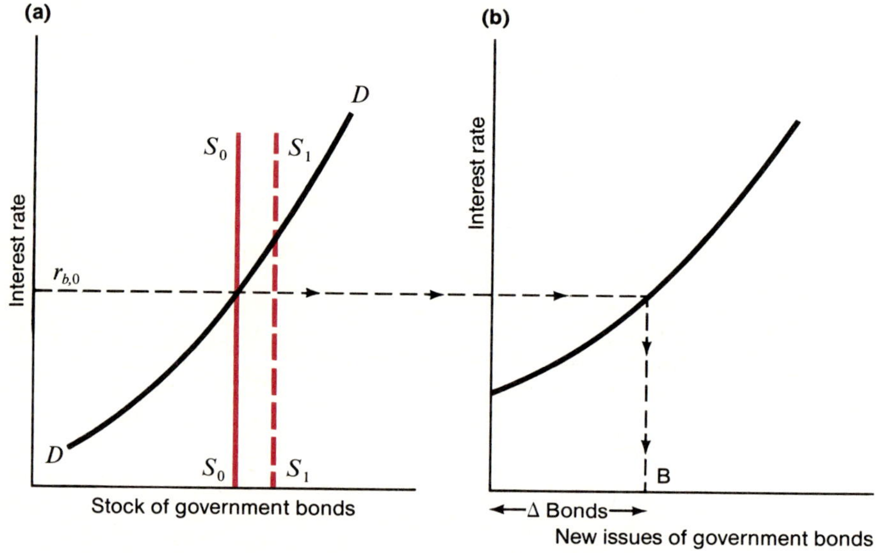

The Supply of Government Bonds

Turning now to the supply of bonds, we must distinguish carefully between the stock of old bonds in the public portfolio and additions to that stock during the time period under consideration. (This is exactly the same distinction we made for the housing market in Chapter 12.) There are two different supplies of bonds. The first is a stock that is on hand at the beginning of the current period. It is composed of bonds issued to finance government deficits and borrowings in previous years. The second is not really a bond supply but rather increments to the bond supply during the current period. Obviously the shorter the time period, the smaller the change in bond supply relative to the initial stock of bonds.

To make things easier analytically, we will define our time period as being so short that the supply of bonds can be treated as independent of new bond issues. This assumption is represented by a vertical bond supply curve in diagram (a) of Figure 13.1. New issues of bonds are shown in (b), which we could label the flow market. The upward-sloping curve in (b) shows new government bonds as a positive function of the bond interest rate. Bonds are issued to finance government deficits.

There are two reasons why deficits rise with the interest rate. First, interest costs are a government expense, and a rise in interest rates tends to increase the government deficit, which has to be financed by bond sales.[7] Second, a rise in interest rates is contractionary. It tends to reduce the level of aggregate demand because it discourages investment, as we saw in the last chapter. Since tax revenues rise and fall with income, a rise in interest rates should lead to falling government revenue and hence rising government deficits. If the money supply is held constant, this rise in the deficit leads to an increase in new bond issues.

Now let us put our two markets together. The interest rate is determined in the short run in the asset market, shown in (a). Interest rates rise or fall until the public is just willing to hold the outstanding stock of bonds inherited from the past; clearly that is at $r_{b,0}$, the intersection of DD and S_0S_0. But this is not the end of the story. For at $r_{b,0}$ we find from the flow market that new government bonds, in the amount 0B, will be issued during the current period. While these new bonds do not influence the interest rate this year, they will be added to the bond supply next period. Increments to the bond supply move the supply curve in (a) out to the right over time (from S_0S_0 to S_1S_1 and so on). Over time, if everything remains the same, continued government deficits, financed by bond sales, will drive the bond interest rate higher and higher.

We have treated the bond supply as if changes could come only through government deficits financed by new issues of government debt. There is another way in which the supply of publicly held bonds can be altered. This is through *open market operations.* As we shall see in the next chapter, the Federal Reserve System makes a practice of buying and selling government bonds in the New York bond market. This transaction is called an open market operation. Such an operation changes the supply of bonds and money held by the public and therefore influences the bond interest rate. However, as open market operations are part of monetary policy, we shall defer a full discussion until the next chapter, when we investigate both the money market and monetary policy.

The Corporate Securities Market

The two main corporate financial securities are stocks or equities and bonds. Both are issued by corporations to finance capital formation. Both are traded on national and regional exchanges. Like government bonds, corporate bonds are loan agreements that pay the holder a fixed number of dollars per year (the coupon interest rate) and promise to repay the principal of the loan at some declared future date (the retirement date). Corporate equity, as the name implies, gives the owner a share of the net profits of the corporation. It does not give a guaranteed annual payment as does the bond.

[7]This is assuming that deficits are not monetized.

The Rate of Return on Corporate Assets

Let us now define the relevant rate of return on these two assets. Like government bonds, the rate of return on corporate bonds is the coupon payment plus capital gains or losses:

(13.9)
$$r_{cb} = \frac{C}{P_{cb}} + \Pi_{cb}.$$

r_{cb} = rate of return on corporate bonds
C = coupon payment
P_{cb} = corporate bond price
Π_{cb} = change in bond price

Likewise, the rate of return on corporate equities can be defined as either the dividend plus expected capital gain or as the ratio of earnings to price per share. Thus:

(13.10)
$$r_s = \frac{D}{P_s} + \Pi_{se}, \text{ or}$$

$$r_s = \frac{E_s}{P_s}.$$

r_s = rate of return on equity
D = dividend
Π_{se} = expected change in equity price
P_s = price per share
E_s = earnings per share

Which definition of r_s in Equation (13.10) is a better predictor of equity demand is an empirical question. If corporations invest their retained earnings wisely, price appreciation should be highly correlated with retained earnings per share. The corporation that pays out little in dividends, choosing instead to plow back earnings into corporate expansion, rewards its investors with capital gains rather than dividends. In other words, retained earnings per share should be a good observable proxy for expected capital gains. Of course, many other factors also affect the expected price of equities, and this must be taken into account by the public in calculating Π_{se}, but we shall assume for simplicity that r_s can be measured by the ratio of earnings to price per share. This ratio, E/P, it will be noted, is just the inverse of the widely followed price-earnings ratio.

Corporate Equities and Bonds as Substitutes

A useful and traditional assumption in the portfolio literature is that corporate bonds and equities are viewed by the public as very close substitutes. Both are long-term financial assets, sharing in any risks associated with the corporate sector. Their major difference is with respect to inflation. Bond returns are fixed in money terms, while earnings per share should rise with inflation. One might therefore expect that any increase in expected inflation would lead to a shift from bonds to equity.

However, there is an important reason why this may not have occurred during our recent inflation. Inflation has two effects on corporate earnings, one positive and the other negative. On the positive side, inflation reduces the real interest cost of corporate financial liabilities. Corporations, just like other borrowers, may gain from inflation if their interest costs do not fully rise with inflation. On the negative side, under our tax system corporate assets are valued for depreciation and tax purposes at historical cost rather than replacement value. But that part of gross earnings that is needed, for example, to replace machines as they wear out should not be thought of as earnings but rather as deferred expense. Thus, whenever there is a rise in the cost of machinery due to inflation, corporations are forced to understate their true expenses, because they are required to use historical cost in calculating depreciation.

Thus, true corporate earnings, net of depreciation, may be adversely affected by inflation, which would imply that neither bonds nor stocks is a particularly good inflation hedge. This may be one reason why the rise in inflation in recent years has not, as expected, led to a portfolio shift in favor of equity.

For simplicity we are going to assume that corporate and government bonds are regarded as perfect substitutes and both are good substitutes for corporate equities. If that is the case, we should expect their two rates of return to move together, differing at most by a constant, k, which reflects the higher uncertainty attaching to equity prices. Hence, using k and k' as risk premiums, we will write:

$$r_s = r_{cb} + k = r_b + k'. \tag{13.11}$$

Equation (13.11) implies that equities and all bonds are good substitutes and that their rates of return move together. How realistic an assumption is this? The answer can be found in Figure 13.2, where we present a historical series of bond rates and the ratio of earnings to equity on the New York Stock Exchange. As the reader can see, the series move together most of the time so that the substitution assumption appears to be defensible.

Substitution has the important implication that the corporate bond rate is equal to the government bond rate plus a risk premium and that both are equal to the rate of return on equities adjusted by an additional risk premium. The key thing about the substitution assumption is that the government bond rate is a good proxy for the rate of return on corporate bond and equity issues: Anything that affects r_b affects r_{cb} and r_s as well. That has significant implications for investors on the stock market.

Equations (13.9) and (13.11) tie together the bond interest rate and stock prices. Let us see why. Look back at the definition of r_s as E_s/P_s in Equation (13.10). Equation (13.11) tells us that a rise in r_{cb} must lead to a rise in r_s. But if expected earnings remain the same, that can happen only if P_s, the price of equities, falls. In other words, rising interest rates imply falling prices on Wall Street, a

Figure 13.2
Selected Interest Rates and Yields on Corporate Equities

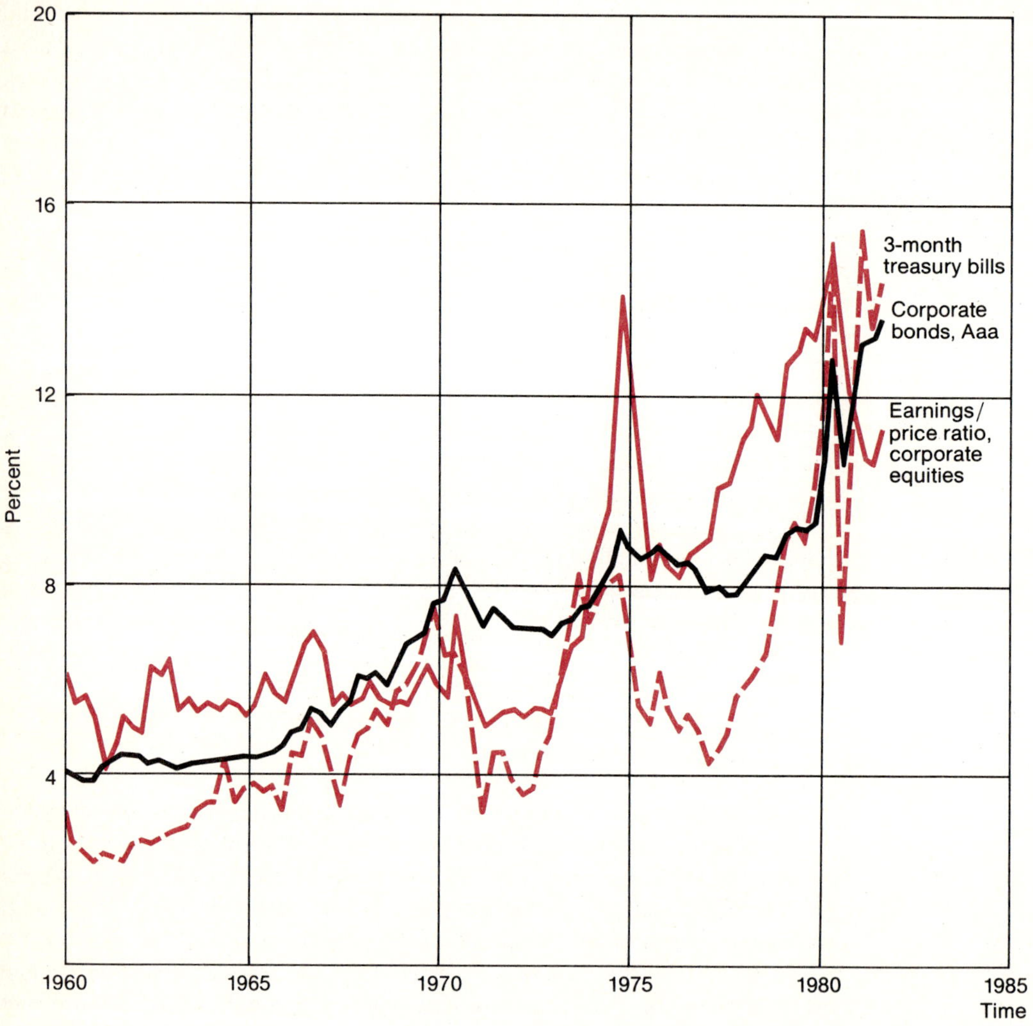

lesson that investors have learned all too well during the last several years.[8]

Another important implication is that we can for all intents and purposes combine the corporate equity and bond markets in our portfolio model and represent the two markets together by the single rate of return r_{cb}. This has an advantage when we consider changes in the supply of corporate debt.

[8]Prices of stocks are even more sensitive than this analysis implies. For as interest rates rise, the economy generally goes into a recession. That reduces earnings, giving a second downward push to equity prices.

Figure 13.3
The Corporate Asset Market
In (a), the demand for corporate bonds and equities and the given stock both determine the market clearing rate of return, $r_{cb,0}$. At that rate of return, we can see from (b) the number of new issues that will be made (I_0). Over time these new issues are added to the stock of corporate assets that must be held by the public. The supply curve in (a) moves to the right over time, and the rate of return rises until the supply curve intersects demand at $r_{cb,e}$, an interest rate at which no further new investment takes place.

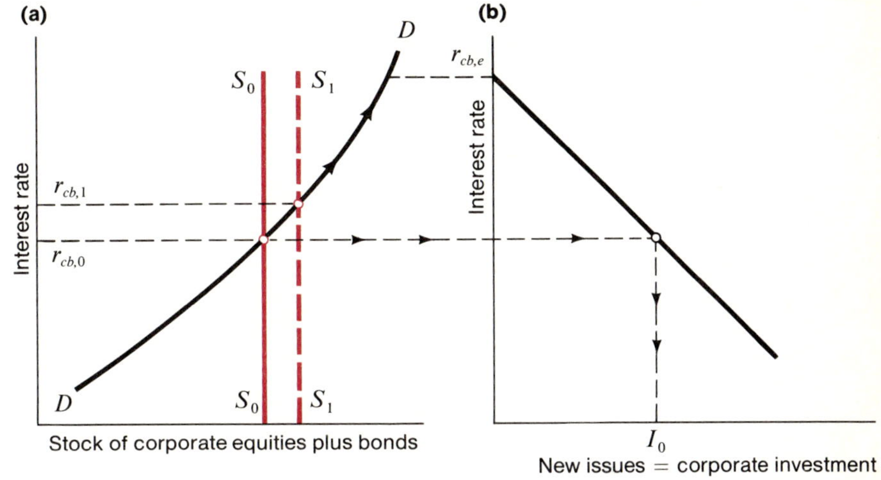

The Corporate Asset Market

Consider now the supply of corporate stocks and bonds. Just as we found for government bonds, here too supply is made up of two parts: one a stock of old assets issued in previous periods to finance corporate investment in those periods; the other this period's new issues, sold by corporations to finance this year's investment. We are going to assume, as we did for the government bond market, that the period of analysis is short enough so that the stock of old assets is very large relative to new issues. This allows us to treat supply at any moment as fixed and not appreciably affected by new issues.

Let us now draw a diagram of the two parts of the corporate asset market.

In diagram (a) of Figure 13.3, we show the demand and the supply of bonds as a positive function of the bond interest rate. The demand curve DD is a picture of Equation (13.4), specified for corporate bonds and stock. D is a positively sloping function of r_{cb}, because the public will want to hold more bonds in its portfolio if the interest rate is higher. Supply is the vertical line S_0S_0. S_0 is the number of shares of equity and bonds outstanding. Because of our definition of time period, this number is so large relative to new additions that supply can be thought of as constant for the time period under consideration (a vertical supply curve).

In the period under consideration, equilibrium in the corporate asset market occurs when demand and supply are equal, at an interest rate of $r_{cb,0}$ and S_0. This, however, is not the end of the story. Consider diagram (b). Here we show new issues of corporate bonds and equities. We are going to assume that all new corporate investment is financed by issues of stock and bonds. Therefore, the horizontal axis can be labeled investment. In the last chapter, we learned that investment is negatively related to the borrowing rate. The borrowing rate is r_{cb}. Thus, we have the negatively sloping investment function curve in (b).

Now let us tie the two diagrams together to see the link between the asset markets and new investment. The interest rate set in the asset market is $r_{cb,0}$. At that interest rate, investors will issue I_0 of new bonds or equity. As the reader can see, in the short run the asset or stock market (diagram [a]) determines the interest rate, which in turn influences the level of new investment.

Now let us look forward. In the short run the supply of bonds and stock was fixed at S_0. But this period an additional I_0 of new bonds is issued. Next period those new bonds will become part of the supply of assets that the public will be required to hold. In (a), the supply curve will slowly move to the right as new issues swell the asset supply. We show this process by moving the supply curve to the right over time. In period 1 it moves to $S_1(S_1 = S_0 + I_0)$, and the interest rate rises to $r_{cb,1}$. If nothing else changes, over time supply will continue to expand until the interest rate reaches $r_{cb,e}$. There the investment curve in (b) intersects the vertical axis, which means that no further investment takes place. This point could be called the long-run equilibrium, because the asset supply is constant; there are no further bond or equity issues. The short-run equilibrium is determined in the asset market by the intersection of each period's supply and demand curve. The long-run equilibrium is determined in the flow market by the condition that new investment go to zero.

The Effect of Changes in Asset Demand in the Short and Long Run

Now we analyze the effect of changes in asset demand in the short and long run, shown in Figure 13.4. Suppose that there is an increase in demand because of an increase in wealth coming from an expansion in the supply of some other asset. Such a change shifts the bond-equity demand curve to the right, from D_0D_0 to D_1D_1. Since the supply of bonds-equities is fixed in the short run, the increase in demand lowers the interest rate from $r_{cb,0}$ to $r_{cb,1}$. That change leads to an increase in investment (new issues) from I_0 to I_1. In other words, the increase in demand leads first to a fall in the rate of return on equities or, equivalently, leads to a rise in their price. That is the signal that the public wishes to hold more of this particular asset. Over time, as new investment takes place, new corporate debt and equity are issued to finance it. These issues satisfy the increased demand. One could say, therefore, that an increase in investment is triggered by an increase in the public's demand for the assets corporations issue to finance investment. When the portfolio demand for that type of asset rises, there will be a fall in r_s, a rise in P_s, and a rise in investment.

It may seem counterintuitive that a rise in the demand for an asset would cause a decline in its rate of return. After all, didn't we say that the rate of return had a positive effect on demand? Here one must distinguish between movements *along* a curve and movements *of* the curve. An increase in demand means a shift in the entire demand curve. At any rate of return people want a greater quantity

Figure 13.4
The Effect of Changes in Asset Demand

The market clearing rate of return on corporate bonds is determined in the asset market. If demand is at D_0D_0, the market clearing rate of return is $r_{cb,0}$. If the demand for corporate assets increases, demand shifts out to D_1D_1. This drives the market clearing rate of return down to $r_{cb,1}$. In (b), we see the effect of changes in asset demand on new issues. If demand increases in the asset market, causing a reduction in r_{cb}, we see that investment rises from I_0 to I_1. If demand falls, investment declines to I_2.

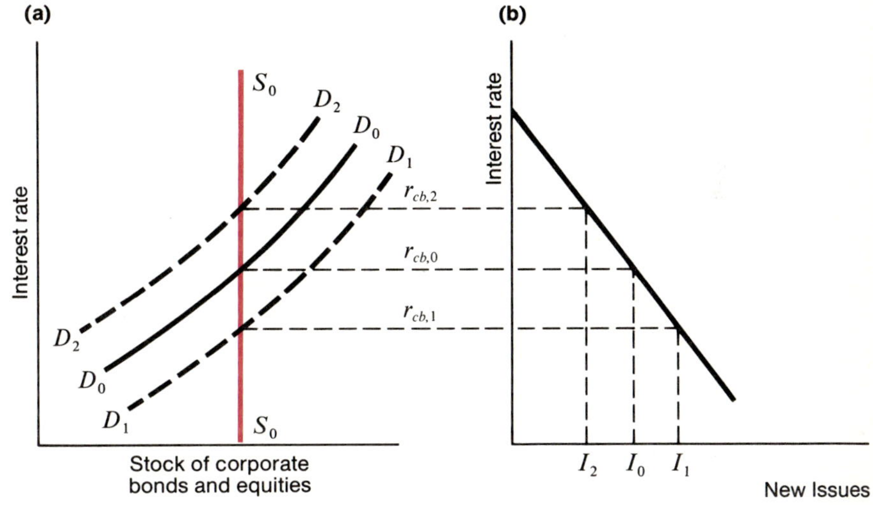

than before. Since the total quantity is fixed, the price is bid up and the rate of return is bid down.

An example of this was the stock market boom of the late 1960s. Because of the increased demand for equities, prices of existing equities were bid up, and the ratio of earnings to price fell to about 5.5 percent (that is, the price-earnings ratio rose to almost 18:1). Conversely, in the late 1970s there was a fall in the demand for equities due to rising interest rates on bonds. As a result, prices on Wall Street fell, and the price-earnings ratio rose to 13.5 percent.

Crowding Out in the Corporate Asset Market

One of the important influences on any asset is the supply of close substitutes. In the case of corporate bonds and equities, the closest substitute is probably government bonds. Let us see what happens when the government issues more bonds, say to finance government deficits. If corporate and government bonds are substitutes, as we assume they are, new bond issues satisfy a part of the public demand for this form of asset. We show what happens in Figure 13.5. In the corporate bond market the new issues shift the asset supply curve to the right, causing an increase in the interest rate on government bonds from $r_{b,0}$ to $r_{b,1}$. In the corporate equity-bond market the demand curve falls, because the public is

Figure 13.5
The Effect of an Increase in Supply of Government Bonds

This diagram shows the effect of an increase in government bonds. This shifts the supply curve in (a) to the right, which causes a rise in the government bond rate. Because private securities and bonds are close substitutes, the increase in bonds reduces the demand for private securities. As a result, r_s rises in (b), causing a reduction in investment in (c).

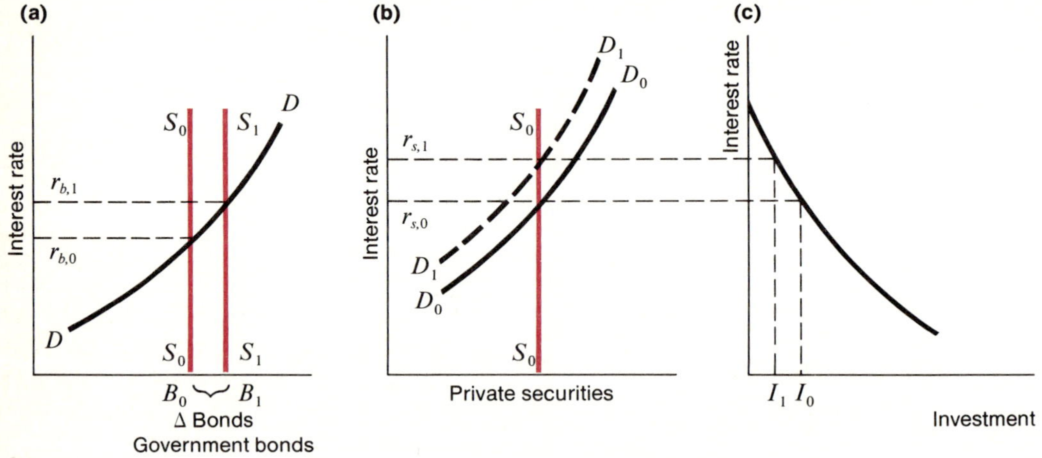

being forced to hold more government securities. As a result, the rate of return on corporate liabilities rises from $r_{s,0}$ to $r_{s,1}$, exactly parallel to the rise in r_b. This, of course, is implied by Equation (13.11), which tells us that these two rates must move together.

What we are describing here is the asset market side of crowding out. Quite literally, the increased supply of government bonds crowds private bonds out. The public is induced to hold the additional supply of government bonds by a rise in r_b; that reduces the demand for corporate bonds. In the short run, r_s rises to get the public to hold the existing supply of corporate securities. However, in the long run new issues decline and the equilibrium amount of capital, financed by those securities, falls.[9] In this way, government deficit financing crowds out private capital formation.

[9]For an interesting attempt to apply this type of model to explain the decline in corporate investment, see George M. von Furstenberg, "Corporate Investment: Does Market Valuation Matter in the Aggregate?" *Brookings Papers on Economic Activity* (1/1975): 347–397. The idea is that rising interest rates drove down the valuation of corporate equities to the point where the price of shares, representing ownership of existing assets, was lower than the replacement cost of the assets themselves. It was therefore cheaper for corporations to buy shares (titles to existing assets) than to build new assets. In this way, the decline in prices on Wall Street could explain the decline in corporate investment. However, von Furstenberg found that market valuation of corporate equities was not a particularly good explanation of investment in recent years.

Physical Capital Markets

The last class of assets that we will analyze in this chapter is the physical capital market, comprised of nonfinancial, reproducible durable goods such as housing, art works, and jewelry. For housing, we developed the theoretical apparatus in the last chapter. However, in that analysis we expressed housing demand in terms of the price of housing. Here we are using rates of return. Clearly, by the way we defined the rate of return on housing, the two are equivalent. For, by Equation (12.15), r_h, the rate of return on housing, was defined as:

$$r_h = \frac{\text{rent}}{P_h} - \delta + \Pi_{he}.$$

If, for simplicity, we assume constant rents, an increase in the demand for housing drives up the price or, equivalently, drives down r_h. That, of course, leads to an increase in construction and an expansion of the housing stock.

For art objects and jewelry, the rate of return presumably is an expected capital gain. When there is a rise in expected inflation, there should be a public portfolio switch to such inflation hedges as houses and art objects. That will drive up the price of paintings, for example, which will induce artists to produce more. Over time the portfolio of the public gradually changes to one holding more inflation-proof assets. Unfortunately, if the portfolio switch to jewelry, gold, and art objects comes at the expense of corporate securities, the rise in expected inflation will lower investment altogether as productive resources are switched into gold mining and jewelry making and out of factories and machines. This sort of switch, which is a very serious one for capital formation and worker productivity, may well have occurred in the United States in recent years.

Summary

In this chapter we have developed a model to explain how the public holds the assets in its portfolio. We showed that the demand for any asset depends positively on its own rate of return, negatively on the rate of return on competing assets, and positively on the total value of the portfolio or wealth. Two factors, income and expected inflation, have an indeterminate sign in the general asset demand equations.

On the supply side we distinguished between the stock and flow markets. For short time intervals, supply in the stock market is fixed. Hence in the short run, the market-clearing rate of return is determined in the stock market. However, that rate of return has an effect on the flow of additions to the stock of assets, since in every case increments to the supply of assets are related to their rates of return. In this way, the set of assets available and the demand for them, at each point in time, determine a pattern of rates of return, which in turn determines how the portfolio will be changing due to additions to the stocks of the various assets in the portfolio.

We singled two asset markets out for particular attention. They are the corporate equity and housing markets. Both are important because additions to the stock of either of these assets are counted as investment, and so have an impact on the goods markets. Since all assets compete in the public portfolio, our general theory tells us that any change in any asset market will have an effect on investment, provided only that it affects the market clearing rate of return for either housing or corporate equities. This is the link between the asset and goods markets.

We have now completed our discussion of the determinants of demand and supply in the various nonmonetary asset markets. What remains to be analyzed is the money market itself. This is a market which has received a great deal of attention and research in recent years. In the next chapter we integrate the money market into our portfolio theory and show how the Federal Reserve, through monetary policy, can act on this and the other asset markets to affect aggregate demand.

Key Concepts

risk
wealth constraint
portfolio substitutes
portfolio theory
bond
short- versus long-run effect of changes in the demand for assets
effective interest rate

Problems and Questions for Discussion

1. In the short run, why can't a reduction in the demand for bonds cause a reduction in the quantity of bonds held? What happens when there is a reduction in the demand for bonds?

2. What does it mean to say that with the wealth constraint one of the asset demand equations can be derived from the other asset demand equations? What important implications follow from this fact?

3. Suppose that a bond was issued in 1967 when the market interest rate was 7 percent. What was the initial price of the bond, and what was its coupon payment? If interest rates rise to 12 percent, what do you expect to be the price of the 1967 bond? Can you think of any reason why the price may not fall as far as our simple model might predict in response to the rising interest rates? For example, how might nearness of maturity affect the interest sensitivity of bond prices?

4. Discuss the stock and flow notions of asset supply presented in this chapter. If there is an increase in the demand for an asset, how does this affect the stock and flow supply of the asset?

5. Distinguish between the short- and long-run effects of a change in the demand for bonds or corporate equities. How is the change in demand accommodated in the short run and in the long run? What is the difference between the two?

6. Discuss and compare the way that the economy creates the different assets government bonds, corporate equities, and housing.

7. Why do rising interest rates lead to falling prices on Wall Street? What is the short- and long-run effect of falling equity prices on the supply of corporate equity?

8. How is the short-run equilibrium interest rate in the corporate equity-bond market determined? How is it determined in the long run? What happens to each of the two interest rates when there is an increase in the demand for corporate equities or bonds?

9. Our asset theory tells us that the demand for any asset is positively related to its own interest rate. Why then does an increase in the demand for an asset lead to a decline rather than an increase in its interest rate?

10. Suppose that the Federal Reserve, through open market operations, increases the supply of government bonds to be held in the public portfolio (it sells bonds to the public). Using the diagrams of the government bond and corporate equity markets, show the short-run effect of this contractionary open market operation on the government bond market and the corporate equity market. Be sure that you show what happens to the interest rate and the supply and demand curves for these two assets.

Chapter 14

Monetary Policy and the Money Market

Having analyzed nonmonetary assets in Chapter 13, we now turn to the money market, the final market in our portfolio theory. This market has always had a special importance in macroeconomic theory—indeed, there is a group of economists who believe that the demand and supply of money are the principal determinants of aggregate demand and the price level. Before studying theories of the demand for money, however, we must first define what it is we are talking about when we say money.

Money and Money Substitutes

Narrowly defined, money consists of those assets that are accepted as means of payment; that is, currency plus bank deposits upon which checks can be drawn. However, in the portfolio definition, there are many other assets that are close substitutes of money. While they cannot technically be used for transactions, such assets as savings accounts and **money market funds** are as liquid as money and so should perhaps be grouped with currency and bank deposits when we formulate the portfolio demand for money.

One of the striking developments in U. S. financial markets in recent years has been the proliferation of money-like assets, most developed by depository institutions so that they could compete for savings in a time when steadily rising interest rates made their traditional savings accounts unattractive to savers. Up until new legislation was passed in 1980, none of these new financial instruments were subject to any reserve requirements. Thus, they were not directly controllable by the Federal Reserve, which meant that the financial system was able to create close money substitutes whenever the Federal Reserve attempted to reduce the rate of growth of the money supply. In this section we will look more closely at the new assets and the recent legislation that has been enacted to give the Fed a measure of control over their rate of growth.

New Money Substitutes

Table 14.1 shows at a glance which assets are included in the various current measures of money. **M1** is the total of all deposits on which checks can be written. **M2** adds small, private savings accounts at depository institutions plus money market fund shares, and M3 adds large savings deposits, commercial repurchase agreement accounts (RPs), and certificates of deposit (CDs). Finally, L adds short-term liquid financial instruments, such as commercial paper, U. S. savings bonds, and bankers acceptances.

Among the new assets, with which readers may or may not be familiar, are the following:

NOW accounts (Negotiated Order of Withdrawal) These are accounts that pay interest and upon which checks can be drawn. NOW accounts were originated by a Massachusetts savings and loan association in 1972. Gradually the practice spread from Massachusetts to surrounding states and from savings and loans to all depository institutions. Prior to 1980, commercial banks in the Federal Reserve System were not permitted to pay interest on checking accounts, but by 1978, the Fed permitted banks to cover overdrafts on checking accounts by automatic transfer from savings accounts (ATS). Finally, in the Deregulation and Monetary Control Act of 1980, all depository institutions were given the right to offer NOW accounts.

ATS accounts (Automatic Transfer Savings) ATS accounts are savings deposits in commercial banks that may be automatically transferred to a customer's checking account. In effect, they permit the payment of interest on a large fraction of the deposits subject to check writing privileges. ATS accounts were the commercial bank substitute for the NOW account and will probably diminish in size and importance after 1981, because under the Monetary Control Act of 1980, banks are now free to offer NOW accounts.

RPs (Repurchase Agreements) RPs are loans from corporations with bank-held government securities as collateral. The corporation gets the equivalent of a checking account, upon which interest is paid subject to the condition that funds may not be withdrawn prior to some agreed-upon date. The duration of these loans may be very short, often overnight. The RP is a way for the corporation to earn money on idle cash balances. The advantage to the bank is that the RP is not considered to be a deposit subject to reserve requirements. Thus, the RPs allow the banking system to increase loans even if the Federal Reserve does not increase reserves.

CDs (Certificates of Deposit) CDs are loans from individuals or corporations to banks. They are sold by the bank with a specific maturity date, although early withdrawal is permitted for small CDs upon payment of an interest penalty. CDs

Table 14.1
The Composition of the Monetary Aggregates

Component	M1	M2	M3	L
Currency	X	X	X	X
At commercial banks:				
Demand deposits inclusive of deposits due to foreign commercial banks and official institutions	X	X	X	X
Demand deposits exclusive of deposits due to foreign commercial banks and official institutions	X	X	X	X
NOW accounts[a]	X	X	X	X
ATS accounts[a]	X	X	X	X
Overnight RPs		X	X	X
Savings deposits		X	X	X
Small time deposits (<$100,000)		X	X	X
Large time deposits				
Other than large negotiable CDs			X	X
Including large negotiable CDs			X	X
Term RPs			X	X
At thrift institutions:				
Demand deposits	X	X	X	X
NOW accounts[a]	X	X	X	X
ATS accounts[a]	X	X	X	X
Credit union share draft balances	X	X	X	X
Savings deposits (mutual savings banks and savings and loan associations)		X	X	X
Small time deposits (<$100,000)		X	X	X
Large time deposits (>$100,000)			X	X
Term RPs (commercial banks and savings and loan associations)			X	X
Other				
Overnight Eurodollar deposits of U. S. nonbank residents[b]		X	X	X
Money market mutual funds shares		X	X	X
Term Eurodollars held by U. S. nonbank residents				X
Bankers acceptances				X
Commercial paper				X
U. S. savings bonds				X
Liquid Treasury securities				X

[a]These accounts were included previously in the savings deposit component of the definitions.
[b]Overnight Eurodollars issued by Caribbean branches of member banks.
Source: Federal Reserve Bank of St. Louis, *Review* (February 1980).

are not limited by interest rate ceilings but instead earn the money market interest rate at the date of sale. Like RPs, certificates of deposit are not subject to reserve requirements, because technically they are not deposits. Both are new financial investments invented by the banking system to make credit available at a time when savings deposits are less attractive to lenders.

Growth of Money Substitutes

In Figure 14.1 we show a historical time series of each of the alternative definitions of money. It is immediately obvious that there has been a very significant growth in M2, M3, and L relative to the narrowly defined money supply in recent years. The change reflects the effort by the financial system to satisfy the demand for money at a time when the Federal Reserve was trying its best to control the growth rate in the money supply by fairly severely limiting the growth in the monetary base.[1] As the reader can see, M1 follows closely the growth in the base. That is because, prior to the Monetary Control Act of 1980, these were the only money-like assets that were subject to reserve requirements. When the Fed tightened up, the banking system turned to new assets, such as CDs and RPs, to satisfy the demand for credit. Also, money market funds were invented to tap the saving of small savers. These new developments were brought about for two reasons. First, the development of cheap, fast electronic funds transfer systems made it feasible to transfer funds between accounts at low cost. Second, the general rise in interest rates, coupled with interest rate ceilings on savings accounts, made it profitable to create higher-yielding liquid, or money-like, assets. Depository institutions, particularly banks, were forced to create new types of liabilities such as CDs and RPs in order to compete with money market funds and maintain a flow of funds to their borrowers.

However, all of this created a problem for the Federal Reserve. If the financial system could create money-like assets, which were not subject to Reserve requirements, how could the Fed carry out its responsibilities for monetary policy? As we have just seen, it was able to control the growth of M1 by slowing the expansion of the monetary base. But that seemed to have little effect on the growth of the more inclusive monetary aggregates.

The Depository Institutions Deregulation and Monetary Control Act of 1980

The first attempt to solve the problem of controlling monetary assets was the Depository Institutions Deregulation and Monetary Control Act of 1980. This act transformed, in a very fundamental way, the rules under which all of the nation's depository institutions function. The key features of the act are:

1. All depository institutions are now required to hold reserves on all of their demand deposits and NOW accounts, plus their nonpersonal time deposits. This requirement extends reserve requirements to banks that had previously not been members of the Federal Reserve System and to thrift and other savings institutions. Effectively, this means that all the assets in M1 are subject to reserve requirements, which solves the problem of assets and banks leaving the System whenever the Fed holds down the growth of reserves. However, the new set of reserve requirements will not make it easier to control the more inclusive mea-

[1] Further on in this chapter we will study how the Fed controls the monetary base and what effect this has on the money supply, narrowly and broadly defined.

Figure 14.1
Time Series of Monetary Aggregates

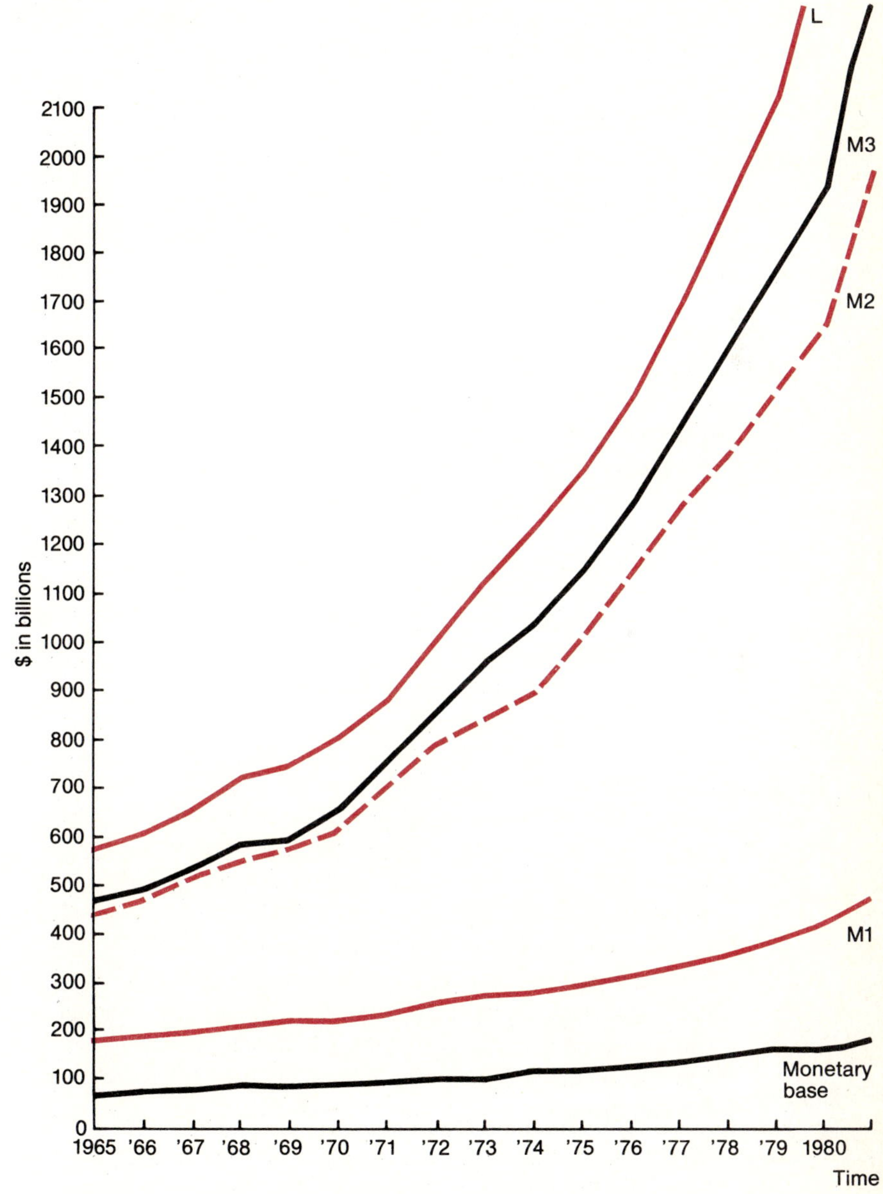

Source: *Economic Report of the President* (Washington, D.C., 1983).

sures of the money supply, M2, M3, and L, because most of the assets in these measures are not subject to reserve requirements. We shall return to this problem in a moment.

2. Interest ceilings on all types of deposits are to be phased out over a six-year period. This effectively decontrols prices in the banking industry and makes the interest rate available to small depositors a function of the competitive forces of the marketplace.

3. All institutions are authorized to offer NOW accounts, which were previously limited to savings and loan associations in and around New England.

4. All depository institutions are to be allowed access to Federal Reserve services on a fee basis. In particular, they will be allowed to borrow at the Fed's discount window, a service previously available only to member banks.

What is important to remember about the new act is that all checkable deposits, regardless of source, are now made subject to reserve requirements. However, other assets (those in M2 and M3 but not M1), such as money market fund shares and savings account deposits, do not have reserve requirements. This obviously gives banks a fairly strong incentive to create such assets when there is a high demand for credit.

The Demand for Money

We turn now to the demand for money. Before we can make an analysis, however, we have to decide which definition of money we wish to use.[2] If one thinks of the demand for money as principally a transactions demand, M1 is undoubtedly the correct definition of money. However, if one thinks of money as simply the least risky and most liquid of the assets in the public portfolio, then one of the expanded definitions is more appropriate. We are going to perform the analysis for both M1 and M2. For our purposes, the key difference between them is that the assets in M1 earn either a zero or very low rate of return while the assets in M2 or M3 earn a rate that is much higher. In the case of money market fund shares, the rate rises and falls with the interest rate on bonds and is almost as high. This makes a good deal of past discussion of the demand for money and the interest rate quite irrelevant if one is thinking of M2 as the appropriate definition of money. For the new, high-interest savings accounts and mutual fund shares allow one to hold money and earn interest at the same time.

[2]There has been an extensive discussion of the appropriate definition of money. For a review of that literature, see Thomas M. Havrilesky and John T. Boorman, *Monetary Macroeconomics* (Arlington Heights, IL: AHM Publishing, 1978), 169–175; Allan H. Meltzer, "The Demand for Money: The Evidence from the Time Series," *Journal of Political Economy* 71 (June 1963): 219–246; and V. K. Chetty, "On Measuring the Nearness of Near-Moneys," *American Economic Review* 59 (June 1969): 270–281.

According to our portfolio theory, the demand for any asset depends positively on its own rate of return and negatively on the rate of return on competing assets. Money should be no exception to this rule. For the narrowly defined money supply we shall assume that the rate of return is zero, whereas for the broader definition the rate will be r_m, a weighted average of the rate paid on savings account and money market fund shares. All the assets at the risky end of the portfolio are portfolio substitutes for money. Thus, we would expect money demand to be negatively related to the rate of return on government and corporate bonds, on corporate equity, and even on housing.

In general, asset demands are negatively related to the rates of return on competing assets. But one could reasonably ask why anyone would hold non–interest-earning money or low—interest-earning savings accounts beyond the base minimum required by transactions if higher interest rates are available on other relatively safe assets, such as government bills or certificates of deposit. In other words, why should money demand vary with the interest rate? Economists have given three alternative explanations: the demand by speculators expecting changes in the interest rate; diversification of assets; and the cost of making transactions. We will now look at each in turn.

The Speculative Demand for Money

J. M. Keynes divided the demand for money into **transactions demand** and **speculative demand.**[3] He granted that the former was not interest-sensitive but argued that the latter ought to be. His idea was based on the simple notion that often speculators hold idle cash balances when they expect that the price of assets they are interested in buying will fall in the near future. They expect to make a speculative profit by waiting to buy.

Let us see how this is related to the interest rate. As we showed earlier, the interest rate and the price of bonds are inversely related by the expression $P_{cb} = C/r_{cb}$. Hence, when we say that speculators hold cash when they expect prices to fall, that is equivalent to saying that they hold cash when they expect interest rates to rise. One might expect that the number of speculators expecting rising interest rates would increase the lower the observed rate. If that is true, then the lower the rate, the greater the number of speculators who hold idle cash expecting a fall in bond prices. Hence, in the aggregate, the demand for money would be a negative function of the interest rate on bonds.

A number of later theorists have pointed out some difficulties in Keynes's theory. In the first place, it seems artificial to split money balances into two parts, one for transactions and one for speculation. Second, the theory implies that any individual is either fully invested, if he expects interest rates to go lower, or fully in cash, if he expects them to go higher. But observation of actual portfolio behavior shows that most people hold cash and assets at the same time, the proportion depending on the interest rate.

[3] John Maynard Keynes, *The General Theory of Employment, Interest, and Money* (London: Macmillan, 1936), Chapter 15.

Diversification and Risk

James Tobin developed a very ingenious portfolio model to try and explain the **diversification of assets** in the typical portfolio.[4] Some assets, such as bonds and stocks, have high but uncertain rates of return. The uncertainty results from the possibility of capital loss. Money is the asset that offers the greatest certainty and the lowest expected rate of return. The investor, according to Tobin, chooses the portfolio that offers the best possible combination of risk and return. Usually he can do this by diversifying. He holds some money in his portfolio, exactly because it is riskless (ignoring losses due to inflation), and he balances this by holding some high-yielding but riskier assets. When the rate of return on any of the risky assets goes up, the investor shifts his portfolio slightly in favor of that asset. Hence the demand for money, the riskless asset, should be negatively related to the rate of return or the interest rate on bonds, equities, or any other risky asset.

Transactions Demand

Yet another reason for a negative relationship between the demand for money and the interest rate was developed independently by William Baumol and James Tobin.[5] Transactions balances, they argued, are held for convenience. Theoretically at least, it would be possible to eliminate all idle cash balances by cashing in an interest-bearing asset at the exact moment when each purchase had to be made. The reason people don't do this is because of the inconvenience and expense of either selling bonds or transferring funds between accounts. The new ATS accounts make this rationale a good deal less plausible than it used to be.

If it is possible to economize on cash balances, it should follow that the higher the interest rate, the more effort will be devoted to economizing on cash balances. Both Tobin and Baumol, using this notion of cost minimization, derive exact formulas in which the demand for transactions balances depends negatively on the interest rate.

Drawing together all of these explanations, we have at least three different reasons to expect a negative relationship between the demand for money and the whole complex of rates of return on risky assets represented by the bond rate, r_{cb}. They are the speculative rationale of Keynes, the portfolio approach of Tobin, and the interest-sensitive transactions balances of Tobin and Baumol.

Therefore, following the example set in Equation (13.4), we will write the demand for money as:

$$M_d = f(\overset{-}{r_b}, \overset{-}{r_{cb}}, \overset{-}{r_h}, \overset{+}{Y}, \overset{+}{W}, \overset{-}{\Pi_e}). \qquad (14.1)$$

[4]James Tobin, "Liquidity Preference as Behavior towards Risk," *Review of Economic Studies* 25 (February 1958): 65–86.

[5]William J. Baumol, "The Transactions Demand for Cash—An Inventory Theoretic Approach," *Quarterly Journal of Economics* 66 (November 1952): 545–566; and James Tobin, "The Interest Elasticity of Transactions Demand for Cash," *Review of Economics and Statistics* 38 (August 1956): 124–131.

As we have just seen, the demand for money depends negatively on the rates of return on competing assets. It also depends negatively on the rate of expected inflation, Π_e, because inflation is a tax on moneyholders. Inflation can be thought of as a negative rate of return or cost for holding money. Hence the higher the expected inflation rate, the lower should be the demand for money.

The other terms in Equation (14.1) have already been alluded to in Chapter 13. Money demand is positively related to income because money is used for transactions. Wealth positively affects the demand for money as it does for all assets in the public portfolio. Other things being equal, an increase in wealth should lead to roughly proportional increases in the demand for all assets.

Drawing all of this discussion into a diagram (Figure 14.2), we can represent the demand for money as a negative function of any of the rates of return shown in Equation (14.1). We will use the government bond rate, r_b. Each of the other factors influencing the demand function, Y, W, and Π_e, are shift variables in Figure 14.2. An increase in income, for example, increases the demand for money and therefore shifts D_1D_1 up to $D_1'D_1'$. An increase in wealth has the same effect, an increase in expected inflation the opposite effect.

In Figure 14.2 we show separate demand curves for M1 and M2 (D_1D_1 and D_2D_2). The curve for M1 is drawn as flatter than that for M2.[6] As we learned in Chapter 4, that means that the demand for the narrowly defined money supply is more sensitive to interest rates than is the demand for M2. The reason for this assertion is that M1 and M2 are close substitutes. Yet so are the interest-bearing assets in M2 fairly close substitutes for short-term Treasury bills, certificates of deposit, and the like. When r_b rises, therefore, so does the interest paid on money market fund shares and several of the other assets that comprise M2. This should cause a shift out of M1 into both M2 and other assets. But the shift from M1 to M2 means that the reduction in M2 per increase in the bond rate is less than the reduction in M1. As we shall see further on, this difference has important implications for monetary policy and the controllability of the money supply.

The Supply of Money

We turn now to an analysis of the supply of money. Since the supply of money includes deposits at commercial banks, we shall have to include banks in our analysis. What we shall show is that the supply of money is a positive function of the interest rate.

[6]Several studies confirm that the interest elasticity of the demand for money is higher for the narrower definitions of money. For example, Brunner and Meltzer found an interest elasticity of −.7 to −.9 for M1, −.5 to −.6 for M2, and −.4 for M3 in their paper "Predicting Velocity: Implications for Theory and Policy," *Journal of Finance* 18 (May 1963): 319–354.

We should note, however, that these studies were all done prior to the recent changes in banking legislation and the innovations in banking practice. Both should increase the interest sensitivity of M1, since the assets in M2 now earn so much higher an interest rate and are so easy to switch back and forth between accounts in response to interest rate changes. Historical data are of limited use in predicting behavior when there is a change in the institutional rules, as there has recently been in U. S. financial markets.

Figure 14.2
The Demand for Money

The two demand curves, D_1 and D_2, show the demand for M1 and M2. The demand for M1 is more sensitive to interest rate changes because the public switches part of its asset holdings to or away from M2 in response to a change in the interest rate. An increase in income will increase the demand for both monetary assets, thus shifting each demand curve out to D'. An increase in expected inflation reduces the demand for money and shifts the demand curves inward to D''.

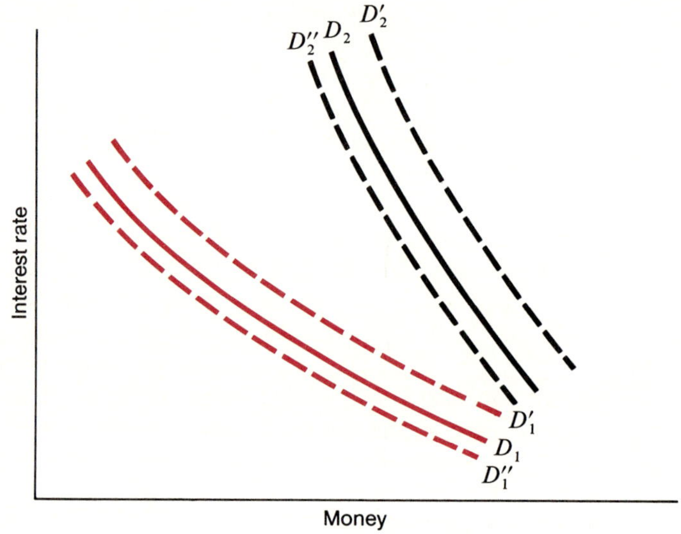

For the purposes of this discussion, let us use M2 as our definition of money. Recall that M2 is composed of currency plus demand deposits subject to reserve requirements plus savings accounts (and mutual fund shares) on which banks determine their own reserves.

(14.2) $$M = Cu + D.$$

Cu = currency in public hands
D = total deposits in commerical banks

Equation (14.2) implies that both the private sector, the commercial banks, and the government have an influence on the supply of money. The private sector determines the fraction of the money supply that it wishes to hold as currency, while banks determine the size of total deposits.

The government, or more properly the Federal Reserve, does not determine the money supply directly. But it does have an enormous influence on the money supply by its control of what is called either **high-powered money** or the **monetary base.** High-powered money, which we shall call H, is defined as currency in public hands plus bank reserves.

Before we see how the Federal Reserve actually controls H, let us see the relationship between H and M2. By definition:

(14.3) $$H = R + Cu.$$

R = bank reserves, both required and voluntary

Now we develop the right-hand side of Equation (14.3). First we will define the reserve ratio, v, as the ratio of total bank reserves to total bank deposits.[7] It follows that:

(14.4) $$R = vD.$$

Next we define the currency ratio, cu, as the ratio of currency to money:

(14.5) $$Cu = cuM.$$

Substituting Equations (14.5) and (14.4) into Equation (14.3), we have:

(14.6) $$H = vD + cuM.$$

By the definition of money in Equation (14.2):

(14.7) $$D = (1 - cu)M.$$

Substituting Equation (14.7) into Equation (14.6) and collecting terms, we have:

(14.8) $$H = [v(1 - cu) + cu]M.$$

This gives us the basic relationship between M2 and the stock of high-powered money:

(14.9) $$M = \left[\frac{1}{v(1 - cu) + cu}\right] H.$$

The term in brackets is called the **money multiplier.** It is the amount by which a given change in high-powered money will change the money supply.

In the United States in 1982 the reserve and currency ratios for M2 are about 2.2 percent and 6.6 percent, respectively. Substituting these values into Equation (14.9), we see that for the United States the money multiplier is about 11.5. Because the multiplier is so much greater than 1, the Federal Reserve has a great deal of leverage in controlling the money supply. A one-dollar change in high-powered money has a magnified effect on the money supply.

[7]We will ignore here money market fund shares even though they are an important component of M2. The reserve requirement argument does not apply to this particular asset. We are not distinguishing here among the separate reserves held against checking and savings accounts. We will do so in the following section.

To make matters more complex for the Fed, the money multiplier is not constant but rather varies with both the reserve and currency ratios. As the reader can see from Equation (14.9), a rise in the reserve ratio, v, will reduce the multiplier. That is because a higher level of reserves will not allow banks to expand loans and deposits as much in response to an increase in reserves. In the limit, if banks were forced to hold 100 percent reserves, as some critics have urged, the money multiplier would be equal to 1.

Similarly, a rise in the currency ratio also reduces the money multiplier. The reason is that a rise in cu denies the banking system a larger fraction of the stock of high-powered money. It is only the banking system that is able to expand money by some multiple of its part of the monetary base. Hence, reducing the fraction of money in the banking system reduces the money multiplier.

To show just how much variation there has been in the money multiplier, we have drawn a time-series picture of the currency and reserve ratios and the money multiplier in the United States (see Figure 14.3).

Determination of the Average Reserve Ratio

In this section we are going to show that the reserve ratio is a function of the rate of interest. The reason is that as the interest rate changes, the public shifts deposits from checking accounts, upon which a certain level of required reserves must be held, over to savings accounts, for which banks themselves set the level of reserves. Since the level of reserves held on savings accounts is almost certainly lower than the level required by the Federal Reserve on checking accounts, any such shift in the composition of M2 resulting from changes in the interest rate must change the **average reserve ratio,** v.

To see how this works, we split up the assets in M2 into currency, checkable deposits or checking accounts (DD), and time deposits or savings accounts (TD). Furthermore, suppose that banks hold only the legal minimum reserves against checkable deposits. Then, if we set re equal to the **required reserve ratio,** we can write required reserves on checking accounts as:

(14.10) $$RE = reDD.$$

re = required reserve ratio
RE = required reserves
DD = demand or checkable deposits

Banks themselves determine the level of reserves they wish to carry on time deposits. We will call that the **voluntary reserve ratio,** rv.[8] Then, the level of reserves on time deposits is:

(14.11) $$RV = rvTD.$$

[8]Note that rv is not necessarily constant. As we show in a moment, it falls when the interest rate rises.

Figure 14.3
Reserve Ratios, Currency Ratios, and the Money Multiplier

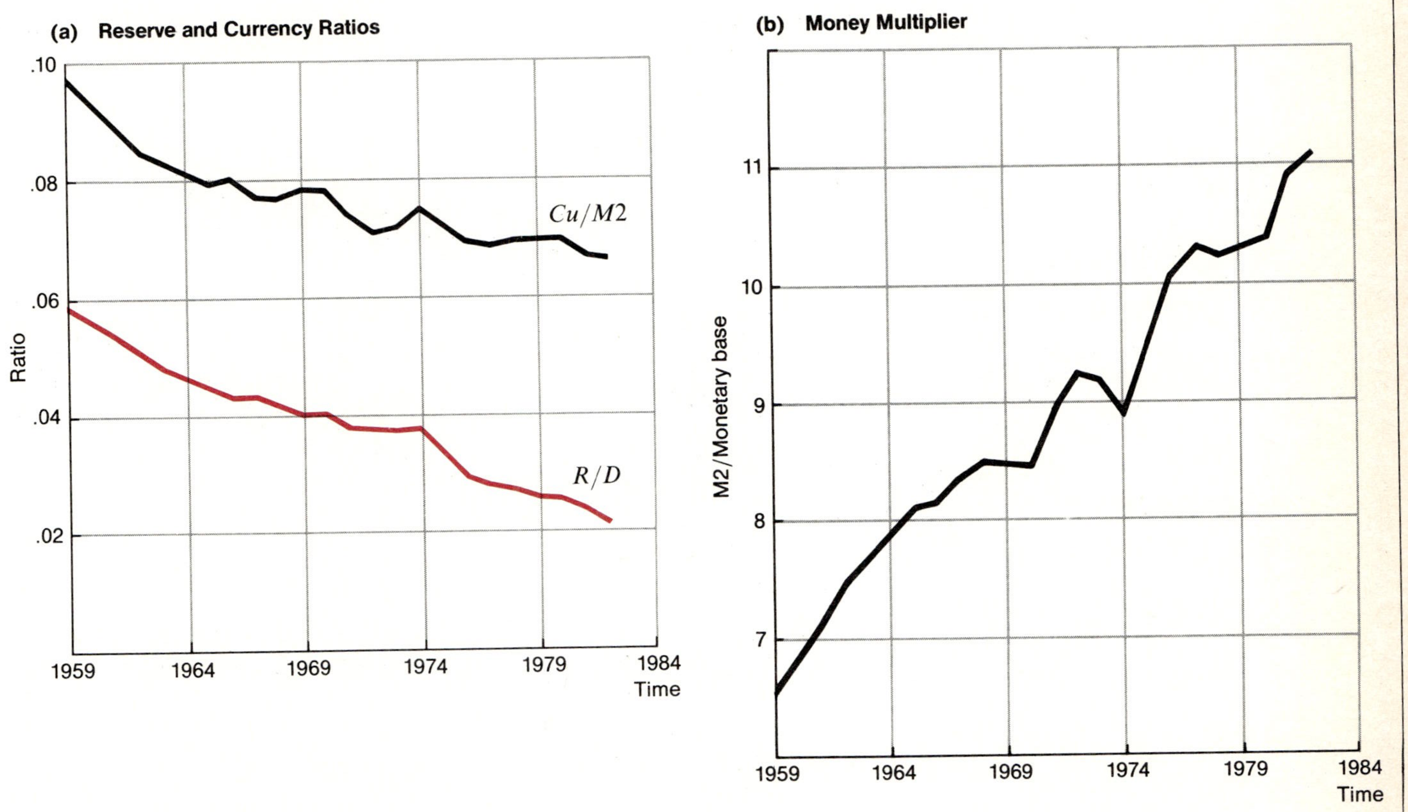

RV = voluntary reserves
rv = voluntary reserve ratio
TD = time deposits

Now if we let d and t represent the ratio of demand and time deposits in M2, we can write the total level of reserves, which is the sum of $RE + RV$, as:

(14.12) $$R = RE + RV = (red + rvt)M.$$

Note that by definition, $d + t = 1 - cu$.

Now we bring currency back into the picture and derive a money multiplier. We know that $H = R + Cu$. But using Equations (14.5) and (14.12), this can be rewritten as:

(14.13) $$H = (red + rvt + cu)M.$$

This gives us a new money multiplier analogous to Equation (14.9):

(14.14) $$M = \left[\frac{1}{red + rvt + cu}\right]H.$$

The two multipliers are equivalent except that Equation (14.14) makes explicit the components of the reserve ratio. The term $v(1 - cu)$ in Equation (14.9) is equal to the term $red + rvt$ in Equation (14.14). The average reserve ratio v is a weighted average of the required reserve ratio on demand deposits and the voluntary reserve ratio on time deposits where the weights are the proportions of M2 held in each of these two assets.

What is relevant here is the effect of shifts between time and demand deposits. Assuming that rv is smaller than re, any increase in the time deposit ratio t coming from a reduction in d must reduce the average reserve ratio and therefore increase the money multiplier. That says that if people shift their assets from DD to TD, the average reserve ratio will go down.[9] To put it another way, the total money

[9]This is easy to show formally. According to the definitions,

$$v = \frac{R}{TD + DD}.$$

Substituting Equation (14.11) and the definition TD and DD, we see that

$$v = \frac{red + rvt}{d + t}.$$

But since $d + t = 1 - cu$, this can be rewritten as:

$$v = \frac{d(re - rv) + (1 - cu)rv}{1 - cu}.$$

This expression varies directly with d when $re > rv$.

supply supportable by a given level of reserves will go up if people shift their deposits from those requiring high reserves over to those requiring low reserves.

How, you may be asking, is this related to the interest rate? The answer is through the differential effect of interest rates on the demand for M1 and M2. Look again at Figure 14.2. It says that when there is an increase in r, there is a more than proportional drop in the demand for non–interest-bearing M1 and a shift of deposits into M2. That is equivalent to saying that when interest rates rise, d falls and t goes up. That increases the money multiplier, as we have shown in footnote 9.

There is a second reason why the money multiplier should vary with the rate of interest. Reserves held at the Fed earn an interest rate much smaller than they would if they were lent out. Raising the interest rate gives banks a reason to economize on idle reserves, just as it gives the public an incentive to economize on idle cash. Therefore, one might expect that the higher the interest rate, the lower the level of rv.

We will summarize this discussion in the form of an equation for the reserve ratio:

(14.15) $$v = t(\overset{-}{r}, \overset{+}{re}).$$

Equation (14.15) tells us that the average reserve ratio is negatively related to the interest and positively related to the required reserve ratio. The reason is that higher rates shift deposits from demand to time deposits where they carry a lower reserve ratio. Higher rates also give banks an incentive to economize on idle reserves by reducing rv itself.

Now substitute Equation (14.15) into Equation (14.9) to derive the relationship between the money multiplier and the interest rate. Since the interest rate and the reserve ratio are inversely related, and since the reserve ratio is inversely related to the money multiplier, it follows that the money multiplier is *positively* related to the interest rate. A rise in interest rates induces the public to shift assets from high to low reserve accounts and induces banks to reduce rv. Both actions will increase the money supply derivable from a given monetary base. A rise in required reserves re would have the opposite effect.

Figure 14.4 gives the reader a visual picture of what has been happening to the deposit ratios in recent years. As the reader can see, there has been a dramatic increase in t and a decline in d, one that corresponds quite closely to the increase in interest rates that has also occurred over the same period. The result, of course, has been a sharp increase in the money multiplier.

Determination of the Money Supply Curve

We now return to the main purpose of this section, which is the determination of the money supply. According to Equation (14.9), the money supply depends on the reserve ratio v, the currency ratio cu, and the monetary base, H. According to Equation (14.15), v is a function of the interest rate and the required reserve ratio. Substituting Equation (14.15) into Equation (14.9) and using r_b as a representative

Figure 14.4
Trends in Demand and Time Deposit Ratios

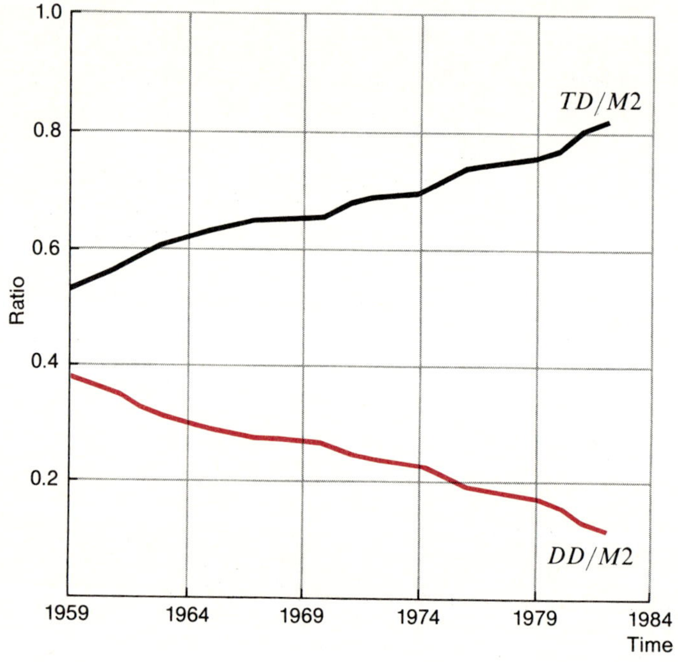

interest rate, we can write a general equation for the money supply in terms of r_b, H, and re. It is:

(14.16) $$M_s = m(\overset{-}{re}, \overset{+}{r_b}, \overset{+}{H}).$$

This equation tells us that the money supply is positively related to both the interest rate and the monetary base and negatively related to required reserves. Using these relationships we can now add a money supply curve to our basic diagram of the money market (see Figure 14.5). Because interest rates increase the money multiplier, the money supply must be positively related to the interest rate, which is why we show the supply curve S_0S_0 in Figure 14.5 as upward sloping.

Equilibrium in the Money Market

Equilibrium in the money market is determined as usual by the intersection of demand and supply, at the interest rate $r_{b,0}$ and the money supply M_0.

Figure 14.5 shows only the relationship between the demand and supply of money and the interest rate. All the other variables appearing in Equations 14.1

Figure 14.5
The Money Market

Supply is an increasing function of the interest rate, because it pays for banks to increase their lending and to economize on reserves when the interest rate goes up. An increase in the monetary base causes the rightward shift in supply shown in the diagram. Since demand is negatively related to the interest rate, an increase in the monetary base must cause a reduction in the interest rate.

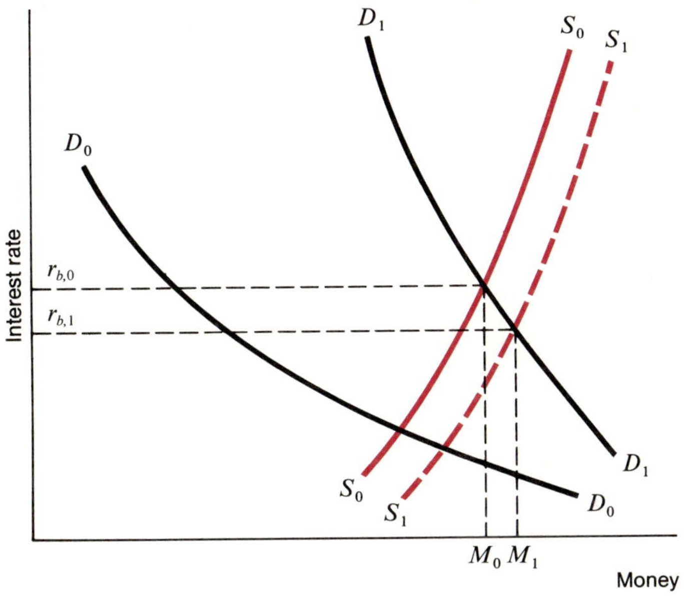

and 14.16 will be shift variables in Figure 14.5. A change in any one of them shifts either the money supply or demand curve. Take the monetary base, H, for example. Since H is positively related to the money supply, an increase in H will shift the supply curve to the right, to the dashed curve S_1S_1. That will lower the equilibrium interest rate and increase the money supply, to $r_{b,1}$ and M_1, respectively. Similarly, an increase in income will increase the demand for money, leading to an increase in both the interest rate and supply of money. Both of these changes will also affect the composition of M2.

Monetary Policy

We turn now to monetary policy, the second major instrument by which the federal government attempts to control the level of aggregate demand. Monetary policy is conducted by the Federal Reserve, which is the United States' central bank. The Fed has three instruments with which to conduct monetary policy. These are the setting of required reserve ratios for demand deposits, the **rediscount rate,** and open market operations. All three affect the position of the money supply curve, in this way influencing the **market-clearing interest rate.**

The Required Reserve Ratio

The Federal Reserve has the legal authority to set required reserve ratios for demand deposits in all financial institutions.[10] Since any change in the required reserves changes the amount of money that can be supported by a given monetary base, this instrument affects the money supply. An increase in *re* reduces the money supply (shifts S_1S_1 to the left in Figure 14.5), and a reduction in *re* has the opposite effect.

Theoretically, the control of bank reserve ratios is a fairly powerful instrument. For example, if required and actual reserves were equal and if the currency ratio were at its normal level, an increase of 5 percentage points in the reserve ratio would decrease the money supply by 15 percent. Perhaps because it is so powerful, the Fed has been somewhat reluctant to use this tool. Between 1963 and 1979, the reserve ratio was changed less than a dozen times, and most of these changes were by less than 1 percentage point.

The Rediscount Rate

The second instrument of monetary policy is the rediscount rate. This is the rate at which member banks may borrow from the Federal Reserve. Since any bank borrowing from the Fed creates bank reserves, that is, increases H, raising the rediscount rate shifts the money supply curve of Figure 14.5 to the left, because it reduces member bank loans. In practice banks do not borrow large amounts from the Fed, so that the changes in the money supply from this source are relatively small. Many feel that the rediscount rate is more important as an indication of Federal Reserve intentions than as a direct influence on the money supply.

Open Market Operations

The most important instrument available to the Fed to control the money supply is *open market operations*. The Fed has a large portfolio of government bonds. An open market operation is the sale or purchase of government bonds on the New York bond market. An open market purchase of bonds by the Fed increases the stock of high-powered money, H, thus increasing the money supply; an open market bond sale reduces H and the money supply. In effect, an open market operation is a way by which the Fed changes the two important components of the public portfolio, namely, government bonds and money. Let us see how the process works and what its effect is.

[10]Prior to the Monetary Control Act of 1980, the Fed set reserve requirements on demand and time deposits of member banks only. Naturally, when the Fed tried to tighten up, banks tended to drop their membership in the Federal Reserve System to escape the mandatory requirements.

Table 14.2
Changes in Balance Sheets as a Result of a $1000 Open Market Bond Purchase by the Fed

Assets		Liabilities	
Public			
Bank deposits	+$1000	No change	
Bonds	− 1000		
Banks			
Reserves	+ 1000	Deposits	+$1000
Federal Reserve			
Bonds	+ 1000	Bank reserve accounts	+ 1000

Suppose the Fed purchases a $1000 bond on the New York bond market. It does this by writing a check on itself, which it exchanges for the bond. When the bond seller deposits the check in his or her bank account, the bank presents the check for payment at the Fed. The Fed honors the check by crediting the account of the bank at the Fed with +$1000. Since bank accounts at the Fed are a part of high-powered money, H, the open market purchase increases H by $1000.

In accounting terms, the open market purchase results in the following (first-round) changes in the balance sheets of the public, the banks, and the Federal Reserve (see Table 14.2).

The public has exchanged a $1000 bond for a bank deposit. The banking system receives an additional deposit, to which corresponds an additional $1000 in reserves. The Fed has an additional asset (the bond) and a matching liability (the added $1000 in bank reserves, which is also the change in H).

The net result of the open market transaction is thus to change the portfolio held by the public. The total stays the same, but it now contains $1000 less in bonds and $1000 more in high-powered money. In this way the Fed is able to directly change H.

What we have analyzed here is only the first-round effect of an open market operation, not the end of the story. As we showed earlier, banks make a multiple expansion of any change in H because of fractional reserve banking (see Equation [14.14]). After the open market bond purchase, banks have excess reserves. They will adjust to the increase in reserves by increasing loans, which will further expand the money supply. In this way the open market bond purchase will lead to an expansion of the money supply by some multiple of the amount of the bond purchase.

Effect on Market-Clearing Rate of Return Because an open market operation disturbs the public portfolio, it must have an effect on the market-clearing rates of return for each asset. In particular, it will affect the rate of return on corporate assets. That is important, as we learned in Chapter 13, because any change in this market affects new capital formation or investment. It may seem strange that a government bond purchase by the Federal Reserve could affect private investment, but it does. The reason is that all the asset markets are linked together, because all assets are portfolio substitutes. Hence, a change in the rate of return on any asset has an effect on the demand for all other assets, particularly on the demand for corporate assets.

Let us look more closely at the effect of the open market bond purchase on r_{cb}, the corporate asset rate of return. For simplicity, we will drop the demand curve for M1 in the money market.

Figure 14.6 shows the three main asset markets that we have been analyzing in the last two chapters. Each is in short-run equilibrium at the initial portfolio of M_0 of money, H_0 of high-powered money, $B_{b,0}$ of government bonds, and $B_{cb,0}$ of corporate bonds. Given total wealth and income, the demand curves in the three markets determine an initial pair of market-clearing rates of return, $r_{b,0}$ and $r_{cb,0}$. Note that $r_{cb,0}$ differs from $r_{b,0}$ by a risk factor that reflects the greater risk of holding corporate assets. Note also that the demand curves in the money and government bond markets are exact mirror images, since they are drawn with respect to the same rate of return.

Now consider the effect of an expansionary open market operation, the purchase by the Federal Reserve of government bonds. This moves the supply curve of money to the right, by the amount of the bond purchases times the money multiplier, and contracts the government bond supply by the amount of the purchases. Hence, $S_{H,0}$ moves to the right to $S'_{H,1}$, and $S_{b,0}$ moves to the left. This, of course, drives down the rate of interest on government bonds from $r_{b,0}$ to $r_{b,1}$ (and raises the prices of outstanding government bonds).

What about the corporate securities market? Here there has been no change in supply. But there is a change in demand. Why? Look back at our general demand Equation (13.4). It says that if the rate of return on an alternative asset declines, demand increases. To put it another way, the increase in money increases the demand for other assets. We show this as a rightward shift in the demand for corporate securities. Since the supply of these securities has not changed, the effect of the increase in demand is to lower the rate of return on corporate securities—or, equivalently, to raise their prices. In this way the open market operation causes a reflexive movement in rates of return throughout the asset markets.

Tracing the process on out to the investment market, we reproduce the relationship between the borrowing rate (r_{cb}) and new investment. Since the bond purchase lowers r_{cb}, it will cause an increase in corporate investment. This is why bond purchases by the Federal Reserve are an expansionary monetary policy. They lower all interest rates and increase the demand for corporate equities. This in turn causes an increase in investment. The reader can easily show that the purchase should also increase the demand for housing, thus stimulating an increase in new housing construction as well.

A contractionary open market operation by the Federal Reserve would have exactly the opposite effect. To contract the level of aggregate goods demand, the Federal Reserve should *sell* some of its government bonds. This will contract the money supply while increasing the government bond supply held by the public. As the reader should be able to show, r_b will rise. This will reduce the demand for all

Figure 14.6
The Effect of Expansionary Open Market Operations on r_b and r_{cb}

An expansionary open market operation shifts the money supply function to $S'_{H,1}$ and the government bond supply back to $S'_{b,1}$. The market clearing interest rate on government bonds falls to $r_{b,1}$. The reflection of this in the corporate securities market is an increase in the demand for corporate securities. That is due to the fact that the public finds itself with more money and fewer government securities than it had initially. The result is a decline in the corporate bond rate from $r_{cb,0}$ to $r_{cb,1}$. Reading over to (d), we see that this causes an increase in new investment from I to I'.

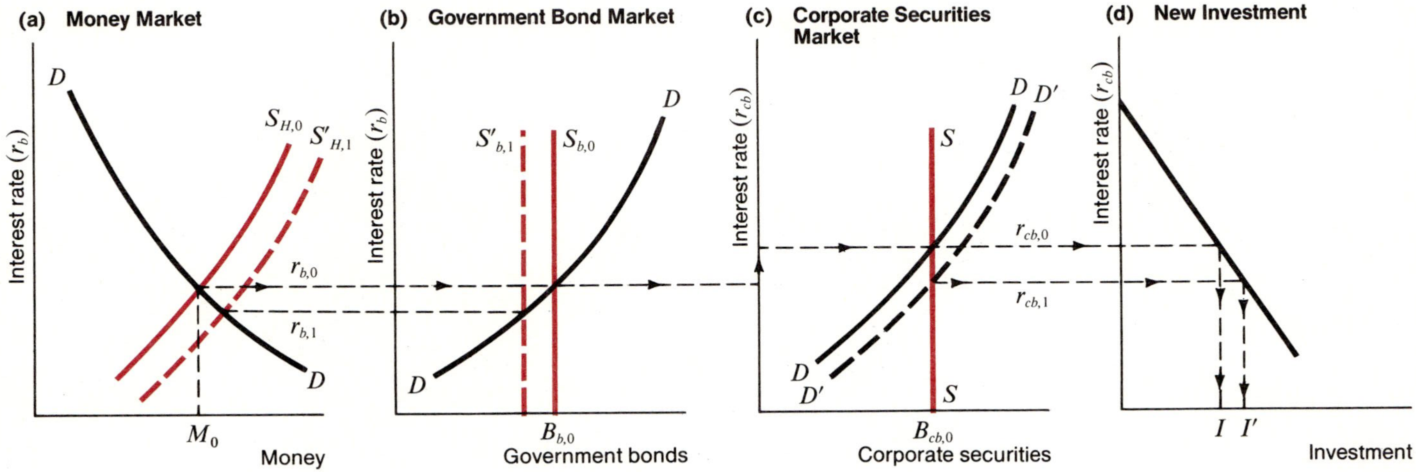

corporate securities (shift the demand curve in Figure 14.6 to the left), raising r_{cb} and lowering total investment. In this way, through open market operations the Federal Reserve has a tool with which to change rates of return, capital formation, and hence the level of aggregate demand.

The Long-Run Effect of Open Market Operations The changes we have been analyzing that occur in response to an open market operation are short-run effects. What about the long run? As we just showed, in the short run equilibrium is determined by the available stock of assets and the demand for it. However, over time the composition and size of that stock can and will be changed by investment because it adds to two particular assets, corporate securities and housing, that the public holds in its portfolio.[11]

Consider the expansionary open market operation once again. As we have just seen, in the short run, giving the public more money and less government bonds increases the demand for corporate securities and housing. That raises investment and is therefore expansionary. Over time this new investment is added to the public portfolio. If, as before, we define the long-run equilibrium as the point when the addition of new assets comes to a stop—when net investment equals zero—then the long-run effect of the expansionary open market operation is an increase in the capital stock, not in investment.

We illustrate this point in Figure 14.7. For simplicity, we will omit the government bond market. We show the asset markets initially in long-run equilibrium at $r_{b,0}$, $r_{cb,0}$. As before, the interest rate r_{cb} exceeds the government bond rate by the risk premium and is at just the level at which net investment is zero ($r_{cb,0}$ is the intercept of the investment function in Figure 14.7).

The expansionary open market operation is shown by the dashed lines S' in the money market and D' in the securities market. In the short run, as we showed earlier, $r_{cb,0}$ falls to $r_{cb,1}$, and net investment rises to I'.

But that is only the beginning of the process. Over time this new investment is added to the stock of corporate securities that the public must hold. In Figure 14.7, security supply moves slowly to the right over time until finally it reaches $S''S''$. This is the new long-run equilibrium at which new investment returns to zero.

The reflection of this in the money market is a slow rise in the demand for money over time until it reaches $D''D''$ in diagram (a). The demand for money increases because investment adds to the value of corporate equities in the public's portfolio, which increases public wealth. That, as we have shown, increases the demand for money.

In the long run, therefore, the system adjusts the asset portfolio by investment until the interest rate r_{cb} returns to $r_{cb,0}$. Therefore, we can see that the long-run effect of expansionary monetary policy is an increase in the capital stock, not an increase in investment. Investment is only the short-run adjustment of the econ-

[11]For a more extended discussion of the long-run effects of monetary policy, see Samuel A. Morley, "The Relationship Between Money, Income and Prices in the Short and Long-run," *Journal of Finance* 28 (December 1973): 119–130.

Figure 14.7
The Short- and Long-Run Effects of Expansionary Open Market Operations

An expansionary open market operation increases the money supply from SS to $S'S'$. In the short run the interest rates on government bonds and corporate securities both fall; r_{cb} declines from the long-run equilibrium level $r_{cb,0}$ to $r_{cb,1}$. I' of new investment takes place. Over time, as this investment is added to the capital stock, supply moves out to $S''S''$ in (b). Long-run equilibrium is reestablished when the interest rate has returned to $r_{cb,0}$. That happens when enough additional investment has occurred to move supply out to S''. At that point, the demand for money has increased to D'', which is just enough to absorb the initial increase in money at the equilibrium interest rate $r_{cb,0}$.

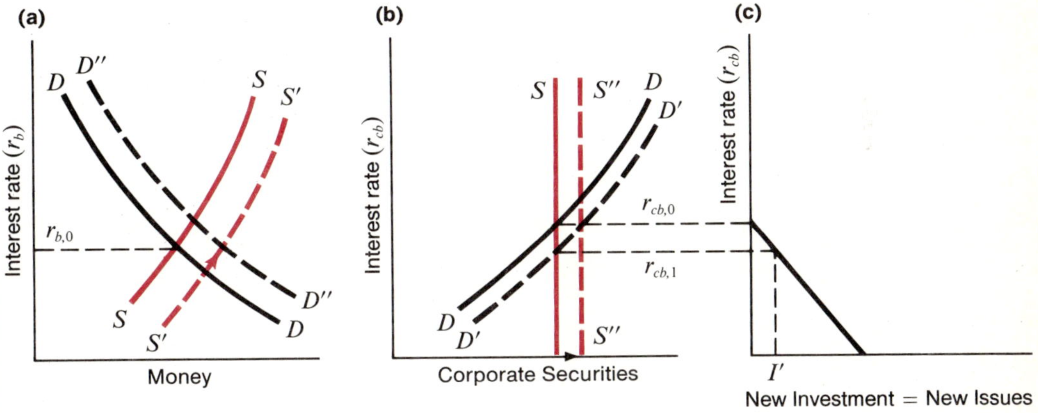

omy to a change in the demand for capital (or securities, which are issued when investment occurs). An increase in the money supply increases the demand for capital. That is expansionary in the short run because it causes capital formation.

In the long run, the increase in demand for capital is satisfied by an increase in the supply of capital. We could say, therefore, that in the long run the effect of open market operations is on the capital stock of the economy. Expansionary open market operations, or, as it used to be called, a low-interest-rate monetary policy, will increase capital formation in the short run and capital intensity in the long run. Contractionary open market operations will reduce investment in the short run and capital intensity in the long run.

Thus, the short- and the long-run effects of monetary policy are dramatically different. In the short run, monetary policy affects investment and therefore aggregate demand. But its long-run effect is on supply, not demand. Since in the long run net investment goes back to zero, the demand effect disappears. But the change in the capital stock that has occurred has a lasting long-run effect on productivity or supply. Expansionary monetary policy increases the capital stock, which should increase capacity; contractionary monetary policy should have the opposite long-run effect. The importance of this distinction between the short- and the long-run effects of monetary policy will become clearer when we discuss supply-side economics and antiinflation policies.

Figure 14.8
The Effect of an Increase in Expected Inflation on Income and Investment

The solid lines in each diagram show the initial full-equilibrium position, A, where net investment in housing is limited to replacement and the interest rate is r_0. An increase in expected inflation changes the relationship between the price of housing and the nominal interest rate as shown in Equation 14.17 and in (c). Specifically, the increase in Π_e shifts the curve in (c) out to the right by the change in expected inflation. In the bottom diagrams, the change in r relative to P_h shifts both the IS curve and the investment function upward by the change in Π_e. The new short-run equilibrium depends on what happens in the money market. It can be shown that the demand for money increases slightly, from D to D'. Nominal interest rates rise but not as much as $\Delta\Pi_e$. As a result, real interest rates decline and investment takes place. The new short-run equilibrium is at point C. Over time, as the new housing is added to the stock of housing, the supply curve in (a) moves rightward to H'. Interest rates rise from r_0 to r_1, and investment falls back to replacement. The rise in housing increases the demand for money, shifting the demand curve rightward in (f) and the LM leftward in (g). Long-run equilibrium is reestablished at point D, when the nominal interest rate has risen by the full change in Π_e, which is at r_1.

The Effect of a Change in Expected Inflation on the Goods and Asset Markets

We would now like to use the framework we have developed to analyze the effect of an increase in expected inflation on the goods and asset markets. As we have already seen, such a change in expected inflation will cause the public to attempt to sell assets whose return is fixed in nominal terms and buy assets whose return tends to move with inflation. Money is a prime example of the former and housing a good example of the latter type of assets. In the short run, however, these attempted portfolio switches cannot take place, because the composition of the public's aggregate portfolio is fixed. Thus, the change in expected inflation must cause a change in rates of return on alternative assets. Those that are inflation hedges will have their prices bid up (or their rates of return bid down), while those that are not inflation hedges will have their prices bid down (or their rates bid up). We should therefore expect a rise in the nominal rate of return on financial assets and a corresponding decline in the rate on nonfinancial assets such as housing. This is not the end of the story, however. As is usually the case when there is a change in portfolio preferences, this switch will trigger an investment response. The public demands more inflation-proof assets. Over time these will be produced by an increase in investment.

To show all this graphically, we select two assets, money and housing. For the latter we show the stock and the flow markets, so that we can see visually how the change in expectations causes an increase in investment. Finally, we show the entire IS-LM diagram, so that we can trace out the effect of the change in inflationary expectations on aggregate demand. Note that we have not chosen corporate fixed investment as an example of an inflation hedge. That, as we discussed before, is because inflation has both positive and negative effects on cor-

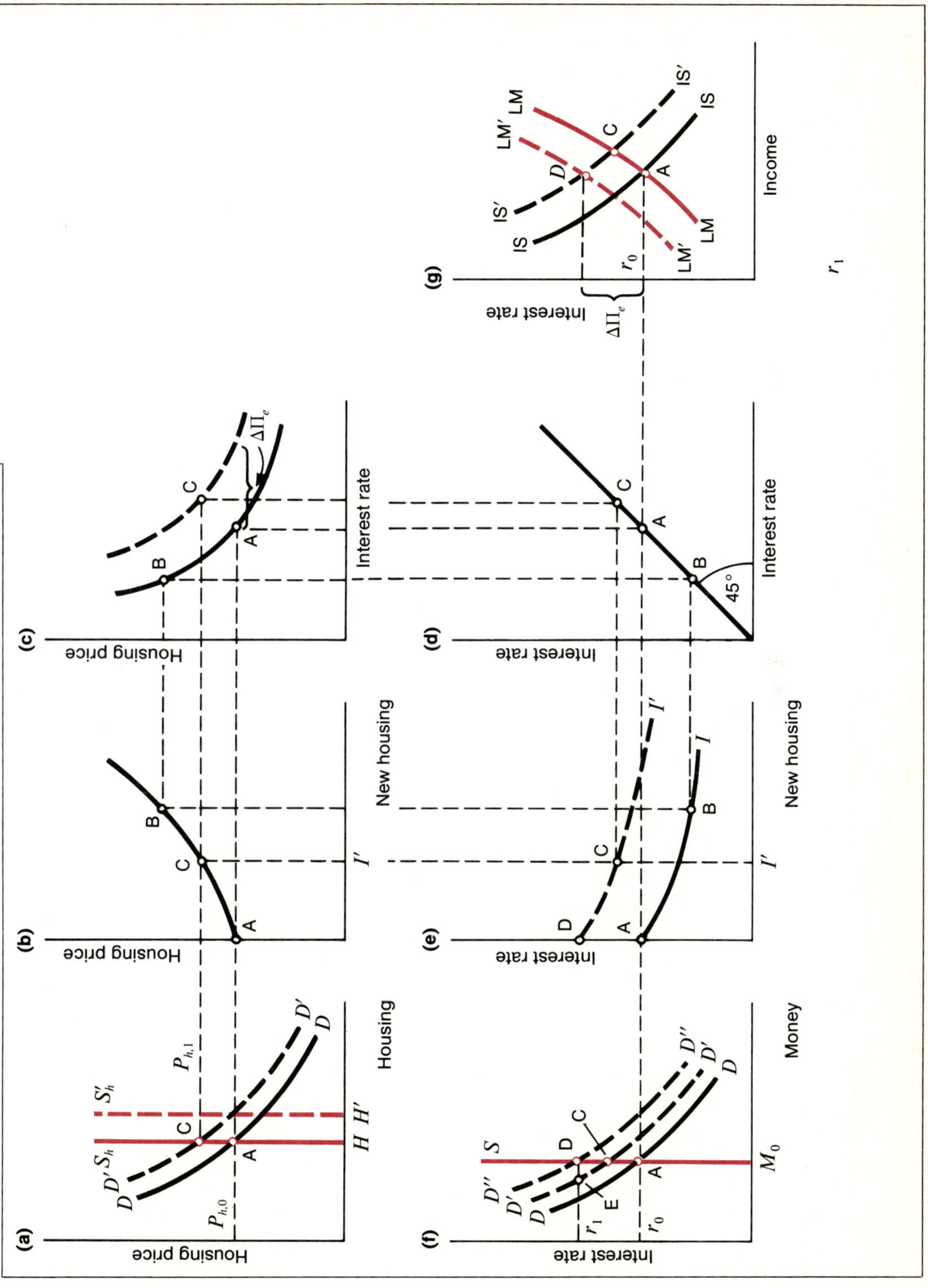
(a)
Housing price
Housing
S_h
S'_h
H
H'
$P_{h,0}$
$P_{h,1}$
D
D'
(b)
Housing price
New housing
I'
(c)
Housing price
Interest rate
$\Delta\Pi_e$
(d)
Interest rate
Interest rate
45°
(e)
Interest rate
New housing
I
I'
(f)
Interest rate
Money
S
M_0
r_0
r_1
D
D'
D''
(g)
Interest rate
Income
IS
IS′
LM
LM′
r_0
r_1
$\Delta\Pi_e$

porate profits, and it is not clear empirically which effects dominate. There is no such ambiguity for housing.

Figure 14.8 shows the effect of an increase in expected inflation. In our chapter on investment we derived the housing investment function in terms of the price of housing; that is the upward-sloping function in diagram (b). We would now like to derive the implicit relationship between investment and the nominal interest rate, using diagrams (b)–(d). The point here is that expected inflation acts as a positive shift variable in (e), which shows investment as a function of the nominal interest rate. To see that, consider the relationship between the price of housing and the nominal interest rate. For simplicity, suppose that investors make the real rates on financial assets and housing equal. Assuming that housing prices rise with inflation, the real return on housing is:

$$r_h - \Pi_e = \frac{\text{rent}}{P_h} - \delta.$$

But if the real return on financial assets and housing are equal, $r_h - \Pi_e = r - \Pi_e$. It therefore follows that:

$$P_h = \frac{\text{rent}}{r - \Pi_e + \delta}. \tag{14.17}$$

Equation (14.17) says that P_h and r are inversely related. Diagram (c) is a picture of this inverse relationship for a given level of rents, depreciation, and expected inflation. Given Equation (14.17), we can now construct a relationship between investment and the nominal interest rate. Since investment is positively related to P_h and since P_h is negatively related to r, housing investment must be negatively related to r. One can construct the investment function in (e) by taking various points on the supply curve of the construction industry in (b) and finding the corresponding points in the r-I diagram. Two such points, A and B, are shown in (e). One can also use this same procedure to construct the IS-LM diagram shown in (g). Since investment is negatively related to r, the IS curve is downward sloping. The LM curve is upward sloping for the usual reasons.

Point A in Figure 14.8(e) is a full equilibrium. The public portfolio of money and housing is such that no net investment is taking place. Now suppose that this portfolio equilibrium is disturbed by a rise in expected inflation. This change increases the demand for housing and drives up the price of housing. In (a), demand shifts up to the dotted line, and $P_{h,0}$ rises to $P_{h,1}$. In (c), the increase in Π_e shifts the entire function up to the dashed lines (see Equation [14-17]), which means an equivalent upward shift in the investment function in (e) and in the IS curve in (g). In both cases the reason is that a given nominal interest rate now corresponds to a lower real interest rate. Since we know that investment is a function of the real rather than the nominal rate, it is reasonable to expect that investment would be larger for any given nominal rate the higher the expected rate of inflation.

In order to see what happens to nominal rates and to investment as a result of the change in expectations, we have to look at the money market and the IS-LM diagram. The demand for money is subject to two conflicting influences. The increase in Π_e should reduce the demand for money. But at the same time, the increase in income, caused by the increased housing investment, tends to increase the demand for money. It can be formally shown that the second influence must outweigh the first and therefore that the demand for money shifts slightly to the right, to D' as shown in (f). As a result, equilibrium shifts from point A to point C. At C investment has increased to I' and nominal interest rates have risen, but not as far as expected inflation. Thus, while housing prices and nominal interest rates have increased, real interest rates have gone down. The rise in r is not as great as the change in Π_e. There has also been an increase in aggregate demand, implying that the aggregate demand function is positively related to Π_e.

This, of course, is not the end of the story. The change in expectations has led to a change in portfolio preferences. The public wants more of its portfolio to be secure against inflation. In the short run the price of inflation hedges, such as housing, rises relative to the price of other assets. In the long run the economy will provide more of such assets. That is the process that is beginning with the rise in investment. Over time, as this new investment is added to the public portfolio, the supply curve of housing shifts to the right in (a), and the demand curve for money shifts to the right in (f), due to the rise in total wealth. That process continues until the housing stock has increased to H' in (a). At that point P_h has fallen back to its initial level.

What happens to the nominal interest rate at the end of this adjustment process? To see that, look at the lower set of diagrams. In the new long-run equilibrium the demand for money has shifted out to D'' which intersects the money supply at D. At D the long-run equilibrium interest rate is r_1. r_1 differs from the initial interest rate r_0 by exactly the change in expected inflation. Looking finally at the LM curve, the increase in the demand for money due to the growth in the stock of housing shifts the LM curve to the left until it finally intersects the dashed IS curve at point D, where the interest rate has risen to r_1 and income has fallen back to its original level. To repeat: The difference between r_0 and r_1 is the change in Π_e.

So far we have carried out the analysis assuming that prices are constant, or the aggregate supply curve is flat. If we go to the other extreme and assume a vertical supply curve, the change in expectations has a rather different outcome. As before, the IS curve shifts up to IS′. However, now this increase in demand simply raises prices. That lowers the level of real balances, shifting the supply curve in (f) back until it intersects D' at point E. As before, the LM curve in (g) shifts to the left, to the long-run intersection with IS′ at point D. Again, as before, the nominal interest rises to r_1.

In both cases the rise in Π_e causes the public to wish to reduce the share of wealth held in financial assets and increase that held in inflation hedges. If prices are constant, that is accomplished over time by building more inflation-proof assets. When prices go up, the same shift is accomplished more rapidly by a fall in the real value of financial assets through inflation.

Summary

In this chapter we examine in detail how the money market works and, in particular, how two important changes in it—namely changes in the money supply caused by monetary policy and changes in the expected rate of inflation—affect the goods market. First we examined the various different concepts of money. Then we looked at the portfolio theory of the demand for money and showed that it depended positively on income and wealth, negatively on the rates of return on competing assets, and negatively on the rate of expected inflation, since inflation is a kind of tax on money holders.

Next we developed a theory of the supply of money. The Federal Reserve controls the monetary base. However, the banking system and the public determine the quantities of money which the monetary base will support. This is done by switching deposits from checking accounts on which a minimum reserve is required to savings accounts on which there is no such reserve requirement. Whenever interest rates increase, the public switches from checking to saving accounts, which reduces the total of required reserves and allows for an increase in the money supply. In this way, the supply of money is a positive function of the interest rate.

One of the two principal control mechanisms in the economy is monetary policy, which is carried out by the Federal Reserve largely through open market operations that alter the composition of the public's portfolio by the purchase or sale of government bonds. This affects the economy by affecting the market clearing rates of return on corporate equities and housing. An expansionary open market operation is a purchase of government bonds from the public. That drives down the rates of return on all competing assets, including corporate equities and housing, which in turn triggers an increase in investment.

A change in expected inflation affects portfolio equilibrium because it affects the demand for money and inflation-proof assets such as housing. An increase in Π_e increases the demand for housing. We showed that if prices are constant, nominal interest rates rise but real interest rates decline. As a result there is an increase in investment. In the long run, the additions to the stock of housing increase the demand for money and drive up nominal interest rates by exactly as much as the change in expected inflation. Hence in the long run the only effect of a rise in expected inflation is an increase in the stock of housing and a rise in the nominal interest rate.

Key Concepts

money market funds
M1
M2
transactions demand
speculative demand
diversification of assets
high-powered money
monetary base
money multiplier
average reserve ratio
required reserve ratio
voluntary reserve ratio
rediscount rate
market-clearing interest rate

Problems and Questions for Discussion

1. What is the difference between M1 and M2 from the public's point of view? From the Federal Reserve's point of view? Is the difference significant?

2. What was the main purpose of the Monetary Control Act of 1980? Why was the act thought to be necessary?

3. Under current arrangements the Federal Reserve tries to control the money supply by controlling the monetary base. However, the control is not perfect, because the money multiplier may vary in response to conditions in the private sector. As a remedy some have proposed 100 percent reserve money. Such a measure would allow the Fed to perfectly control the money supply. Do you think this would be a good idea? Why or why not?

4. Credit cards are accepted in payment of many bills. One definition of the money supply is the means of payment. Should we therefore include credit card balances in our definition of money? Why or why not? Would an increase in credit limits on all credit cards be equivalent in its effect to an increase in M1? Why or why not?

5. Suppose that the required reserve ratio for checking accounts is 10 percent and for savings accounts 5 percent. Suppose also that the public holds 30 percent of money balances (M2) in the form of currency. If the ratio of time deposits, t, is related to the interest rate by the equation

$t = .25 + i,$

where i is the interest rate expressed as a decimal,

- **a.** What is the money multiplier when the interest rate is 10 percent?
- **b.** What happens to the money multiplier when the interest rate falls to 5 percent?

6. For the monetary system described in Problem 5, calculate the money supply when the interest rate is 10 percent and the monetary base is 1000. By how much does the money supply decrease when the interest rate falls to 5 percent? (This demonstrates that the money supply is positively related to the rate of interest.)

7. Describe the process by which an open market purchase of government bonds by the Fed leads to an increase in the money supply?

8. Using diagrams, show the effect of a contractionary open market operation on the money market, the government bond market, and the corporate equity market. What is the difference between the short- and the long-run effect of such a policy?

9. A rise in expected inflation changes the public's portfolio preferences. There is an increase in the demand for inflation-proof assets and a reduction in the demand for assets that are not protected against inflation. How does this change in portfolio preferences affect the goods and money markets in the short run? In the long run? How will your answer to this question differ if the aggregate supply curve is vertical?

10. The demand for money has always been thought to be negatively related to the interest rate. Yet during 1980 and 1981, the money supply rose quite rapidly, while at the same time interest rates rose to their highest levels in over a century. Has the theory of the demand for money been disproved by the events of 1980 and 1981? If not, how can the combination of rising interest rates and rising M be explained?

PART FIVE

PROBLEMS IN DEMAND MANAGEMENT AND THE CONTROL OF INFLATION

Chapter 15

Policy Rules versus Policy Activism

In the previous chapters of this book we developed models of aggregate demand and supply and showed how variations in demand lead to changes in prices and output in the short and the long run. We also learned how monetary and fiscal policies affect aggregate demand. We should now be ready to use this knowledge of how the economy works to devise a strategy by which monetary and fiscal policies can be used to keep the economy at some desired level of employment and output.

Earlier models of the economy would suggest that this would be a simple task, predicting that countercyclical monetary and fiscal policies would effectively control the economic cycle. However, the vast structural changes that have occurred in our economy since these models were developed have made successful implementation of such policies far more difficult than expected.

In this chapter we will closely examine countercyclical demand policy and the various arguments among economists over its desirability and effectiveness.

Should the Government Try to Stabilize through Active Demand Management

Twenty-five years ago, when the first complete models of the economy were developed, optimists predicted that policymakers would soon eliminate the economic cycle by countercyclical monetary and fiscal policies. These expectations have not been fulfilled. The 1970s have been a period of wide fluctuations in output, accelerating inflation, and several serious policy errors. Forecasting errors and apparent changes in the structure of the economy have made the operation of countercyclical policy much more difficult than expected. While we have avoided major recessions in the postwar period (at least up to 1982), we have not kept the economy very close to full employment, nor have we avoided very serious periods of inflationary excess demand. To make matters worse, government policy has often been a source of instability. Instead of reducing instability coming from the private sector, the government has often exacerbated instability by spending too much during booms and contracting too far during recessions. For this reason, a large and increasingly influential group of economists who call themselves **monetarists** argue that the government should stop trying to actively control the economy and should instead base its fiscal and monetary policies on a set of automatic rules.[1] The monetarists want the government to stop trying to keep the economy at full employment, because they think that government efforts to do so, however well intentioned, too often make the situation worse instead of better.

The monetarists argue that left to itself, aggregate demand in the private sector is quite stable, and therefore activist stabilization by the government is probably unnecessary. Even if that were not the case, monetarists do not think that we will ever know enough to manage countercyclical policy successfully. They think that the government, far from stabilizing the economy, has actually been a major source of instability, particularly inflationary instability. One of the reasons for this is political. Now that government policymakers have learned how to control demand, they face continuous pressure to reduce unemployment through expansion. This explains a good deal of the tendency towards inflation in many western economies.

An opposing group of economists, whom we shall loosely label **Keynesians,** emphatically disagree with this pessimistic view of government countercyclical demand managment.[2] While they acknowledge that the government has made numerous policy errors in the past, Keynesians do not think that complete abandonment of countercyclical policy is advisable. They think that the economic record of the U. S. economy since the government has engaged in such policies is far

[1] The name "monetarism" was introduced by Karl Brunner in "The Role of Money and Monetary Policy," *Review of the Federal Reserve Bank of St. Louis* 50 (1968): 9–24. It refers to the central influence of money in the economy. The philosophical founder of monetarism was Milton Friedman. For a good discussion of monetarism, see Thomas Mayer, ed., *The Structure of Monetarism* (New York: Norton, 1978) and William Poole, *Money and the Economy: A Monetarist View* (New York: Addison Wesley, 1978). See also Robert J. Gordon, ed., *Milton Friedman's Monetary Framework: A Debate with His Critics* (Chicago: University of Chicago Press, 1980).

[2] There has been a long and energetic debate between the monetarists and the Keynesians that used to focus on the relative potency of monetary and fiscal policies. Recently the debate has turned to the more significant questions of stability and policy activism that we shall be covering in this chapter. For a good statement from a Keynesian perspective of the recent issues that separate the two schools, see Franco Modigliani, "The Monetarist Controversy, or, Should We Forsake Stabilization Policy?" *American Economic Review* 67 (March 1977): 1–19. See also Peter McClelland, "A Layman's Guide to the Keynesian-Monetarist Debate," in Peter McClelland, ed., *Introductory Macroeconomics 1980–81* (Ithaca, NY: Cornell University Press, 1981).

better than it was before. They doubt that the private sector is as stable as the monetarists believe it is, and they point out that we really have no idea how stable an economy would be if it were operated under the sort of policy rules proposed by the monetarists. In the following sections, we shall look more closely at arguments of these two groups of economists over the need and desirability of activist countercyclical demand management.

Inherent Stability of the Private Sector

Monetarists think that private sector aggregate demand is quite stable and that the government itself has been the main source of cyclical instability in the economy. They are convinced that the private sector has several built-in corrective feedback mechanisms that keep the economy close to full employment and that government stabilization efforts are therefore superfluous or even harmful. The three main stabilizing mechanisms are consumption, taxes, and prices.

Consumption

Personal consumption, as we learned in Chapter 11, is based on permanent income or a lifetime consumption plan. It is not totally based on this year's income. Therefore, whenever there is an increase in aggregate demand coming from any source, households react mainly by varying saving, not consumption. The short-run or transitory propensity to save is high. This tends to stabilize aggregate demand because consumption does not follow, and therefore magnify, demand disturbances.

Taxes

The countercyclical behavior of saving is similar to and complementary with the automatic stabilizer features of our tax and transfer system. As we have seen, both taxes and transfers depend on income. When income increases, taxes automatically go up and government transfer payments go down. By the definition of government saving, this implies that government saving rises in booms and falls in recession, exactly the pattern followed by private saving according to the permanent income hypothesis. Both of these feedbacks are stabilizing. They tend to make the IS curve steep, and they also make it less sensitive to shifts in autonomous expenditure. Because of this, the monetarists expect private demand to be relatively stable, which should make active government stabilization efforts less necessary and therefore less desirable.

Prices

Price flexibility converts changes in nominal aggregate demand into price level changes rather than real fluctuations in output and employment. Price flexibility is equivalent to a steeply sloped short-run supply curve. An economy with price flexibility is one that stays near to full employment regardless of fluctuations in demand. Whenever there is an increase in demand, prices will rise. That will automatically cause some reduction in spending, which tends to offset the initial increase. Reductions in demand should have the opposite effect. When prices are flexible, no government policymaker has to make any decision; the process is entirely automatic.

If one believes that the goal of government stabilization is to keep the economy close to full employment, supply-side price flexibility will achieve that goal. Of course, it will do so at the cost of price fluctuations, which are not entirely costless. But if one thinks that price variability is less harmful than fluctuations in real output, one has less reason to favor government efforts to regulate aggregate demand. For if the supply curve is steep, such efforts mainly stabilize the price level and not the level of output.

Keynesians disagree with the monetarist view of price flexibility. They tend to think that wages and prices are much less flexible and the aggregate supply curve much flatter than the monetarists do.[3] Many Keynesians would subscribe to the supply-side model that we have labeled the disequilibrium model in previous chapters. If the supply curve is relatively flat, as they think it is, cycles in demand will be primarily reflected in output and employment and not in prices. In the short-run, flat supply curves imply substantial divergence from the full employment level of output. Given the high real cost of such divergences, Keynesians tend to be persuaded that government countercyclical demand management makes sense and has benefits that far outweigh costs.

Monetarists counter by arguing that even if such countercyclical policy might be desirable in an ideal world of perfect information and short lags, it is not desirable in the imperfect world that we actually inhabit. The long lags between the time policy changes are needed and the time those changes actually begin to have an effect on the economy, coupled with our rather poor forecasting record, make it likely that government stabilization efforts will make instability worse instead of better. Indeed, the monetarists argue that the government has more often than not been a source of instability rather than stability in the past. Let us look more closely now at the problems of lags and forecasting errors.

Lags

In order to operate countercyclical policy of any sort successfully, government policymakers have to know how long it will take for policy measures to affect the economy. They also have to know policy multipliers and be able to predict what the economic situation will be in the future when proposed policy changes begin to

[3] Friedman himself argued that the distinction between the monetarist and the Keynesian models was that the monetarist model assumes that aggregate supply is independent of demand-side factors (that is, the supply curve is vertical), while the Keynesians believe that price is independent of demand-side factors (that is, the supply curve is flat). See Milton Friedman, "A Theoretical Framework for Monetary Analysis," *Journal of Political Economy* 78 (March–April 1970): 193–239.

affect the economy. Unfortunately, our knowledge about all three of these elements is both imprecise and unsatisfactory. That is primarily because of the long lags between the time when a policy change is first needed and the time when the change begins to affect the economy.[4] One can distinguish three different components or stages of this lag.

Recognition Lag

The **recognition lag** is the length of time between the moment when a policy change is needed and the moment when policymakers realize this fact. This lag is generally at least four to six months long. Statistics about the economy are collected and published with a delay. Despite the fact that economists have developed fairly dependable leading indicators, that is, series that forecast what the economy is going to do three to six months in the future, there is still uncertainty about the exact timing of cyclical turning points. To give an example, in the early part of 1980, the government was attempting to cool off a superheated economy in which inflation had risen to almost 20 percent. Although economists expected a downturn sometime during the year, they were still taking contractionary measures as late as March, in the belief that the boom still had some time to run. It was not until June that it was learned that the economy had actually peaked in January. There was a recognition lag of almost five months for this particular turning point, which is about the average length of time that it takes to be sure where the economy is headed.

Administrative Lag

The second source of delay in any policy change is the time period between realizing that a change is needed and getting that change enacted. We shall call this the **administrative lag,** a period that is obviously far longer for fiscal than for monetary policy. As the reader can imagine, this lag is usually longest when contractionary fiscal policy is called for, since Congress is always reluctant to raise taxes or cut off cherished government programs.

The most egregious example of an administrative lag came in the mid-1960s, when the Vietnam War made some sort of contractionary fiscal policy imperative. By 1965 the unemployment rate had dipped below 4 percent, and evidences of excess demand and rising inflation appeared. Government economists realized that a surtax was needed to slow down the economy. However, the Congress was unwilling to cut taxes without an equilivalent cut in government spending. As a result, President Johnson delayed his surtax request until 1967. Even then the tax was not passed until mid-1968, 3½ years after its need was first noted. Not all administrative lags are this long, but there generally is a period of at least six months between the recognition of a need for changes in fiscal policy and the time when a program is put into effect.

[4] See Milton Friedman, "A Monetary and Fiscal Framework for Economic Stability, *American Economic Review* 38 (June 1948): 245–264. See also Michael J. Hamburger, "The Lag in the Effect of Monetary Policy: A Survey of the Literature," Federal Reserve Bank of New York, *Monthly Review* (December 1971).

Effect Lag

The final lag is the time it takes for a change in fiscal or monetary policy to begin to affect behavior in the private sector. This is called the **effect lag.** For government expenditure changes, people have to be hired or fired, while for tax changes, consumers take time to react to a change in tax liabilities. For monetary policy changes, investors take a good deal of time to react to changes in interest rates, since investment plans are made with a long lead time. Until recently it has been thought that the effect lag was longer for monetary policy than for fiscal policy. However, events in the last several years suggest that investors react to monetary policy much more rapidly now than they used to.

When we add together these three lags, we have a total period of not less than one year for fiscal policy and probably at least nine months for monetary policy between the time when a policy is needed and the time when remedial action can begin to affect the economy. During that period, of course, conditions may change in the private sector in a way that makes the policy totally inappropriate. For instance, policymakers may perceive a recession and change to expansionary monetary or fiscal policy. However, by the time the policy takes effect, the economy may have pulled out of the recession on its own and be entering a boom. Thus, expansionary policy may just increase already excessive private sector demand. In this case, active government attempts to stabilize the economy may actually make the situation worse instead of better.

Forecasting Errors

Because of the lag between the time when a policy is needed and the time when it actually begins to affect the economy, the government needs to design policy for events at least a year in the future. To do that, it needs forecasts of the economy that are accurate and reliable. Unfortunately, despite our great advances in computer technology, our forecasting models are not yet good enough to give reliable forecasts that far in advance. Since 1973 a series of unforeseen structural changes in our economy has caused several very large and serious forecasting errors, some of which have misled policymakers and caused them to make bad policy choices.

Stephen McNees, an economist at the Federal Reserve Bank of Boston, has made a careful study of the forecasting record over the 1970s of five of the leading forecasters.[5] These forecasts are based on formal models complemented by the judgment of the model builders. McNees compared the mean one-year-ahead forecast of these five models with what actually happened in the economy. His results are shown in Figure 15.1. As the reader can see, the track record of our

[5] Stephen S. McNees, "The Forecasting Record for the 1970's," *New England Economic Review* (September–October 1979), 33–54. See also Victor Zarnowitz, "On the Accuracy and Properties of Recent Macroeconomic Forecasts," *American Economic Review* 68 (May 1978): 313–321.

Figure 15.1
Prediction Errors in GNP and Inflation

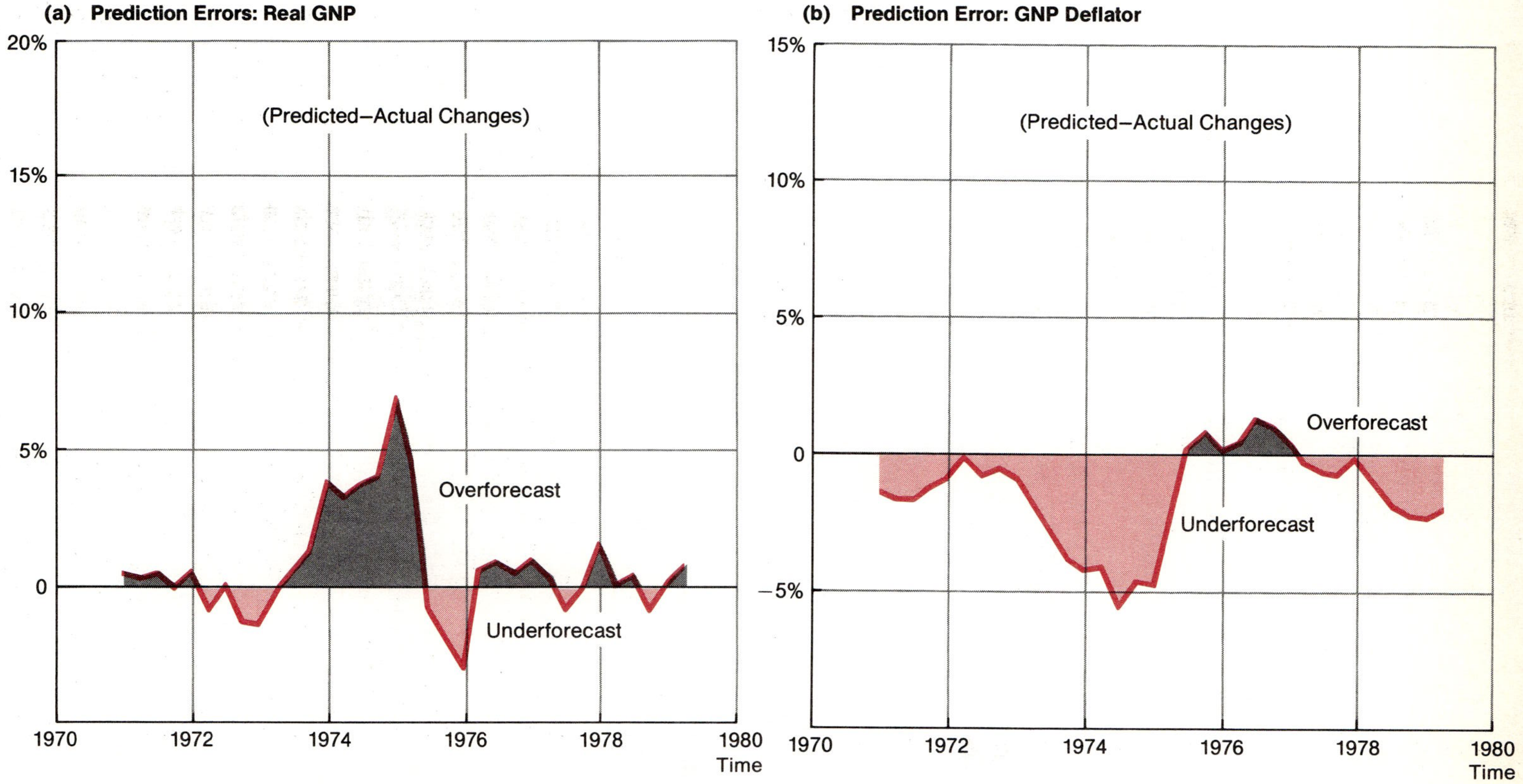

leading forecasters was not a very good one in the 1970s. A severe supply shock in 1974 caused a serious underforecast of inflation and an even more serious overforecast of the level of economic activity. Economists had no previous experience with supply shocks, and they were almost completely unprepared for the 1974–1975 recession, the most severe in the entire postwar period. Because of these forecasting errors, the government took almost no measures to counteract the decline.

The apparent reason for the forecasting errors was changes in the structure of the economy. Alan Greenspan, coming to Washington to assume the chairmanship of the President's Council of Economic Advisors in September 1974, said in an interview:

The last forecast I made out of my model before I left for Washington was for a mild recession in 1975. And I thought I was a pessimist.[6]

When asked why there were such forecasting errors, Greenspan answered,

In all instances the models were wrong. You cannot construct what happened in the next year (1975) or the next six months from the structure of any model then extant. Now it is certainly true that all of our models have been rejiggered to factor in that particular sequence, and the effect has been to very dramatically increase the impact of monetary policy in the models . . . As it turned out, there was a massive shutdown of the capital investment process. All of a sudden capital investment collapsed and that triggered the inventory collapse . . . What was missing in all of the models was the ability to see what premiums could do to capital investment.[7]

In recent years our predictions do not appear to have gotten better. To show this, we supplement the McNees data in Figure 15.1 with the annual forecasts of the President's Council of Economic Advisors for the period since 1978 (see Table 15.1). These forecasts are presented in the form of ranges of expected real GNP growth, inflation, and unemployment. For policy purposes these are the forecasts that matter, since they represent the predictions of those who are actually designing policy.

As one can see from Table 15.1, there has been a systematic and serious underforecast of the inflation rate in the period since 1978. That was mainly caused by the second oil price shock in 1979 and its aftermath. But it was also caused by a prolonged underestimate of demand pressures by the Carter Administration during the years 1978–1980. That error caused a long delay in applying restraint to the economy, a delay during which inflation accelerated to over 15 percent.

By 1978 the economy had been expanding for almost four years. At such a point in the business cycle, it is normal to expect a slowdown in spending. Writing in January of 1978, Carter said:

[6] Alan Greenspan as quoted in Samuel A. Morley, "The CEA and Macroeconomic Policymaking in the United States" (Vanderbilt Institute of Public Policy Studies Working Paper: February 1980), 22.

[7] Ibid., p. 22.

Table 15.1
Predicted and Actual Growth Rates of Macro Variables (in percent)

	1978		1979		1980		1981	
	Prediction	Actual	Prediction	Actual	Prediction	Actual	Prediction	Actual
GNP Real	4½–5	4.7	2–2½	1.6	−¾ to −1¼	−.01	1½–2	0.7
CPI	5¾–6¼	9.0	7½	13.3	10.4	12.3	12	9.4
GNP Deflator		8.1	7¼–7½	8.0	8¾–9¼	9.7	10.0	8.6
Unemployment	6–6¼	5.8	6–6½	5.9	7¼–7¾	7.5	7.5	8.3
Consumption	4¼–4¾	4.8	1¾–2¼	2.0	−½ to −1	+.6	1–1½	1.2
Investment	7–8	9.0	4–4½	2.9	0 to −½	−4.3	1–1½	1.4

Source: Economic Report of the President (various years).

While it is difficult to determine precisely when economic growth would slow, the underlying trends in the economy—together with the effects of fiscal policy—point clearly to a reduction in the pace of expansion later this year or early in 1979.[8]

In order to forestall this decline, in January 1978 the Carter administration proposed cuts in individual and corporate income taxes. These tax cuts were enacted and were to take effect in October 1978. However, by May 1978, with inflationary pressures and demand rising above the forecast levels, it became increasingly clear that restraint rather than fiscal expansion was called for. The tax reduction was scaled down and delayed until January 1979. In retrospect, however, it is clear that more decisive moves to restraint should have been taken. The reason that they were not was that the Carter administration, as well as most forecasters, was sure that the economy would slow down, or even go into a mild recession, on its own. It thought that contractionary policies would only exacerbate the cyclical downturn that was expected.[9] It was to counteract this slowdown as well as to offset the rising social security taxes that took effect in 1979 that Carter proposed his personal income tax reductions.

From Table 15.1 it appears that the Carter forecast for 1979 was accurate, indeed even optimistic, since the economy did slow down, with a growth rate of 1.6 percent, well below the forecast. But keep in mind that this forecast was made at the beginning of the year, before the doubling of the price of oil. During the difficult year of 1979 it was the resiliency of the economy, not the slowdown, that was surprising. As Carter put it, looking back at 1979 at the beginning of 1980:

[8] *Economic Report of the President* (Washington, D. C., 1978), 73.

[9] In January 1979, Carter predicted that the economy would grow about 2¼ percent in 1979, below the long-run growth trend for the United States. That slowdown was expected to be sufficient to take demand pressures off product markets and therefore to moderate inflationary pressures. See *Economic Report of the President* (Washington, D. C., 1979), 92.

In 1979, despite rising inflation, restraint on aggregate demand from monetary and fiscal policy, and a huge 'oil tax' levied by OPEC, the economy continued to move forward . . . The oil drag at year's end was reducing consumer spending power by almost $55 billion at an annual rate, or about 3 percent of personal after-tax income. The magnitude of this restraint has no parallel in any postwar year, including 1974, when the first big OPEC price increase rocked the economy.[10]

Yet in spite of everything, demand continued to increase.

While it is still not entirely clear what caused the overforecast of demand, one of the main reasons appears to have been the behavior of consumers. During the three years 1978–1980, consumers maintained a very high level of spending despite a decline in disposable income by drawing the rate of personal saving down to the lowest level ever recorded in the United States. There is still a good deal of doubt about why this happened, but there is no doubt at all about its effect. It meant that the United States stubbornly refused to go into a stabilization recession. It was not until the emergency monetary measures of March 1980 that Carter finally got the recession he had been expecting for the previous two years. During those two years, a great deal of inflationary damage had been done by our unwillingness to restrain demand.

Unfortunately, forecasting has not improved in the most recent two years for which we have data. The yearly performance does not look too bad in Table 15.1. However, when one reads more carefully what administration economists expected quarter by quarter over the years 1980–1981, it seems clear that no one had an accurate idea of where the economy was going. In 1980 the administration expected a mild slowdown in the first half of the year, followed by mild upturn.[11] What happened was a strong first quarter, with output rising by 3.3 percent, then a very sharp decline in the second quarter, −9.9 percent, and then a surprisingly strong recovery in the third and fourth quarters. The decline in the second quarter was caused by the emergency monetary measures, particularly selective credit controls, put into effect by the Fed in March. Those measures were enacted because the economy was so much stronger than expected. To quote again from the President's economic report,

Early in 1980, there were few signs of recession. If anything, activity seemed to be picking up. The evidence available at the time hinted that households, far from retrenching, were on a buy-in-advance spending spree. Retail sales, which had risen at an annual rate of 13 percent from October 1979, to January 1980, accelerated to an annual rate of nearly 43 percent in January 1980.[12]

When the selective credit controls were removed in the summer of 1980 demand picked up again, and real GNP grew at a 3.1-percent rate for the second half of the year. Reading the record, one has the strong feeling that policymakers simply did not have a forecasting model good enough to enable them to predict what was going to happen in the economy.

[10] *Economic Report of the President* (Washington, D. C., 1980), 29.

[11] Ibid., p. 67.

[12] *Economic Report of the President* (Washington, D. C., 1981), 134.

That impression continued in 1981. In January of that year, the administration forecast that output would be essentially flat during the first half of the year and that an expansion would start in the second half.[13] What happened was again almost exactly the opposite of the forecast. Output rose in the first half of the year and then declined sharply in the final quarter. That decline continued through 1982.

It may appear that recent model builders and administrations in Washington have just been particulary unlucky or incompetent. However, that is probably unfair and untrue. What has happened instead is a series of fundamental changes in the structure of the economy that makes forecasting very difficult. The economy has been confronted by new events such as supply shocks and double-digit inflation. We do not know exactly how those changes will affect behavior, because they have never happened before. Nor can our econometric models tell us. Those models are based on observed experience, most of which was recorded before the structural changes took place.[14] It should not be a surprise that policymaking in the 1970s was more difficult than it was in earlier, more stable times.

Policy Multipliers

As if the forecasting problems were not enough, there is also a very wide range of uncertainty over the absolute size of the basic policy multipliers. Gary Fromm and Lawrence Klein compared the predictions of various leading macromodels about how much a one-dollar increase in government expenditure would increase real income.[15] The multiplier estimates range from almost $3 for the Keynesian Brookings and Bureau of Economic Analysis models to −$.20 for the monetarist model of the St. Louis Fed (after two years). Obviously, policymakers need more exact answers than these if they are to change fiscal or monetary policy so as to hit a given target level of income. They are not going to get much help when the models can't even agree on whether government spending should rise or fall in order to raise the level of demand, let along by how much.

Government as a Source of Instability

Because of the long lags and the uncertainties of forecasting noted in the previous sections, government countercyclical policy could exacerbate private sector instability rather than reduce it. By the time that the need for a discretionary policy is recognized and acted upon, it may well be that underlying conditions have

[13] Ibid., p. 165.

[14] For a pessimistic view of what we can expect from econometric model forecasts, see George Jaszi, "The Role of the Economist in Government: An Economic Accountant's Audit." Paper delivered at a conference on the role of the economist in government, in Royamont, France, 1974. Quoted in David Naveh, "*The Political Role of Professionals in the Formation of National Policy: The Case of the President's Council of Economic Advisors*" (Ph. D. thesis, University of Connecticut, 1978), 168–169.

[15] Gary Fromm and Lawrence R. Klein, "A Comparison of Eleven Econometric Models of the United States," *American Economic Review* 63 (May 1973): 385–394.

changed, making the change in policy inappropriate. Unfortunately, say the monetarists, this has often happened in the past. Monetarists argue that the best we can do, in our present state of knowledge, is stop the government from being an additional source of instability. The way to do that is to take away the government's ability to pursue discretionary policy by forcing it to follow some sort of preset policy rule.

The best-known such rule is the one favored by Friedman, the **constant percentage rate of growth rule.**[16] Friedman wants to require the Federal Reserve to expand the money supply by a constant percentage amount each year. The rate of growth of M would be publicly announced, and it would not vary with conditions in the economy. We will examine this rule more closely in Chapter 17.

For our purposes here we note that such a rule would take away the ability of both monetary and fiscal authorities to engage in countercyclical policy. For monetary policy, the reason is obvious. For fiscal policy the reason is that any change in government spending or taxes would require a compensating change in bond finance, which would tend to offset the direct effect of fiscal policy. Take an expansionary fiscal policy. If the money supply grows at a constant rate, the government budget identity tells us that any countercyclical increase in government spending or tax reduction must be financed by increased bond sales. As we learned in Chapter 5, this tends to contract private sector demand, offsetting part or all of the effect of the expansionary fiscal policy. In this way, Friedman's constant growth rule installs an automatic feedback mechanism, ensuring that discretionary government spending will not become an additional source of instability (or stability) in the economy. We will come back to this question in the next chapter.

Procyclical Government Demand Management

In the debate over discretionary government policy, Keynesians agree that on many occasions in the past the government has been a source of instability: It has acted procyclically. The most famous example is the Great Depression. Friedman's own painstaking research has shown that misguided Federal Reserve policy during that period led to a contraction of the money supply. That made the depression far more serious than it would have been had the monetary authorities adopted his strategy of expanding the money supply at a constant rate.[17]

Another example of procyclical government policy occurred during the Vietnam War in the late 1960s. Because of wartime spending, fiscal policy became highly expansionary after 1965. Instead of providing an offset to this stimulus, monetary policy was also expansionary. Except for a short period in 1966, rapid growth in the money supply helped finance the expansion and exacerbate the cycle. Not until 1969 did both monetary and fiscal policies finally turn contractionary—but by that time, the unemployment rate was 3.2 percent and the inflation

[16] Friedman first proposed this rule in his *A Program for Monetary Stability* (New York: Fordham University Press, 1959).

[17] For Friedman's examination of the causes of the Great Depression, see Milton Friedman and Anna J. Schwartz, *A Monetary History of the United States* (Princeton, NJ: Princeton University Press, 1963).

rate had accelerated to over 5 percent. Government procyclical spending and monetary policy had increased private demand when it should have reduced it.

There is no doubt that government policy in the 1960s and 1970s was erroneous and procyclical. However, Franco Modigliani, in defending countercyclical policy, correctly points out that there is a difference between saying that the government has often been a source of instability in the past and saying that countercyclical government demand management is a source of instability.[18] Most people would agree that the Federal Reserve made a mistake in the Great Depression. Its policies were destabilizing—but that was not because they were trying to stabilize the economy. Had that been the intention, the depression would undoubtedly have been milder.

Similarly, during the late 1960s, the reason the government did not act more energetically to curtail aggregate demand was not that policymakers were trying mistakenly to cure a recession. Rather, it was that they overestimated the effect of tax cuts and underestimated the resiliency of the private sector.[19] Neither of these policy errors were the result of misguided countercyclical policy. They do not prove the point that government countercyclical policy has been destabilizing. But they do support the monetarist point that if government authorities have to determine the level of policy variables, they often make destabilizing errors. Whether those errors are due to misguided attempts at countercyclical policy or not is irrelevant. If the government were forced to follow a fixed rule, such as the one proposed by Milton Friedman, authorities would not be free to make such errors. They would therefore be protected from the effects of their bad judgment.

The Continuing Debate over Discretionary Policy

In the final analysis, two policy questions have to be answered in order to resolve the debate over the advisability of activist government demand management. First: Is government discretionary policy destabilizing, whether it be countercyclical or not? Second: How stable will the economy be it the government follows some set of predetermined rules, such as those suggested by the monetarists?

To these questions we can offer no clear-cut answers. Despite a good deal of effort, no one has been able to devise a test for the effectiveness of countercyclical policy. However, one should note that the period since 1945, when we first started applying such policies, has been overall the most stable in our history. To quote one of the founding fathers of business cycle analysis, Arthur Burns, writing in 1959:

> *Since 1937, we have had five recessions, the longest of which lasted only 13 months. There is no parallel for such a sequence of mild—or such a sequence of brief—contractions, at least during the past hundred years in our country.* [*By now we can add to that list the recessions of 1961 and 1970.*][20]

[18] Franco Modigliani, "The Monetarist Controversy, or Should We Forsake Stabilization Policy?"

[19] See Samuel A. Morley, "The CEA and Macroeconomic Policymaking in the United States."

[20] As quoted in Franco Modigliani, op. cit., p. 14.

Of course, it is possible that the changes in the postwar period were simply lucky structural changes that had nothing to do with policy. Such an interpretation might draw support from our difficulties since 1974, when we have had a quick succession of relatively serious recessions. However, up until the very recent past, there have been few economists who did not think that government countercyclical policy should take some of the credit for increased stability.

There is a more subtle point regarding discretionary policy. Suppose we grant that discretionary policy can be stabilizing when properly used. Can we be sure that it will be properly used? Will government authorities, if empowered to make discretionary decisions, be able to resist political pressures to overexpand the economy? Will they be able to reduce the money supply or raise taxes when the situation calls for that? Such questions are not technical, they are political. They ask whether popularly elected governments have the patience to wait for recoveries and the forbearance to cut off booms before inflationary pressure gets out of hand.

On this score, the record of the United States is not particularly encouraging. As one might expect, it has been relatively easy to get a political consensus to raise the money supply or cut taxes to get out of a recession but far harder to get an agreement to restrain the economy when that is what should be done. For this reason, many pessimists claim that democratic governments with discretionary power over monetary and fiscal policies tend to have a bias toward overexpansion. Knowing how to reduce unemployment by expansion, governments are likely to face great pressures to do so, regardless of whether or not it is wise. One could make a quite convincing case that the temptation to overexpand is the main reason that the economies of democratic governments have exhibited such a strong tendency toward inflation since the invention of countercyclical demand management in the 1930s. There would be far less inflation if we stripped the government altogether of its discretionary decision-making power.

Granting the great difficulties that governments have had using demand management successfully, we really cannot say how the economy would act if the government followed a growth rate rule of the type proposed by Friedman. No one disagrees that such a rule would reduce the danger that the government might be a source of instability. But that does not mean that the economy would be stable. Nor does it imply that the economy would be more stable then it would be under activist government demand management. We simply do not have enough historical experience to tell us how our economy would behave under a rigid set of rules for monetary and fiscal policies.

It may seem obvious that the economy would be more stable if the monetary authorities followed a stable rule for expanding the money supply. However, such a conclusion is not necessarily justified. The verdict depends on the duration and the source of the disturbance. If disturbances come from the demand side, and if they last a long time, then it is likely that the government can help to stabilize the economy by active intervention. That was the case in the 1930s and the late 1960s. However, when disturbances are transitory, probably no purpose is served by such policy.

We should make it clear that in our discussion we have been implicitly assuming that all of our difficulties come from demand-side disturbances. However, many of our most recent cycles have been caused by supply-side shocks, such as the oil price increase in 1979. As we shall see in Chapter 20, supply-side shocks require an entirely different set of policy responses. Countercyclical demand management in response to supply shocks is probably unwise under any circumstances. Suppose, for example, that oil price increases push the economy into a recession. Here the government should probably not try to counteract the recession by expansionary policy. Some decline in output is inevitable, because the capacity level of the economy has been diminished. Expansionary policy only blurs that unpleasant reality in the short run, at the cost of a higher rate of inflation.

To summarize, the basic issue is whether the government should be granted the power to engage in countercyclical demand management. Those who do not think so base their argument on both the technical and the political difficulties of operating discretionary policy correctly. Those who do think so grant the difficulties cited by the pessimists. They acknowledge that we shall never know enough to be able to fully control the economy or to avoid overexpansion on occasion. But that does not mean that we must never actively intervene to change policy, or that we must dogmatically rely on a set of rules under any circumstances. It is one thing to argue against intervention to counteract small fluctuations in unemployment and output. It is quite another to refuse to adjust policy in the face of obvious and persistent deviations from full employment.

Rational Expectations

Recently a strong new attack on policy activism has been mounted by a group of economists whose work on expectations seems to prove conclusively that the government is powerless to affect the level of economic activity in the economy unless it acts completely randomly.[21] The theory upon which this assertion is based is called **rational expectations**. The reader will recall that both of our short-run macromodels depend crucially on the differences between actual and expected prices. Expected prices themselves were assumed to be formed adaptively, which means that they are based on past actual values of prices. The trouble with this adaptive theory of price expectations is that it ignores information and is therefore likely to lead to systematic forecasting errors. For example, if there is an expansion in the money supply, those basing their price forecasts on past actual prices will underforecast the price level. They will make a forecasting error because they are ignoring the fact that the money supply is increasing.

[21] Two good introductions to the writings on rational expectations are Rodney Maddock and Michael Carter, "A Child's Guide to Rational Expectations," *Journal of Economic Literature* 20 (March 1982): 39–51; and a symposium on rational expectations published as a special issue of the *Journal of Money, Credit and Banking* 12 (November 1980, part 2). See also Bennet T. McCallum, "The Significance of Rational Expectations Theory," *Challenge* (January–February 1980): 37–43.

Two of the important early contributors to this literature were Neil Wallace and Thomas Sargent. Their papers are quite technical. See, for example, their "Rational Expectations and the Theory of Economic Policy," *Journal of Monetary Economics* 2 (April 1976): 169–183.

The new theory, whose implications we shall examine here, is based on the assumption that expectations are formed rationally rather than adaptively. What that means is that economic actors use all the information available to them when making price forecasts. One of the key items of information is knowledge of how the economy works and what determines prices. Suppose, for example, that people know that prices are related to the money supply. If so, it is not rational for them to ignore information about the money supply when predicting the future price level. The rational expectations model assumes that price forecasts are based on a model of the economy rather than on lagged prices.

The effect of this change in assumptions is dramatic. It implies that variations in output from the full equilibrium level must be caused by either random shocks or unexpected deviations of policy from the levels expected by the public. The reasoning is straightforward. If prices and output are a function of exogenous policy variables, as our models say they are, and if the public knows both the model and the values of those variables, then the public's price predictions will be accurate except for random shocks or mistakes in forecasting the policy variables.

Mathematical Derivation of the Rational Expectations Model

We now develop this idea more formally. Consider the following simple model of the economy, similar to that used earlier in the book. Aggregate demand is positively related to the money supply and fiscal policy (F) and negatively to prices. Thus, we write our demand equation as:

(15.1) $$Y_d = y(\overset{+}{M}, \overset{+}{F}, \overset{-}{P}).$$

For convenience, we will rewrite Equation (15.1) as an equation relating price to these same variables:

(15.2) $$P = p(\overset{+}{M}, \overset{+}{F}, \overset{-}{Y}).$$

On the supply side, output is a function of the capital stock and unexpected inflation. Thus, we write our supply equation as:

(15.3) $$Y_s = s\left(\overset{+}{K}, \overset{+}{\frac{P}{P_e}}\right).$$

We close the model by setting supply equal to demand:

(15.4) $$Y_s = Y_d.$$
$$Y_s = Y.$$

In our previous models of the economy, we have treated expected prices as a function of past prices. The rational expectations model is based on the assertion that if prices are determined by Equation (15.2), then so should expected prices be based on that equation. To assume otherwise is to say that forecasters ignore information or make systematic forecasting errors.

The rational expectations model replaces the adaptive price expectations equation with a price forecast based on Equation (15.2). That forecast equation is:

(15.5) $$P_e = p(M_e, F_e, Y).$$

Expected prices are based on the expected value of the money supply (M), fiscal policy, and income.

Now we substitute Equations (15.2), (15.4), and (15.5) into Equation (15.3) to get an expression for income. This is:

(15.6) $$Y = s\left(K, \frac{p(M, F, Y)}{p(M_e, F_e, Y)}\right).$$

Equation (15.6) says that real income is a function of actual and expected levels of monetary and fiscal policies and the capital stock, which determines capacity. Note that neither expected nor actual prices enter this equation. Under reasonable assumptions about functional form, we can simplify Equation (15.6) to:

(15.7) $$Y = v\left(\overset{+}{K}, \overset{+}{\frac{M}{M_e}}, \overset{+}{\frac{F}{F_e}}\right).$$

Equation (15.7) expresses one fundamental result of the rational expectations model. It is that income is not a function of unexpected inflation and deflation but rather of unexpected monetary and fiscal policies. Furthermore, it should be the case that when monetary and fiscal policies are predicted accurately, actual and expected prices should be equal, and therefore the economy should be in full equilibrium. That is, if $M = M_e$ and $F = F_e$, $Y_s = Y_d = Y_{FE}$.

What all of this says is simply that deviations from full equilibrium output are a result of deviations of monetary and fiscal policies from their expected settings, for that is what causes expected and actual prices to differ. When one stops to think about it, this result is a perfectly consistent implication of the entire rational expectations approach. If people forecast prices with a model of the economy, and if the model is a good one, the only way there can be price forecasting errors leading to deviations of Y from Y_{FE} is if there are errors in forecasting the exogenous policy variables or if there are random shocks to the economy.

It follows that the only way the authorities can influence the level of economic activity is to do something that the public does not expect. For example, if they want output to rise above Y_{FE}, they must expand the money supply faster or run a fiscal policy more expansionary than people expect.

Policy Implications of the Rational Expectations Model

We return to our policy activism question: Can and should the government operate countercyclical monetary and fiscal policies? That depends on whether the public can predict monetary and fiscal policies accurately. As we have just learned, when

$M_e = M$ and $F_e = F$, the economy will be at its full equilibrium level, regardless of what monetary and fiscal policies actually are. Therefore, in order to affect output and employment, policy has to be different than the public expects it to be. Thus, the debate on the feasibility of policy activism boils down to the question of whether the government can devise a way of conducting countercyclical monetary and fiscal policies that will not eventually be learned by the public. The rational expectations economists do not think this is possible.

Given the importance to the private sector of accurate forecasts, it seems reasonable to suppose that considerable resources would be devoted to learning how the government sets monetary and fiscal policies. Therefore, if policymakers follow any sort of systematic countercyclical policy rule, the public should eventually learn it. When that happens, the public will be able to forecast M and F accurately, and income will go to the full employment level regardless of what rule the authorities follow. To put it another way: Once the public has learned to forecast government policy, that policy can no longer have any real effect on the economy. Therefore, one can say that any systematic method of conducting monetary and fiscal policies is as good as any other, and all methods are equally irrelevant to the determination of real income. Under rational expectations any policy, if and when it can be forecast, will be completely neutral with respect to output and employment. Of course, the authorities could still "surprise" the public by setting monetary and fiscal policies at random, but that does not seem like a very sensible way to manage policy.

The rational expectations model in essence asserts that the economy supply curve is vertical. Once the public learns to forecast M and F expected and actual prices will be equal, and the economy will be on the full equilibrium vertical supply curve. As we know, on that curve demand management does not affect output, it only affects prices. Thus, according to the rational expectations model, governmental operation of monetary and fiscal policies will have a big impact on prices but little or no effect on output. If, for example, the government runs expansionary monetary policy, the economy will not expand; prices will go up instead (assuming the policy was not unexpected).

It follows from this that if the authorities want to reduce the inflation rate, they should follow a contractionary policy, and they should widely announce this intention. If they do this, M_e and F_e will fall along with M and F, and that will reduce expected inflation and allow the economy to enjoy a reduced actual inflation rate without an extended stabilization recession.

For the rational expectations school, the reason we have long stabilization recessions is not that price expectations are slow to adapt. Rather, it is that the government's determination to stabilize is not credible.[22] The public overforecasts the inflation rate because it overforecasts the rate of monetary expansion, not

[22] On the credibility hypothesis, see William Fellner, "The Credibility Effect and Rational Expectations: Implications of the Gramlich Study," *Brookings Papers on Economic Activity* (1/1979): 167–178. See also his *Towards a Reconstruction of Macroeconomics* (Washington, D. C.: American Enterprise Institute, 1976) and his "The Case of the Controversy about Reducing Inflation: An Introductory Analysis," in William Fellner, ed., *Contemporary Economic Problems 1978* (Washington, D. C.: American Enterprise Institute, 1978), 1–13.

because it bases its inflation forecasts on lagged values of the price index. Therefore, according to this line of thought, the key to reducing the inflation rate is to convince the public that the government is serious. When that happens, M_e will fall to M, which will reduce inflationary expectations at a much lower cost than will the long stabilization recessions implied by the adaptive expectations model.

There are two strong policy implications of the rational expectations model. First, active countercyclical policy is useless, because it will eventually be forecast by the public. Any automatic rule, such as the one Friedman proposed for the money supply, will stabilize the economy just as well, if not better. Second, to fight inflation, one need only reduce the growth rate of the money supply and get the public to believe that the reduced rate is permanent. The secret to successful stabilization is credibility. If the public believes the government when it says it is going to reduce M, the program becomes a self-fulfilling prophecy. Actual inflation rates fall while the economy stays at, or close to, full employment.

Criticisms of the Rational Expectations Model

It is clear that the rational expectations model offers powerful theoretical support to those who argue against policy activism and for antiinflationary stabilization. Those who are convinced that demand management does affect real output criticize the rational expectations theory for its lack of realism and applicability to actual economies.[23] No one disagrees that *if* economic actors used a price model in making predictions, and *if* there were no long-term contracts, the economy would tend to stay on its full equilibrium supply curve. But are people that sophisticated? Do union negotiators check the expected money supply when they set their wage demands? Critics of rational expectations think that they probably use some sort of rule of thumb instead. Perhaps they base their wage demands on which other unions in their area are demanding, or on inflation in previous periods. No rule of thumb is rational in a world of perfect certainty, but such a rule may be when information about the economy is uncertain, hard to understand, and costly to obtain.

Even if everyone were to form his or her price expectations rationally, the supply curve would still not be vertical in the short run. In our economy long contracts and staggered wage setting impose a good deal of inertia into the economy's ability to react to changes in conditions. Suppose, for example, that all contracts last three years and that one-third are negotiated each year. In such an economy, any change in monetary or fiscal policy, even if it is known by everyone, will have a real effect on output, because it will change the real terms of all contracts in force. Unless the public can accurately forecast policy out into the future, at least as far as the longest contracts will reach, policy changes will have real effects on the economy.[24]

[23] See James Tobin, "Are New Classical Models Plausible Enough to Guide Policy?" *Journal of Money, Credit and Banking* 12 (November 1980, pt. 2): 788–800.

[24] See John Taylor, "Staggered Wage Setting in a Macro Model," *American Economic Review* 69 (May 1979): 108–113. Taylor shows that if the contracts are overlapping, policy changes have effects for even longer than the contract length.

Another difficulty for the rational expectations models is the continued existence of booms and recessions. According to the model, deviations from full employment should occur only when there are random shifts in either private sector demand or public sector policy. Random shocks cannot explain booms or recessions. For both of these are persistent deviations of actual from full equilibrium output. Such deviations cannot be the result of purely random fluctuations. The rational expectations model has no clear explanation of how such persistent deviations could occur unless the public systematically, over a period of years, over- or underforecasts either private demand or government policy.

To critics of the rational expectations approach, such an explanation for recessions and booms seems contrived and unrealistic. The disequilibrium economist argues that markets do not necessarily clear in the short run, because workers and businesspersons set their wages and/or prices on the basis of some sort of rule of thumb or markup over cost. Then, it is variations in nominal demand, not price, that primarily determines quantity sold and employment in the short run. One could say that this behavior is not rational, in the sense that if sellers know demand conditions, and if their prices or wages are set at a level that will lead to recession, they should adjust those prices and wages.[25] Perhaps they should. But if actual participants in the economy behave as the disequilibrium economists say they do, the economy will have a relatively flat supply curve. In that case, fluctuations in demand will cause booms and recessions rather than variations in the price level.

Once again we come down to a disagreement over how our economy works. The rational expectations school is an extension of the full equilibrium view that prices are flexible and markets clear. The disequilibrium view says that prices and wages are determined by sellers, probably by rules of thumb, and often at levels inconsistent with full employment. They believe that demand management can and does have effects on income in our real economy, even though it would not in a world of price-takers and rational expectations. While that would be an ideal economy to live in, policymakers have no choice but to deal with our actual economy. And in that economy, if the critics are right, demand management does still matter.

Summary

Having examined how monetary and fiscal policies work, in this chapter we addressed the fundamental question of when and if they should be used. A large group of economists who call themselves monetarists do not think that the govern-

[25] James Tobin has pointed out that in a world of imperfectly competitive "coalitions" of firms and their workers, there is no guarantee that each coalition will set its prices in such a way that quantity sold will equal capacity, even if each coalition knows the future path of nominal income. The key problem here is the dispersion of decision makers and markets. If each seller knows total demand but does not know what prices other sellers are going to set, it is not clear what the "rational" price should be. Tobin shows that there are good reasons to expect price and wage adjustments to be rare in such a world. See his "Are New Classical Models Plausible Enough to Guide Policy?", loc. cit..

ment should use its policy instruments in a discretionary way to control the level of aggregate demand. They think that the private sector of the economy is inherently self-stabilizing, that the government has been a significant source of instability in the past, and that greater stability could be achieved by forcing the government to give up discretionary policy and follow a set of rules instead. One reason for their pessimism stems from the long and variable lags between the time when a policy change is needed and the time when the change begins to affect the economy. Another reason stems from the inherent difficulties in forecasting with enough accuracy to fine-tune the economy and rests on the conviction that the economy will do acceptably well if the government just leaves it alone.

Rational expectations provides an additional reason for following a policy rule. If individuals form their price expectations using a model of the economy, it can be shown that only unforeseen changes in policy can have any real effect. Since the public is likely to learn of any discretionary stabilization rule that the government might adopt, active countercyclical policy will not have its desired effect.

Opponents of the monetarist-rational expectations school make three points. First, they do not think that the private sector is all that stable. Second, they doubt that the public forms expectations rationally. Third, while they accept the argument that forecasting is difficult and the government has often made policy errors in the past, they do not think that this proves that the economy would be more stable were the government to forsake activist demand management altogether. Thus, while they are willing to abandon fine-tuning, these economists are unwilling to tie policymakers' hands in cases of severe recession or inflation. They are convinced that countercyclical, activist demand management will be beneficial in such cases.

Key Concepts

monetarist
Keynesian
recognition lag
administrative lag
effect lag
constant percentage rate of growth rule
rational expectations
automatic stabilizers

Problems and Questions for Discussion

1. Why do the monetarists think that government macropolicymakers should be obliged to follow policy rules instead of attempting to engage in countercyclical monetary and/or fiscal policy? Do you think their position is defensible? If so, why? If not, why not?

2. Do you think that a demonstration that government has been a source of instability in the past is a proof that the economy will be more stable if the government follows a rule rather than attempting to stabilize the economy? Why or why not?

3. What are the stabilizing feedbacks in our economy that tend to limit the cyclical fluctuations of output around its long-run trend? Can you think of ways in which we might increase the potency of these automatic stabilizers?

4. Discuss examples of and reasons for poor forecasting during the 1970s. Can you think of any general explanation for the problem? What does it imply for policy-making?

5. Many monetarists argue that if the government is free to choose its monetary and fiscal policies to combat inflation and unemployment, the result will be a tendency toward inflation. What is the basis for this monetarist position? Do you think it is a sound one? Can you think of historical instances that either support or contradict the monetarist position?

6. If the monetary authorities were forced to follow the constant percentage growth rate rule for the money supply, monetary policy could not be a source of instability. But monetarists claim that the rule helps counteract procyclical fiscal policy as well. Explain their argument. Do you think they are correct?

7. "If expectations are formed rationally, the government is powerless to affect the level of output in the economy unless it acts completely randomly." What does this statement mean? Do you think it is correct? Why or why not?

8. According to the rational expectations hypothesis, under what conditions does output in the economy rise above Y_{FE}? Under what conditions does output fall below Y_{FE}? How does this explanation for booms and recessions compare with that for the partial equilibrium model?

Chapter 16

The Operation of Fiscal Policy

In the last chapter we considered in general terms the issue of whether or not the government should try to actively control the level of aggregate demand. We now wish to consider specifically how to manage fiscal and monetary policies. In this chapter we shall focus on the operation of fiscal policy.

Fiscal policy consists of changing government expenditures or tax rates in order to influence the size and the composition of private sector demand. What tax rate should the government set? Should it try to coordinate fiscal policy with monetary policy, and if so, how? If the government runs deficits, how should they be financed? These are some of the questions that we shall take up in this chapter.

The Measurement of Fiscal Policy

Before we can intelligently discuss fiscal policy or judge actions by policymakers, we need an indicator that will tell us what fiscal policy is. Specifically, we need to know when fiscal policymakers are trying to restrain the economy with contractionary policy and when they are trying to stimulate it.

The Government Deficit

The most popular and most misunderstood indicator of the direction of fiscal policy is the **government deficit,** defined in Equation (16.1).[1] Since the deficit depends positively on government expenditure and transfers and negatively on taxes, it

[1]Note that the government deficit defined in Equation (16.1) is simply the negative of government saving as defined in Chapter 2.

would seem logical that an increase in the deficit is a signal of expansionary policy and reduction a signal of contraction. Certainly that is the way that deficits are interpreted in the popular press.

(16.1) $$Def = G - tY + R.$$

Unfortunately, this simple interpretation of the government deficit is incorrect. The government deficit is not a good indicator of fiscal policy, mainly because it is a function of both government policy and private demand. That is because tax receipts and transfers both depend on income. Therefore, anything that influences the level of income will affect the size of the government deficit, even if there is no change at all in fiscal policy. Technically, the government deficit is an endogenous variable; that means that it is not fully under the control of the government. Clearly, the government can influence the size of the deficit by changing G, R, or t. But those are not the only factors that can change the deficit.

Suppose, for example, that investors become more pessimistic, so that the level of autonomous expenditure falls. This, as we have learned, will reduce Y, which will in turn reduce government tax receipts and increase the deficit even though the government has not changed G, R, or t. If we were to judge fiscal policy on the basis of the size of the actual deficit, we would think that such a change indicated expansionary fiscal policy, since the deficit increased. But the rising deficit, in this case, indicates nothing of the sort. All it shows is that private sector demand has fallen.

Another important factor that can change the government deficit without changing the fiscal policy variables is monetary policy. Expansionary monetary policy tends to increase the level of income, while contractionary policy tends to reduce income. Either, according to Equation (16.1), will affect the level of tax receipts and thus the government's deficit. For example, contractionary monetary policy will tend to reduce tax receipts and raise the deficit. If one is using the deficit as an indicator of fiscal policy, one might mistakenly conclude that an expansionary fiscal policy was taking place.

To see the connection between monetary policy and the government deficit more clearly, consider Figure 16.1. Diagram (a) is the IS-LM diagram, which we derived in Chapter 4. Diagram (b) is a picture of Equation (16.1). The deficit function in (b) is downward sloping, because tax receipts are positively related to income. If the money supply is M_0 and tax rates and government expenditures are t_0 and G_0, equilibrium income is Y_0, and the government budget is balanced.

Now suppose the monetary authorities reduce the money supply. Their action will shift the LM curve back to LM′ which will cause income to fall to Y_1. What is relevant to our discussion here is that the fall in income will cause the government deficit to rise to D_1. Contractionary monetary policy increases the government deficit.

This particular policy mix can cause some serious interpretation problems for those who focus on government deficits as indicators of fiscal policy. For example, deficits are thought by most people to be inflationary or at the very least expansionary. Some deficits are, but not the ones we are examining here. A government

Figure 16.1
Monetary Policy and the Deficit

Diagram (b) is a picture of Equation 16.1. It is downward sloping because tax revenues are positively related to income. This says that the government deficit is negatively related to income. Therefore, a contractionary monetary policy of the sort depicted in (a) by the shift in the LM curve to LM′ will cause the deficit to rise from 0 to D_1.

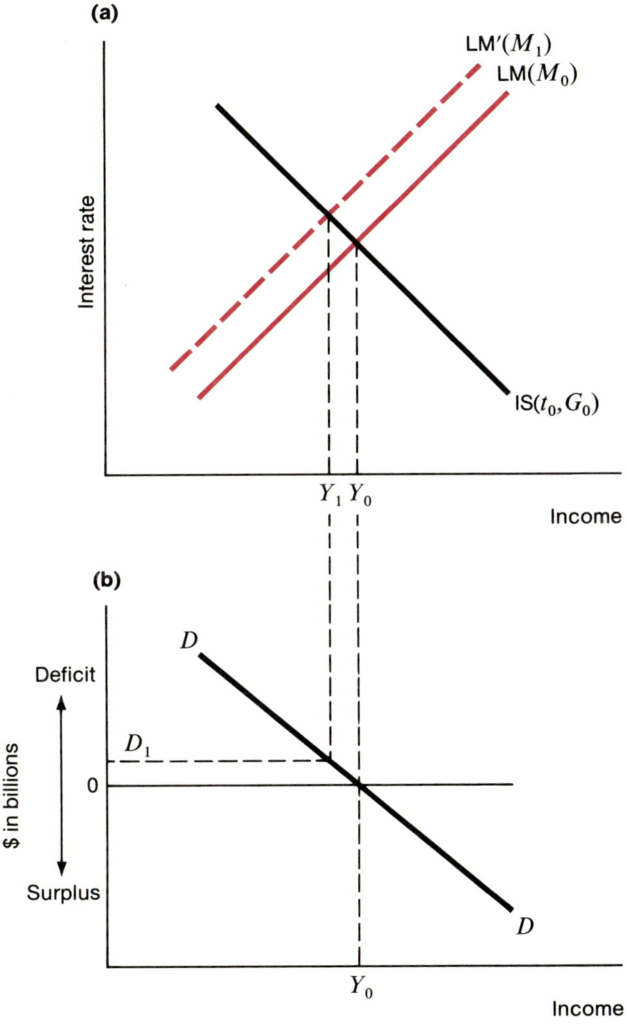

deficit that is caused by contractionary monetary policy could hardly be thought of as an inflationary deficit. Surely no one worried about inflation would criticize the government if it reduced the money supply to help control inflation. Yet that action will increase the deficit too. Such a deficit is not an inflationary deficit. Quite the contrary, it is a deficit that *results* from the government's efforts to curb inflation by controlling the money supply.[2]

The Full Employment Deficit

What we have said so far should be enough to convince the reader that we need a better indicator of fiscal policy than the actual deficit, a measure that depends only on the government's fiscal policy instruments. One such measure that goes a long way in this direction is the **full employment deficit.**[3]

The full (or high) employment deficit ($DEFF$) is defined as the deficit the government would incur if the economy were producing the full employment of output Y_{FE}; that is:

(16.2) $$DEFF = G - tY_{FE} + R.$$

Since $DEFF$ uses the hypothetical government revenues at full employment output, it is unaffected by changes in actual demand. Hence, the main influence on $DEFF$ is changes in the three government fiscal policy instruments, t, G, and R. This is what makes $DEFF$ a good indicator of fiscal policy.

We show the actual deficit and the full employment deficit diagrammatically in Figure 16.2. If the income level is Y_a, the actual deficit is distance AB. If income is at the full employment level, Y_{FE}, the deficit is distance CD. By definition, distance CD is the full employment deficit. For the tax and expenditure rates shown in the diagram, $DEFF$ is a surplus.

Consider now the effect of a change in fiscal policy instruments. Expansionary fiscal policy either raises G or lowers the tax rate. In either case, the line D shifts up in the diagram to line D'. As the reader can see, the actual deficit probably will increase, although this depends on how much actual income responds to the expansionary stimulus. The full employment deficit unambiguously increases. Usually, whenever fiscal policy becomes more expansionary, $DEFF$ increases; when-

[2]Ronald Reagan had exactly this interpretation predicament in 1981–1982. Monetary policy was exceedingly tight, and the economy was operating far below its normal capacity. Also, the government was running very large deficits. While the Reagan tax cuts may have added somewhat to the deficits, the largest part of the government's red ink was a result of the recession, a recession that was brought about by the antiinflationary program of the Federal Reserve. Those decifits, therefore, were a result of the fight against inflation. They were not the result of expansionary fiscal policy, and they were not inflationary.

[3]The concept of the full employment budget deficit was introduced by the Committee for Economic Development in 1947. For a full discussion of the full or high employment deficit concept, see Herbert Stein, *The Fiscal Revolution in America* (Chicago: University of Chicago Press, 1969), especially chapter 9. See also Alan S. Blinder and Robert M. Solow, "Analytical Foundations of Fiscal Policy," in Alan S. Blinder, *et al.*, *The Economics of Public Finance* (Washington, D. C.: Brookings Institution, 1974), 3–119, especially 14–33. For a discussion of how the full employment deficit is currently being measured and the most recent estimates, see Frank DeLeeuw, Thomas M. Holloway, Danvin G. Johnson, David S. McClain, and Charles A. Waite, "The High Employment Budget: New Estimates, 1955–1980," *Survey of Current Business* 60 (November 1980): 13–44.

Figure 16.2
Actual and Full Employment Deficits

The actual government deficit depends on the level of income. At income Y_a, the deficit is distance AB. At the full employment income, Y_{FE}, the full employment deficit is CD. Changing tax rates or expenditures clearly changes the full employment deficit but may not change the actual deficit.

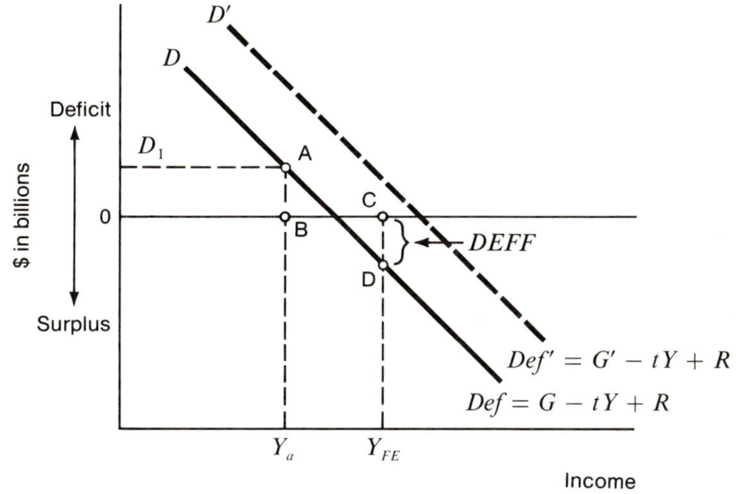

ever it becomes more contractionary, *DEFF* declines. Note that it is not the choice of full employment output that makes *DEFF* a better indicator of fiscal policy than *Def*, but simply the choice of a particular level of *Y*.

Unfortunately, even *DEFF* is not an entirely unambiguous indicator of fiscal policy.[4] In the first place, it is affected by changes in the price level. Since our tax system is progressive, when there is an inflation real tax receipts go up and *DEFF* falls, even though there has been no specific change in fiscal policy. Second, since tax receipts are sensitive to the level of output, economic growth, which increases Y_{FE} over time, will reduce the full employment deficit. Like the effect of inflation, this change in *DEFF* does not indicate a change in discretionary fiscal policy. Third, and most important, taxes, government spending, and transfer payments have different income multipliers. It is thus possible for the government to stimulate or contract the economy through fiscal policy even though *DEFF* is unchanged.[5]

[4]For a full discussion of these difficulties of the *DEFF* measure, see Blinder and Solow, op. cit., pp.14–33.

[5]In addition, of course, *DEFF* is sensitive to the level of unemployment considered to be full employment. At present, *DEFF* is calculated on the basis of a 5.2-percent unemployment rate. See DeLeeuw, et al., op. cit., p. 17.

Suppose, for example, that the government raises G and raises tax rates by just enough to cover the extra revenue at full employment. We know that this will increase income—it is expansionary. Yet $DEFF$ will be unchanged. To get around this problem in the measurement of the full employment deficit, a number of economists have proposed that we use a weighted full employment deficit, where the weights would be related to the multipliers and shares of different expenditures and taxes in the total government budget.[6] The goal is to find a measure that goes up *only* if fiscal policy is expansionary and goes down *only* if it is contractionary. We will ignore this complication in the discussion that follows.

Opposite Movements of Def *and* DEFF

Is it possible for the full employment deficit and the actual deficit to go in opposite directions? The answer is yes, as we shall demonstrate in the following example. Suppose the economy is operating with a substantial amount of slack, which the government decides to cure with a tax cut. Suppose, in addition, that the monetary authorities complement the tax cut with expansionary monetary policy. We show the net effect of this particular set of policies on income and the deficit in Figure 16.3. In diagram (a), we show both the IS and LM curves shifting to the right because of the tax cuts and the rise in M. Income rises from Y_0 to Y_1. The more interesting question is what happens to the deficit. To see that, look at (b). A fall in the tax rate from t_0 to t_1 rotates the deficit line counterclockwise. As the reader can see, the full employment deficit rises from zero to a positive number. But the actual deficit goes down, from D_0 to D_1. The reason is that income increases by so much that the revenues at the lower rate actually increase, because the expansionary monetary policy complemented the tax cut. Had the money supply not increased, the actual deficit would almost surely have increased.

The case we have been discussing here, where Def and $DEFF$ move in opposite directions, is not merely a hypothetical one, as the reader can see from Figure 16.4.

The government has run a deficit every year since 1973. But the actual deficit figures do not tell the story of fiscal policy during this period. Look at 1974. That was the year when the Ford and Nixon administrations struggled to contain the inflation sparked by the OPEC oil price increase of 1973. Fiscal policy became sharply tighter, as we can see by the reduction of $19 billion in the full employment deficit. Mostly this reflected the effect of high inflation rates on individual and corporate tax liabilities, rather than discretionary tax decisions by the government. Whatever the cause, the data tell us that in 1974, fiscal policy became quite sharply contractionary. At the same time, the rate of growth of the money supply was curtailed. As a result, the economy was pushed into the 1974–1975 recession, the sharpest and deepest since the 1930s. One can see from Figure 16.4 what that recession did to the government's finances. The actual deficit began to rise in 1974, and then in 1975 it shot up to the highest level ever recorded in peacetime. That deficit was not the result of expansionary fiscal policy. Rather, it

[6] See Blinder and Solow, op. cit., especially pp. 14–33.

Figure 16.3
Tax Reductions May Lower the Deficit

These two diagrams show the effect of a reduction in the tax rate financed by an increase in the money supply. The rate reduction shifts both the deficit line and the IS curve counterclockwise to the dashed lines. What happens to the deficit depends on the slopes of the curves and the monetary policy. In the case shown, the expansion in the money supply is sufficient to increase income and tax revenues, despite the lower tax rate. As a result the deficit declines from D_0 to D_1.

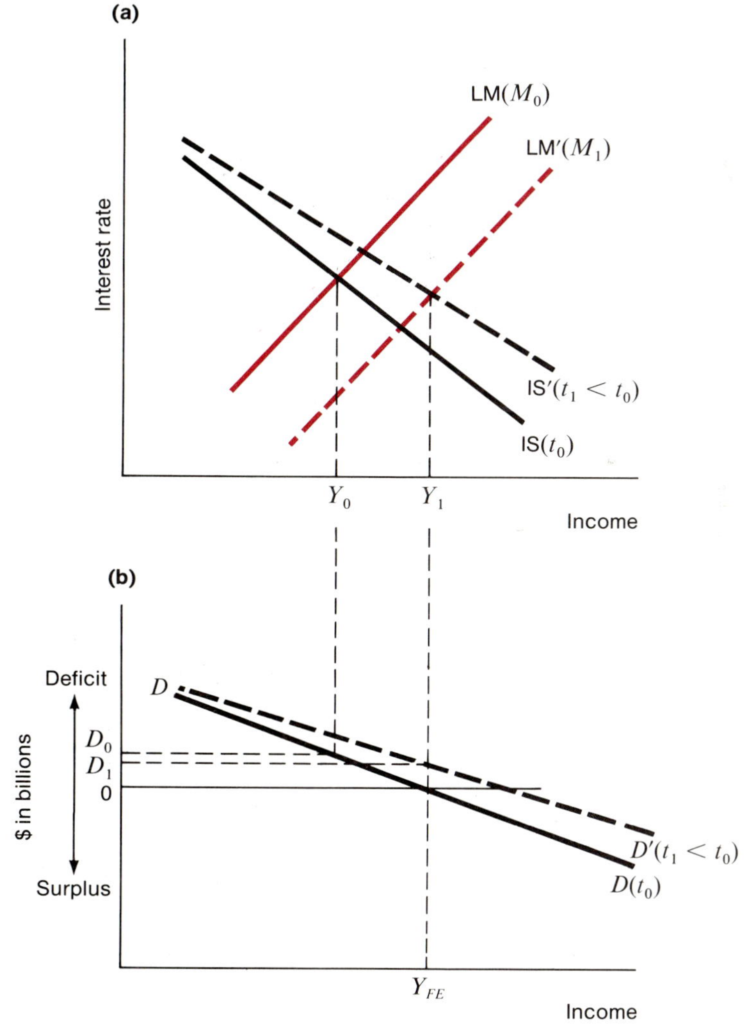

Figure 16.4
Actual and Full Employment Deficit As a Fraction of GNP

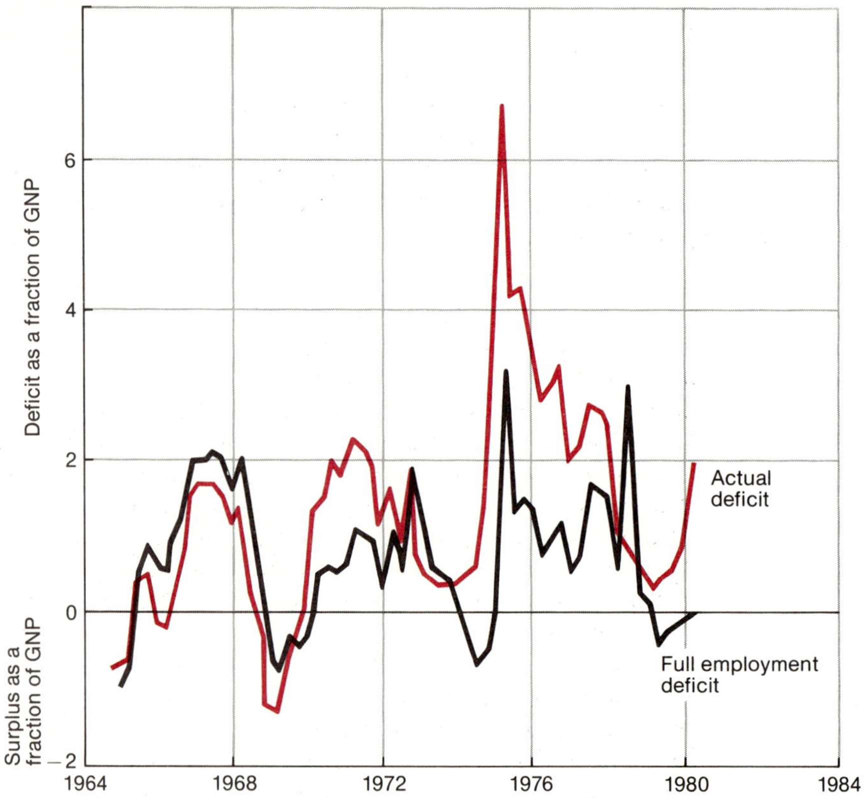

was the result of contractionary monetary policy carried out to curb inflation. One would get a totally misleading picture of fiscal policy had he or she focused on the actual deficit during that year.

Furthermore, the notion that the 1975 deficit was an inflationary deficit is also misleading. As we mentioned earlier, some deficits are the result of a fight against inflation using restrictive monetary policy. The 1975 deficit was one of them. Indeed, as one can see from Figure 16.4, a large proportion of the total amount of deficit spending in the post-1973 period is a result of our having operated our economy at less than full employment. We did that knowingly, in order to curb inflation. Therefore, one might paradoxically say that a substantial part of our deficits was the *result* of our fight against inflation rather than a *cause* of inflation, as so many critics of government spending would have us believe.

Rules for Fiscal Policy

Having defined an acceptable measure of fiscal policy, we would now like to discuss several different policy rules that the fiscal authorities might adopt. We shall assume that the case against an activist fiscal policy is a strong one, and therefore that a discretionary countercyclical policy is not advisable. We take it as given that the goal of policymakers is to keep the economy operating as close to full employment output (Y_{FE}) as possible at some desired level of prices and to avoid destabilizing the economy through perverse policy interventions. Note that since full employment output can always be reached by letting prices eliminate any differences between it and aggregate demand, our policy goal can be restated as keeping aggregate demand as close as possible to full employment at some desired level of prices. The reason that we wish to use fiscal and monetary policies to avoid such price adjustments is that all price changes are costly. Where aggregate demand is excessive, price increases can cause an inflationary spiral; where aggregate demand is deficient, necessary price reductions can cause recessions and also may be difficult to bring about in the disequilibrium-type economy.

Each of the rules we will discuss relies on the automatic stabilizers that are built into our tax and transfer system. In the U. S. economy, most of our taxes are a function of income. Therefore, tax receipts automatically increase when income increases. Transfers behave in an equally desirable fashion. Welfare and retirement payments, food stamps, and so forth generally fall during booms and rise during recessions. This means that government deficits tend to fall in booms and rise in recessions. This tends to choke off private demand in a boom and support demand in a recession, in this way automatically stabilizing the economy. The great advantage of all this is that it is automatic. It does not require lengthy and difficult government countercyclical policy decisions. For this reason, income-related taxes and transfers are called automatic stabilizers. If the government does not wish to engage in active countercyclical fiscal policy, it may wish to make its tax and transfer system depend, to as great an extent as possible, on income, and then let the automatic stabilizers reduce, as much as they can, the magnitude of fluctuations in private sector demand.

Assuming the government decides to rely on automatic stabilizers, it still must set a tax rate. What rate should it set?

Rule One: Balance the Budget

The simplest rule would probably be to set government expenditures on the basis of the merits of the various programs, or the needs of the citizenry, and then set a tax rate that balances the budget—that is, make taxes equal to expenditures: $T = \bar{G} + \bar{R}$. The appropriate tax rate, therefore, is:

$$t = \frac{\bar{G} + \bar{R}}{Y}.$$

This is the rule being proposed by those in favor of a constitutional amendment to balance the budget every year. Unfortunately, such a rule would not work very well in practice. The main reason is that it would require the government to intervene procyclically over the business cycle. Let us see why.

The rule would require the government to raise the tax rate any time income goes down and lower it any time income goes up.[7] But that is procyclical. The government would find itself raising taxes in recessions and lowering taxes in booms. That would surely exacerbate private sector instability and make cycles worse. Furthermore, since the rule would require changes in tax rates over the business cycle, it would not satisfy the opponents of an activist fiscal policy. For these two reasons, most economists are opposed to the goal of balancing the budget as an appropriate target for fiscal policy.

Rule Two: Balance the Budget at Full Employment

A more persuasive variant of the budget balance rule would be to set the tax rate so that the budget is balanced at full employment—that is, set the tax rate so that the full employment deficit is zero. Once again, government expenditures would be determined on the basis of need or merit, and the tax rate would be set so that those expenditures are just paid for when the economy is on its trend output line.[8] This rule could be expressed as: Set t^* such that $DEFF = 0$. This implies that

$$t^* = \frac{\bar{G} + \bar{R}}{Y_{FE}}.$$

The full employment balanced budget rule is shown diagrammatically in Figure 16.5.

If the economy stays at full employment, the budget will be balanced. However, if private sector demand declines, the automatic stabilizers will guarantee that government receipts decline too. Tax receipts will fall during recessions and rise during booms. Hence, the feedback mechanisms of the tax and transfer system automatically adjust fiscal policy in a countercyclical fashion. This will help dampen saving or cycles in private sector demand, which is obviously a big improvement over the annual balanced budget rule. This rule also meets the objections to activism, for it does not require discretionary countercyclical decisions by the government. Furthermore, it helps to reduce the magnitude of the economic cycle.

Thus, setting $DEFF = 0$ passes two of the tests we might wish to apply to any fiscal policy rule we adopt. But it flunks a third test. Only by chance does this rule stabilize the economy around the full employment level of output. The rule dampens oscillations in the economy coming from the private sector. However, it does not guarantee that the output level around which the oscillations are reduced will be Y_{FE}. Thus, if the goal of policy is to find a rule that keeps output as close to

[7]An alternative to tax rate variation is changes in government spending. But that is subject to the same procyclical objection that we raise for tax rates, with the additional complication that expenditures are harder to turn on and off than taxes.

[8]We assume, for simplicity throughout the remainder of this section, that transfers are not a function of income.

Figure 16.5
Budget Balance at Full Employment
Here the tax rate is set so that the budget is balanced at full employment.

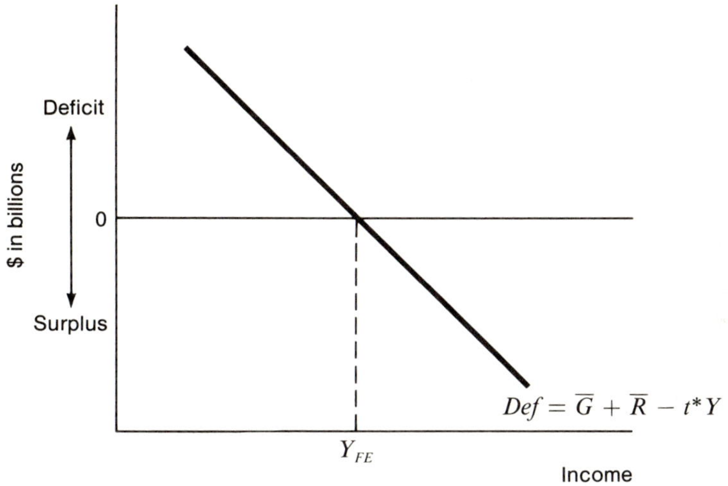

Y_{FE} as possible without the use of discretionary policy and without a change in prices, this rule is not adequate. Let us see why.

Suppose the government, following the rule, sets $t = t^*$. Unfortunately, there is nothing that guarantees that private sector demand or monetary policy will be such that setting $G = \overline{G}$, $R = \overline{R}$, and $t = t^*$ will lead to an equilibrium level of income, Y_{FE}, at the desired price level.

When the government sets its policy parameters, it affects both the IS and the deficit curves as shown in Figure 16.6. But fiscal policy is not the only thing that affects the position of the IS curve; that is also influenced by private sector demand. Furthermore, setting the IS curve does not alone determine the level of aggregate demand in the economy. That is affected by the position of the LM curve too. As we have drawn Figure 16.6, private sector demand and the LM curve are both so low that with $\overline{G}$, $\overline{R}$, and t^*, aggregate demand is Y_a at $\overline{P}$ rather than at Y_{FE}. Thus, setting $DEFF = 0$ does not lead to the desired level of income and prices. If, in spite of this difficulty, the tax rate is set at t^*, and if the supply curve is as drawn in diagram (c), output will temporarily settle at Y_a rather than Y_{FE}. If the government maintains the tax rate t^*, full equilibrium will be eventually reestablished at Y_{FE} by a decline in prices. That decline will increase demand by increasing real balances and shifting the LM curve in (a) out to LM′. At the same time, the price reductions will shift the short-run aggregate supply curve down until it intersects with the demand curve at point E on the long-run supply curve. Thus, even if a tax rate is chosen that does not lead to the desired level of income in the short run, prices will eventually correct the error if given enough time for adjustment.

Figure 16.6
The IS-LM and the Government Deficit

If the government sets the tax rate at t^* income settles at Y_a, because the money supply is too small to support a full-employment level of output and the price level $\overline{P}$. If the money supply were increased until the LM curve shifted out to LM′ and the aggregate demand curve shifted right to D', the economy would go to full employment at the price level $\overline{P}$ and the tax rate t^*. Note that if the supply curve is upward sloping, this will require a rightward shift to reduce workers' wage demands. If the money supply is not increased, the aggregate supply curve must shift down to S'' S'' to reestablish full equilibrium.

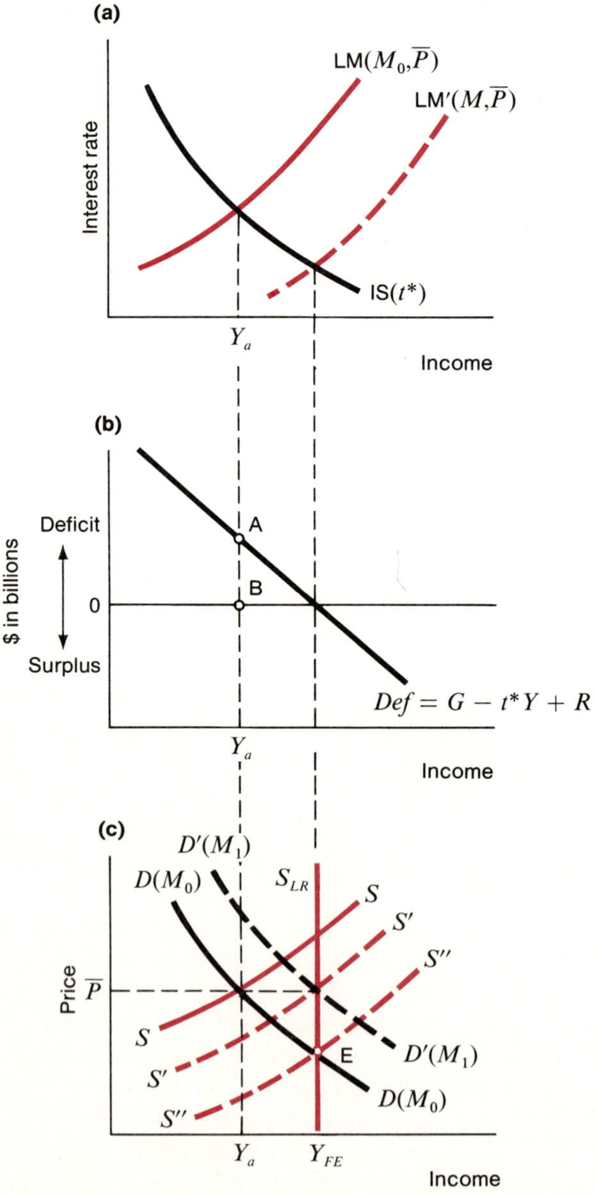

Recall that our goal was to find a rule for tax policy that would avoid the need for such price adjustments. Can we do better than choosing the tax rate t^*? The answer is yes. There are at least two improvements we can make. One of them is to change monetary policy. Look back at Figure 16.6. An alternative interpretation of the situation pictured there is that monetary policy is too restrictive to allow the $DEFF = 0$ rule to work properly. If the monetary authorities were to expand the money supply enough to shift the LM curve out to LM′, the economy would reach Y_{FE} with no change in prices. Thus, if monetary and fiscal policies were coordinated, $DEFF$ could be set equal to zero, and the automatic stabilizers would stabilize the economy around Y_{FE} at the desired level of prices. However, if monetary and fiscal policies are treated as independent of each other, we cannot follow the rule of balancing the budget at full employment unless we are willing to endure price adjustments. We need to look for a better fiscal rule.

The Full Employment Tax Rule

One of the reasons our various rules have not succeeded in keeping the economy at Y_{FE} is that we have not defined the policy in terms of this goal; we have been thinking too much in accounting or budget balancing terms. What if we change our outlook and say that the goal of macropolicymakers should be to control the level of aggregate demand rather than balance the budget? Then our fiscal policy rule becomes quite different: It is to set the tax rate such that when $P = \bar{P}$, the expected level of income in the economy is Y_{FE}, given private sector demand and monetary policy. We will call this tax rate t^{**}. This rule abandons budget balance altogether and says, instead: Set the tax rate to get the economy to the desired level of income and prices. We shall call this rule the **full employment tax rule,** because usually the target level of output will be Y_{FE}. There are cases, such as persistent inflation, in which the government may wish to aim at a slightly lower level of income instead. This does not affect the rule at all, for one simply substitutes another target level of income for Y_{FE} in the equations that determine t^{**}.

Let us see how the full employment tax rule would work for the low-demand economy pictured in Figure 16.7. For this economy we should lower the tax rate from t^* to t^{**}. This will shift the deficit line upward from Def^* to Def^{**} and, at the same time, shift the IS curve out to IS′. Aggregate demand shifts outward from DD to $D'D'$ in (c), and equilibrium income increases from Y_a to Y_{FE}. Note that monetary policy is assumed to be exogenously set, such that the LM curve is fixed at LM($\bar{P}$). Basically, we are using fiscal policy alone to hit a target level of income and prices, by adjusting the tax parameter to offset deficient private sector demand.[9] At Y_{FE}, the government will run a full employment deficit equal to distance DE in diagram (b). This deficit may appear to be an unacceptable drawback to the full employment policy. There are two responses to this sort of criticism. The first is that producing less than Y_{FE} is worse than running a deficit. The second is that the deficit could always be eliminated by simultaneously expanding the money supply and setting the tax rate at t^*. In diagram (a), the expansion in M would have to be enough to make the LM curve intersect IS at point C.

[9]See the next section for the derivation of t^{**}.

Figure 16.7
The Full Employment Tax Rule

Here the fiscal policymakers set the tax rate so that the economy will be at full employment except for fluctuations in private demand. In the economic conditions pictured here, this requires setting a tax rate, t^{**}, at which the economy runs a full employment deficit equal to distance ED. The rate t^{**} is lower than t^{*} by enough to shift the IS curve out to IS′. IS′ intersects the LM curve at the full employment income level, Y_{FE}. Note that Y_{FE} could be achieved by expanding the money supply until the LM shifted out to intersect the IS at point C. As in Figure 16.6, the supply curve must shift rightward until it intersects $D(t^{**})$ at point F. This is brought about by a reduction in worker expectations.

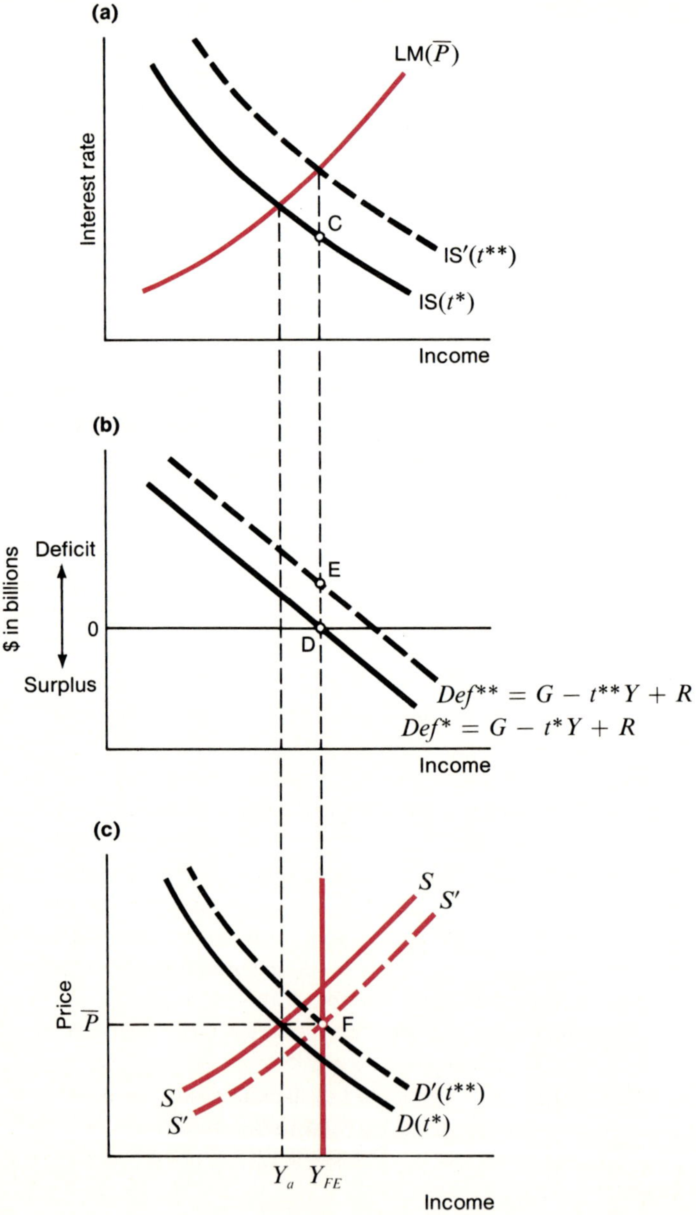

An Algebraic Derivation of Fiscal Policy Rules

We would like to stop here and demonstrate more formally the points we have been making about fiscal policy. For that purpose we use the linear form of the IS and LM curves that we derived in Chapter 5. In Equation (5.8), repeated here for convenience, we showed that for a lump sum tax model, aggregate demand could be expressed as a linear function of M/P, G, T, and W/P:

(5.8)
$$Y = \frac{q(G - cT) - ui\dfrac{W}{P} + i\dfrac{M}{P}}{q\,(1-c) + in}.$$

The equivalent expression for aggregate demand when taxes are a function of income can be found by substituting the expression $T = tY$ in place of T in Equation (5.8) and then solving for Y. Making that substitution, we get:

(16.3)
$$Y = \frac{qG - ui\dfrac{W}{P} + i\dfrac{M}{P}}{q(1-c[1-t]) + in}.$$

Equation (16.3) shows how aggregate demand varies with M/P, W/P, G, and the tax rate, t. This expression will tell us the level of aggregate demand corresponding to any of our alternative rules for fiscal policy.

Suppose first that we set the tax rate so that $DEFF = 0$. That requires that $t^* = G/Y_{FE}$. We now substitute this value for t in Equation (16.3) and solve for the level of aggregate demand. Thus we get:

(16.4)
$$Y = \frac{qG - ui\dfrac{W}{P} + i\dfrac{M}{P}}{q\left(1 - c\left[1 - \dfrac{G}{Y_{FE}}\right]\right) + in}.$$

From this equation it should be clear that there is nothing guaranteeing that aggregate demand will equal Y_{FE} for any particular values of W, M, G, and P. Setting the tax rate to balance the budget at full employment will not make $Y = Y_{FE}$ at $P = \overline{P}$, except by accident.

If in spite of this deficiency we set $t = t^*$, prices will be left to make aggregate demand equal to Y_{FE}. Using Equation (16.4), it is easy to see how that happens. A reduction in price increases the value of both W/P and M/P, one of which reduces aggregate demand and the other of which increases it. Since $u < 1$, the net effect of a price reduction is to increase demand. Thus, if $Y < Y_{FE}$ at t^*, prices will fall and demand will increase. It is obvious that if we wait long enough, we can reach Y_{FE} with t^*. In effect, we wait for price declines to increase real balances by enough to bring demand up to Y_{FE}. The alternative method, discussed just prior to this, is to directly increase the money supply by enough to make $Y = Y_{FE}$ at the initial price level.

If we are unable to coordinate monetary and fiscal policies in this way, and we do not wish to wait for price-caused demand adjustments, we can set the tax rate so that $Y = Y_{FE}$ at $P = \bar{P}$. To do this we substitute Y_{FE} for Y in Equation (16.3) and then solve for t^{**}. This gives:

$$t^{**} = \frac{qG - ui\dfrac{W}{P} + i\dfrac{M}{P} - (in + (1 - c)q)Y_{FE}}{cqY_{FE}}. \tag{16.5}$$

If the government sets its rate at t^{**}, aggregate demand will be at Y_{FE} when $P = \bar{P}$. To put it another way: The aggregate demand curve in diagram (c) of Figure 16.7, for t^{**}, M, G, and W, will go through the point Y_{FE}, $\bar{P}$ (point F).

Another point worth noting from Equation (16.5) is the connection between monetary and fiscal policies that is necessary if the government wishes to set its policy parameters to reach a certain level of income and prices. Clearly, the right value for t depends on the money supply (and vice versa). Since the relationship between t^{**} and M in Equation (16.5) is positive, the lower the money supply, the lower the full employment tax rate should be. That being the case, there obviously is a value for the money supply at which the tax rate t^{**} would lead to a balanced budget at Y_{FE}. That is only another way of saying that we can always achieve a balanced budget and Y_{FE} at the same time if we are willing to coordinate monetary and fiscal policies.

Constraints on Government Spending

There is a good deal of confusion over exactly what, if anything, limits government spending. As we all know, the rest of us cannot spend more than we earn or can borrow. The federal government is different. It, and it alone, can create money to acquire purchasing power and cover its expenditures. That is because the government has the exclusive right to issue money. When the central government runs a deficit it can finance that deficit, either directly or indirectly, by borrowing from its central bank. The bank, in turn, "pays" for the loan by simply creating money. Thus, the government as a whole, lumping central bank and Treasury together, can print money to finance a deficit.

It may appear that the ability to print money frees the government from any sort of budget constraint, enabling it to choose a level of expenditure without worrying how that expenditure is to be financed. Certainly, that is the way many governments seem to act. However, we will argue that this is wrong: The government does have budget constraints that limit its freedom of action. The government budget constraint, however, operates less directly than by the usual requirement that spending must be equal to revenue. Hence, the government may ignore the constraint in the short run. If it does this, however, there will usually be an upsurge of inflation.

The discovery that government can print money to finance its deficits has a large potential for both good and bad. On the positive side, it has allowed government to use automatic stabilizers to dampen economic cycles. On the negative side, there is no obvious bookkeeping discipline to keep government deficits under control. Western societies are still in the process of learning to deal with the discovery that governments can create money to finance expenditure.

Many wish to restrain government by forcing it to balance its budget. That, we think, is pushing the clock back: trying to pretend that the government does not have a power that everyone knows it does have. A better course is to inquire more carefully into the true constraints that face the government, so that we may fashion a set of guidelines for fiscal policy that account for its new powers and possibilities.

Government Budget Identity

We will argue that the government faces two constraints, one of which limits it in an accounting sense and the other of which limits it in an economic sense. The accounting identity is the **government budget identity,** which we introduced in Chapter 5. This says that government expenditure must be financed by either taxes, bond sales, or the creation of high powered money. We reintroduce the government budget identity here for convenience:

(16.6) $$G + R = T + \Delta B + \Delta H.$$

ΔB = change in bonds in public hands

ΔH = change in high-powered money

What sets the identity apart from other budget constraints is the last term on the right, ΔH. All other units must limit their expenditure to revenue, plus borrowing. The federal government can create money to pay for its expenditure as well. Thus, this bookkeeping identity does not appear to be a constraint at all. Yet it does have important implications for the composition of output and the cost of government, which we shall consider in a moment. First, however, consider the other constraint limiting the government.

The National Income Identity

The true economic constraint limiting government expenditure is the **national income identity**, which we first saw in Chapter 2. It is:

(2.1) $$Y \equiv C + I + \Delta INV + G + E - M.$$

This identity limits government in a more fundamental sense than the budget identity. It basically says that rising government expenditures must either increase income or reduce private sector demand. This can be seen when we convert Equation (2.1) into differences and ignore the foreign sector and possible changes in inventories:

(16.7) $$\Delta G = \Delta Y - \Delta C - \Delta I.$$

To put Equation (16.7) another way: Unless output can be increased, the cost of increased government spending is the private consumption or investment that has to be curtailed because of it. In some cases, an increase in G can be met by raising income; that happens when the economy is operating at less than full employment. At any other time, a rise in G must cause, one way or another, a reduction in either C or I. Taxes, bond sales, and inflation are the three ways of accomplishing this reduction.

Equation (16.7) is the real budget constraint facing the government. Given the ability of the government to create money, it is the capacity of the economy and the needs of the private sector that limit G, not the government's ability to finance its deficits. The cost of government is not the taxes or the bonds that are levied to pay for it. Rather, it is the private sector spending that is *crowded out* by the government. Lower consumption or investment is the true cost of government. Society bears that cost even if government spending is financed by printing money.

Equation (16.7) has several surprising implications. One is that there is a difference between the amount of revenue that the government should levy to pay for expenditure in a bookkeeping sense and the amount of such revenue in an economic sense. Suppose the government decides to levy taxes to pay for an increase in expenditure. The bookkeepers, using Equation (16.6), will say: Make $\Delta T = \Delta G$. The economists would say: Raise taxes by enough to make $\Delta C = \Delta G$. That will certainly require an increase in taxes greater than the increase in government expenditure. Why? Because consumption changes by less than taxes. From the consumption function, we know that $\Delta C = c\ \Delta T$. Hence, $\Delta C < \Delta T$.

What would happen if the government ignored the economists and made $\Delta T = \Delta G$? Then there would be excess demand, because the reduction in C would be less than the increase in G. Either income would go up or, if capacity had already been reached, prices would rise until the reduction in consumption required by Equation (16.7) had taken place. From this example it should be clear that, for the government, accounting identities are not the only thing that is relevant. The government must worry about economic constraints, too. They determine the cost of government and the amount of taxes or bond sales that have to be levied to pay for government expenditure.

It may appear from the above discussion that since the national income identity is the important economic constraint, the government need not worry about the budget identity (Equation [16.6]). That is not true. How the government finances its deficits has important implications for asset market equilibrium, which are only recently beginning to receive attention from economists.

The government budget identity tells us that the government must "finance" its expenditures in one of three alternative ways: by taxes, by bond sales, or by printing money. Each has a different effect on the economy. As we showed in Chapter 5, bond sales shift the LM curve to the left, which drives up interest rates and crowds out interest-sensitive expenditures. Tax increases reduce disposable income and drive down consumption. Printing money to finance a deficit is the most expansionary of the three. It does not directly cause crowding out at all—quite the contrary, aggregate demand increases. However, if it is not possible to increase supply, there will still be crowding out; the national income identity tells us that. What happens, of course, is that the increase in the money supply drives up prices until a volume of price-sensitive expenditure equal in value to the increase in G has been crowded out. Thus, the crowding out caused by each different type of financing may be summarized as follows:

Type of Finance	Crowding Out
Bond sales	Interest-sensitive expenditure, primarily investment
Taxes	Consumption
ΔM	Price-sensitive private expenditure: exports and consumption

When Should Fiscal Policy Changes be Bond-Financed and When Should They Be Monetized?

The government budget identity tells us that each different method of financing changes in the government deficit has different effects on the economy. Therefore, whenever we make a change in either taxes or government expenditure, we must also decide what type of financing we prefer. If we say that we wish to hold the money supply constant we are, in effect, choosing bond financing. As we have seen, expansionary fiscal policy with a constant monetary base implies that the Treasury sells bonds to the public to finance its deficit. When should one choose this form of financing? Since the effect of bond financing is to reduce the level of aggregate demand, one should choose it when the increase in G (or reduction in T) is not undertaken to increase demand. That is, bond financing is appropriate when the change in fiscal policy is not countercyclical.

We as a nation increase government spending for either of two basic reasons: either because the new programs are desirable or because we want to expand the level of aggregate demand. The first purpose is what we can call structural, the second, countercyclical. We have raised questions about the effectiveness of countercyclical policy in previous chapters. But assuming such a policy is chosen, and G is raised or taxes lowered primarily to increase aggregate demand, then it does not make much sense to finance that increase by selling bonds, because that contracts demand. Conversely, if we are reducing G (or raising taxes) to reduce aggregate demand, it doesn't make sense to allow this to lead to a contraction in the outstanding bond supply, because that is expansionary. Our financing rule should, therefore, be:[10]

1. If the change in G or T is countercyclical, monetize it; that is,allow the stock of high-powered money to vary with the deficit.

2. If the change in G or T is structural, bond-finance it; that is, allow the outstanding stock of debt to vary with the deficit.

We have said that one should use bond financing when G is increased for structural reasons (such as a need for added defense expenditures) but we do not wish to

[10]For an early discussion of the various ways of financing government expenditures and when each is appropriate, see Abba Lerner, *The Economics of Control* (New York: Macmillan, 1944), chapter 24. The approach taken here owes a great deal to the Lerner discussion.

increase aggregate demand. Bond sales to finance such an increase in G will reduce the level of aggregate demand by driving up interest rates and crowding out private spending. We do this when the level of aggregate demand might otherwise be excessive. A good example of when such a strategy made sense was during World War II, when we most assuredly were not increasing G to fight recession but rather to fight the Axis powers. The government sold debt to reduce private sector demand, because it was unwilling to raise taxes by the amount that would have been necessary to reduce consumption by the full increase in G.

When the economy is operating at its desired level, Y_{FE}, the real budget constraint facing the government is not the accounting identity we have been discussing—rather, it is the national income identity:

$$Y_{FE} = C + I + G + E - M.$$

If income is to remain at Y_{FE}, any positive change in G must, by definition, cause a reduction in either C or I. The real cost of government here is not the taxes that pay for it—rather, it is the reduction in either C or I that must take place in an economy constrained to stay at Y_{FE}. Taxes and bond sales are alternative ways to achieve this reduction, or crowding out, of private sector spending. If the government uses taxes, consumption will primarily fall. If it uses bond sales, investment will suffer the main reduction. Thus, the choice between taxes and bond sales depends upon which—consumption or capital formation—is regarded as more expendable. If the government elects neither to raise taxes nor to sell bonds, the budget identity tell us it must monetize the deficit—that is, print money to pay for the government spending. In this case inflation, rather than taxes or bond sales, reduces private sector demand by the amount required by the national income identity. Unfortunately, there is no way to escape from one of these three unpleasant ways of paying for government expenditure in an economy where income cannot increase.

The Problem of the Government Debt

We cannot leave the subject of fiscal policy without discussing government debt and the apparent burden that it imposes on future generations.[11] The United States now has an accumulated government debt of over $1 trillion. Most of that debt has been incurred because the government has run countercyclical deficits during periods of recession, deficits that were financed by bond sales rather than by printing money. Those who advocate a continuation of government deficit spending during recession or who do not worry about balancing the budget appear

[11] For a fuller discussion of the burden of the debt, see Franco Modigliani, "Long-Run Implications of Alternative Fiscal Policies and the Burden of the National Debt," *Economic Journal* 81 (December 1961): 730–756; and W. G. Bowen, R. G. Davis, and D. H. Kopf, "The Public Debt: A Burden on Future Generations," *American Economic Review* 50 (September 1960): 701–706.

Figure 16.8
Gross National Debt/GNP

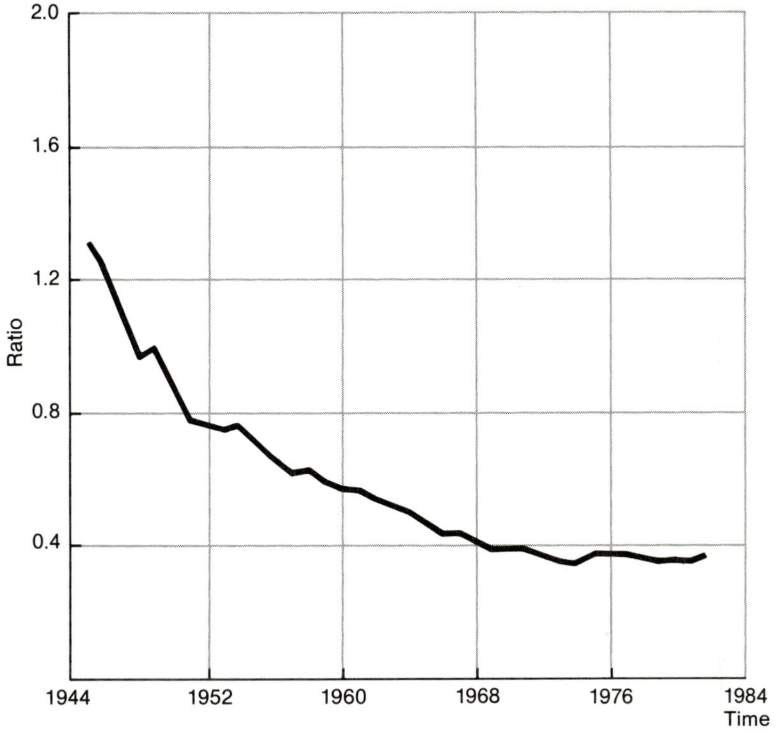

to be advocating a continually rising government debt. Won't such a policy be a burden on future generations? Is there not something wrong with a policy that lets our generation pile up debt that it will be up to future generations to pay off?

A Historical Perspective on Government Debt

The U. S. government has run very large deficits in recent years. As a consequence, the gross volume of outstanding U. S. government debt is now over $1 trillion. While that is a very large number, it is not nearly as large relative to our GNP as smaller quantities of debt were in the past. Figure 16.8, which shows the ratio of debt to GNP, tells the story. As the reader can see, the United States emerged from World War II with a debt/GNP ratio of 1.31, four times what it is today. That ratio was brought down steadily, until around 1970, by a combination of rapid economic growth and small government deficits. Even the large absolute deficits since 1974 have not significantly increased the ratio. By historical standards, the public debt is clearly not excessive relative to our level of income.

The Burden of the Debt

Returning to the question of the burden of the debt on future generations—let us first define what we mean by a burden. By that we mean a load, something that a generation would be better off not having to carry. In that sense, is government debt a burden on future generations?

Government debt is not like private debt, because we owe the former to ourselves. Some taxpayers owe the debt, and other taxpayers (perhaps even the same ones) are liable for the taxes that would be used to pay off the debt. Paying off the debt requires no net transfer of resources away from the society, only transfers within the society from taxpayers to bondholders. Note here that we are speaking of government debt held by its own citizens rather than foreigners. Using this logic it would appear that internally held public debt should impose no burden on future generations.

Furthermore, any generation could if it wished, at any moment, wipe out the outstanding debt by monetizing it. That is, the Federal Reserve could exchange the public's bonds for an equivalent amount of high-powered money through an expansionary open market operation. The reason the Fed does not get rid of the debt in so direct and simple a way is obviously that it would be highly expansionary to do so. But if it did, would the generation in which it happened be better off because it no longer had an outstanding, interest-bearing debt? It certainly isn't obvious that it would be, if one defined well-being in terms of lifetime consumption levels.

Clearly we need to think more carefully about just what the burden of the debt might be. In doing this, an example might perhaps be instructive. Suppose that the government is forced to wage a war that it is not willing to finance by raising taxes. Since the economy is at full employment, the Treasury sells bonds to finance its war-related expenditures. If we set ΔG = wartime expenditures, and if we ignore exports and imports, and since $\Delta Y = 0$, the national accounting identity tells us that:

$$\Delta G = -(\Delta C + \Delta I).$$

We have argued that the true cost of government expenditures is the private sector spending that is crowded out to pay for it. We argued further that taxes and bond sales were two alternative ways to effect this crowding out. To simplify things a bit, suppose taxes affect consumption while bond sales drive up interest rates and reduce investment. In that case, the two methods of financing this change in G have different intergenerational impacts. If taxes are levied to pay for the war, the same generation that fights the war pays for it by reduced levels of consumption. But if the war is paid for by bond sales, it is investment that suffers. In that case future generations bear the cost of the war, because they inherit a smaller capital stock than they would if the war had been paid for by taxes.

Here then is the burden of government debt on future generations. Because government bonds and titles to capital are substitutes in the public portfolio, any time the government issues debt it will tend to crowd out private investment and therefore make the stock of capital that we pass on to our children smaller than it would have been under an alternative financing method. The burden of our trillion-dollar debt is the capital formation that has been crowded out by that debt.

Note that it is extremely difficult to know how large an amount that is, since different types of debt may have different effects on capital formation. Short-term debt could in fact increase the demand for capital instead of reducing it. Also, debt sold during recessions probably has relatively little effect on capital formation.

Note also that contractionary bond sales by the Fed impose exactly the same cost on future generations in lower capital formation as does bond financing of government deficits. Any time either the Treasury or the Federal Reserve sells bonds to the public, it drives up interest rates and chokes off investment. That tends to reduce the capital stock that will be available in the future.

This is one reason why it does not make very much sense to sell bonds to finance government deficits in recession. To the extent that those bond sales choke off investment they cause a completely unnecessary reduction in the future capital stock. When the government runs a deficit in a recession, there need be no crowding out of private expenditure. Indeed, all private expenditure could be higher, because the spending multiplier is greater than 1. One should sell bonds and incur the cost in capital formation only when a reduction in private sector expenditure is required because of inflationary pressures. At any other time, bond sales impose a completely unnecessary burden on the future.

To make a complete analysis of the burden of the debt, it is not enough to ask if the future generation is worse off because of the debt; to that we know the answer is yes, because of the reduction in the capital stock. We also have to ask what the government expenditure was used for. If the government sold bonds to finance its own investment expenditure, and if that investment had as high a rate of return as the investment that was crowded out, then overall the future generation is better off than it would have been without the government debt and the government investment it financed. For the government, of course, it is hard to draw the line between consumption expenditures, which benefit only the current generation, and investment expenditures, which benefit future generations. For example, take education expenditures. They are classified as consumption, but surely they create human capital, which benefits future generations, too. As another example, take expenditures to maintain our system of national parks. Here again there is an element of investment in what our national accountants classify as government consumption. In both cases, the investment component may well compensate future generations for the private capital that was crowded out by government bond sales to finance these types of expenditure.

Summary

In this chapter we described features of fiscal policy that help determine what the government should and should not do in different economic situations. Our principal findings were five:

1. Actual deficits are a poor measure of fiscal policy because they depend on the level of income, an endogenous variable that is influenced by many things other than fiscal policy. A better measure is the full employment deficit, $DEFF$.

2. If the government decides to rely on the automatic stabilizers built into the tax system, it must choose a tax rate. We considered several alternative rules and concluded that if one wishes to stabilize around some particular level of income, one should set the tax rate so as to achieve that income level rather than achieve some particular deficit or surplus.

3. The real cost of government is the private sector expenditures that are crowded out because of it. Taxes, bond sales, and money are the three alternative ways of financing government expenditures. Each causes a different type of crowding out. Taxes on households reduce disposable income and crowd out consumption. Bond sales crowd out interest-sensitive expenditure, which we assumed to be primarily investment. Monetizing deficits crowds out price-sensitive private expenditure, but only when the economy is close to full employment and prices increase.

4. The government budget identity tells us that all fiscal policy has monetary side effects. Government expenditure must be financed by either taxes, bond sales, or the creation of high-powered money. Either of the last two affects the LM curve. Deficits should be bond-financed when they are structural and monetized when they are countercyclical. It does not make much sense to run deficits to stimulate demand and then finance those deficits by selling bonds, because that reduces demand by reducing capital formation, which is costly to future generations.

5. Government debt is a burden to future generations because it crowds out capital formation. Therefore, debt financing should be used only when the expenditure being financed is also beneficial to the future generation. Bond financing of government expenditure in a recession imposes a completely unnecessary cost on future generations, assuming that one does not wish to stay in recession to dampen inflationary pressures.

In the next chapter we investigate the conduct of monetary policy. There we shall perform the same analysis of problems, guidelines, and goals that we have done for fiscal policy in this chapter.

Key Concepts

rules for fiscal policy
full employment deficit
full employment tax rule
economic constraints on government spending
burden of government debt

Problems and Questions for Discussion

1. Why is the government deficit a poor measure of fiscal policy?

2. The full employment deficit has been proposed as a better measure of fiscal policy than the actual deficit. Why is it better? Is it an entirely unambiguous indicator of fiscal policy? If so, why? If not, why not?

3. Suppose the government accounts record the following changes over two years:

			Surplus (or Deficit)	
Year	G	T	Actual	Full Employment
1	100	105	5	0
2	105	85	(20)	10

a. Would you view fiscal policy as more expansionary or contractionary in year 2 than year 1? Why?

b. How should the government "finance" the $20 billion deficit in year 2?

4. Should the government set the full employment deficit at zero? What are the advantages and disadvantages of such a target?

5. Consider an economy with the following behavioral equations:

$$C = .8(Y_d)$$
$$G = 200$$
$$I = 100$$
$$Y_d = (1 - t)Y$$
$$t = .25$$
$$Y_{FE} = 800$$

a. Derive the equilibrium level of income for the tax rate and level of G specified above.

b. What are the actual and full employment deficits?

c. What should the full employment deficit be if the government decides to increase G so that $Y = Y_{FE}$?

d. What private expenditure is crowded out by the rise in G required to make $Y = Y_{FE}$?

6. In Problem 5, suppose the government decides to lower taxes rather than increase G as a way of pushing the economy to full employment.

a. At what rate should t be set?

b. What will the full employment deficit be for this setting of t?

c. Can you explain why the full employment deficit is different for the expansion through tax reduction than it is for the expansion through the increase in G?

7. Should the target full employment deficit adopted for fiscal policy be influenced by the target set for monetary policy? Demonstrate your answers using the IS-LM and *DEFF* diagrams.

8. "A rise in the government budget deficit is always inflationary." Discuss this statement, indicating the conditions under which it is true and under which it is false.

9. Suppose an economy is operating at less than full employment output:

$$Y_{FE} = 100$$
$$Y = 95$$
$$C = 60$$
$$G = 20$$
$$I = 15$$

Suppose the government decides to increase its spending to 30.

a. What are the three ways that this increased spending can be financed?

b. Which would you choose under the conditions described? What would be the effect on consumption and investment of the method you choose?

c. By how much do consumption and/or investment have to be reduced because of the planned increase in G?

10. "The purpose of bond sales and taxes is not to finance government expenditures but rather to reduce private demand." Explain what this statement means, and indicate its relevance to the question of how government deficits should be financed over the business cycle.

11. The United States has a gross public debt of over $1 trillion. Is this debt something we should worry about? Is it a "burden on future generations"? Are our grandchildren going to be worse off because of the government debt? Explain.

Chapter 17

The Operation of Monetary Policy

In Chapter 14 we learned how the Federal Reserve conducts monetary policy through open market operations, the setting of reserve requirements, and the rediscount rate. In this chapter we will consider the practical problem of how the Federal Reserve should carry out its responsibilities. Major questions about monetary policy are currently unresolved. Should the Fed actively try to counteract cycles in the private sector? If not, what sort of policy rule should it follow? Should it try to control interest rates or the money supply? Which definition of the money supply should it use, given that there are now at least four different candidates? Should there be coordination between monetary and fiscal policies? These are the principal questions that we will address in this chapter.

Carrying Out Monetary Policy

Before discussing issues in the operation of monetary policy, one should know exactly how monetary policy is carried out.[1] The Fed sets policy through decisions of the **Federal Open Market Committee (FOMC).** This committee is composed of the seven governors of the Federal Reserve System, the president of the New York Fed, and the presidents of four of the other eleven Federal Reserve banks, who serve on a rotating basis. The FOMC meets on a monthly basis, or more often if conditions require it. For each meeting, staff economists prepare two briefing books that contain a complete description of the current situation in financial mar-

[1] For a good discussion of how monetary policy is actually carried out, see Lawrence S. Ritter and William L. Silber, *Money*, 4th ed., rev. (New York: Basic Books, 1977).

kets and the economy and recommendations for policy actions. At these meetings, the members of the FOMC review the state of the economy and decide on an appropriate monetary policy. Their decision is embodied in the FOMC directive. The directive tells the manager of the Federal Reserve Open Market Account at the New York Federal Reserve Bank, the person who is responsible for carrying out open market operations, what the Fed wants him or her to do. The directive is couched in general rather than specific terms. For example, it does not tell the account manager to sell a certain quantity of bonds; it says that the Fed wants monetary policy to be easy or tight and that it wants the growth of bank reserves to be kept within a certain target range. The important thing about this procedure is that it leaves the account manager a good deal of latitude for deciding just exactly what conditions are, and therefore what sort of open market operations are called for on a day-to-day basis.

Changes in Federal Reserve Procedures

Up until 1979, the Fed used the federal funds interest rate as both the main indicator of conditions in the money market and the main target for monetary policy. In effect, the FOMC directive was carried out by controlling the federal funds rate. This procedure came under sharp criticism from the monetarists, as we shall see in the next section. They argued that by its excessive concern for stability in the interest rate, the Fed was allowing an excessive expansion in the money supply. The monetarists wanted the Fed to concentrate on monetary targets and let the interest rate fluctuate.

Under the pressure of monetarist criticism, there has been a movement away from interest rates and general money market conditions in the FOMC directive and towards specific monetary targets. Up until the 1960s, the directive was expressed solely in terms of money market conditions. In 1966, however, it was enlarged to include a proviso clause. The account manager was instructed to "conduct open market operations" with a view toward firmer conditions in the money market, provided that bank credit was not deviating from projections. The second half of this directive was the first attempt to set limits on the range of decision-making authority of the account manager. The next change came in early 1970, when the money supply was added to bank credit in the proviso clause. In 1972, bank reserves were added to money market conditions as an operating target.

Despite these changes, control of the money supply did not noticeably improve. Throughout most of 1976–1977, money growth exceeded the targets set out in the FOMC directive. The reason was that the Fed continued to use interest rate targets in its effort to control the money supply. A rate was chosen that was thought to be consistent with the desired rate of growth in the money supply. The account manager was directed to keep the market rate within a narrow band, which he accomplished by buying or selling bonds when the rate moved to either the upper or lower limit. That worked only so long as the Fed chose the interest rate that was consistent with the demand and supply of money. However, when the demand for money changed, the system broke down. For in general, it is not possible to control both the price and supply of money at the same time. During the late 1970s, under the pressure of rising inflation, the federal funds rate kept bumping up against its target ceiling. The account manager responded by pumping reserves into the system, in effect allowing the money supply to exceed its target. When the choice came, the Fed chose to meet the interest rate target and abandon the money supply target. Unfortunately, constant interest rates were not what the economic situation called for in 1979.

In October 1979, in an important reversal of policy, Paul Volcker, the chairman of the Fed, announced that henceforth monetary policy would concentrate on monetary growth targets rather than the interest rate. The account manager would be instructed to carry out his policy in such a way that the target rates of growth of the money supply and bank reserves were met. This, of course, meant that the interest rates would be left to fluctuate, because the Federal Reserve would no longer intervene in the market to keep the rate within a narrow band, as it had before. It is still too early to evaluate the effect of this latest change in monetary policy. However, it is certain that it has resulted in much wider variations in the interest rate than would have been thought conceivable in the recent past.

The Choice of Targets: Interest, Money, or Reserves

We now turn to a fuller discussion of the basic issue behind the change in Fed operating instructions. That issue is: What target should the Fed shoot for—interest, money, or some measure of reserves? The Fed controls three policy instruments: the discount rate at which reserves may be borrowed from the Fed, the reserve requirement, and the monetary base. The ultimate goal of Fed policymakers is to operate monetary policy so as to help stabilize aggregate demand. At the very least, they want to avoid making monetary policy a source of disturbance.

Interest versus Money Targets Unlike fiscal policymakers, who set the budget only one or two times per year, authorities at the Federal Reserve can continuously affect the financial markets through open market operations. Thus they can, if they wish, pursue a policy of active and discretionary stabilization. However, in order to do this, they need an indicator or signal to tell them what they should do. Traditionally, the interest rate has been that signal. It is like a temperature gauge for the nation's financial markets. When it is high, conditions are tight; when it is low, the supply of credit is relatively ample. If the authorities wish to adjust monetary policy to conditions in the financial markets, interest rates are the obvious indicator to use. When they are higher than is considered desirable, the Fed can order expansionary open market operations. When they are too low, bond sales can be undertaken. This is how discretionary monetary policy with an interest rate target or indicator would function.

Milton Friedman and the monetarists have long criticized the Fed for using interest rate targets.[2] The problem is that interest rates, an endogenous variable in

[2] Milton Friedman, "The Role of Monetary Policy," *American Economic Review* 58 (March 1968), 1–18. See also his "Money—Tight or Easy?", reprinted from *Newsweek*, March 1, 1971, in Milton Friedman, *An Economist's Protest* (Glen Ridge, NJ: Thomas Horton, 1972), 59–61.

the economy, are influenced by many factors other than monetary policy. Thus, a rise in interest rates could result from many different causes, each of which requires a different response from the Fed.

Consider two examples. Suppose that the economy is operating at full employment output and is disturbed by a random increase in private sector spending. This is shown in diagram (a) of Figure 17.1 as the rightward shift in the IS curve. As we have learned, this increases income from Y_0 to Y_1 and raises the interest rate from r_0 to r_1. What should the response of the Fed be? If Y_0 is the desired income level, and if the Fed wants to engage in deliberate countercyclical policy, it should contract the money supply. This will shift the LM curve to LM′. This action will exacerbate the rise in interest rates, but it will also counteract the rise in demand.

But there is another and completely different reason why the interest rate may be rising. Rather than an increase in the demand for money due to rising output, it may be that there is a change in portfolio preferences leading to a rise in the demand for money and a fall in the demand for other assets. This is shown in diagram (b), as a shift in the LM curve. In this case output will fall unless the monetary authorities expand the money supply, which is just exactly the reverse of the policy they should follow for the first case.[3]

Which policy should the Fed follow? In answering, keep in mind that, while it knows what is happening to interest rates, it will probably not know what is happening to output and employment, because these figures come with a significant lag. All the Fed knows is that there has been a rise in rates and a tightening in the financial markets. In the one case, that tightening should be accentuated; in the other, it should be offset. Thus, the interest rate target contains, from the monetarists' point of view, a fatal flaw. It requires judgment by the authorities on which policy is appropriate. The monetarists are not very confident that government policymakers are ever going to know enough to make such judgments successfully. Furthermore, they are philosophically opposed to expansions of the governmental role in the economy in general. Therefore, they have argued forcefully against the interest rate target approach to monetary policy. At bottom, the dispute is really over whether the Fed should attempt to actively stabilize the economy. Those who believe that it should argue for some indicator of financial market conditions, like the interest rate, upon which to base their policy decisions. Those who want the government to follow rules rather than judgments in macropolicy are against the interest rate target and favor a monetary target instead.

To summarize this discussion: Whether or not it is better to use interest rates or money as a target depends on the source of instability in the private sector. If the instability comes from the goods market, the money target is preferable. However, if the instability comes from the asset markets, we would be better off with interest rate targets.

[3]For a further discussion of when interest rates or the stock of money is the appropriate target of monetary policy, see Benjamin M. Friedman, "Targets, Instruments and Indicators of Monetary Policy," *Journal of Monetary Economics* 1 (October 1975): 443–473; and William Poole, "Optimal Choice of Monetary Policy Instruments in a Simple Stochastic Macro Model," *Quarterly Journal of Economics* 84 (May 1970): 197–216.

Figure 17.1
Two Reasons for Rising Interest Rates

A shift in goods market demand shifts the IS curve to IS′ and raises the interest rate to r_1. An increase in the demand for money in (b) has the same effect on the interest rate.

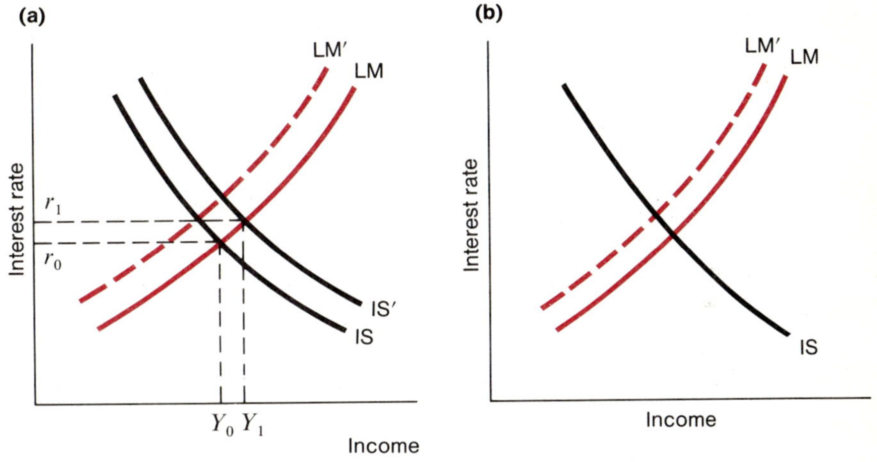

An example of the sort of error that the use of interest rate targets can cause has been the confusion between nominal and real interest rates. This had led to a serious tendency to overstate the degree of restraint in financial markets due to high nominal rates. As we all know, interest rates in recent years have risen to unprecedented heights. Despite the fact that some policymakers know that the relevant indicator of financial ease or tightness is the real rather than the nominal rate, they have tended to think that high nominal rates meant that money markets were tight, when in fact the real rate of interest was not tight at all and monetary policy was anything but restrictive. By focusing on the interest rate, which was rising because of inflation, they tended to overexpand the money supply.

The effect of a rise in the inflation rate on the interest rate is shown in Figure 17.2. A rise in the inflation rate shifts the IS curve out, because any given nominal interest rate now corresponds to a lower real rate and thus a higher level of investment demand. If the Fed leaves the money supply unchanged, the nominal rate rises from r_0 to r_1. This is another example of a rise in the interest rate resulting from a shift out in goods demand. It is not one that calls for expansionary monetary policy—on the contrary, it should trigger contractionary monetary policy to control the level of aggregate demand and slow down the inflation. However, as we have already indicated, in the late 1960s the Fed thought the high interest rates were undesirable and failed to follow a contractionary policy.

It is easy to sympathize with the Fed. Everyone's perception of interest rates is influenced by past rates. Thus, it is hard not to think of a 20-percent prime rate as a high rate even if the inflation rate is 18 percent, as it was in the beginning of

Figure 17.2
The Effect of a Rise in the Inflation Rate on the Interest Rate
An increase in the inflation rate, with the interest rate kept constant, increases demand in the goods market. That shifts the IS curve out to IS′ and raises the interest rate from r_0 to r_1.

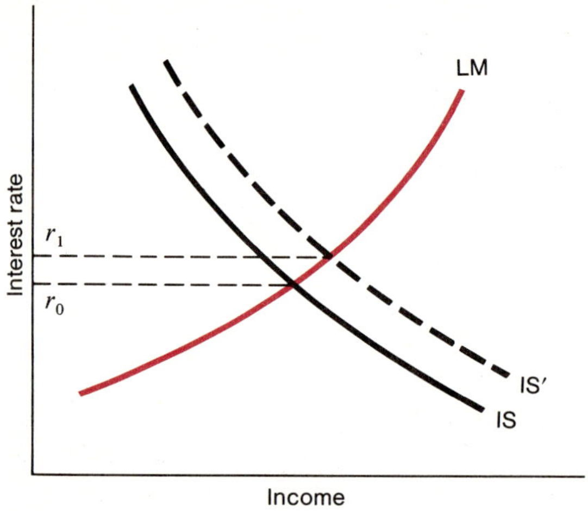

1980. Furthermore, high rates cause disintermediation for savings and loan associations and a rise in the interest cost on the outstanding government debt for the U. S. Treasury. For all these reasons, the Fed has tended to interpret high rates as a signal for monetary ease, when the opposite policy was probably more appropriate for the conditions of the late 1970s.

Reserve Targets There are a number of reserve targets that the Fed might use as a policy objective.

Total Reserves These are the sum of currency in public hands plus the reserves of member banks.[4] Total reserves is also called the *monetary base*. It is directly controlled by open market operations.

Excess Reserves These are the difference between required and total reserves of banks. Excess reserves are an indicator, like interest rates, of the degree of tightness or ease in financial markets. When markets are tight, excess reserves should decline.

[4]Starting in 1981, all banks and savings and loan associations were required to keep reserves against checkable deposits. Both member and nonmember banks can now borrow from the Fed.

Borrowed Reserves These are the quantity of credit borrowed by banks and savings and loans from the discount window of the Fed. The higher the level of borrowed reserves, the greater the demand for credit and the tighter the financial markets.

Free or Unborrowed Reserves These are the difference between excess and borrowed reserves of banks and yet another indicator of tightness or ease in financial markets.

As targets, excess, borrowed, and free reserves all suffer from the same fault as the interest rate. All are affected by shifts in conditions in the private sector and require discretionary decisions from the Fed. An increase in demand, which shifts the IS curve out, raises interest rates and reduces both excess and free reserves. Borrowing from the Fed should go up, but this should not cause the Fed to pump reserves into the system—if anything, the Fed should engage in contractionary open market operations. Thus reserve targets, like the interest rate, will mislead the Fed if it interprets a fall in reserves as signal calling for a easier policy.

Advantages of Money as a Target The monetarists have a solution for the target problem. They insist that the Fed should adopt a money supply target and hit it by expanding the monetary base in a steady, predictable fashion. The advantage of the monetary base as an instrument and the money supply as a target is that neither are much affected by the private sector. Thus, they can be controlled without having to compensate for changes in conditions in the financial markets. Furthermore, if the Fed follows the second half of the monetarist policy recommendations, namely, that the money supply be expanded at a constant rate, then all discretionary power can be removed from those actually in charge of day-to-day open market operations. From the monetarist point of view, this is probably the biggest benefit to be gained by the adoption of the money target.

The monetary base has two other advantages. First, it is unambiguous and controllable by the Fed. Second, since it is not affected by the private sector, it is a good indicator of what the Fed is doing. Interest rates and all reserve measures, other than the monetary base, change because of conditions in the private sector. They suffer from exactly the same fault as the actual government budget deficit as an indicator of fiscal policy: Each reflects influences other than government policy. That is not true of the monetary base. It is an exact indicator of what the Fed is doing. When it rises, one knows that the Fed has engaged in expansionary open market operations.

The money supply is also a pretty good indicator of Fed actions. However, as we shall see in a moment, there have been some fairly sharp changes in the money multiplier in recent years, which has made the money supply rise at a rate quite different from either the rate of growth of reserves or the rate of growth desired by the Fed.

As we observed earlier, the Fed has moved closer and closer to the monetarist goal of expressing its targets in terms of monetary growth rates rather than interest rates. The most recent change in Fed operating procedures in October 1979 appears to have been a complete victory for the monetarists, because interest rates were officially demoted and replaced by monetary targets. The victory, however, may be a hollow one. Just when the Fed has finally been convinced to concentrate on controlling the money supply, profound inventions in the financial system have made it more and more difficult for the money supply to be controlled. We turn next to a discussion of this important problem.

Which Money Supply Should the Fed Control?

During recent years financial markets and institutions have created a vast array of assets having many of the characteristics of money. M1 includes all deposits on which checks may be drawn. M2 adds private small savings accounts and money market fund shares. M3 includes all these assets, plus large savings accounts, plus commercial repurchase agreements. If the Federal Reserve decides to try to control the money supply, on which of these alternative money supplies should it concentrate?

The answer to that question depends on how money affects the economy. As we have just seen, the monetarists think about the effect of money in terms of the equation of exchange ($MV = PY$). Thus, it should follow that if one wants to control aggregate demand by controlling M, he or she should choose that M for which velocity has been roughly constant.

We show velocity for M1, M2, and M3 in Figure 17.3. As one would expect, V_1, the ratio of income to M1, has risen steadily over the last 16 years as the financial system developed money substitutes in a period of rising interest rates. Yet, V_2 and V_3 are relatively constant, exhibiting a range of less than 10-percent variation over the period. This suggests that either M2 or M3 is the appropriate definition of money and the right target for Federal Reserve policymakers. The constancy of V_2 and V_3 suggests that if the Fed can control M2 and M3 it will be able to control the level of nominal income.

Here is where a dilemma arises. The assets in M1 are all subject to reserve requirements. Therefore, it is a fairly simple matter for the Fed to control M1 by regulating the monetary base. But M1 does not appear to have a constant relationship with income. Yet, the monetary aggregates that do have such a relationship with income are only loosely related to the monetary base, the Fed's policy instrument. Therefore, it would appear that the financial inventions of recent years have made the problem of controlling the economy through monetary policy a far more complex and difficult one than it used to be. The Fed is still struggling to develop procedures to deal with this problem.

The Fed's problem was readily apparent in 1980. During that year the Fed wanted to follow a restrictive monetary policy. Accordingly, it allowed the monetary base to expand by only 3.9 percent. But M2 grew at 9.5 percent and M3 at 10.1 percent.[5] Those growth rates do not suggest a very restrictive policy. It seems that the financial system is able to create money substitutes faster than the Fed can learn to control them, with the result that the traditional instruments of monetary control have lost a good deal of their effectiveness.

[5] Even M1 grew at over 6 percent during 1980.

Figure 17.3
Measures of Velocity 1964–1982.

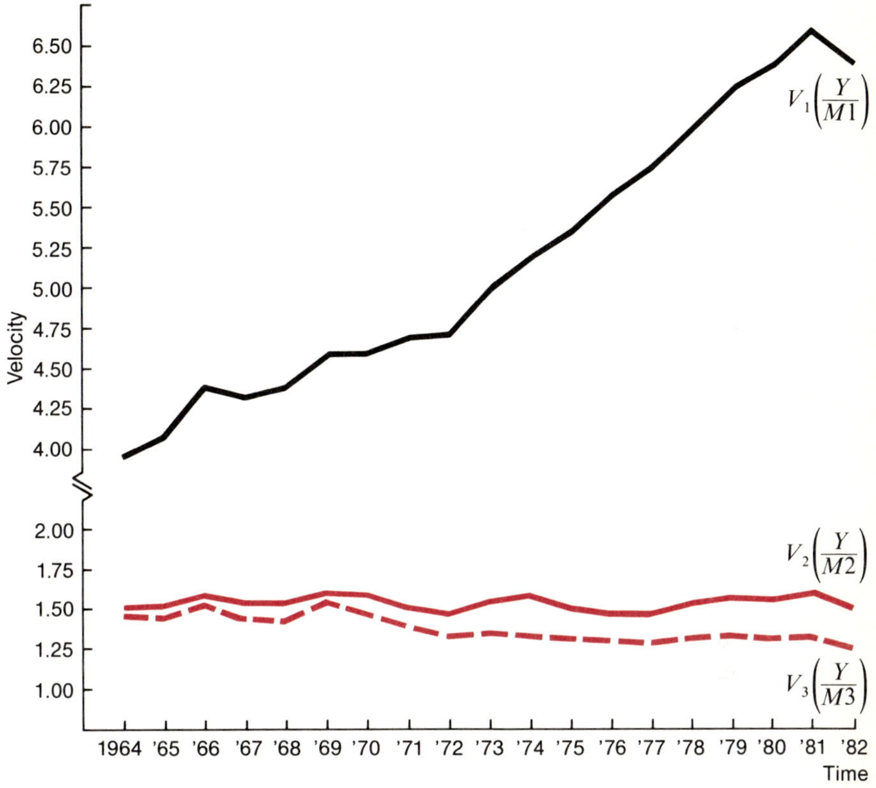

If we look at this same issue of monetary control from the portfolio balance point of view, we appear to be in the midst of a period of major innovations in the financial system. More efficient electronic funds transfer systems have made it possible to eliminate the distinction between demand and time deposits. The invention of money market funds, repurchase agreements, and certificates of deposit have created assets with many of the portfolio qualities of money that can be issued by borrowers to finance capital formation. Thus, in effect, the financial system has indirectly transferred much of the public demand for money into an indirect demand for capital. This is exactly what fractional reserve banking did in an earlier age. It is not surprising that, during the period when these innovations were taking place, the monetary authorities appeared to lose control, or that aggregate demand continued at a high level in spite of the fact that the monetary base grew at a relatively slow rate.

There is a question of how far this process can go. Many critics are worried that the financial system has become dangerously fragile and overextended. After all, borrowers are creating short-term liabilities (savings accounts, CDs, money market shares) to finance long-term assets. If a severe downturn were to come, there would be no way to pay off all the short-term lenders. In the meantime, however, the nation has been able to subvert the intention of monetary policy and to maintain capital formation at a high rate (except in housing) despite a slow growth in the monetary base.

The Constant Percentage Rate of Growth Rule (CPRG)

Let us leave aside the question of defining the money supply and turn back to the basic question with which we started this chapter: How should the monetary authorities carry out monetary policy? In view of the Fed's apparently procyclical policy record, and also in view of the problems of forecasting and lags, more and more people have come to accept Milton Friedman's prescription for the Fed. He argues very persuasively that the Fed should abandon discretionary policy altogether and instead should simply expand the money supply at some constant, preannounced rate. Granted, this will not eliminate economic cycles, but at least it will neutralize the Fed as a source of instability which, Friedman argues, it often has been in the past. In this section we will examine some complications that would arise from following the Friedman **constant percentage rate of growth rule.**

At the outset, one should note that the CPRG rule is not an optimal rule. It is a second-best approximation for a world in which we do not know enough to do better. Granting, for the purposes of this discussion, that some sort of rule is preferable to discretionary anticyclical policy, what sort of rule should be followed? There are a great many possibilities, out of which we shall look at three. First is the constant interest rate rule, second, the CPRG rule, and third, the feedback rule, in which fluctuations in aggregate demand influence monetary expansion.

CPRG Rule versus a Constant Interest Rate Rule

As we have already noted, the CPRG rule is better than the interest rate rule if the major sources of private sector instability come from the goods market rather than the money market (see Figure 17.1). If there are random fluctuations in goods demand, a constant rate of monetary expansion will automatically help offset them. In this case, the CPRG would make the financial markets into an automatic stabilizer, which tightens up when aggregate demand increases and loosens up when it falls. For goods market disturbances, an interest rate rule is inferior to the CPRG. It would commit the Fed to a procyclical monetary policy, because in its effort to hold interest rates constant, the Fed would have to expand the money supply when goods demand increased and contract money when it fell.

But what if the source of instability is the money rather than the goods market? Here the interest rate target is better. If, for example, the demand for money randomly increases for some reason, the appropriate policy is to increase the supply of money and keep interest rates constant. That will allow the economy to avoid a needless recession. Conversely, if the demand for money declines, the monetary authorities should reduce the supply. That is what they would do using interest rate targets.

Figure 17.4
The Effect of Money Substitutes on the LM Curve

An increase in money substitutes reduces the demand for M1, thus shifting the LM curve out to LM′ and lowering the interest rate. Note that the LM curve is defined here in terms of M1.

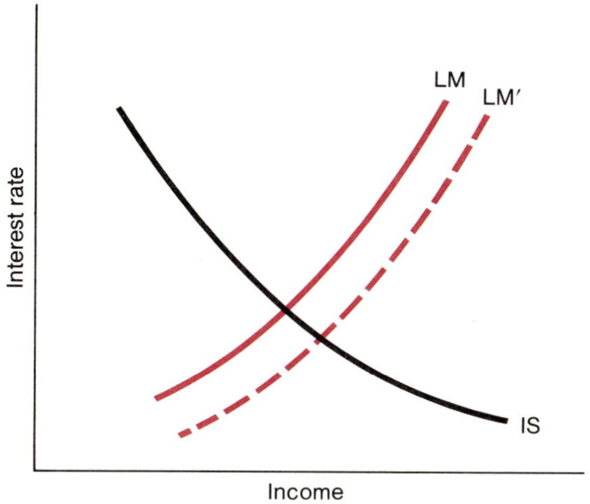

The issue, then, between these two rules is: Which is the major source of random disturbance—the goods or the money market? The jury is still out on this question, but one might point out that the financial innovations to which we alluded in the previous section do appear to represent significant shifts in the demand for money. If we draw the LM curve in terms of M1, the quantity of money that the Fed controls through open market operations, then the creation of CDs, money market shares, and time deposits, which have many of the qualities of money, will reduce the demand for M1 relative to income. In terms of the IS-LM diagram, these new assets cause the LM curve to shift out, lowering the rate of interest and increasing aggregate demand. (See Figure 17.4.) If the monetary authorities use a CPRG rule, these targets will not respond to this change in conditions. However, the appropriate policy is to reduce the rate of expansion of the monetary base. This the authorities would do if they used the interest rate target rather than the CPRG rule.

One should add that the right interest target must be chosen, in particular, one corrected for inflation. Under recent conditions in the United States, the inflation rate complicated the picture by driving the interest rate up. Not many policymakers would have been willing to reduce the expansion of the money supply so as to raise the interest rate in the conditions of 1975–1980. Yet in retrospect, that would have been the appropriate policy. High as the interest rate was, it was low in real terms and should have been raised. If the demand for M1 declines, the authorities should reduce supply. That happens automatically under an interest target, so long as the target is adjusted for inflation.

The CPRG versus a Feedback Rule

The basic issue is not over discretion versus rules. Rather, it is over whether, among all the possible rules that one could devise, the CPRG rule is best. One can think of many feedback rules that are nondiscretionary and yet might be better because they allow for some interaction between aggregate demand and monetary expansion. We shall develop one obvious example. We will write a rule in which the money supply grows faster than normal whenever output is lower than desired and slower than normal whenever output is higher. Such a rule might be written as follows:

(17.1) $$\frac{\Delta M}{M} = k + a\frac{Y_{FE} - Y_t}{Y_{FE}}.$$

k = CPRG, equal to long-run growth rate of the economy plus permissible rate of inflation

Y_{FE} = desired output level, presumably at full employment level under normal circumstances

Equation (17.1) is the CPRG when output is at its desired level. When output falls short of Y_{FE}, monetary expansion is faster than normal, and vice versa. Note that if changes in actual output are the result of supply-side rather than demand-side shocks, Y_{FE} must be adjusted to reflect changes in capacity output; otherwise, our rule will lead to an overly expansionary monetary policy and a permanently higher rate of inflation. A serious problem with this rule, as with all such rules, is lags. Money affects the economy with a six- to nine-month lag. Also, we only find out about output levels with a lag. Hence, we cannot be sure that this rule will not exacerbate cycles instead of reduce them. It will if cycles are short in duration, but it will improve things if cycles are long.

Several economists have constructed macro experiments comparing the CPRG rule with variants of Equation (17.1). Unfortunately, there is no clear verdict on which of the rules is superior, since the results depend crucially on the assumptions made in the policy simulations.[6]

The CPRG and Fiscal Policy

One of the curious attributes of the Friedman CPRG rule is that it ignores fiscal policy altogether. In doing this it follows an old tradition in macropolicy analysis, namely, that monetary and fiscal policy authorities should be independent of each other. One may argue over the wisdom of this separation. In this section, we shall consider the effect of applying the CPRG rule at the Fed and a nondiscretionary fiscal policy rule at the Treasury. We will show that the two nondiscretionary rules do not fit together well because the automatic stabilizing effects of the one will be automatically neutralized or offset by the other.

[6]See J. Phillip Cooper and Stanley Fischer, "Stabilization Policy and Lags: Summary and Extension," *Annals of Economic and Social Measurement* (October 1972): 407–418.

As we saw in Chapter 15, there is a growing consensus that we are not yet able to conduct discretionary stabilization policy effectively. Many now support as a second-best alternative for fiscal policy reliance on the automatic stabilizers inherent in the tax and transfer system for countercyclical dampening of random shocks in private spending. If one accepts this alternative, the appropriate rule is to set the tax rate at that level which produces full employment at normal levels of private demand. Deficits will then be higher than normal when private sector demand declines, and vice versa.

On the Incompatibility of the CPRG and Automatic Stabilizers

How would such a rule for fiscal policy fit together with the CPRG rule for monetary policy? A moment's reflection indicates that they would work together very badly. In recessions, when deficits are higher than normal, the Treasury will have to sell bonds, which is contractionary. In a boom the Fed would have to buy bonds, which is expansionary. This follows from the government budget identity, re-presented here for convenience:

(17.2) $$G + R = T + \Delta H + \Delta B.$$

H = high-powered money
B = government bonds

Suppose for simplicity that the tax system is set so as to produce a balanced budget at full employment. Then, positive exogenous shocks in private spending will generate a surplus. According to Equation (17.2), the surplus must be matched by a reduction in either high-powered money or government bonds. But under the CPRG rule, the high-powered money supply is exogenously set so as to guarantee a preset rate of growth in the money supply. Therefore, the tax surplus will effectively be used to retire bonds. This can happen in two different ways. Either the Treasury uses the surplus to retire bonds directly, or the Federal Reserve makes expansionary open market bond purchases. For if the Fed were to do nothing and the Treasury were not retiring bonds, the surplus would reduce the money supply, which would violate the CPRG rule. Either method of reducing the bond supply is expansionary, because it reduces the demand for money and shifts the LM curve to the right. The public is forced to hold a portfolio with a higher proportion of money. That will happen only if interest rates decline or the level of income increases. In this way, the CPRG rule implies that the LM curve will shift procyclically whenever the tax system is automatically dampening spending during a boom.

In a recession, the CPRG rule does not cause a perverse open market operation, but the monetary effect is still procyclical. Here the government runs a deficit. According to the government budget identity, either the money or the bond supply must expand more rapidly than usual. The Treasury sells bonds to finance the deficit. If the Fed follows the CPRG it will not do anything, since Treasury bond sales to finance deficits do not affect the money supply after the proceeds have been spent by the government. Hence, in a recession the public is forced to hold a portfolio with more bonds than usual. As we learned in Chapter 5, government

Figure 17.5
The Procyclical Effect of the CPRG Rule

When the CPRG rule is combined with an automatic stabilizer fiscal policy, the result is procyclical. In booms the government runs a surplus, as shown in (b). This surplus is used to retire government bonds, which reduces the ratio of bonds to money, as shown in (a). This in turn tends to drive down interest rates, which stimulates investment and increases aggregate demand, as shown in (c). The situation is exactly reversed in recessions. Thus, aggregate demand tends to be pushed up by this set of rules in a boom and pushed down in a recession.

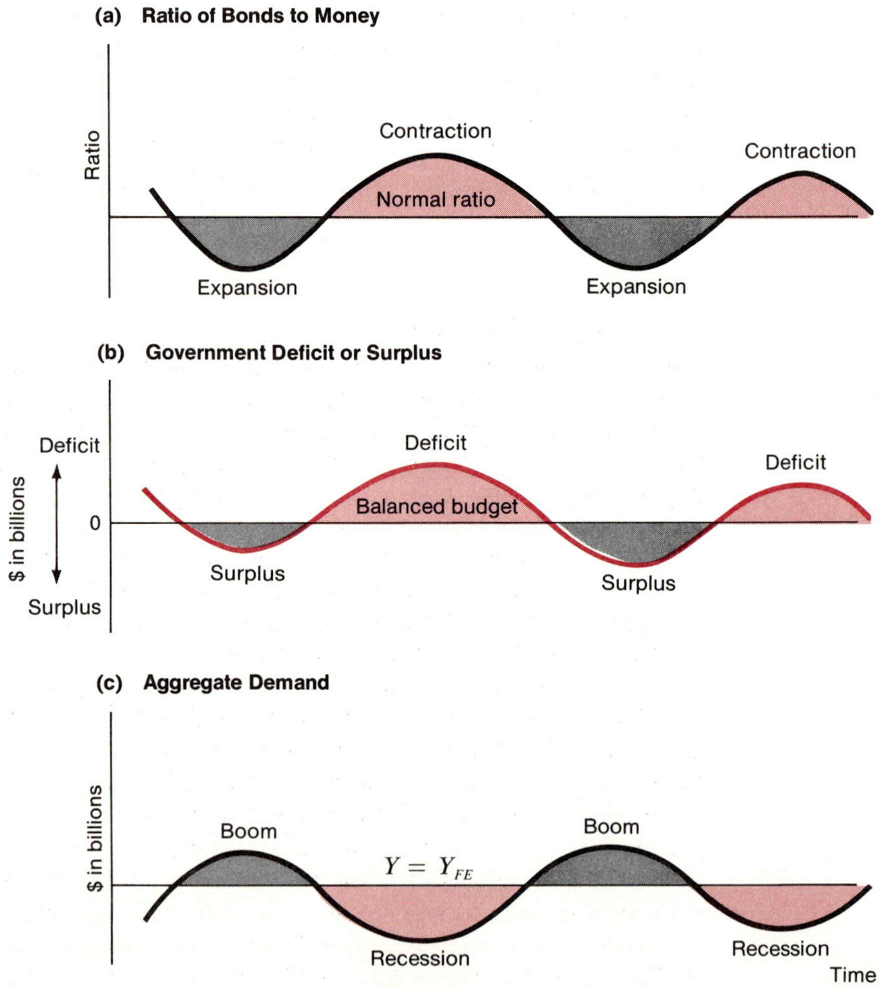

expenditures financed by bond sales rather than money crowd out private expenditures. Thus, bond financing offsets at least part of the direct expansionary effect of countercyclical fiscal policy.

We can summarize all of this in Figure 17.5. In booms the government runs a surplus, in recessions a deficit. In diagram (a), we show the effect of these deficits and surpluses in the financial markets by tracing out the ratio of government bonds to the money supply. If the Fed follows the CPRG rule, the bond supply will be negatively related to private spending. Hence, the ratio of bonds to money will be lower than normal in booms and will be higher than normal in recessions. We learned in Chapter 5 that if we hold the money supply constant and increase the stock of bonds that the public is forced to hold, the demand for money increases; this shifts the LM curve to the left and is therefore contractionary. The opposite happens when the bond supply falls relative to money. Hence, we may think of the areas above the normal bond-to-money ratio as times when monetary management is exerting a contractionary pull on the economy, while the areas below the line are times when monetary policy is expansionary. When one now compares diagram (a) with diagrams (b) and (c), it is clear that debt management and monetary policy are perversely procyclical. Whenever the economy is above its normal capacity monetary policy is expansionary, and whenever it is below Treasury debt sales are contractionary.

If we were able to put together the debt sales by the Treasury and the open market operations by the Fed and call the combination monetary policy, we could say that monetary policy defined in this way is expansionary in booms and contractionary in recessions. Now it may seem strange to say that monetary policy is contractionary in recession, since the Fed carries out no open market sales of bonds. But the public is being forced to absorb additional bonds into its portfolio by the Treasury. From the public point of view, it makes no difference whether this is done by the Fed through open market operations or by the Treasury through bond sales to finance deficits. The effect is the same: Interest rates go up, and private sector demand is reduced.

Lags and the Compatibility of CPRG and Automatic Stabilizers

In comparative statistics, one cannot justify a set of rules that offset one another. However, there are several different lag structures under which offsetting rules may be appropriate. First, the lag between automatic tax collections and changes in public spending may be so long that the automatic stabilization of the tax system will be perverse. During the boom the government runs a surplus, but the reduction in private spending does not occur until the economy is heading into a recession. Here even the automatic stabilizers are destabilizing, and the Friedman rule is appropriate because it offsets a perverse fiscal policy. An alternative way of achieving the same end would be to make the tax system independent of the level of economic activity.

A second lag structure under which the CPRG rule might work is one where the lag for monetary policy is significantly longer than that for fiscal policy and long compared to the business cycle. Then it would be rational to be carrying out expansionary monetary policy and contractionary fiscal policy at the same time, because the fiscal policy would be dampening things in the short run while the monetary policy would be counteracting the ensuing recession.

Compatible Rules for Monetary and Fiscal Policy

Except for the above two lag structures, the CPRG rule for the monetary authorities is a perverse one if the government also uses fiscal automatic stabilizers. We can remedy this perversity very easily, however, without abandoning the principle of rules. One way is simply to reverse the CPRG rule. Instead of having the money supply grow at a constant fixed rate and treating bonds as a residual, hold the bond supply constant (or make it grow at a constant rate), and treat high-powered money as a residual. Set the tax system to function automatically at the tax rate that keeps the economy at full employment under normal conditions. Finance all deficits by printing money, and use all surpluses to reduce the money supply. (We are assuming here that the level of government spending is based on the desires of the electorate and is independent of the level of output.) This rule operates on the principle that since deficits occur only when private spending is below its full employment level, they should be financed in as expansionary a way as possible, namely, by printing money. The opposite is true for surpluses. Using this rule there, the money supply would automatically behave countercyclically; therefore, if private spending were related positively to the stock of money, monetary and fiscal policies would always be pulling in the same direction.

The Long-Run Effect of Open Market Operations

There is still another complication that the monetary authorities must bear in mind as they decide how to conduct monetary policy, and that is the long-run effect of their policies on the stock of capital and the level of capacity output. In the short run, asset market equilibrium is determined by the available stock of assets and the demand for it. However, over time the composition and size of that stock can and will be changed by investment, because it adds to two particular assets, corporate securities and housing, that the public holds in its portfolio.[7]

Consider an expansionary open market operation. In the short run, giving the public more money and fewer government bonds increases the demand for corporate securities and housing. That raises investment and is therefore expansionary. Over time this new investment is added to the public portfolio. If, as earlier, we define the long-run equilibrium as the point where the addition of new assets comes to a stop—where net investment equals zero—then the long-run effect of the expansionary open market operation is an increase in the capital stock, not in investment.

We illustrate this point in Figure 17.6. For simplicity, we will omit the government bond market. We show the asset markets initially in long-run equilibrium at $r_{b,0}$ and $r_{cb,0}$. As before, the interest rate r_{cb} exceeds the government bond rate by a risk premium and is at just the level at which net investment is zero ($r_{cb,0}$ is the

[7] For a more extended discussion of the long-run effects of monetary policy on capacity, see Samuel A. Morley, "The Relationship Between Money, Income and Prices in the Short and Long Run," *Journal of Finance* 28 (December 1973): 119–130.

Figure 17.6
The Short- and Long-Run Effects of Expansionary Open Market Operations
An expansionary open market operation increases the money supply from SS to $S'S'$ in (a). In the short run the interest rates on government bonds and corporate securities both fall, the latter from $r_{cb,0}$ to $r_{cb,1}$. At $r_{cb,1}$, I' of new investment takes place. Over time, as this investment is added to the capital stock, the supply of corporate issues moves out to $S''S''$ in (b). Long-run equilibrium is reestablished when the interest rate has returned to $r_{cb,0}$; that occurs when enough additional investment has occurred to move supply out to $S''S''$. At that point the demand for money has increased to $D''D''$, which is just enough to absorb the initial increase in the money supply at the equilibrium interest rate, $r_{cb,0}$.

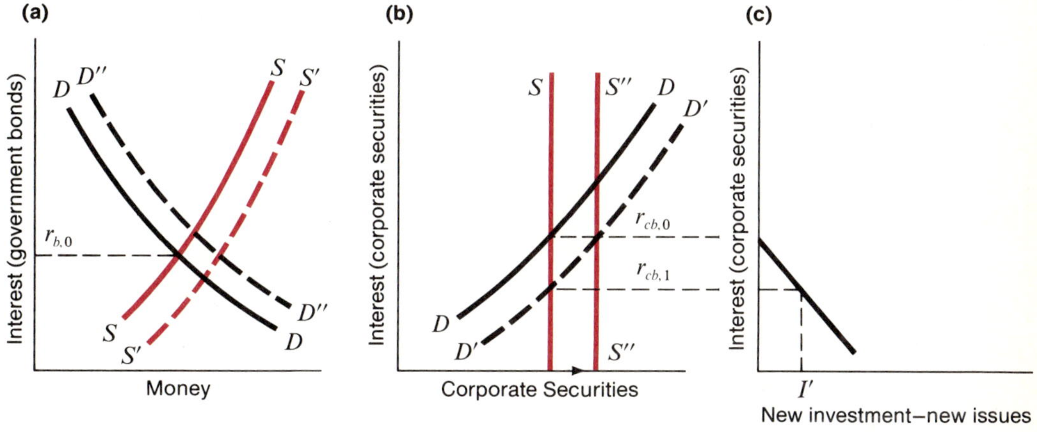

intercept of the investment function in diagram [c]). The expansionary open market operation is shown by the dashed curves $S'S'$ in the money market and $D'D'$ in the securities market. In the short run, $r_{cb,0}$ falls to $r_{cb,1}$ and net investment rises to I'.

But that is only the beginning of the process. Over time this new investment is added to the stock of corporate securities that the public must hold. In Figure 17.6, security supply moves slowly to the right over time, until finally it reaches $S''S''$. This is the new long-run equilibrium at which new investment returns to zero. The reflection of this in the money market is a slow rise in the demand for money over time until it reaches $D''D''$ in diagram (a). The demand for money increases because investment adds to the value of corporate equities in the public's portfolio, which increases public wealth. Increased wealth, as we have shown, increases the demand for money.

In the long run, therefore, the system adjusts the asset portfolio by investment until the interest rate $r_{cb,1}$ returns to $r_{cb,0}$. Therefore, we can see that the long-run effect of expansionary monetary policy is an increase in the capital stock, not an increase in investment. Investment is only the short-run adjustment of the economy to a change in the demand for capital (or securities that are issued when investment occurs). An increase in the money supply increases the demand for capital. That is expansionary in the short run because it causes capital formation.

In the long run, the increase in demand for capital is satisfied by an increase in the supply of capital. We could say, therefore, that in the long run, the effect of open market operations is on the capital stock of the economy. Expansionary open market operations or, as it used to be called, a low-interest-rate monetary policy, will increase capital formation in the short run and capital intensity in the long run. Contractionary open market operations will reduce investment in the short run and capital intensity in the long run.[8]

In deriving the long-run positive relationship between money and capacity, there is an important distinction to be made between economies with upward-sloping and those with vertical supply curves. The analysis we have just made is appropriate for an economy with an upward-sloping supply curve. In such an economy, monetary policy is not neutral; it has profound effects, one of which is to affect capital accumulation. In sharp contrast, if the supply curve is vertical, monetary policy has no real effect. Prices rise or fall in the same proportion as the nominal money supply rises or falls. Real balances are unchanged, with the result that the demand for either capital or fixed investment is unaffected by the change in the nominal supply of money.

The short-run and the long-run effects of monetary policy are dramatically different in the case of the upward-sloping supply curve. In the short run, monetary policy affects investment and therefore aggregate demand. But its long-run effect is on supply, not demand. Since in the long run net investment goes back to zero, the demand effect disappears; but the change in the capital stock that has occurred has a lasting long-run effect on productivity or supply. Expansionary monetary policy increases the capital stock, which should increase capacity; contractionary monetary policy should have the opposite long-run effect. The importance of this distinction between the short- and long-run effects of monetary policy will become clearer when we discuss supply-side economics in Chapter 20.

Summary

This chapter has been concerned with the practical problems of operating monetary policy. Like any other discussion of monetary policy, this one had to confront the increasingly influential ideas of the monetarists. Their ideas were summarized in the belief that (1) monetary policy is the key to controlling aggregate demand and (2) the government will never know enough to conduct discretionary stabilization policy successfully. From these two points follow their main policy prescriptions: The Fed should concentrate on controlling the money supply rather than

[8] The economics of money and growth in the vertical supply curve case has been worked out by numerous authors. The result is sharply different than the one we just derived. Basically, if money and capital are the only two assets in the public portfolio, the opportunity cost of holding more money is that the public holds less capital. Money and capital, according to this view, are substitutes. See Harry G. Johnson, "Money in a Neo-Classical One-Sector Growth Model," *Essays in Monetary Economics* (London: George Allen & Unwin, 1967), 143–178.

interest rates, and it should do nothing beyond making the money supply grow at a constant rate.

This CPRG rule sounds attractive, clear-cut, and simple. It has, however, several difficulties in execution. First, it is not clear which of the four money-supply assets the Fed should control. Unfortunately, the one over which the Fed has the most control, M1, is not the one that is most tightly linked to output. New financial inventions have expanded the number of near-monies. Measures of money, including these new assets, are highly correlated with aggregate demand but not closely linked to M1, let alone the monetary base, the Fed's policy instrument.

A second problem with the CPRG is the relationship between it and fiscal policy. Monetary and fiscal policies are not independent of each other; because of the government budget identity, they are tied together. If the authorities of both wish to follow automatic, nondiscretionary policy rules, the CPRG will work at cross-purposes with fiscal automatic stabilizers. This defect could be remedied by having the government bond supply, rather than the money supply, grow at a constant rate.

Key Concepts

short- versus long-run effects of monetary policy

constant percentage rate of growth rule

coordination of monetary and fiscal policy rules

Problems and Questions for Discussion

1. Does a rise in interest rates indicate restrictive monetary policy? If so, why? If not, why not?

2. Suppose there is an increase in interest rates in the money market. Under what conditions should the monetary authorities respond by expanding the money supply? Under what conditions should they contract the money supply?

3. Empirical evidence suggests that whenever the money supply changes, velocity changes in the opposite direction. Does this mean that monetary policy is ineffective in controlling the level of aggregate demand?

4. Why has velocity measured by $Y/\text{M1}$ increased so sharply in recent years while velocity measured by $Y/\text{M2}$ has been fairly constant?

5. Assuming that the Fed wants to use some sort of policy rule, under what conditions should it use the interest rate as a target and under what conditions should it use the money supply?

6. Suppose that we wish both monetary and fiscal policies to be guided by nondiscretionary policy rules. What rule should we set for fiscal policy? What rule should we set for monetary policy? Explain how the two rules would work together to dampen random fluctuations in private sector demand.

7. Suppose that the government decides not to use discretionary fiscal policy, instead setting a constant tax rate, t, and a marginal transfer rate, tr, such that the government deficit is the following function of income:

$$
\begin{aligned}
Def &= G + R - T \\
R &= Z - trY \\
T &= tY \\
Def &= G + Z - (t + tr)Y.
\end{aligned}
$$

If monetary policy is determined by the CPRG rule,

$$M_t = (1 + g)M_{t-1},$$

show what happens to the IS and LM curves during recessions caused by a reduction in private sector demand. What happens during booms?

8. Trace out the steps by which the economy reacts to a once-and-for-all change in the money supply in the short and the long run. Why is there a difference between the short and the long run?

9. If the full equilibrium supply curve of the economy depends on the capital stock, what is likely to be the long-run effect of a one-time reduction in the money supply on the long-run output level in the economy? What is the likely effect on the price level in the short run and in the long run? Show your argument in terms of the goods market diagram.

Chapter 18

The Theory and Practice of Stopping Inflation

One of the most difficult problems facing macropolicymakers is the control of inflation. Stopping the rise in prices after an extended period of inflation is probably the most delicate and difficult economic maneuver that a government can attempt, for it inevitably means a cutting back in some direction with undesirable consequences—falling output and consumption and increased unemployment. Stopping inflation is the morning-after following an economic blast. What is the best way to get through this unpleasant morning-after?

The goal of antiinflation policy is to return to a desired rate of increase in prices with the least possible loss in production during the transition period. There are essentially two ways to do this: orthodox reductions in aggregate demand and/or some form of incomes policy. Which approach to use depends fundamentally upon whether the economy behaves like our partial equilibrium model or our disequilibrium model. If the economy's short-run supply curve is upward sloping, orthodox measures are preferable; if the supply curve is flat, incomes policies are better.

In this chapter we shall examine the theory upon which each of the antiinflation strategies is based. At bottom, however, which to choose is an empirical matter, for it depends on the shape of the short-run supply curve. To shed some light on that question, we shall examine U. S. experience with antiinflation programs. This should gives us some idea of which inflation remedies work and which do not.

Theories of Inflation Control

Before making its choice about how to control its inflation, a government ought first to consider whether controlling it is worthwhile. The cost of controlling inflation through demand reduction is a period of dislocation, falling output, and high employment. Fighting inflation through price and wage controls is costly in terms of government bureaucracy and of the possibility of inefficient and inequitable price and wage decisions. In the United States during recent years, we have found this cost to be high.

Costs of Inflation

What are the costs of inflation? Here one must carefully distinguish between expected and unexpected inflation. The latter causes redistribution of income from wages to profits and from lenders to borrowers, both of which are socially divisive and undesirable. Expected inflation does not have these costs. Why then should we not simply accept whatever rate is being forecasted by labor and adjust the entire system to it? Not attempting to reduce expected inflation is a policy alternative that deserves to be seriously considered, especially if the costs of inflation are judged to be small.

One cost of inflation is that it causes the economic system to operate inefficiently. Inflation induces people to reduce their money holdings and to change their saving behavior in ways that make less productive capital available to the economy. People devote time, and business devotes labor, to avert inflationary redistributions of real wealth. Such action is inefficient. Moreover, inflation is discriminatory. Unless inflation is perfectly anticipated, it can cause rather dramatic changes in real income shares in the short run.[1] These attributes are undesirable.

The government has to balance the inefficiencies and inequities introduced by an inflation against the temporary costs of reducing that inflation to some desired level. Quite clearly, the longer the inflation continues, the longer will be the period of adjustment to a lower actual rate. The reason for this is that the public, and especially labor, has become accustomed to that rate of inflation. It will expect that rate to continue in the future, and it will take some time before its expectations adjust to the lower rate. During the adjustment period the levels of output and employment are undoubtedly going to be lower than normal, because actual real wages rise above their long-run equilibrium levels.

Once again we should stress the fundamental difference between controlling inflation with and without expected inflation. When labor expects no future change in prices, wages need rise only enough to offset previous inflation. There is a one-time further increase in prices and an elimination of involuntary overemployment, and the process ends. There is no period of more-than-normal unemployment and no period of excess capacity. Reducing inflation involves nothing more than giving up higher-than-normal output levels.

When inflationary expectations have become embedded in wage decisions, the cost of fighting inflation rises dramatically. Now the antiinflation program must produce an actual rate of inflation lower than expected. We have not learned any other way of doing this except through a temporary recession. Thus, if an inflation

[1] For an estimate of the redistributional effects of inflation, see G. L. Bach and James B. Stephenson, "Inflation and the Redistribution of Wealth," *Review of Economics and Statistics* 61 (February 1974): 1–13. Bach and Stephenson estimated that between 1945 and 1971 inflation reduced the value of household wealth by around $500 billion.

has gone on long enough so that expected inflation is positive, the public must expect any inflation program to lead to a period of greater-than-normal unemployment, excess capacity, and unused resources while the economy adjusts to the lower rate. The longer the inflation, the higher the likely unemployment during the antiinflation program.

Our analysis implies that the cost and the difficulty of fighting inflation vary directly with the length of the preceding inflation and the degree of price rigidity in the economy. There must be cases where the history of inflation is so long or the price inflexibility so high that reducing inflation per se is not an optimal policy—that is, the cost of continuing the inflation may well be less than the cost of reducing it. Price stability is not an end in itself. It is just one characteristic of an economy whose benefit may or may not be worth the cost of achievement.

It may seem politically naive to imagine that a society would ever prefer to live with, rather than eliminate, an inflation. We have all read about the costs imposed by inflation on the retired, on lenders, on the poor, and on other groups. It is these costs that gave President Reagan his mandate to adopt a fairly stringent antiinflationary program in the United States.

When one thinks further about the costs of inflation, however, it is clear that most are caused by unintended redistributions of income within the private sector and between it and the government. Most of these could be eliminated by what is called **indexing.**

Indexing

Indexing simply means a legal requirement to adjust contracts written in nominal or dollar terms for inflation.[2] Indexing holds out the hope of insulating the distribution of income from changes in the price level or the inflation rate. There are three forms of contracts that could be indexed.

Wage Indexing The most important contract to be indexed is wages. Workers and their employers would bargain and settle on whatever wage they wished. Over the life of the wage contract that wage would be automatically adjusted for inflation by formulas calculated by the government. This would stop inflationary redistributions of income between workers and their employers.

Wage indexing is not the same as wage control. It requires no elaborate bureaucracy and does not interfere with the setting of wages. Note also that indexing would eliminate the need for cost-of-living adjustments, because the index would take their place. Note further the very important point that the adjustment would come after the inflation, not before it. With an indexing system wages would not go up in anticipation of future inflation but only as an adjustment to past inflation. In

[2] A good introduction to the economics of indexation and inflation can be found in American Enterprise Institute, *Essays on Inflation and Indexation* (Washington, D. C.: American Enterprise Institute, 1974.) See also Jo Anna Gray, "Wage Indexation: A Macroeconomics Approach," *Journal of Monetary Economics* 2 (April 1976): 221–235; and Stanley Fischer, "Wage Indexation and Macroeconomic Stability," *Journal of Monetary Economics* 3 (supplement, 1977): 107–147.

this way wage increases could not be an independent cause of inflation as expected inflation is a root cause of wage increases under our current arrangements.

Debt Indexing Debt contracts, such as mortgages, bonds, and even bank accounts, can also be indexed. Remember that the idea of indexing is to stop inflationary redistributions from one side of a contract to the other. This applies as much to debts as to wages. Under our current system, the rate of interest has a component that pays the lender for the loss in purchasing power of the money he or she has lent. It is a sort of premium for expected inflation, just as cost-of-living adjustments are on wages. Under indexing the interest rate represents the real cost of borrowing money. Debt indexing aims to prevent the inflationary redistribution of wealth between borrowers and lenders. It has been applied with some success in other countries.

Tax Indexing The final form of indexing, which actually will go into effect in the United States in 1984, is tax indexing. As we indicated in Chapter 6, inflation has caused a very significant redistribution of income from the private sector to the government because our tax system is progressive and the income brackets and exemptions are written in nominal terms. Inflation pushes people into higher tax brackets and thus increases their real tax burden. All this will be eliminated after 1984, because the tax brackets and exemptions will, henceforth, be adjusted for inflation. This is an extremely significant change in fiscal policy, for it eliminates the increase in real tax rates due to bracket-creep. No longer will the government be able to raise its tax revenues without our permission by simply causing an inflation.

In general, a comprehensive system of indexing of wages, debt instruments, and taxes would eliminate most of the inflationary redistribution of income that does so much to raise the cost of inflation.

Despite these apparent advantages, economists are not particularly enthusiastic about indexing. They claim three drawbacks. First, indexing seems to imply a willingness to accept inflation. Second, it is likely to make the inflation rate far more erratic in response to supply shocks, such as crop failures. Finally, indexing cannot really eliminate an inflationary redistribution of income when relative prices change—indeed, it could make it worse. Businesspersons do not sell the consumer price index, they sell a particular product, whose price behavior may be different than the CPI. If workers in a particular firm are getting automatic wage adjustments related to the CPI but prices are rising at a slower rate, profits will suffer. The greater the variability of prices among sectors, the greater the risk due to the dispersion of relative prices. While this defect could be alleviated by allowing only a partial inflation correction, it appears to be a serious drawback in any indexing scheme.

The Orthodox Antiinflation Program

The orthodox way of reducing the rate of inflation is by lowering the level of aggregate demand through some combination of higher taxes, lower government spending, or a reduction in the money supply. This will shift the aggregate demand curve of the economy to the left. Business will find that it cannot sell its output for as high a price as it could if the government had not reduced demand. Rates of inflation will decline. At the new price level, business will find it unprofitable to hire laborers whose wage demands will now be unrealistically high, given the lower rate of inflation. After a period in which rates of inflation have been lower than those expected by labor, the unemployed workers will begin to lower their expectations and their wage demands. This will put pressure on the wage rates of the workers who are still employed, and the average rate of increase of wages will begin to decline. In terms of the Phillips curve, reducing aggregate demand moves the economy to the right along a short-run Phillips curve. As expectations adjust downward, wage demands decline, employment begins to rise, and the stabilization phase draws to a close.

We have seen in previous chapters that there is a significant disagreement among economists about the shape of the short-run supply and Phillips curves. Because of markup pricing, monopoly power, and labor stockpiling, there may be a kink in both of these curves, such that both become flat at less than full employment. When demand is reduced in a disequilibrium economy with a flat supply curve, the inflation rate does not fall, at least not rapidly, Instead, unemployment increases dramatically. One would expect that the presence of supernormal unemployment would lead employed workers to moderate wage demands, allowing prices to decline. But in reality that may not happen to any significant extent. As we have learned, when there is a recession, companies may not lay off their skilled labor in proportion to the decline in output that they suffer. If they expect the downturn to be a short one, it may be cheaper for them to maintain their skilled labor force even though some of the workers are partially idle in the short run. This can be explained by the importance of firm-specific training in the skilled labor force. During recessions, therefore, the unemployment rate of skilled labor may remain quite low. Big increases in unemployment occur among the marginal labor force, but that does not put much pressure on the wages of skilled workers. With excess labor already, companies may simply stop hiring—that is, they may engage in job rationing at the going wage rather than driving wages down and hiring the unemployed.

If the short-run aggregate supply curve has a significant change of slope or kink at some level of output, the cost of fighting inflation through reductions in aggregate demand depends on the position of the economy. Above the kink such a program does what it is intended to do. However, below the kink, reductions in demand mainly drive up the unemployment rate. They have little effect on either inflation or expectations. For if prices and wages are not very flexible downward, the effect of the antiinflation program will be reflected primarily in reductions in output and employment, not prices. Inflexible prices turn an intended deflation of prices into a depression of output. Clearly, the flatter the supply curve of the economy, the more severe will be the real costs of the orthodox program in terms of lost output, unemployed people, and wasted resources.

A factor that is relevant to the debate on the relative flexibility of prices and wages is the degree and duration of unemployment. Probably few of the proponents of wage and price rigidity would care to argue that prices and wages would remain inflexible in the face of really severe unemployment. When unemployment rates were driven up to over 10 percent during the Reagan administration and held there for a long time, wages and prices did respond. That proved that an orthodox policy, pursued with sufficient determination, could slow down the inflation rate. Prior to Reagan, no president has been willing to put the economy through such a wringer as the United States has endured during the 1980–1982 period because the political and economic costs have been thought to be too high. Therefore, we have had a series of stop-go cycles instead, each of which has caused a mild recession. None of those recessions was severe enough to bring inflation under control before the political implications of high unemployment required the government to take action to get out of the recession. The Reagan-Volcker program is the first antiinflation program carried through despite the political cost (which, as shown in the 1982 election, was high).

Economists who believe that wages and prices are inflexible downward do not support the **orthodox antiinflation program** beyond a certain point (the kink in the supply curve). They acknowledge that such a program may reduce inflation if it is drastic enough, but they feel that the costs in lost output and unemployment will be exorbitant. Such economists favor an entirely different approach to inflation control. Essentially they argue that if prices and wages are inflexible out to a high unemployment rate, we should not use the orthodox antiinflation program except to eliminate excess demand. To reduce inflation further, we should use some sort of incomes policy instead.[3] Incomes policies come in two varieties: voluntary and mandatory. Voluntary programs include wage and price guidelines and guideposts. Mandatory incomes policies include wage and price controls. In the next section we shall consider some of the different types of compulsory wage and price control programs that have been proposed and used in the United States.

Wage and Price Controls

What we mean by a wage-price control program is some intervention by the government to force labor and management to set prices and wages below the level they would otherwise have chosen. The aim of the intervention is to bring the rate of inflation down to an acceptable level without the necessity of an unemployment-producing recession. In terms of our supply and Phillips curve diagrams, the government forces the economy down from one flat supply or Phillips curve to a lower one. Under the orthodox program, this downward motion is supposed to come about through the pressures of unemployment and idle capacity upon wages and prices.

Economists are not particularly fond of **wage and price controls**. Such programs mean government bureaucracy, inefficiencies, shortages, prices set at the wrong level, and other undesirable effects. Advocates simply believe that these costs are less than those of any alternative antiinflation program. Consider now the general kinds of programs that have been proposed. Disregarding voluntary guidelines, there are three types of control programs, one of which controls both prices and wages, another of which controls only wages, and a third of which uses tax incentives to reduce the rate of increase of wages and prices. Since wage controls

[3] For one such proposal, see Arthur M. Okun, "The Great Stagflation Swamp," *Challenge* 20 (November-December 1977): 6–13.

are common to the first two, let us first consider the wage component of each of them.

Wage Control Systems The general form of most of the wage control systems that have been proposed is that average wages for each firm should be allowed to rise at the national rate of increase of productivity plus the target rate of inflation. If such a policy were strictly adhered to, and if there were no increase in profit margins, the actual inflation rate would equal the target rate.[4] Thus, if the price controllers want to arrive at a 2.5 percent rate of inflation, and if they expect labor productivity to rise by 3 percent per year, they allow wages to rise by 5.5 percent. Labor costs, prices, and profits all rise by 2.5 percent. Note that under this formula profits remain constant in real terms.

But we know that there are intrasectoral differences in productivity. Should not the wage increase granted to workers in each sector reflect this? The answer appears to be no, but over the long run there should not be too much difference between the national and the sectoral systems. Under either system we should note that wages must reflect supply and demand conditions as well as productivity in the labor market. Under the uniform productivity rule, wage costs and relative prices rise in low productivity sectors; that means that either prices fall or profits rise in high productivity sectors. In either case capital, production, and jobs gradually flow from the low to the high productivity areas of the economy. Relative profits and prices encourage both consumers and producers to take advantage of variations in productivity across sectors.

When wages follow sectoral rather than national productivity trends, the adjustment is shifted from prices and profits to wages. If wages rise with productivity in each sector, neither relative prices nor profits change; rather, wages rise in high productivity sectors. This should draw workers away from low productivity areas, tending to equalize wages and expand output in the more productive sectors of the economy.

Thus, it would appear that the final effect of the two different wage systems on the economy is the same: Output and employment shift toward the more produc-

[4] Mathematically, this idea is expressed:

$$P = R + WL,$$

$$L = \frac{1}{APL},$$

$$R = \lambda P.$$

P = price
R = profits
W = wage
L = labor inputs
APL = average product of labor
λ = profit share

Hence,

$$\frac{\Delta P}{P} = \frac{\lambda \, \Delta P}{P} + (1 - \lambda)\frac{\Delta(WL)}{WL}$$

or,

$$\frac{\Delta P}{P} = \frac{\Delta W}{W} - \frac{\Delta APL}{APL}.$$

tive sectors. However, the paths followed and the beneficiaries are different. Under the national productivity rule, consumers and capitalists benefit from differential productivity; workers do not. Under the sectoral productivity rule, the opposite is true. In the first case, the force for expansion is consumer demand and relative profit rates; in the second, that force is the attraction of high relative wages on sectoral labor supply. Whether one prefers the national or the sectoral system depends upon whether one wants workers or consumers to benefit from changes in productivity in the short run.

Price Control Programs We now turn to a far more complex question: price controls. Before one even starts thinking about the design of any program, it is good to recognize a few fundamental facts about prices and the price system. Prices are the basic transmitter of information in a market economy. They are signals, telling producers about the desires of consumers. As such, they play a central role in the allocation of the economy's productive resources. Any price control system will make prices lower than they would have been in the open market. Employment and output decisions will be affected. There should be compelling reasons for intervention in such a key element of our economic system.

Deciding upon the right price or the right system of prices is an incredibly difficult job. The government must keep track of literally millions of price and wage decisions. It has to know the right level for each price and how that level should change over time. Suppose, for example, that the government sets a target rate of inflation of 4 percent. Does this mean that all prices should be rising by 4 percent? Not at all. If there is any real growth going on in the economy, some products are expanding. Even in the absence of any greater-than-normal price increases in the raw material costs or wages, prices may rise in the industry because of diminishing returns. How much they rise depends on just how hard it is to expand output. In a growing economy the demand for different products grows at different rates, and the ability to supply that increased demand varies by industry. The government would have to know each industry's supply curve to determine the justifiable price increase it should be granted.

Another problem immediately comes to mind: What signal does the market have for raising output other than profits? If demand rises in the industry, prices are raised, profits increase, and business in that industry is prompted to expand its facilities and to increase its output. The short-run rise in prices is the legitimate signaling device of the market economy by which more output will later be supplied. If the government short-circuits the signal, no extra output will be forthcoming. This is all right if government sets the right price. If it sets one that is too low, the substitute for inflation is a smaller total output and perhaps rationing. One sees examples of this in public utilities and cities with rent controls. Prices set at artificially low levels have created long-run shortages in electric power, natural gas, and housing.

Other problems with price controls are the possibilities of cheating and customer discrimination that are introduced. Manufacturers can downgrade the quality of their products to cut costs when prices are set at the wrong level. They can create new products for which no price controls exist and stop making the old products. An amusing example of this occurred in the United States in 1972. Price controls were applied to 4×8 plywood sheets. In response, the plywood manufacturers cut $\frac{1}{16}$ inch off their sheets and started selling a new product, $4 \times 7\frac{15}{16}$ plywood sheets, for which there was no price ceiling. They also exported lumber to Canada, where the prices were higher, and then bought it back again because price controls did not apply on imported products. There is probably no system that could be devised that would eliminate all such loopholes.

Because of the enormous complexity of the economy, all feasible price control programs limit their coverage in one way or another. Typically the limitations are either by the importance of the product or by the degree of monopoly power of the firm producing the product. Since there is a crude relationship between monopoly power, or price-setting ability, and firm size, most programs reserve the closest scrutiny for the largest firms. The argument is that, since prices are administered in such firms anyway, one might as well substitute a public for a private administrator; he or she at least has the public interest in mind when price decisions are made.

Suppose that the government has selected the group of firms whose prices are to be monitored. What criteria should it use in setting the firm's prices? For example, do we let the firm pass on all costs on a dollar-for-dollar basis or on a percentage basis? The former will keep dollar profits constant, while the latter will allow profits to grow at the same percentage rate as costs. The disadvantage of the latter is that it gives the firm an incentive to be inefficient. All it must do is show a cost increase, whether this be executive airplanes, paneling in corporate headquarters, or a wasteful use of labor, in order to get permission to raise prices and profits. Cost pass-through on a dollar-for-dollar basis is a system by which prices are allowed to rise only by the same number of dollars that cost per dollar of sales goes up. Thus, if labor and raw material costs amount to 75 percent of sales and if they rise by 10 percent, product prices will be allowed to rise by only 7.5 percent. Profits per dollar of sales are thus constant. The only problem with this rule is that it penalizes profits if there is general inflation. Profits, after all, represent the payment for capital and entrepreneurial services. They must be sufficient to cover depreciation and to induce businesspeople to take risks. Some adjustment of nominal profits must therefore be allowed under general inflation even if full cost pass-through is not permitted.

The TIPS Scheme Because of the administrative difficulties encountered in operating a full-fledged price and wage control system, several economists have suggested using a system of tax incentives or penalties to encourage wage restraint by business.[5] These plans are called **tax incentives for price stability (TIPS)** plans. The basic idea is to vary an individual corporation's tax rate according to the rate of increase of wages that it grants its employees. Corporations granting highly inflationary wage settlements would pay a high tax rate. Thus, under a typical TIPS scheme the tax rate for the ith corporation would be:

(18.1) $$t_i = b + m\,(w_i - n). \quad (m > 0)$$

[5]The basic TIPS proposal was developed by Henry Wallich and Sidney Weintraub in "A Tax-Based Incomes Policy," *Journal of Economic Issues* 5 (June 1971): 1–19. See also Abba Lerner, "Stagflation—Its Cause and Cure," *Challenge* 20 (September-October 1977): 14–19. A careful discussion of problems in the application of TIPS-type schemes can be found in Laurence S. Seidman, "Tax-Based Incomes Policies," *Brookings Papers on Economic Activity* 2/1978): 301–363.

b = base tax rate
m = the TIP multiplier, a policy parameter
w_i = average rate of wage increase
n = target rate of wage increase

The attraction of the TIPS scheme is that it does not require an extensive bureaucracy as do the other forms of wage and price controls. Each corporation simply counts up its employees and multiplies that number by its permissible average wage level. That will be the average paid the previous year, plus the permissible wage increase set by the federal government. Wages above that level trigger a penalty tax.

Administratively and politically, the TIPS plan does have certain problems. One is what to do about new firms or firms whose employment structure changes. A second is what to do about prices; the TIPS scheme appears to put the onus for inflation on excessive wage demands. What about profits? What is to prevent corporations from using TIPS plans to force down wages while they keep right on raising prices? We can say only that profit margins have always been quite stable in the United States, and there is no reason to expect this to change under a TIPS plan. Also, workers could be protected against excessive inflation by a wage insurance program of the type proposed by Carter. This would work as follows. If workers in a firm signed up for the TIPS program, they would receive a payment from the government if inflation were higher than the rate consistent with the wage target (n in Equation [18.1]). This would insure workers who cooperated in the program against unexpected reductions in their real wage caused by rising markups.

Theoretically, one could design a TIPS system for prices as well as wages. However, the technical problems of defining, measuring, and insuring compliance are much greater for prices than for wages. Thus the wage TIPS system, accompanied by some sort of real wage insurance, appears to be a way of reducing the inflation rate without excessive interference in the price system or a long stabilization recession. It should speed up the process by which the economy goes from a high to a low rate of inflation and eliminate much of the waste caused by recession in orthodox stabilization.

Case Study:

Stabilization in the United States, 1967–1982

The period since 1967 offers an invaluable lesson in alternative ways to fight inflation. During this period most of the policies we have just discussed have been tried in a long and frustrating battle with increasing prices. The record shows with depressing clarity how hard it is to bring inflation under control once a serious inflation has been allowed to continue long enough to affect people's expectations. It took three major recessions, and over $700 billion of lost output, before the inflation rate finally began to show signs of slowing down. In this section we will briefly describe the U. S. efforts to fight inflation.

Broadly speaking, this long fight against inflation has had five phases: a period of orthodox demand-side restraint in 1968–1971; a period of wage and price controls in 1971–1974; a period of contraction (1974–1975) in response to our first supply-side inflation; a five-year period of continuous expansion under Presidents Carter and Ford; and a period of stringent contraction in 1980–1982 after Paul Volcker took over at the Federal Reserve. In this study we will briefly describe U. S. efforts to fight inflation during each of these periods. The reader may find it useful to refer ahead to Figure 18.1, which gives a visual picture of the cycles in output and inflation that occurred during these years.

An Orthodox Program to Stop Inflation, 1968–1971

The 1960s were a time of great hopes followed by bitter disappointment for economic policymakers. By a judicious use of tax cuts, budget deficits, and expansionary monetary policy, they had apparently broken the inevitable boom-recession business cycle. In December 1965, the economy was entering its 58th month of economic expansion, the longest peacetime boom in U. S. history. Unemployment was down to 4.1 percent, the lowest since 1957, and profits were at their highest levels since the Korean War. Yet the rate of inflation was less than 2 percent. One could have been forgiven for believing that the United States was entering a new era of progress and uninterrupted prosperity.

This pleasant picture was exploded by the Vietnam War. The war came at a most unpropitious time. By 1965 the economy was already at or close to full employment. This was not a time when a major new government spending program could be introduced without either a contraction in some other area or an increase in taxes. But President Johnson was unwilling to cut his Great Society programs or raise taxes because of the war. The result was a rise in federal government expenditures in real terms by over 25 percent in 1965–1967 and a corresponding increase of $14 billion in the federal deficit. These fiscal developments helped to fuel a large increase in aggregate demand at a time when the economy had little idle capacity in either workers or machines. The rate of inflation rose to 3.4 percent in 1966, capacity utilization rose to over 90 percent, and unemployment fell below 4 percent for the first time since the Korean War.

Belatedly the government mobilized to fight the inflation. Its first actions were traditional orthodox demand restraint. Both fiscal and monetary policies were used. Because the fiscal authorities were reluctant to request a tax increase in 1966 for political reasons, the monetary authorities were the first to act. In the early months of 1966, they produced a short but sharp contraction in the nation's money supply. Six months later, there was an unmistakable slowing down in demand and production. What would have happened had the Federal Reserve maintained its restrictive stance is a fascinating question that we will never answer satisfactorily, because the Federal Reserve backed off. The money supply, which had grown only 2.2 percent in 1966, was allowed to grow by 6.6 percent in 1967 and 7.2 percent in 1968.

Meanwhile the government had reluctantly come to the conclusion that an increase in taxes was necessary. In his economic report for 1967, President Johnson asked Congress to enact a temporary 10 percent income surtax. Despite the mounting evidence of inflationary pressure in the economy, the bill was not signed until June 1968. Even though the tax was retroactive to January for corporations and to April for individuals, a full year went by between the request for the surtax and its implementation by a reluctant Congress. And this was only one of a series of lags between the time when the tax was first needed and the time when it finally affected spending. For between the last half of 1968 and the first half of 1969, the public reacted to the new surtax by reducing saving, not consumption, just as our theory of permanent income would predict. Eventually, as the surtax was extended for a full year to June 1970, private consumption did fall, a major factor in the downturn in economic activity that began in the fourth quarter of 1969. But the lag between the first presentation of the tax surcharge and its effect spread over two years. During that time, the consumer price index rose by 11 percent. A policy that is that slow is not a very effective inflation-control tool.

As we have seen, during the two years 1967 and 1968 the monetary authorities had permitted an expansionary monetary policy. In 1969, as inflation accelerated, they switched back to restraint. During the eight months from July 1969 through February 1970, the money supply rose by less than 0.5 percent, which meant a decline of 3 percent in real terms. Interest rates soared to their highest levels in over one hundred years. Finally, fiscal and monetary policies were pulling in the same direction, and both were working strongly toward restraint. Slowly, demand began to contract. Throughout 1969, the rate of growth of the economy fell while unemployment held at the abnormally low level of 3.5 to 3.8 percent; inflation worsened significantly. In 1970, the induced recession began in earnest. Unemployment rates climbed rapidly throughout the year, going from 3.5 percent in December 1969 to 6.2 percent one year later. Gross national product declined in real terms. Monetary and fiscal policies had successfully broken the boom by reducing aggregate demand.

Driving the country into a recession was not the final goal of government economists. They were using the orthodox antiinflation model and saw the recession as an unpleasant first step toward the achievement of a lower rate of inflation. The administration saw unemployment and recession as a way of reducing the rate of actual inflation and thus bringing expected inflation to a lower rate. Once expectations had fallen to an acceptable level, the economy would be allowed to return to full employment.

For more than eighteen months the government resolutely played by this orthodox game plan. At first it was gratified by reductions in the rate of inflation. The seasonally adjusted annual rate of increase of the consumer price index, which had been 5.9 percent in the second half of 1969 and 6.0 percent in the first half of 1970, was 4.6 percent from June to November 1970. However, unemployment rose to a reported 6 percent of the labor force by December. Such an unemployment rate cannot be maintained unless it yields fairly quick results in reductions in wage and price increases—and that did not seem to be happening. Listen to the Council of Economic Advisors:

The behavior of prices from the end of 1970 to mid August (1971) and especially after April heightened concern about inflation. Although the rise in consumer prices continued to decelerate for several months early in the year, it quickened

Table 18.1
Changes in Consumer Prices for All Items and All Items Less Food and Mortgage Interest[a]

	All Items	All Items Less Food and Mortgage Interest
December 1968–December 1969	6.1%	5.2%
December 1969–December 1970	5.5	5.9
December 1970–March 1971	2.8	3.8
March 1971–June 1971	5.3	6.1

[a] All inflation rates are annualized.

in the spring, as did the rise in wholesale industrial prices . . . The 1970 improvement (in the CPI) had been due mainly to a slower rise in food prices. There was a further slowdown in early 1971. The improvement proved to be short lived as the second quarter brought a rise of 5.3 percent (annual rate) in the CPI. Not only was there some step-up in the rise of food prices, but non-food commodities also rose more rapidly, at about their 1970 rate.[6]

If food and interest rate effects are removed from the CPI, one gets a more accurate measure of prices that should directly respond to aggregate demand. Here the picture was not comforting, as Table 18.1 shows. Except for the first quarter of 1971, there was no deceleration in inflation at all. Keep in mind that all this was occurring at the same time that capacity utilization had fallen to 75 percent and the unemployment rate had risen from 4 to 6 percent, hovering at the latter rate for the entire six-month period from December 1970 through May 1971. Orthodox policy was either not working to reduce expected inflation or was working much more slowly than expected. With the 1972 election only a year away, political pressures mounted to try some other policy.

Even the economic advisers split. One group, pointing to the slow decline in the rate of increase in the CPI, contended that the inflation program was working and should be resolutely continued. A second group, headed by Arthur Burns, the new chairman of the Federal Reserve, argued that prices and wages were too unresponsive to demand conditions and that a switch to an incomes policy—that is, some form of price and wage controls—must be considered. Here is Burns speaking in May 1971:

During the past year and a half, our unemployment rate has risen from 3½ percent to about 6 percent. Labor is now readily available across the range of skills and in most sections of the country. Virtually, all industries have substantial amounts of excess capacity. In such circumstances, past experience would have led us to expect a substantial reduction in the rate of increase of costs and

[6] *Economic Report of the President* (Washington, D.C., 1972), 41.

prices, if not actual declines. In fact, however, the improvement thus far has been modest . . . Cost-push inflation cannot be dealt with effectively by using monetary and fiscal tools alone. In today's environment, efforts to do so would inevitably reduce output and employment far beyond the limits that our governments can accept or their citizens tolerate. On the other hand, I fear that cost pressures may become so intractable in our countries that they will ultimately weaken democratic institutions, besides stifling economic progress.

Over a year ago, I reluctantly came to the conclusion that monetary and fiscal instruments needed to be supplemented for a time by incomes policy in the United States—that is, policies designed to enable labor and commodity markets to approximate more closely the competitive model.[7]

We have argued that the orthodox program should be applied only in an economy with an upward-sloping short-run supply curve. Burns's statement reflects the dawning realization by many economists and policymakers that the short-run supply curve was apparently much flatter than they had imagined for low levels of output and employment. Many reluctantly concluded that a new antiinflation strategy was called for. That strategy was wage and price controls.

The U.S. Experiment with Wage and Price Controls, 1971–1974

In August 1971, confronted by a worsening balance of payments situation and inflationary recession at home, President Richard M. Nixon jettisoned his three-year-old orthodox program and embarked on the first peacetime price and wage controls in U. S. history.[8] Unlike previous guidepost systems and many European incomes policies, the program was not voluntary. The price and wage ceilings had the force of law, and violations could be rolled back and penalties assessed.

Nixon's program set up a Cost of Living Council (CLC), which in turn delegated its authority to a number of different committees composed mainly of private citizens. The two most important were the Pay Board and the Price Commission. These two bodies were to set permissible standards for wages and price and decide their application in particular cases. Verification of compliance was left in the hands of the Internal Revenue Service.

The goal set by the CLC was to get the inflation rate down to 2 to 3 percent by the end of 1972. To this end the Pay Board set permissible wage increases for all workers at 5.5 percent. Since labor productivity on average had been growing at

[7] Arthur Burns, "Two Key Issues of Monetary Policy," *Federal Reserve Bulletin* (June 1971): 452–453.

[8] The Economic Stabilization Act of 1971, which established wage and price controls, required an annual report by the President describing actions taken and their effects. These reports are included in the annual *Economic Report of the President.* For a more detailed description of the Nixon program see: Arnold R. Weber, *In Pursuit of Price Stability: The Wage-Price Freeze of 1971* (Washington, D. C.: The Brookings Institution, 1973); Robert F. Lanzilotti, Mary T. Hamilton, and R. Blaine Roberts, *Phase II in Review: The Price Commission Experience* (Washington, D. C.: The Brookings Institution, 1975); and Arnold R. Weber and Daniel J. B. Mitchell, *The Pay-Board's Progress: Wage Controls in Phase II* (Washington, D. C.: The Brookings Institution, 1978).

about 3 percent in the postwar period, this should have led to an inflation rate of 2 to 3 percent.[9]

On the price side of the controls package, the general features were the following:

1. Firms were allowed to raise their prices by the same percentage amount that allowable costs had increased. Profits were therefore positively related to costs.

2. Maximum profit margin rule: Even if otherwise justified, price increases were not allowed if the firm's profit margin (profit as a percentage of sales) exceeded the average of the best two of the fiscal years preceding August 15, 1971.

3. Many large, multiproduct firms were allowed to negotiate special agreements with the Price Commission. These agreements specified a maximum by which the average of all the firm's prices might rise over the year.

4. The intensity with which the program was enforced varied by the size of the firm. Firms were divided by size into three groups or tiers, and the large firms were subjected to closer surveillance and more stringent reporting requirements than the smaller ones.

This compulsory program lasted 17 months, until January 1973. On the surface its record was impressive. The inflation rate for 1972 fell to 3.4 percent from the 5 to 6 percent rate of the pre-controls period. At the same time, the authorities were emboldened by the presence of controls to abandon their restrictive fiscal and monetary policies. Fiscal policy was deliberately expansionary, and the money supply rose by 8.2 percent over the year 1972. In other words, the government shifted from orthodox restraint with no price or wage interference to price and wage controls coupled with expansionary monetary and fiscal policies. The results were heartening. At the same time that inflation seemed to be winding down, the unemployment rate fell from 6.1 percent to 5.1 percent from December 1971 to December 1972, and production rose by 7.6 percent. With the advantage of hindsight, it now appears that 1972's expansion was excessive. For just as the economy reached approximately full employment, it was confronted with a completely new problem: real scarcity. It was a problem that was to make a shambles of the controls program and generate a new round of inflation far more virulent than anything seen in the United States up to that time.

On January 11, 1973, in a masterpiece of bad timing, the control system was switched from a compulsory to a voluntary one. The government continued to set standards for "reasonable price and wage behavior" to which it requested that business and labor conform. (No advance approval for price increases was required for the large firms, however.) The new voluntary program appeared to be a disaster. The CPI, which had been so well behaved in 1972, began to rise—at an 8-percent rate during the first two quarters of 1973. The situation in the wholesale price index was equally bleak. Prices of crude industrial raw materials rose by 12

[9] Note that this rule gave all workers national rather than sectoral productivity wage increases. Exceptions to the general ceilings were allowed for groups whose pay was grossly out of line with other comparable groups when the program began and for workers whose pay had increased at less than 7 percent per year during the previous three years.

percent in just the first six months of 1973—a 28-percent annual rate. (Those were the prices that would be reflected in consumer prices with a three-to-six month lag.) Thus, no relief on the price front was in sight. A superficial observer of the economic situation would have concluded that either the rapid expansion of 1972 had generated a new round of inflation or compulsory controls had only delayed the inflation. A more careful look at the evidence reveals a rather different story.

Supply-Shock Inflation, 1973–1975

The year 1973 was the United States' first experience with supply-shock inflation. During the first half of that unfortunate year, a worldwide constellation of economic misfortunes combined to drive up prices.[10] In the agricultural sector there was a reduction of 36 million tons in the world production grains in 1972 due to simultaneous crop failures in India, Russia, and China. The situation was complicated by a decline in the production of animal feed supplements—notably soybeans and fishmeal. The result was an explosion of feed grain prices and a fall in the production of livestock. By the beginning of 1973, experts were warning that food prices would rise by 25 percent over the year—a prediction that turned out to be conservative. Aside from food, there were rapid increases in the prices of key industrial raw materials, such as lumber, oil, copper, and aluminum. This was a result of a construction boom, rapidly rising levels of economic activity, and the devaluation of the dollar in March of 1973. The result of all these events was a sharp commodities inflation in the first half of 1973. It would have been followed by rising wage demands and a general round of price increases under the best of circumstances. But to make matters worse, in the winter of 1973 war in the Middle East led to an oil embargo and then a quadrupling of oil prices in 1974. Clearly, no controls program could have stopped inflation under these unpropitious circumstances.

By summer it was obvious that a major explosion in food and fuel prices was occurring. In August 1973, the government abandoned the voluntary program and returned to a compulsory system very similar to the 1972 system, except that it imposed a freeze on profits.

The period between August 1973 and April 1974, when controls were abandoned, was dominated by crop failures, the oil boycott, and the Middle East War. Energy and food prices marched inexorably upward, drawing the inflation rate for the year to over 11 percent. Clearly, no controls system could have worked under this combination of booming production and sectoral supply bottlenecks. Belatedly the government moved to reduce aggregate demand by restrictive monetary and fiscal policies. The money supply fell 4.6 percent in real terms in 1974, and the full employment surplus rose by more than $35 billion. Most of this increase resulted from an inflation-caused increase in tax rates rather than any new tax or spending program.

This new round of orthodox restraint produced the sharpest recession recorded in the United States up to that time. Unemployment rates rose steadily

[10] This section relies heavily on John A. Schnittker, "The 1972–73 Food Price Spiral," *Brookings Papers on Economic Activity* (2/1973): 498–508.

throughout the unhappy year of 1974, peaking in May 1975 at the unprecedented level of 9 percent. Capacity utilization in manufacturing hit 71 percent, the lowest rate since the Korean War.

Expansion, 1975–1980

The period since the recession of 1974–1975 has been one of stop-and-go policy shifts. First, in response to the recession Presidents Ford and Carter used expansionary policy. Taxes were reduced in March 1975, and the money supply was allowed to increase, although not at too rapid a rate. As a result of these stimuli, by the fall of 1975 a recovery was under way. For the next four years the economy was allowed to slowly expand back toward full employment (see Figure 18.1). The idea was to regain full employment without igniting a new round of inflation.

The cautious expansionary policy seemed to be working fairly well until, in 1979, the economy was hit by its second major supply shock, the doubling in the price of oil due to the oil cutoff by Iran. As in 1973, this set off a new burst of inflation and caused confusion among policymakers.

Stringent Contraction, 1980–1982

In 1980 Paul Volcker took over at the Federal Reserve, and the government adopted a policy of stringent contraction. As in all previous uses of orthodox restraint, the economy fell into a recession—a recession that, after an uncomfortable lag, was accompanied by a significant reduction in both inflation and wage demands. What was different about this most recent use of the orthodox inflation medicine was the determination with which it was applied. Despite the highest unemployment rates since the 1930s (an unprecedented 10.4 percent in October 1982) and a recession that lasted longer than any experienced in the postwar period, the Federal Reserve refused to change its policy. It was determined to bring the inflation down to an acceptable level and to break inflationary expectations before it would allow a recovery to occur. While it is still too early to tell with certainty what the final outcome will be, it is clear that there has been a very significant decline in the inflation rate. It is also clear that the cost of this success, in terms of lost output and unemployment, has been enormous. Whether one decides that the gain has been worth the cost depends on how much one dislikes inflation compared to unemployment. But the Reagan-Volcker policy does show one thing for sure: It is possible to bring inflation down if one pursues a restrictive policy long enough.

Lessons from the Long Fight Against Inflation

In the previous section we described in some detail the actual history of the U. S. attempts to control inflation. What lessons can this history teach us about this difficult problem? I draw five main conclusions, each of which will be discussed in turn. First, democracies have a very difficult time adopting any meaningful inflation control program; when they do, they are likely to give up after recessions too short to have much effect on inflation. Second, the U. S. supply curve is relatively flat, as implied by the disequilibrium model. This implies that a really serious orthodox program to fight inflation will cause fairly severe recession. Third, the sequence of events just described makes it exceedingly difficult to decide whether or not wage and price controls are or are not helpful in fighting inflation. Fourth, orthodox anti-inflation policy will slow down the inflation rate if it is maintained long enough, but it will have a high output cost, and finally, for economies with kinked supply curves, an efficient program to control inflation should combine some mild form of incomes policy with what I will call the optimal demand curve.

Fighting Inflation in a Democracy

The evidence suggests very strongly that democracies have great difficulty in adopting meaningful contractionary demand management policies. It is easy to use discretionary policy when expansion is called for, but it is next to impossible to get public acceptance of the need for surtaxes and tight money when there is excess demand. As we saw in the 1960s, it took President Johnson two years to call for a surtax and another year for the surtax to be enacted, despite the fact that inflation was accelerating, unemployment had dropped to 3.2 percent, and the Vietnam War had pushed the economy into an unsustainable boom. Similarly, every attempt by the Fed to choke off inflation has been met by resistance and threats to reduce the Fed's authority and independence. Perhaps the only exception to this behavioral rule was Fed policy during 1980–1982. In this period the Fed maintained its tight money policy regardless of the pressure and regardless of the fact that the fiscal authorities made life much more difficult by simultaneously passing the largest tax cut in our history. Even here, we find it unlikely that the Fed could possibly have maintained its contractionary policy for as long as it did had it been more directly responsible to the electorate. We conclude that if we are ever to fight inflation by orthodox policy, we will have to depend on the monetary rather than the fiscal authorities to do it.

Evidence on the Shape of the Supply Curve

We think that the empirical evidence pretty clearly supports the notion of a relatively flat supply curve. Since 1967 we have been through two complete cycles and are currently completing our third. In each cycle the government forced the economy into recession in the hopes of curing our inflation. But did these recessions cure inflation? Up until 1982, the answer is clearly that they did not. Inflation rates have been very insensitive to recession, at least up to the levels deemed acceptable prior to the Volcker program in 1980–1982.

To see this fact visually, in Figure 18.1 we have plotted the quarterly inflation rate against the rate of capacity utilization in manufacturing. The latter, closely related to Y/Y_{FE}, is a proxy for excess demand in the economy, for it measures the level of output relative to capacity. Because there is a good deal of mothballed capacity in the economy, normal capacity utilization seldom exceeds 85 to 87 percent; 83 to 85 percent is considered approximately normal in the same way that

Figure 18.1
Capacity Utilization and Inflation

This figure shows the U. S. experience in three contractionary cycles since 1967. As indicated in the text, acceleration of inflation in all three cycles occurs at the right-hand side of the figure at high rates of capacity utilization. Note that the acceleration begins at successively lower rates of capacity utilization in each cycle. Furthermore, in each cycle the economy seems to move almost straight west in contraction and straight east in expansion. The only exceptions to this pattern are the two sharp reductions in the inflation rate in the second quarter of 1975 and the first quarter of 1982, both of which were the result of the adaption to higher oil prices by moving to higher price levels but not higher inflation rates. All of this evidence suggests a kinked supply curve, rising at high levels of capacity utilization and relatively flaı at low rates of utilization.

(a) The Contraction 1967:1–1971:2

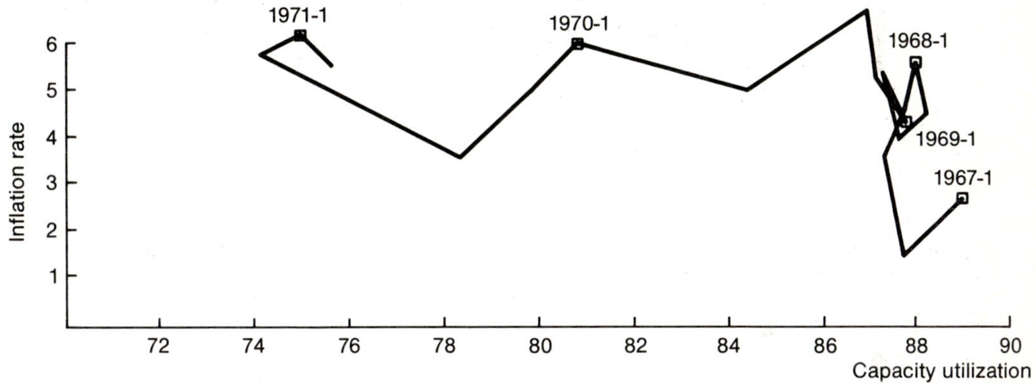

(b) The Supply Shock Cycle 1973:1–1978:1

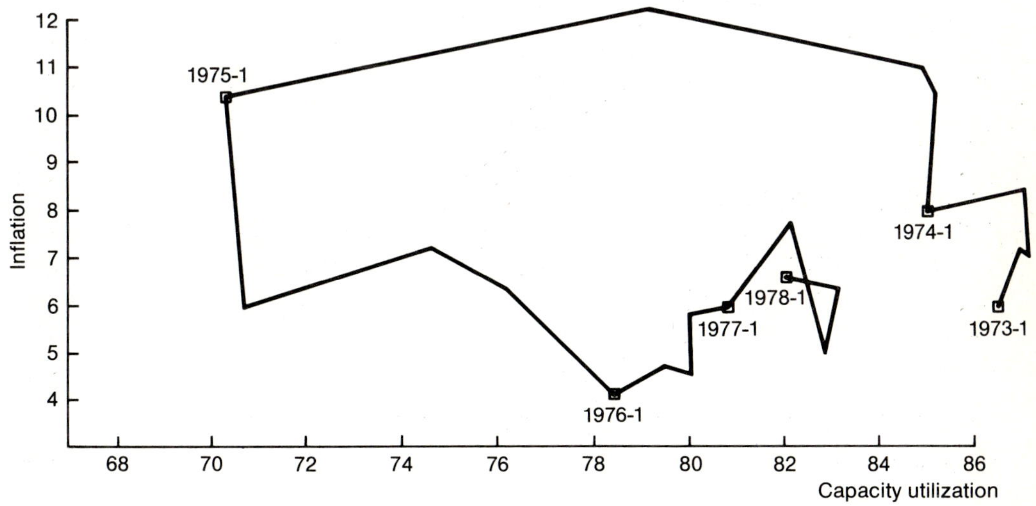

Figure 18.1 *(continued)*
Capacity Utilization and Inflation

(c) An Inflationary Cycle 1975:4–1982:4

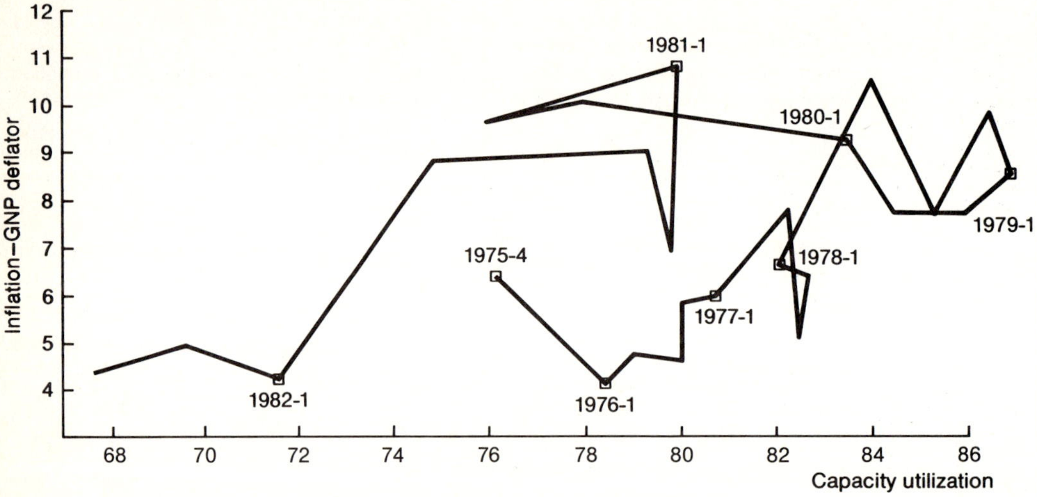

5 to 5.5 percent unemployment is considered to be normal or frictional. We have separated the three stabilization cycles in the diagram, the first at the top of the figure prior to wage and price controls in August 1971, the second after these controls were removed in 1973, and the third after the second oil shock in 1979.

If one follows the dated pathways traced out by the economy in Figure 18.1, it is possible to see exactly the relationship between demand and the inflation rate. In all three cycles, note first the acceleration of inflation that occurs at high rates of capacity utilization in 1967–1969, 1973–1974, and 1978–1980. That strongly suggests that the supply curve is upward sloping at its right-hand end. It also appears that there has been a shift downward in the point at which this acceleration of inflation occurs. In the 1967–1969 episode, inflation accelerated when the economy reached a capacity utilization rate of around 88 percent. In 1973, that point was reached at an 86 percent rate, and in 1978 it occurred when capacity utilization was only 82 to 83 percent. This poses a serious dilemma for policymakers.

The figure also suggests that our supply curve is relatively flat at its left-hand end. If it were upward sloping in that region, we would expect the economy to move southwest in recession and northeast in expansion. But that is not what it did. Rather the economy seems to have moved straight west in contraction and straight east in expansion—just what you would expect if the supply curve were flat. There are two exceptions to this pattern: the sharp reduction in the inflation rate in the second quarter of 1975 and the first quarter of 1982. Both of these cases were the result of the interaction of higher oil prices and restrictive monetary policy. The United States reacted to the two oil shocks with a neutral to contractionary monetary policy. As a result our prices rose, but we did not permit a permanently higher inflation rate. Therefore, once that higher price level was reached, the inflation rate dropped back to a floor of around 5 to 6 percent. As the reader can see, expansion in 1975–1976 did not increase that rate, nor did further contraction in 1982 reduce it.

Other Studies on the Insensitivity of Prices to Demand The apparent insensitivity of wages and prices to demand fluctuations shown in Figure 18.1 has been confirmed in a number of recent studies. Arthur Okun reviewed the implicit relationship between economic slack and the reduction of inflation in a number of such studies. In his words:

They all point to a very costly short-run trade off. For an extra percentage point of unemployment maintained for a year, the estimated reduction in the ultimate inflation rate at equilibrium unemployment ranges between one-sixth and one-half of 1 percentage point, with an average estimate of 0.3. Or to put it another way, the average estimate of the cost of a 1 point reduction in the basic inflation rate is 10 percent of a year's GNP with a range of 6 percent to 18 percent. The extra 3.5 years of unemployment and the sacrifice of $200 billion of output buys, according to these estimates, a reduction of between 0.6 and 1.8 points in the basic inflation rate of the 1980's.[11]

In another study, George Perry found that prices in a large part of the economy are set on the basis of a markup over costs, a markup that is insensitive to the state of demand.[12] Wages do vary with the unemployment rate, but not by very much. As a result, the response of inflation to high rates of unemployment is distressingly small. For example, Perry's results imply that an extra percentage point of unemployment maintained for one year would reduce inflation by about 0.3 percentage points and, even if maintained for three years, would lower inflation only by 0.7 percent.

Otto Eckstein, who has probably studied empirical price behavior as intensively as any economist, confirmed our idea that the U. S. economy supply curve is kinked. As he puts it:

First, in the short-run, the inflation rate does respond to the level of aggregate demand, and does so in a quite non-linear fashion. In particular, when excess demand develops, even if it is only for some sectors of the economy, inflation gets much worse. Second, there are major elements of monopoly in both product and labor markets which slow down the conversion of demand weakness into lower prices. Business prefers price discipline and the resultant shared quantity variations to competitive price-cutting which would let recession produce a higher anti-inflation benefit.[13]

[11] Arthur M. Okun, "Efficient Disinflationary Policies," *American Economic Review* 68 (May 1978): 348.

[12] George L. Perry, "Slowing the Wage-Price Spiral: The Macroeconomic View," *Brookings Papers on Economic Activity* (2/1978): 259–301.

[13] Otto Eckstein, "The Core Inflation Rate and an Analysis of Stagflation," in Allen R. Sanderson, *DRI Readings in Macroeconomics* (New York: McGraw-Hill, 1981), 69.

Eckstein distinguishes demand- and supply-shock inflation from what he calls core inflation, a notion analogous to what we have been calling residual inflation. He defines core inflation as the trend rate of increase in the price of aggregate supply.[14] That trend has been rising steadily since the mid-1960s. Eckstein, using an 800-equation macromodel, simulates alternative ways to bring down the core inflation and concludes that using monetary and fiscal policies alone would require a prolonged and deep depression, with unemployment rates over 10 percent. U. S. experience in 1981–1982 confirms his judgment. He concludes that policies other than demand management are preferable.[15]

Phillip Cagan has confirmed the small direct relationship between capacity variables and the inflation rate.[16] For example, he estimates that the annual inflation rate would be reduced by only 0.37 percentage points per year for each 1 percentage point of slack maintained over an entire business cycle. But, he points out, the total effect of slack could be much greater if it was actually maintained long enough to change price expectations. What has kept the expected inflation so high, according to Cagan, is the tendency of government authorities to use expansionary policy in recession, thus guaranteeing that all recessions are short, and also government's tendency to overshoot the level of full employment during recovery.[17] This observation appears to have been confirmed in the Volcker-Reagan program, though one cannot be sure whether it is the pressure of the unemployed or the reduction in expectations that has reduced the rate of inflation.

There is a good deal of evidence that the degree of wage and price rigidity has increased in the postwar period, which is one reason why postwar recessions seem to have had less effect on the inflation rate than recessions used to fifty years ago. Two separate studies, one by Phillip Cagan and the other by Jeffrey Sachs, measure the changing cyclical flexibility of wages and prices.[18] Both find that in the postwar period, wages and prices show more downward rigidity in recession than they used to. Cagan and Sachs hypothesize that this is due to both the increased duration and the coverage of collective bargaining agreements in the postwar economy and to the belief that macroauthorities will always promptly counteract recession by expansionary policy. Contract duration affects short-term rigidity by lengthening the time it takes for downward adjustments in workers' inflation expectations to get incorporated into wage contracts, while the duration of recessions affects both union willingness to negotiate lower wages and business willingness to lower prices or reduce labor stockpiling.

[14] For a more complete version of Eckstein's work on inflation, see Otto Eckstein, *Core Inflation* (Englewood Cliffs, NJ: Prentice-Hall, 1981). For a definition of core inflation see p. 7.

[15] Ibid., pp. 3–4.

[16] Phillip Cagan, *Persistent Inflation: Historical and Policy Essays* (New York: Columbia University Press, 1979), chapter 9.

[17] Ibid., pp. 247–248.

[18] Ibid., chapter 3; Jeffrey Sachs, "The Changing Cyclical Behavior of Wages and Prices: 1890–1976," *American Economic Review* 70 (March 1980): 78–91.

Robert Gordon has also studied the changing responsiveness issue, but he comes to different conclusions than Sachs and Cagan.[19] He does not find an increase in price rigidity in the postwar period. But he does find that almost one-half of the total price response to economic slack is now lagged by at least a year or more. Thus, prices look more rigid in the short run. He hypothesizes that this is probably due to the increase in multiyear labor contracts in the postwar economy. If Gordon is right, the greater apparent inflexibility of prices in recent years is only a short-run phenomenon.

The Effectiveness of Wage-Price Controls

The historical evidence suggests substantial wage and price rigidity, which implies that orthodox inflation fighting is costly in terms of unemployment. What about the other antiinflation medicine, wage and price controls? What sort of success did they have when they were applied between 1971 and 1974? That is a very difficult question to answer, because so many things were changing at the same time; thus, it is hard to identify the separate effects of the controls program. The fact that controls were established after two years of orthodox restraint further complicates the matter. If the rate of inflation went down during the control period, that could be nothing more than the lagged effect of the preceding policy.

Most econometric attempts to quantify the effect of wage and price controls on inflation imply that they had a modest and temporary effect. For example, Jon Frye and Robert Gordon built an econometric model of prices and used it to predict what prices would have been in the absence of controls if all variables, such as the money supply, had been set at their historic levels.[20] Their results show that the compulsory control program in 1971–1972 lowered the inflation rate about 1.3 percent relative to what it would have been, but the removal of controls in 1974 allowed inflation to be about 1.6 percent higher than it would have been predicted to be on the basis of the other explanatory variables in the model. Their conclusion is that controls had, at most, a temporary effect that was soon dissipated by rising inflation in the post-control period.[21]

I find such econometric demonstrations somewhat unconvincing. In 1973, four things happened together: Inflation accelerated, the United States switched from compulsory to voluntary controls, the economy operated at a high rate of capacity utilization, and there were severe supply shocks. It is very difficult to sort

[19] Robert J. Gordon, "Output Fluctuations and Gradual Price Adjustment," *Journal of Economic Literature* 19 (June 1981): 493–530.

[20] Jon Frye and Robert J. Gordon, "Government Intervention in the Inflation Process: The Econometrics of 'Self-Inflicted Wounds,'" *American Economic Review* 71 (May 1981): 288–294.

[21] Frye and Gordon's pessimistic assessment of the long-run effectiveness of controls is echoed by other studies. See in particular Edgar Feige and Douglas Pearce, "Inflation and Incomes Policy: An Application of Time Series Models," in Karl Brunner and Alan H. Meltzer, eds., *Economics of Wage and Price Controls*, supplement to *Journal of Monetary Economics* 2 (1976): 273–302.

Table 18.2
Sectoral and Aggregate Inflation Rates During and After Controls

(a) Aggregate Price Indices

		CPI	GDP
1971	II	4.8%	4.4%
	III	4.4	3.0
	IV	1.6	1.5
1972	I	4.0	5.1
	II	2.9	1.8
	III	3.2	3.2
	IV	3.9	4.0
1973	I	5.5	5.5
	II	9.3	7.2
	III	11.4	7.4
	IV	7.9	8.8
1974	I	11.8	9.8
	II	11.8	10.0
	III	12.7	12.5
	IV	12.3	13.4

(b) Sectoral Price Indices

	Components of WPI				Components of CPI	
			Final Goods			
	Farm Products + Processed Feed	Crude Materials	Producers Finished Goods	Consumer (Excluding Food)	All Items	All Items Less Food
December 1972	132.6	136.8	120.3	114.6	127.3	127.6
March 1973	149.0	142.5	121.7	116.6	129.8	128.4
June 1973	163.6	152.8	123.4	118.4	132.4	130.3
September 1973	173.5	161.0	124.2	119.0	135.5	131.8
December 1973	168.0	179.8	126.7	123.1	138.5	134.8
Inflation rate in 1973	26.7%	31.4%	5.3%	7.4%	8.8%	5.0%

Note: In (a), the inflation rate is annualized rate over the quarter.

out econometrically how much of the rise in inflation was due to each one of the latter three factors. To get more perspective on the issue, it is useful to take a closer look at the historical record.

In sorting out these questions, the timing and sectoral nature of price increases is crucial. Recall that the compulsory program lasted from August 1971 until January 1973. During 1972 the inflation rate fell to 3.5 percent, while the economy simultaneously moved rapidly towards full employment. Subsequently, after the changeover to a voluntary control system, the inflation rate exploded. But, as we just indicated, and as one can see from Table 18.2, price increases were sector specific. They were caused by shortages in particular commodities markets, particularly food and raw materials for industry.[22] They were not the result of lifting controls; the problems were in supply. Crop failures, a commodities boom, excess aggregate demand, and a large devaluation in March 1973 all combined to cause a resurgence of inflationary pressure. We think that the evidence supports the conclusion of a recent study by Bosworth and Vroman that the rise in inflation during 1973 and 1974 was not the delayed effect of the lifting of controls—rather, it resulted from independent supply shocks and excess demand unrelated to the controls program.[23]

A subtler criticism of the controls program is that it encouraged the authorities to adopt too expansionary a policy in 1972–1973. There is some merit in this position. Clearly the economy was expanded too rapidly in 1972, and this exacerbated the effects of supply shocks on the price index in 1973 and 1974. However, remarks by economic policymakers of the time suggest that the overexpansion in 1972–1973 was not the result of underestimating the danger of inflation—rather, it was a failure to realize just how fast the economy was expanding in that period. The models of the time underestimated the responsiveness of private demand and overestimated full employment output.[24] Government economists thought there was more slack in the economy than there was, and they were criticized for not being sufficiently expansionist.

Whether or not there was a connection between controls and excessive expansion in 1972, the point is clear that controls should never be thought of as a substitute for conservative fiscal and monetary policies. They are a complementary weapon, to be used *after* orthodox stabilization has pushed the economy down to the flat part of the supply curve. With the advantage of hindsight, we can see that the Nixon administration erred in pushing the economy too far toward full employment. But one should not blame all controls programs just because in this one case excess expansion on the demand side, coupled with severe supply interruptions, caused an outbreak of inflation after the controls program was lifted.

The Costs and Benefits of the Orthodox Anti-Inflation Program

Those who believe either that short-run supply curves are upward sloping or that downward wage and price rigidity is a temporary result of people's skepticism about the government's determination to control inflation think that a firm policy of demand restraint carried on long enough will successfully control inflation. Our experience since 1980 shows that they are right. One can reduce inflation if one is

[22] This point is emphasized in John A. Schnittker, "The 1972–73 Food Price Spiral," loc. cit. See also Marvin H. Kosters, "Controls and Inflation," in Joel Popkin, ed., *Analysis of Inflation: 1965-1974* (Cambridge, Mass.: National Bureau of Economic Research, 1977), 121–189.

[23] Barry Bosworth and Wayne Vroman, "An Appraisal of the Wage-Price Control Program," in Joel Popkin, ed., op. cit., pp. 67–112.

[24] See the quotations by Herbert Stein in Samuel A. Morley, "The CEA and Macroeconomic Policymaking in the U. S.," Vanderbilt Institute of Public Policy Studies working paper (February 1980), 21.

willing to carry out a contractionary policy consistently and for a long enough period of time. No one, however, should be deceived into thinking that progress comes quickly or at low cost. Over the period 1980–1982 the U. S. inflation rate was brought down about five percentage points. The cost in terms of lost output was over $300 billion.

A Program for Efficient Inflation Control in Economies with Kinked Supply Curves

Those who think that our economy has a kinked supply curve believe that the orthodox way of fighting inflation is simply too costly. They think that there is a more efficient way. They argue that demand management is a necessary but inadequate tool for controlling inflation. The government must eliminate excess demand by restrictive monetary and fiscal policies, but it should not try to eliminate inflation by going further. For if the economy has a relatively flat short-run supply curve (beyond the kink), the cost of orthodox stabilization is too high.

The Optimal Demand Curve If the supply curve does have a kink, the goal of policymakers should be to make the demand curve intersect supply as close to the kink as possible. This is what we shall call the optimal demand curve. In Figure 18.2 the **optimal demand curve** is one which intersects the full equilibrium aggregate supply curve in region a. This will yield all the inflation abatement possible from demand management alone. In region c, the economy will be subject to accelerating inflation; in region b, there will be a very costly recession (costly in the sense that output will be lost without producing much reduction in inflation rates). We do not know exactly the limits of region a, clearly an area for future research. But they undoubtedly lie somewhere in the range of 98 to 101 percent for Y/Y_{FE}, 82 to 85 percent for manufacturing capacity utilization, and 5.5 to 6 percent for unemployment. Those are pretty broad targets for government authorities to shoot at.

The sort of demand management we are advocating here will not eliminate what one might call the residual or core inflation left over from previous supply shocks and periods of excess demand. It will eliminate excess demand as a source of further inflation, but it will do next to nothing to reduce the inflationary expectations, which are the root cause of residual inflation. If we are not satisfied with that level of residual inflation, what can we do? Economists know of only two possibilities: restrictive monetary and fiscal policies or some form of wage and/or price controls. The economists who believe that the short-run supply curve is upward sloping, or who do not believe in the efficacy of wage and price controls, will argue for a continuation of the orthodox program, even if it means a fairly long recession. Those who believe the supply curve is relatively flat out to the acceptable limits of unemployment will argue for some sort of incomes policy.[25] Incomes policies are drastic medicine, but many think that inflation is a drastic disease, too.

[25] For an eloquent statement of this point of view see James Tobin, "Stabilization Policy Ten Years After," *Brookings Papers on Economic Activity* (1/1980): 19–71.

Figure 18.2
The Optimal Demand Curve

Government authorities should try to manage monetary and fiscal policy so as to keep the aggregate demand curve in region a. In region c there will be accelerating inflation and in region b there will be recession, which will do little to moderate the residual or base inflation.

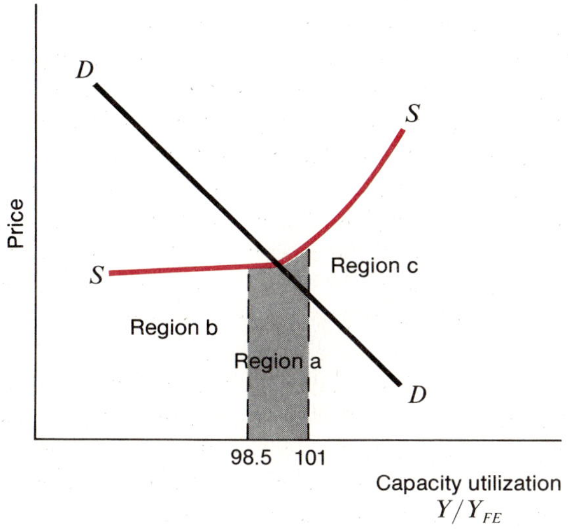

Of the three interventions that we discussed, some sort of TIPS program is the least drastic and should probably be tried first. TIPS requires no large bureaucracy and allows prices and wages to be set in the marketplace. The scheme insures only that the public's interest in wage restraint will be transmitted to wage-setters by tax penalties and incentives.

Other Measures to Control Inflation A number of other measures have been proposed by economists, most of which are intended to shift the supply curve downward and to the right. It is well known that the government itself is a major source of cost pressure in the economy. Sales and payroll taxes directly raise costs. Arthur Okun has proposed that they be partially replaced by income taxes as a way of lowering the supply curve.[26] Government regulations, import quotas, tariffs, and farm price supports also tend to raise prices. The government could lower inflation fairly costlessly if it redesigned such programs. Finally, in the long run, another way to lower the inflation rate is to increase worker productivity. That will allow a higher rate of growth of real output and a correspondingly lower

[26] Arthur M. Okun, in "The Great Stagflation Swamp," *Challenge* 20 (November-December 1977): 6–13 and Arthur M. Okun, "Efficient Disinflationary Policies," *American Economic Review* 68 (May 1978): 348–352.

rate of growth of prices for a given rate of increase in nominal income. Increasing productivity requires that we devote a greater share of our resources to capital formation. Thus, proponents of this method of increasing supply favor investment tax credits, accelerated depreciation, and lower taxes on capital gains.[27] We shall explore these supply-side questions more thoroughly in Chapter 20.

Summary

There are three ways to deal with the problem of inflation: restrictive monetary and fiscal policies, some form of wage and price controls, and indexing. The last is more a way to adapt to inflation than a way of controlling it. The first, or orthodox, remedy causes a recession in the short run, but it should also drive down inflationary expectations and wage demands, thus leading to a lower rate of inflation in the longer run. The only question is how long the process takes and how severe the recession has to be. Disequilibrium economists expect the adjustment period to be long and severe, because they think the short-run supply curve is quite flat, while the followers of Friedman expect the adjustment to lower inflation rates to be fairly rapid. An examination of the record of the U. S. economy in three antiinflationary recessions since 1967 suggests a fairly flat supply curve at low levels of output. This means that we have had to pay a good deal in lost output and employment for fairly modest progress in lower inflation.

We argued that if the short-run supply curve is indeed kinked at some particular level of output, the goal of demand management ought to be to keep aggregate demand close to the kink in the curve. That is likely to achieve the optimal amount of inflation control at the lowest cost in terms of lost output and employment. If one wishes to make further progress on inflation, some kind of incomes policy, such as a TIPS program, should be used.

The other remedy for inflation is wage and price controls. The most recent U. S. experience with such a system was the Nixon controls program between 1971 and 1974. It was far more elaborate than the TIPS program. How effective were the Nixon controls? The record shows some early moderation of inflation, but that gave way after 1973 to a combination of excess demand, supply shocks, and inflation, all of which had been repressed during the period of compulsory controls. While there is some disagreement among economists about the effectiveness of the controls program due to the difficulty of disentangling the various factors that caused prices to rise so rapidly after 1973, most believe that the controls had only a small and temporary effect on the inflation rate.

[27] Otto Eckstein estimates that a combination of accelerated depreciation and investment tax credits costing about $16 billion per year would, in five years, boost fixed investment by 9.8 percent, raise real wages by 0.9 percent, and reduce the core inflation rate by 1.0 percent. That is a far lower cost than would be required to make an equivalent reduction through orthodox stabilization. See Otto Eckstein, *Core Inflation*, pp. 4–5.

Key Concepts

indexing
wage and price controls
tax incentives for price stability (TIPS)
optimal demand curve
orthodox antiinflation program

Problems and Questions for Discussion

1. Compare the process by which orthodox antiinflationary policy reduces the inflation rate in the partial equilibrium and the disequilibrium economy. Pay particular attention to the roles of unemployment and expectations in the determination of wages and prices during the process.

2. Why is a recession almost invariably required to bring down the inflation rate?

3. Are cost-of-living clauses inflationary? If so, why? If not, why not?

4. Indexing has been described as a way of adjusting the economic system so that it is easier to live with inflation. Yet Milton Friedman has argued that indexing should also make it easier to reduce the inflation rate. Can you think what his argument might be? (Hint: What should be the shape of the aggregate supply curve in the indexed economy?)

5. Suppose that you were going to institute a system of price controls. Would you allow any price increases? Would you make exceptions for firms that are increasing output? How would you decide the right price for each industry?

6. Wage and price controls have clearly been effective in the United States, because the rate of inflation fell after they were imposed and rose after they were removed. Discuss.

7. Suppose that a government decides to institute some type of incomes policy. What complementary monetary and fiscal policies should the government choose to go along with the incomes policy?

8. Does the fact that the inflation rate fell substantially during 1982 invalidate the claim of the disequilibrium model that the short-run aggregate supply curve is quite flat at less than full employment? If not, what might explain the reduction in the inflation rate?

9. Using the latest quarterly data on GNP and the GNP deflator, prepare an updated version of Figure 18.1 for the period since 1980. Can you think of a sequence of shifts of the short-run supply and demand curves that will explain the observed time paths of inflation and output? Does the experience confirm or contradict either or both of our basic short-run models?

PART SIX

EXTENSIONS

Chapter 19

Productivity and Economic Growth

Up to this point we have been concerned exclusively with the factors accounting for the fluctuations of income around its capacity level. We now turn to the perhaps more important and fundamental question: What determines the level and growth rate of capacity itself? Because we are all myopic, it is easy to become overly concerned with the short-run problems of recession and inflation. But in the long run, the success or failure of our economy is more likely to be measured by its ability to generate sustained increases in per capita income over long periods of time than by its avoidance of either recession or inflation.

Our recent macroeconomic record is not very encouraging. The growth rate of per capita income has declined dramatically since 1973, due to a corresponding decline in labor productivity. The wage-productivity problem is a particular example of a more general question: What are the long-run determinants of economic growth? To answer this question, we first develop a theoretical framework within which to examine the sources of economic growth and the causes for the productivity slowdown of recent years. Next, we derive a simple model of the growth process based on the growth of the capital stock. With this model we examine the effect of changes in the saving rate on levels and growth rates of output and consumption per capita. We conclude the chapter with a discussion of the question of whether or not the United States saves too little and whether deficient capital formation is, in fact, the main cause of our recent productivity slowdown.

Sources of Economic Growth

We cannot begin this discussion without a glimpse at our record of per capita income growth since the beginning of this century (see Figure 19.1). From this perspective, the record of the U. S. economy is remarkable. From 1900 to 1982, real income grew eighteen-fold, from $75 billion to over $1400 billion, a growth rate

Figure 19.1
The Growth of Actual and Capacity GNP (1900–1982)

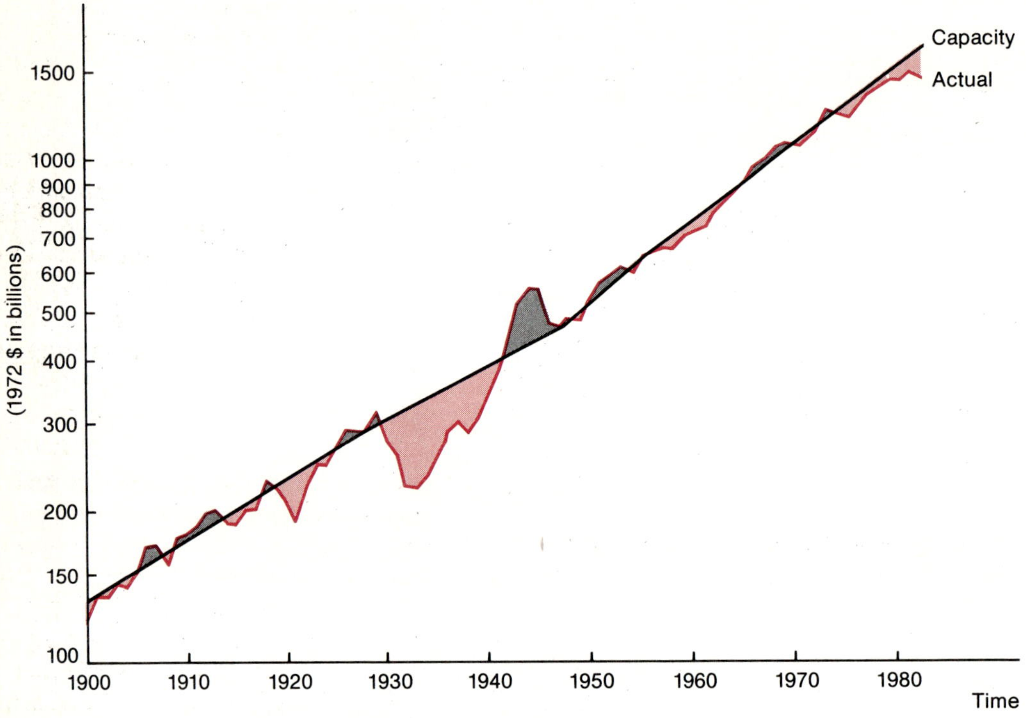

of about 3.3 percent per year. Per capita real income increased more than five times over the same period.

What factors explain this record? In particular, how important are the contributions of capital accumulation, labor force growth, and productivity to our long-run growth performance? If we can answer this question, we can perhaps answer another important, related question: Why has labor productivity slowed down so markedly since the late 1960s?

The Labor Productivity Problem

One of the worrisome features of our recent macroeconomic performance is a significant reduction in the growth rate of **labor productivity.** Whereas national income per employed worker grew at about 2.1 percent per year between 1948 and 1973, between 1973 and 1978 it grew only 0.1 percent per year. This is a striking change, and it has some rather pessimistic implications if it continues. First of all, it means that real wages can no longer increase at the rapid rates of the past, for, as we have learned, real wages are determined by labor productivity. Second, stagnant productivity makes any attempt to control inflation much more difficult.

What explains our reduced growth rate of productivity? Is capital accumulation lower than it was in the past? Have American workers gone soft? How important as contributing factors are government safety regulations, pollution control requirements, and other regulations? To get some perspective on these questions we now develop a theoretical framework for determining the sources of economic growth.

Contributions of Technology, Capital, and Labor to Economic Growth

To derive a theory of economic growth, we shall proceed in two steps. The first is essentially accounting. Starting with the production function that we developed in our theory of aggregate supply, we decompose the sources of growth into components resulting from the growth of labor, from capital, and from technical change. To convert this into a theory of growth in output/capita, we then develop an economic explanation for the growth rate of capital per worker.

Recall from Chapter 6 the aggregage production function, re-presented here:

(19.1) $$Y = f(N, K).$$

In our work up to now we have assumed that the capital stock is constant. We now analyze the effects of the growth of both labor and capital on output. In this analysis, we are concerned with the long run as opposed to the cyclical variation of income around its capacity level. Thus the labor input which we now write as N_t should be understood as the full-employment labor supply at time period t. At any point in time, N_t is a constant. In the long-run time frame we are now considering, N_t will be growing.

At any point, technology is given. Therefore, we may write the production function as we did in Equation (19.1). However, if there are technical changes occurring over time, it will probably be the case that an economy can get more output from a given amount of labor and capital inputs. Thus, the production function in Equation (19.1) ought to have a time subscript. One particularly simple way to write this dependence on time is as follows:

(19.2) $$Y_t = A_t f(N_t, K_t).$$

Equation (19.2) says that capacity at time t depends on the normal labor force and capital stock at time t and on a shift variable, A. A_t is a variable that represents technology at time t. If A increases, the economy gets more output from a given amount of capital and labor. Economists have called this sort of growth in A **disembodied technical change,** since it implies that there will be an increase in output irrespective of any change in factor inputs. A picture of the production function and of the influence of a change in A can be found in Figure 19.2.

It may well be the case that a good deal of what we put into A is actually a result of changes in the other inputs. For example, if there are changes in the skill level of the labor force or if inventions make the capital stock more productive, these improvements will not be realized unless the new capital is actually built or the more skilled workers enter the labor force. In other words, the improvements that we measure as changes in A probably are not as independent of growth in the

Figure 19.2
The Production Function

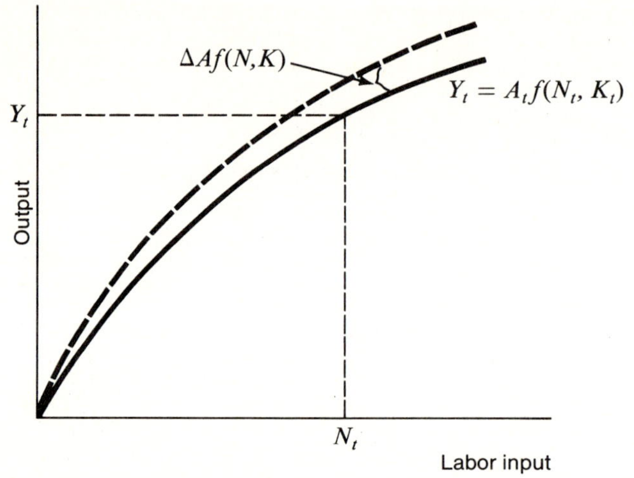

other factors as Equation (19.2) implies. Nonetheless, Equation (19.2) provides a good starting point for our classification of the sources of income growth.

First, let us split up the growth of output into three possible sources: technical change and growth in the two factor inputs, capital and labor. We have already defined the marginal product of labor as the change in output per change in labor input ($\Delta Y/\Delta N$). Let us define the marginal product of capital, MPK, in a way exactly parallel to $\Delta Y/\Delta K$. Using these definitions, the effect of an increase in labor, ΔN, on output is $(MPL)\Delta N$, and the effect of an increase in capital is $(MPK)\Delta K$. The pure effect of technical change is measured by a change in A. Looking at the production function in Figure 19.2, one can see that the change in production resulting from a change in A is $\Delta Af(N,K)$. Now we add these three sources of output growth together to get a complete classification of the possible sources of growth in capacity output:

(19.3)
$$\Delta Y = \underbrace{\Delta Af(N, K)}_{\text{Technical change}} + \underbrace{(MPK)\Delta K}_{\text{Capital contribution}} + \underbrace{(MPL)\Delta N}_{\text{Labor contribution}}.$$

Equation (19.3) could be used directly to examine the sources of growth. However, it is useful to make a simple transformation of the equation to express output growth in terms of variables that are easier to observe and measure than those in Equation (19.3). To do this, we divide both sides of the equation by Y to convert the expression from absolute to percentage output growth. Thus:

(19.4)
$$\frac{\Delta Y}{Y} = \frac{\Delta A f(N, K)}{Y} + \frac{(MPK)\Delta K}{Y} + \frac{(MPL)\Delta N}{Y}.$$

We now rewrite the three terms on the right-hand side of the equation to express the contributions of the three sources:

$$\frac{\Delta A f(N, K)}{Y} = \frac{\Delta A f(N, K)}{A f(N, K)} = \frac{\Delta A}{A}.$$

$$\frac{MPK\,\Delta K}{Y} = \frac{(MPK)K}{Y}\cdot\frac{\Delta K}{K} = \frac{Z\Delta K}{K}.$$

$$\frac{(MPL)\Delta N}{Y} = \frac{(MPL)N}{Y}\cdot\frac{\Delta N}{N} = \frac{(1 - Z)\Delta N}{N}.$$

A word about the last two transformations. If we multiply and divide the capital equation by K, we get an expression that has a ready economic interpretation. If capital earns its marginal product, then $(MPK)K$ is the gross profits earned by capital, and $(MPK)K/Y$, which we are calling Z, is the share of profits in national income. Thus, the contribution of capital to growth is the growth rate of capital weighted by its share in output. Following the same logic, the contribution of labor is its growth rate times its share in income.

If we now combine all of these results, we have:

(19.5)
$$\frac{\Delta Y}{Y} = \underbrace{\frac{\Delta A}{A}}_{\text{Technical change}} + \underbrace{\frac{Z\,\Delta K}{K}}_{\text{Capital contribution}} + \underbrace{\frac{(1 - Z)\Delta N}{N}}_{\text{Labor contribution}}.$$

Equation (19.5) says that the growth in capacity output is the sum of pure technical change plus the growth of capital and labor, each weighted by its share in national income.

Let us see how Equation (19.5) might work in practice. Suppose that capital's share in income is about 0.35, as it is in the United States, that capital and labor grow at 4 percent and 1.5 percent, respectively, and that the rate of growth of technical change is 1 percent per year. Then, the growth of output will be:

$$\frac{\Delta Y}{Y} = 1\% + 0.35\ (4\%) + 0.65\ (1.5\%)$$
$$= 1\% + 1.4\% + 0.975\%$$
$$= 3.37\%.$$

The sources of growth in percentage terms will be:

	Absolute Contribution	**Percentage Contribution**
Technical Change	1.00%	0.30
Capital	1.40	0.41
Labor	.97	0.29
	3.37%	1.00

Before proceeding to an examination of the sources of growth in the United States, it is useful to express Equation (19.5) in terms of output per worker, Y/N, which we shall write as y. For many purposes y is a more significant variable than Y itself. Output per worker is what most people mean when they talk about productivity. It is the ratio that determines living standards in a country and is the number that has stopped growing in recent years.

By definition, the rate of growth of output per worker, which we shall write as $\Delta y/y$, is equal to the difference between the rate of growth of output and the rate of growth of labor. Thus:

(19.6) $$\frac{\Delta y}{y} = \frac{\Delta Y}{Y} - \frac{\Delta N}{N}.$$

Substituting Equation (19.6) into Equation (19.5) we get:

(19.7) $$\frac{\Delta y}{y} = \frac{\Delta A}{A} + \frac{Z\Delta K}{K} + \frac{(1-Z)\Delta N}{N} - \frac{\Delta N}{N}.$$

(19.8) $$\frac{\Delta y}{y} = \frac{\Delta A}{A} + Z\left(\frac{\Delta K}{K} - \frac{\Delta N}{N}\right).$$

(19.9) $$\frac{\Delta y}{y} = \frac{\Delta A}{A} + \frac{Z\Delta k}{k}.$$

To get Equation (19.9), note that $(\Delta K/K) - (\Delta N/N)$ is the rate of growth of capital per worker, which we will write as $\Delta k/k$. Equation (19.9) has the very simple interpretation that the rate of growth of labor productivity is equal to the rate of growth of pure productivity plus the rate of growth of the capital-labor ratio, weighted by the share of profits in national income. The great advantage of Equation (19.9) is that it tells us to look for productivity growth from two basic sources: growth in capital per worker and pure technical progress.

In our example we found that output grew at 3.37percent when the labor force was growing at 1.5 percent. Thus, per capita income was growing at 1.87 percent. Let us see how this can be calculated according to Equation (19.9). By substitution:

$$\frac{\Delta y}{y} = 1\% + 0.35\ (4\% - 1.5\%)$$
$$= 1.87\%.$$

In this example, just a bit over one-half of the growth rate in per capita income comes from pure technical change, the rest from the growth rate in the capital-labor ratio.

Case Study

Sources of Economic Growth in the United States

The present high levels of income and living standards in the United States are based on sustained increases in production that have been going on for over two centuries. With our accounting framework, we can examine this growth record more closely to see what have been the main sources of growth. When we do that, several important facts stand out. First, there has been a striking increase in the contribution of technical change to growth in the period since World War II. Second, this source of growth has fallen dramatically since 1973. Third, there has been a large change in the relative growth rates of capital and labor since the late 1960s. The coming to age of the baby-boom generation and the increased participation of women in the labor force have raised the rate of growth of labor and halved the growth in the capital-labor ratio. The result of both of these trends has been a sharp decline in the rate of growth of labor productivity. In effect, we have maintained the growth rate of total income in recent years only by increasing the growth of labor inputs.

We now look more closely at the data underlying this broad description. Table (19.1), drawn from the work of Edward Denison, allows a decomposition of the sources of growth as indicated in Equation (19.5).[1] Both before and after 1948, about 40 percent of the increase in national income was a result of the growth in output per unit of input, which is what we called pure technical change and denoted by $\Delta A/A$ in Equation (19.5). That means that almost one-half of the growth in national income is not accounted for by the growth in conventional inputs. Denison estimates three sources of improved productivity. The first is changes in the production structure, which move people from low average productivity sectors to high, thus improving the overall allocation of resources in the economy. The main such structural change in the U. S. economy has been the transfer of labor from agriculture to industry and services. The second component of A is economies of scale. Increasing the scale of production as our economy has grown has allowed producers to take advantage of cost saving due to specialization and size. Finally, advances in knowledge resulting from our substantial investments in research and development have played an increasingly important role in raising output in the postwar period.

Because of its high weight in national income, labor growth is the most important single cause of increases in national income. Since Denison's measure of labor is people and not hours, he has to make a negative correction in his calculations for the reduction in average hours worked since 1929. A second negative factor is the change in the composition of the labor force. In the period since 1948, as the baby-boom generation has grown to maturity and entered the labor force, the composition of the labor force has changed. The proportion of young workers with low average salaries has increased, which has tended to drag down the average productivity of the entire labor force. The same thing has resulted from the

[1] Edward F. Denison, *Accounting for Slower Growth: The United States in the 1970's* (Washington, D. C.: The Brookings Institution, 1979), 104.

Table 19.1
Sources of Economic Growth in Total Actual National Income

	Annual Growth Rate		Percentage Contribution	
	1929–1948	1948–1973	1929–1948	1948–1973
National Income	2.49%	3.65%	100	100
Total Factor Input	1.52	2.13	61	58
Labor ($[1 - Z][\Delta N/N]$)	1.42	1.42	57	39
Employment	1.01	1.22		
Change in hours worked	−0.22	−0.24		
Age-sex composition	0.01	−0.14		
Education	0.38	0.41		
Miscellaneous	0.24	0.17		
Capital ($[Z][\Delta K/K]$)	0.10	0.71	4	19
Output per Unit of Input ($\Delta A/A$)	0.97	1.52	39	42
Advances in knowledge and miscellaneous determinants	0.46	1.10	18	30
Improved resource allocation	0.28	0.29	11	8
Pollution abatement and safety	0.00	−0.04	—	−1
Economies of scale	0.21	0.32	8	9
Other	0.02	−0.15	1	−4

Source: Edward F. Denison, *Accounting for Slower Growth: The United States in the 1970's* (Washington, D. C.: The Brookings Institution, 1979), Table (8–1), p. 104.

increasing participation of women, because their average wage rates tend to be lower than males'. These two negative components are just about offset by the improved productivity resulting from the educational upgrading of the labor force that has also been occurring.

The final source of growth is the capital stock. Capital has had a relatively small direct impact on the growth of national income. This was particularly true in the 1929–1948 period, because the growth rate of capital was so low during the depression and World War II. To some extent the apparent unimportance of capital is a statistical artifact. Recall that we calculate the contribution of capital by multiplying the growth rate of the capital stock by the share of capital in national income; the latter is around 20 percent in Denison's calculations. Recall further that the reason we use the capital share is because of our assumption that capital is actually paid its marginal product. However, if capital gets less than that, Denison's estimates will underestimate the true contribution of capital.

Another reason why the contribution of capital might well be larger than appears in the table is that Denison assumes that all of the advances in knowledge would have occurred even without investment. Many economists believe that a good many of the so-called advances in knowledge come embedded in new machinery and that therefore they are not usable until the new machinery is put in place. New computers may be more productive than old ones, but we won't get the

Table 19.2
Labor Productivity Growth
(Percent Change per Year)[a]

	1948–1965	1965–1973	1973–1979	1978 IV–1979 IV	1979 III–1980 III
Private Business	3.2	2.4	0.8	−0.9	−0.1
Nonfarm Business	2.6	2.2	0.6	−1.1	0.1

[a] Data refer to output per hour for all persons.
Source: *Economic Report of the President* (Washington, D. C., 1982).

benefit of that extra productivity until we acquire the new machines. Unless the price of new machines fully reflects their productivity advantage over old machines, a good deal of the contribution that capital makes to growth will end up in our measure as an increase in A.

Why Has Productivity Slowed Down?

A very important feature of the period since 1965 has been a sharp slowdown in the rate of growth of labor productivity, shown in Table 19.2. Whereas in the years immediately after World War II output per hour grew at over 3 percent per year, this growth rate fell to 2.4 percent between 1965 and 1973, then fell to less than 1 percent between 1973 and 1978. Even more worrisome, since 1978 labor productivity has been essentially constant. This is an unprecedented and exceedingly unfortunate situation, because growth in labor productivity is so critically important to insuring growth in future per capita income.

Despite the importance of the declining productivity trend, no one is entirely sure what its cause is and therefore what we as a nation should do about it. Equation (19.9) tells us that declining productivity growth stems from two causes: reduced growth in A and reductions in the rate of growth of the capital-labor ratio. Both have occurred since 1965.

The Capital-Labor Ratio The fall in the growth rate of the capital-labor ratio is not, despite many statements to the contrary, due to a decline in investment in the United States. Rather, it is a result of the big increase in the labor force that has been occurring as the postwar baby-boom generation and an increasing number of women have gone to work. Consider Table 19.3. The first column is the ratio of net business investment to real GNP. It shows clearly that we as a nation have actually increased the share of our national income that we devote to investment. Yet, because the labor force has been growing by more than 2 percent per year since 1974, and because the depreciation rate has apparently increased, this new investment has been sufficient to only approximately maintain the capital-labor ratio rather than allow it to increase by 3 percent per year, as was the case prior to 1974.

Table 19.3
Growth Rates of Capital and Labor

		Percent Change, Average Annual Rate (End of Year to End of Year)				
Period	Real Business Fixed Investment as Percent of Real GNP[a]	Net Capital Stock (Nonresidential)[b]	Employment[c]	Hours[c]	Capital-Employment Ratio	Capital-Hours Ratio
1949–1959	9.1	4.0	1.1	0.7	2.9	3.2
1959–1969	9.8	4.6	1.6	1.2	3.0	3.3
1969–1974	10.5	4.2	1.2	0.5	2.9	3.7
1974–1979	10.3	3.0	3.1	2.8	−0.1	0.2

[a] Average annual investment-GNP ratio, in percent.
[b] Net fixed nonresidential business capital, 1972 dollars, end of year.
[c] For private business, all persons. End of year calculated as average of year's fourth quarter and following year's first quarter.
Sources: Department of Commerce, Bureau of Economic Analysis; Department of Labor, Bureau of Labor Statistics.

Table 19.4
Estimated Sources of Growth of Labor Productivity
(Average Annual Growth Rates)

	1948–1966	1966–1973	1973–1978	1973–1978 (Less 1948–1966)	1980–1990 (Predicted)
Real Product/Unit of Labor	3.5	2.1	1.1	−2.4	2.1
Sources of Growth					
Growth in k	0.7	0.5	0.3	−0.4	0.5
Growth in A	2.8	1.6	0.8	−2.0	1.6
Advances in knowledge	1.4	1.1	0.8	−0.6	0.9
Changes in labor quality	0.6	0.4	0.7	0.1	1.0
Education	0.6	0.7	0.8	0.2	0.8
Health	0.1	0.1	0.1	—	0.1
Age/sex composition	−0.1	−0.4	−0.2	−0.1	0.1
Resource reallocation	0.8	0.7	0.3	−0.5	0.3
Volume changes	0.4	0.2	−0.1	−0.5	0.4
Regulation	−0.1	−0.2	−0.4	−0.3	−0.2
Miscellaneous	−0.3	−0.5	−0.3	—	−0.5

Source: John W. Kendrick, "Productivity Trends and the Recent Slowdown: Historical Perspectives, Causal Factors and Policy Options," in William Fellner, ed., *Contemporary Economic Problems* (Washington, D. C.: American Enterprise Institute, 1979): 33–34.

We may infer that the depreciation rate has increased by noting that even though the investment ratio has increased, the growth of the net capital stock has declined. That is because more of our gross investment is now being used for replacement. There are some who argue that using net capital in the capital-labor ratio overstates the loss in efficiency of old capital, and therefore that the fall in the growth rate of k in Table 19.3 is somewhat overstated.[2] However, there is no doubt that there has been a sharp slowdown in that growth rate.

Empirical Estimates Several economists have made an attempt to account for the slowdown in productivity growth. One such estimate is shown in Table 19.4.[3] This table is not directly comparable to Table 19.1 because of differences in the definition of capital and labor and differences in endpoints. However, because of internal consistency, it can be used to see why there has been a fall of 2.4 percent in the rate of growth of labor productivity.

Consider the fourth column of the table. As the reader can see, the fall in the growth rate of K/N, large as that has been, has contributed only 0.4 percent, or 16 percent to the fall in labor productivity. That is because Z, the share of profits in national income, is so small. To discover why productivity has declined, one must explain why there has been a decline of 2 percent in the growth rate of A. That, according to Kendrick, has three main causes. First, there has been a reduction in research and development in recent years, as well as a slowdown in the diffusion of new inventions. Retardation from this source contributed 6 percent to the overall slowdown, the largest single factor in the decline. Second, the United States no longer is benefiting in any important way from the shift of resources out of low productivity sectors, such as from agriculture to industry and services. Third, because of lower rates of growth, we no longer are enjoying the benefits of economies of scale. On the contrary, in the most recent period cyclical factors have actually offset the positive scale factor, causing a reduction of productivity.

Of particular interest are Kendrick's estimates of the effect of several widely suspected culprits in the productivity puzzle. Many people think that the growing burden of regulation must have been a main factor, since it occurred at precisely the same time that productivity growth came to a halt. Not so, says Kendrick, and other researchers appear to back him up. Regulatory burden explains no more than 12 percent of the decline in labor productivity (0.3%/2.4%).[4] Furthermore,

[2]Martin Baily makes the opposite claim. He argues that rising energy prices and the inroads of imports into many industries have made much of our capital stock obsolete and caused its retirement. If we were to measure the capital stock by its current market value, the decline in the capital-labor ratio would be sufficient to explain all the decline in productivity growth. See Martin N. Baily, "Productivity and the Services of Capital and Labor," *Brookings Papers on Economic Activity* (1/1981): 1–67.

[3]For other viewpoints on the productivity slowdown, see Edward F. Denison, op. cit. For a summary of Denison's views, see his "Explanations of Declining Productivity Growth," *Survey of Current Business* vol. 59, pt. 2 (August 1979): 1–24; J. R. Norsworthy, Michael J. Harper, and Kent Kunze, "The Slowdown in Productivity Growth: Analysis of Some Contributing Factors," *Brookings Papers on Economic Activity* (2/1979): 387–421; and Peter K. Clark, "Capital Formation and the Recent Productivity Slowdown," *Journal of Finance* 33 (June 1978): 965–975.

[4]Denison estimates that pollution abatement, worker safety, and the rise of crime altogether subtracted about 0.26 percent from the growth rate of A in the period 1969–1975. The subtraction is higher in recent years, but since the total decline in A in the Denison calculation is only 2 percent, this estimate appears to be in broad agreement with Kendrick's. See Edward F. Denison, "Effects of Selected Changes in the Institutional and Human Environment upon Output per Unit of Input," *Survey of Current Business* 58 (January 1978): 21–44.

this factor probably represents a one-time loss. Whatever losses are being sustained, the volume of regulation is not increasing; hence, we should not suffer any further losses from this source.

There appears to be little evidence that the decline in labor productivity has much, if anything, to do with a decline in willingness to work or with the idea that American workers aren't as good as they once were. There has been a decline in labor quality due to the growth in the proportion of young, inexperienced workers of both sexes in the labor force. However, as the reader can see from Table 19.4, that factor was most significant in the 1966–1973 period, and it will surely turn positive in the years ahead as all of those workers gain experience. Even in the 1973–1978 period increases in education more than compensated for the negative impact of changing labor force compensation, so that changes in labor quality is the only variable whose contribution to productivity growth was greater in the 1973–1978 period than it had been earlier.

The Role of Energy Prices

Finally, what has been the contribution of higher energy prices to falling rates of productivity improvement? The effect of this variable cannot be seen directly in Table 19.4 because most of its effect will come about through the adoption of less energy-intensive production techniques. If capital and energy are complements, while energy and labor are substitutes, a rise in energy price should lead to a reduction in the use of capital and an increase in the use of labor. If that happens, one should observe a rise in output per unit of capital and a fall in output per unit of labor. In effect, labor is used to save energy. Hudson and Jorgenson have attempted to measure this affect.[5] According to their calculated estimates, a large part of the slowdown in the growth of K/N is a result of more expensive energy. If this is so, energy has played a major role in changing the growth trend in productivity.

Outlook for Productivity Growth

Despite the drop in the growth of Y/N since 1973, there are fairly good grounds for believing that this trend will not continue. First, the last of the baby-boom generation will soon be in the labor market. Thus, there is no doubt that the future growth of the labor force will be slower than it was in the 1973–1978 period. Experts predict that the growth rate of the labor force will gradually decline from around 2 percent per year up until 1983 to just over 1 percent for the balance of the decade. If we continue our current rate of investment or even accelerate it slightly, we should soon observe a resumption in the growth of the capital-labor ratio; Kendrick estimates that this will add 0.5 percent to the growth in Y/L over the 1980s. Furthermore, the absorption of the baby boom will have a positive effect on labor quality. As these young workers gain experience and as the proportion of new

[5] Edward A. Hudson and Dale W. Jorgenson, "Energy Prices and the U. S. Economy, 1972–76," *Data Resources Review* 7 (September 1978): 1.24–1.37.

entrants to the labor force declines, the average productivity of the labor force will increase. Meanwhile, our increased expenditures on education will continue to give us a strong positive productivity boost. As a result of these improvements, Kendrick estimates that we should be able to resume a growth rate of about 2 percent in labor productivity over the 1980s, which is about equal to our record during 1966–1973. Other experts are somewhat less optimistic than Kendrick, but there appears to be a consensus that labor productivity should grow by at least 1.5 percent per year over the decade.

The Theory of Economic Growth

We have now looked at the growth record of the U. S. economy from a historical perspective. We have seen that there are two sources of growth in output per capita, technical progress and capital per worker. We now build a theory of economic growth based on the second of these two sources.[6]

We should say at the outset that the theory of economic growth that we shall develop is not a very complete or satisfactory one, because it does not give us an explanation for the rate of growth of technical change. Since technical change in the past has contributed almost one-half of the growth in per capita income, this is obviously a serious shortcoming. But the theory we shall develop is not entirely useless. It will give us an explanation for the growth of capital. That in turn will allow us to explore the question of the relationship between the saving rate, the capital stock, and the economy's growth rate. It is widely believed that an increase in the saving rate will allow the economy to grow more rapidly. That, we will show, is true only in the short run. In the long run it is the level of per capita income, not its growth rate, that is influenced by the saving rate. This being the case, our growth theory will give us some interesting insights into the optimal saving rate, or what fraction of its income a society should set aside for capital formation.

To develop a theory of growth, we go back to the basic production function of the economy:

(19.1) $$Y = f(N, K).$$

Because we shall be concerned with growth in per capita income, it is useful to convert Equation (19.1) into per capita terms. This we may do by dividing both sides of the equation by N:

(19.10) $$\frac{Y}{N} = f\left(1, \frac{K}{N}\right).$$

(19.10a) $$y = g(k).$$

[6]For a more extended discussion of the theory of economic growth, see R. M. Solow, *Growth Theory: An Exposition* (New York: Oxford University Press, 1970).

Figure 19.3
The Production Function in Per Capita Terms

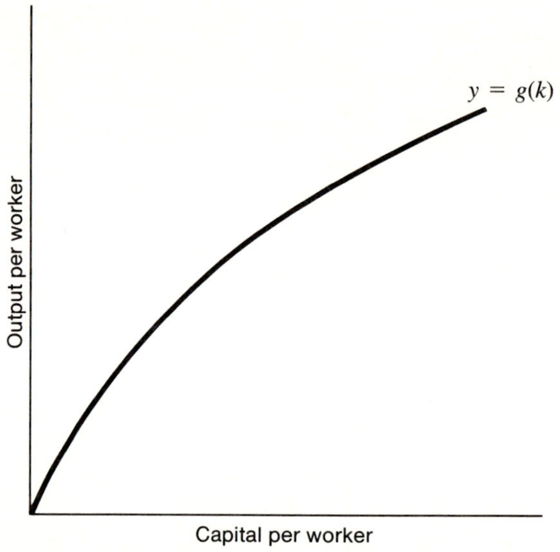

Equation (19.10a) tells us that per capita income is a function of the capital-labor ratio.

It is useful at this point to draw a picture of the production function (see Figure 19.3). We have drawn the function under the standard assumption of diminishing returns. Diminishing returns means that the slope of the production function gets flatter as we go to the right in the diagram—that means that as we increase k, we get smaller and smaller increments of y. This assumption will play a central role in determining the characteristics of long-run equilibrium for the economy.

As we indicated at the outset, since we do not have an adequate theory for the technical change we shall leave it out of the theory that follows, concentrating our attention on the relationship between the growth of k and y. Recall Equation (19.9). There we showed that the growth in per capita income was equal to the growth in A plus the growth in k, weighted by the share of profits in national income. Since we are now assuming that there is no technical change ($\Delta A/A = 0$), our basic growth equation becomes:

(19.9) $$\frac{\Delta y}{y} = \frac{\Delta A}{A} + \frac{Z\Delta k}{k}.$$

(19.11) $$\frac{\Delta y}{y} = \frac{Z\Delta k}{k}.$$

Equation (19.11) says that the growth in per capita income depends entirely on the growth in the capital-labor ratio. Thus, to get a theory of growth, all we need is a theory of the growth of k. That, fortunately, we can derive.

Recall first that k is the difference between the growth rate of the capital stock and the growth rate of the labor force. Thus, if n is the latter growth rate, we may write:

(19.12) $$\frac{\Delta k}{k} = \frac{\Delta K}{K} - n.$$

In Chapter 2 we learned that additions to the capital stock are investment and that in equilibrium, saving must equal investment. Therefore, the growth in the capital stock must be equal to gross saving less depreciation, which is the amount of capital that wears out each year. If d is the depreciation rate and saving is proportional to income, the net change in K can be written:

$$\Delta K = I - dK$$

(19.13) $$\Delta K = sY - dK.$$

Equation (19.13) is simply a definition of net investment. However, it does highlight the all-important fact that an economy must save more to increase the growth rate of the capital stock.

Now we substitute Equation (19.13) into Equation (19.12) to get an expression for the growth rate of the capital-labor ratio. It is:

(19.14) $$\frac{\Delta k}{k} = \frac{sY - dK}{K} - n.$$

This can be simplified as:

(19.15) $$\frac{\Delta k}{k} = \frac{sY}{K} - d - n.$$

The first term on the right-hand side of Equation (19.15) shows the growth in k generated by gross saving. Some of that saving (d) must go to replace capital as it wears out; some is also used to equip new entrants to the labor force. The net growth in k is the difference between the two terms.

It is convenient to transform Equation (19.15) into per capita terms by dividing the first term on the right-hand side by N. Thus:

(19.16) $$\frac{\Delta k}{k} = \frac{sY/N}{K/N} - d - n.$$

The percentage change in the capital-labor ratio is:

(19.17) $$\frac{\Delta k}{k} = \frac{sy}{k} - d - n.$$

The absolute change in the capital-labor ratio is:

(19.17a) $$\Delta k = sy - (d + n)k.$$

Equations (19.17) and (19.17a) represent our theory of the growth of the capital-labor ratio, expressed equivalently in either percentage or absolute terms. In order to understand the theory, consider Equation (19.17a). What it says is this: The absolute growth in k is equal to the sum of the two terms, one positive, the other negative. The first, sy, is the amount of gross investment per capita resulting from saving. The second tells us the amount of this gross saving that is needed to replace worn-out or depreciated capital (dk), plus the amount needed to equip new entrants to the labor force (nk).

To complete the growth theory, we simply substitute Equation (19.17a) into our basic growth Equation, (19.11), to get:

(19.18) $$\frac{\Delta y}{y} = Z\left[\frac{sy - (d + n)k}{k}\right].$$

Equation (19.18) is too complex to analyze directly. However, we can make some progress by looking more closely at the numerator of the equation's right-hand side. Clearly, if gross saving is just equal to $(d + n)k$, the numerator will be zero and there will be no growth in y. Similarly, if gross saving is greater than $(d + n)k$, per capita income will be increasing. Thus, we can write the following three general rules:

If: $sy > (d + n)k$, $\Delta y/y > 0$.

$sy = (d + n)k$, $\Delta y/y = 0$.

$sy < (d + n)k$, $\Delta y/y < 0$.

What these rules say is straightforward. When gross saving is just sufficient to replace capital as it wears out and equip new labor force entrants, net investment will be zero, and therefore both k and y will be constant. The economy will be in a long-run equilibrium. If saving is more (less) than sufficient for replacement and new entrants, the capital-labor ratio and per capita income will be growing (falling).

To see how this growth system works visually, consider Figure 19.4. The diminishing returns production function is the same as in previous diagrams. However, we have added two new functions. The first is the saving function, sy. Since we have assumed that saving is a constant fraction of income, sy has the same concave shape as the production function itself. The saving function shows the amount of gross saving per capita at various capital-labor ratios. The second new function is $(d + n)k$. It is a straight line through the origin with a slope equal to $d + n$. We will call this line the *capital requirements line*. It shows the amount of capital that is needed to replace depreciated equipment and equip new labor force entrants. The capital requirements line shows the amount of saving required to just

Figure 19.4
The Long-Run Equilibrium Solution

Gross output per worker is given by the production function. Gross saving is shown by the saving function. Since in this long-run model we assume that saving equals investment, the saving function also shows gross capital formation per worker. The straight line shows the capital required to replace depreciated capital and to equip new entrants to the labor force. Thus, if saving is greater than capital requirements, as it is at point A, the capital-labor ratio is growing, which means that the economy will be moving to the right, as shown by the arrows. Full equilibrium occurs at the intersection of the saving and capital requirements functions, at k^* and s^*.

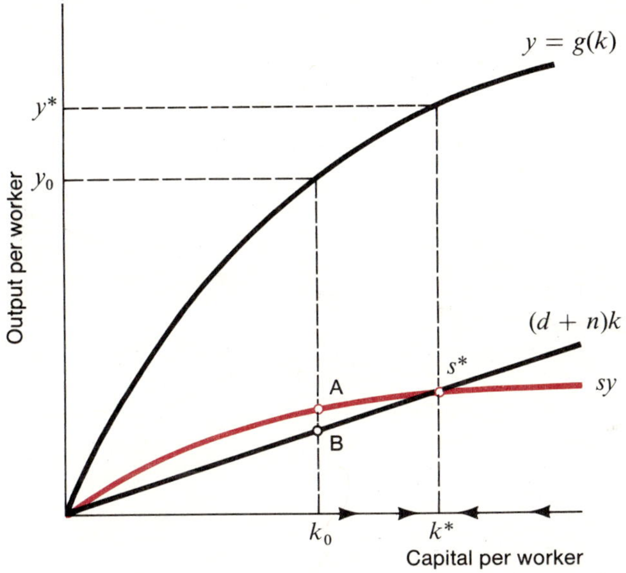

hold the capital-labor ratio constant. This function and the saving function provide a visual representation of the two components on the right-hand side of Equation (19.17a).

Let us now see how our model works. Suppose an economy starts with a capital-labor ratio, k_0. Its income per capita is y_0, and its gross saving is represented by the vertical distance k_0A. But, as the reader can see, capital requirements are only the distance k_0B. Gross saving is greater than what is required to replace worn-out machines and equip new labor force entrants ($sy > (d + n)k$). Hence, the capital-labor ratio must be growing. Over time, k will move to the right as indicated by the arrows in the diagram, and per capita income will increase until the economy reaches k^*. At k^*, gross saving is just equal to capital requirements. The economy is no longer able to save enough to generate further growth in k (or y), and so the economy must come to a halt at this point. For this reason we shall call k^* the long-run equilibrium point for this growing economy. At k^*, per capita income is y^* and gross saving is s^*.

Figure 19.5
The Effect of a Change in the Saving Rate

Suppose that an economy in full equilibrium at k_0^* with saving rate s_0 is disturbed by an increase in the saving rate from s_0 to s_1. Over time, the capital-labor ratio grows to k_1^*, and per capita income grows from y_0^* to y_1^*. When the economy reaches the new equilibrium, the growth rate returns to its original rate, which is the growth rate of the labor force. Thus, in the long run a change in the saving rate affects per capita income, not the growth rate.

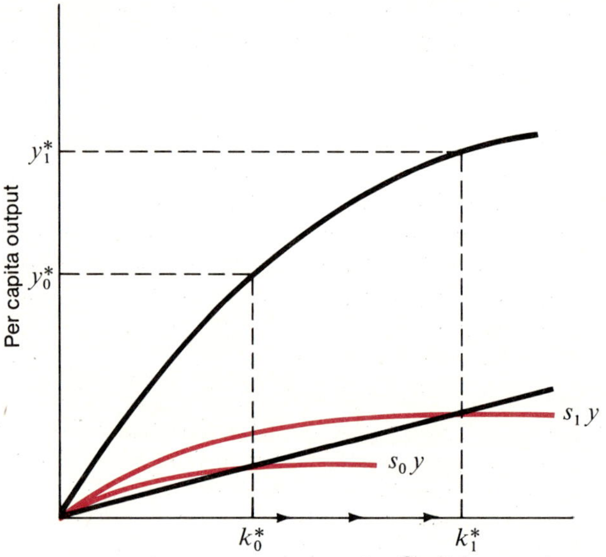

It should be clear that if we had started our economy to the right of k^*, the capital-labor ratio would have declined until we reached k^*, since in that case saving is less than capital requirements. Thus, k^* is the long-run solution. This equilibrium is always found at the intersection of the gross saving and capital requirements functions.

The long-run solution for the growing economy that we have found has one surprising implication: Per capita income and capital are constant. That, of course, means that both income and capital are growing at the same rate as the population. In other words, the long-run growth rate of the economy is n. This growth rate does not appear to depend on the saving rate. To check that, let us examine what happens to our long-run solution when we change the saving rate.

The Effect of a Change in the Saving Rate

Let us see what happens to our long-run equilibrium solution if we increase the saving rate from s_0 to s_1. This change is shown in Figure 19.5. The increase in the saving rate rotates the saving function counterclockwise to s_1y. According to the rules we developed in the previous section, the long-run equilibrium for the

Figure 19.6
A Time Profile of Changes in Capital and Income Per Capita in Response to an Increase in the Saving Rate

When there is an increase in the saving rate, the growth of income rises above its long-run rate, which is n, the growth rate of the labor force, as shown in (b). Thus, over time both per capita income and capital rise from their initial levels, y_0^* and k_0^*, until they reach their new equilibrium values, k_1^* and y_1^*.

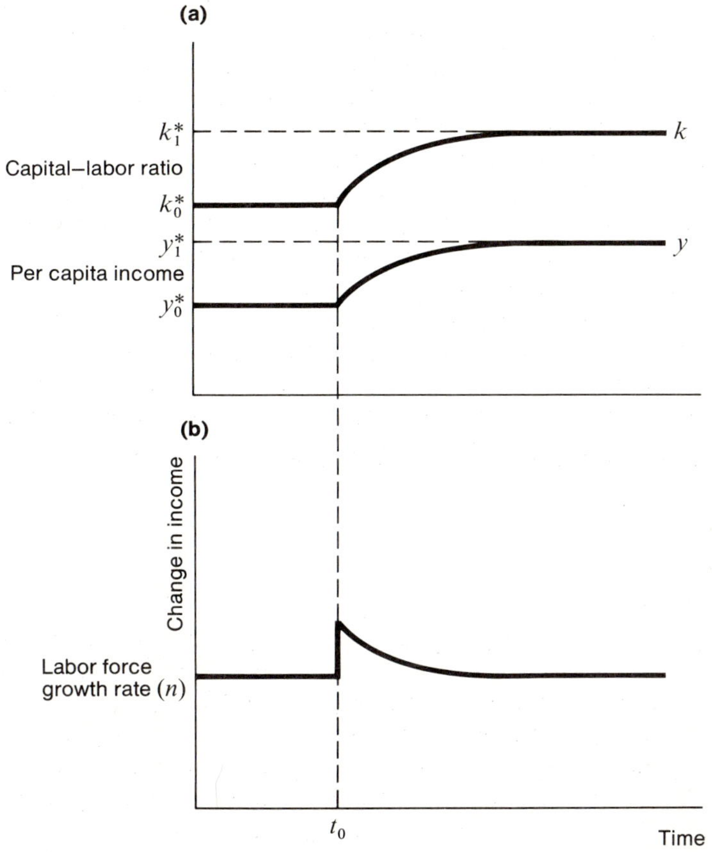

economy is k_0* if the saving rate is s_0. That equilibrium shifts outward to k_1* when the saving rate rises to s_1, since that is the capital-labor ratio at which the new saving function intersects the capital requirements curve.

If the economy was in long-run equilibrium at k_0* prior to the change in saving, there will be a transition period during which the growth of the economy and its capital-labor ratio both increase. However, after a period of time this growth spurt will come to a stop as higher capital requirements once again completely absorb the increase in saving made possible by higher levels of production.

A time profile of these changes is shown in Figure 19.6. As the reader can see, there is a short-run burst of growth and capital accumulation, but in the long run the growth rate of income settles back to the rate of growth of the population. What this demonstration says is that the saving rate determines the long-run income *level* of an economy, not growth rate of income. Of course, in the short run saving affects growth too. As we just saw in our example, a rise in s does increase the growth rate of income during the transition to the new long-run equilibrium.

The long-run independence of an economy's growth rate from its saving rate seems paradoxical. After all, the rate of growth of capital is equal to I/K. Since $S = I$, one would think that the higher the saving rates, the higher the growth rate would be. The reason that does not happen is diminishing returns. We have assumed that as one raises the capital-labor ratio, one gets a smaller and smaller increment of output. Since saving is proportional to output, diminishing returns implies a decline in the additional saving one gets to meet capital requirements. Since those requirements increase in proportion to the change in k, eventually there will come a time when new saving is no more than sufficient to satisfy capital requirements. That is the long-run equilibrium.

In Figure 19.5, diminishing returns is expressed in the concavity of both the production and the saving functions. That concave shape guarantees that eventually the saving function will intersect the capital requirements function, since the latter is a straight line. If there were no diminishing returns, the saving function would be either linear or convex. In either case, there would be no stable long-run equilibrium.

The Optimal Rate of Saving

A natural outgrowth of our analysis of long-run equilibrium and the saving rate is an inquiry into what the **optimal saving rate** should be. How much of our income should we set aside for capital formation? Are we saving too little, enough, or too much? These questions bring us to a more fundamental question, which is: What are the factors that determine the saving choice? What does the society accomplish when it saves? We have learned that increasing the saving rate raises per capita income; therefore, by its decision on how much to save a society determines its long-run per capita income. But the problem is more complicated than this. Is it really per capita income that is of interest to society, or is it per capita consumption? We think that it is consumption, not income. Saving is the part of income that has to be set aside to build new capital. It is not directly useful except to the extent that it makes possible a higher level of consumption. A natural goal for a society might well be to choose the saving rate that maximizes long-run per capita consumption.[7]

We can easily determine what this saving rate would be. Consider Figure 19.7. According to the previous section, long-run equilibrium is at the intersection of the saving line and the capital requirements line. By its saving choice, the soci-

[7]The notion of the optimal saving rate and growth path was introduced by Edmund S. Phelps in his article, "The Golden Rule of Accumulation: A Fable for Growth-Men," *American Economic Review* 51 (September 1961): 638–643. See also Phelps's later paper, "Second Essay on the Golden Rule of Accumulation," *American Economic Review* 55 (September 1965): 793–815.

Figure 19.7
The Optimal Saving Rate

If a society wishes to maximize per capita consumption, it should choose a saving rate at which the saving function intersects the capital requirements line where the latter is furthest away from the production function. This occurs at point B, where the production function and the capital requirements lines are parallel. At this point, consumption is the distance CB and saving is AB.

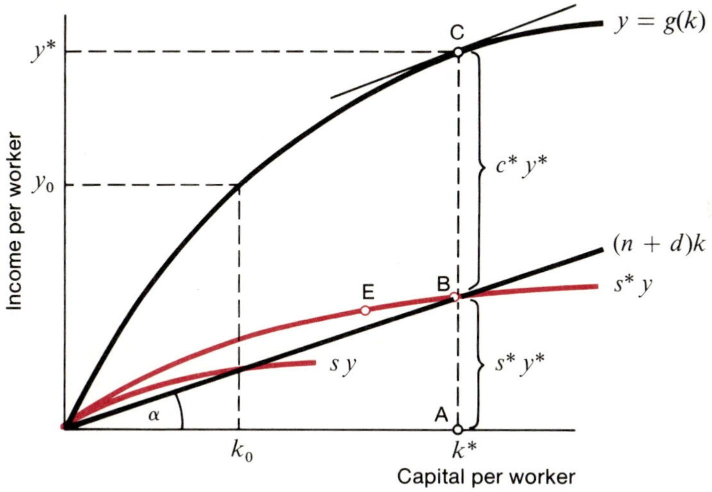

ety determines per capita income. If it saves a fraction, s, income will be y_0; if it saves s^*, income will be y^*.

This same saving decision also determines per capita consumption. Let us see how. Consumption per capita equals income per capita minus saving per capita. Therefore, in Figure 19.7 per capita consumption is the vertical distance between the income and the saving functions. For example, if the saving rate is s^*, per capita consumption is the distance BC. Clearly, therefore, when the society decides on a rate of saving, it determines both per capita income and consumption.

The problem, then, is to choose a saving rate that maximizes per capita consumption. We know that geometrically equilibrium is at the intersection of the saving and capital requirements functions. Therefore, to maximize per capita consumption, the society must choose the saving function that intersects the capital requirements function as far as possible below the production function. This happens where the slope of the production function is just exactly equal to that of the capital requirements line. In Figure 19.7, consumption is maximized at point B, where the capital requirements line is just parallel to the production function. At this point per capita consumption is c^*y^*, which is the distance BC; per capita saving is s^*y^*, the distance AB; and per capita income is y^*. If society sets aside s^* of income, it will maximize the long-run living standard of the society.

A natural question now occurs: How does our actual saving rate compare with s^*? Are we saving too much or too little? To answer that, we have to know what s^* is. Is there any way to do this? The answer is yes, provided our assumptions about production and factor shares are reasonable.

We can now derive a useful identity. Recall Equation (19.11), an expression for the rate of growth of per capita income when $\Delta A/A = 0$:

(19.11) $$\frac{\Delta y}{y} = \frac{Z\Delta k}{k}.$$

From Equation (19.11) we can derive an expression for the slope of the production function in Figure 19.7. It is:

(19.19) $$\frac{\Delta y}{\Delta k} = \frac{Zy}{k}.$$

We also know the slope of the capital requirements line: It is $n + d$. We have argued that maximum per capita income is achieved when the slopes of these two functions are equal. Hence, maximum consumption is achieved when:

(19.20) $$\frac{\Delta y}{\Delta k} = \frac{Zy^*}{k^*} = n + d.$$

Now consider angle α in Figure 19.7. That angle is equal to the slope of the capital requirements function, $n + d$. But by the definition of the tangent, the tangent of α is also equal to the ratio s^*y^*/k^*. Therefore, setting these two slopes equal, we have:

(19.21) $$n + d = \text{tan angle } \alpha = \frac{s^*y^*}{k^*}.$$

Now set Equation (19.21) equal to Equation (19.20) to get the simple condition:

(19.22) $$\frac{Zy^*}{k^*} = n + d = \frac{sy^*}{k^*}.$$

This reduces finally to:

(19.23) $$Z = s^*.$$

Equation (19.23) is a very simple rule of thumb. It says that a society maximizes consumption when the gross saving rate just equals the share of profits in national income. If saving is less than profits, a society can increase per capita consumption by saving more; if the saving rate is greater, it is probably saving too much.

The Effect of Technical Progress on Productivity

So far we have ignored technical progress. But as we showed earlier, technical progress has been responsible for about ⅖ of the increases in income in the United States since 1948. What happens to our analysis if technical change is incorporated?

This turns out to depend on the form taken by technical change. In our simple formulation, we assumed that technical change was completely independent of the growth rate of either capital or labor. It was simply a shift factor that increased the amount of output obtainable from a given quantity of inputs. If technical change takes this form, there will be no steady-state long-run equilibrium growth rate. Because the production function continuously shifts outward, the economy may continue forever growing faster than capital requirements. Here technical progress offsets the dampening effects of diminishing returns. If it is large enough, per capita income may increase indefinitely.

Another type of technical change affecting productivity is one that makes labor more effective. In this case technical change simply enhances the growth rate of labor inputs expressed in units of constant efficiency. Here a steady-state long-run equilibrium does exist, but it is one in which income and capital per worker both grow at the same rate of growth as technical progress.

Is the United States Saving Enough?

We can now address the question with which we began this inquiry: Is the United States saving too much or too little according to the maximum consumption rule?[8] To tentatively answer that question, we have collected some recent data on profits and investment for the U. S. economy, presented in Table 19.5.

Profits in the national accounts are composed of rent, interest payments, profits, and some part of the income of proprietors. Since there is no way of knowing what share of the last is the implicit profit from capital owned by proprietors and what share comes from their own labor, we show the profit share under various assumptions. These estimates provide an outside range of what the true profit share is.

In the last column of the table we show the ratio of gross investment to GNP. This is the equivalent of the saving share, since gross saving = investment. We report the ratio in terms of investment because so much of private saving at present is being offset by government dissaving (deficits). In the United States, after financing government deficits, we save and invest about 16 to 17 percent of GNP. But the profit share is at least 20 percent. Therefore, according to our rule of thumb, it appears that the United States is indeed not saving enough.

Before we jump to the conclusion that we should increase the saving rate, there are two things that we ought to remember. First, in a situation such as the

[8] For a more sophisticated attempt to show that the United States is indeed saving too little, see Martin Feldstein, "Does the United States Save Too Little?" *American Economic Review* 67 (February 1977): 116–121.

Table 19.5
Profit Share under Different Assumptions about Proprietors' Income

	All Profits	½ Profits	0 Profits	Investment/GNP
1968	28%	24%	19%	15%
1972	32	28	24	16
1976	25	21	18	15
1977	25	21	18	17
1978	26	22	19	17
1979	26	22	19	17

Source: *Economic Report of the President* (Washington, D. C., 1982).

one shown in Figure 19.7, since both y and k are still growing, we are probably not in long-run equilibrium; we may be at a point such as E. If that is the case, the profit share could fall to s^* when we reach the long-run equilibrium appropriate to our saving rate. Second, the gains in per capita consumption are not instantaneous. The generation who initiates an increase in the saving rate probably will suffer a reduction in its per capita consumption.

Figure 19.8 shows the time path of per capita consumption in response to an increase in the saving rate. Suppose an economy starts out in long-run equilibrium at y_0. At this point consumption is the distance AB in diagram (a). Now suppose the society decides to increase the saving rate enough to reach the maximum consumption income level, y^*. That requires an increase in the saving rate from s_0 to s^*. At the time of the increase, per capita consumption falls by the shift up in the saving function. The reason is that the society is diverting production away from current consumption in order to build more capital. In the short run, the production from those additional capital goods is not equal to the loss of consumption goods required to build them.

Over time, the economy will move from its initial equilibrium at k_0 to a new equilibrium k^*. At this point, per capita consumption will be the distance CD, which is greater than distance AB. The time path of per capita consumption can be seen in (b). The society has a short-run decline in consumption in return for a long-run gain. Whether or not a particular generation in a particular country wishes to make this short-run sacrifice for the long-run gain of future generations is an ethical question that cannot be answered by economists.

Summary

In this chapter we examined the sources of growth in the United States and developed a simple model of the growth process. Growth comes from three sources: growth in labor inputs, growth in capital, and pure technical change. During the postwar period, income has grown by a little over 3.5 percent per year. About 40

Figure 19.8
Time Profile of Per Capita Consumption in Response to an Increase in the Saving Rate

Diagram (b) shows the response of per capita consumption to the increase in the saving rate shown in (a). At k_0, per capita consumption is c_0 and the saving rate is s_0. Now suppose that saving is increased to s^*. Initially consumption falls, because the amount of income that must be set aside to build new capital is greater than the extra production of that capital. Eventually the increase in saving will lead to an increase in per capita consumption, but if a society has a very high rate of discount, the short-run loss in consumption in the immediate future may outweigh the long-run gains. In this case, increasing the saving rate is not optimal.

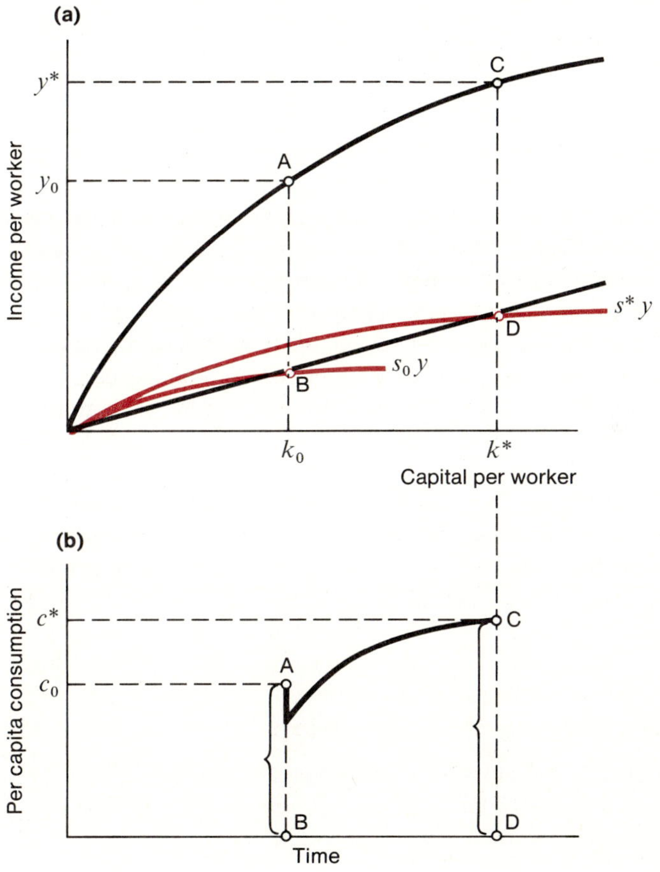

percent of that growth comes from increases in the labor force, about 40 percent from technical change, and only about 20 percent from the growth in the capital stock.

In recent years, there has been a sharp slowdown in the growth of labor productivity or income per worker in the United States. This slowdown has coincided with, but apparently not been caused by, a fall in the growth of capital per worker. Instead, there has been a sharp decline in technical progress. Prior to 1966, technical improvements in production, higher labor quality, and the movement of labor out of agriculture added 2.8 percent per year to the growth of per capita income. In the 1970s, that figure fell to less than 1 percent, a phenomenon that pulled the overall growth rate of per capita income down to about 1 percent per year. Serious as this situation appears to be, there is evidence that the slowdown may be over. Economists expect a resumption of productivity growth, at about 2 percent per year, over the 1980s, with big improvements coming from the rising educational level of the labor force and more rapid growth in capital-labor ratios after the baby-boom generation of the 1950s has been absorbed into the labor force.

In the final sections of this chapter, we developed a model of the growth process, based on growth in the capital-labor ratio. Using that model we showed that in the long run the growths of capital and income both converge to the growth rate of the labor force, which implies that both the capital-labor ratio and per capita income are constant. This implies that in the long run the saving rate, not the growth rate, affects the level of per capita income, a fact that suggests the policy question: How much should a society save? We showed that if a society wishes to maximize consumption per capita, it should save an amount exactly equal to profits in national income. However, for any particular generation, it may not be worthwhile to move to the saving rate that maximizes long-run consumption. For in the short run, an increase in the saving rate does reduce the consumption level of the generation initiating the change, and the long-run benefits to future generations may not compensate for the loss in consumption in the short run.

Key Concepts

disembodied technical change
labor productivity
reasons for declining productivity
optimal saving rate

Problems and Questions for Discussion

1. Suppose the share of income going to profits is 25 percent and to labor 75 percent. If the labor force grows at 3 percent per year and the capital stock at 4 percent per year, and if technical change is 1 percent per year,

a. What is the rate of growth of income?

b. What is the rate of growth of per capita income?

c. What are the contributions of productivity growth and increases in k to the growth in per capita income?

2. What are the main reasons for the slowdown in productivity growth in the United States? Will any of these factors change in the future?

3. Suppose that there is a substitution of labor for capital in production due to rising energy costs. What will happen to measured productivity? Do you think this change is an accurate indicator of what is happening to productivity in this case?

4. Since an increase in the saving rate increases capital formation, why doesn't such a change increase the growth rate of income? What does it do instead? Using diagrams, show how the level and the growth rate of per capita income change over time in response to the increase in the saving rate.

5. Developing countries are often criticized for having such high rates of population growth. It is usually argued that high rates of population growth make more difficult the attainment of satisfactory rates of growth of per capita income. Discuss this position in light of the theory of growth presented in this chapter. What is the relationship between population growth and either the growth or the level of income?

6. Discuss the effects of each of the following changes on both the level and the growth rate of the per capita income in the short and the long run:

- **a.** A once-and-for-all increase in productivity (an upward shift in the production function).
- **b.** A tax cut financed by bond sales.
- **c.** A reduction in the rate of growth of population.

7. Show that a society maximizes per capita consumption when saving equals profits.

8. If we maximize per capita consumption when saving equals profits, does it therefore follow that we can increase per capita consumption by increasing the share of profits in income?

Chapter 20

Supply-Side Economics

Seldom, if ever, has an idea advanced so rapidly from the realm of theory to policy as has supply-side economics. Until the late 1970s it was little more than a gleam in the eyes of people like economist Arthur Laffer and Representative Jack Kemp. Yet, by 1980 it became the chief theoretical support behind President Reagan's 30 percent personal income tax cut. In this chapter we will take an extended look at supply-side economics. We shall try to answer the questions of just what it is, how it is related to the theories we have been developing throughout the rest of the book, and whether it offers a way out of our current inflation-recession dilemma.

Supply-Side Versus Demand-Side Economics

We shall define **supply-side economics** as the analysis of the effects of government policy on capacity output in the economy.[1] The key idea here is the connection between policy and supply. This is a fundamental reversal from Keynesian economics, which was concerned almost exclusively with **demand-side economics.** Notice also that we are talking about capacity rather than actual output. We do so because we want to distinguish between the demand- and the supply-side effects of policy. Many government measures, such as tax cuts and monetary expansion, lead to increases in output. But they do this by increasing demand, not

[1] For a more extended discussion of supply-side economics see J. Dewey Daane and Samuel A. Morley, "Supply Chic," *Across the Board* 17 (November 1980): 45–49; Herbert Stein, "Some Supply-Side Propositions," *The Wall Street Journal,* March 19, 1980, 24; and John A. Tatom, "We Are All Supply-Siders Now," *Review of the Federal Reserve Bank of St. Louis* 63 (May 1981): 18–30.

Figure 20.1
The Supply and Demand Effects of a Tax Cut

A cut in taxes has both demand- and supply-side effects. As we have learned, the tax cut shifts the aggregate demand curve out from D_0 to D_1. It also increases capacity from $Y_{FE}(t_0)$ to $Y_{FE}(t_1)$ and shifts the short-run supply curve out to S_1. The demand-side effect of the tax cut is the distance $Y_2 - Y_0$, whereas the supply-side effect is $Y_1 - Y_2$.

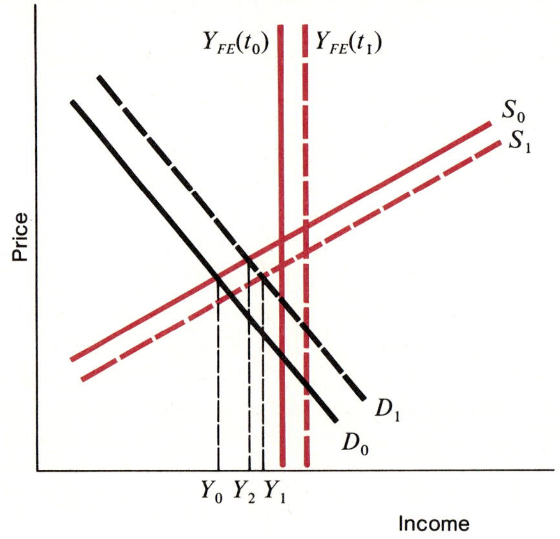

supply. There is an outward shift in the aggregate demand curve leading to an increase in output if the economy is below full employment. This is not a supply-side effect. Rather, it is a result of expansionary demand management. By contrast, supply-side economics confines its attention to the effect of policy on the long-run aggregate supply curve.

To see more closely the distinction we are drawing between the demand-side and the supply-side effects of policy, suppose the government reduces income taxes. Provided that monetary policy accommodates this change, aggregate demand will increase. In the short run, output will go up. But that is not a supply-side effect. That is a straightforward, expansionary fiscal measure designed to move the economy closer to full employment. The supply-side effect, if there is one, will be the increase in full employment income that comes about because of the tax cut. For example, if the tax cut increases work effort or leads to an expansion of the labor force, supply will increase. That is the supply-side effect. Typically, such effects are far smaller than the demand-side effects that we have been accustomed to analyzing.

Consider Figure 20.1. It shows an economy in short-run equilibrium at Y_0 with a tax rate of t_0. Now suppose the government cuts taxes to increase the level of income. As we have learned, aggregate demand shifts to D_1 and aggregate supply to S_1. Income rises to Y_1. Proponents of the tax cut may point to the increase in income as evidence in support of supply-side tax cuts. But most of the increase in income is a straightforward result of demand stimulus, not supply. Using Figure 20.1 we can see exactly how much of the rise in income is supply and how much is demand induced. The supply-side effect, according to our definition, is the change in capacity resulting from the tax cut—that is, $Y_{FE}(t_1) - Y_{FE}(t_0)$. If there had been no increase in capacity when taxes were reduced, income would have risen to Y_2, the intersection of D_1 and the initial short-run supply curve S_0. Therefore, one can say that $Y_2 - Y_0$ is the increase in income coming from the simple expansion of demand, while $Y_1 - Y_2$ is the supply-side effect.

Since Keynes, most economists have concentrated on the demand side. Supply-side economics is a return to the older and more fundamental concerns about the forces determining capacity, productivity, and growth in the economy. As such, it is a healthy development. However, one should not overestimate supply-side effects by combining them with the results of demand stimuli.

According to the production function, capacity is a function of capital, labor, and productivity. Thus, we can decompose supply-side effects into three different types: those that increase the supply of capital, those that increase the supply of labor, and those that increase the productivity of a given supply of labor and capital. Let us look more carefully at different government policies and their effects on each of these three factors. While all government policies undoubtedly have some effect on capacity, we shall confine our attention to three policies: regulation, monetary policy, and fiscal policy.

Effect of Government Regulation on Supply

The government has always exercised a degree of control over business activity. However, a rising tide of reform in the 1960s extended government regulatory authority to safety standards, consumer protection, and pollution. Economists were, of course, aware that such regulation would tend to diminish productivity and raise costs. However, the recent decline in worker productivity has spurred interest in determining just how costly such regulation is.

In the last chapter, we presented John Kendrick's estimate that increased regulation had reduced the growth rate of productivity by 0.4 percent per year between 1973 and 1978 (see Table 19.4). In evaluating this number, one should remember that our output measure does not include the value of clean air and water, or debit GNP for worker and consumer accidents. Thus, we do not know whether or not the new regulations were worth the cost they imposed.

Another form of regulation with important capacity effects is government-sanctioned limitations on competition. In banking, airlines, and trucking, to name three examples, the government has cooperated with producers to fix prices and control entry. The result has been higher prices and lower output than would be observed in a more open, competitive environment. Deregulation in this area started under President Carter, who opened up competition in airlines, banking, and trucking. Such deregulation measures will increase productivity. They may also encourage more capital formation in industries subject to extensive regulation.

Figure 20.2
Personal Tax Rates in the United States

Source: Steven Braun, "Discussion of the Evans Paper," *The Supply-Side Effects of Economic Policy* (Federal Reserve Bank of St. Louis and Center for the Study of American Business, 1981), p. 95. The marginal tax rate series is that computed by Michael K. Evans. Both series include state and local taxes and social security taxes.

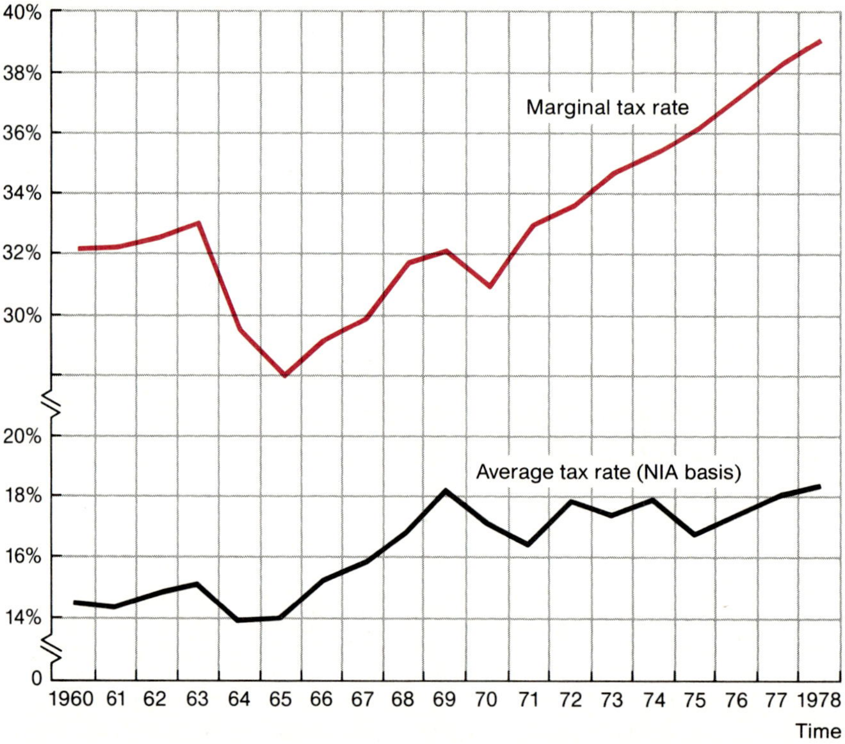

Effect of Taxes on Labor Supply

Most of the discussion of supply-side economics has centered on the effects of tax cuts on the supply of labor and capital. The argument in favor of positive supply-side effects is a simple one. Income taxes reduce the incentive to work, hence they may reduce the supply of labor. Corporate income taxes reduce net corporate profits, which reduces the incentive to invest. The first reduces N and second reduces K, both of which effects will shrink capacity output.

It is easy to understand the concern over the disincentive effects of our tax system. Since 1965 there has been a sharp increase in both the marginal and the average tax rates in the United States, as can be seen in Figure 20.2. Yet the

Figure 20.3
Female Labor Force Participation Rate
Source: U. S. Department of Labor

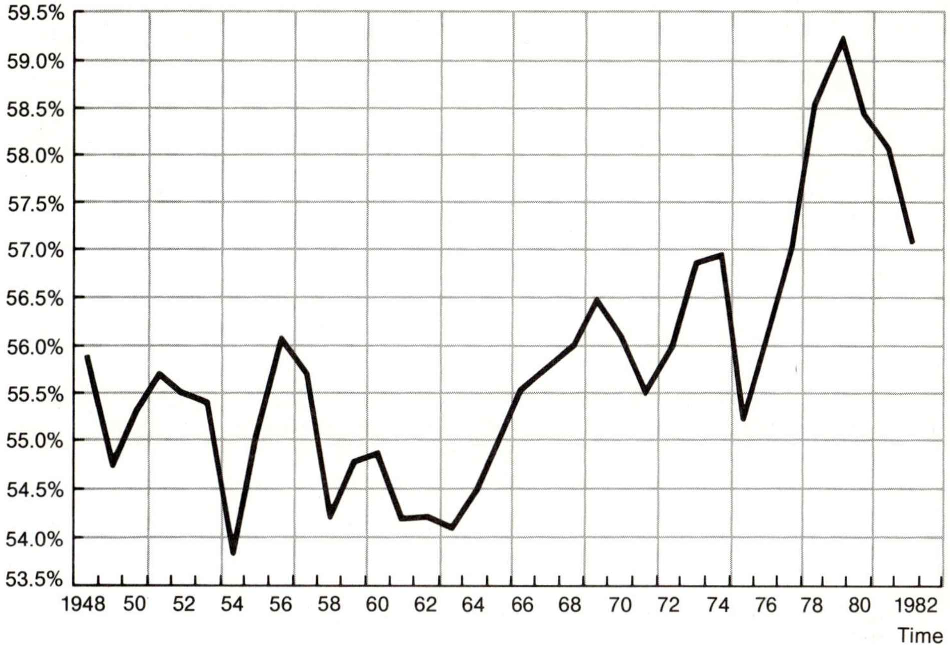

relationship between taxes and work is more complex than it first appears to be.[2] Lowering taxes has two effects on work. It makes the return for working greater, which is an incentive for people to work more. But at the same time, it gives people more disposable income for the same amount of work. Some may take this windfall and buy leisure; since they earn more per hour, they may work fewer hours rather than more. People do that when they work toward an income goal. Higher wages allow such people to achieve the goal with fewer hours of work.

Such a seemingly perverse reaction to higher wages has been observed in numerous agricultural societies, where the supply curve of labor responds negatively to rising real wages. Whether the situation is so extreme in the U. S. economy is not known. However, everyone should bear in mind that the perverse income effects of higher disposable income will reduce the net amount of extra labor induced by a tax cut.

[2] For a more extended discussion of the relationship between taxes and the supply of labor, see Jerry A. Hausman, "Labor Supply," in Henry J. Aaron and Joseph A. Pechman, eds., *How Taxes Affect Economic Behavior* (Washington, D. C.: The Brookings Institution, 1981), 27–83.

One should also bear in mind that if there is an expansion of labor supply it has to come from either more hours worked by current labor force members or an expansion of the labor force. For the great majority of jobholders, the first option is not possible without moonlighting. Jobs require a certain number of hours of input. Thus, people are not free to vary the hours they work, except by moonlighting, in response to a tax cut. Therefore, it seems unlikely that changing taxes will have much effect on hours worked. As for expansions in the labor force, these will have to come mainly from women, teen-agers, and retired people, since nearly all employable adult males are already in the labor force. Judging by the behavior of women's participation rates in the recent past, reducing taxes is not likely to add much to labor supply. As the reader can see from Figure 20.3, there has been a dramatic increase in the female participation rate in the last 15 years, at exactly the same time that tax rates have been rising, not falling.

We do not know to what extent the expansion of the female labor force is a response to rising real wages or to the desire to maintain family income in response to a recent period of falling real wages, rising inflation, and rising taxes. Putting together all of these possible effects, the Council of Economic Advisors recently estimated that a 10-percent cut in the personal income tax would increase the labor force by at most 1 percent, which in turn would increase capacity output by 0.6 percent.[3]

Effect of Government Policy on Supply of Capital

We turn now to the first of several interactions between government policy and the capital stock.[4] The willingness and ability of corporations to invest are sensitive to tax policy, monetary policy, and the level of aggregate demand. Any government concerned about inflation and productivity growth must take these interactions into account in designing policy.

Of the three areas of policy, maintaining the level of aggregate demand is clearly the most important. As we saw in Chapter 12, the single most significant determinant of fixed investment is the level of demand relative to capacity. A recessionary economy is a low-investment economy. This is confirmed in all studies of investment and could be seen clearly in Figures 12.1 and 12.2. The late 1950s and the years 1975–1976 were years of low rates of capacity utilization and investment, while the mid-1960s and the years 1978–1979 were just the opposite. If the government wishes to increase the investment rate, the best thing it can do is manage demand so as to keep the economy close to full capacity utilization.

Among other things, this implies that stabilization recessions are directly contrary to the supply-side policies of capacity expansion. Many who favor stabiliza-

[3] *Economic Report of the President* (Washington, D. C., 1981), 81–82.

[4] For a survey of the relationship between government policy and investment, see George M. von Furstenberg and Burton G. Malkiel, "The Government and Capital Formation; A Survey of Recent Issues," *Journal of Economic Literature* 15 (September 1977): 835–879.

tion recessions argue that investment is negatively related to inflation, because inflation makes all investment more risky. Thus, antiinflation policy should have a long-run positive supply-side effect. However, this benefit must be weighed against the low investment that stabilization recessions also cause.

Monetary Policy

Supply-side economists have concentrated their attention on the effects of tax policy and regulation. But the same considerations apply to monetary policy, too. When the Federal Reserve contracts the money supply and raises interest rates, capital formation is discouraged. That has a negative effect on capacity or supply—indeed, it is precisely the point of contractionary monetary policy to reduce aggregate demand somewhere by raising interest rates. In the very simple models we have used in this book, investment is the variable that is affected by interest rates. In a more realistic model consumption too would be affected. Be that as it may, if monetary policy has an effect on investment, it must have an effect on the capital stock. In Chapter 13 we called this the long-run effect of monetary policy. We showed there that in the short run monetary policy affects investment, and in the long run it affects the size of the capital stock. Contractionary monetary policy reduces investment in the short run and capacity in the long run. The latter is the supply-side effect of monetary policy.

Consider an obvious recent example of this effect. In 1980–1981, a sharp rise in interest rates reduced the rate of new housing construction in the United States to the lowest level in 20 years. That means that in the future, the stock of housing will be lower than it would have been under a less restrictive policy. The same thing is true for corporate investment. Raising interest rates reduces the profitability of investment, which tends to make the capital stock lower.

This analysis may appear to imply that if the monetary authorities are interested in enhancing capacity they should always operate expansionary policy. This does not follow at all. For if the money supply expands too rapidly there will be an inflation, and that is likely to discourage investment, too. Thus, what the supply-side factors suggest is a proper mix of monetary and fiscal policies, one that controls aggregate demand yet minimizes the perverse effects of policy on capacity. Before we can discuss what this mix should be, we must consider the effect of taxes on investment and saving.

Taxes, Saving, and Investment

From a national income accounting point of view, if we wish to increase capital formation we must increase the supply of saving. As we have seen, the United States is a relatively low-saving country. We set aside a smaller fraction of our disposable income for saving than practically any other developed country. Recently, there has been a good deal of interest in the possibility that we could increase the supply of saving by reducing the income tax. At first glance, the argument seems compelling. Since private saving is a function of disposable income and since tax reductions increase disposable income, surely tax cuts will also increase private saving.

While this may be a popular argument, it is a most misleading one. In Chapter 3, we learned that it is *total* saving, not private saving, that must be equal to investment. And while tax reductions definitely increase private saving, at the same time they usually reduce public saving. Every dollar that the government loses in tax receipts leads to an increase in the government deficit. Unless this extra deficit is matched by increases in private saving, total saving and total investment will be reduced by a tax cut. There is only one possible case in which personal tax cuts do not reduce investment, and that is when a tax cut causes an increase in income large enough to offset the lower tax rate.

Here the reader must distinguish between tax cuts to get the economy to full employment and tax cuts to increase capacity income. As supply-side economists, we should be talking only about the latter. The former group of tax cuts is intended to stimulate demand. Those cuts may well reduce the government deficit and increase private saving, but that is only because they push the economy closer to full employment.

As an example, consider the Kennedy-Johnson tax cut of 1964. Personal income tax rates were lowered in stages by about 20 percent at a time when the government was running a deficit. Yet two years later tax receipts had increased by 10 percent, and the deficit had fallen by $5.5 billion. But this was not a supply-side effect. This tax cut was introduced at a time when the economy was operating far below capacity. The unemployment rate had been 1 to 2 percent above the normal level ever since 1958. The economy had substantial slack and a very low inflation rate. As a result of the tax cut and a complementary expansionary monetary policy, the economy moved rapidly toward full employment, which it reached during 1965–1966. Most of the increase in tax receipts came from the demand stimulus, not the supply. This was a straightforward Keynesian remedy for a stagnant economy. It should not be used in support of supply-side tax cuts to stimulate saving and investment.

Let us consider a bit more carefully the conditions under which a cut in tax rates leads to an increase in total savings. Ignoring business saving for simplicity, we write the saving-investment equilibrium condition as:

(20.1) $$S = S_h + S_g = I.$$

(20.2) $$S_h = -a + (1 - c)(Y_{FE} - T).$$

Note that we solve for full employment income here because we are interested in supply-side effects. S_g is:

(20.3) $$S_g = T - G.$$

If we assume that taxes at full employment are proportional to Y_{FE}, we have tax receipts:

(20.4) $$T = tY_{FE}.$$

Figure 20.4
The Effect of Tax Reductions on Total Saving

Total saving is a function of income. Since taxes are a part of saving, the tax rate is one of the determinants of the slope of the saving function. A reduction in the tax rate from t_0 to t_1 rotates the saving function downward. If there were no change in income, total saving would necessarily fall when taxes were reduced. But income may go up for two different reasons: demand-side and supply-side effects. Here we analyze only the supply-side effects. We look at the increase in saving at capacity income. Because of supply-side effects, capacity income rises from Y_{FE} to Y_{FE}'. Since the reduction in saving is greater than the increase in income, total saving falls from S_0 to S_1. Only if the supply-side effect raised income to Y_{FE}'' would total saving not fall.

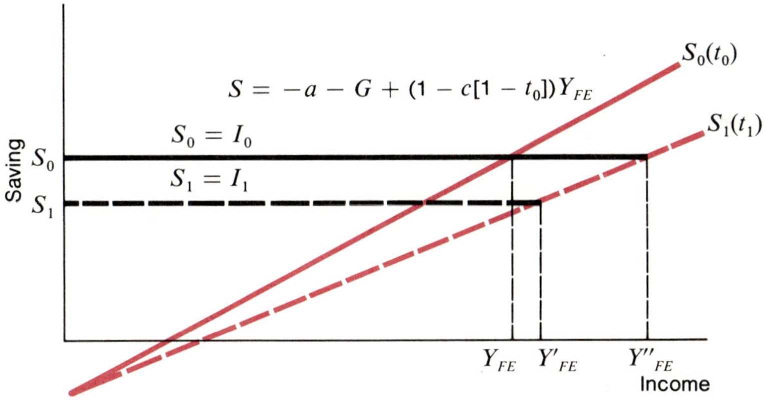

Substituting Equations (20.2), (20.3), and (20.4) into Equation (20.1), we find that total saving is positively related to the tax rate. Thus:

(20.5) $$S = -a + (1 - c)(1 - t)Y_{FE} + tY_{FE} - G.$$

(20.6) $$S = -a - G + (1 - c[1 - t])Y_{FE}.$$

Equation (20.6) only expresses formally the point we have already discussed. When one includes government saving into the accounting, as one should, taxes are positively related to saving, not negatively as some proponents of tax cuts would have us believe.

It is still possible for a tax reduction to increase total saving. For that to happen, the tax reduction has to increase Y_{FE} by enough to offset the direct effect of reduced taxes on saving. That could happen if Y_{FE} is quite sensitive to tax rates. We can see all of this in Figure 20.4. Line $S_0(t_0)$ shows total saving as a function of income; its slope is equal to $1 - c(1 - t)$. Y_{FE} is a certain income level in the diagram. Since the equilibrium condition is that $S = I$, we can add a horizontal investment line (because investment is not a function of income) to the diagram and find equilibrium at the intersection of the saving function and the horizontal investment line. Thus, if investment is I_0, equilibrium will be at Y_{FE}.

We now use Figure 20.4 to analyze the effect of a reduction in taxes on both saving and Y_{FE}. To see that, suppose we lower the tax rate from t_0 to t_1. This rotates the saving function downward to the dashed line. Now, if people work harder and more people enter the labor force in response to the tax cut, Y_{FE} will increase. Suppose the increase shifts Y_{FE} to Y_{FE}'. In that case, total saving at full employment falls to S_1, because the reduction in tax rates is not offset by rising revenues. Sooner or later investment must decline to I_1, because if it did not there would be excess demand ($Y > Y_{FE}'$). In this case, tax reductions reduce investment spending and lead to a lower long-run capital stock. The reason is that increased private saving is more than offset by increased government deficits. Here, tax cuts crowd out private investment by increased government borrowing to cover its deficit.

It should be clear that what happens to total saving depends on how much induced expansion there is in Y_{FE}. If Y_{FE} is relatively sensitive to the tax rate, saving may rise rather than fall. In Figure 20.4, if Y_{FE} rises to at least Y_{FE}'', then saving and investment will not fall. Thus at bottom, the sign of the relationship between saving and tax rates is an empirical question of the sensitivity of Y_{FE} to the tax rate. Several rough estimates have been made of this sensitivity, and they suggest that in our tax system total saving is negatively related to taxes. If that is so, tax reductions are not a good way to increase capital formation.

The Laffer Curve

A question related to the one we have been discussing is the relationship between tax rates and government receipts. Arthur Laffer, an economist at the University of Southern California, was the first to express this relationship with his now-famous **Laffer curve.**[5] The Laffer curve says that the relationship between tax rates and tax receipts is an inverted U, which means that there is some tax rate at which receipts are at a maximum (t^* in Figure 20.5). If rates are raised above this point, receipts will fall. Furthermore—and this is more important from a policy standpoint—Laffer asserts that the U. S. tax rates are above t^*. If Laffer is right, reducing the tax rate will increase government revenues, lower whatever deficit we have, and by definition increase total saving and capital formation as well.

No one can reasonably dispute the general shape of the Laffer curve. After all, tax receipts would be zero at a tax rate of zero, and probably would be so at a rate of 100 percent as well. Obviously, in between these two extreme rates, receipts are higher. Hence, there must be some rate t^* at which receipts reach their maxi-

[5] Tradition has it that the Laffer curve was first developed on the back of a napkin in a Washington restaurant where Arthur Laffer was trying to convince Jude Wanninski of the negative effect of high tax rates on the economy. Apparently Wanninski was convinced, for he became one of Laffer's strongest supporters. See his article "Taxes, Revenues and the Laffer Curve," *The Public Interest* 50 (Winter 1970): 3–17. For more formal and more critical comments on the empirical relevance of the Laffer curve see James Tobin, "The Reagan Economics Plan: Supply-Side, Budget and Inflation," *Economic Review of the Federal Reserve Bank of San Francisco* (May 1981): 5–14.

Figure 20.5
The Laffer Curve

The relationship of tax receipts to tax rates is an inverted U shape. When the supply-side elasticity of income with respect to taxes is less than 1, tax receipts rise with tax rates, because the percentage reduction in income is less than the percentage increase in the tax rates. At t^* the supply-side elasticity is equal to 1. Research suggests that t^* occurs at a rate much higher than actual tax rates in the United States.

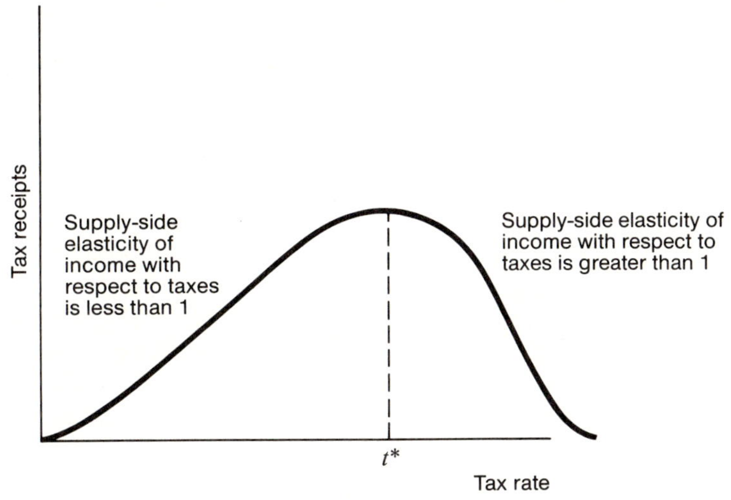

mum. Empirically the question is: How high is that rate t^*? Why might tax receipts rise when the tax rate is lowered? Because, according to Laffer, taxes inhibit capital formation and work effect and drive people into the so-called underground economy. In our terms, Laffer is counting on the positive supply-side effect of tax cuts to more than offset the cut in rates.

Expressing this formally, we write tax receipts as:

(20.7) $$T = tY_{FE}(\overline{t}).$$

Equation (20.7) expresses the fact that tax rates affect receipts in two opposite ways. The direct way is through t, holding Y_{FE} constant; that effect is positive. The indirect way is through the supply-side effects of taxes on Y_{FE}. That effect, as the equation indicates, is negative. Which effect dominates is the key empirical question.

We can say this much formally: If the percentage increase in Y_{FE} is greater than the percentage reduction in taxes, total receipts will rise as taxes decline; otherwise, receipts will fall. If we define the absolute value of the percentage change in Y_{FE} with respect to a 1-percent change in tax rates as the supply-side elasticity with respect to tax rates, receipts rise if this elasticity is less than 1 and fall if it is greater than 1. The rate at which the supply-side elasticity is equal to 1 is t^*.

The next empirical question is whether we are above or below t^* in our economy. No one has a firm and definitive answer to this question yet, but one rather casual estimate puts t^* at somewhere around 75 percent, far above our current tax rates. While that may be a bit high, few people think that the supply-side elasticity is anywhere close to 1. As we pointed out above, the Council of Economic Advisors estimated that a 10-percent income tax cut would increase Y_{FE} by at most 0.6 percent per year. That implies an elasticity of .06, obviously far less than 1.

We show the derivation of the Laffer curve diagrammatically in Figure 20.6. In (a) we show the supply-side effect of taxes on Y_{FE}. Higher tax rates reduce Y_{FE}. Since tax receipts are equal to the tax rate times Y_{FE}, total receipts for any tax rate are represented by the appropriate rectangle under the curve in (a). In (b), we plot the area in the rectangles in (a) against the tax rate. Diagram (b) is the Laffer curve. The curve peaks at t^*, which is the rate at which the elasticity of the curve in (a) is just equal to 1.

There has been a great deal of misleading talk about the Laffer curve. Most of the confusion stems from a failure to distinguish the effect of tax cuts on observed income as opposed to capacity income. Tax cuts increase aggregate demand. If there is idle capacity, this will obviously lead to an increase in income. Tax receipts are likely to rise as well in such a situation. But that is because of demand-side multipliers, not induced supply-side effects, and is a straightforward application of Keynesian fiscal policy. It has nothing to do with the new notions of supply-side economics.

We have shown that the relationship between taxes and total saving is somewhat less obvious than it may appear in popular discussions. While tax cuts increase private saving, they generally reduce public saving at the same time. For the tax rates in our economy it is unlikely that the supply-side elasticity is greater than 1, which means that we are still on the positively sloped portion of the Laffer curve. Reducing tax rates increases government deficits by more than it increases private saving. Cutting taxes, therefore, is likely to crowd out private investment. While lower taxes may increase work effort, they are also likely to lead to lower rates of capital formation.

The Direct Effect of Taxes on Investment

Apart from its effect on saving, the tax system also has a direct effect on investment. Corporate taxes reduce the profitability of investment; hence the higher the corporate tax rate, the lower investment should be. Another tax factor affecting investment is the tax treatment of depreciation. Corporations are allowed to treat the depreciation of their capital stock as a cost. Since no one knows exactly how fast capital goods wear out, depreciation accounting uses general average lifetime rules for buildings and equipment. The average lifetimes are set by the Internal Revenue Service. If the government reduces the average lifetime of capital, it allows corporations to deduct a greater amount from their gross profits as depreciation. This lowers taxable net income and the corporate tax liability and thus increases gross after-tax corporate profits. Since investment is a function of after-tax profits, increasing depreciation should lead to greater investment.

Figure 20.6
Deriving the Laffer Curve

Diagram (a) shows the relationship between capacity income and the tax rate. The curve is negatively sloped because of the negative supply-side effects of raising tax rates. Since tax revenues are equal to the tax rate times Y_{FE}, tax receipts are the area under the curve in (a). This area is graphed in (b), where the curve traces out the Laffer curve. At t^*, the elasticity of the curve in (a) is just equal to -1.

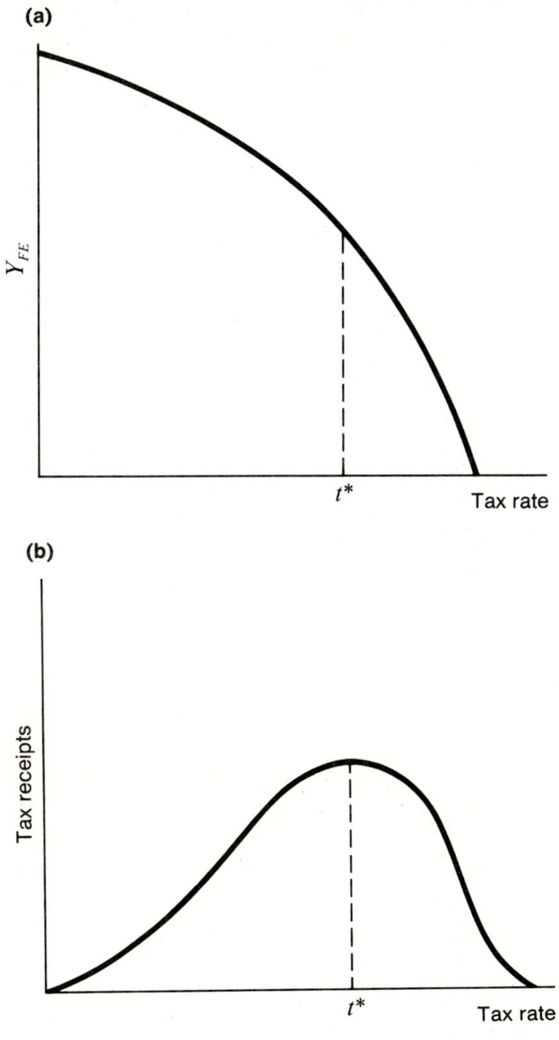

Still another obvious way to affect investment is to grant tax credits for investment. First used in 1962 under President Kennedy, tax credits allow a firm making an investment to deduct some portion of the investment cost from its tax liability. In this way the government pays part of the investment, thus lowering its direct cost and raising its profitability to the investor. Clearly, investment tax credits should encourage more investment, and they seem to have done so whenever they have been tried in the past.

Corporate Profitability As we have pointed out several times, the rate of capital formation in the United States is not particularly high. Contrary to popular belief, however, it has not declined in recent years—but neither has it grown much. Given the link between productivity growth and investment, there has been a good deal of interest in ways to stimulate investment. One fairly common belief is that the reason investment is not higher is because of a decline in corporate profitability in recent years. People who believe this generally favor some lowering of the corporate tax rate. Is there any truth to the claim that corporate profits have declined? Or, to put it another way, do we really need to cut corporate taxes in order to encourage more investment?

The question of profitability trends is not an easy one to answer. The gross rate of return measured by the rate of return on depreciable assets has declined (see column 4 in Table 20.1); however, the rate of return on stockholder equity has not. Indeed, in the three years since the economy came out of the 1974–1975 recession, this rate of return has been higher than it had been previously at comparable stages of the business cycle (see, for example, 1979 versus 1964 or 1956).

There are two reasons for the dispersion between the rate of return for depreciable assets and stockholder equity. One is corporate taxes. Because of a number of changes in the tax law, there has been a fairly substantial decline in corporate tax liabilities. The other is corporate borrowing. The denominator in the return-to-equity formula is net worth, which is the value of capital less than value of debt. Obviously, for the stockholder interest payments are a cost and are not included in after-tax profits. The divergence between these two measures of profits means that stockholders were able to borrow at less than the rate of return on capital to finance a large part of their capital formation. Investment was profitable, because a good deal of it was financed at low interest rates in an inflationary environment. The rate of return on assets fell but the rate of return to stockholders did not, because corporations were able to borrow so much at low rates. Whether that will continue to be true in the future will have a large effect on the net profitability of investment.

Whether or not the net trend in corporate profitability is up or down, it is clear from Table 20.1 that one very significant determinant of profitability is the level of aggregate demand. Profits are high in booms, low in recessions. If the government wishes to stimulate investment, a full employment policy, including cuts in corporate tax rates, is likely to do more than anything else.

Legislation Affecting Corporate Tax Rate When supply-siders call for reductions in taxes to stimulate investment, they seem to ignore the fact that there has already been a series of significant changes in the tax system, all of which have tended to shift taxes away from corporations and onto individuals. In 1962 an investment tax credit of 7 percent was granted on all new and used property other than buildings. The same act shortened the depreciation lifetimes of machinery by

Table 20.1
Measures of Corporate Profit, 1955–1980

	Pretax Corporate Profits/National Y	Corporate Tax/National Y	After-Tax Profit/New Investment	Rate of Return on Depreciable Assets	Rate of Return on Stockholder Equity
1955	13.8%	6.6%	7.2%	14.3%	6.2%
1956	12.5	6.3	6.2	12.2	5.5
1957	11.9	5.9	6.0	11.1	5.0
1958	10.5	5.2	5.3	9.5	3.9
1959	12.4	5.9	6.5	12.2	4.9
1960	11.4	5.5	5.9	11.1	5.0
1961	11.3	5.3	6.0	11.2	4.4
1962	12.2	5.2	7.0	12.9	5.9
1963	12.7	5.4	7.3	13.8	6.4
1964	13.2	5.3	7.9	14.7	7.6
1965	14.0	5.4	8.6	16.1	9.3
1966	13.6	5.4	8.2	15.8	9.1
1967	12.4	4.9	7.5	14.0	8.0
1968	12.3	5.4	6.9	13.8	7.8
1969	10.9	5.1	5.8	12.1	7.2
1970	8.8	4.2	4.6	9.5	4.6
1971	9.5	4.3	5.2	10.1	5.4
1972	10.0	4.3	5.7	10.7	6.7
1973	10.0	4.5	5.5	10.6	9.3
1974	8.2	4.4	3.8	8.1	8.7
1975	8.9	4.1	4.8	8.8	5.4
1976	10.0	4.6	5.4	9.6	4.9
1977	10.6	4.7	5.3	10.1	6.3
1978	10.6	4.8	5.8	9.9	7.1
1979	10.0	4.5	5.5	9.0	7.8
1980	8.6	3.8	4.8	—	—

Source: *Economic Report of the President* (Washington, D. C., 1982).

around one-third. Two years later, in 1964, the basic corporate tax rate was lowered from 52 percent to 48 percent. In 1975, as a part of the plan to stimulate demand, the corporate tax was reduced again, and the investment tax credit was raised to 10 percent. Then in 1978, the Revenue Act of 1978 reduced the corporate tax rate from 48 to 46 percent. It also made permanent the investment tax credit. The same act liberalized the treatment of long-term capital gains, lowering the effective rate on this form of income by about one-third.

In 1981, the Tax Reduction Act lowered the corporate tax rate again—to 45 percent—and, more important, substantially liberalized depreciation. In the so-called 10-5-3 scheme, the lifetime of buildings has been lowered to ten years, equipment to five years, and cars and trucks to three years. Furthermore, corporations not earning a profit are allowed to sell their tax deductions to profitable corporations. It is estimated that these measures will significantly reduce corporate tax liabilities. It should be clear from this long recitation of tax history that the idea of stimulating investment has already been used to substantially reduce the corporate tax rate. Whether we should go further in this direction is a question that future policymakers will have to decide.

Supply-Side Economics and the Fight Against Inflation

When one considers methods of fighting inflation, demand-side and supply-side policies stand in direct conflict.[6] To fight inflation by demand management, one raises taxes or reduces the growth rate of the money supply; that reduces demand. But supply-side theory has just shown us that those same policies have an adverse effect on supply, too. Higher taxes cut work effort, and restrictive monetary policy cuts capital formation. This leads to the paradoxical possibility that the effects of demand-side policies intended to reduce inflation might be perverse. If such policies reduce supply or raise costs by more than they lower demand, they could conceivably produce an increase in prices rather than the desired reduction.

Figure 20.7 shows the effect of an antiinflationary income surtax, such as we imposed in the United States in 1968–1969. As we learned earlier in the book, a surtax should cause the aggregate demand curve to shift downward, from D to D'. That obviously would lower the price level or inflation rates *if* supply were unaffected by the surtax. But supply-side economics tells us that supply is affected, and in a perverse way—it contracts. Both the long- and the short-run supply curves shift to the left. As the reader can see, if the demand shift is bigger than the supply shift, prices will fall. If it is smaller, the surtax will raise, not lower, prices. As we have drawn the diagram, the demand shift is bigger so the surtax, on balance, is antiinflationary. P_1, the price level after the surtax, is lower than the original price level, P_0. But the size of relative curve shifts could be reversed. Surtaxes could be inflationary.

Exactly the same considerations apply to monetary policy. Its demand-side antiinflationary effects are well known. Less well known are the opposing supply-side effects we looked at in the last section. Monetary policy reduces demand; that helps to lower inflation. But at the same time, capital formation is discouraged by higher interest rates; that tends to reduce capacity and is inflationary. Just as in the case of taxes, if the supply-side effect dominates prices go up; if the demand-side effect is larger, prices go down.[7]

[6]For a succinct discussion of inflation and supply-side economics, see Martin Feldstein, "Inflation and Supply-Side Economics," *The Wall Street Journal,* May 20, 1980, 22. See also J. Dewey Daane and Samuel A. Morley, "Supply Chic," loc. cit.

[7]This argument is developed at greater length in Samuel A. Morley, "The Relationship between Money, Income and Prices in the Short and Long Run," *Journal of Finance* 27 (December 1973): 1119–1130.

Figure 20.7
Supply and Demand Effects of an Antiinflationary Surtax

An antiinflationary surtax shifts the demand curve from DD to $D'D'$. The supply curve also shifts leftward because of the negative supply-side effects of higher tax rates. As a result, equilibrium shifts from point A to point B. In this diagram, since the demand-side shifts are greater than the supply-side shifts, the surtax lowers prices. If the supply-side effects were greater, a surtax could actually raise, rather than lower, prices. It is believed by most economists that demand shifts are larger than supply shifts, which implies that surtaxes are still an effective weapon against inflation, in spite of their perverse supply-side effects.

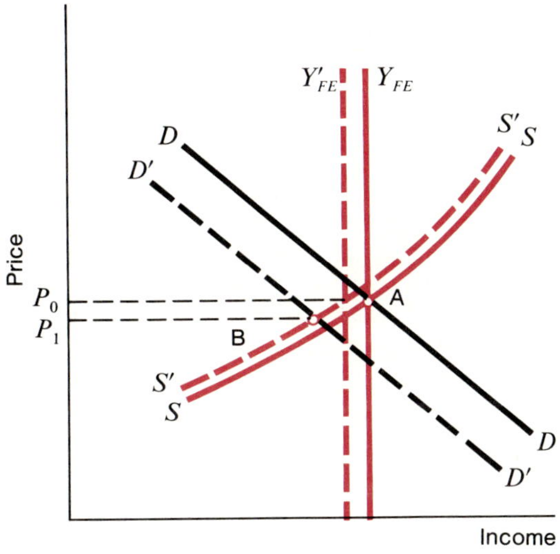

At bottom, the question of which effect is bigger is an empirical one that must be decided by investigation of behavior. Among economists there is pretty widespread agreement that, in the short run, the demand effects dominate. For all the policies affecting capital formation the reasoning is straightforward: Investment creates capacity, but the amount of capacity created per dollar of investment is generally far smaller than one dollar, simply because it usually takes more than a dollar of machinery to produce a dollar of output. (In the language of economics, the capital-output ratio is larger than one.) Hence, if investment is reduced by hiking the corporate income tax or by raising interest rates, the reduction in capacity is much smaller than the reduction in investment. Since the demand effect is the change in investment and the supply effect is the change in capacity, one can see that the demand effect is larger.

The relative magnitudes are less obvious for household taxes. Increased income taxes and sales taxes reduce consumption—that is the demand effect. They also reduce labor supply and saving—the supply-side effect. Otto Eckstein, to our knowledge, is the only economist to have attempted to quantify these two effects.

According to him, the labor supply effects of higher taxes, while significant, are not nearly so great as the reduction in consumption. Once again demand factors dominate.

The assertion that supply factors are less important than demand factors, however, is an argument about the short run. When the government lowers business taxes, which raises the demand for capital, capital formation goes up. This is the demand effect. In the longer run, after the economy has adjusted to the change, capital formation returns to its previous level, but the economy now has a larger capacity. That is the supply expansion stressed by supply-siders. In the short run, the tax reduction for investment increases net demand—that is inflationary. In the long run, it increases supply more than demand—that reduces inflation.

Typically, economists look at the short run. But if policy is being designed for a long period, one cannot afford to take so narrow a view. For example, if the government is planning a ten-year antiinflationary program, the supply factors may be exceedingly relevant. Several stabilization programs currently under discussion in the United States call for a decade of above-normal unemployment and excess capacity. This is sure to lower capital formation. A decade of such a policy would have a noticeable effect on our capacity and productivity. The same would obviously be true if we follow the prescription of many inflation fighters to have a decade of tight money.

Case Study

Reaganomics

The Reagan economic program has been billed as the nation's first application of supply-side economics. It couples large tax and expenditure cuts for the government with a fairly contractionary monetary policy. The program has been advocated as a simultaneous cure for stagnation and inflation[8]—it promises to bring greater economic growth and a lower rate of inflation at the same time. If it is successful, it will be a truly revolutionary change in policy. Higher growth and greater price stability are two goals that have never before been simultaneously achieved.

Expressed in our language, **Reaganomics** is based on the belief that the expansionary supply-side effects of this particular package of monetary and fiscal policies will be greater than the expansionary effects on demand. In the public discussion of the program, it was generally assumed that the fiscal element of tax and expenditure cuts would be expansionary, because the cuts in taxes were so

[8]There has been a large volume of literature on Reaganomics. In particular, see David Stockman, "How to Avoid an Economic Dunkirk," *Challenge* 24 (March-April 1981): 17–21; and Henry Kaufman, "Reaganomics: Why Isn't Wall Street Convinced?" *Challenge* 24 (September-October 1981): 43–48. For critical views, see James Tobin, "The Reagan Economic Plan," loc. cit., and Alfred S. Eichner, "Reagan's Doubtful Game Plan," *Challenge* 24 (May-June 1981): 19–27.

much greater than the cuts in expenditure. However, most of this discussion ignored monetary policy. It should not have. For if fiscal policy was expansionary, it was working directly at cross-purposes to contractionary monetary policy. As we learned in Chapter 5, that particular policy combination leads to large government deficits, which must be financed in the bond market. That drives up interest rates and crowds out private investment. Overall, demand may still expand, but it is clear that the main effect of expansionary fiscal policy coupled with contractionary monetary policy is to change the composition rather than the level of aggregate demand. Consumption is increased, investment is reduced. This is why the monetarists on the Reagan economic team insisted that the tax cut would not be inflationary. Without a complementary increase in the money supply, the tax cut would not have a large effect on the overall level of aggregate spending.

Where the Reagan economists were not right was in their analysis of supply-side effects. They expected a substantial rightward shift in the supply curve because of the tax cuts and lowered expectations about inflation. But they seem to have overlooked the negative effect of recession and tight money on supply. Their program was introduced in an economy in recession. Since the combined effect of monetary and fiscal policies was not expansionary, there was little to pull the economy out of recession—and a great deal to push it further in. Under the best of circumstances, expansionary fiscal policy and tight money would have crowded out investment. But capital formation was further reduced by the prospect of extended recession. As we showed earlier, capital formation always falls in recession, and this was no exception.

Recession also tempers the labor supply effect of lower tax rates. With an unemployment rate of over 8 percent by the fall of 1981, there was no guarantee that any extra workers would be able to find work. Indeed, if there is a labor supply effect from lower taxes, its size is undoubtedly related to the level of economic activity. In recessions it is hardly obvious that the effect is operative. Under the best of circumstances supply-side effects are fairly small, at least in the short run. But with a severe recession, such as the one in 1981–1982, they are likely to be even smaller than usual.

We have drawn a diagram of the Reagan program in Figure 20.8. The solid lines show aggregate supply and demand as it was in the summer of 1981, before the application of Reaganomics. The economy was well below full employment at Y. The dotted lines show what the Reagan economists hoped would happen to supply as a result of their program. They thought that demand would expand slightly to D' and supply would increase a great deal to S', because of the supply-side effects of their tax cuts, lower inflation expectations, and the preferential tax treatment given to investors. As the reader can see, an expansion of supply to S' would have allowed a simultaneous increase in income to Y' and a reduction in the rate of inflation.

If we are correct, however, Reaganomics has, if anything, reduced rather than increased supply. Rather than shifting outward to S', the short-run supply curve has probably shifted back slightly to the dashed line S''. As a result, income stagnated but inflation continued at a high rate throughout 1981. Subsequently, in 1982, inflation declined, but that was the result of the favorable effect of high unemployment on wage rates and not supply-side economics.

Figure 20.8
The Effect of Reaganomics

Reagan inherited an economy operating below full employment at Y. Tax cuts shifted demand out slightly to D'. The Reagan administration believed that the supply-side incentives of its program would have a great effect on supply, shifting the supply curve out to S'. Had this happened, output would have increased from Y to Y', while simultaneously the rate of inflation would have declined from P to P'. However, if we are correct, the supply-side effects from recession and the continuation of restrictive monetary policy are likely to have shifted the supply curve to the left, to S'', leading to only a slight increase in output, to Y'', and an exacerbation of inflationary pressures.

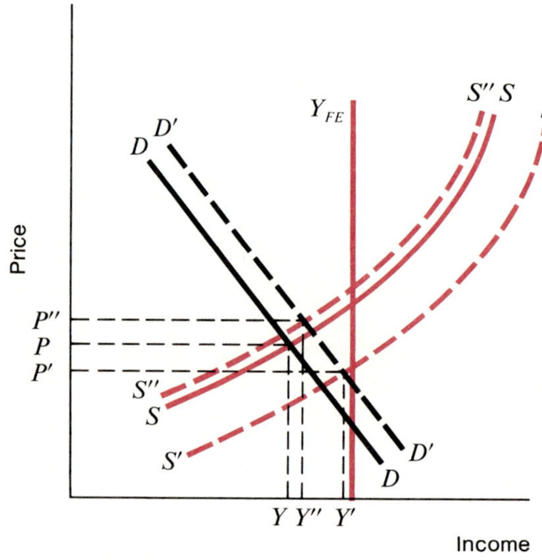

Overall, therefore, despite its label as supply-side, the Reagan program was very much like any other orthodox anti-inflation program. Because of its tight monetary policy, it kept the economy in recession. That brought down inflation, but it was through recession, not supply-side effects. Unfortunately, we have not enjoyed many positive supply-side effects from Reaganomics, partly because the positive effects of tax cuts were offset by the investment-reducing effects of tight money and partly because the program, on balance, did not give us enough expansion to get out of recession.

Combining Monetary Fiscal Policies to Maximize Positive Supply-Side Effects

Supply-side economics makes life more difficult for macroeconomic policymakers. If they are trying to control inflation through restrictive demand management, supply-side effects produce wholly unwanted reductions in supply at the same time. If demand management is neutral, and if policymakers wish to maximize supply-side benefits, certain mixes of monetary policy and fiscal policy are called for. Based upon what we have learned, let us see if we can develop some general guidelines that would be helpful to policymakers. These guidelines all depend on behavioral relationships in the economy about which not enough is known. If behavior were different, the optimal policy mix would change.

1. Economists believe that demand-side effects of both monetary and fiscal policies are larger than supply-side effects in the short run. That means that one cannot fight inflation with expansionary monetary or fiscal policies. While both will shift supply curves to the right, the shifts they will cause in the demand curves will be greater. Expansionary policy, therefore, will raise prices, even taking into account supply-side effects. There does not appear to be any combination of monetary and fiscal policies that increases supply by more than it increases the level of demand. Therefore, supply-side economics does not change in any fundamental way our beliefs about ways to control inflation.

2. One maximizes the positive supply-side effects of any policy by keeping some demand pressure on capacity. Empirical studies show that the single most important determinant of investment is capacity utilization. Hence, if we want a high-investment, rapid-growth economy, we should use demand management to keep the economy close to full employment. Not only should such a policy increase investment, it also should maximize the positive benefit of any inducements to an expansion in labor supply. Supply-siders have taught us to be concerned with the effect of taxes on labor supply. But when the government lowers taxes in order to increase the supply of labor, this will have little effect in a slack economy. There cannot be much of an increase in work effort on the part of the labor force in the face of high rates of unemployment.

From all of this, the message is clear: a demand policy that aims at the kink in the short run supply curve is also a high-growth, high-productivity policy. Put the other way, orthodox stabilization programs may fight inflation, but they are also recipes for low investment and slow growth of both productivity and income.

3. For a given level of aggregate demand, the mix of monetary and fiscal policy that maximizes positive supply-side effects depends on the relative strength of tax effects on labor and the effects of monetary and fiscal policies on investment. To simplify the following discussion, let us suppose that tax policy affects only labor supply, while monetary policy affects only investment.

Consider Figure 20.9. Suppose the authorities wish to keep aggregate demand at Y^*. They can do this by combining an easy fiscal with a restrictive monetary policy, an easy money with a restrictive fiscal policy, or some combination of the two. Which should they choose? Our rule says that the choice depends on the relative strength of supply-side effects on labor and capital formation.

The authorities can keep aggregate demand at Y^* by choosing either the solid or the dashed IS-LM curves. The solid curves represent a combination of easy fiscal policy counterbalanced with relatively contractionary monetary policy. Presumably there is a high level of government expenditure and deficits that must be financed by bond sales. Interest rates are high, and the share of investment in GNP is low.

Figure 20.9
Combinations of Monetary and Fiscal Policy to Affect the Composition of Aggregate Demand
The solid IS-LM curves represent a policy mix of easy fiscal and tight monetary policy. This policy mix keeps income at Y^*, but because it has relatively high interest rates the investment ratio, I_1/Y^*, is lower than the policy mix represented by the dashed IS-LM curves. Here a more restrictive fiscal policy is offset by an easier monetary policy. Aggregate income is still Y^*, but the new investment ratio, I_2/Y^*, is larger because interest rates are lower.

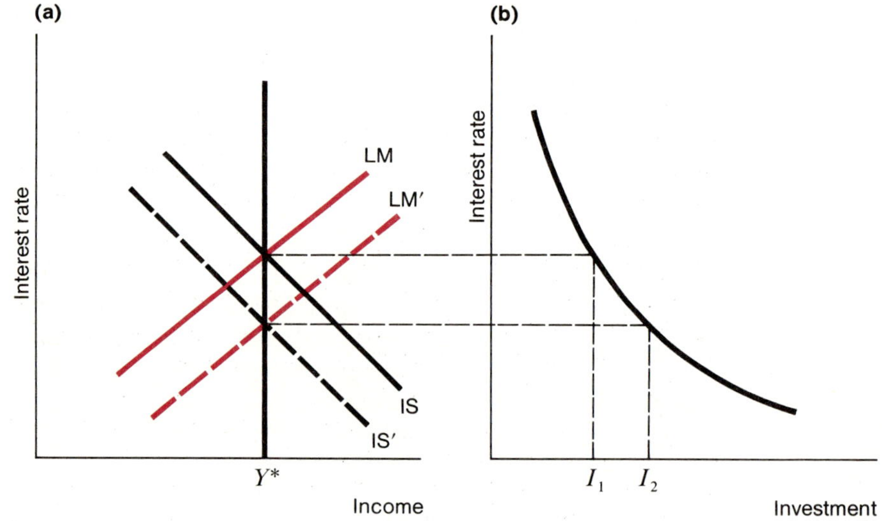

The dashed IS-LM curves represent the opposite policy—restrictive fiscal combined with expansionary monetary. Here tax rates are high, government expenditures are low, and the monetary authorities expand the money supply by enough to lower interest rates and increase private investment by enough to maintain the overall level of demand. As the reader can see, this is obviously the high-investment policy. If the authorities wish to raise the rate of capital formation, they should use the tight fiscal-easy money policy combination.

There is a complication, however. We have ignored the effect of taxes on labor supply. If we raise taxes and have easy money we will increase investment, but we may also discourage labor supply. It could be that the effect on capacity of lower labor supply outweighs the favorable effect of higher investment—that is, the supply-side effects of fiscal policy may be more important than the supply-side effects of monetary policy. When that is the case, authorities should use the tight money-easy fiscal combination. When it is not, the tight fiscal-easy money policy is best.

Under current conditions in the United States, capital appears to be more of a constraint than labor, for the labor force is growing rapidly and the capital-labor ratio is not. Hence, the supply-side effects of monetary policy on investment are likely to be greater than those of taxes on labor supply. If this is so, supply-side considerations call for the tight fiscal-easy money policy. They call for raising taxes on households, lowering taxes on business, and giving investment tax credits. They also call for reducing nonessential government expenditure, since it crowds out private investment when monetary policy does not accommodate it. Finally, monetary policy should be sufficiently expansionary to keep aggregate demand close to full employment.

In the United States we have not followed this policy package during the 1970s—indeed, we have done almost exactly the opposite. We have cut taxes, increased government expenditures, and run large deficits, but we have relied on the Federal Reserve to keep the lid on demand. Politically, this was the easy thing to do. Various administrations could cut taxes and fight recession with large spending programs and government deficits, meanwhile blaming the contractionary Fed for our failure to keep the economy closer to full employment. This approach may have been an effective way to fight inflation (although I am doubtful), but it certainly was not a good way to increase capital formation and the rate of growth of productivity. Indeed, as one commentator pointed out, with respect to investment, the mystery was not why investment was so low in the late 1970s but rather why it was as high as it was, given the degree of slack in the economy and the high interest rates.[9]

Summary

In the popular view, supply-side economics means accounting for the positive effect of lower taxes and less regulation on labor supply, capital formation, and labor productivity. However, we defined the term more generally as the effect of all government policies on the level of capacity output in the economy. Most macroeconomic government policies have both demand-side and supply-side effects; heretofore, our analysis has focused only on the demand side. Supply-side economics looks at the effect of those same policies on the long- and short-run supply curves.

Supply-side effects can be decomposed into those affecting labor supply, capital formation, and productivity. Of the many government policies that one could examine, we focused on regulation, taxes, and monetary policy. Regulation primarily affects productivity and capital formation. Income taxes reduce the supply of labor, since they reduce after-tax income. Business taxes and restrictive monetary policy reduce investment. Each of these tends to reduce long-run capacity in the economy.

One of the reasons that supply-side economics gained such rapid acceptance was its promise that we could have our cake and eat it too. The supply-siders told us we could cut taxes and not worry about the inflationary consequences, because

[9] Peter K. Clark, "Investment in the 1970s: Theory, Performance, and Prediction," *Brookings Papers on Economic Activity* (1/1979): 103.

the supply-side effects of lower taxes on capital formation, labor supply, and saving would more than outweigh the inflationary impact of higher demand.

Unfortunately, a closer look shows this view to be either wrong or seriously misleading. First, it ignores monetary policy. If monetary policy is not adjusted, lower taxes almost certainly imply higher government deficits. The resulting increase in private saving is more than offset by a reduction in government saving. Hence, lowering taxes almost certainly reduces capital formation rather than increasing it. Those same tax cuts may increase the supply of labor, but whether the net effect is positive or negative depends on the relative strength of labor supply and capital formation effects on capacity. There are tax rates so high that lowering taxes does increase capacity income enough to lower the government deficit and, therefore, increase total saving. This is what the discussion of the Laffer curve is all about. However, there is fairly wide agreement that tax rates in the United States are not nearly that high. For us, lower taxes most probably lower rather than raise government revenues and total saving.

Can supply-side effects help in the fight against inflation? Unfortunately, it is likely that they cannot. When one uses the standard orthodox antiinflation program of demand restraint, supply-side effects are perverse; they tend to reduce capacity, which is price increasing. Nor does supply-side economics give us a new and less painful way to fight inflation. It is very unlikely that the supply-side effects of expansionary policy are large enough to outweigh the direct effect of demand growth on price. Instead, what supply-side economics does is remind us that our standard orthodox remedies are less effective than we had previously thought.

Rather than a short-run weapon to be used against inflation, supply-side economics should be thought of as a set of theories to help us design a longer-run strategy to increase the growth rate of capacity. In this light, it gives us several simple but important policy maxims. First, the government should strive to keep the economy close to Y_{FE}; allowing the economy to stagnate, whatever the reason, means slow growth in both productivity and income. Second, the aim of monetary and fiscal policies should be to achieve a given degree of restraint or expansion with maximum positive supply-side benefits or minimum supply-side costs. The optimal policy combination depends upon the relative strengths of supply-side effect on labor supply and capital formation. If the latter effects dominate, as we would expect them to in the United States, the government should use restrictive fiscal policy coupled with easy money. That will increase the share of investment in the short run and raise the level of national income in the long run. The Reagan administration apparently believes that the labor supply effects are more important than the effect of tight money on investment, for it has lowered taxes and counterbalanced with restrictive monetary policy. It is still too early to tell whether this policy, taken in the name of supply-side economics, will actually lead to a faster rate of growth of capacity.

Key Concepts

supply-side economics
taxes and labor supply
Laffer curve
Reaganomics
recession and investment
taxes and the saving rate

Problems and Questions for Discussion

1. Why is the net effect of income taxes on labor supply indeterminant? Under what conditions will a rise in taxes reduce the supply of labor?

2. What are the different ways in which monetary and fiscal policies affect the supply of capital? Which do you think is the most important?

The following model of the economy will be used in Problems 3–6. Note that the level of aggregate demand is assumed to be determined by the simple quantity theory, which means that any change in government deficits is financed by bond sales.

Production Function

$$Y_{FE} = \tfrac{1}{3}KL.$$

Aggregate Demand

$$MV = PY.$$

Government Saving

$$S_g = tY - G.$$

Private Saving

$$S_h = -\overline{C} + s(1 - t)Y.$$

3. If

$G = 250$	$K = 3000$
$t = .25$	$L = 1.0$
$s = .20$	$M = 500$
$\overline{C} = 10$	$V = 2$

a. Find Y, I, S_g, and S_h.
b. Derive an expression for total saving.
c. What happens to total saving and investment if the government lowers the tax rate from 25 percent to 20 percent?

4. In Problem 3 we calculated the effect of tax cuts on investment. Now we calculate the effect of these changes on the growth rate of income. According to the production function, capacity income is a function of the capital stock and the labor force. If we ignore depreciation, we know that the change in the capital stock is equal to investment:

$$K_{t+1} - K_t = I_t.$$

a. Using the production function, calculate the growth rate of income for the tax rate of 25 percent. Assume that L is constant and that there is an increase in M proportional to the increase in Y.

b. How does the growth rate of the economy change when the tax rate is reduced to 20 percent? (This demonstrates the long-run negative effects of crowding out on the capital stock and the growth rate.)

5. In Problems 3 and 4 we found that reductions in the tax rate adversely affect the growth rate of income. That was partially because we ignored the positive effects of tax reductions on the supply curve of labor. We now make the supply of labor a function of after-tax disposable income and recalculate the supply-side effects of tax cuts.

Suppose labor supply is the following function of disposable income:

$$L = .03651\ (Y[1 - t])^{\frac{1}{2}}.$$

All other functions are the same as in Problem 3.

a. Derive a reduced-form expression for Y as a function of the capital stock and the tax rate.

b. What is labor supply, income, and investment when $K = 3000$ and $t = 25\%$?

c. Calculate Y, S_T, I, S_g, and S_h for a tax rate of 20 percent. Does income increase or decrease when taxes are cut from 25 percent to 20 percent? Why?

d. Does the growth rate of income increase or decrease when taxes are cut from 25 percent to 20 percent? How can you tell?

e. On balance, would you say that the supply-side effects of tax cuts are positive or negative in this case? Why?

6. For the economy represented in Problem 5, plot total tax revenue as a function of the tax rate. The curve you will have plotted is the Laffer curve for this particular economy. At approximately what tax rate does tax revenue reach a maximum?

7. Once the government has decided upon the level of expenditures it desires, its problem is to finance these expenditures in a manner that has the fewest effects on supply. Discuss the alternatives that are available and the likely effects of each on aggregate supply. Which method of financing do you favor? Why?

8. Consider an economy in which the supply of labor is a negative function of the tax rate. Suppose this economy is operating at less than full employment. Using the aggregate goods market diagram, show what happens to actual and full employment income if there is a tax cut accompanied by an expansion of the money supply. Identify in your diagram that part of the increase in income which is due to the supply-side effects of the tax cuts. How much is due to the stimulus of demand?

9. Are there any conditions under which a reduction in the money supply, undertaken to restrain inflation, could actually lead to an increase in prices? If so, demonstrate how this anomalous result could happen using the aggregate goods market diagram. Does your answer differ in the short and the long run?

10. The orthodox antiinflation program reduces aggregate demand and causes a recession in the short run. What are the effects of this type of policy on the aggregate supply curve? Are there circumstances under which the orthodox policy could be counterproductive? If so, what are they? If not, why not?

11. Reaganomics was designed and explained to the American people as a supply-side program.

- **a.** Describe briefly what the fiscal and monetary implications of the program were.
- **b.** Under what conditions could the program have increased supply?
- **c.** Why didn't it lead to an increase in income (at least in the first two years)?
- **d.** On balance, was the effect of the program supply-enhancing?

Chapter 21

The International Sector

Up to this point we have ignored the fact that the United States is part of a world economy. We have conducted our analysis as if the rest of the world had no influence on our economy or our policymakers. While that used to be a fairly defensible assumption years ago when we imported and exported less than 5 percent of GNP, it no longer is. Foreign markets have become increasingly important to American business and American workers, and foreign sources of supply now play a critical role in determining our economic health. At present, foreign trade comprises over 11 percent of GNP and one out of eight jobs in U. S. manufacturing depends, directly or indirectly, on export sales.

The foreign sector adds another complicating dimension to the tasks of macroeconomic policymakers. Internally they must try to control the level of aggregate demand and the inflation rate. Externally they have to worry about the balance of payments. Maintaining the balance of payments equilibrium is the third in the triad of goals that macropolicymakers must try simultaneously to achieve.

In this chapter we shall investigate the balance of payments mechanism and the dollar market. We start off with some formal definitions of the balance of payments. We then go on to examine the foreign exchange markets and the various factors determining the exchange rate. Finally, in the next chapter, we incorporate the dollar market into a macromodel of the open economy to see what effect the foreign sector has on the operation of macroeconomic policy.

The Balance of Payments

Basic to an understanding of the foreign sector is a set of accounting definitions for our transactions with the rest of the world. This accounting, shown in Table 21.1, is called the **balance of payments.** It is essentially the difference between the demand and supply of dollars. Dollars are demanded to buy U. S. goods or to make

Table 21.1
U. S. International Transactions in 1979
(U. S. dollars in billions)

	Supply of Dollars (to Foreigners)		Demand for Dollars (from Foreigners)		Balance
Current Account					
1. Goods and Services	−281.5	Goods and Services	+286.5	Goods and Services	+5.0
Imports	−211.5	Exports	+182.1		
Services	−36.5	Services	+38.4		
Investment income and other payments to/from foreigners	−33.5	Investment income and payments by foreigners	+66.0		
2. Net Transfers	−5.7		—	Net Transfers	−5.7
Government grants	−3.5				
Government and private pensions and remittances	−2.1				
3. Current Account Total (1 + 2)	−287.1		+286.5	Current Account	−0.7
Capital Account					
4. Private Investment	−56.9	Private Investment by foreigners in U.S.	+51.8	Private investment	−5.1
5. Government	−3.8		—	Government	−3.8
6. Capital Account Total (4 + 5)	−60.7		+51.8	Capital Account	−8.9
7. Statistical Discrepancy				Statistical Discrepancy	+23.9
Total (3 + 6 + 7)	−347.8		338.3	Total (official reserve transactions balance	+14.3[a]

[a] Financing of the surplus:

Reduction in foreign official reserves	−14.3
Increase in U. S. official reserves	− 1.1
Increase in U. S. special drawing rights	+ 1.1

Source: *Survey of Current Business,* March 1981.

investments in the United States. Dollars are supplied by Americans wishing to buy foreign commodities or securities. If these two flows are not equal, central banks are forced to take corrective action. Either they must buy up the excess supply of dollars or foreign currency, run down international reserves, or allow the exchange rate to adjust to reestablish equilibrium. Maintenance of balance of payments equilibrium is a major task of our macropolicymakers.

There are two main components of the balance of payments: the **current account** and the **capital account.**

The current account shows our trade in goods and services plus transfer payments. The account has positive and negative entries. The positive entries are items that improve our balance of payments and that represent a demand for dollars. Examples are exports, profits remittances by U. S. corporations abroad, and spending by foreign tourists in the United States. Negative entries in the current account represent the corresponding supply of dollars to buy foreign currencies. Imports, spending by U. S. tourists abroad, interest payments to foreigners, profit remittances by foreign corporations, and aid to foreign governments are the main entries on the negative side of the current account. As the reader can see, the United States imports far more than it exports. This is due in large part to two items, oil ($61 billion) and automobiles ($25.6 billion). However, this large deficit is almost completely offset by earnings on U. S. overseas investments. The balance of payments on goods and services alone (line 1 in Table 21.1) is the amount that goes into the national accounts as net exports.

The other component of the balance of payments, the capital account, records foreign investment in the United States and investments by Americans abroad. The positive entry in the capital account is the demand for dollars by foreigners to buy assets in the United States, while the negative entry is the supply of dollars spent by Americans to buy foreign assets. In 1979, as in almost every other year in the postwar period, Americans have invested more abroad than foreigners have invested here.

The final item worth noting is the so-called **statistical discrepancy.** Not all of the transactions between U. S. citizens and foreigners are carried on through official channels where they can get recorded. When there is a difference between the measured current and capital account transactions and official reserve transactions, the difference is reconciled by the statistical discrepancy entry. In 1979 this item was +23.9 billion, an amount so large that it pushed our entire balance of payments into surplus by $14.3 billion.

The sum of the current and capital account balances is the best measure of the overall balance of payments. Formally it is called the *official reserve transactions balance,* since any deficit or surplus must be settled by official transactions between central banks. Whenever there is a deficit or a surplus, as there was in 1979, the dollar market is not in balance. The demand for dollars either exceeds or falls short of the supply. When that happens, either foreign central banks or our own Federal Reserve must step in to absorb the excess. If there is an excess supply of dollars (called **BOP deficit**), foreign central banks absorb the excess by increasing their official reserves; if there is a surplus, foreign central banks run down their reserves, or the Federal Reserve increases its official reserves. These equilibrating transactions are called **official reserve transactions** (ORT). Thus, the item official reserve transactions measures the overall deficit or surplus in the balance of payments. If the ORT is positive, as it was in 1979, the United States has run a surplus, and our net official reserve position has improved. A negative ORT means that the United States is running a BOP deficit.

There are three ways to finance a balance of payments deficit (or surplus). The United States can transfer gold to foreigners, a method that was quite common in the 1950s before we depleted our gold supply. We can draw down our official reserves with the International Monetary Fund (IMF). Finally, because other countries hold dollars as a part of their reserves, we may be able to finance our deficits by getting foreign central banks to hold more dollars. This method was a fairly common one before foreigners realized that they were in effect giving the United States interest-free loans.

Let us look back at Table 21.1 to see how our balance of payments surplus was financed by foreigners in 1979. Our surplus was $14.3 billion. To finance this, foreign central banks ran down their official dollar reserves in the United States by $14.3 billion. At the same time, the United States received an additional line of credit of $1.1 billion at the International Monetary Fund called **Special Drawing Rights,** which we used to increase our official reserves.

The Economic Significance of the Balance of Payments

Over the last 20 years, the typical balance of payments position of the United States was one in which we ran a current account surplus that was more than offset by a capital account deficit, with the result that in most years the ORT was negative. The year 1979 was an exception to this rule because of the large statistical discrepancy item. A record of the three accounts over this period is shown in Figure 21.1. This implies that throughout most of the postwar period the total supply of dollars has been greater than the demand for dollars. As a result there has been continuous pressure on the exchange rate and constant problems in the foreign exchange market. Just what is the significance of such balance of payments deficits?

There are two different types of balance of payments deficits that should be distinguished. One is the result of a deficit in the current account, while the other comes from a deficit in the capital account. The United States has had the second sort of deficit. It is a good deal less serious than the first. Let us see why.

If a country runs a surplus in its current account, by definition it must be accumulating assets abroad. Why? Since the country is exporting more than it imports, buyers of its products must be "paying" for part of their purchases with IOUs rather than exports. (Since its imports are smaller than its exports, those IOUs are an asset that can be cashed in at any time to increase imports.) Thus, a current account surplus is a form of investment that builds up assets abroad that may one day be cashed in to increase a country's own standard of living.

But, you may ask, what about a country like the United States, which historically has run deficits in its capital account that were larger than its current account surplus? Are these deficits not a cause for alarm? Definitionally, our capital account deficit simply means that in addition to accumulating assets from the current account surplus the United States has also invested more abroad than foreigners have invested here. During most of the postwar period, U.S. corporations have

Figure 21.1
The U. S. Balance of Payments

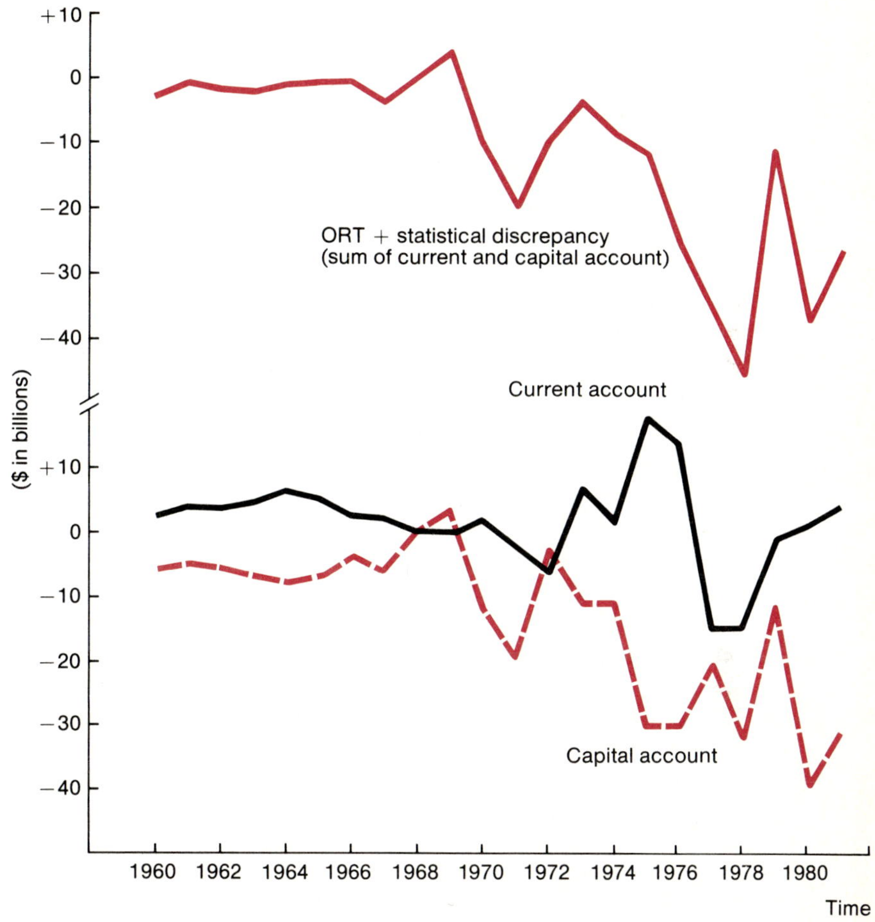

embarked on a massive buildup of their overseas assets. **Direct investment,** which is what this form of transaction is called, is exemplified by the purchase or construction by General Motors of a plant in Belgium or the oil explorations by U. S. oil companies in the Middle East. A massive surge of direct investment in response to the Common Market in Europe, and to a lesser extent to secure natural resource supplies in other countries, is largely responsible for the U. S. capital account balance of payments deficit.

When one thinks about the significance of this type of deficit, it is clear that the balance of payments accounting leaves out something, namely, the value of U. S. assets abroad. A capital account deficit means that the supply exceeds the demand for dollars. But it does not mean that the United States does not have assets to exchange for those dollars if it should choose to do so. The assets it has are primarily the foreign assets of U. S. corporations. In total value they far exceed the supply of dollars or dollar-denominated assets held by foreigners, because part of their value has been paid for by current account surpluses.

Suppose General Motors decides to make an overseas investment by transferring capital from the United States. Assuming previous balance and no offsetting foreign capital movement, this sort of direct investment causes a deficit in the capital account, which will be financed in one of the three ways we described. The United States may transfer gold or international reserves to the accounts of the foreign central bank, or the foreign central bank may hold the excess supply of U. S. dollars. Let us look at the transaction. General Motors has its overseas factory, in exchange for which the central bank of the recipient country has either gold, international reserves, or dollars. In effect, the United States has traded the foreign government a liquid asset—gold or reserves—for a factory. There is no transfer of wealth, simply a change in the portfolio of the two countries: The United States has a greater stock of physical capital, and the foreign country has a greater stock of liquid assets.

An entirely different sort of balance of payments problem is one in which a country runs a current account deficit that it finances by a capital account surplus. In this case, the overall balance of payments may well be positive, but the country builds up net liabilities rather than assets abroad. It is, in effect, living beyond its means and financing the excess by borrowing. Sooner or later those loans will have to be repaid, at which time the supply of output for domestic consumption must decline.

We would argue that in the long run, the current account balance is economically more significant than the capital account balance because it shows whether a country is accumulating assets or liabilities abroad. It is natural for developing countries to run current account deficits and to be net debtor countries. Over time, as their need for credit diminishes, they begin to pay back those loans and even to extend credit to other countries.

The Foreign Exchange Market

Because American sellers won't accept marks and foreigners don't generally accept dollars, Americans who want to buy Porsches or factories on the Rhine or Germans who want to buy Levis or shares in General Motors each have to exchange their own domestic currency for foreign exchange. Americans who wish to import, travel, or invest abroad get foreign exchange from American banks, which in turn are supplied by the Federal Reserve. Foreigners who wish to buy things in the United States go to their banks and exchange their currencies for dollars. Foreign banks get those dollars from foreign central banks. In this way, transactions among countries with different currencies create what we will call a market for foreign exchange. The idea of a market obviously is an abstraction that represents a complex network of banks, central banks, and companies specializing in the purchase and sale of foreign exchange.

Two aspects of this foreign exchange market are central. One is the key role played by central banks. Since they provide foreign exchange for their citizens, they can and do control the exchange rate, which is nothing but the price of foreign exchange. Thinking now specifically of the dollar market, the second thing to remember is that demand in the dollar market is composed of foreigners wishing to buy either U. S. goods and services or U. S. assets. Hence, the demand for dollars represents exports plus foreign investment in the United States. Dollars are supplied by Americans who wish to buy things abroad, be they imports, hotel rooms in Paris, or foreign assets.

The Effect of Exchange Rates and Prices on the Demand and Supply of Dollars

We now wish to analyze the main economic variables that determine each of the components of the demand and supply of dollars (see Table 21.2).

The Relative Price of Domestic and Foreign Goods One of the main determinants of both imports and exports is the relative price of U. S. and foreign products, P_{REL}. This relative price is written:

$$\frac{eP}{P_f}.$$

e = exchange rate in foreign currency/U. S. \$
P = U. S. price
P_f = foreign price

The variable e will play an important part in our analysis. It is called the **exchange rate,** which we shall define as the price of dollars; e is the number of marks, yen, or pounds that foreigners have to pay for dollars. Note that e is the inverse of what Americans usually think of when they think of exchange rates. We are more accustomed to thinking of the exchange rate in terms of how much we have to pay for foreign currency. Thus, we usually express the dollar-pound exchange rate as \$2.30 per pound. But we shall write the exchange between dollars and pounds as:

$$e = \frac{1}{2.30} = .43.$$

This says that Englishmen pay .43 pounds for 1 dollar. The reason for reversing the usual way of writing the exchange rate will be clear in a moment.

In the expression for P_{REL}, since e is the price of dollars and P is the price of commodities the numerator of this expression, eP, is the price in foreign currency that foreigners have to pay for U. S. commodities. When we divide this by the price of foreign commodities, we see that the entire expression represents the relative price of U. S. products to foreigners.

Table 21.2
Factors Affecting the Demand and Supply of Dollars

	Effect		
	Positive	**Negative**	**Uncertain**
Supply of Dollars			
Current Account			
Imports	$\uparrow$ U. S. Income		$\uparrow P_{REL}$
Capital Account			
U. S. direct investment		$\uparrow \Pi_{US}/\Pi_f$	
Portfolio investment		$\uparrow r_{US}/r_f$	
Demand for Dollars			
Current Account			
Exports	$\uparrow$ Foreign Income	$\uparrow P_{REL}$	
Capital Account			
Foreign investment in U. S.	$\uparrow \Pi_{US}/\Pi_f$		
Foreign portfolio investment in U. S.	$\uparrow r_{US}/r_f$		

Definitions:
e = exchange rate in foreign currency/\$
Π_{US} = U. S. corporate profit rate
Π_f = foreign corporate profit rate
r_{US} = U. S. interest rate
r_f = foreign interest rate

Let us look at an example. Suppose we wish to compare the relative prices of Volkswagens and imported Chevrolets in Germany. Suppose further that Chevys cost \$7000 while Volkswagens in Germany cost 10,000 marks. If the exchange rate is 2 marks per dollar, and if we ignore transportation costs, then:

$$P_{REL} = \frac{eP}{P_f} = \frac{2 \times 7000}{10{,}000} = 1.4.$$

Chevys are 1.4 time as expensive as Volkswagens in Germany.

Relative Prices and the Demand for Imports and Exports Given the definition of P_{REL}, it should not be surprising that a rise in P_{REL} reduces U. S. exports. We show this in Table 21.2 by the placement of P_{REL} in the negative effects column. A rise in P_{REL} can be caused by an increase in e—that is, a rise in the price of dollars, a rise in U. S. prices, or a fall in German prices. Any of these three will tend to reduce U. S. exports because our goods become more expensive.

Let us now see how relative prices influence imports. Perhaps surprisingly, P_{REL} is also the relative price of foreign products in the United States. Let us see why. When Americans buy foreign currency, they pay $1/e$. Hence, the price of foreign products in the United States is $1/e \times P_f$. If we now calculate the relative price of U. S. and foreign products in the United States, we get the same expression we just used for the relative price of U. S. exports—for the relative price of imports and U. S. products for Americans is:

$$\frac{P}{P_f/e} = \frac{eP}{P_f} = P_{REL}.$$

To see this more clearly, consider our Volkswagen-Chevy example again. What is the relative price of VWs in the United States?

Price of VWs in U. S. = $\frac{1}{2} \times 10{,}000 = \$5000$.

Thus:

$$P_{REL} = \frac{\$7000}{\$5000} = 1.4.$$

Thus, P_{REL} represents the relative price of foreign and domestic commodities in either country.

Given this equivalence, P_{REL} should be positively related to imports. For if P_{REL} rises, U. S. commodities become more expensive relative to imports, which should induce some Americans to buy more imports. And yet, in Table 21.2, we see that the effect of a rise in P_{REL} on the supply of dollars to buy imports is uncertain. The reason is that there is a distinction between the quantity of imports and the quantity of dollars. When P_{REL} rises, the quantity of imports goes up. But the quantity of *dollars* to buy imports may not. The supply of dollars to buy imports is the product of the price of foreign exchange, which is $1/e$ for Americans, and the value of imports expressed in foreign currency. Formally, the supply of dollars can be written:

$$S_\$ = \frac{1}{e} \times M\overset{+}{\left(\frac{eP_{US}}{P_f}\right)}.$$

Import Elasticity Now suppose there is a reduction in e. That should reduce the quantity of imports, since foreign products become more expensive; but at the same time it should make foreign exchange purchases more expensive, since $1/e$ rises. Thus, it is entirely possible that a reduction in e, on balance, will increase rather than reduce the number of dollars Americans have to pay for imports. Whether this happens or not depends on the *elasticity* of import demand. That **import elasticity** is defined as the percentage change in the quantity of imports demanded per 1-percent change in the exchange rate. The condition for the supply of dollars to be positively related to e is that the import elasticity be greater than 1, which means that the quantity of imports declines by more than the decline in the exchange rate.

An example might be helpful at this point. Suppose that the United States imports 4 million Japanese cars per year when their average price is 15,000 yen and the exchange rate is 2.5 yen per dollar, or \$.40 per yen. The United States will be spending 15,000 × $.40 × 4,000,000 = $24 billion on Japanese auto imports. Now suppose that the United States devalues by 25 percent in order to reduce the outflow of U. S. dollars to buy Japanese cars. That means that after the devaluation Americans have to pay 25 percent more or $.50 per yen rather than $.40. The devaluation makes Japanese cars 25 percent more expensive for Americans, since the U. S. price rises from $6000 to $7500.[1]

If the import elasticity is less than 1, the quantity of Japanese cars imported will fall by less than 25 percent. Suppose it drops by 10 percent to 3,600,000. Now let us calculate the total number of dollars that will be used to purchase imported cars after the devaluation:

Before devaluation: 4,000,000 × 15,000 × .40 = $24 billion.

After devaluation: 3,600,000 × 15,000 × .50 = $27 billion.

As the reader can see, devaluation actually causes an increase rather than a reduction in the supply of dollars, because the elasticity of import demand is less than 1.

In practice, the elasticity of import demand depends a good deal on the time horizon of the analysis. The longer the time horizon the bigger the elasticity will be, because there will be more time for buyers to switch from imports to domestic substitutes and to change their consumption patterns to use fewer imported products. The influence of the other components of P_{REL} on imports is straightforward. A rise in U. S. prices increases imports or the supply of dollars, while a rise of foreign prices has the opposite effect.

Other Factors Influencing the Dollar Market

The other factors influencing the demand and supply of dollars are U. S. and foreign incomes and the relative rate of return on investments. U. S. imports are positively related to U. S. income, since imports are some of the things we buy in greater quantity as our incomes rise. Empirical studies suggest that in the long run a 1 percent increase in our income increases imports by a little over 1 percent. By the same reasoning, U. S. exports and the demand for dollars are related to foreign income. Recessions in foreign countries hurt our export sales, while recessions in the United States drive down sales of imports here.

The capital account is comprised of U. S. direct and portfolio investment abroad and foreign direct and portfolio investment in the United States. All of these capital flows are influenced by relative profit rates. In the case of U. S. direct investment, the relevant variables are the profit rates in the United States and abroad: The higher the relative profit rate in the United States, the smaller will be the supply of dollars of U. S. corporations to purchase overseas assets. By the same token, a high rate of profit in the United States should stimulate direct invest-

[1] 15,000 × $.40 = $6000; 15,000 × .50 = $7500. We assume that the devaluation has no effect on the price in yen of Japanese cars.

ment by foreigners. Thus, Π_{US}/Π_f should be negatively related to the supply of dollars and positively related to the demand for dollars, which is what we show in Table 21.2

The same reasoning explains the relationship between portfolio investment and the relative interest rate, r_{US}/r_f. When U. S. interest rates are high relative to foreign rates, U. S. portfolio investors tend to buy U. S. securities; so do foreign investors. Hence, as r_{US}/r_f rises, the supply of dollars to buy foreign securities falls and the demand by foreigners to buy U. S. securities rises. In this way interest rates have an important effect on the dollar market and on the U. S. balance of payments. As we shall see, short-term portfolio investment has become an extremely significant and volatile factor in the market for dollars and other currencies. In many cases, capital movements have had more influence on the level of exchange rates than imports, exports, or any other factor.

The Dollar Market Diagram

We summarize this discussion of the dollar market with a diagram of the demand and supply of dollars (see Figure 21.2). In this diagram we show demand and supply as functions of the exchange rate. We show supply as a positively upward-sloping function of e, which means that we are assuming that the import elasticity is greater than 1. (If the elasticity were less than 1, as it might well be in the short run, the supply curve would be negatively sloped.) The demand curve is downward sloping, since exports clearly decline when e rises.

All of the other variables in Table 21.2, such as income and relative rates of return, are shift variables in Figure 21.2. They shift the supply or demand for dollars in the direction indicated by the signs in Table 21.2. For example, take U. S. income. A rise in U. S. income shifts the supply curve of dollars to the right; the demand curve is unaffected. An increase in U. S. interest rates reduces the supply of dollars but increases the demand for dollars; hence, the supply curve shifts left and the demand curve right.

There are two distinct types of foreign exchange regimes, one in which exchange rates are fixed and the other in which they are floating. In the **fixed exchange rate** regime central banks determine the exchange rate, while in the **floating exchange rate** regime the rate is determined by the market, at the level at which the demand and supply of dollars are equal. In Figure 21.2, for the given interest rates and income levels the equilibrium exchange rate is e_0. That is the rate that will be reached under the floating rate regime when there is no intervention by the authorities.

Suppose that the exchange rate is fixed at e_1 rather than being allowed to float down to e_0. At e_1 there is an oversupply of dollars, which means that the United States is running a balance of payments deficit—to put it another way, the price of dollars is too high. In the language of central bankers, the dollar is overvalued. Just like any other price control scheme, this one can be maintained only if foreign central banks absorb the excess supply of dollars. This, as we have seen, is done by either a transfer of gold and official reserves from the Federal Reserve to foreign central banks or by foreign central banks accumulating dollar reserves in their accounts at the Federal Reserve. In any case, this can go on only so long as the

Figure 21.2
The Foreign Exchange Market

The supply of dollars represents the demand by U. S. citizens to buy things abroad. The demand for dollars represents the demand by foreign citizens to buy things in the United States. The supply (demand) for dollars is positively (negatively) related to the exchange rate. All other factors influencing the demand and supply of dollars are shift variables on the demand and supply curves. Under flexible exchange rates, equilibrium occurs when the balance of payments is in equilibrium at e_0. Under fixed rates, the exchange rate may diverge from e_0. We show an overvalued rate, e_1, at which the supply of dollars is greater than the demand. There is a balance of payments deficit equal to the distance between the curves, AB.

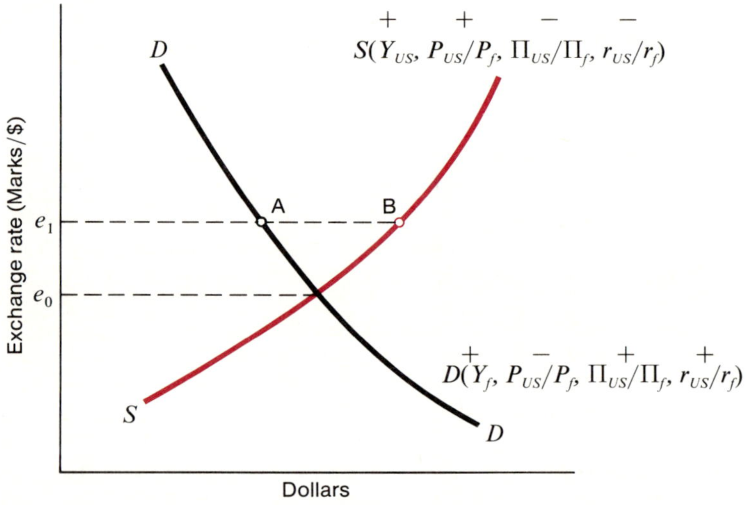

United States has international reserves or gold to exchange or so long as foreign central banks are willing to accumulate the excess dollars.

We now use the diagram to analyze the effect of changes in income and interest rates on the balance of payments or the exchange rate. The effect of such a change will be on the exchange rate when it is floating; when it is fixed, the effect will be on the balance of payments. Note that when rates float, a rise in the rate is called a **rate appreciation,** while a decline is a **rate depreciation.**

Let us now see what happens in the foreign exchange market when U. S. income or interest rates increase. Both of these changes are shown in Figure 21.3. In both diagrams the solid lines show the situation before the change and the dashed lines the effect of the change. In (a), if income increases from Y_0 to Y_1 the supply of dollars to buy imports increases, causing the supply curve to shift outward to S_1. If rates float, this increase in imports causes the exchange rate to depreciate from e_0 to e_1. A rise in U. S. interest rates has the opposite effect on the

Figure 21.3
The Effect on the Dollar Market of Changes in Interest and Income.

An increase in U. S. income shifts the supply of dollars out to S_1, because it increases the demand for imports. If exchange rates are flexible, the rate drops from e_0 to e_1. Hence, a rise in income causes a depreciation of the exchange rate. If rates are fixed, the rise in Y causes an increase in the balance of payments deficit from AB to AC.

A rise in domestic interest rates shifts the demand curve to the right and the supply curve to the left, because it reduces the outflow of U. S. dollars and increases the inflow of foreign capital. If exchange rates are flexible, the rise in r causes e to rise from e_0 to e_1. If rates are fixed the change lowers the deficit, from distance AB to distance DE.

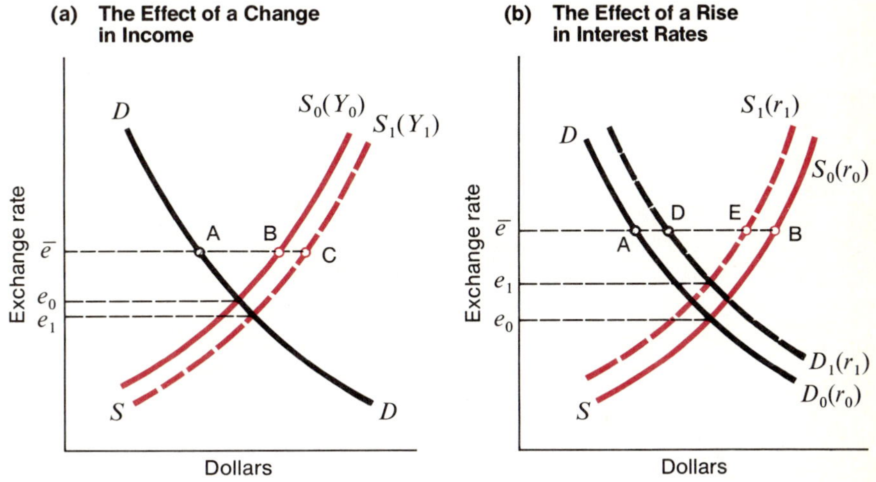

exchange rate, as one can see in (b). There is a reduced outflow of U. S. investment and an increased inflow of foreign investment to the United States. The supply curve shifts left to S_1, while the demand curve shifts right to D_1, causing a rise or appreciation of the exchange rate from e_0 to e_1.

If exchange rates are fixed, the changes we have been looking at in Figure 21.3 will have their effect on the balance of payments rather than the exchange rate. Suppose the economy starts with an overvalued exchange rate, $\bar{e}$. The initial balance of payments deficit is AB, the horizontal distance between the solid supply and demand curves. As we have already learned, an increase in income shifts the supply curve to the right in (a). Rather than affecting the exchange rate, the change in income now increases the balance of payments deficit to AC; similarly, the rise in interest rates diminishes the deficit to DE in (b). Thus, we can conclude that an increase in income increases a balance of payments deficit while an increase in interest rates reduces it. The effect on the exchange rate or the balance of payments of each of our other variables is shown in summary form in Table 21.3.

Table 21.3
The Effect of Different Variables on the Exchange Rate and the Balance of Payments

Rise	Floating Rate Effect on e	Fixed Rate Effect on BOP
Y_{US}	Depreciation	Negative
Y_f	Appreciation	Positive
P_{US}	Depreciation	Negative
P_f	Appreciation	Positive
Π_{US}, r_{US}	Appreciation	Positive
Π_f, r_f	Depreciation	Negative

The Short- and Long-Run Effects of Devaluation: the J Curve

When a country on a fixed exchange rate devalues, the effect in the short run is likely to be counterproductive. The **devaluation** is quite likely to make the balance of payments worse rather than better. Let us see why. In the short run, the elasticity of imports with respect to relative prices is almost certainly less than 1. As a result, the country will find itself spending more of its domestic currency to buy imports, rather than less. In terms of our diagram of the foreign exchange market, the short-run dollar supply curve is likely to be negatively sloped (see Figure 21.4). It is also true that the short-run demand curve is a good deal steeper than the long-run curve. Just as it takes time for domestic buyers to react to changes in relative prices, so will it also take time before U. S. producers begin to produce more exports and before foreign buyers switch their buying patterns to take advantage of cheaper U. S. commodities. Thus, in the short run the demand curve for dollars is steeper, and the supply curve has a negative slope.

The effect of these two changes is shown in Figure 21.4. Because the supply curve has a smaller negative slope than the demand curve, a devaluation increases the deficit. For example, a devaluation from e_0 to e_1 increases the deficit from distance AB to CD rather than reducing it. Over time as buyers, both abroad and in the United States, change their buying patterns, and as producers alter their production as well, the supply curve will make a clockwise rotation while the demand curve will do the opposite. As the two curves shift, the initial worsening in the balance of payments reverses itself, and the balance of payments deficit disappears. Hence, the reaction of the balance of payments to a devaluation takes the form of the capital J shown in diagram (b). At first the balance of payments deteriorates. Then, as buyers react to the change in relative prices, the balance of payments improves. Because of the shape of the balance of payments time curve in (b), this phenomenon, called the **J curve,** makes life frustrating for central bankers who try to manipulate the exchange rates in order to correct balance of payments deficits. The J curve tells us that in the short run, exchange rate fluctuations may have perverse effects on the balance of payments.[2]

[2]The reason for the J curve is that the short-run effect of changes in relative prices on the quantity demanded of imports and exports is much smaller than the long-run effect. On this see Rudiger Dornbusch and Paul Krugman, "Flexible Exchange Rates in the Short Run," *Brookings Papers on Economic Activity* (3/1976): 558–566.

Figure 21.4
Short- and Long-Run Effects of Devaluation

In the short run the supply of dollars may be negatively related to the exchange rate, because the quantity response of imports may be insufficient in the short run to offset the change in the price of foreign currency. Hence, a devaluation may increase rather than decrease the number of dollars that Americans have to pay for imports. Also, because it takes time to change buying habits, the short-run demand curve may be steeper than the long-run curve. Over time, both the supply and demand curves should change slope as indicated by the arrows in (a). The supply curve should rotate in a clockwise direction around point B, while the demand curve should rotate in a counterclockwise direction around point A. When one traces out the time response of the balance of payments to a devaluation, one gets the so-called J curve shown in (b). The deficit is AB at time 0 (zero) and exchange rate e_0. When the rate is devalued to e_1, the balance of payments at first deteriorates to distance CD, as shown by the two short-run curves in (a). Over time, as the two curves approach their long-run slopes, the balance of payments improves and finally goes into equilibrium at point E.

(a) Short- and Long-Run Demand and Supply Curves

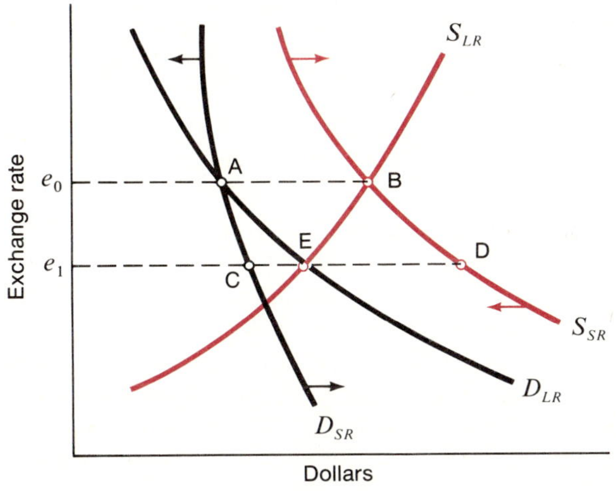

(b) The J Curve

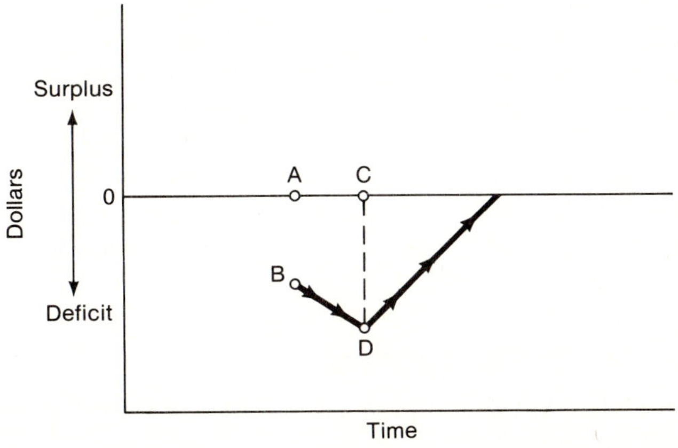

Summary

In this chapter we began the task of incorporating the foreign sector into our economic model. The balance of payments measures our transactions with the rest of the world. It is composed of the current account, which measures our imports and exports of goods and services, and the capital account, which measures the capital flow into and out of the United States. The sum of the two is the balance of payments, measured by or financed by official reserve transactions between the Federal Reserve, other central banks, and the International Monetary Fund.

One can visualize the transactions between the United States and other countries in the context of the dollar market. In this market the supply of dollars is composed of imports plus capital outflows from the United States; the demand for dollars is made up of our exports plus capital inflows into the United States. The exchange rate is the price of dollars. We showed that the supply of dollars is a positive function of the exchange rate while the demand for dollars is a negative function, because both imports and exports depend on the relative price of U. S. and foreign goods. Since a rise in the exchange rate (an increase in the price of dollars) makes U. S. goods more expensive for foreigners and foreign goods cheaper for Americans, a rise in the exchange rate should reduce exports and increase imports. This will be truer in the long run that in the short, because it takes time for both suppliers and buyers to react to changing prices. Hence, the short- and long-run supply and demand curves in the dollar market may have quite different slopes.

Some countries fix their exchange rates, while others allow them to float. In the former case, disturbances in either the U. S. economy or foreign economies will affect the balance of payments; in the latter, they will affect the exchange rate.

When a country with a fixed exchange rate runs a balance of payments deficit, it should be able to correct the situation by devaluing, since that should increase the demand for its currency and reduce the supply. However, this improvement may not occur in the short run. Because it takes time to reduce imports and increase exports, a devaluation may well worsen the balance of payments in the short run.

Key Concepts

balance of payments
current account
capital account
BOP deficit
official reserve transactions
Special Drawing Rights
direct investment
exchange rate
import elasticity
dollar market
rate appreciation
rate depreciation
devaluation
J curve

Problems and Questions for Discussion

1. Which of the following items are reported in the current account, which in the capital account, and which as official reserve transactions?

a. Repayments of foreign debt.

b. Purchases by Americans of assets in foreign countries.
c. Profit remittances.
d. Government aid grants to foreign countries.
e. Government loans to other countries.
f. Gold sales to foreigners.
g. Changes in the U. S. account at the IMF.

2. What is the difference between running a balance of payments deficit in the current account and in the capital account? Which do you think is more serious? Why?

3. Suppose that the exchange rate between yen and dollars is 225 yen per dollar.
a. How much does an American pay for 100 yen?
b. If a Toyota Corona costs 1,350,000 yen and a Chevrolet Citation costs $7000, what is the relative price of Toyotas and Chevrolets in Japan?
c. What is the relative price of the same two goods in the United States?

4. If there is a devaluation of the yen, what will happen to e? What will happen to P_{REL}? What will happen to U. S. exports to Japan? To imports from Japan?

5. Under what conditions is the supply curve for dollars positively related to e, or upward sloping in the dollar market diagram? Will the dollar market be unstable if these conditions are not met?

6. Suppose that in a certain year the United States imports $10 billion and exports $9 billion. Suppose also that the average exchange rate $e = 2.00$, that the elasticities of imports and exports with respect to e are $+0.5$ and -1.0, respectively.
a. If the United States devalues by 10 percent, what happens to the quantity of exports and imports?
b. What happens to the demand and supply of dollars?
c. What happens to the U. S. balance of payments?

7. Show what happens in the dollar market diagram when each of the following changes occur.
a. An increase in U. S. income.
b. A rise in U. S. interest rates relative to foreign interest rates.
c. An equal, proportional increase in foreign and domestic prices.
d. An increase in U. S. profit rates.
e. An increase in U. S. aid to foreign countries.

8. Indicate the effect of each of the changes shown in Problem 7 on:
a. The exchange rate if exchange rates are flexible.
b. The balance of payments if exchange rates are fixed.

9. Why is a devaluation likely to worsen the balance of payments in the short run? What happens over time to reverse the situation?

10. Discuss the different methods that a government could use to correct a balance of payments deficit. What are the advantages and disadvantages of each method?

Chapter 22

Equilibrium in the Open Economy with Fixed and Flexible Exchange Rates

In the last chapter we examined the operation of the dollar market. We learned which factors tend to improve the balance of payments or cause the exchange rate to appreciate and which lead to depreciation or a worsening of the balance of payments. But we ignored the feedback between the dollar market and the rest of the economy. Imports and exports directly affect supply and demand in the goods market. Changes in the exchange rates have an impact on domestic prices, and changes in the balance of payments affect the money supply. These are some ways in which the foreign sector influences the rest of the economy.

In this chapter we will add to our understanding of how a modern macroeconomy works by incorporating these features into our model. To do so, we shall integrate the balance of payments into our basic IS-LM model to see what influences the foreign sector, with its fixed and flexible exchange rate systems, has on both equilibrium and the choices facing government policymakers.

Fixed and Flexible Exchange Rates

To begin our expansion of the basic macroeconomic model, we shall analyze separately two different foreign trade regimes: **fixed exchange rates** and **flexible exchange rates.** Fixed rates simply mean that the exchange rate is set by the government rather than the market. Fixed rates obviously can be and are changed fairly often. The basic difference between the two systems is that when rates are fixed, the exchange rate is a policy variable under control of the government, while when rates are flexible, it is an endogenous variable determined by supply and demand in the foreign exchange market. In the fixed rate system, it is the balance of payments, rather than the exchange rate, that is endogenous. For simplicity, we will examine each exchange rate regime under an assumption, first of constant, then of flexible, prices.

Fixed exchange rates were the rule prior to 1973. When there were balance of payments deficits or surpluses, central banks were forced to intervene to maintain the rate by either acquiring or giving up reserves. There was widespread dissatisfaction with this system, particularly among Europeans. The reason was that they were unable to untie their domestic monetary policy from that of the United States. We ran fairly large and continuous deficits. That forced foreigners to either devalue, which they were reluctant to do, or accumulate international reserves. The latter, as we shall see in a moment, causes an increase in a foreign country's money supply. Thus, balance of payments deficits by the United States forced an unwanted expansion of the money supply in other countries. Under fixed rates, domestic monetary policy is not entirely under the control of the central bank; it depends critically on the balance of payments as well.

In order to unlink domestic money supplies from the dollar and the balance of payments most countries, led by Germany and France, changed over to a system of flexible rates. It was hoped that the new system would lead to less extreme swings in the balance of payments, less currency speculation, and a more stable international environment. Unfortunately, it has not worked out quite as proponents had planned—if anything, there has been less stability under flexible rates than there was under fixed rates. Wide fluctuations in the exchange rate have created a climate of uncertainty in international trade. Furthermore, in some countries currency devaluations seem to have generated a vicious circle in which devaluation has led to a rise in domestic prices and wages. This, in turn, has caused a further worsening in the balance of payments, requiring further devaluation. Some of these difficulties may well be due to the oil price shocks.

To begin our exploration of how an economy operates under fixed and flexible exchange rates, we return to our IS-LM diagram.

The Expanded IS-LM Diagram for the Open Economy

The basic tool for the analysis we are about to make is an expanded IS-LM diagram. In it we show how both the IS and LM curves are affected by the foreign sector.[1] In addition, we shall derive another curve, which represents equilibrium in the dollar market.

The IS Curve for the Open Economy

Consider first the IS curve. It represents all pairs of income and interest rates at which the goods market is in equilibrium. Since the goods market now includes

[1] For two excellent surveys of the current thinking on how the foreign sector should be integrated into the macromodel, see Rudiger Dornbusch, "Exchange Rate Economics: Where Do We Stand?" *Brookings Papers on Economic Activity* (1/1980): 143–185; and Ronald I. McKinnon, "The Exchange Rate and Macroeconomic Policy: Changing Postwar Perceptions," *Journal of Economic Literature* 19 (June 1981): 531–557.

both imports and exports, it follows that anything that influences either of these variables must affect the IS curve too.

For the open economy, the basic equilibrium condition for the goods market is:

(22.1) $$Y = C + I + G + E - M.$$

Equation (22.1) says that production must now be sufficient to supply all domestic demand plus net exports, $E - M$. In the closed economy, we used the equality of sales and production to derive the IS curve. We now do the same thing for the open economy.

In previous chapters we showed that consumption is a function of income and interest rates, that investment is a function of the interest rate, and that exports and imports are functions of relative prices and domestic income. Therefore, we can rewrite Equation (22.1) to reflect these behavioral relationships:

(22.2) $$Y = c(\overset{+}{Y}, \overset{-}{r}) + I(\overset{-}{r}) + G + E(\overset{-}{eP/P_f}) - M\left(\overset{+}{\frac{eP}{P_f}}, \overset{+}{Y}\right).$$

In the closed economy, the functional relationship between saving and income and between private spending and the interest rate determines an implicit relationship between Y and r at which the goods market is in equilibrium. We called this relationship the IS curve. It is downward sloping, because an increase in income increases private and public saving, and that requires an increase in investment or a reduction in r to maintain the basic equilibrium between saving and investment.

In the open economy an increase in income causes an increase in imports, which is another form of saving. Therefore, when income rises not only does investment have to increase by enough to equal the rise in domestic saving, it has to offset the increase in imports as well. Since investment has to increase more, it follows that r will have to fall further in the open economy to offset an increase in income. All of this implies that the IS curve for the open economy, shown in Figure 22.1, is downward sloping and steeper than it was for the closed economy.

We have learned that IS curves are steeper in open economies because imports are positively related to income. But that is not the only effect that opening the economy has on the IS curve. It should be clear from Equation (22.2) that a change in any of the components of P_{REL} will shift the IS curve.

Consider first a fall in the exchange rate. That will increase exports and reduce imports. Devaluation or depreciation of e leads to an expansionary increase in the demand for domestic output and, therefore, causes the IS curve to shift rightward to the dotted lines in Figure 22.1. Obviously, a rise in the exchange rate would have the opposite effect. Another way to express this is to say that a fall in the exchange rate reduces foreign saving, which we defined in Chapter 2 as $M - E$. Therefore, in order to maintain the equilibrium of total saving and investment, income has to rise by enough to induce an equivalent increase in domestic saving. However one puts it, it should be clear that devaluation is expansionary, because it increases demand in the goods market.

Figure 22.1
The Effect of Devaluation on the Open Economy IS Curve
Devaluation shifts the open economy IS curve to the right because it increases the demand for domestic output.

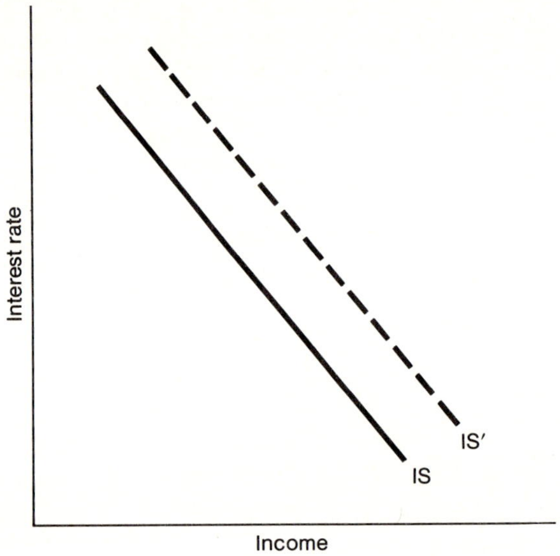

A rise in domestic prices has the opposite effect from a devaluation. It is contractionary, because it causes exports to decline and imports to increase. Therefore, a rise in the price level will shift the IS curve to the left. This effect of prices on imports and exports simply complements and strengthens the negative relationship between aggregate demand and prices that we have already discussed and used in previous chapters. We leave the reader to work out the effect on the IS curve of changing foreign prices.

The LM Curve for the Open Economy

The inclusion of the foreign section affects the LM curve as well. That is because balance of payments deficits and surpluses affect the supply of money. When a country runs a balance of payments surplus, the money supply will usually increase; when there is a deficit, it will decline. Thus, BOP deficits should be accompanied by a leftward shift in the LM curve and surpluses by a gradual movement of the LM to the right. Let us see why.

In Chapter 14 we learned that the domestic money supply is equal to some multiple of the stock of high-powered money, H. H, in turn, is equal to the total assets of the central bank. In a closed economy, central bank assets are government bonds and gold. In the open economy, the central bank also holds interna-

Table 22.1
First-Round Changes in the Balance Sheets of Banks and the Fed When There Is a BOP Surplus ($ in millions)

	Banks		Federal Reserve	
	Assets	Liabilities	Assets	Liabilities
	Reserves +$1000	Deposits +$1000	Bonds	Bank reserves +$1000
	Loans		International reserves +$1000	Currency
Total	+$1000	+$1000	+$1000	+$1000

tional reserves, comprised of holdings of foreign currencies, credit balances at foreign central banks, and reserves at the International Monetary Fund. Thus, in an open economy one could write the basic accounting identity of the central bank as:[2]

Liabilities Assets

(22.3) $$H = B_G + IR.$$

B_G = government bonds
IR = international reserves

It follows from Equation (22.3) that whenever there is an increase in IR, the stock of high-powered money will increase. This will, of course, cause a multiple expansion in the money supply.

In order to see clearly how surpluses and deficits affect the monetary base, consider Table 22.1, which shows how a surplus in the balance of payments affects the balance sheets of the Fed and the banking system. Suppose Americans sell $1 billion more abroad than they buy from abroad. When they exchange their export earnings in yen, marks, and pounds for dollars, domestic bank deposits and bank reserves rise by $1 billion. High-powered money, H, also rises by $1 billion. In the Fed balance sheet, this new liability is counterbalanced by an increase in international reserves. This is, of course, only the first-round effect. Subsequently, the banking system will expand the money supply by making new loans. This is the way in which a BOP surplus causes the money supply to increase. Obviously, a BOP deficit would have exactly the opposite effect.

It is possible for the Fed to circumvent the link between the BOP and the money supply by open market operations. If the country runs a BOP surplus, the Fed can sterilize this surplus by contractionary open market operations. In our example, the Fed could sell $1 billion worth of government bonds to the public, in this way holding the level of high-powered money constant. Conversely, if the country is running a deficit, which tends to reduce the money supply, the Fed can

[2]For simplicity, we shall ignore gold holdings throughout this chapter.

buy bonds back from the public to keep the money supply constant. If the Fed takes no action, BOP surpluses shift the LM to the right and deficits shift it to the left.

The BP Curve

In the closed economy we had two markets, the money and goods markets, for each of which we had equilibrium conditions that generated the LM and IS curves. In the open economy, we add the foreign exchange market. Equilibrium in this new market generates a third curve called the **BP curve.** The BP curve shows the pairs of interest rates and income levels at which the balance of payments is in equilibrium (see Figure 22.2). It is upward sloping, like the LM curve. A rise in income increases U. S. imports and worsens the balance of payments. To keep BOP equilibrium, interest rates must be raised enough to induce an offsetting inflow of capital. Thus, increases in income require an increase in interest rates in order to maintain BOP equilibrium.

The BP curve may be flatter or steeper than the LM curve. Which it is depends on the income elasticity of imports and the interest sensitivity of capital inflows and outflows. The more sensitive capital movements are to domestic interest rate changes, the flatter the BP curve will be. If there were a perfect integration of domestic and foreign capital markets—that is, if domestic and foreign bonds were perfect substitutes—the BP curve would be flat. In that case, any change in the current account deficit, because of a change in income, would immediately cause an equivalent reverse flow in the capital account, with no change in interest rates.

At the other extreme are developing countries whose capital markets are completely separate from the world capital market. They can raise domestic interest rates and get no inflow of foreign capital. For such countries, the BP curve is vertical. The United States falls somewhere between the extremes of perfect integration and perfect separation, lying closer to the former than the latter. We shall assume that for the United States, the BP curve is flatter than the LM curve.

Any point to the right of the BP curve represents a deficit in the balance of payments, since the higher level of income will cause an increase in imports. For the same reason, points to the left are surpluses.

Any factor that influences the balance of payments, other than income or interest rates, will shift the BP curve to the left or right. Those factors improving the balance of payments shift it to the right; those worsening it shift the BP to the left. For example, suppose there is a devaluation. That reduces imports and increases exports, thus improving the balance of payments. Hence, if income and interest rates are unchanged, there will be a balance of payments surplus. To regain equilibrium either interest rates must fall or income must increase, which implies that the BP curve shifts down and to the right to BP′ in Figure 22.2 in response to a fall in e.

Other factors shifting the BP curve are U. S. and foreign prices and foreign incomes. An increase in U. S. prices shifts the BP to the left, because it worsens our balance of payments. Increases in foreign incomes and prices both increase our exports and reduce our imports. This improves our balance of payments and thus shifts the BP to the right.

Figure 22.2
The BP Curve

The BP curve is the collection of all pairs of income and interest rates at which the dollar market is in equilibrium. It is upward sloping because a rise in income increases the demand for imports. Balance of payments equilibrium can be maintained only by an increase in interest rates, which increases the inflow of capital. As one moves up the BP curve, the current account balance gets worse and the capital account balance improves. The dashed BP′ line shows the effect of devaluation. Since devaluation improves the balance of payments, the BP shifts to the right in response to a reduction in e.

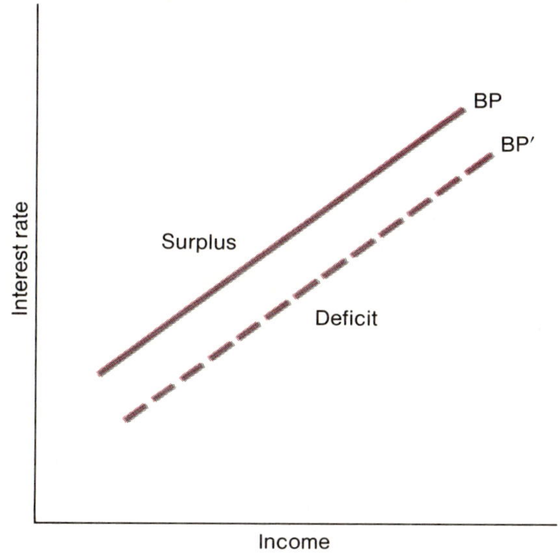

Equilibrium in the Open Economy with Fixed Exchange Rates

We now put our three markets together and examine the additional constraints that the new foreign exchange market imposes on policymakers. At the outset, it should be clear that there is no guarantee that the three equilibrium curves will intersect at a single point. When they do not, as at point A in Figure 22.3, we shall assume that the short-run equilibrium is at the intersection of the IS and LM curves, which implies that the balance of payments condition may not be met. In other words, we shall assume that, with fixed exchange rates, it is possible to run balance of payments deficits or surpluses. At point A, there is a deficit.

How does the economy get to a full equilibrium? If there is no intervention by policymakers, the deficit causes a reduction in the money supply. That, as we have learned, shifts the LM curve to the left, as shown by the arrows in Figure 22.3. The process goes on until the deficit is eliminated and the LM has shifted back to LM′. Full equilibrium is then reestablished at point B, the intersection of the BP and IS

Figure 22.3
Partial and Full Equilibrium in the IS-LM-BP Diagram
With fixed exchange rates, it is possible for the economy to run a balance of payments deficit, that is, be off the BP curve in the short run. Point A represents a deficit in the balance of payments. Barring an intervention by the Fed, this balance of payments deficit leads to a decline in the money supply, which shifts the LM curve to the left until full equilibrium is reached at point B.

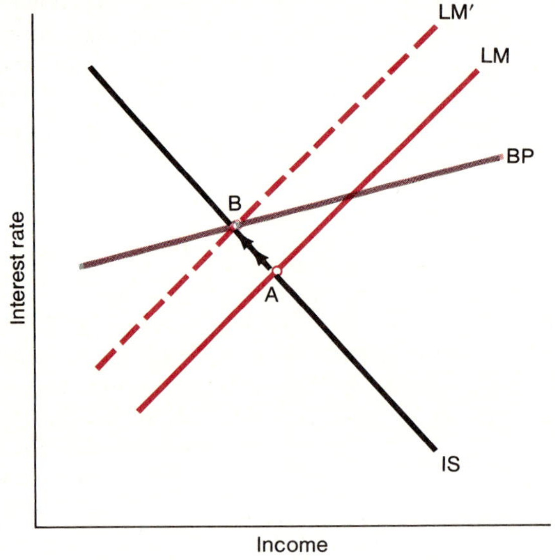

curves. We are assuming here that the monetary authorities do not make an expansionary open market operation to stop the contraction of the money supply.

What this discussion shows is that in a fixed exchange rate economy: first, full equilibrium is at the intersection of the IS and BP; second, that the automatic response of the money supply to BOP deficits and surpluses is the mechanism that moves the economy to full equilibrium.

Fiscal and Monetary Policies under Fixed Rates

Let us now examine the operation of fiscal and monetary policies under fixed rates in the open economy.[3] In doing this we shall, for the moment, assume that prices are fixed. As we shall see, the differences between monetary and fiscal policy

[3] A pioneer in adapting the theories of monetary and fiscal policy to the open economy was Robert Mundell. See in particular his "The Appropriate Use of Monetary and Fiscal Policy for External and Internal Balance," *IMF Staff Papers* 9 (March 1962): 70–77; and his "Capital Mobility and Stabilization Policy under Fixed and Flexible Exchange Rates," *Canadian Journal of Economics and Political Science* 29 (November 1963): 475–485.

Figure 22.4
Fiscal Policy in the Open Economy with Fixed Exchange Rates
Expansionary fiscal policy moves the economy from point A to point B. At B there is a BOP surplus (assuming the LM curve is steeper than the BP). That is because the rise in interest rates causes an inflow of capital. As a result of the surplus, the money supply expands, shifting the LM curve to the right until full equilibrium is reached at point C.

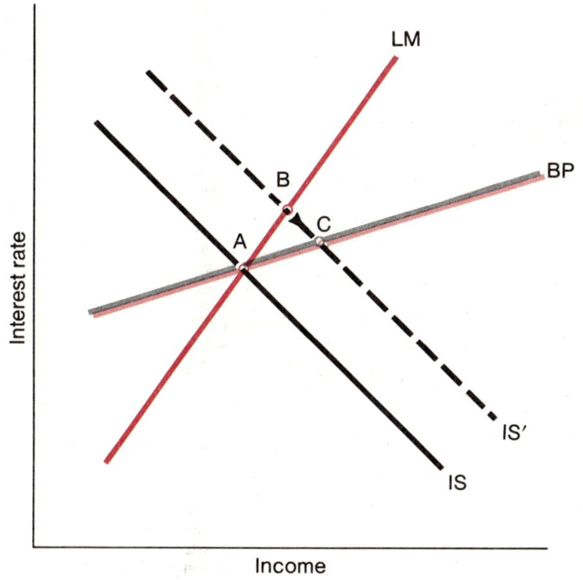

under fixed and flexible rates are much greater under fixed than under flexible prices. Suppose that an economy starting in full equilibrium at point A in Figure 22.4 is disturbed by a cut in taxes. This expansionary fiscal policy measure shifts the IS out to IS′. In the short run the economy moves out to point B, the intersection of the LM and IS′. But at B, the economy runs a balance of payments surplus. That causes an expansion of the money supply and income until a new full equilibrium is reached at point C. Thus, in the open economy under fixed exchange rates, the effect of fiscal policy on income appears to be enhanced. Rather than moving from point A to point B, the economy expands further to point C. That is because expansionary fiscal policy moves the economy up the LM curve in the short run, causing a rise in interest rates and an inflow of capital. This in turn causes a balance of payments surplus and a complementary expansion of the money supply. In effect, the government can generate more external borrowing and an expansion of the money supply through expansionary fiscal policy.

The picture is reversed for monetary policy. It is less effective in the fixed rate open economy than it was in the closed economy. Let us see why. In Figure 22.5 we show the effect of expansionary monetary policy. The authorities increase the money supply, which shifts the LM curve to the right to LM′. In the short run the

Figure 22.5
Monetary Policy in the Open Economy with Fixed Exchange Rates
An increase in the money supply has only a temporary effect. In the short run, the economy moves from point A to point B. However, at B the economy has a BOP deficit. This causes a reduction in the money supply. The LM shifts leftward until it returns to its original position, and the economy returns to point A.

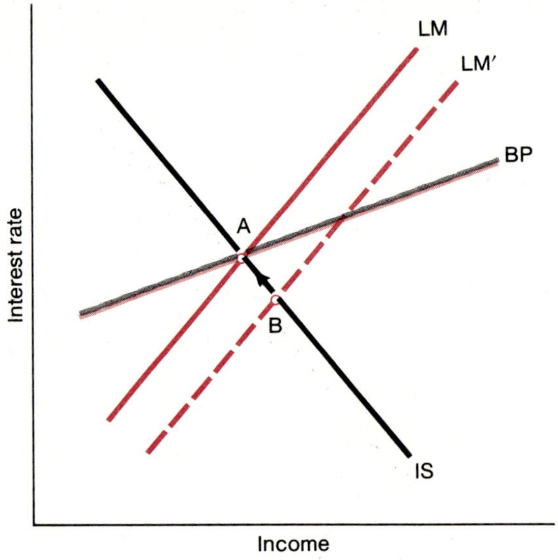

economy expands outward to point B, the intersection of LM′ and IS. But, unfortunately, this is not the end of the story. For at B there is a balance of payments deficit. This, as we have learned, tends to contract the money supply, causing the LM curve to shift back. If the monetary authorities do nothing, the LM will continue to shift back until full equilibrium is reestablished at point A, as indicated by the arrow in the diagram.

Of course, the Fed could counteract this reversal by expansionary monetary policy, but if that does not happen monetary policy has, at most, a temporary effect on income. In a world of fixed exchange rates, the balance of payments constraint determines the money supply. The money supply is not an exogenous policy variable, at least in the long run. Thus, discretionary monetary policy has, at best, a short-run effect on income in the fixed rate open economy.

As we said, the Fed could counteract the reduction in H by expansionary open market operations. This, in fact, is what the United States did for long periods prior to the abandonment of fixed exchange rates in 1973. We kept our money supply constant or growing, despite our balance of payments deficits. Since other countries did not sterilize the extra international reserves they were receiving from the United States, their money supplies also grew. Thus, our unwillingness to allow the balance of payments to determine our money supply caused an increase in

Figure 22.6
Increasing Income and Investment in the Open Economy

The goal here is to simultaneously increase income and investment. That requires a southeasterly move in the diagram from point A to B. To do this, the authorities must devalue by enough to push the BP line out until it intersects Y_{FE} at point B. This devaluation shifts the IS to IS′. The authorities then engage in expansionary monetary and fiscal policies sufficient to shift the IS and LM out until they both intersect the BP at point B.

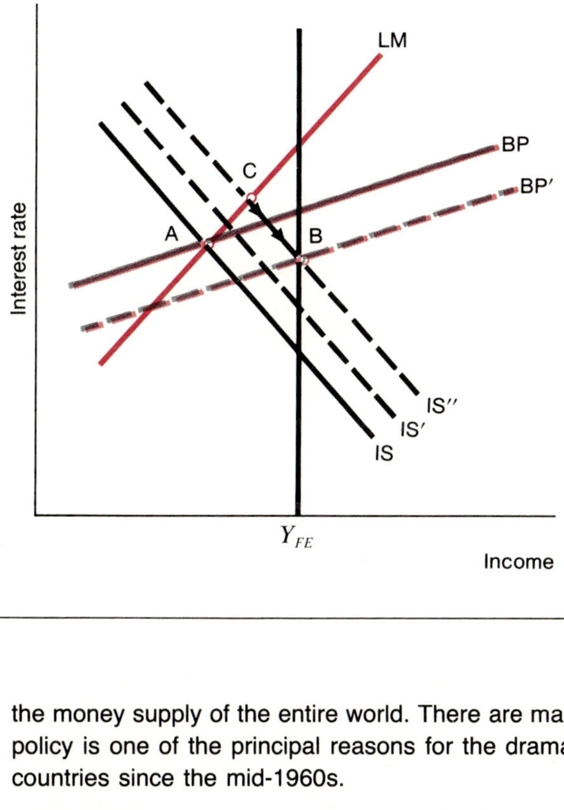

the money supply of the entire world. There are many who believe that this U. S. policy is one of the principal reasons for the dramatic increase in inflation in all countries since the mid-1960s.

Controlling the Level and Composition of Output with Fixed Exchange Rates

Suppose that an economy is in full equilibrium at point A in Figure 22.6. However, this equilibrium is at less than full employment. Suppose that the authorities wish to move the economy to full employment but to do it without driving up interest rates and choking off investment—that is, they wish to move from point A to point B. In the closed economy, that is a relatively easy problem to solve: the government would simply expand the money supply. That will not work here except in the short run, because the resultant BOP deficit will tend to contract the money supply, thus offsetting the initial increase in M. Fiscal policy will not work either. Cutting taxes or raising government expenditures can increase income, but it cannot do that without crowding out investment—for, since the BP curve is upward sloping, expansionary fiscal policy must drive up the interest rate.

What, then, should the government do to get the economy from point A to point B? Neither fiscal nor monetary policy alone, or in combination, is sufficient to achieve this goal. The government must use its third policy instrument, the exchange rate, as well. We have shown that the BP curve is a function of e. Therefore, the government should devalue. Assuming the import elasticity is greater than 1, that will improve the balance of payments and shift the BP curve to the right. The exchange rate is reduced until BP shifts out to BP′, a situation in which the balance of payments will be in equilibrium at point B.

This lower exchange rate also affects the IS curve. As we have learned, devaluation is expansionary. It lowers imports and increases exports, both of which shift the IS curve to the right, to IS′. There is, of course, no guarantee that the BP and IS shift out by the same amount—it is likely that the IS moves less. In that case, devaluation must be augmented by a slightly expansionary fiscal policy to shift the IS out to IS″, which intersects BP′ at B. This is the new full equilibrium. If the monetary authorities do nothing, the economy moves first to point C, at which there is a surplus in the balance of payments. As the money supply increases, the economy moves on to full equilibrium at point B. The monetary authorities could hasten the convergence to B by expanding the money supply through open market operations.

The main point of this exercise is that in an open economy with fixed exchange rates, monetary policy becomes relatively ineffective. It is still possible to control the level of income and investment at the same time (that is, move from any point to any other point in the IS-LM-BP diagram). However, that generally requires simultaneous use of both of the other policy investments available to the government, fiscal policy and the exchange rate.

In many cases, a policy that corrects a balance of payments disequilibrium conflicts with internal goals. For example, a country running a balance of payments deficit can cure that deficit by reducing income or raising domestic interest rates to attract capital from abroad. But both of these remedies have unfortunate side effects—rising unemployment in the one case and falling investment in the other. It is possible to avoid these unpleasant side effects only through use of the exchange rate policy instrument. To correct a BOP deficit without reducing income or driving up domestic interest rates, the government has to make foreign goods relatively more expensive by devaluation. This should correct the BOP deficit while avoiding either a domestic recession or a contraction of domestic credit.

Equilibrium in the Open Economy with Flexible Exchange Rates

We turn now to an analysis of the currently more relevant case of an open macroeconomy with flexible exchange rates. In such an economy the exchange rate is not controlled by the government but is allowed to float to that level at which the demand is exactly equal to the supply of dollars. Ideally, one would never observe a balance of payments deficit in such a world. In practice, central banks in coun-

Figure 22.7
Fiscal Policy under Flexible Exchange Rates

Fiscal policy is less effective under flexible rates than under fixed rates. The reason is that it causes an offsetting change in the exchange rate. Here we show the effect of expansionary fiscal policy. The expansion shifts the IS out to IS′. If exchange rates were fixed, the short-run equilibrium would be at point B. At B, however, there is a surplus. That causes an appreciation of the exchange rate from e_0 to e_1, which shifts both the IS and the BP curves to the left, to BP′ and IS″. The final equilibrium is at point C.

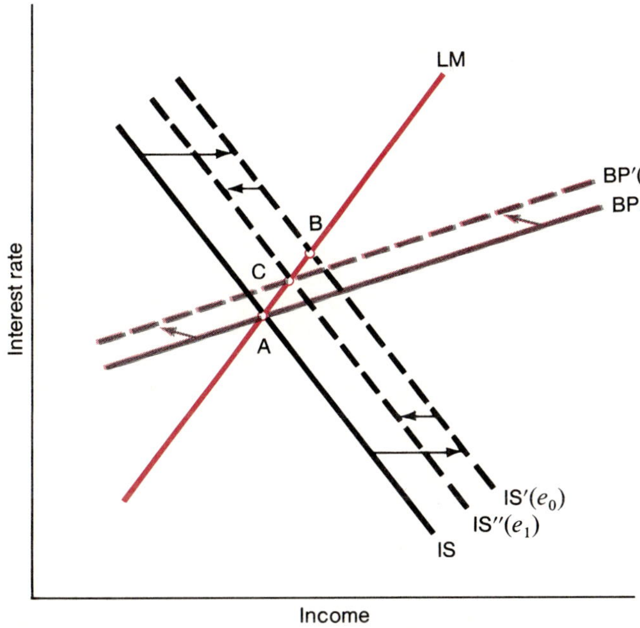

tries whose currencies are freely floating intervene in foreign exchange markets in the short run in order to prevent excessive instability in their exchange rate. This type of intervention has come to be called a dirty float. If there are persistent BOP deficits or surpluses, the exchange rate gradually appreciates or depreciates, but at the same time BOP deficits and surpluses are observed in the short run. Full equilibrium is attained through exchange rate movements rather than changes in the money supply. In the analysis that follows, we shall assume that exchange rate adjustments are automatic and fast enough so that deficits and surpluses have no effect on the money supply.

Fiscal and Monetary Policies under Flexible Exchange Rates

We shall first examine the effect of monetary and fiscal policies in an economy with flexible exchange rates and fixed prices. Suppose that the economy starting in full equilibrium at point A in Figure 22.7 is disturbed by an increase in government

Figure 22.8
Monetary Policy with Flexible Exchange Rates

Monetary policy is more effective with flexible rates than with fixed rates. Suppose the money supply increases, shifting the LM out to LM′. At point B there is a BOP deficit. That leads to a depreciation of the exchange rate, shifting both the BP and the IS to the right. Full equilibrium is established at point C.

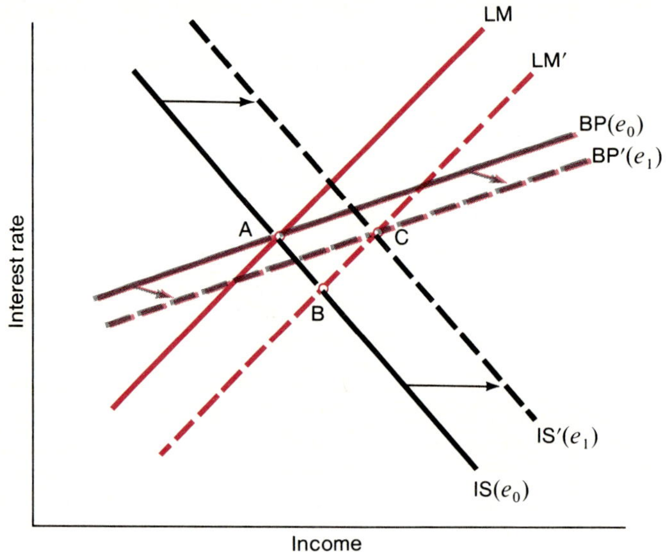

expenditures financed in such a way that the LM curve stays constant. This rise in G pushes the IS curve out to IS′. Before the exchange rate adjusts, the economy moves out to point B, where there is a BOP surplus and an expansion of income.

Under flexible rates, the short-run BOP surplus resulting from expansionary fiscal policy causes an appreciation of the exchange rate. This, as we learned in the last section, causes both the IS and the BP curves to shift to the left. The IS curve moves because exchange rate appreciation is contractionary; it reduces exports and increases imports. For the same reason, appreciation worsens the balance of payments, which moves the BP curve to the left. In reaction to the surplus the exchange rate rises, and the two curves shift leftward until they intersect on the LM curve. This occurs at exchange rate e_1 and at point C in Figure 22.7. (We should note here that, for the moment, we are holding domestic prices constant; that assumption will be relaxed later.) From this exercise, we can see that fiscal policy is less effective than it is under either fixed exchange rates or a closed economy. For so long as the LM is steeper than the BP expansionary fiscal policy causes a surplus, and that leads to a contractionary appreciation of the exchange rate.

The situation is reversed for monetary policy. It becomes more effective than it was under either fixed rates or a closed economy. Take our same economy and disturb it with expansionary monetary policy, as shown in Figure 22.8. Before the exchange rate reacts to the change, the economy expands to point B, at which the country is running a BOP deficit. Under flexible rates, that deficit causes a depreciation of the currency. But depreciation, we have learned, is expansionary. Lowering e shifts the IS and BP to the right, the former because exports increase and imports decline and the latter because depreciation improves the balance of payments. The depreciation must be such that the IS and BP shift out until they intersect on the LM curve at point C. (Again, we assume for the moment no change in domestic prices.)

As the reader can see, monetary policy is more effective here than it would be under fixed rates or a closed economy. The reason is that monetary expansion lowers the domestic interest rate. That sparks an outflow of capital which, in turn, causes a depreciation of the exchange rate. Monetary policy, therefore, is doubly expansionary. It lowers domestic interest rates, which stimulates investment, and it also causes depreciation of the exchange rate, which stimulates exports and contracts imports. Both increase demand in the domestic goods market.

Policy in the Open Economy with Flexible Prices

So far, we have examined policy options in the open economy when prices were fixed. But generally, any policy that increases income also increases the price level. Since relative prices appear in both the export and the import equations, the price feedback has an effect on the final equilibrium that will be observed in response to any policy changes. In some cases, the response to policy is quite different when price changes are included in the analysis.

First, we examine the effect of a change in prices on the IS-LM-BP diagram (see Figure 22.9). As we have already noted, a rise in price makes U. S. products more expensive for everyone. This tends to reduce our exports and increase our imports, both of which reduce the demand for domestically produced goods. Hence, a rise in price shifts the IS curve to the left. Because of this same effect on exports and imports, the rise in price makes the balance of payments worse, which shifts the BP curve to the left. Finally, the price increase reduces the real money supply, and that shifts the LM curve to the left as well. In short, a rise in price shifts all three curves to the left, not necessarily by equal amounts. Therefore, if an economy starts in equilibrium at a point such as A in Figure 22.9, a rise in price will shift the LM curve to LM′, the IS to IS′, and the BP to BP′, leading to a new equilibrium at point B. Obviously, a fall in price would have exactly the opposite effect.

Monetary and Fiscal Policies with Flexible Exchange Rates and Prices

Ignoring prices, equilibrium in the open economy requires the simultaneous intersection of the IS, BP, and LM curves. Allowing prices to change is equivalent to bringing in an additional equilibrium condition—namely, the economy should be on its long-run supply curve, $Y = Y_{FE}$. As we learned in our study of inflation, at

Figure 22.9
The Effect of a Rise in Price

A rise in price shifts all three curves to the left. The LM curve shifts because of the reduction in real balances. The IS curve shifts because of the effects of price on consumption and imports. The BP shifts because a rise in price worsens the balance of payments.

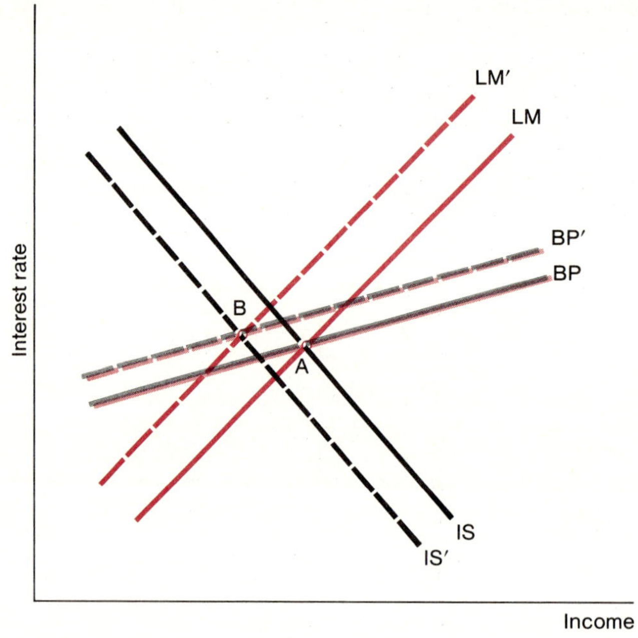

any other income level inflation rates are either rising or falling; that will tend to shift the IS, BP, and LM curves. Thus, any equilibrium point that is not on the long-run economy supply curve must, at best, be temporary. When we bring in prices, full equilibrium requires the simultaneous intersection of four curves: the IS, BP, LM, and vertical long-run supply curve, $Y = Y_{FE}$.

From our analysis of supply, we know that any intersection to the right (left) of Y_{FE} implies rising (falling) prices or inflation rates, just as any intersection below the BP curve implies BOP deficits and a falling money supply. Let us now see what the introduction of this new definition of full equilibrium does to our analysis of policy options in the open economy. We shall first examine monetary and fiscal policies under flexible exchange rates and flexible prices.

Monetary Policy Suppose we have an economy in full employment equilibrium such as at point A in Figure 22.10. Now we disturb the equilibrium with an expansionary monetary policy, which shifts the LM curve out to LM′. Recall that when prices were fixed, monetary policy was doubly effective with flexible ex-

Figure 22.10
Monetary Policy with Flexible Exchange Rates and Prices
An expansion of the money supply, if exchange rates were flexible, would move the equilibrium out from point A to point B so long as prices were fixed. However, if point B is above Y_{FE}, prices will start to rise. This shifts all three curves back and to the left until they all once again intersect at point A. Thus, if prices are flexible, an expansion in the money supply leads only to a rise in price and a depreciation of the currency by the same percentage amount. It has no effect on either output or the interest rate.

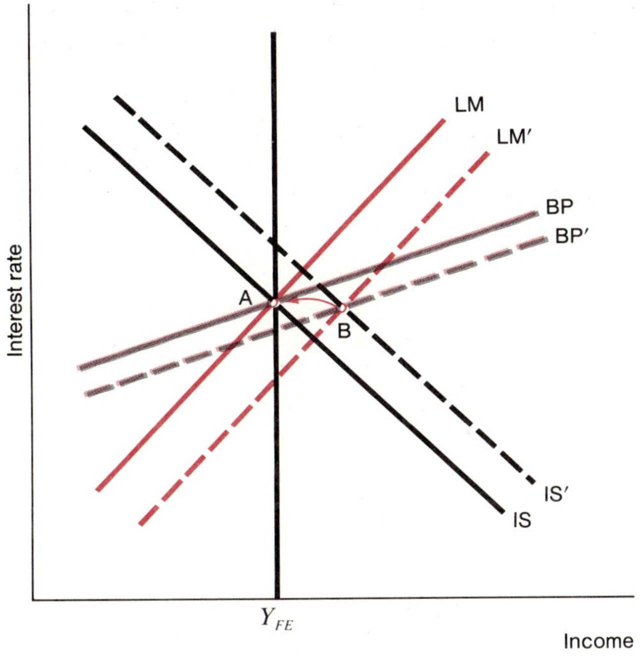

change rates—for the monetary expansion triggered a currency depreciation, and that increased the demand for exports and import substitutes, leading to a new equilibrium at point B.

Things are different when prices are flexible. At point B there is excess demand, and that means that prices will start to go up. As we have just shown, rising prices shift all three of our curves to the left. Over time, the rise in price will wipe out the entire effect of both the monetary expansion and the depreciation of e. The economy will return to point A, as shown by the arrow in the diagram. Indeed, it can be shown that if prices are perfectly flexible, prices will rise and the exchange rate will fall by exactly the same percentage amount as the original expansion in the money supply. As a result, the original level of relative prices between U. S. and foreign goods will be restored, which implies that the BP and IS curves will return to their original positions, as will the LM curve. The only permanent result of expansionary monetary policy is a higher price level and a lower exchange rate. The real

Figure 22.11
Fiscal Policy with Flexible Exchange Rates and Prices

Expansionary fiscal policy would move the economy from point A to point B if prices were fixed. But if B is above Y_{FE}, prices should begin to rise. That again shifts all three curves to the left. The process should stop when all three curves intersect on Y_{FE}, at a point such as C. Here fiscal policy leads to an increase in prices, an appreciation of the exchange rate, and a rise in r. While the level of output is unaffected by fiscal policy, the composition is. Consumption or government expenditures go up, investment and exports go down.

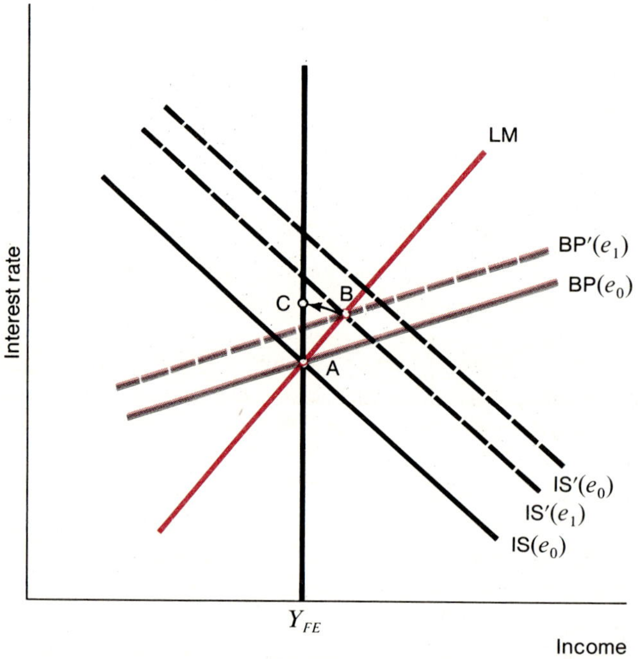

economy is as neutral with respect to monetary policy in the open economy as it is in the closed economy. This is strikingly different from our conclusions regarding monetary policy when exchange rates were flexible but prices were fixed.

Fiscal Policy Now consider the effect of expansionary fiscal policy in an economy starting in full equilibrium such as at point A in Figure 22.11. Expansionary fiscal policy shifts the IS curve out to IS′. In the fixed price model, this caused an appreciation of the exchange rate, which tended to offset part of the initial expansion because appreciation shifted both the IS and BP curves to the left. The fixed price economy moved from point A to point B in response to expansionary fiscal policy.

That is not the end of the story when prices are flexible. Since point B is to the right of Y_{FE}, prices begin to rise. That, as we have learned, shifts three curves to the left. The process continues until the economy reaches a point such as C, at which all three curves again intersect at Y_{FE}.

The effect of prices on the solution is in some ways like the reaction to monetary policy. Rising prices are contractionary; they drive the economy back to Y_{FE}. But in one way, the two cases are different. Fiscal policy is not neutral. Since prices rise and the money supply is constant, we know that the LM curve must shift to the left. That means that interest rates will be higher at point C than they were at point A. Hence, investment will be crowded out by expansionary fiscal policy.

That is not the only change. Because expansionary fiscal policy causes an appreciation of the exchange rate and a rise in U. S. prices, it must worsen the balance of payments on current accounts. Exports will fall and imports will rise. The current account deficit is matched by an increase of capital inflows, due to the higher interest rates. Therefore, it is clear that expansionary fiscal policy does have real effects on the composition of production in the open economy. Income returns to Y_{FE}, but the increase in government spending crowds out both investment and exports.

Monetary and Fiscal Policies with Fixed Exchange Rates and Flexible Prices

We turn now to an examination of the effect of macropolicy in an economy with fixed exchange rates and flexible prices. Recall that when both exchange rates and prices are fixed monetary policy is completely ineffective, because any change in the internal money supply is soon offset by an equal change in international reserves. In contrast, fiscal policy has a double effect. Not only does it shift the IS curve; it also causes BOP deficits or surpluses, which lead to complementary expansions or contractions in the money supply. Let us now see what happens to those results when prices are flexible. We look first at fiscal policy.

Fiscal Policy As before, let us disturb an economy in full equilibrium by an expansionary fiscal policy. In the fixed price world shown in Figure 22.12, this change would shift the IS curve out to IS′, and the BOP surpluses would gradually shift the LM curve out to an intersection with IS′ at point B. This point is no longer a full equilibrium. Because the income level at B is greater than Y_{FE}, prices rise; this shifts all three curves to the left. After an adjustment period, the economy reaches a new equilibrium at a point like C. Point C must lie above point A on Y_{FE}, because the rise in prices reduces exports and shifts the BP curve up and to the left. To counteract the worsening in the current account, interest rates must rise enough to improve the capital account by an equal and offsetting amount.

The net result of expansionary fiscal policy is, therefore, to drive up prices, reduce the current account balance, and crowd out investment. This was precisely the same effect we found for fiscal policy when exchange rates and prices were both flexible. Whether exchange rates are fixed or flexible, expansionary fiscal policy simply changes the composition of output at Y_{FE}. Exports and capital formation decline while government spending or private consumption increase, depending on whether the fiscal stimulus comes from the expenditure or revenue side.

Figure 22.12
Expansionary Fiscal Policy with Fixed Exchange Rates and Flexible Prices

As in Figure 22.11, expansionary fiscal policy moves the economy out to a point such as B. Then, rising prices shift all three curves until they intersect on Y_{FE} at a point such as C. If prices are flexible, the net effect of expansionary fiscal policy does not depend on whether exchange rates are fixed or flexible.

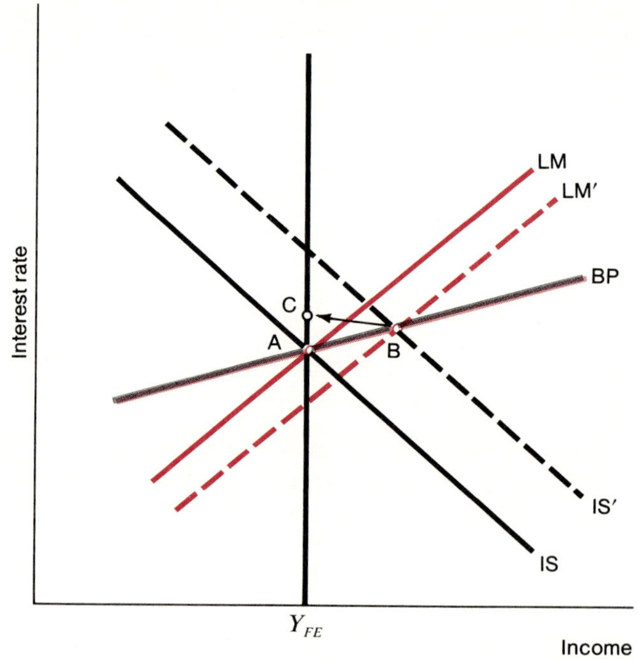

Monetary Policy We turn now to monetary policy under flexible prices and fixed exchange rates. Recall that in the fixed price case monetary policy has no long-run effect, because deficits and surpluses in the balance of payments lead to offsetting changes in the money supply. The same thing is true when prices are flexible, but the pathway back to full equilibrium is somewhat more complex.

As before, we disturb an economy at full equilibrium such as at point A in Figure 22.13 by an expansion in the money supply. In response to this monetary expansion, the economy moves out to point B. That obviously is not an equilibrium, for there is both a BOP deficit and excess demand in the goods market. In response, the money supply falls and prices increase. As a result, all three curves shift to the left. Where does the economy end up? The somewhat counterintuitive answer is back at A. That requires the money supply and prices to return to their original level. Let us see why.

The initial rise in prices shifts the BP and IS curves to the left. This, along with the fact that the economy runs a BOP deficit, contracts the real money supply. At

Figure 22.13

Expansionary Monetary Policy with Fixed Exchange Rates and Flexible Prices

An expansion in the money supply shifts the LM curve out to LM′. If prices were fixed, the new equilibrium would be at point B. However, at B there is a balance of payments deficit; that should cause the money supply to contract. If, at the same time, excess demand in the goods market causes prices to increase, both the IS and the BP will shift to the left. If that happens, the economy cannot simply return to A, as it would if prices were fixed. Instead, there must be a time during the adjustment process when the economy is at a recession point, such as C. Prices decline and all three curves shift to the right until equilibrium is reestablished at A. Thus, so long as prices are flexible, the final equilibrium after monetary expansion is unchanged whether exchange rates are fixed or flexible.

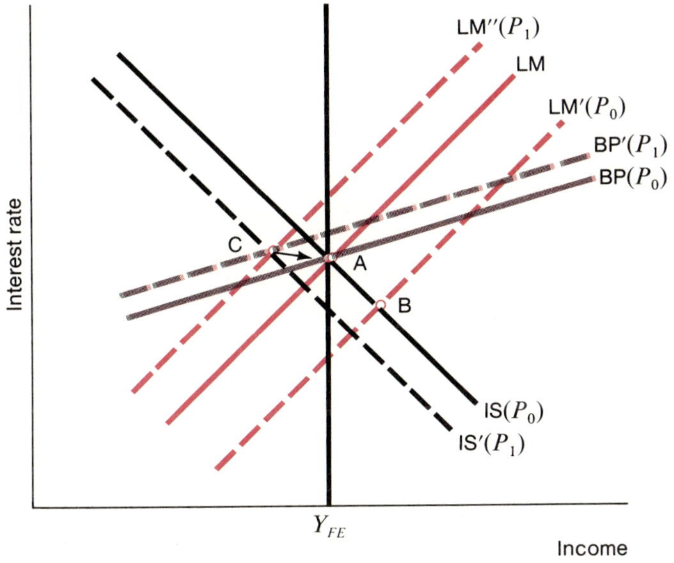

some point the real money supply falls back to its original level, meaning the economy is back on the original LM curve. Can the intersection of this LM curve and Y_{FE} at A be a full equilibrium? Obviously not, for the leftward shifts in the IS and BP caused by the rise in prices assure us that all three curves cannot intersect at A until prices return to their initial level. Therefore, we know that the contraction process will continue until the LM moves back to a curve like LM″, which intersects with the IS and BP at point C. But C is not a full equilibrium either, because income is less than capacity. Now, assuming that prices are flexible, prices begin to fall, shifting all three curves to the right. This process continues until the real money supply and prices return to their original levels. At this point, the BP, IS, and LM curves have shifted back to their initial levels, and the economy is back in full equilibrium at point A.

Table 22.2
Effect of Policy Changes under Different Assumptions about Prices and Exchange Rates

	Fixed Rates	Flexible Rates
Expansionary Monetary Policy		
Fixed prices	No real effects: real money supply held constant by outflow of reserves	Output rises, e falls
Flexible prices	No real effects: prices rise but return to initial level; real money supply held constant by outflow of reserves	No real effects: prices rise; e falls in same proportion as money supply increases
Expansionary Fiscal Policy		
Fixed prices	Output rises, money supply rises, interest rate rises	Output rises, e rises, current account deteriorates
Flexible prices	Output is constant, prices rise, interest rates rise, exports and investment both fall	Output is constant, prices rise, e rises, interest rises, exports and investment both fall

To summarize: Monetary policy has no long-run effect on the economy in a world with fixed exchange rates. There is only one difference between the fixed and flexible exchange rate economies. When exchange rates are fixed, the money supply is reduced by an outflow of international reserves in response to the BOP deficit. When exchange rates are flexible, prices go up and there is an equivalent compensating devaluation. In either case, monetary policy has no *real* long-run effect. Bringing in the supply-side equilibrium condition and price feedbacks eliminates the apparent difference between the effect of monetary policy on the economy under fixed and under flexible rates. This difference holds only when prices are constant; it does not hold when they are flexible.

Our results are summarized in Table 22.2. Most analysis of policy in the open economy draws a distinction between the effectiveness of monetary and fiscal policies in economies with fixed and flexible exchange rates. Monetary policy is thought to be more effective when rates are flexible and fiscal policy more effective when they are fixed. This distinction disappears when prices too are flexible. There is little difference between the effect of monetary and fiscal policies under the two exchange rate regimes.

Look at lines 2 and 4 in the table. When prices are flexible, the sharp distinction is blurred between the effectiveness of policy across either exchange rate regime. According to line 2, under either regime the long-run effect of expansionary monetary policy is a rise in prices but no change in any real variable, such as income, investment, or employment. There is a difference between monetary policy under fixed and flexible exchange rates, but it is limited to price and exchange rate movements and international reserves. Likewise, expansionary fiscal policy under either exchange rate regime affects the composition of output in the same way. Output is constant, but investment and exports both decline. In short, when one includes prices in the analysis, the long-run results of policy changes are just

Figure 22.14
Curing a BOP Deficit by Changes in Domestic Prices
Suppose that an economy starts at point A. There is full employment but a BOP deficit. If prices were rigid, the money supply would contract until a full equilibrium was reached at B. However, at B, $Y < Y_{FE}$. This should cause prices to decline, leading to a rightward shift in all three curves. Full equilibrium will be reestablished at point C, at which interest rates are higher, investment is lower, and exports are higher than they all were initially at point A.

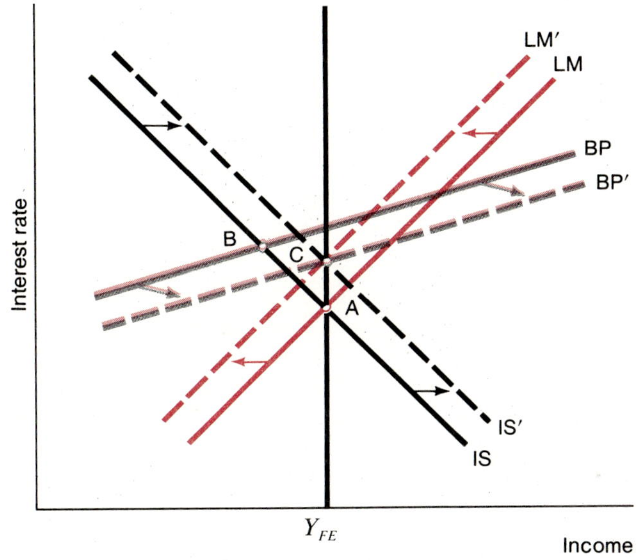

what they were in the closed economy and differ little across exchange rate regimes. Monetary policy is neutral, affecting only prices and exchange rates; fiscal policy changes the composition of output, but not its level.

Correcting BOP Disequilibria When Prices are Flexible and Exchange Rates are Fixed

So far we have examined how an economy in full equilibrium reacts to a change in monetary or fiscal policy. It remains to be seen how an economy that is not in full equilibrium can get to full equilibrium, either through price or exchange rate adjustment.

Automatic Price Adjustment Suppose an economy starts at a point such as A in Figure 22.14. At A, the economy has full employment, but it is running a BOP deficit. How is this disequilibrium eliminated by price changes in the fixed exchange rate economy?

Since there is a deficit in the balance of payments, the money supply declines. If prices were fixed the economy would move to point B, the intersection of the BP and IS curves. But since income at B is lower than Y_{FE}, prices decline. This causes a rightward shift in all three curves. Eventually, the economy reaches a new long-run equilibrium at a point such as C. Because prices are lower, we know that exports increase. Because the real money supply declines from its initial level, we know that interest rates increase and investment declines. The balance of payments is equilibrated without any change in income by an increase in exports, a decline in imports, an increase in capital flows, and a decline in domestic investment. One could say that the cost of putting the balance of payments into equilibrium is borne by domestic capital formation.

Devaluation to Cure a BOP Deficit Let us now see what happens if the government attempts to cure a BOP deficit through devaluation, as shown in Figure 22.15. Again the economy starts at point A, where there is full employment and a balance of payments deficit. Now suppose that the government attempts to cure the problem by devaluation. The devaluation shifts both the IS and BP curves out to point B, assuming that import elasticities of demand are greater than 1. But at B, $Y > Y_{FE}$, and therefore prices will increase—devaluation is inflationary. As prices increase, all three curves shift to the left until the economy reaches a new full equilibrium at point C. Since prices have increased, we know that the real money supply declines and the LM curve shifts to the left. That, in turn, implies that the interest rate at point C must be higher than it was at point A.

The net effect of the two methods of adjustment does not appear to be to dissimilar. In both cases, interest rates rise, net exports increase, and some domestic investment is crowded out by exports and the domestic production of import substitutes. However, in one respect the two methods are dramatically different. With devaluation prices go up and there is a short-run expansion, while with the other prices go down and there is a short-term recession. Price adjustment requires recession and domestic deflation; exchange rate adjustment generates an expansion, which causes inflation.

There are cases where the inflationary impact of devaluation is so severe that the devaluation could worsen the BOP situation rather than improve it. Such cases could simply exacerbate the perverse effects we noted in our discussion of the J curve. Some economists refer to these cases as vicious circles in which devaluation drives up prices so much that the balance of payments gets worse instead of better.

The method of adjustment by recession assumes that recession will in fact drive down prices and so make the country more competitive. When prices are inflexible downward, curing a balance of payments deficit without devaluation means a contraction in the money supply and a recession. Whether recession or devaluation is a better way of curing a BOP problem in a particular country depends on the inflationary implications of devaluation versus the downward inflexibility of prices. Most countries appear unwilling to accept domestic recession as the price for curing a BOP deficit. We therefore tend to see devaluation as the accepted response to BOP deficits. This cure, unfortunately, has inflationary costs, particularly when the economy is close to full employment.

Figure 22.15
Devaluation to Cure a BOP Deficit

We start again at point A, at which the economy is running a BOP deficit. The authorities devalue, causing both the IS and the BP to shift rightward to IS′ and BP′, respectively. If prices were rigid, a new equilibrium would be established at point B. However, at B prices begin to rise. This shifts all three curves to the left, to IS″, LM″, and BP″. The process continues until a new full equilibrium is reached at point C. We know that C must be above A because real balances must have declined due to the increase in prices. As in Figure 22.14, the real effect of the adjustment has been to increase exports and reduce investment. In this case the adjustment process leads to domestic expansion and a rise in prices, whereas in Figure 22.14 it led to a recession and a reduction in prices.

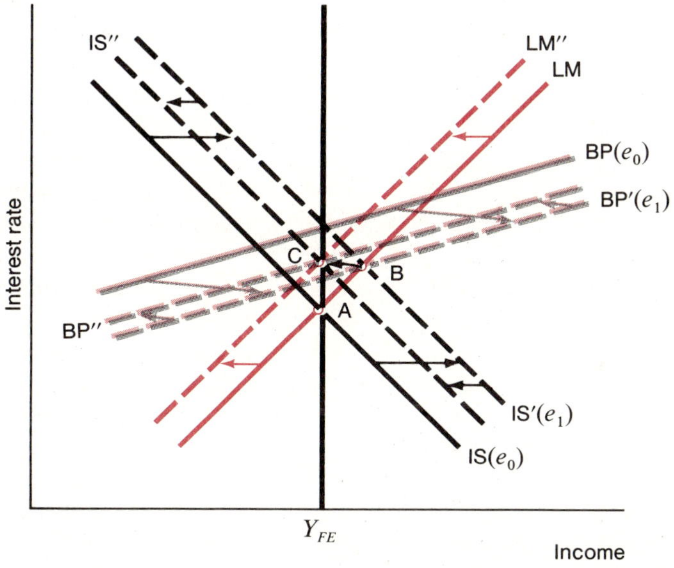

Summary

In this chapter we first integrated the balance of payments into a model of the open economy. Exports and imports affect the goods market, making the IS curve steeper in the open than in the closed economy. In the money market, since international reserves are incorporated into the monetary base, any balance of payments surplus increases the money supply and shifts the LM curve to the right. A balance of payments deficit does the opposite.

The dollar market adds another constraint line, the BP curve, to our basic IS-LM diagram. The BP curve represents different interest rate-income combinations at which the balance of payments is in equilibrium. It is upward sloping because an increase in income, which causes a current account deficit, can be offset by a rise in interest rates, which causes a capital inflow.

We next analyzed policymaking in the open economy. In several cases the effects of policy in the open economy are dramatically different. For example, when prices and the exchange rate are both fixed, the money supply is an endogenous variable, and therefore monetary policy is ineffective. If the central bank attempts to increase the money supply, the resulting balance of payments deficits will cause M to contract again. In contrast, fiscal policy is doubly effective under fixed exchange rates, since any expansion will cause a rise in interest rates, an inflow of capital, and hence an increase in the money supply.

When exchange rates are flexible, the situation is reversed. Monetary policy is more effective than fiscal, because any expansion in M leads to a balance of payments deficit. This causes a devaluation, a rightward shift in both the IS and BP curves, and hence an expansion in income. Expansionary fiscal policy would be less effective than monetary policy under flexible rates, because it would cause a contractionary appreciation of the currency.

The situation is different when prices are flexible rather than fixed. In this case, there is no difference across exchange rate regimes in the effect of either monetary or fiscal policy. For example, in a fixed exchange rate regime, an expansion in the money supply causes an outflow of reserves but no change in either the level or the composition of income. In the flexible rate case, prices rise and the exchange rate falls, both in proportion to the change in M, but again there is no real effect on either the level or composition of income.

For fiscal policy we observe the same pattern. Under fixed exchange rates and flexible prices, an expansionary fiscal policy causes an increase in price, a rise in interest rates, and crowding out of exports and investment. Exactly the same pattern should be observed when exchange rates are flexible.

Key Concepts

fixed exchange rate
flexible exchange rate
BP curve
effectiveness of fiscal and monetary policy in the open economy

Problems and Questions for Discussion

1. Why is the slope of the IS curve in the open economy steeper than in the closed economy?

2. Show how each of the following changes affects the IS and LM curves.
- **a.** A devaluation.
- **b.** An increase in foreign income.
- **c.** An increase in U. S. prices.
- **d.** A balance of payments deficit (under fixed exchange rates).

3. What conditions determine the slope of the BP curve? What do you think the BP curve for Nigeria would look like relative to the BP curve for the United States?

4. Why is monetary policy relatively ineffective when exchange rates and prices are fixed?

5. The money supply is supposedly endogenous in a fixed exchange rate economy.

a. Describe the process by which balance of payments deficits and/or surpluses affect the money supply.

b. Could the Federal Reserve maintain control over the money supply if the United States ran continual balance of payments deficits? If so, describe how the Fed would do so and what the effect of its policies would be on the U. S. balance of payments and on the economies of other countries.

6. Suppose that the United States has a fixed exchange rate, is at full employment, and is running a balance of payments deficit. Describe two sets of policies that would simultaneously eliminate the deficit while keeping the economy at full employment. (Hint: Remember that the exchange rate is a policy variable.) Show your two solutions in the IS-LM-BP diagram.

7. In the situation described in Problem 6, suppose the government does nothing. Can the economy reach full external and internal equilibrium on its own? If so, show how this would happen, using the IS-LM-BP diagram. Why might a government be unwilling to accept this remedy for a BOP deficit?

8. Show that when prices are flexible there is no difference between the effect of monetary policy across exchange rate regimes. What is the net effect of expansionary monetary policy in these circumstances?

9. Assuming flexible exchange rates, what is the effect on the exchange rate, the price level, the level of income, and the level of imports of an increase in government expenditures? Show your solution in the IS-LM-BP diagram. Does your solution depend on the shape of the aggregate supply curve? If so, how?

10. How could policymakers in an open economy with fixed exchange rates increase defense spending, lower taxes, increase investment, increase income, and eliminate the BOP deficit all at the same time? (If you can answer this, you get a year as an intern on the Council of Economic Advisors).

11. In Problem 10, could you produce the same results holding income constant? If so, how? If not, why not?

Glossary

accelerator The theory that investment is a linear function of a change in output. It implies that investment is procyclical, meaning that it will rise in booms and fall in recessions.

accommodating demand policy One possible policy response to a supply shock. Aggregate demand is allowed to increase by enough to support the rise in prices and wages caused by the supply shock.

actual measured investment The observed investment expenditure.

actual unemployment The observed level of unemployment.

adaptive expectations Price expectations that are based on past prices.

administrative lag The time between the recognition of the need for a policy and the adoption of that policy.

aggregate demand The total demand for newly produced goods and services by all the spending units in the economy: households, business, and government.

aggregate supply The total amount of output that producers are willing to produce at the current price level.

appreciation A rise in the exchange rate. It means that the price of dollars goes up, which implies that Americans can buy foreign goods more cheaply and U. S. goods become more expensive for foreigners.

asset crowding out The reduction in interest-sensitive expenditure caused by bond sales required to finance expansionary fiscal policy.

automatic stabilizer Any government expenditure transfer or receipt that tends to make the government deficit bigger when the economy is in recession or smaller when it is in a boom. Income taxes and unemployment benefits are the most important automatic stabilizers.

average propensity to consume The ratio of household consumption expenditures to disposable income.

average reserve ratio The ratio of total bank reserves to total deposits, both demand and time. It is a weighted average of the reserve ratio on demand deposits and the reserve ratio on time deposits.

balance of payments The difference between a nation's receipts from other countries and its expenditures in other countries for goods, services, assets, dividends, interest, and transfer payments.

bond A financial agreement between the borrower (issuer) and the lender (owner) specifying the number of dollars per year that will be paid to the owner and the date on which the original loan will be repaid.

BOP (balance of payments) deficit A situation in which the total receipts from other countries for the sale of goods, services, assets, and investment income are less than a nation's expenditures to other countries for the same items.

BP curve A schedule showing all the pairs of interest rates and income at which the dollar market is in equilibrium.

bracket-creep The movement of people into higher income tax brackets caused by the increase in their income due to inflation. Bracket-creep will be eliminated by indexing the tax system.

capacity GNP The amount of GNP the economy would produce at full employment. It is equivalent to the full equilibrium level of output.

capital account That part of the balance of payments which includes the purchase or sale of assets. Portfolio and direct investment are the two principal components of the capital account.

capital stock The amount of plant and equipment available to produce output. The growth in capital through investment is one of the main determinants of the growth of GNP per capita.

comparative statics In an economic model, the study of how changes in exogenous variables affect the equilibrium values of the model's endogenous variables.

constant interest rate rule A policy rule for monetary policy that would direct the Fed to keep the interest rate constant.

constant percentage growth rate rule The rule proposed by Milton Friedman directing the Federal Reserve to make the money supply grow by a constant percentage rate each year. Friedman argues that by following this rule, the government could not be a source of instability.

consumer price index A price index that measures changes in the cost of a market basket of goods purchased by the average urban consumer.

core inflation The trend rate of increase in the price of aggregate supply. It is a key notion in the work of Otto Eckstein.

cost-push inflation An inflation in which costs, particularly wage costs, are rising faster than prices. The symptom of cost-push inflation is rising prices accompanied by falling output.

crowding-out effect The reduction in interest-sensitive private expenditure that occurs when the government engages in expansionary fiscal policy but holds the money supply constant.

current account That portion of the balance of payments which includes all transactions with foreign countries other than the purchase or sale of assets. Principal components of the current account are imports, exports, dividends, interest, and transfer payments.

demand-pull inflation An inflation caused by an increase in demand relative to supply. The symptom of demand-pull inflation is rising prices accompanied by rising output.

demand-side economics The study of the ways in which the government can control the level of aggregate demand.

depreciation A fall in the exchange rate. It means that the price of dollars declines, which implies that foreign goods become more expensive for Americans and U. S. goods become cheaper for foreigners.

desired capital stock The profit-maximizing capital stock that a firm would like to have given its level of output.

devaluation A reduction in the exchange rate by a country on a fixed exchange rate. It reduces the price that foreigners pay for that country's currency.

diminishing returns The opposite of increasing returns to scale. It means that output increases by less than the percentage increase in inputs as the scale of production increases.

direct investment The investment by corporations in operating subsidiaries abroad.

dirty float An exchange rate regime in which exchange rates are neither fixed nor perfectly flexible. Rates are partially determined in the foreign exchange market, but the government intervenes to keep fluctuations in the exchange rate within permissible bounds.

disembodied technical change An increase in the quantity of output producible by a given quantity of capital and labor.

disequilibrium theory A short-run theory of aggregate supply that is based on markup pricing. The main implication of the theory is that there is involuntary unemployment in the labor market and relatively inflexible prices during recessions.

disintermediation The outflow of funds from financial intermediaries, particularly savings and loan associations, in response to high interest rates.

diversification of assets The holding of a number of different assets in a portfolio in order to reduce the variability or uncertainty of the portfolio's return.

double counting The use of the value of total sales as a measure of total production. It is called this because if some firms sell to other firms, their production will be counted twice in the total value of sales.

dynamic analysis The study of how the economy moves from one equilibrium to another in response to a change in an exogenous variable.

economies of scale An increase in efficiency due to an increase in the scale of operations. It means that output increases by a greater percentage than increases in capital and labor.

effect lag The time between the adoption of a policy and the time when it begins to affect the economy.

effective interest rate The interest rate on old bonds. It is equal to the coupon paid by the bond plus capital gains, all expressed as a percentage of the current price of the bond.

endogenous variable A variable whose values are determined within the model being analyzed.

equation of exchange The equation upon which the quantity theory is based. It says that nominal income is proportional to the money supply.

equilibrium The solution for an economic model. It is a set of values for each of the endogenous variables that simultaneously satisfies all the equations in the model.

exchange rate The relative price of foreign and domestic currencies. It can be expressed either as the price in marks or yen that foreigners pay for dollars or as the price in dollars that Americans pay for marks or yen.

exogenous variable A variable whose value is determined outside the framework of the model being analyzed.

expansionary phase The initial phase of the inflationary cycle, during which output and prices are both rising. It is caused by unexpected inflation resulting from an unexpected increase in aggregate demand.

Federal Open Market Committee The policymaking unit of the Federal Reserve. It meets monthly to decide on monetary policy and is composed of the seven governors of the Federal Reserve System, the president of the New York Fed, and representatives from four of the other eleven Federal Reserve banks.

feedback rule Any policy rule in which conditions in the economy have an effect on policy.

firm-specific The quality of being unique to a particular firm.

fiscal policy The manipulation of government expenditures, taxes, or transfers in order to influence either the size or the composition of GNP.

fixed exchange rate An exchange rate regime in which the exchange rate is set or controlled by the government. In effect, the exchange rate becomes a policy variable that the government can try to use to influence the balance of payments.

flexible exchange rate An exchange rate regime in which the exchange rate is determined by the forces of supply and demand in the foreign exchange market.

floating exchange rate An exchange rate system in which the exchange rate is determined by the supply and demand for foreign exchange rather than being set by the government.

F-P model An economic model based on the theories of Milton Friedman and Edmund Phelps. See *partial equilibrium theory*.

frictional unemployment Refers to workers who are between jobs when the economy is operating at its normal or full employment rate. Frictional unemployment is voluntary and consists mainly of people who are searching out their best job opportunities.

full employment deficit The deficit that the government would run if the economy were at the full equilibrium or full employment level of output. It has been proposed as a better measure of fiscal policy than the actual government deficit, because it does not depend on the actual level of income.

full employment tax rule A rule for fiscal policy that requires that the tax rate be set so that the economy will go to full employment, given the money supply.

government budget identity An accounting equation that states that the difference between government expenditures and tax revenues must be equal to the change in bonds plus the change in the stock of high-powered money. The identity implies that government deficits must lead to an increase in either the bond supply or the money supply, either of which will have an effect on the money market.

government deficit Total government expenditures minus total tax revenues.

GNP deflator The price index for GNP. It is defined as the ratio of nominal to real GNP and tells how much of any change in GNP is due to changing prices.

gross business saving The amount that business retains from gross profits for reinvestment. It is equal to depreciation plus retained earnings.

gross national product (GNP) The value of goods and services produced by the economy over a certain time interval.

high-powered money The monetary base that is controlled by the Federal Reserve through open market operations. It is defined as the sum of currency in the hands of the public plus reserves of the banking system.

idiosyncratic An attribute of a certain job meaning that the skills required are useful only in that job. The job market for idiosyncratic jobs will tend to be internal to the firm. Furthermore, workers with idiosyncratic skills have a strong tie to their firms; they tend to be laid off rather than fired during recessions.

import demand elasticity The percentage change in the quantity of imports demanded per 1-percent change in the relative price of imports.

incomes policy Any policy by which the government intervenes in the setting of prices and/or wages. Incomes policies run all the way from voluntary guidelines for wage increases to full-blown systems of mandatory wage and price controls.

indexing A mechanism used to adjust contracts written in nominal terms for inflation that occurs over the life of the contract. Bonds, mortgages, debts, taxes, and wage contracts can all be indexed. The aim of all indexing is to prevent a redistribution of income between the two parties to the contract because of inflation.

inflationary cycle The response by the economy to a one-time increase in demand. The typical pattern is an expansion in output and a rise in prices followed by a return to the full equilibrium supply curve coupled with a further increase in prices.

internal labor market Describes a labor market in which many jobs tend to be internal to or specific to the firm. In such a market many jobs would have specific requirements of either trust or skill that would give the firm's own employees a large advantage over outsiders.

International Monetary Fund (IMF) An international organization founded by the Bretton Woods agreement in 1944. It extends credit to member countries when they run temporary balance of payments deficits. It has a major responsibility for insuring the smooth and effective operation of the international financial system.

investment Expenditures on new construction, new machinery, and changes in inventories. Gross investment less depreciation represents additions to the capital stock.

IS curve A schedule showing all the pairs of interest rates and income at which the goods market is in equilibrium. At all points along the IS curve total saving equals investment.

J curve A schedule showing what happens over time to the balance of payments after a devaluation.

Keynesian A term describing the economic beliefs of the followers of John Maynard Keynes. It is generally associated with the belief in the efficacy of active countercyclical policy and an unwillingness to let price and wage decreases cure recessions.

kinked supply curve The nonlinear supply curve that is implied by the disequilibrium model. The change of slope or kink occurs at the normal operating capacity level of the economy.

labor stockpiling The practice of retaining the skilled labor force in the face of a decline in sales that is viewed as temporary. It results from the desire of firms to avoid losing their trained labor force. The practice leads to declining profits, rising costs, and declining labor productivity during recessions.

Laffer curve A schedule named after Arthur Laffer showing tax revenues as a function of tax rates. It has an inverted U shape.

life-cycle hypothesis A theory of household consumption behavior developed by Franco Modigliani and others. It asserts that households make a lifetime consumption plan in which they maximize lifetime utility by saving during high income years to finance consumption during retirement. The theory implies that an increase in wealth will reduce saving.

liquidity trap The flat portion of the LM curve. In the liquidity trap the demand for money is so sensitive to interest rates that changes in the supply of money can be absorbed without any change in the interest rate. Thus, monetary policy loses its ability to influence interest rates.

LM curve A schedule showing all the pairs of interest rates and income at which the money market is in equilibrium. At any point on the LM curve, the demand for and the supply of money are equal.

macroeconomic model A formal representation of how the economy works. It is usually written in the form of a system of behavioral equations and definitions, which can be solved for an equilibrium.

macroeconomics The study of aggregate economic phenomena such as income, employment, and the price level.

marginal physical product of labor The change in the value of production produced by an additional worker.

marginal propensity to consume The change in consumption spending per one-dollar change in disposable income.

marginal propensity to save The change in household saving per one-dollar change in disposable income.

marginal revenue product The change in the value of sales produced by an additional worker.

market-clearing interest rate The rate of interest at which the demand for and supply of money and bonds are equal.

modified accelerator The accelerator theory of investment that takes account of the fact that investment takes time to complete. It implies that investment is a function of both current and lagged changes in output.

monetarism The beliefs of a group of economists who are followers of Milton Friedman. Key ideas are that money is the main determinant of aggregate demand, that the government should not engage in active countercyclical demand management, and that all inflations are caused by excessive monetary expansion.

monetary base See *high-powered money*.

monetary policy The manipulation of the money supply through open market operations and changes in the rediscount rate and the bank reserve ratio. Monetary policy is undertaken to control the level of aggregate demand and its composition as well as price level.

monetizing the deficit Financing the government deficit by increasing high-powered money. This requires that the Federal Reserve buy bonds through an open market operation in the same amount that the Treasury sells bonds to finance the deficit.

money market funds Institutions that borrow from individuals and invest these funds in short-term financial securities. Offer limited check-writing privileges to the individual and higher interest rates than are available at banks. Is included in M2.

money multiplier The ratio of the money supply to the monetary base. It tells by how many dollars the money supply will change when there is a one-dollar change in the monetary base.

multiplier The change in an endogenous variable with respect to a one-unit change in an exogenous variable.

national income The sum of payments to the three factors of production—land, labor, and capital—that combine to produce output.

national income identity An identity that states that gross national product must be equal to consumption plus government expenditure plus total investment plus net exports. It can be used to show the cost of increases in government expenditure in terms of either consumption or investment.

natural unemployment The unemployment that occurs when the labor market is in full equilibrium. It can also be thought of as the level of unemployment at which there is no tendency for the inflation rate to either accelerate or decelerate.

net investment Gross investment less depreciation.

net national product (NNP) Gross national product less depreciation.

neutral demand policy A possible policy response to a supply shock. Aggregate demand is left unchanged, and prices rise by only the fall in capacity. Such a policy response is likely to cause a recession to keep wages from rising along with prices.

nominal GNP The value of goods and services produced by the economy valued at current prices.

nominal rate of return The rate of return uncorrected for losses in purchasing power due to inflation.

nonaccelerating inflation rate of unemployment See *natural unemployment*.

official reserve transaction A transaction between central banks or the International Monetary Fund to settle balance of payments surpluses or deficits. When a country runs a balance of payments deficit, it must run down its reserve balances in other central banks or at the IMF.

Okun's law An empirical relationship between the unemployment rate and the level of production originally discovered by the late Arthur Okun. According to Okun's findings, a reduction of 1 percent in the unemployment rate is associated with an increase of about 3 percent in the ratio Y/Y_{FE}. Current research puts the relationship at closer to 1:2.

open market operation The buying or selling of government bonds by the Federal Reserve. Open market operations are the primary way by which the Federal Reserve influences the stock of money.

optimal saving rate The saving rate at which per capita consumption is maximized.

orthodox stabilization policy A contractionary monetary and/or fiscal policy aimed at reducing the rate of inflation.

partial equilibrium theory A short-run theory of aggregate supply developed by Milton Friedman, Edmund Phelps, and others. Its main points are that supply equals demand in all markets and that booms and recessions are caused by price forecasting errors.

permanent income The level of income that people expect to earn apart from random fluctuations. It is the basis for household consumption decisions, and it is usually measured as a weighted average of past measured income.

permanent income hypothesis Milton Friedman's theory of household consumption behavior. It asserts that consumption is based on permanent rather than measured income and implies that temporary changes in income through tax cuts or recession will primarily affect saving, not consumption.

personal disposable income The income received by households to spend or save. It is equal to GNP less all taxes and gross business savings plus all transfer payments.

Phillips curve A negative relationship between wage changes or the inflation rate and the unemployment rate.

planned investment The amount of investment that a firm makes plans to undertake. It is a key component of the modified accelerator theory of investment.

portfolio theory A theory of the household demand for all the different assets that together constitute household wealth.

price fixing The determination of price by sellers rather than by supply and demand in the goods market.

producers price index A price index based on the wholesale prices of produced goods. It used to be called the wholesale price index.

production function A function that relates output to inputs of labor and capital.

profit maximization rule The rule that determines the employment level that will maximize profit. It requires business to make the real wage equal to the marginal physical product of the marginal or last employee hired.

progressive tax A tax that is relatively higher for those in higher income brackets. Income taxes are progressive; sales taxes are not.

quantity theory The theory that nominal income is proportional to the money supply. It is based on a theory of the demand for money. The quantity theory can be converted into a theory of real income by making prices exogenous or to a theory of the price level by making real income exogenous.

rational expectations The theory that price expectations are based on a model of the economy rather than on past behavior. If price expectations are formed in this manner, policymakers can affect real output only when the public is unable to predict what policy will be.

Reaganomics A name applied to the economic program of the Reagan administration. It promised a cure for inflation without a recession and was composed of tax and expenditure cuts by the government coupled with a fairly restrictive monetary policy to reduce inflationary expectations.

real GNP The value of goods and services produced by the economy at constant prices. It is the best measure of production in the economy.

real interest rate The nominal interest rate minus the rate of inflation. It measures the real cost, in terms of resources, of borrowing or lending.

real money balances The value of nominal money balances held by the public, deflated by the price index. It is the command over goods represented by the nominal stock of money.

real rate of return The nominal rate of return on an asset less the rate of inflation.

real wage The nominal wage deflated by the price index. It represents the amount of goods and services that can be purchased with the nominal wage.

recognition lag The time it takes for policymakers to realize that a change in policy is needed.

rediscount rate The rate of interest at which banks may borrow from the Federal Reserve.

reduced-form equation An equation, derivable from an economic model, that relates an endogenous variable to a set of exogenous variables. It contains no more than one endogenous variable. The coefficients of each of the exogenous variables in this type of equation are the multipliers of the endogenous variable with respect to each of the exogenous variables.

required reserve ratio The ratio of reserves to demand deposits that banks are required to maintain. It is set by the Federal Reserve.

risk The possibility of capital loss arising from fluctuations in the price of assets held in a portfolio. It is often measured by the variability over time of the price of the asset.

secondhand bond A bond that has been resold by the original lender. The fact that bonds can be resold means that secondhand bond prices are sensitive to current interest rates.

special drawing rights (SDRs) Rights of members of the IMF to borrow up to a certain amount from the IMF for the discharge of balance of payments deficits. These were first created in 1969 in response to the need for international reserves beyond what was available in the form of gold, sterling, and dollars.

speculative demand A demand for money by speculators or wealthholders who expect the prices of assets to decline, enabling them to gain more by waiting to buy than they would lose in interest earnings forgone. This type of money demand is negatively related to the interest rate.

stabilization recession The part of the inflationary cycle that occurs when wage earners adjust to higher prices. It generally involves inflation coupled with falling output as workers demand catch-up wage increases to compensate for the unexpected rise in prices during the expansionary phase of the inflationary cycle.

stagflation The simultaneous occurrence of rising inflation and falling output.

structural unemployment Unemployment that is not curable by an increase in aggregate demand. It is caused by a mismatch between the skill structure of the labor force and the skill requirements of the jobs available in the economy.

supply-shock inflation An inflation caused by the sudden reduction of capacity due to an increase in the price of a key input, such as imported oil. The inflation is triggered by the inward shift of the supply curve relative to the demand curve, and it is accompanied by falling output.

supply-side economics The economic analysis of the effects of government policy on capacity output. It has generally been limited to considerations of the effects of taxes and regulation on supply, but it can be extended to include monetary policy.

tax incentives for price stability (TIPS) A tax plan proposed by Henry Wallich and Sidney Weintraub that would make the corporate tax rate a positive function of the rate of increase in wages granted by a firm. The plan would impose a penalty tax on firms whose wage settlements were overly generous.

total autonomous expenditure The part of aggregate demand that is not a function of GNP.

transaction demand The demand for money to make purchases. It should be positively related to income.

transfers Government and business payments to individuals that are not in return for services rendered. The main examples are interest payments, medicare, social security, and unemployment benefits.

transition equation In a dynamic model, an equation that shows how variables that are exogenous in each period change between one period and another.

transitory income The difference between measured and permanent income. It is the income (or loss) arising from random fluctuations in earnings.

user cost The cost of holding a capital good. It is equal to the nominal rate of interest plus the depreciation rate less capital gains all relative to the price of the capital good.

velocity The ratio of income to the money supply. It tells how many times the average dollar is spent per year.

voluntary reserve ratio The ratio of reserves to time deposits that banks elect to maintain at the Federal Reserve.

Index